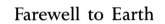

Farewell to Earth

Photo by Tullio Inglese, Amherst, Mass., USA, 1982

Farewell to Earth

The Collected Writings of
ARTHUR K. DAVIS

Volume I

Published by
ADAMANT PRESS
ADAMANT · VERMONT 05640 · USA
1991

First Edition

Library of Congress Cataloging-in-Publication Data

Davis, Arthur Kent.
    Farewell to earth: the collected writings of / Arthur K. Davis.
      p. cm.
    Includes bibliographical references and index.
    ISBN 0-912362-09-X (v. 1). (Alk. paper) : $45.00, US or Canadian
    1. Social history—20th century. 2. Historical sociology.
    3. Social sciences. 4. North America—Social conditions.
    I. Title.
    HN16.D38 1991
    301'.09—dc20   91-39085
                                             CIP

Dustjacket design: The Laughing Bear Associates, Inc., Montpelier, Vermont 05602
Dustjacket illustration: Edward Epstein
Typeset by Asterisk Typographics, Inc., Barre, Vermont 05641
Printing and printing production by Backman & Backman, Inc., Printing Specialists,
    Montpelier, Vermont 05602

Published by Adamant Press, Box 7, Adamant, Vermont 05640 USA

Dedication

To My Children

Carol Anne Davis Marino (1943–)
Randall Foster Davis (1955–)
Meredith Annette Davis (1974–)

And My Two Grandchildren

Peter Arthur Marino (1971–)
Emily Anne Marino (1973–)

And to the Memory of Annette Harrison (1942–1972)
from St. Annes-on-Sea, Lancashire, England

Clubbed at Selma, Alabama, marching with Martin Luther King, 1965.
Brilliant graduate student and university teacher at Liverpool,
Calgary, Minnesota and Wisconsin (River Falls Campus).

"Yet what binds us friend to friend
But that soul with soul may blend."

−A.H., 1966

Contents

PART II — From Western Canada:
Toward Cross-Disciplinary Holistic Analysis.
Cases and Disciplines of Change

Preface

THIS ANTHOLOGY, *Farewell to Earth*, is a selection of my short papers, travel notes, book reviews and public letters, written 1933–1991. Arranged in rough chronological order, most are self-contained as to content. But they share a common aim and a common method.

The paramount aim is to develop and convey in non-technical language an understanding of the contemporary world, or aspects thereof. How did things become what they are? What are the options for the future? What basic concepts seem useful in this kind of social-historical analysis?

This is not an exercise in orthodox North American academic sociology – the field inscribed on my three degrees from Harvard University – 1937, 1938 and 1941. Perhaps my field of operations might be called historical sociology, but that is not really broad enough.

Toward a Holistic World View

Every aspect of knowledge and collective behavior is needed: an holistic worldview, no less. Literature, sport, art, music, drama, dance, economic history, geopolitics, architecture, landscape, rituals, urban-rural differences and relationships, religion and philosophy – all these and other aspects lead to an holistic worldview.

No one can fully achieve such an in-depth and massive overview. Certainly I did not succeed. But that is the direction in which I sought to move. Most important, I believe, were the many exchanges I had with people from various cultures and social classes – including the great number of books and landscapes I experienced. Indeed, one of the best things that happened to me was getting pushed out of the ivy tower of academia in the late 1930s, first by World War II, later by travel ventures to a number of foreign countries. The latter reinforced my slow emancipation from the ivy tower begun by wartime service in western Europe and China. I came to realize by the 1950s what a tremendously revolutionary age we live in. Books on history and social change doubtless helped to pave the way, yet the decisive factor surely has been going abroad to see other societies (or aspects thereof) for myself.

Personal Background

To assess this book, readers need some information about the author. In class terms, we belonged to the petty bourgeoisie, "new" wing. The old wing includes skilled workers and small entrepreneurs, without the control of capital that defines the dominant elite in capitalist societies. The new wing has made a few upward small steps by virtue of education in the professions and middle administrative levels of large bureaucratic organizations: corporations, universities and school systems, hospitals, governments, the mass media, the arts both literary and performing. These people may or may not be celebrities in some cases; but they are not policymakers. The term "intelligentsia" is appropriate; it originated in Czarist Russia during the later 19th century, as that class slowly gained self-consciousness and social respectability.

Thus, my father was an engineer graduated from the Massachusetts Institute of Technology in 1911; my mother went through a four-year course in music (piano) and academic subjects at the New England Conservatory of Music in Boston. Looking back, I believe that she was greatly frustrated by the contradiction between her education and her role as a housewife. This is still a general contradiction in capitalist societies. The socialist countries have done significantly better in this matter by pioneering large-scale daycare programs, and in related institutional restructuring. But even socialists have serious problems remaining in this area.

Development of Basic Concepts

The great capitalist depression of the 1930s made me a socialist. "Poverty in the midst of plenty" was both unjust and irrational. I knew vaguely that the Five-Year Plan had begun in the USSR. But the Spanish Civil War became far more immediate to me in the mid- to late 1930s. Clearly the Spanish Republic, duly elected in 1936, was overcome by aid from the fascist States of Italy and Nazi Germany, while the capitalist States of France and England—or their upper-class elements—watched. Communist-led volunteers from western Europe and North America made up the International Brigades which came to aid the Spanish Republic. The conflict was fierce. During the summer evenings on the

Vermont farm, I would hurry down the hill road a short mile to North Calais to get the Boston paper that came in on the daily mail stage from Montpelier, 15 miles south. Early in 1939 the Republic collapsed, and the Spanish fascists ruled Spain for a generation. The USSR sent materials, but was too far away, and too preoccupied with its own industrializing drive, and its own rearming against the German menace – to have any effective leverage. It was apparent that this conflict was a prelude to a much greater struggle. This broke out in September, 1939, but did not become intense until the Nazis invaded the USSR in July, 1941.

By then I had completed my Ph.D. thesis on the Social Theory of Thorstein Veblen (1857–1929). Veblen was basically Marxist with a broad streak of philosophical anarchism. My focus became comparative institutional change. Institutions meant family and kinship, class structure, the power structure, economic organization including technology, and basic value orientations (nationalism, religion and the like). The war had taken me to the China ports – a new dimension. I became interested in the emerging Chinese revolution.

My background in Unitarianism was non-theistic, oriented to social justice. It made it easy to cut loose from the static world-view and ideology of capitalism. I saw that the capitalist world was founded on imperialism, and that the socialist world had a great task of catching up – building socialist institutions in the face of attacks and invasions by capitalist armies. Revolutions are not pink tea parties – I read enough history to realize that fundamental truth. The class struggle was perhaps most intense in its international aspects. The First World (capitalist) confronted the Second World (socialist). The Third World, as it decolonized itself, brought me into final touch with the global reality in which I lived.

Related Interests

Landscape was one, especially in mountains. I climbed many mountains in Vermont, New Hampshire, the Adirondacks. At Harvard I learned to take some easy courses so that I could branch out into history and literature – Russian, American, comparative world literature – fields wherein I could study widely. I specialized in the history of social thought from Greek times to the present, but always in an institutional and historical context. It is essential, for example, to know that Plato was a conservative landowner, not simply an idealist philosopher. His class background was all-important to a full comprehension of his dialogues. In the Boston Public Library on Copley Square is a mural of Plato lecturing to his students, with the Parthenon and the Acropolis in the distance. Such a painting, however beautiful, has to be transcended. And the *Utopia* of St.

Thomas More has to be placed in its class and historical context. In the Frick Collection in New York City the portrait of More by Holbein has always been one of my favorites. But it has to be set against the social life and squalor of that day.

Museums have always attracted me all over the world. In the Anthropology Museum of Mexico City one can see both the social life and the artifacts of the various historical epochs of Aztec and modern Mexican times. But equally important are the fly-ridden villages and the poverty one sees en route to climb the great snow volcano, Popocatapetl. The glamour of the Paseo de la Reforma is no more important than the grinding poverty of the slums that fester in most of the remainder of the National Capital outside the "Pink Zone."

I did no real climbing until I moved to western Canada in 1958. Real climbing means ropes, pitons and ice axe. What I did in the Green Mountains and the Adirondacks was simply strenuous hiking, not real climbing. I joined the Alpine Club of Canada to attend the annual summer camps in the Rocky Mountains of Alberta and southeastern British Columbia. This is where one learns what small-group co-operation really means. The Alpine Club emphasizes safety. In the high snowfields I observed some crazy foolhardiness. That is not my idea of climbing. Nor is the extreme use of stone drills to get past overhanging ledges by the most direct route. That is better styled "engineering" rather than real climbing. Often it involves bravado flaunting of common-sense safeguards.

In the mid-1970s I would attend the May weekend training camps of the Alpine Clubs on the edge of the Rockies east of Jasper, Alberta. I would take a half-dozen beginners in tow in order to teach them simple rope-management and safety. My task was to climb up a rock face and tie a rope to a secure rock ledge about 50 to 60 feet up, then rappel down, having established an experienced climber tied to the top anchor rock to handle the rope of the other ascending climbers. We all wore crash helmets of course. Once back down, I would check the beginners as they started their upward ascent. It was de rigueur, of course, to avoid knocking down loose rocks onto ascending climbers. Rules, however, may not always be observed. Nature is recalcitrant. A beginner named (let us say) Monique from France kicked down a loose rock the size of my fist onto my helmet. It had a free fall of 60 or 70 feet through the air. I felt my head settle suddenly into my neck. To this day my helmet has a dent squarely in the middle of the top, the size of a fifty-cent piece. Without a helmet, I would have had a hole in my skull. Later I had a few quiet words with Monique–enough to emphasize the safety aspect, but not to discourage her from further climbing activity.

Other Holistic Influences

Union College, Schenectady, New York, was a good small institution for men; it was partly engineering and partly liberal arts. I spent six years there, 1946–1952. The city was dominated economically and politically by the General Electric plant, where the union leadership was leftwing. The college dated from 1795; its domed library had architectural style. Its lacrosse team was excellent. The social science faculty held informal discussion sessions periodically at someone's home. We were a group of generalists primarily, rather than specialists. I was teaching Economics as well as Sociology. Discussions were invariably transcending discipline boundaries.

In 1949 we acquired an Austin small car. Carol, my firstborn, was six. With her mother, Anne, we could now make short ventures into the Catskills, Adirondacks and Vermont. Carol chugged up the summer slopes like a tireless steam engine. Meanwhile, I was beginning to write for the *Monthly Review*, an independent Marxian Socialist magazine in New York City. My occasional public letters to the local Schenectady newspaper may be found later in this collection. Though they dealt mainly with local municipal problems, I also challenged the basic premises of American foreign policy: the Cold War, the alleged Communist threat in Europe (although some local petty bourgeois Republicans imagined that many Reds were hiding under their beds). I was active in the local Council of Social Agencies Board of Advisors as press secretary. Policymaking posts, of course, were reserved for the Dutch elite. When U.S. President Harry Truman launched his abortive medicare plan, based on universal prepaid insurance, I became an active campaigner for that plan. The plan was defeated in due course by the dinosaurs who headed the American Medical Association. A limited medicare plan for seniors over 65 eventually emerged, years later. But in 1949–50, medicare was a hot issue attended by much hysteria.

On one occasion a free public lecture on health insurance was announced by the local medical society in Schenectady. I immediately telephoned the president of the Medical Society, to ask what provision was planned to hear the "other side." I was informed that the visiting speaker, a publicist hired by the American Medical Association, would handle both sides of the issue. This was more than I could stomach. I offered to provide myself and one or two other professors as additional speakers – 10 minutes for each speaker. Or, I suggested, we could air the controversy in the local press. After all, the meeting was to be held in the Union College Chapel. The offer was accepted, perhaps not too happily. We had the report of the U.S. Presidential Commission, five or six paperback volumes, as ammunition. I had that report well in hand. The turnout was excellent. No vote was taken; we simply aired the options—just what I believe a university should do. The visiting AMA publicist turned out to be a pleasant fellow, indeed likable. He never tried to answer us directly; he simply would say—"Well, that's democracy for you." By that I mean—he rolled with the punch.

On another venture in Schenectady, I prepared a plan for introducing dental care for school children on a preventative basis starting in grade I. The health care reports available made it clear, at least to me, that there was a large backlog of needed dental care not being met. I wrote off the older children—with regret—in order to seek out a new approach for younger children that would over the years lift the level of dental health in a significant way. This got nowhere in Schenectady. It was simply a loaf cast upon the waters. In Canada since 1962, thanks to the pioneering struggle of Saskatchewan progressive people, we now have all these benefits: universal compulsory health insurance. But the die-hards still try to chip away at Medicare, even in Canada.

New York; Philadelphia; Vermont Sojourn

I left Schenectady in 1952, by mutual consent. Union was not ready for a community activist. I was not prepared to settle into an orthodox academic role—meeting classes and rocking no boats. My first of three divorces complicated matters. Union gave me a year's salary to go away. There was no public fuss.

I moved to Columbia University for a half year, spending most of the other half in Vermont. Then a year at the University of Pennsylvania in Philadelphia. Both of these posts were temporary replacements of other staff on leave. So too, was my 1955 spring term at Vassar College in Pough-keepsie. Two senior faculty there, Emily Brown and Mabel Newcomer, had been students of Thorstein Veblen in the early 1920s at the New School for Social Research in New York City. From Vassar anthropologist John Murra I learned much about Latin America.

Those three years broadened and deepened my grasp of the Marxian key. In New York I could attend the meetings of the Monthly Review Circle—Paul Sweezy, Leo Huberman, Carey McWilliams, specialist in American ethnic minorities, editor of the *Nation*—a socialist, although he did not publish a socialist magazine. And then there was Paul Baran, Stanford economist and Marxist, and a commuting consultant to the so-cialist Government of Poland. There were others. My ongoing study of China put me in touch with Owen Lattimore (*Inner Asian Frontiers of China*, 1940) and especially with Joseph Needham and his Cambridge University circle (*Science and Civilization in China*, 1955 ff.). For hours in 1954 and 1955, I sat in the New York City Public Library studying books suggested by Joseph Needham and Solomon Adler. My often revised papers on China appeared in the *Monthly Review* in 1956.

In Philadelphia, life was not without its exciting moments. For example, that Memorial Day observance of homage to Walt Whitman (1819–1892), in my opinion America's greatest poet. It was held at Whitman's grave in Camden, New Jersey, across the river from Philadelphia. Hardly a dozen attended, half of them I estimated to be Federal plainclothesmen. One of the latter followed me home. Such was life in the McCarthyite era.

In mid-1955 I moved to the University of Vermont with a three-year contract. At Vermont there was an outstanding social-science professor: Paul Evans in History. His course on the French Revolution drew my full attention. I attended all his lectures, did all the assigned reading and much more.

Anther event worth noting is the exhibition of Thorstein Veblen's books in the small University Library on the occasion of the 100th anniversary of Veblen's birth in 1857. I supplied most of the books, and a sentence or two about each one. I do not know whether anyone bothered to look at the exhibition. No matter. Where one or two persons are gathered in my name, there also am I. . . .

At Vermont I had the privilege of contributing a monthly volunteered column, "In Perspective," 1957–58, printed in the Swanton *Courier* and its associated weekly newspapers, all published in Franklin County, northwestern Vermont.

Saskatchewan: The Shining Land

In mid-1958 I moved to Saskatchewan in Canada, where I became Chief Research Officer of the newly founded Centre for Community Studies in Saskatoon. Our job, funded by the Co-operative Commonwealth Federation (CCF) government of the Province, was to study social change on the western prairies, and clarify the options confronting villages and towns, in non-jargon language. My six years in Saskatchewan were in many ways the height of my professional career. I felt that I was doing something socially useful for the people of Saskatchewan whose hard-earned dollars paid my salary. My work took me all over the Province and into the northern bush country peopled only by Métis and Indians – in sharp cultural contrast to the agrarian southern half of the Province, where co-operatives were powerful enough to push back the town businessmen thought by many to be exploiters of the farms. The Premier, 1944–61, was Tommy Douglas, the greatest orator in North America, and father of medicare. Always he stayed a little ahead of his followers, but never out of touch.

In Saskatchewan I broke out of the ivy tower of academia. I won the confidence of so many people in rural Saskatchewan. I felt that I could be myself. And indeed, I fell in love with that beautiful Saskatchewan landscape, with its grain elevators 10 miles apart on the net of rail lines. Summer and winter, spring and fall, in mud and sunshine, ice and rain – I travelled the back roads, digging myself out whenever that was necessary. Those small town and country people I met – they were the sharpest and most friendly people that ever crossed my path. When I drove into a farmyard, they looked first at my cleated hiking shoes, then at my unpressed pants, then invited me in for coffee. No one refused me an interview; and never, not ever did I violate their confidence. That was Saskatchewan. When the people suffered, so did I. I came to understand the cost-price squeeze – that farmers had to sell their grain in a world market they did not control, yet they had to purchase their farm machinery in a closed monopolistic market that skinned them in the name of private profit. My sense of social justice was outraged.

Fired from Saskatchewan

My dilemmas were two – if we oversimplify. The first was the effort by the Director of the Center for Community Studies to get me to revise my research results of our studies in Northern Saskatchewan. I refused. This is described in "A Prairie Dust Devil" reprinted from *Human Organization*, 1968, and reproduced in Part II of this book. The other was the medical classification of my son Randy in 1961 as autistic. That is referred to later, in Vol. II. In the fall of 1961, Randy's mother twice abducted Randy, then age six, from Saskatoon to New York City, where she sought to institutionalize him – having said nothing to me about her plans. Twice in the fall of 1961, I recovered Randy and put him back in his special community-oriented program. In March, 1963, the Saskatoon Court of Queen's Bench awarded exclusive custody of Randy to me, with no visitation by the mother. She ran screaming from the courtroom on hearing the judgment, and returned to New York City within a few days. As for me, it was time to leave Saskatchewan. In early 1964, Randy and I packed what household effects we could carry, and drove through the wintry Rogers Pass to Bellingham, Washington, where I had a semester of teaching at Western Washington State University.

The star of the social sciences faculty at Western Washington was Herbert C. Taylor, chairperson, and holder of a double Ph.D. in archeology and social anthropology from the University of Chicago, 1951. His brilliance as a teacher and researcher is legendary, equalled only by his skills in administration. My office in Old Main had real atmosphere. I would still be there if only Western Washington had been located in Canada.

But my life has been a series of arrivals and departures. In July of 1964 I taught in the summer session of the University of Alberta, Edmonton, and then moved to Calgary as Professor of Sociology and Anthropology. I was proud of that joint title, though it slighted my interests in economics and history.

Calgary and Annette Harrison

The University of Calgary had a small Master's degree program in the social sciences, which attracted students mainly from southern Alberta and the West. In 1963, however, two graduate students arrived in Alberta from England. One was assigned to the University of Alberta at Edmonton; the other came to Calgary. The latter was Annette Harrison, who grew up in St. Annes-on-Sea, Lancashire, and took her undergraduate work at the University of Liverpool.

I saw her first in my class on the history of social thought, September, 1964. It was impossible to miss her. She was blond, beautiful, highly intelligent, witty. She was already recognized by the faculty as the most able student in the Department. The first thing she said to me, after the first meeting of my class, was–"Professor Davis, you left us absolutely floundering." A gentle wipe-out!

This 1964–65 course was my only direct teaching contact with Annette. Her thesis work was directed by another faculty committee on which I did not sit. We were simply friends after the course ended; we met as equals. Our common interests were many and deep. Indeed, she was the high point of my adult life in so many ways. I cannot write what she meant to me. Perhaps she said it best herself: "Yet what binds us friend to friend, / But that soul with soul can blend." She wrote these lines in February, 1966, in a copy of *The Innocents at Cedro*, by Robert L. Duffus (Macmillan, 1944). To find this out-of-print book, Annette had scoured the bookstores of St. Paul and Minneapolis.

Our time together was woefully short. Annette left Calgary in September, 1965, headed for the University of Minnesota to study for a Ph.D. She drove down by herself in her red British roadster MG. On January 2, 1965, I had acquired my black Volvo 1800S, which we took turns driving to Banff and Lake Louise, and to other places in the Rocky Mountains. Annette liked the Volvo because it "cornered" so well. Once indeed two or three years later she put the car in the ditch near Lethbridge as I was escorting her to Shelby, Montana, and the train to Minneapolis. No damage, however. A truck soon stopped to pull us back onto the highway, which was covered with bumpy ice ridges. And a year or so later, I myself, driving back to Calgary from visiting my oldest daughter Carol in her final year at the University of Alberta, Edmonton, allowed the car to edge onto the highway shoulder, where wet snow grabbed my outer wheels and pulled the car into the ditch. Again, no damage.

Annette returned to visit me in Calgary during her long vacations—a fortnight each at Christmas and Easter, and four to six weeks during the summer. I would meet her in Shelby or Great Falls, Montana. We agreed that either of us could go off alone as circumstances might determine. We carried on a vigorous mail correspondence, and I often phoned her evenings. Our commitment to each other was as nearly absolute as it could be—still giving us both a large measure of freedom. Marriage? My status after the 1963 custody trial in Saskatoon was a judicial separation. Technically I was not free to marry. But that was a secondary reason. The primary reason was more complex. In a relationship such as marriage, equality is difficult to achieve. Someone in terms of career or income or child-care is number one; the other party is usually number two. There was no way I could see Annette, with her energy and generosity and activist commitments, placed in a number two status. Not by me, certainly. I loved her too much. And my own career was circumscribed by my job requirements: I would always have to go where the job led me. Does this mean that professional couples should not marry? Perhaps so, in some cases. Not necessarily, in other cases. Let me add: Annette managed beautifully with Randy: she accepted him as he was, and Randy responded warmly to her human touch.

Annette could and did get involved in social movements—especially the quest for women's rights. She travelled widely. Beneath that facade of witty charm, there was a bedrock sense of tragedy. This I understood, because I share that characteristic. She admitted that herself, whenever we discussed it. Is not the essence of human life tragic?

On January 24, 1972, Annette died of monoxide poisoning in her garage at St. Croix, Wisconsin. She was aged 30, and a tenured assistant professor of Sociology at the River Falls campus of the University of Wisconsin. By faculty and students alike, she was considered the finest teacher in her field. But an accident cut her off: early that winter morning, having skipped breakfast, she started her car without opening the garage door first; when she got out to do so, she fainted before the door was opened. After careful inquiries among her friends, I concluded her death was accidental, and not a suicide. Annette was indeed accident-prone; she had fainting spells. Once at my Calgary house, I had to kick open a locked door and drive her quickly to hospital emergency. Suicide was entirely out of character; all her friends agreed on that point.

News of the tragedy reached me at the University of Regina several days after the event. I was shattered. I have never fully recovered. Her ashes rest in the Protestant Cemetery in Rome, a city she loved so well.

That fact alone tells me how much of Annette's life I did not share. Notwithstanding, she was the "wisest soul of all my days and lands . . . There in the fragrant pines and the cedars dusk and dim." (Whitman)

The Cost of Modernity to the Human Race: Self-Destruct

In 1851, an exiled Russian nobleman, Alexander Herzen, published a long letter to and about Russians. His book, *From the Other Shore*, urged his readers to cross the bridge to modernity.

Given the conditions of 1851 in Europe and its offshoot imperialisms, Herzen had an irresistible case. But looking back from 1989 as I write these lines, something has gone dead wrong.

By modernity we can mean only urban-industrial society, large-scale and therefore bureaucratized like a modern corporation or army or government. This form of socio-economic organization generates immense power, against which only another bureaucratic pattern can prevail or even survive.

Inequities are built into, and generated by this modernity-bureaucratized system. Modernity captured the capitalist Western nations first. To that enormous expansion of western Europe over the last four centuries (more or less, here and there)–the rise of socialism is a direct response. Hard on in close pursuit follows the Third World, rooted in poverty, desperately bent on escaping its poverty, once the universal way of life of people the world around, but now rejected by the endless tide of rising aspirations for material goods and services.

It took the capitalist world perhaps four centuries to achieve its current unfair and uneven standards of living, both within and among its component nations. As Marx so clearly saw in the 1840s, the rich get richer and the poor get poorer. Catching up is a long and grinding task. It is also a vain task, because the goal of material plenty is itself a death potion. Urban-industrialism generates a hinterland-against-metropolis form of organization. The metropolitan elites require the resources and the labour and the markets of the underclass hinterlands. Modernity thus feeds upon itself; it is a self-consuming cannibalism. It is massive self-destruction.

Friends, look around you. Do you really believe that it is possible to automobilize the world? Even if this dreadful prospect were realistically possible, is it socially desirable? Now turn to the Epilogue of these books, and read the 1899 poem of a little-known Canadian poet, Archibald Lampman, "The City of the End of Things."

> Beside the pounding cataracts
> Of midnight streams unknown to us
> 'Tis builded in the leafless tracts

And valleys huge of Tartarus.
Lurid and lofty and vast it seems;
It hath no rounded name that rings,
But I have heard it called in dreams
The City of the End of Things.

. . . .

The roar shall vanish at its height,
And over that tremendous town
The silence of eternal night
Shall gather close and settle down.
All its grim grandeur, tower and hall,
Shall be abandoned utterly,
And into rust and dust shall fall
From century to century;
Nor ever living thing shall grow,
Nor trunk of tree, nor blade of grass;
No drop shall fall, no wind shall blow,
Nor sound of any foot shall pass:
Alone of its accursèd state,
One thing the hand of Time shall spare,
For the grim Idiot at the gate
Is deathless and eternal there.

The Title of this Book: Farewell to Earth

This is borrowed from the last aria of Verdi's opera *Aida.* The hero
and the heroine are entombed underground. In a few minutes the air
will run out. They sing that great duet, first sung in 1871 in Cairo. To
me in 1990, that aria sums up our present world dilemma and heritage – a
fatal one.

For the cost of modernity is death, by the self-destruction of the human race. Consider waste, pollution, the looming exhaustion of non-
renewable resources, the nuclear arms race running wildly out of control, racism, poverty. All these festering ongoing developments are built
into our most fundamental social structures. Ask the kids; they know
that the future is stacked against them – and against us. The warming
of the planet – already underway – but everyone thinks this will not happen to me. Like hell it won't.

A special responsibility attaches to North Americans. We made this
world; others only react to it, usually by seeking to copy our mistakes.
In our own day, since World War II, we have gone through one crisis
after another. In the 1950–53 Korean War, some 5 million people died
(*Encyclopedia Britannica* estimate, 1985), including 33,000 U.S. military. In
Vietnam, 1955–75, another dirty war. After the French were smashed out

of Vietnam by the revolutionary forces of Ho Chi Minh at the Battle
of Dien Bien Phu in early May, 1954, the nine-year effort of France to
recapture its colony collapsed. I was then in Philadelphia. I sensed that
an era of imperialism had ended in southeast Asia—almost. For I reck-
oned without the United States.

The imperialist attempt to reconquer southeast Asia was picked up
by the United States, slowly escalating to an all-out war—which was lost
decisively in the spring of 1975. I recall listening to the broadcasts on
Canadian Radio, on Easter Sunday, describing the helicopters lifting off
from the roof of the American Embassy in Saigon. Vietnamese stooges
of the U.S.A. were clinging desperately to the departing helicopters. The
debacle was an historical milestone in the exposure of the United States
as a defeated would-be colonial imperialist power in southeast Asia.
Domination of the metal resources of southeast Asia was a prime aim
of American intervention. Yet the crushing defeat made little impression
in American homes, except among those receiving the coffins of the
56,000 U.S. fatalities and the care of 303,000 U.S. wounded. (Canadian
Encyclopedia, Hurtig Publishers, Edmonton, 1988, 2nd edition, vol. 4).

And how can we count the millions of deaths rained down on Vietnam, Laos and Cambodia by the American carpet-bombing assaults in
air-conditioned planes safely aloft above any countervailing attack from
the victim populations below. Fair fight? Fair play? What the world so
desperately needs is a socialist revolution in the United States. We need
an army to cleanse the world of the excrescence of American capitalism.
An army like Cromwell's Puritans; like the French Revolutionary army
of "le grand Carnot"; like the Soviet Army that conquered Nazi Germany in World War II, at an incredible cost. Who among us can weigh
the 21 million deaths suffered by the USSR—including the 7 million military deaths? The rest were civilians—old people, women and children.

Marxism

My interpretations involve the Marxian key, as I use that concept.
This is further discussed later in these volumes. However, at this point
I should sketch my understanding of Marxism.

I rely mainly on the Communist *Manifesto* of 1848, plus the other numerous writings of Marx. But Marx wrote between the 1840s into the
1880s: times have changed since then. In 1848, capitalism was still competitive; now it is monopolistic. The pre-capitalistic social orders still
important in 1848 Europe have largely disappeared except in the Third
World. But class struggle between the owning corporate bourgeoisie and
the proletariat as core antagonists still remains. Intervening between
them is still the petty bourgeoisie, old and new, a few struggling to make

it into the real bourgeoisie, and the relative newcomers, the new petty bourgeoisie, who hold a moderately privileged status as educated experts and trained administrators—but who are not key policymakers. Socialism still remains as the inevitable outcome of capitalist evolution, as in Marx's day; but the development of out-of-control technology in this nuclear age has thrust upon us a new alternative: self-destruction of the human race. It is in the latter direction that I tilt. A reversion to fascism—the dictatorship of last-ditch capitalists, or of elements acting in their name and on their behalf (e.g., Hitler's Germany or the like) would bring on that last final war. Assuming an ever larger importance, perhaps a decisive one, is the awakening of the Third World—a marginal concern of Marx in his day—indeed a great void in his theory, on hindsight from 1990.

In his day, Marx could pay little attention to China and India, although he wrote some brilliant essays on India. The less said about his foray into analysis of China, the better. For perceptive insights about China, we turn—not to Marx—but to Thomas T. Meadows and Augustus Lindley (mid-nineteenth century analysts) and above all to Mao Tse-tung, as creative as Marx, but drawing upon Chinese history rather than European history for his insights and inspiration.

Marxism is a developing intellectual and historical tradition; it is not static or mechanical, but dynamic. We should speak of "socialisms," like "capitalisms," to allow for variations in time and place—stemming from changing and often unique factors that modify regional and national evolution.

In my case, I read widely in the classics of Marxism, increasingly with regard to the historical situations from which those written works emerged. Paul Sweezy's essays were penetrating and crucial—especially *The Present as History* (Monthly Review Press, New York, 1953). Moving to a different society—Canada in 1958—reopened another type of learning—observation of a different set of concrete social institutions and systematic historical analysis thereof. Travel accompanied by such analyses became the basis of my immersion in comparative institutional change. Although I had a university background in such studies, extending it into praxis was both exhilarating and painful. Holistic social analysis was a prime goal and method. Marxism was an indispensable aspect of that analysis, but it was not the only aspect.

Letters to the Editor

This type of public statement is one of the few available to academics who do not wish to confine their written communications to stuffy professional journals read only by other academics. I devoted time and effort to the cultivation of short capsules of information and opinion that could convey my specialized professional data and insights to non-specialized readers on public issues relevant to all or many of us as fellow citizens. Such communications must be clear, non-jargonized and above all – condensed. Editorial space in newspapers is necessarily limited. Editors regard captions as their special sphere, and likewise such technical editing as the use of sub-captions, paragraphing, punctuation and the like. Short sentences and short paragraphs is a good rule of thumb, as I learned many years ago. How well I learned is not for me to say. I usually got published with cuts sometimes of about 10 or 15 percent, and with paragraphing adjustments which in the net I felt were beneficial.

Since most North American newspapers like to foster public forums in their columns, subject to limitations of space and related journalistic usage, I believe that academics with something to say on public issues should make a serious effort to cultivate the art of writing letters to the editor. This is, needless to add, an unpaid voluntary activity. But it is, when well done, an educational project in the public interest.

Rounding Out

This book began several decades ago in New Hampshire and Vermont. It seems fitting to close the project there. Adamant is a small place in the northern Vermont hill country. Yet it can encompass the world. And how often have I seen myself as confronting choices between a rock and a hard place? I have roots there in more ways than one.

The world was in turmoil when this book was begun in 1933. Today in 1991 the world has greatly changed, and the nature of the turmoil also, though not its intensity. During the interim six decades, I have seen much of the globe, both physically as landscape and conceptually as evolving history. Perhaps I understand better this many-faceted social earth, its predatory human societies seemingly bent willy-nilly on self-destruction. But that is not for me to say.

Yet are there no affirmations that sustain me? Of course there are. My family, relatives, friends and students, widely scattered notwithstanding. Especially Carol west of Boston, with my son-in-law, Fabio Marino, and my two grandchildren, Peter Arthur and Emily Anne Marino; Randy here with me in Edmonton, Canada; and Meredith nearby. My love and honour to them all.

» «

One chilly spring afternoon in 1991, sitting in my kitchen workplace, Meredith, just turned 17, dashed off the following lines. They fit some themes of this book.

Mother Earth

We live in a world being rapidly destroyed
   In a society full of people and their industrial toys
   Car exhausts and chain saws turning our sky black.
We've hit a point of no return
   Where we may never be able to turn back.
As life on earth becomes extinct
   No one seems to know exactly what is on the brink.
What is more important—money and power
   Or the life of our earth that is dying
   Just like the life of a flower.

                                     —Meredith Annette Davis
                                         April 23, 1991

PART I

Wide Horizons and Key Ideas

The Present as Tragedy

Toward a Critique of Sorokin's View of North American Society*

I.

WHEN I TOOK my first course in sociology as an undergraduate at Harvard College some three decades ago, the professor was Pitirim Sorokin, already a world famous scholar. He had been publishing in a dozen languages for about thirty years, and he would go on publishing for thirty more. His fantastic energy turned out nearly 40 books – some of them comprising multiple volumes – and more than 200 papers. The count is still incomplete. Not in any sense were they machine-made "sausages." The more important of his books quickly became standard works in their particular fields, and they have continued to be so regarded, despite the fact that they did not kow-tow to the idol of quantification that has dominated modern social science. For Sorokin dealt with ideas and interpretations as well as with facts. Indeed, he recognized that these two categories are really inseparable. An empirical fact is definable only in terms of a partly non-empirical conceptual scheme. The myth of "value-free sociology" received short shrift from him. He knew that a scholar can be objective without being neutral.

It is difficult to grasp the extent of Sorokin's productivity. Yet it was not simply his immense scholarship that made him such a memorable figure. He set us an impossible example. The Professor had read everything, and he expected his students to do likewise. This was a standard,

The second Sorokin Memorial Lecture delivered October 30, 1969 at the University of Saskatchewan, Saskatoon, Canada. Copyright © 1970 by, and reprinted with permission of, the University of Saskatchewan.

* Dedicated to Jim F. C. Wright, 1904–1970: investigator, historian and native son of the Canadian Prairie hinterland.

I must confess, that none of us ever realized – there was just no way – but the "press" was real.

Equally important, in my opinion, was Sorokin's role as a public critic. He sharply attacked various aspects of contemporary society, both social and political. His caustic comments on the materialistic customs of his time were usually made from a conservative point of view. He was critical of some of the American New Deal reforms of the 1930s, because from his knowledge of world history he was aware that similar experiments had often failed before. However, the stereotyped categories of political "right" and "left" did not fit Sorokin. His early hostility toward the Bolshevik government of the Soviet Union which had severely persecuted him abated in time, until by the 1940s he could recognize the virtues and achievements of the Russian revolution as well as its terrible costs. During World War II, he was active in Russian war-relief agencies around Boston.

The myth of scholarly detachment and impartiality was not for him; he knew that silence and seclusion in the academic ivy tower can also be a form of partisanship favoring the status quo. When the great majority of his contemporaries were swaddling, ostrich-like, in their mantles of middle-class conformity, Sorokin vigorously spoke out against the insanities of American foreign policy after World War II. Nowadays, when the enormities of American activities abroad are being hideously revealed on television, at least in Canada, it has suddenly become almost popular to join the critics. Twenty years ago, however, only one senior member of the Harvard faculty besides Sorokin had the temerity to speak out. Sorokin had far more insight – and guts – than the overwhelming majority of North American academics.

At certain times in his career, Sorokin became even more deeply involved in the social movements of his time. He was important enough in the Russian Social Revolutionary Party and in Kerensky's short-lived regime in 1917 to attract occasional hostile lines from Lenin and other Bolshevik writers. Earlier he was arrested three times by the Czarist police and, later, three times by the Bolsheviks. In 1922, he barely escaped from Russia with his life. From his 1924 book, *Leaves from a Russian Diary*, and from his 1963 autobiography, *A Long Journey*,[1] we may gain some vivid impressions of what he experienced. Dangerous and at times indescribably horrible as were some of his experiences, they probably contributed much to his insights and to his later analyses of the basic trends of our times.

Still another major influence from Sorokin was the kind of sociology department he built at Harvard during the years of his chairmanship, in the 1930s and early 1940s. It was a very small department, as those things go today—about a half-dozen faculty members with perhaps eight or ten graduate students employed as teaching assistants. For the years of my stay, which included time both before and after the Second World War, Sorokin was the only full professor. But there was also a small number of distinguished visiting scholars, usually one each term or one each year. In addition, we were encouraged to take courses in such other departments as psychology, anthropology, history, economics, and law. We were expected to know something about the social thought of India and China. There was nothing parochial about the graduate training we were offered in Sorokin's department. The real problem was overcoming the parochialism of the junior staff and of us graduate students. All the Professor could do was to sow some germinal seeds. The dubious harvest was our responsibility, not his.

Although Sorokin was easily the leading figure in Harvard sociology at that time, he never sought to dominate his students. I can bear witness to the truth of the following lines from *A Long Journey*:

> As founder and chairman of the departments of sociology at Leningrad and Harvard, I never pressed students to accept my theories uncritically but, rather, repeatedly advised them to follow the path of independent investigation and formulation of their own views regardless of their agreement or disagreement with my or any other conceptual schemes, methods and conclusions.[2]

The small size of the department in my student days made for easy contact with the faculty in small classes, seminars, and informal gatherings. And once or twice a year we would be invited to the home of the Professor and his gracious wife, Helen, herself an eminent scientist in the field of biology. These informal parties featured wideranging conversations and the Professor's smooth but highly deceptive punch, which consisted (if my memory is correct) of two parts tea, two parts fruit juices, and one part pure grain alcohol long since unobtainable on the open market.

Nonetheless, Sorokin was a very exacting teacher. The drafts of my term papers and thesis, the latter of which was written mainly under the supervision of Talcott Parsons, are scattered through with Sorokin's blunt and terse marginal comments—such as "Superficial flap!" or, "Read Confucius and revise your statement."

In his classroom from time to time the Professor would review the emerging trends of the present era, and he would announce with a grim smile that, "History is going according to schedule." The Sorokin view of the contemporary world would thus be vindicated once again. For example, he wrote in volume III of his magnum opus, *Social and Cultural*

Dynamics (1937), that "the curse or privilege of being the most devastating or most bloody war century belongs to the twentieth."[3] On occasion it was evident that Sorokin judged other theorists of social change—Danilevsky, Spengler, Toynbee—by how closely their theories approximated his own. This was apparent during the memorable 1946 confrontation between Sorokin and Toynbee in Cambridge, Massachusetts. It may, safely be said that Sorokin had great confidence in his own ideas, once they were formulated. Yet this would be an incomplete judgment. Looking back at the five years of his life that went into the production of *Social and Cultural Dynamics*, the author wrote:

> In this long labor there were, of course, many dark moments of feeling it a failure, of finding myself in a blind alley, of doubt as to the importance of the study and the advisability of its continuation.[4]

Perhaps the main image of Sorokin that stands out in my mind is that of the universal scholar pursuing his own way, but now and then pausing to chastise his colleagues, his students, and the secular powers of the world. This is a large judgment. But it is illuminated by a small incident. At the August, 1969, meetings of the American Sociological Association in San Francisco, some unknown persons, doubtless young and iconoclastic, took the trouble to procure and freely dispense some large yellow lapel badges, on which in black letters were inscribed the words, SOROKIN LIVES. I do not know whether these altruistic persons were anticipating the verdict of posterity; or whether they were simply echoing Tolkien's magical saga, *The Lord of the Rings*, which is a book about the hobbits, those half-mythical inhabitants of the Shire—the eternal hinterland. I would guess that they were doing both, but that verdict is not for me now to render. I shall leave that badge in the Sorokin collection in the University of Saskatchewan Library.

Some day, perchance, someone may do for Sorokin what R. L. Duffus did for Thorstein Veblen in *The Innocents at Cedro*. Duffus grew up near Waterbury, Vermont, three generations ago. In 1907/08, he was a student at Stanford University, California. For a year he lived in Veblen's household at Cedro Cottage, out in the countryside, near the campus where Veblen taught. That Veblen was one of the greatest American-born social thinkers is neither here nor there. Duffus gave us a live portrait in depth of one of his professors, and there lies my present point. It is an insightful judgment by an average student about one of his more significant teachers. In the context of this Sorokin memorial lecture, I should like to read to you what Duffus wrote about Thorstein Veblen.

> I cannot say precisely what the Veblen mark is. I did learn from him to examine human institutions and to some extent human motives with a

measure of scepticism. . . . I learned to think in terms of a changing, not a static society. And this was well for me. The tides of change were running faster and faster. . . . One needed some preparation and fore-warning to ride that surf. Veblen gave us some.

I learned, too, to respect workmanship. And by workmanship I mean, and I think Veblen meant, all work, humble or ambitious, demanding a little skill or all the power of genius, done with the hands or with the head, that men do for work's sake. It is a thing all good workmen under-stand, and in it they are brothers. . . .[5]

II.

LET US NOW TURN to another aspect of the occasion of the present essay: Sorokin in Saskatchewan. At first glance, a more unlikely con-nection could hardly be imagined. Never did it occur to me in my stu-dent days at Cambridge that one day we would be celebrating Sorokin's work on the Saskatchewan prairies. Yet today the Sorokin library, his manuscripts and papers rest in the custody of the University of Saskatch-ewan at Saskatoon. How did this come about?

This very question is a measure of the blind parochialism of metrop-olis. It reminds me of the letter I received from the east in 1961, soon after the death of Ernest Hemingway in Idaho was announced. The let-ter asked, what was this famous writer, this Nobel prize winner, doing out in the boondocks of Idaho? An answer to that type of inquiry should take us to the heart of our problem.

I suggest that part of the answer lies in the changing relations be-tween metropolis and hinterland. Another part lies in the nature of this particular hinterland province, with special reference to the university which is and has been, ever since its founding, such an integral com-ponent and reflection of the Saskatchewan thrust and drift.

Concerning the relation between the University and the people of Saskatchewan, the former Premier, Tommy Douglas, spoke as follows at the Golden Jubilee celebration of the University on September 28, 1959 – some of you probably were present at that oration, or perhaps you heard it (as I did) on the Saskatoon radio:

> The real heroes of this university are the little people of Saskatchewan who have made it possible, the people who, out of their taxes, have helped to build this university. . . . I know of no university that has been more closely integrated with the life of a province than has our university. . . . It has gone out into the highways and the byways . . . This is a university which has woven itself into the very fabric of the province and into the life of our people.

So said Tommy Douglas. One of his political successors has learned that he can disturb this mutual relationship only at his own peril.

The main answer to the question, how should we understand the presence of the Sorokin papers in Saskatchewan, is therefore to be found in the dynamic relationship between metropolis and hinterland. Here you must allow me a backward glance.

It has been some ten years since I came from New England to these high Canadian plains. I think I learned something from my Saskatchewan incarnation. Certainly I shed some encapsulating illusions. Before I came, Saskatchewan in my mind was little more than a strange-sounding place-name. I learned, first-hand, that during the post-war years of escalating Cold War, and of shrinking social horizons in the United States, Saskatchewan had remained the last progressive beachhead in North America. Of course, in Seymour Lipset's somewhat misnamed *Agrarian Socialism* (Berkeley, 1950) we in the East had read that out in the Canadian West there still survived an unusual multitude of voluntary organizations, activist "publics," and periodically surging social movements with broadly based grass-roots support. I came to see for myself that this was true. All this stood in sharp contrast with the state of affairs in New England, allegedly the home and stronghold of town meeting democracy, but actually a region long ago encapsulated in suburban apathy and conformity to its metropolitan masters. Yet I did not see New England or the United States clearly until after I came to Saskatchewan.

Saskatchewan in brief was a paradox. A generation ago it was relatively rural, underdeveloped and semi-colonial. Yet after World War II it pioneered in progressive, welfare-state legislation, especially in health services and in bringing to the countryside and to small communities a number of social services and public utilities not otherwise available at the same cost. Moreover, there is a long history of populist, grass-roots striving to bring the amenities of modern life to the Saskatchewan hinterland, as the works of Vernon Fowke, Jim Wright, and Jim McCrorie have shown. Then in 1962 came medicare, and the doctors' quixotic strike by one of our most highly educated and most insulated professions. That story is well known, and it needs no repeating here. The matter has been dramatically presented by Robin Badgley and Samuel Wolfe, in *Doctors' Strike*, published by Macmillan, Toronto, in 1967.

Less widely acceptable, perhaps, at least in Saskatchewan, is my view that populism (not socialism) is the key to understanding not only the Saskatchewan Co-operative Commonwealth Federation (CCF) but also Social Credit in Alberta. Populism means a revolt, or an attempt, on the part of the small producer, the small business man, the family farm, to achieve, by collective efforts with others of his kind, a larger place in the national sun. An important populist doctrine among rural and small-town colonials, in both the Canadian and the American west, is the belief in "direct democracy"–in the use of government to restrain and circumvent the eastern plutocrats and giant corporations. C. B. Macpherson wrote in 1953:

> The radicalism of both [the United Farmers of Alberta provincial government of 1921–35, and the Social Credit government that took over in 1935] was that of a quasi-colonial society of independent producers, in rebellion against eastern imperialism, but not against the property system.[6]

And on the subject of American populism in the 1890s, John D. Hicks had this to say:

> Implicit in the Populist conception of government intervention in economic affairs was the assumption that the government itself should be truly representative of the people, that the long-established control of the plutocrats should be broken.[7]

The social histories of Saskatchewan and Alberta are not the same. But surely they have much more in common than otherwise. I have become convinced, after living a half-decade in each province, that the social movements known as the CCF in Saskatchewan and as Social Credit in Alberta embody many basic similarities in motivation, in broad general goals, in their "social-gospel" ancestry, and even in some of their instrumental public policies, particularly in their use of governments to achieve benefits for small producers like farmers. Their differences, though real, seem to have been exaggerated by pressures stemming from proximity, from routine political competition, and from distortions inherent in a short-run, close-up view.

In general, since World War II the key process on the Canadian Prairies has been urbanization, the basis of which has been economic expansion and diversification. These are terms which obviously include too many components to analyze here. Suffice it to say that this on-going transformation has its educational and cultural aspects. Higher education has burgeoned; many new amenities have come to the urban centres, large and small, and in lesser degree to the countryside.

Clearly, however, the goodies have not come equally to everyone. Groups like the aged, the small farmers, the Indians and the Metis have not shared in the feast, and even the larger farmers are now painfully caught once again in the chronic cost-price squeeze that is inherent in North American agriculture. At least one Canadian in five exists below the poverty line, as that line is conservatively defined by federal agencies. Don Willmott's studies of Esterhazy in the early 1960s revealed that the

economic expansion and diversification which attended the development of the potash industry in that area also entailed a sharpening of
class–and interest–group conflict.[8] Of course, the sharpening of class
lines and the increase of socio-economic distance between top and bottom groups are most apparent in northern towns. In southern Canada,
these trends are obscured, and also in part counteracted, by the growth
of the "new" middle classes–those white collar and professional categories which are employed by the corporations, government agencies,
universities, school systems, hospitals, and so on. If certain hard-pressed
groups have no way up or out, at least their sons and daughters can make
it into the new middle classes by means of higher education. Besides
the expansion of the new middle classes, in Canada, there are the ever-
beckoning opportunities for the skilled occupations south of the border:
emigration is still another safety valve. Nonetheless, it can be argued
that, underneath these surface waves and cross currents, the gap between the core upper-class and the core under-class groups in Canada
is widening, not decreasing.

However, this is not the immediate point I wish to develop, except
as a background idea. For those favoured sectors of the population
which have significantly profited from the post-war surge into urbanization, the frosting on the cake of affluence is sweet indeed. The leading
artists, orchestras, ballet companies, and theatre groups now visit our
prairie cities at regular intervals, whereas formerly they could be seen
and heard only in the largest cities of eastern Canada or of the United
States. All sorts of metropolitan influences have reached out into the
prairie hinterland.

One phase of the post-war expansion of the universities has been the
spread of interest in the social studies, especially sociology. Although
this field had been established in most of the older American universities
since the turn of the century, it was not until the early 1950s that the
first full-time graduate Ph.D. sociologist was appointed at the University
of Alberta, and the middle 1950s at the University of Saskatchewan. Since
then, growth has been rapid. By the late 1950s there were enough people
around to organize a regional professional association. The Western Association of Sociology and Anthropology, drawing its members chiefly
from the prairie provinces and Montana, was founded in 1959, three
years before the corresponding national society was separately established. Indeed, for some years the largest sociology department in Canada has been the one at Edmonton, not Toronto. By the middle 1960s,
graduate programs leading to the M.A. were appearing at several prairie
universities and a Ph.D. program in both sociology and anthropology
was underway at Edmonton. A quarterly journal, the *Canadian Review*

of Sociology and Anthropology, has been appearing for about five years, edited first at Toronto and now at McMaster University. Last year the Western Association of Sociology and Anthropology decided for the first time to publish its annual proceedings,[9] something the Canadian Sociology and Anthropology Association has not yet done.

It is in this context of educational, cultural and professional expansion that we should view the migration of the Sorokin library and papers from Cambridge to Saskatoon. This in no way detracts from the credit properly due to the University of Saskatchewan for acquiring these papers. It was a notable coup, as every sociologist in North America will acknowledge with admiration and no doubt with a dash of envy.

III.

NOW TO STILL ANOTHER question: what is the nature and significance of Sorokin's view of North American society?

In general, Sorokin looked upon North American society as a part of a much larger entity: Western society or Western culture. Further, he took a very long perspective. Starting with the early societies of the eastern Mediterranean region, Western society, according to Sorokin, has alternated between two types of mentality – sensate and ideational. Each phase lasted several centuries, and then gradually gave way to its opposite. By *ideational*, Sorokin meant a culture emphasizing otherworldly values, supersensory faith, and absolute ethical principles. Sensate culture, on the other hand, stressed worldly and materialistic values, utilitarian and hedonistic ethics, and sensory sources of knowledge. For example, cognition in an ideational age depends heavily on divine revelation; in a sensate era, cognition is based mainly on sensory perception and empirically oriented science. Historically speaking, ancient Greece and Rome from approximately the fourth century B.C. to the fourth century A.D. constituted the first major sensate epoch. The second sensate age emerged about the fourteenth century and is still continuing. The European middle ages Sorokin classified as ideational, and likewise the period before the sixth century B.C. in ancient Greece and the Near East.

The scope of Sorokin's theory of change in cultural super-systems is conveyed by the following lines:

> In the course of the historical unfolding of the Graeco-Roman and Western cultures, its supersystem has twice repeated the triple rhythm of Ideational-Idealistic-Sensate phases, from the twelfth century B.C. to the end of the Middle Ages, and after the fifteenth century for the third time entered the sensate phase, which is seemingly declining at the present

time. . . . Moreover . . . we have traced somewhat similar rhythms even
in several other cultures, like the Hindu, the Chinese, the Arabian, and
a few others. . . .

In regard to the nature of the true reality—the number of possible answers is very limited. . . . first, the nature of true reality is supersensory
(Ideational premise); second, it is sensory (Sensate premise); third, it has
both aspects inseparable from one another (Idealistic premise). . . . The
same can be said of the main styles of art: Ideational (Symbolic), Visual
(Sensate), and Idealistic (Integrated Symbolic-Visual). . . .

So also in regard to the main forms of ethics. Any integrated system of
ethics may be either that of Absolute Imperative or the ethics of Sensate
Happiness in its eudemonistic, utilitarian, and hedonistic varieties. . . . [10]

This is no more than an over-simplified sketch of Sorokin's theory of
social change, which was set forth in detail in a four-volume work, *Social
and Cultural Dynamics* (1937–1941), with applications to art, philosophy,
law, ethics, and social relationships. The important characteristics of this
approach, for present purposes, are the very long time—several
centuries—allocated to each phase of the cycle; the alternation between
the two main types; and the primary focus upon values, ideas, meanings—
upon what the Marxians would call "super-structural" elements—rather
than on such other components as socio-economic organization or
institutions.

Sorokin's third type of cultural mentality, the "idealistic," has not
been mentioned here, because it is simply a comparatively short-lived
blend of the other two. He found only two such periods in Graeco-
Roman and European history: the fifth century B.C. in Greece; and the
thirteenth century A.D. in western Europe. Both marked the transition
from ideational to sensate culture. For the reverse transition—sensate to
ideational—the phenomenon does not occur, although in his last publications Sorokin came back to the idealist blend, now restyled "integral
culture."

Sorokin interpreted the mounting crisis in Western society today as
signs of a collapsing sensate era and the beginning of a shift back toward
an ideational age. Remarking in 1937, a depression year in North America, that optimism about the future was shrinking even in the United
States, he went on to say:

Every important aspect of the life, organization and the culture of Western society is included in the crisis. . . . We are seemingly between two
epochs: the dying Sensate culture of yesterday and the coming Ideational
culture of the creative tomorrow. . . . The night of the transitory period
begins to loom before us and the coming generations. . . . [11]

And in 1941, he wrote:

> Contrary to the prevalent opinion [in the United States during the 1920s
> and early 1930s] in my works I indicated that wars and revolutions were
> not disappearing but would grow in the twentieth century to an abso-
> lutely unprecedented height . . . that democracies were declining, giving
> place to various kinds of despotism; that the creative forces of Western
> culture were drying up . . .[12]

This is surely a very different spirit and prospect from those expressed
by many previous Western social thinkers. The growing optimism of that
earlier day was never more strongly voiced than by Antoine-Nicholas
de Condorcet, Marquis of France. Writing about 1793, during the Great
French Revolution, which in another year or two would claim his own
life, Condorcet declaimed as follows:

> Our hopes for the future condition of the human race can be subsumed
> under three important heads: the abolition of inequality between nations,
> the progress of equality within each nation, and the true perfection of
> mankind. . . . Is there on the face of the earth a nation whose inhabitants
> have been debarred by nature herself from the enjoyment of freedom and
> the exercise of reason? . . . In answering these questions we shall find
> in the experience of the past, in the observation of the progress that
> science and civilization have already made, the strongest reasons for be-
> lieving that nature has set no limit to the realization of our hopes. . . .
> All the causes that contribute to the perfection of the human race . . .
> by their very nature exercise a perpetual influence and always increase
> their sphere of action.[13]

This optimism conveyed the self-confidence of a rising middle-class
urban industrial social order which still had all the world before it. As
the nineteenth century wore on, it became the prevailing view in western Europe and North America. There were other currents of opinion,
of course, but they remained in the minority until the First World War
in Europe, and perhaps until the Second World War in North America.
Even in the late 1940s Henry Luce in LIFE Magazine, a voice of imperial
America, could trumpet the future of the "American Century." However, Europe had suffered by the 1920s what Toynbee called a "loss of
nerve." Even before that time, such writers as Spengler and Pareto had
turned their backs on linear theories of progress of the "onward and
upward forever" variety. They were working on cyclical conceptions of
history. Indeed, a comparison of the poet Tennyson's "Locksley Hall
Sixty Years After" (1883) with the much earlier "Locksley Hall" suggests
that his disillusionment with the new industrialism was already far
advanced—a straw in the wind of changes yet to come. Let us glance
briefly at the change in Tennyson.

From "Locksley Hall" (written before mid-century):

> Men, my brothers, men the workers,
>   ever reaping something new;
> That which they have done but earnest
>   of the things that they shall do.
>
> Till the war-drum throbb'd no longer,
>   and the battle-flags were furl'd
> In the Parliament of man,
>   the Federation of the world.
>
> Not in vain the distance beacons.
>   Forward, forward let us range,
> Let the great world spin for ever
>   down the ringing grooves of change.

From "Locksley Hall Sixty Years After":

> "Forward" rang the voices then,
>   and of the many mine was one.
> Let us hush this cry of "Forward"
>   till ten thousand years have gone.
>
> Is it well that while we range
>   with Science, glorying in the Time,
> City children soak and blacken
>   soul and sense in city slime?
>
> Far away beyond her myriad
>   coming changes earth will be
> Something other than the wildest
>   modern guess of you and me.

In contrast to the optimists of perpetual progress Sorokin may perhaps be classified as a pessimist, at least to the extent that he foresaw an indefinite time of troubles immediately ahead. For the long run, he forecast an ideational revival, and he wrote about it in glowing, almost ecstatic terms. I think he was a deeply religious man, though not a church-goer according to his autobiography. In his later writings, after his "retirement"[4] to emeritus status in 1955, he referred increasingly to the possibility of an "integralist" culture emerging sometime after an era of continued sensate decay. In the early 1960s, as he spelled it out in *The Basic Trends of Our Time*,[5] integral culture is clearly another name for his concept of "idealistic" culture. It involved an ideational revival, but one that retained certain sensate elements like science and rationality, perhaps under the auspices of the Oriental societies. For the East–India, China, Japan–had already made extensive progress toward adapting such western patterns as science and technology to their own ancient culture heritages, and their obvious success in "kicking out the white man" seemed promising to Sorokin. But he left us no detailed predictions.

The scale of Sorokin's analysis was too vast to permit of much attention to particular societies. Because he was primarily concerned with ideas, with broad value premises of a philosophical nature, his conceptual scheme is too large a mesh to catch concrete social institutions. In such books as *Russia and the United States*[16] (published in 1944 to further Soviet-American understanding, and quickly relegated to oblivion by the subsequent emergence of the Cold War), we can obtain a slightly better picture of how he would have gone about analyzing a particular society as a whole. He found a number of similarities between the two nations, and concluded that this fact was conducive to "unbroken peace" between them. The general approach, however, still rested heavily upon value-orientations rather than on an organizational framework. Sorokin's description of North American society can be deduced, for the most part, from his general theory of cultural super-systems.

I should now like to compare an organizational and historical analysis of North American society with Sorokin's cultural frame of reference. In so doing, I see the former as complementary to the latter, not a substitute for it. In the course of this discussion, it will be argued, among other things, that Sorokin's seemingly pessimistic view of North American society was not pessimistic enough.

IV.

As a comparative exercise, it is interesting to take a dialectical approach to the social and economic development of North America. Let us assume that major changes in the social structure of a society result from oppositions. From a dialogue or collision of incompatible interest-complexes may eventually emerge a new institutional pattern which is not like either of the original complexes, but which probably includes elements from both—most likely in unequal proportions, depending on the particular case.

For example, in his well-known study of four modern social revolutions, *The Anatomy of Revolution*,[17] the historian Crane Brinton concluded that the end-result of these four great upheavals, once they had run their course, was neither a restoration of the *status quo ante*—though in every case some important elements of the old order clearly reasserted themselves—nor was it something new like the interim revolutionary regime. And, of course, each of his four cases had a number of unique aspects. Brinton wrote his book under the influence of Pareto, but our dialectical premise is borrowed from Marx.

Our first concern in this discussion must be with the United States sector of North American society, because it is by far the largest, the wealthiest, the most powerful, the most nearly sufficient unto itself. In truth, Canadian history, possibly since American independence but certainly since the mid-nineteenth century, has been in great part a secondary reaction to American developments, a pale reflection of American strategems and American drift. I hope this interpretation will not offend this Canadian audience, but the chips must fall where they may.

Moreover, having recently visited and read about Mexico, I have come to believe that we ought to broaden our concept of North American society to include Mexico as well as Canada. Their history and institutions are very different, yet in significant respects each may be seen as an exploited hinterland of the American metropolis. Like a knife slicing cheese, the aggressive agrarian and commercial imperialism of nineteenth-century America could carve great chunks of territory out of pre-industrial Mexico—an Indian and peon society itself ruthlessly exploited by the Catholic Church and a small Spanish upper-class of big landlords and military adventurers. But American expansionism northward was effectively staved off by the string of Canadian colonies, occupied by a similarly motivated, ascetic and commercially acquisitive population, and—above all—backed by the mighty British empire. British power soundly spanked the United States in the War of 1812–14, and forced a compromise in the Oregon northwest boundary dispute at mid-century. The decisive Canadian-American confrontation would come later. However, an analysis of the Mexican role in the North American metropolis-hinterland drama must await another occasion.

Since the symbiotic concepts of *metropolis* and *hinterland* play a leading role in this presentation, let me take a moment to clarify their meaning. I use the term *hinterland* to denote relatively underdeveloped or colonial areas which export for the most part semi-processed extractive materials, often including people emigrating from the country to the city. *Metropolis* symbolizes the centres of economic and political control which are located in the larger cities. It may also refer to urban upper-class elites or over-classes of one sort or another. *Hinterland* may usefully include urban under-classes as well as rural peasantries and rural proletariats. Finally, we must think of hierarchies of metropolitan-hinterland relationships. As northern Saskatchewan in key respects may be viewed as a hinterland of southern Saskatchewan, so Saskatchewan itself is a hinterland primarily of eastern Canada: and Canada, of the United States. Needless to say, the United States likewise includes a complicated network of hinterland or under-class groups, regions, marginal "colonials," and so on.

Because hinterlands sooner or later tend to fight back against their metropolitan exploiters in order to gain a larger place in the sun, the metropolis-hinterland frame of reference, like that of over-class and under-class, lends itself well to a dialectical approach to the history and sociology of a society.

» «

We have advanced the premise that major changes in social structure result from oppositions. However, this does not mean that all structural changes in a society come about in this way. At least one other leading mode of structural change suggests itself. That is the impersonal, un-planned[18] evolution of large social processes. As illustrations of this category of change, we may point to the cumulative development of science and technology, many migrations, and the emergence of large-scale corporate organizations in business and the modern state. This type of change seems to consist of the realization of the potentialities inherent in a system, the unfolding of immanent tendencies, as facilitated or retarded by external or local and varying conditions. Max Weber's concept of "rationalization" appears to cover what I have in mind. Sorokin's concept of immanent change is also relevant. However, rationalization, immanence and dialectical oppositions are not necessarily mutually exclusive concepts and processes.

Returning now to the problem of major oppositions and resultant resolutions in United States history, we readily discern at least two during the nineteenth century. The first was that confrontation leading to the American civil war, 1861–65. It consisted of the competitive clash between two increasingly divergent societies – North and South – both based on capitalistic economies which had to expand or perish. By mid-century, the outcome of the contest was no longer in doubt. The Northern coalition of commercial and industrial interests, linked with the western farmers, steadily forged ahead in wealth and power. In 1860, with the election of Lincoln, the control of the national government passed to the new order. It only remained to win the civil war and make the victory official. As usual, the old regime preferred to initiate a desperate counter-revolutionary war rather than to acquiesce in its own displacement.

> Viewed under the light of universal history, the fighting was a fleeting incident; the social revolution was the essential portentous outcome. . . . The capitalists, laborers and farmers of the North and West drove from power in the national government the planting aristocracy of the South. . . . The physical combat merely hastened the inevitable. As was remarked at the time, the South was fighting against the census returns that told of accumulating industrial capital, multiplying captains of industry,

expanding railway systems, widening acres tilled by free farmers. Once the planting and the commercial states, as the Fathers with faithful accuracy described them, had been evenly balanced; by 1860 the balance was gone. . . . Viewed in the large, the supreme outcome of the civil strife was the destruction of the planting aristocracy which, with the aid of northern farmers and mechanics had practically ruled the United States for a generation.[19]

No other war in American history, before or since, ever made such an indelible impression on the people, the memories, and the traditions of the American people and their descendants, both North and South. When the death of latter-day American hero-presidents like Franklin Roosevelt and John Kennedy were memorialized and publicly solemnized, the poem invariably recited was Walt Whitman's great elegy to President Lincoln: "When Lilacs last in the Dooryard Bloomed." The greatest American national crisis evoked the greatest national poem. Subsequent American crises, because they have been lesser, have merely echoed the greatness of that earlier day.

» «

The second great opposition in recent American history began to take shape soon after the end of the Civil War. As the immense expansion of post-war American industrialism got under way, nurtured by the new protective tariff, by public subsidies to transcontinental railroads, and by the fabulous resources of the West, rumblings of discontent and revolt appeared among workers, miners, farmers and various other colonials. Frustrated farmers, excluded from the feast for one reason or another, organized to raise hell instead of corn. Strikers fought pitched battles with police and militia-men across the country. Socialist splinter groups sprang up here and there, and numerous other strange counsels and cults alarmed the ruling burghers. By 1900, a fledgling indigenous Socialist movement led by Gene Debs was under way. In 1912, the various Socialist groups together received 6.3 percent of the popular vote for the Presidency. But since then, the combined Socialist percentage of the American presidential vote has steadily declined. It was seven-hundredths of one per cent in 1956.

What happened? Why did the emerging opposition collapse? Why did the opposition to capitalism, generated by capitalism as predicted by Karl Marx, collapse immanently in the United States, where the lack of non-capitalistic alternatives and the absence of anti-capitalistic traditions should theoretically have made for a classic case of socialist displacement of capitalism? The basic reason seems to have been the over-success of American capitalism.

The fantastic resources of the American heartland; the absence of any competing traditions or rival aristocracy; a vast domestic market protected by a high tariff; an endless supply of cheap immigrant labor; friendly politicians in control of the national government (which owned more than half of all land in the nation in 1860), eager to help, and to share; these are the factors pointed out by the historians Charles and Mary Beard as the key elements in the "triumph of business enterprise."[20]

And when, much as Marx had predicted, capitalism began to generate the resisting forces of labor organizations and populist agrarian revolts toward the end of the nineteenth century, those thrusts, in the case of the United States, were turned aside by a combination of sharing the goodies at home and imperialistic expansion abroad. The crisis of the 1890s threatened by the closing of the frontier was resolved in part by extending an investment frontier beyond the national boundaries. Indeed, as William A. Williams,[21] another American historian, has shown, it was the rural colonials—farmers and small-town processors in the American hinterland—who pressed most strongly for market expansion abroad. Some of the disappointed colonials moved to the Canadian prairies for a second try.

In other words, interest-groups that feel deprived strive first and foremost to improve their position in the going economic system. With a few adjustments, the system then carries on—with a few new faces at the head table. A parallel conclusion was reached by McCrorie in his recent study of the Saskatchewan farmers' movement in the twentieth century.[22] The American farmers got markets; later they got subsidies. American labor turned to "business unionism." The real process was much more complex, naturally.

The foreign expansion of business was decisively and irreversibly reinforced by the effects of two relatively cheap world wars that brought still further economic growth. On another level, the Keynesian and social-security reforms have likewise bolstered the fairy-tale American version of capitalism since the 1930s. In our own generation, the military and space budgets, which Thorstein Veblen would have called waste, have operated as additional investment frontiers. In truth, the limitless sky has become the limit. It all adds up to the most fantastic success story in human history. It staggers the imagination.

My central concern, however, is not the dynamics and contours of American history, but certain consequences that appear to follow from them, in the light of our dialectical premise. Since the First World War, there has been an absence of great oppositions in American society. Competition has been sharp, often nasty, sometimes violent. But no new phi-

losophy, with organizational resources and potentially decisive mass support, has arisen to challenge seriously the prevailing pattern of corporate
structures and middle-class style of life. The hippies have opted out for
their own encapsulated thing; some student groups may drop out, turn
on, or even sit in; the Blacks—so far—simply riot; the old left is largely
defunct; the new left—at least in the foreseeable future—has far less organizational and mass support than has George Wallace's reassertion of
traditional white racism. Practically everyone that matters, power-wise,
in the United States accepts the American way of life. The protests seem
negative; none of them sounds positive.

The absence of major oppositions acts as a block to the necessary
structural changes that might adapt the United States to the modern
world. The investment frontiers abroad are successively being closed out
by the rising revolutionary tides of nationalism and communism. The
Soviet revolution of 1917, the Chinese upheaval of 1949 have slammed
the door on American expansion in those vast and heavily populated
heartland regions. Latin America could follow suit any day, any year. Yet,
in this mounting crisis, there is no dialogue, no positive opposition in
American society. On the contrary, there is rigidity and nativistic revivalism. In this perspective, the decline of American society may have
set in two or three generations ago. It is interesting to note that Toynbee,
in his study of civilizations, puts very early in his grand cycle the shift
from a creative to a dominant (i.e. uncreative) minority, even though a
long period of increasing national power and glory may follow.

The oppositions to American society and to the American ethos are
today external rather than internal. This further impedes meaningful dialogue between Establishment and Opposition, by virtue of the emotional barriers of nationalism and racism. Yet without such a dialogue,
without massive and positive oppositions, the United States may well
become increasingly obsolete, like the dinosaurs that in a long-ago age
failed to meet the challenge of their own time. Unfortunately, the
United States still bestrides the world like a muscle-bound and inflexibly
programmed colossus. It holds the fate of all of us in a finger-tip poised
above a nuclear push-button.

The problem of the United States in 1969 is not primarily Vietnam.
"Uncle Sugar" could get out of Vietnam tomorrow without fundamentally altering his underlying dilemma. Moreover, the real problem of
American society is not even the ghetto-encapsulated blacks. The crisis,
the failure of nerve, the Achilles heel of American civilization surely lies
in the colossal, almost indescribable failure—and need—to face up to
itself.

The central issue of the mid-twentieth century is how to sustain democracy and prosperity without imperial expansion and the conflicts it engenders. . . . The way to transcend tragedy is to reconcile the truths which define the tragedy. . . . To transcend tragedy requires the nerve to fail. . . . For the nerve to fail has nothing at all to do with blustering and self-righteous crusades up to or past the edge of violence. . . . For Americans, the nerve to fail is in a real sense the nerve to say that we no longer need what Turner calls "The gate of escape" provided by the frontier. . . . The traditional effort to sustain democracy by expansion will lead to the destruction of democracy.[23]

Using different terminologies, a number of writers have come to similar verdicts—Veblen, Sorokin, Walter Lippmann, Paul Sweezy—to name but a few.

"Over-success as failure"—that is just another label for the same thing.

Once there was a way to get back homeward,
Once there was a way to get back home . . .

sang the Beatles in their *Abbey Road* recording of 1969. Once upon a time it was not too late to retreat. But not any more.

» «

The case of Canada, in the light of our dialectical premise, appears somewhat different from that of the United States. Regional and class oppositions have always been prominent in Canadian history. Above all, today we have Quebec and the Anglo-French confrontation. It is not entirely impossible that Quebec may yet be the salvation of Canada, especially if she secedes, as seems increasingly likely.

In several important senses, the development of Canadian society may be seen as a reaction to and reflection of events in the United States. Confederation in 1867 was a belated response to the obvious economic successes achieved by American independence and unification of the colonies, especially in exploiting the resources of the West. The Hudson-Mohawk route from New York to the interior proved superior to the St. Lawrence route. The business and financial interests of Toronto and Montreal slowly realized that they could look only to Western Canada for their new investment frontier.

Accordingly, in the third quarter of the nineteenth century, the "National Policy" gradually took shape. It has been admirably described in the works of the late Vernon Fowke, who surely needs no introduction here. Suffice it to say that the National Policy comprised western agricultural settlement, large-scale immigration to the west, a heavily subsidized transcontinental railroad, a protective tariff, an easy land policy to facilitate settlement, and the research necessary to adapt agriculture to semi-arid prairie conditions. There were a few other incidentals, too. Rupert's Land had to be acquired at a handsome purchase-price from the Hudson's Bay Company, and the Indians had to be brushed out of the way by means of low-cost treaties and a bargain-basement reserve system. This latter coup, a worthy echo of the Elizabethan poor law, has come back to haunt us today.

To see the Canadian National Policy as a secondary reaction to American developments is not to detract from the Canadian achievement. The remarkable thing is that so much was accomplished. Resources were less; obstacles were greater. South of the Great Lakes, for example, the land was fertile, and hospitable to farms, towns and commerce. But north of the Lakes was a thousand miles of rocks and bush.

We should avoid any notion that the American and Canadian developments we have been discussing were mainly or perhaps even largely planned ventures. Probably the most we can say is that some insightful entrepreneurs in both societies successfully read some of the signs of the times, and acted accordingly. But long-run impersonal forces surely account for much of what happened. You may have noted that in speaking of the disappearance of oppositions in the United States, I avoided the term co-optation. This was because it implies the idea that "someone planned it that way." I suggest, instead, that this was simply the way the system or situation worked out. Fowke has put the matter in this way:

> The National Policy was not by itself sufficient to make Western development possible on the scale eventually attained. The establishment of the prairie wheat economy, which may be regarded as its first major economic triumph, was accompanied by tremendous economic expansion throughout the entire Canadian economy, and was an integral part of a complex of dynamic forces which pervaded the western world. Professor Mackintosh has spoken of the "conjuncture of favourable circumstances" which marked the transition from the nineteenth to the twentieth century and which gave to Canada three decades of unprecedented expansion. This conjuncture of world circumstances created the opportunity for Canadian expansion, but a half-century of foundation work along the lines of national policy had prepared Canada for the opportunity.[24]

Canada has reacted, in part, to the fantastic American economic expansion of the past generation by a considerable degree of assimilation to the American empire. The economists describe this process as "continentalism." George Grant has attacked that development as a key decision, taken without public debate, by the eastern establishment in his *Lament for a Nation*.[25] Once again, I suggest that this in large part is simply the way the situation works out. Certainly the ongoing expansion of the American empire in Canada materially lessens the needed opposition between Canada and the United States. Like the colonials of an earlier day, Canada appears to have sought a better place in the sun by opting into the dominant system.

Moreover, even for the United States, that "conjuncture of favorable circumstances" which carried forward so profitably the American and Canadian sense of manifest destiny no longer holds:

> For the common attribute of contemporary events is not their responsiveness to our designs, but their indifference to them. . . . History less and less presents itself as something we find or *make*, and more and more as something we find made for us.[26]

Afterthoughts are now arising in Canada with respect to the ongoing American economic takeover of Canada. The old National Policy no longer serves to provide Canadian enterprise with a distinctive, Canada-oriented focus. What is to take its place?

Only two alternatives seem possible. One – doubtless the most likely – is a continued drift toward continentalism as is now occurring. The other is a Canadian Castro. However unrealistic this may at first appear, I see nothing between these two extremes. Here we may revert again to Quebec. Some years back, the Province of Quebec nationalized an American-owned corporation – Quebec Hydro – and borrowed the money from the Americans to pay for the takeover. We should all reflect at length upon this event. We might just possibly make it financially worthwhile for the Americans (who know a good business deal when they see one) to finance Canadian independence. And we can always hope to scale down the interest rate in due time.

The real leader of the opposition in Canada today is not Mr. Stanfield, but René Lévesque, leader of the moderate faction of Quebec separatists and a socialist by inclination. It is a far-out speculation on my part that an independent Quebec might precipitate significant confrontations both in Canada and the United States. I feel sure only about two points: first, large, bold and risky confrontations will be necessary, and soon, if we are to avoid the catastrophe toward which we are drifting in the wake of the American decline. Small compromises will hardly do. Second, we have nothing whatever to lose.

» «

My conclusion, then, is that an organizational, dialectical approach to North American society is a useful supplemental to the supersystem mentality perspective used by Sorokin. It also produces much more pessimistic results. By Sorokin's method, one may see the present as a tough transition to something better—that is, more integrated and harmonious than contemporary sensate society. By the dialectical method, as applied to the particular North American context at this particular time—for the results in this case are not merely a function of the method, but also of the specific time and place—by the dialectical method, then, one can scarcely escape a grim picture of the North American present as stark tragedy.

Notes

1 *A Long Journey: The Autobiography of Pitirim A. Sorokin*, P. A. Sorokin. College and University Press, New Haven: 1963. This book is both a self-portrait and a social history of an era. It should be read by everyone interested in the quest of the human spirit for survival and understanding.

2 *A Long Journey*, p. 249.

3 *Social and Cultural Dynamics*, P. A. Sorokin. 4 Vols., Bedminster Press, New York: 1937–1941 (reissued 1963). Vol. III, p. 342.

4 *A Long Journey*, p. 247.

5 *The Innocents at Cedro*, R. L. Duffus, Macmillan, New York: 1944, p. 160.

6 *Democracy in Alberta*, C. B. Macpherson, University of Toronto Press: 1962, p. 220.

7 *Twentieth Century Populism*, T. Saloutos and J. Hicks. Lincoln: 1951, p. 32.

8 *Industry Comes to a Prairie Town*, D. Willmott. Canadian Centre for Community Studies, Saskatoon: 1963. Organizations and Social Life of Farm Families in a Prairie Municipality, Canadian Centre for Community Studies, Saskatoon: 1964.

9 *Perspectives on Regionalism*, B. Y. Card (ed.). University of Alberta Bookstore, Edmonton: 1969.

10 *Social and Cultural Dynamics*, IV, pp. 737–740.

11 *Social and Cultural Dynamics*, III, 535.

12 *The Crisis of our Age: The Social and Cultural Outlook*, P. A. Sorokin. Dutton, New York: 1941, pp. 13–14.

13 *Sketch for a Historical Picture of the Progress of the Human Mind*, Antoine-Nicholas de Condorcet, London: 1795 (1955 ed, Weidenfeld).

14 Sorokin published more books after his "retirement" than most writers publish in a full life-span.

15 *The Basic Trends of our Time*, P. A. Sorokin. College and University Press, New Haven: 1964.

16 *Russia and the United States*, P. A. Sorokin. Dutton, New York: 1944.

17 *The Anatomy of Revolution*, Crane Brinton. Vintage Press, New York: 1957.

18 Unplanned as a whole, that is, however rationally the component actions may be planned and executed.

19 *The Rise of American Civilization*, Charles and Mary Beard. Macmillan, New York: 1927. Vol. II, pp. 54–99.

20 *The Rise of American Civilization*, Charles and Mary Beard. Macmillan, New York: 1927. Chapter 20.

21 *Roots of the Modern American Empire*, William A. Williams. Random House, New York; 1969.

22 All that my Saskatchewan friend Roy Atkinson, President of the National Farmers' Union, is trying to do by organizing a National Farmers' Union is to give farmers an effective trade association such as most other categories of capitalistic entrepreneurs have long enjoyed. A more conservative, truly capitalistic, goal could hardly be imagined.

23 *The Tragedy of American Diplomacy*, William A. Williams. Dell, New York: 1962, pp. 303, 307–309.

24 *The National Policy and the Wheat Economy*, V. C. Fowke. University of Toronto Press: 1957, p. 70.

25 *Lament for a Nation*, George Grant. McClelland and Stewart, Toronto: 1965.

26 *The Future as History*, R. Heilbroner. Harper, New York: 1959. Torchbook paper edition: 1968, p. 55.

American Decline and Fall

However stifling the policies of the United States since World War II, American progressives have assumed that some bright day, sooner or later, these dreary blunderings must come to an end. Then this nightmarish old regime will give way to a brave new era, and a rejuvenated America will resume its place in the forward march of civilization. Socialism perchance will displace capitalism. Just how this great transition will take place evokes bitter arguments. But that it will somehow occur has seldom been seriously doubted. Long-run optimism has been the common premise of the contending splinters on the American Left.

Seen from afar, the grounds for that optimism look pretty shaky. It is entirely possible that the United States may be unable to generate enough creativity to get out of its present ruts and to set itself a new course. The menace of hydrogen war is a symptom rather than the cause of the sterility that has crept up on American society in recent years.

What are the reasons for doubting the capacity of the United States to free itself from its present straitjacket and to solve its problems constructively?

Progress comes from oppositions. It is made possible, though not necessarily certain, by the emergence of incompatible social conditions and group aspirations. Eras of progressive social development seem to require, at least in their critical initial phases, the confrontation *and* resolution of decisive oppositions among peoples or classes. From the clash of thesis and antithesis comes a new synthesis—if circumstances are favorable—and this may become the basis for a new epoch of more gradual social evolution.

But in the United States today there is precious little opposition to the domestic and foreign policies of the ruling circles. No important faction has yet challenged the cold war. The phony principle of anti-Communism is still the sacred cow of American politics.

By contrast, an organized mass movement committed to ending the cold war, to peaceful coexistence abroad and to renewed social reforms at home—that sort of movement would clash head-on with current American policies.

This is not to say that the American scene is one of harmony. Nasty conflicts chronically flare up among competing business groups, farmers, labor unions, and various minorities. The overriding opposition between capital and organized labor is one of two or three major dynamic forces in American life. But these struggles are waged for bigger shares of pie. They do not call into question the righteousness of the system by which the pie is baked.

For instance, the slogan of Negro movements like the National Association for the Advancement of Colored People has been "Count us in," not "Change the system." The rising Negro bourgeoisie, according to Frazier, has no quarrel whatever with the American way of life, aside from its discriminatory aspects. If Frazier's acid portrait is true, large sections of the black bourgeoisie delude themselves with conspicuous consumption and sham achievements which for pure hokum surpass the white bourgeois standards they ape. The new Negro middle class wants in at the head table. Nothing more.

And was this not also true of the right-wing movement called McCarthyism? This motley collection of Texas oil kings, up-and-coming but still insecure Irish and German groups, and other frustrated social climbers used anti-Communism as a club against the upper-class Eastern aristocracy. When McCarthy rashly took on key figures in the Eisenhower administration, which speaks primarily for the bluechip elements of the Eastern oligarchy, then his wings had to be clipped. McCarthyism, wrote Viereck, with more than his customary perception, "is the revenge of the noses that for twenty years of fancy parties were pressed against the outside window panes."

The main competing interest groups in the United States have a common slogan—"Me too!" As for really fundamental oppositions with mass followings—there aren't any.

Nevertheless, beneath the surface there are great pressures building up for change in the United States. Abroad, United States foreign policy is in a hopeless impasse. The rebirth of Russia and China and their successful transitions to socialism, the advancing rebellion of colonial people against fading Western imperialisms—these irresistible move-

ments, the most decisive of our time, the United States quixotically resists. Leading an inherently unstable coalition of fossilized puppets on
the one hand, and of capitalist powers with acutely divisive interests on
the other, and seeking blindly to negate the chief affirmative tides of the
age, American foreign policy, even in Latin America, seems fated to pass
from one strategic defeat to another.

At home the pressures for change are no less massive than those from
abroad. The American economy leans heavily on war spending and
other forms of systematic waste. So great is the expanding productivity
of this glittering economic machine that its distributive channels are periodically inadequate to accommodate the flow of its goods and services.
Without waste it would collapse. And the amount of waste, even on
today's colossal scale, is not always sufficient.

The looming crisis of the cities seems almost enough by itself to promote revolutionary alterations in the national structure. Faced with rising costs and demands for new services, straitjacketed by archaic financing and administration, American cities are approaching the brink. They
need money, streamlined management, coordinated highway and mass
transit systems, vast housing and redevelopment programs. Schools, universities, and health services need overhauling and expansion. No reasonable authority disputes these points. Never has the country been better able to pay for massive improvements. Yet the United States is merely
nibbling around the fringes of most of its urban problems.

This paradox of the cities' deepening financial crisis in the face of
a steadily growing national income strongly suggests that there is something basically wrong with American society. Most Americans live in
cities or in suburbs. But cities and other local governments are legal creatures of the states, which are dominated by gerrymandered rural minorities. For funds, cities must depend chiefly on the obsolete real estate
tax and on state grants. Urban financial reform requires a reconstruction, not simply of local taxation, but of the entire apparatus of federal,
state, and local public finance. Regressive property and sales taxes need
to be largely replaced by progressive personal and corporation income
taxes, federally collected, then allocated in part to local governments
for spending.

Inseparable from the financial problem, and just as acute, is the administrative crisis. There are about 100,000 unstandardized, uncoordinated, overlapping, inefficient governmental units—school and tax districts, cities and towns, counties, special authorities, and so on. Many
state lines are irrational. Needed are two flexible types of local government: metropolitan areas consisting of a central city and its satellites,
and enlarged rural counties. These should be grouped, not in states, but

in a few great regional authorities – like the Tennessee Valley Authority, only with more powers and functions. At the top should be a stream-lined national government.

The present divisions of powers between the federal and state governments, and between public and private interests, are embalmed in the federal Constitution, adopted in 1789. It is hard to see how the American financial and administrative tangle can be straightened out without writing a new Constitution. How else can political structures and boundaries be revised on the necessary scale? How otherwise can the key powers and functions be transferred from the private to the public sector of the economy? The great questions which confront the United States cannot be resolved, or even faced, except in the framework of a nationally planned – and planning – social order.

Beneath its lush exterior, the American social system is like an engine out of whack, gradually beating itself to pieces. Its imbalances have become so overdeveloped that efforts to repair it along traditional lines may upset it still more. A crash program in education, for example, would cast new burdens on the already archaic public-finance machinery. Piecemeal reform, exalted by the liberals, may actually worsen the situation as a whole.

In view of these mounting foreign and domestic crises, why are there no basic oppositions in the United States? Chiefly, I suggest, because of the overdevelopment of American capitalism.

American society unfolded in relative isolation during the nineteenth century. It waxed great on the limitless wealth of a virgin continent. It grew without competition from earlier social traditions. There was nothing to compare with Europe's carryovers from pre-industrial feudalism. There were only the Indians – primitive hunters and neolithic cultivators, easily brushed aside.

Since the founding of the republic, significant oppositions have appeared only twice in American history. The first was the struggle for the West waged by the agrarian capitalism of the South and the rising commercial-industrial capitalism of the North. This epic contest was settled by the Civil War, 1861–65. The second, never concluded, consisted of the various farm and labor movements which appeared in response to the industrializing boom that followed the Civil War. Let us briefly consider each.

Soon after independence, a picture of the United States as a westward-moving nation began to take shape. Political leaders gave substance to that image. Writers gave it voice.

At first the popular conception of the western utopia was agrarian. Would the West be exploited by large slave-labor plantations or by small freeholds? Two variants of capitalism, both of which had to expand or perish, contended for the mastery of the West. For three generations the southern oligarchy successfully dominated both the domestic and foreign policies of the United States. As wasteful cultivation exhausted the soil of the old South, new lands had to be acquired in the West, while the older plantations turned to breeding slaves for the new estates. Continued southern control of the federal Senate depended upon increasing the number of slave states. This could be done in two ways: organizing new slave states in the American West, and stealing foreign territory—from Mexico, for example, in 1848.

The interests of the more populous commercial and industrial capitalism of the North demanded the expansion of markets and raw materials by new western settlements based on free labor. With the Republican Party as its vehicle, an alliance of the agrarian-commercial Northwest and the commercial-industrial Northeast finally won national power—legally—in the election of 1860. Civil war was then precipitated by the South, just as all other great modern civil wars have been started by discredited Old Regimes. No room for compromise remained. One social system could expand only by restricting the other, and neither system could survive without expanding.

The issues and dynamics of the Civil War were perceived most clearly by a special London correspondent of the *New York Tribune*, which spoke in the 1850's for the radical Northern bourgeoisie. That correspondent was Karl Marx, whose stunning *contemporary* insights into that titanic conflict have stood up far better than those of most later historians.

The second massive opposition in the history of the American Republic began to develop with the industrial boom after the Civil War. As industrial capitalism triumphantly spanned the continent, class conflicts sharpened. Epic labor battles broke out. Agrarian revolts flared. The first seeds of modern socialism took root. By the end of the century, elements of various farm, labor, and other groups were taking up socialist positions.

The beginnings of a mass socialist movement were unmistakable. A socialist newspaper, *The Appeal to Reason*, reached a circulation of 600,000, with special issues running in the millions; Socialists were elected to local offices; Gene Debs running for President in 1912 got 6.2 percent of the popular vote—the best showing a professing socialist has ever made in an American presidential election.

Until World War I, the American economy was running generally true to the course that Marx, a half century earlier, had foreseen as normal for capitalism. Capitalist conditions of production, he had said, would produce a disciplined and eventually anti-capitalistic labor force, which would be driven to reject capitalism and adopt socialism.

Still another symptom of intensifying crisis became evident around the turn of the century. This was the resurgence of imperialism. In the years before the Civil War, as conflict between the rival capitalisms came to a head, there had been aggressive ventures abroad – the steal from Mexico in 1848, filibustering in the Caribbean area, intrigue in the Pacific, and a "me too" policy in the Far East, where England and France were leading the bloody suppression of the Chinese Taiping revolution. Now, a half century later, its fever chart again rising, American capitalism once more turned to beating in the doors of its Latin American neighbors, seizing concessions in the Pacific, and muscling in on the plunder of prostrate China.

What changed this prospect of rising political ferment? What cut off the development of the second American opposition before it could mature?

Wars, hot and cold.

Two world wars, which ruined large parts of rival European powers, brought great prosperity – cheaply – to the United States. Various bush wars and the present cold war have pressed in the same direction. The leftward-moving labor opposition to capitalism has been counteracted and bought off. Enough benefits of economic imperialism and of systematic waste of capitalism's surplus product have filtered down, or have been wrested from Big Business by unions and other interest groups, so that those potentially dissident elements which count have been harnessed to the chariot of the vested interests.

Wars have made it easy to herd would-be critics into conformity by levelling against them the weight of unthinking patriotic emotion and by excommunicating them as "un-American." Today when progressive Americans take part in such movements as nuclear disarmament, they take stands which are usually much too conservative for the crisis at hand. Perhaps they remember past reprisals and their present comfortable jobs. Doubtless they exemplify the isolation of their society – they cannot fully realize the urgency of hungry and hopeful Asians, Africans, and Latin Americans, nor can they grasp the moral callousness of their own society. And is it not also true of other Western nations, England and France in particular, that their left-wing movements have been blunted by sharing some of the benefits of imperialism? One thinks of how the British Labor Party equivocated with colonialism after World War II. One recalls the shameful record of the French Socialists, and the ambivalence of the French Communists toward Algeria.

Today, there is no Left in the United States. There are only left-wing splinters with no apparent prospect of gaining a mass following. In nearly every other Western industrial nation, the political spectrum includes Right, Center, and Left elements – this is the normal state of affairs in late-modern capitalist societies. Socialist or Communist parties, or both, are part of the social landscape in West Germany, France, Italy, England. Even Canada has a small but influential social democratic party.

But the United States has only the two major parties, both dominated by business interests, and both covering about the same Right-to-Center range of the political spectrum. American politics is a complex uneasy compromise among more conservative and less conservative factions of the Right and Center. By means of concessions and piecemeal reforms, the system operates to prevent the emergence of a genuine Left. So effectively has this mechanism worked – given the uniquely favored position of American capitalism in the world situation – that most Americans have no idea of the potentialities afforded by a Left party. They have been conditioned to regard socialism as monstrous. Yet many, if not most, of the basic needs of the United States can be met only by a mass leftist movement committed to socialist reconstruction. That there is no political machinery to express and fulfill those needs is one of the big reasons for believing that the United States may be headed down a one-way, dead-end street.

The table on the next page shows that the socialist movement reached its peak in the United States before World War I. After 1912 it withered on the vine. Each little spurt of life in 1920, 1932, and 1948 was weaker than the preceding one. By 1956 the socialist vote – seven hundredths of one percent – was as infinitesimal as the prohibition vote. The table also shows that the Communist Party, which took over the leadership of American radicalism in the 1920's when the Socialist Party became hopelessly ossified, never became acclimated to the American scene. The notable contributions of the Communist movement to American life lie in the fields of labor organization and special causes and crusades rather than in the party arena.

The widespread idea that the New Deal regime of the 1930's had a socialist underpinning seems basically false. Whatever may have been its intellectual debt to the Socialist Party platforms of a previous generation, the New Deal was no more than a reform of, and within, the existing institutional framework of capitalism. It performed two services for capitalism: it broadened social security, and it made government spending a permanent and primary channel for disposing of capitalism's surplus product. It was assured of success by a timely and cheap world war.

The figures also indicate that, insofar as capitalist-oriented reform movements have taken the form of third parties, they have steadily decreased in scale since 1912. In that year the Roosevelt Bull Moosers won over one-fourth of the popular presidential vote; in 1924 La Follette got

U.S. Presidential Votes by Minor Parties, 1892–1956

	Total Popular Vote for President	Socialist and Socialist Labor Presidential Vote		Communist Presidential Vote		Other Independent Parties	
		000	% Total Vote	000	% Total Vote	000	% Total Vote
1892	12,044	–	–	–	–	1027 (Populist)	8.5
1896	13,813	36 (SL only)	.3	–	–	132	.9
1900	13,965	128	.9	–	–	50	.4
1904	13,524	436	3.2	–	–	115	.9
1908	14,887	435	2.9	–	–	112	.8
1912	15,031	926	6.2	–	–	4126 (Progressive)	27.5
1916	18,528	600	3.2	–	–	46	.2
1920	26,813	927	3.5	–	–	410	1.5
1924	29,091	36 (SL only)	.1	36	.12	4848 (La Follette)	16.7
1928	36,812	289	.8	49	.13	46	.1
1932	39,751	918	2.3	103	.26	65	.2
1936	45,647	197	.4	80	.18	1177 (882 Lemke)	2.6
1940	49,820	110	.2	49	.10	472 (417 ALP)	.9
1944	47,976	106	.2	–	–	1012 (496 ALP, 329 Lib)	2.1
1948	48,834	168	.3	–	–	2488 (1169 Sts Rts, 1156 Prog.)	5.1
1952	61,552	50	.08	–	–	335	.5
1956	62,027	42	.07	–	–	623	1.0

Compiled from *Statistical Abstract of U.S.*, 1957, p. 341.

one-sixth; in 1948 the "progressive capitalism" of Henry Wallace drew only a little over two percent. In the last three presidential elections, reactionary splinter parties have actually attracted more votes than reformist splinter groups.

American politics now seem completely monopolized by two slowly fossilizing parties incapable of meeting the demands of the times. But this decline into impotence and inflexibility began, not with the abandonment of the New Deal in the late 1930's, as many progressives imagine. It began with the first World War, which cut off in its infancy a potentially decisive tendency toward the Left.

» «

The external relations of the United States as well as its internal conditions tend to confirm the suspicion that the United States may have "had it."

During the greater part of history the leadership of world social evolution has fallen mainly to the more urbanized societies of the Near
East, China, and India. This leadership is now returning to the East.
Today's transition from capitalist to socialist industrialism is one of the
great divides of history, comparable perhaps to the development of agriculture in prehistoric neolithic times – comparable also to the emergence of city life, writing, and metallurgy centuries later, at the dawn
of recorded history.

The major oppositions in which the United States is now involved
are external rather than domestic. They will confirm rather than lessen
American isolation. Against outside societies can be mustered the
thought-stifling emotion of blind nationalism. The United States has become dangerously separated from the main drift of world civilization.
Its chief assets – those unique geographic and historical conditions
which nourished it to world power – are now contributing to its undoing.

Many Americans still see their country through the eyes of the "frontier ideologists." The ideology of a frontier Eden, where old-world shackles have been cast aside, was erected on the material foundation of
capitalism developing unhampered in the fabulously rich American
heartland. Today, America still inclines to see herself both as a departure
from, and a lesson to, a decadent Old World. From this viewpoint, the
United States can take either of two attitudes toward Eurasia –
renunciation or Americanization – "fortress America" or "manifest destiny." During most of American history, have not public policy and opinion fluctuated between those two alternatives?

The frontier ideology expresses the uniqueness and superiority of
American civilization as seen by Americans. But the graveyard of history
is littered with the shattered claims of "chosen peoples."

Seen from afar, the problem of the United States is neither to escape
from the Old World nor to Americanize it. The real task is to relate –
peacefully – to the great currents of social regeneration now flooding the
Eurasian heartlands – eastern Europe and China today, the Middle East
and India and Africa – and, yes, Latin America – tomorrow. This will require a rebuilding of American economic and social institutions, for
American institutions are the cause of the disastrous American policies.

It is a measure of the isolation of the United States from reality that
its policy-makers still operate as if "fortress America" or "manifest destiny" are practical choices. But it is a measure of the tragedy of the
United States that the American people respond to such insanity with
indifference – and without opposition.

Freedom Under Socialism:
Summary and Comment

I N WINNING PEOPLE to socialism, no issue is more crucial than that of freedom under socialism. The discussion in recent issues of *Monthly Review* clearly poses the problem and takes us far toward a valid solution. Let us summarize the essential points made by Messrs. Kaminsky, O'Sheel, and Bachrach, and by the editors of MR.

Kaminsky's very capable lead-off article (November, 1950) starts with the contrast between the apparent freedom of Americans to oppose their government and the evident absence of that freedom in socialist countries. If socialism negates freedom, what claim can it have to anyone's loyalty?

The solution of this perennial dilemma is Kaminsky's basic theme: *every social system develops its own version of freedom.* He explicitly rejects the liberal conception of freedom as a natural right, an abstract liberty to do and think as one pleases quite apart from any social order. He equates this "abstract freedom" with the "civil and individual rights" specific to capitalism. Socialist freedom must differ from capitalist freedom, which indeed socialism negates by its revolutionary reordering of society. During the transition, people who cling to capitalist freedom will naturally consider the new order tyrannical, and some of them will be coerced. But eventually recognition of the benefits of socialist discipline will prevail, chiefly through education, as the dissenters are drawn willy-nilly into the forward flow of socialist life. And once acclimated, people will for the most part carry out their socialist duties spontaneously, thus minimizing the need for external authority. Kaminsky's final point denies the validity of what he calls "hodge-podge" socialism which seeks to retain the "good" aspects of capitalism while getting rid of the "bad." Capitalism must be accepted or rejected in its entirety.

In their comment (December, 1950) the editors of MR accept the central Kaminsky thesis that socialist freedom differs from capitalist freedom, and that the transition, while primarily an educational process, is in part coercive. But, they ask, how coercive? Why can't socialism, once consolidated, incorporate at least some bourgeois civil liberties and operate according to the canons of "due process of law?" Isn't Kaminsky unduly inclined to take the socialism of the USSR and eastern Europe as a model for American socialism regardless of significant differences in conditions and background?

To this query Kaminsky responds (February, 1951) that socialist freedom is based on collective ownership of the means of production with maximum central planning and control, whereas bourgeois freedom presupposes a private-enterprise economy with minimum governmental activity. Trying to combine the two implies eating one's cake and having it too.

Like the editors, O'Sheel (February, 1951) endorses the main Kaminsky thesis but enters a qualification concerning the extent of the differences between capitalist and socialist freedoms. That there will be some—perhaps considerable—carryover of capitalist liberties into the socialist era he affirms on three grounds: (1) revolutionary rigor is not permanent; (2) socialist society will not be entirely new but will preserve important elements of capitalist social structure; (3) man's unique biological traits of reasoning and inventing for progress require free communication. Societies restricting communication (civil rights) dangerously hamstring themselves in the competition for progress, and even if some are so short-sighted as to try it, "human nature will break through." (We must discard O'Sheel's biological frame of reference as untenable. But if we read "social" for "biological," the essential idea remains unaffected.)

O'Sheel also takes issue with two of Kaminsky's subsidiary points: that Americans can freely oppose their government, and that under socialism there will be no freedom to err. The latter he attacks as a precise parallel to the "pretensions [to infallibility] by which the shamans of all religions have cowed the masses."

Kaminsky's reply (February, 1951) cites the publication of MR as proof that Americans can oppose not only their government but also their social system. The charge of religious fanaticism he accepts: every era has its basic principles and whoever deviates must pay the price. (Does he not confirm the O'Sheel contention that we cannot *freely* oppose our social system?) On the main question whether there will be a cultural carryover from capitalism to socialism and hence at least a partial survival of bourgeois freedom in socialist society, Kaminsky yields ground: "Socialism, like capitalism before it, marks a step in the perfection of the social order."

Thus far the discussion has merely qualified the original Kaminsky thesis. Bachrach, however, entirely rejects it (February, 1951). Adhering to the abstract definition of freedom, he declares that no socialism is worthwhile unless it preserves bourgeois civil liberties. This, he continues, the USSR has signally failed to do. If we do not denounce the Soviet denial of these liberties, how can we logically attack the Vatican's intolerance? And since, according to Bachrach, Marxism is not an exact science and hence not infallible, all the more reason for preserving bourgeois civil rights to facilitate criticism and change of official dogma. Soviet gains, the reality of which Bachrach does not deny, cannot compensate for the absence of freedom in Russia.

Kaminsky responds (February, 1951) that Bachrach's anti-Soviet axe-grinding completely begs the question of the nature of socialist freedom, that Bachrach is really interested in maintaining bourgeois freedom, not in defining or attaining socialism.

» «

It seems to me that Kaminsky's central thesis, as modified by the editors and by O'Sheel, is fundamentally sound. Certain points deserve sharpening, however, and some additional issues need consideration.

We must clearly distinguish between the general (formal) prerequisites of freedom and the specific social institutions which give freedom its substance in time and place. The ideals and institutions of each social era provide the *content* of freedom. The discussion summarized in the previous section focused exclusively on the content of freedom. In the present section we shall introduce the formal aspect of freedom, returning in the next section to specific versions of freedom.

The formal aspect of freedom refers to those broad functions which every social order must effectively fulfill in order to operate as a reasonably stable going concern. In this sense, freedom is a universal which each epoch realizes in varying degree and through the medium of different specific institutions. For the general functions of a social system can be met by various concrete social structures, depending of course on existing conditions.

Before we get into our subject more deeply, we must rid ourselves once and for all of the naive notion that freedom means the right to do "anything." Kaminsky calls this the liberal or abstract idea of freedom, and he rightly rejects it. Taken at face value, it is anti-social. A society in which anyone could literally do anything would be no society at all, but anarchy—the absence of order. Thus defined as random action, anarchy makes either for the war of each against all, or for apathy—both of which negate social life.

Yet the liberal idea of freedom has too much tenacity and too many adherents to be so easily disposed of. If its explicit formulation—the right to do anything—reduces to an absurdity, what is its underlying substance? Clearly, it can only be the specific freedom of bourgeois society universalized into a mythical absolute as one facet of capitalism's egocentric illusion of its own superiority over other social orders. In the stable phase of capitalism, of course, many individuals feel they *can* do "anything." This really means that they can successfully realize a high proportion of the goals which capitalism teaches people to seek. It means that conflicting values simply do not occur to enough people to upset the prevailing impression of freedom.

The truth is that every society trains its members to seek certain socially approved goals by acceptable means. If those goals are compatible—that is, if the society is well integrated and efficiently organized—then the members *feel* free. They are doing what they want to do—but they learn from growing up and living in their own society what to desire and what to shun. Since behavior patterns differ from one society to another, it follows that what constitutes freedom varies likewise. This is the validation of the Kaminsky thesis that every social order develops its own version of freedom. In the liberal idea of freedom, then, we see bourgeois freedom dressed up as an absolute.

It is of the utmost importance to emphasize that no specific version (content) of freedom has any standing outside its own social setting. But presenting a specific freedom as an absolute, universally valid, is not merely a rank violation of truth and logic. Far more significant from our present point of view is the fact that the ideology of absolute freedom operates to preserve the existing social order. For instance, whoever regards American freedom today as an absolute value, perhaps imperfectly realized but essentially changeless as an ideal, must for this very reason accept capitalism, since in reality that freedom is produced by capitalist society. He will necessarily view any other version of freedom as tyranny; he will react spontaneously against any other social order. In a showdown he is in the capitalist camp, and that is what counts. He may criticize certain features of capitalism—usually its domestic aspects—but ultimately he is bound to its chariot by his commitment to what is inseparable from capitalism. Once bourgeois freedom has been successfully portrayed as absolute freedom, anti-capitalist sentiment is diverted automatically into such harmless channels as paper utopias and verbal reformism which, to the extent that they involve more than mere words, look essentially to the perfection of capitalism. The very possibility of working for a non-capitalist social order is precluded by defining freedom as an absolute. This is the snare into which Bachrach has fallen, along with the cohorts of American reformers–the Republocrat "liberals," the Norman Thomas Socialist Party, the shallow prattlers of the "vital center." Let us call it the *squirrel cage fallacy*–because its unsuspecting victims, like the caged squirrel on his wheel, go blithely through the motions of progress but get nowhere.

A prerequisite of a vital socialist movement in America is breaking the intellectual bondage of the myth of absolute freedom, and recognizing that freedom is a house of many mansions, one for every social order. Once they are clear on this fundamental principle, some of the people now in the reformist wing of the capitalist camp will gain the insight and courage to join in the quest for genuine socialism.

Let us now return to the formal or universal aspect of freedom. Given any social system, what are the general prerequisites of freedom?

To survive, every society must perform certain functions. It must reproduce new members, teach them to carry on its traditions, meet the problem of social change, produce and distribute goods, keep aggression within bounds, and so on. *How* these functions are carried out varies widely. But whatever its specific nature, a given social order is stable to the degree that (1) its social structure is harmoniously integrated; (2) it effectively trains new members; (3) it successfully adapts itself to changing conditions, internal and external; (4) it harnesses the frustration of its members–for no society is perfectly integrated.

Insofar as these conditions are realized, the members of a society well *feel* free and will *consider themselves free*, whether they are African nomads or American capitalists or Russian Communists. In its formal aspect–the only one which can be defined in terms valid for any social system–freedom is a state of mind, a subjective feeling of well-being resulting from the objective fact of living in an effectively functioning society. In this sense, "freedom" is to any social order as "health" is to any biological organism. Both terms refer to the state of a going system; neither can be identified with any particular part of the whole.

From the definition of formal freedom three conclusions follow. *First*, the extent of freedom under socialism depends on how well a socialist order can meet the problems inherent in modern industrial society. On theoretical grounds alone we can recognize that the intense specialization of industrialism requires central planning and control to coordinate the economic system. To larger proportions of the people than under any other system, socialism offers the potentiality of escaping from scarcity and exploitation. But the final proof is life itself. That socialism "works" is clear from the Russian case, which we may cite as compelling evidence because socialism there became a going concern despite a minimum of advantages and a maximum of obstacles. Under the acid test of massive invasion by a Nazi Germany in control of the resources and manpower of most of Europe, the Soviet order retained the intense loyalty of the great majority of its citizens and mustered the strength to defeat the attack. This should dispose of the "Slave State" myth. Not that all Russians were free or felt free. In a revolutionary transition era this could not be true. But the people were clearly sufficiently convinced by past and prospective progress that they were on the right track to remain intensely loyal. What capitalist-trained people think of the Soviet order is largely irrelevant for deciding how much freedom the Russians enjoy. What really matters is what the Soviet citizens themselves think.

Second, socialist freedom differs in content—that is, in its specific rights and duties—from capitalist freedom, because the two social orders are different. But they do not differ throughout. I shall try to show later that we must expect considerable carryover of capitalist behavior patterns (including much of the present substance of "due process" norms) into socialism. In principle, however, we need to underline Kaminsky's strictures against the hodge-podge variety of socialism, which promises the "good" aspects of both capitalism and socialism with the evils of neither. Every system, including socialism, has features that are evil *by its own standards*, since no society can be perfectly integrated. We must remember, too, that how we feel *now* about various actual or prospective socialist institutions is no indication of how we will feel about them after socialism has been fully realized in America. Confusing present with future attitudes is a short cut to the squirrel cage fallacy.

Third, during the transition to socialism freedom will be reduced in rough proportion to such factors as the speed of the transformation, the hostility of the international environment, and the amount of disorganization in the society at the start of the transition. A transition era is unstable, especially if it takes the form of a revolution, which can perhaps be best defined as very rapid and pervasive change in a social system. The old ways no longer function effectively; new ones are not yet worked out. Some of our most ingrained and hard-learned habits and attitudes are abruptly upset by the impact of fast-changing social conditions. To the strain which comes from facing both ways at once there are various responses. Many people reject both competing societies and relapse into apathy. Others latch onto utopian panaceas: in the new Jerusalem are many prophets. Still others over-react and attempt to suppress by force one or the other pattern. The net result is almost sure to be intensified frustration, which negates our four conditions of stability and therefore decreases freedom.

A new social order, once built, is not burdensome if it meets the four conditions, and there is every reason to believe that socialism does meet them. It is the transition which is painful. The sharp curtailing of freedom observable in socialist countries today is due mainly to the inevitable but temporary conditions of social change, not to the socialist system itself. Two facts, then, must be faced realistically: the potential rigors and decreased freedom of the transition, and the distinction between the unstable interim period and the stabilized socialist epoch.

Reviewing the universal aspect of freedom as a subjective feeling of well-being caused by living in any relatively well integrated society, some readers may be skeptical. By definition, whoever feels free is satisfied with the existing order. Since a majority of Germans supported Hitler, doesn't this make Nazi Germany a free society? Within limits, yes. *But freedom under fascism is inherently temporary, because fascism does not solve, but in the long run only intensifies, the problems of capitalism.* Nazism brought a relative freedom to most Germans, who could behave more as they wanted to than before. It also brought extreme oppression to sizable minorities of Germans. But what is most important is that the freedom of the Nazis to act as they wanted to was certain to lead them and everyone else into disaster. Ultimately, the necessary consequence of fascism is foreign imperialism and domestic catastrophe – the very negation of our four prerequisites of freedom.

Socialism, on the contrary, *can* resolve the tensions of capitalism and thus achieve a stable freedom. The degree to which socialist society is unfree – as we have already noted, every social order generates *some* frustration – is largely due to the necessity of preventing people from acting as they want to when what they want to do would be harmful and perhaps even fatal for the vast majority of the people concerned.

» «

We now turn from the form to the content of freedom – from the universal aspects or prerequisites of freedom to the ideals and social institutions which give to freedom its specific meaning in a particular epoch. More precisely, we return to the questions raised in the first section about the concrete nature of freedom under socialism. Here we deal with freedom not as a state of social integration, but as a set of living values. Our main problem is the extent to which bourgeois freedom and toleration can be carried over into socialism. Kaminsky minimizes the possibility; O'Sheel and the editors take a less narrow view of the chances. The second case, I think, is the stronger.

To demonstrate a carryover of capitalist freedom into socialism, it is necessary to show that some approved bourgeois values and behavior patterns are present and approved in socialist society, and that there are no insuperable obstacles to their realization.

The case for expecting the preservation of certain bourgeois freedoms in the era of *stabilized* socialism rests on the fact that capitalism and socialism are variants or successive forms of the same general social type–urban-industrial society. The history of modern times hinges on the post-medieval movement from the self-sufficient peasant community to large-scale industrialism. In the West, developed capitalism is now recognizable as a passing phase of the larger transition to socialism, since a mature industrial society clearly requires central planning and collective ownership of the means of production.

As the industrial order develops through capitalism into socialism, two aspects of social life that become increasingly prominent are bureaucracy and science. On them depends much of the continuity between bourgeois and socialist freedoms. Let us examine them in turn.

By "bureaucracy" we mean any large-scale hierarchy of specialized and coordinated offices, the basic unit of which–the "office"–is a set of impersonal systematized rules spelling out the rights and duties of the incumbent. Authority lies in the office, not in the person of the incumbent, whose powers and procedures tend to be explicitly defined, hence limited. Obedience is to the legal order, embodied in written files and precedents, rather than to the particular office-holder. *Bureaucracy in this sense is obviously the indispensable frame work of the modern industrial world.* States, corporations, armies, and all other large-scale, sustained enterprises require the bureaucratic type of organization to attain the coordination necessary to carry on their work.

Now is it not true that the bureaucratic pattern, with its impersonality and its systematic procedures is the very essence of our contemporary principles of "due process" and "law over men"? Of course it is. To emphasize the organic relationship between bureaucracy and our rational legal system, we may note that the only stable non-bureaucratic type of authority is the highly personal, vaguely defined power of the local lord or elder in a small-scale, self-sufficient economy, where custom and the chief's whim are the main determinants of authority.

By centralizing and streamlining the wasteful hodge-podge of capitalist economic and political bureaucracies, socialism will greatly refine and extend "due process of law." Without a monolithic bureaucratic framework, social planning is impossible. Let us not be misled by the present unpopular connotations of the term "bureaucracy." They are temporary reflections of our frustration by the *transition* toward centralism.

The specific rights and duties of the citizen and job-holder will be partly redefined under socialism. But the legal order, once stabilized, will assure due process and the limitation of arbitrary power. Here is one major element of bourgeois freedom which socialism alone can bring to full flower.

Another is science. It is the cornerstone of any industrial order. Capitalism has made notable advances toward the mastery of nature and the solution of the age-old problem of scarcity. It remains for socialism to extend scientific mastery from nature to society, and to accomplish the final conquest of scarcity.

The feeling of freedom in the formal sense can be realized in *any* society, even the most primitive, provided it functions effectively enough to permit its members to achieve the goals society teaches them to seek. In the modern world the rise of science and industrialism has fostered among us the ideal of maximizing man's rational control of his own destiny. Hence attaining freedom in our time is impossible without the radical extension of science. Primitive and peasant societies according to this standard (though not necessarily by their own original standards, of course) have only a slight degree of freedom because of their rudimentary control over nature. Capitalism broadens the realm of freedom by notably extending our mastery over nature. Socialism further extends the area of freedom by bringing not only nature but also society under rational human guidance. We could in fact say that science is the key to socialist freedom, because freedom in our epoch requires the understanding of necessity—of the laws of nature and society, and how they may be harnessed to social purposes. On this all-important point see the brilliant passage from Engels' *Anti-Dühring* (cf. *MR*, 1951).

Closely related to the goal of control over nature and society is the striving for freedom in the positive sense of the realization of creative self- and social development. Despite its great advances over previous eras, capitalism wins these freedoms for no more than a favored minority. The socialism of the transition may do little better, especially if the transition is abrupt. But the ultimate stabilizing of the socialist order will greatly broaden freedom for the many. In the growth of leisure and security we have for the first time on a mass scale the possibility of offsetting the intense specialism and uncertainty of modern industrialism with a more balanced life pattern, admired since the Greeks but attained only occasionally by elite minorities. Marx clearly expressed the basic relation between leisure and freedom when he said that

> freedom [in production] cannot consist of anything else but of the fact that . . . the associated producers regulate their interchange with nature rationally, bring it under their common control, instead of being ruled

by it as by some blind power. . . . But it always remains a realm of necessity. Beyond it begins that development of human power which is its
own end, the true realm of freedom, which, however, can flourish only
upon that realm of necessity as its basis. The shortening of the working
day is its fundamental premise. (*Capital*, III, 954.)

Socialism thus inherits many of its basic values from Hellenic and
Renaissance humanism, from the rationalism of the Enlightenment,
from the universalism of modern democratic ideals, and from science.
The bureaucratic framework, greater control over human affairs, higher
material standards of living, wider realization of the humanist ideal of
balanced self-development—these major elements of socialist freedom
are carried over from bourgeois, and to a certain extent even from pre-
bourgeois, society. And not just carried over, but greatly developed. In
a very real sense, as O'Sheel suggests, we may speak of socialism as fulfill-
ing the promise of capitalism.

Still another significant carryover will be the chronic ferment that
has long characterized the West. The tradition of primitive messianic
Christianity with its immanent anti-institutional bent; the secularized
utopianism of the eighteenth century and after; the inherent dynamism
of modern science and the drive for "progress"—all have entered directly
or indirectly into Marxism. Revolutionary goals, like "equality" and "fra-
ternity" in 1789, are never completely realizable, but their catalytic role
in producing social change is undeniable. The capitalist epoch has provided a long series of reform tendencies, great and small. What proves
that socialism has a similarly dynamic quality is its projection of Communism as the next, "higher" stage of society. Ideals like the "classless
society" and the "withering away of the State" may be currently unrealistic, but they guarantee ferment. The Russians, who consider themselves now in the stage of socialism, place the greatest emphasis on
achieving Communism. Requirements of organizational stability will naturally harness socialist dynamism, just as they have restricted capitalist
innovation, but they cannot eradicate what is built into Western social
structure itself. Change is always a compromise between the real and
the ideal.

Freedom in modern societies is not static. Its ideals and institutions
change over time, and the degree to which those ideals are realized varies too. We can judge the freedom of a society only by the extent to
which its own standards are *voluntarily* practiced. Coercion and freedom
vary inversely. Judged by its own norms—say, the Bill of Rights and the
philosophy of classical liberalism—capitalism is becoming less free. And
by their own values, socialist societies still have a long road ahead to

freedom, although in one or two of them a fair stretch has already been traversed.

Our next point concerns toleration. Can socialism match the undeniably great achievement of capitalism in tolerating nonconformity?

To compare toleration in socialist and capitalist societies we must take them in similar stages of stability. This we cannot yet do, since the existing socialist countries are still in the transition phase. Although the real Russian Revolution (the social reorganization represented by the Five Year Plans) got "over the hump" by the mid-thirties, final stabilization will take decades. Anti-Soviet diatribes like Bachrach's are therefore irrelevant. But we are not without some genuine insights.

We may expect considerable toleration from *mature* socialism for two reasons. The first is the stability of the post-transition era. No major contradictions in socialist states, beyond those associated with the reconstruction period, are yet in view. The second and more important reason is the complexity of urban-industrial life, with its flow of inventions and fads and its mobility of people and ideas, assuring a cosmopolitan atmosphere directly opposed to the intolerant conservatism found in the peasant world. Toleration has never flourished except in an urban setting. Socialism means an expansion of the industrialization and urbanization featured by capitalism.

But we cannot look for unlimited toleration. Nonconformity in any society must be restricted, or stability and perhaps the very possibility of social life are negated. We must distinguish between *verbal* and *organized* opposition to a social order. Self-confident integrated societies may afford wide scope to verbal criticism, but they react strongly against overt nonconformist activity. And under stress no social order tolerates even verbal opposition: witness the rising thought-control tendencies in America today. In its prime of life, capitalism showed unprecedented tolerance. Marx wrote unmolested for years in London; MR is freely published today. But the O'Sheel contention that capitalism tolerates mainly verbal rather than overt dissent is valid. American history is spattered with repressive sanctions (ostracism, economic and legal disabilities, coercion) against *active* dissenters like Abolitionists, Mormons, splinter parties, labor organizers, Communists.

In summary, there is every reason to expect not merely a carryover of certain basic elements of capitalist freedom into mature socialism, but the positive expansion of those elements. Other aspects of bourgeois freedom of course will be revised or removed. Central planning will remold, but not generally reduce, individualism. For the true bases of individualism are (1) a decreased scope for kinship-based factors like race, clan, nationality, and sex, which decide a person's life chances largely by the accidents of birth; (2) an increased scope for learned interests and activities, vocational and avocational. Developing during post-medieval times, individualism will be further broadened under socialism, as the rules of nature and society are progressively understood and harnessed.

» «

Freedom has many facets. We have discussed them on two levels: freedom as a resultant of social integration, and freedom as a set of specific ideals. The two aspects meet in the famous slogan: "From each according to his ability, to each according to his need." In the one sense this expresses a leading goal of socialism, the achievement of which has been relegated to the next major epoch—Communism. But in another sense it epitomizes the condition of any integrated social system. For people acquire both their skills and their needs from growing up and living in a community. If the society functions effectively, needs and abilities roughly match each other to realize both the necessities of social life and the aspirations of freedom.

There remains one question, the most important of all, the question of war and peace. Capitalism has doomed its achievements, including its own version of freedom, through its growing dependence on war as the main support for an over-producing economy. War is no longer compatible with modern society; war and freedom today are mutually exclusive. Capitalism has irrevocably failed to solve the problem of war. What about socialism?

There are several reasons for believing in the basically peaceful character of socialism. (The problem of peace or war *between socialism and capitalism* is beyond the scope of this article: we are speaking of socialism after it has spread to the major peoples of the world.) In western nations today the dominant groups cannot maintain themselves and their way of life without embarking on a course that inevitably leads to war. Once this war-breeding condition has been changed, once the chief economies of the world are rationally planned and internationally coordinated, once the main populations have passed through the industrial revolution to a common and stabilized cultural pattern—then the roots of modern war should largely atrophy. Not until then will the dream of world government become practically realizable. The peaceful character of socialism, in other words, will then find institutional expression. In the meantime, to demand the form of world federation without the content of world socialism is simply to invite frustration.

When world socialism has finally been reached, the real potentialities of freedom under socialism will unfold in the flowering of a richer, better integrated, and more universal society than the world has known before.

Social Theory and Social Problems*

Fragments for a Philosophy of Social Science

A WIDENING CLEAVAGE between social theory and the study of concrete social problems has been a prominent feature of academic social science–especially of sociology–for some time. This fact was set forth in a keynote statement to the recently organized Society for the Study of Social Problems, an association of professional academicians and researchers. In that statement the Society's first President, Professor Ernest W. Burgess of Chicago, listed the bridging of the gap between social theory and social problems as one of the six general aims of the new organization.[1] The gap still remains, however. Indeed, to venture a broader view, it appears that the social science of the universities, in this revolutionary epoch, has little to contribute either toward the understanding of our many-sided social crisis or toward the mastery of that crisis.

Does this not suggest an unhealthy alienation of academic social science from society? Not only do we academic social scientists today tend to bypass the central question of expanding the control of social forces in order to match the successes of the natural scientists in extending man's mastery of natural phenomena–not only do we thus depart from a traditional humanistic and utilitarian goal of modern science since Francis Bacon–but we also fail to convey a convincing and useful understanding of contemporary social reality to the rank and file of our fellow citizens. It is hardly to the professional journals and monographs that one would turn for meaningful explanations of the changes and conflicts that mold our lives. The inquiring mind would fare better in his search for realistic ideas about society if he scanned the little political

Reprinted by permission. *Philosophy and Phenomenological Research*, 18 (1957): 190–208. Brown University. © 1957, PPR, University of Buffalo.

and literary magazines far removed from the university towers.[2] More than one top-quality graduate student known to the present writer has withdrawn from academic social science, claiming to have found more obfuscation than clarification—more artificially departmentalized knowledge of the embalmed past than unified grasp of the living present.

Yet the universities, as the stronghold of science and learning, form a key institutional complex in Western capitalist societies. The university faculties may therefore be viewed as our nearest counterpart to what Max Weber, speaking somewhat one-sidedly of feudal China's scholar-officials,[3] called a culture-bearing elite. It appears, then, that an important segment of our culture-bearing elite—the segment including our academic social scientists and philosophers—is becoming less culture-bearing. This is simply another way of saying that certain aspects of academic learning are tending to become unduly segregated from some of the basic social trends of our age.

Against this general background, we address ourselves in this paper to four questions, each treated in a separate section. (1) What characteristics of social theory and the study of social problems account for the gap between these two academic fields? (2) How may this cleavage be bridged? (3) What ethical premises, common to *both* disciplines, currently help to maintain the cleavage and to block its bridging? (4) What alternative ethical premises for social science would facilitate a realistic synthesis of social theory and social problems? A fifth section will deal with some implications for the social control of science.

Some Characteristics of American Sociological Theory and the Study of Social Problems

The fields of theory and of social problems are the most abstract and the most concrete branches, respectively, of American sociology. As Karl Mannheim indicated in a 1932 paper,[4] the latter has received far more attention than has the former. To separate scientific theory from fact is of course to set up a false dichotomy. Some sort of theoretical orientation is implicit in every empirical study, and even the most abstract theoretical concepts presumably have empirical referents. In general, however, Mannheim's characterization of American sociology still holds. Studies having primarily theoretical interest have formed a distinctly minor current, flowing usually from European influences. Most of the work, especially in social problems, has been factual and often statistical.

Let us now consider separately some contemporary characteristics of the two fields. Our remarks should not be construed as aspersions either upon sociological theory or upon social problems. Notable advances have been made in both areas in recent years. The point is not that certain topics have been vainly studied, but that certain others have been comparatively neglected.

A. *Social Theory.* In late years the theoretical branches of sociology and of social anthropology, between which no intrinsic distinctions can be drawn, have become increasingly occupied with timeless, structural-functional studies, ideal types (models), hypothetical interrelationships among sociological and psychological variables, and minute analytical refinements of conceptual schemes that owe much more to logical manipulation than to empirical testing. These abstract conceptualizations strikingly resemble the normal-equilibrium schema of pre-Keynesian neoclassical economics, in that they are logical—Veblen would have said "taxonomic"—constructs leaning heavily on a premise of built-in stability and integration of the social system, and in that they fail to describe decisive aspects of the social reality, chiefly its dynamic and "problem" aspects. In brief, theoretical work in sociology has tended to become increasingly abstract, static, and nonhistorical.

Doubtless the most conspicuous theoretical school in recent years has been that developed by Professor Talcott Parsons and his colleagues.[5] We need not attempt to evaluate the Parsonian achievement here, beyond acknowledging it as a major landmark in American sociology, and beyond indicating that its general approach to social phenomena—notwithstanding its great contribution to analytical sophistication—tends to be static and highly abstract. Thus, its theoretical apparatus stresses structure rather than process, ideal types or models rather than concrete institutions, integration rather than conflicting interests. It focuses most effectively upon such relatively minute topics as individual personality, roles, and small groups, the analysis of which lends itself to a sociologized Freudian approach.[6] Applied to large-scale subjects, however, such as social classes and mass movements and entire societies, its analyses become cloudy and cumbersome. Like neoclassical economic theory (Professor Parsons' original field), it is a logically developed theoretical model, not a theory of any concrete society. It escapes no farther from its static approach than to present broad social movements as a series of still pictures—structural analyses each conceived as a more or less unstable equilibrium.[7] In dealing with German fascism, for example, Parsons places particular emphasis on the role of ideas and on Weber's concept of rationalization and its uneven incidence on, and frustration of, different segments of the population. While this helps to correct the Marxian underemphasis on such traditional elements as religion and the family, it is accomplished at the expense of almost completely overlooking the positive Marxian contribution. Some two generations ago, Thorstein Veblen was able to make much the same correction of Marxian neglect of factors making for traditionalism and inertia[8] without going to the extreme of suppressing the exceedingly relevant Marxian contribution to the dynamic analysis of class and economic interests in capitalist societies.

The intellectual antecedents of the Parsonian "theory of action"[9] show a pronounced tendency toward static analysis, and they underscore the unsuitability of Parsons' schema for analyzing social change. Pareto's sociology, which was one of the formative influences on the "theory of action," depended heavily on an equilibrium model. This is true even of his theory of social change, the "circulation of the elite," which Pareto conceived as a highly abstract, self-regulating mechanism. Another important influence on Parsons' work was Durkheim, whose over-riding interest was the problem of order and stability in society, and the key role of ideas therein. Freud, a third source, concentrated upon the microscopic world of the middle-class individual personality. The dynamic portions of his work were mainly limited to the life-cycle of the individual—psychodynamics rather than social dynamics.

Max Weber alone among these forbears dealt consistently with concrete historical processes. Much of his work, and most of his ambiguities, may be understood in terms of his life-long effort to replace Marxian historical materialism with a theory of change assigning causal primacy to ethical and ideal factors. But Weber retained too firm a grasp of history to commit himself unreservedly to a static and idealist approach to social phenomena. His comparative works on China, India, and Judea contain much realistic and dynamic historical analysis. However he might now and then force the role of ideas and ethical factors, his final conclusions on such points were usually stated as tentative suggestions in subjunctive mood. Perhaps it may be said that Weber in certain respects supplemented Marx without displacing him.

On the other hand, the American followers of Weber, lacking the latter's historical grounding, have moved much farther in the direction toward which Weber strove. The result is an intensively refined analytical apparatus that is, by and large, so nonhistorical and abstract as to be replete with concepts having ideal rather than empirical referents.[10] Hence it is not surprising that the Parsonian theory of action has been received by the empirically-minded majority of American sociologists, in part as an admirable *tour de force*, and in part as something of a flight from reality.

But the static tendency in current American social science is by no means confined to Professor Parsons' "theory of action." A much broader influence which, though greatly developed by Parsons and his associates, has profoundly influenced many other sociologists and anthropologists is the structural-functional approach. Since its inception more than a generation ago by the British anthropologists Malinowski and Radcliffe-Brown, functionalism has made for field work portraying nonliterate communities as they operate in the here and now. It depicts the community as being, more often than as becoming. Thus, Malinowski's references to the Trobriand past and future are few and far between, although the impact of European culture had clearly become the central dynamic process in Trobriand Society long before Malinowski began his field work there.

This has become the characteristic pattern for the majority of anthropological studies to this day, and for field studies of modern communities too, now that anthropologists like W. L. Warner have applied their attention and methods to advanced societies. The bulk of the typical field monograph, after a short introductory section on the historical background, is devoted to the statically conceived functioning of the community under investigation. As examples we may cite the main works of Radcliffe-Brown, Boas, Firth, Fortes, Evans-Pritchard, Margaret Mead, Lowie, Kluckhohn, L. Thompson, and Linton's earlier studies – to mention but a few names. It has been something of an exception for a community study to focus upon historical change as one of its major facets. Cases there are, of course, in varying degree – the works of Redfield and H. Kuper, Lynd's Middletown analyses, Leslie White, Bernhard Stern, Linton's posthumous volume on social evolution, and several important books by V. G. Childe. Warner's dynamic analysis of the evolution of the Yankee City economy to the strike of the 1930's, though hardly typical of that author's usual view, is another example.[11] On the other hand, one can read M. Fried's study of a Chinese village in the late 1940's[12] and scarcely become aware, except for an occasional incidental remark, that China was in the throes of a major revolution.

This is not to belittle the achievements of the structural-functional approach. It has taught us to view communities as wholes – at least in theory, for the relative neglect of the dynamic aspects of the whole has surely vitiated the practice. It has also taught us to look for latent as well as manifest functions, and much more besides. In technical development and general maturity, both sociology and anthropology are the better for the functional movement. We only say that an historical as well as a timeless approach is needed, before we can expect another major phase of scientific advance. In fact, much work now underway in social science already takes cognizance of relevant dynamic aspects. The predilection for a static-equilibrium frame of reference does not extend, for example, to those sociological fields which rely on time-series—e.g., population studies. A main problem in population analysis has been to relate demographic variables more adequately to their institutional contexts. The static nature of current institutional theory in sociology, however, seems to have retarded progress in that direction. That demographers have found economic history more helpful seems significant for our present thesis.

B. *Social Problems.* In contrast to social theory, the field of social problems is closely bound up with contemporary social changes and conflicts. Crime, delinquency, ethnic relations, revolution, war, mental disease—indeed, most of the subject matter of social problems—are more or less intimately related to the dynamic processes of modern urbanization and industrialization. This is expressly recognized by nearly every professional scholar in this field. A wealth of factual data, correlations, and empirical generalizations has been accumulated on many aspects of these problems.

A leading weakness of the field of social problems is its avoidance of, and its failure to discriminate, the more basic and controlling elements of the industrial revolution, especially where capitalist institutions are concerned. The scientific study of social problems suffers, not from a lack of touch with empirical reality as does social theory, but from an empiricism that fails to penetrate sufficiently beneath the surface of concrete phenomena. It suffers, in short, from an overabundance of superficial empiricism. Hence many of its correlations, such as that between criminality (as measured by arrests and convictions) and residence in the working-class "zone of transition," are not causal or functional explanations. They are simply statistical associations which have yet to be explained. Associations between parts must be related to the whole in order to be adequately understood. In other words, truly causal or functional explanations—a *sine qua non* of science—can be achieved only by relating the associated variables to a larger group of analytical elements constituting an autonomous or self-sufficient system—in this case, the social system of modern capitalism viewed as a changing whole. Thus, whether criminality causes residence in slums, or vice versa, or whether both variables are responses to a third set of forces, such as perhaps the social class system, are questions which cannot be answered without resorting to a theory of social systems that deals with wholes as well as parts.

Most professional treatises on social problems today hinge their discussions on the key fact of social change, and a few of them use a specific theory of technological change—Ogburn's well-known formulation of culture lag.[13] Probably the commonest theoretical approach to social problems, however, is the catch-all one of "value-conflict," viewed against a backdrop of vaguely conceived social change.[14] The equally heterogeneous "multiple-factor" theory of causation is widely used. So, too, is the "vicious-circle" approach, wherein the factual association of bad housing, crime, delinquency, broken families, and poverty is presented in such a way that each tends to be explained in terms of the others. But none of these methods gets us very far analytically; all of them operate on a relatively superficial level of generalization with respect to causation. The chief exception is the widely used case-history type of analysis, a well developed method which reveals how particular individuals are drawn into "problem" behavior and situations. Here, however, the focus is upon the individual life-history, not upon the problem pattern, which is simply taken for granted.

From the professional literature on social problems, then, we can readily learn how Jack Doe happened to become a delinquent in his youth, but we will learn much less about the deeper relations of juvenile delinquency to the social structure as a whole. Why does delinquency persist in our society, what interests does it serve, what frustrations does it relieve? Such questions tend to be avoided in academic treatments of social problems, although the recent books by M. L. Barron and A. K. Cohen are encouraging exceptions.[15] Cohen argues that delinquency is a subculture which is essentially a working-class response to the frustration stemming from the unattainable middle-class norms of economic and occupational success. He shows that the delinquency subculture consists of behavior that is consciously malicious (especially toward property), versatile, non-utilitarian (unlike much adult crime), and carried out by strongly knit male gangs. It is the opposite of bourgeois individualism stressing long-range career goals, respect for property, "wholesome" recreation, education and self-restraint. Cohen's penetrating analysis is a long step ahead, however, of the typical treatment of delinquency in the field of social problems.

As a summary of this section on social theory and social problems, some remarks by the late Charles A. Beard on American social science are worth recalling:[16]

> The spirit of American scholarship in the social sciences is intensely empirical. . . . It seems to be widely believed also that the selection, amassing, and organization of social data can proceed in a kind of vacuum, beyond the influence of assumptions, hypotheses, and predilections. The belief appears to be held as a truth, rather than cherished as a method or device for escaping the pressure of primitive notions in the community. . . . Every student of the social sciences brings to his choice of areas

for research, his detailed investigations, his selection of data, and his organization of materials some more or less clearly developed assumption and scheme of valuation. . . .

And what schemes of organization and valuation have generally prevailed among American scholars in the social sciences? In the main the system of British Manchesterism has prevailed, with modifications in detail. . . .

But the efforts of American scholars to bring to pass a social synthesis by the application of the empirical method have come to a dead end. This fact is not generally admitted. Indeed, it is stubbornly contested. Yet the guess may be hazarded that on this point the history of American social thought is destined to turn in the not distant future.

Bridging the Gap between Sociological Theory and Social Problems

Doubtless the main reason why the field of social problems has derived relatively little stimulation from sociological theory lies in the static nature of the latter. A predominantly static social theory cannot explain a dynamic social reality. This was the essence of the strictures directed at the orthodox economics by Thorstein Veblen two generations ago.[17] Many of his criticisms are applicable to academic sociology today.

Sociological theory would greatly profit from closer contact with the more empirical and realistic bent that prevails among the students of social problems. It would be favorably affected by the latter's keener awareness of the key importance of a dynamic approach to the ongoing industrial revolution that constitutes modern times.

In turn, the study of social problems would be significantly advanced by a more self-conscious theoretical integration of its empirical data, not only to deepen its insight into phenomena, but also to illuminate the possibilities of social control and remedial action. Such a theory must clearly be a theory of social change and, eventually, of the historical development of types of societies. And just as clearly it must also be a theory which views conflict and crisis as inherent in the changing social system rather than as external and accidental. Only a dynamic theory of society—not of "society in general" which tends to be the object of Parsonian theorizing, but of our specific late-capitalist society—with empirical studies set in a context of an inherently changing and crisis-generating social system—only such a theory can bridge the present chasm between sociological theory and social problems.

So far removed are we now from any such theory that the few contemporary writers who have focused on immanent change and crisis—Sorokin, Toynbee, the Marxians—are not considered proper social scientists by the orthodox majority of sociologists. They are summarily dismissed either as "philosophers" or as "propagandists."

We do not propose to pursue further in this paper the merits and demerits of particular theories of change, but instead to address ourselves to the question, What philosophical preconceptions of academic social science obstruct the emergence of the desired dynamic-realistic theories on the one hand, and at the same time perpetuate, on the other hand, the present vogues of static abstract theory and of superficial empiricism in social problems? In other words, we seek to clarify the premises which, underlying *both* the fields of social theory and of social problems, operate to maintain the mutually stultifying cleavage between the two disciplines and to prevent the bridging of that gap.

These preconceptions, to be explained in the next section, may be called the ethic of neutrality and the ethic of nonideological science. They affect in varying degree all the professional social sciences, and even philosophy. Some of their effects are beneficial for the advancement of the social sciences. Without attempting to assess all their ramifications, we will call particular attention to one of their adverse consequences—a growing separation of academic sociology and philosophy from the great social issues of the age. Some of the symptoms of this dry rot were mentioned in the introductory paragraphs of this paper: the withdrawal of talented graduate students, and the faltering ability of professional scholars to illuminate the current world crisis.

As will appear in the ensuing discussion, we attribute the persistence of these philosophical premises less to intellectual forces than to the inherited cultural inertias and vested social interests which ultimately mold intellectual formulations, though not without being secondarily reacted upon in their turn.

Two Philosophical Premises Perpetuating the Gap between Social Theory and Social Problems

The first may be called the ethic of neutrality, which affirms that social scientists, as scientists (and often as private citizens, too), should avoid taking stands on policy aspects of the more controversial social issues. The second premise, closely related, may be styled the ethic of nonideological science, which means that the two categories, ideology and science, are assumed by orthodox scientists to be mutually exclusive. Science, they say, describes empirical relationships; ideology advocates a significant change in basic social structure and policy.

Together, these two premises form what we will call the "canon of orthodoxy" of modern academic sociology. Tacitly fostered in the main graduate training centers, it is widely held among professional sociologists and other social scientists. It is largely self-enforcing, once internalized by the individual scientist. Should deviation appear, it may often be controlled by such informal sanctions as labelling the transgressing view "philosophical" or "ideological," therefore nonscientific and out of bounds.

One result of these two preconceptions is that scientific orthodoxy in sociology tends to become identified either with small-scale studies of minutely refined empirical variables, or with abstract theorizing in terms of models sufficiently remote from reality to have no practical implications for understanding or controlling the social world we live in. Both fields, social problems and social theory, are thus affected by the canon of orthodoxy. They are affected advantageously by the considerable degree of immunity from political interference which the acceptance of the canon entails, and by the logical precision and control of irrational and emotional bias which they facilitate. They are affected disadvantageously by the restriction of scope and artificial separation from many basic social issues–a separation which, especially in revolutionary eras like the present, invites both the stifling of scientific creativity and the loss of its potential contribution to society, just when the need for the latter is greatest.

Let us now observe how the canon of orthodoxy can operate to obstruct the viewing of social problems as inherent aspects, rather than as accidental by-products, of our social structure. To look upon crime or delinquency or mental disease as immanent products of our evolving society (as some recent studies by Sutherland, Cohen, and Hollingshead indicate) inevitably invites some adverse value-judgments about that society, especially since those pathological phenomena seem to be spreading. But to state the fact that our social class system generates delinquency and mental disease is, according to the prevailing yardstick of orthodoxy, to enter the realm of partisan ideology. Effectively conditioned to avoid this scientific sin, the average social scientist will automatically turn aside. He does not do this, usually, because of any coercion by, or fear of, the beneficiaries of our class system who are ultimately his employers or directors. He turns aside because ordinarily he shares their values decrying "ideological and destructive criticism" and upholding the beneficence of our status system, of which he himself (in terms of relative prestige and even income) is a minor beneficiary. Coercion is generally unnecessary, except for a few atypical recalcitrants. On touchy subjects, therefore, the ordinary social scientist will tend to come up with a formulation so theoretically abstruse as to have no "destructive" implications–and little empirical relevance–or he may more likely find himself drawn into a comparatively innocuous field like small-group research, as Coser has indicated.[18] Veblen once put the matter succinctly, albeit acidly:[19]

> The official leaders of science do commonly reach conclusions innocuous to the existing law and order, particularly with respect to religion, ownership, and the distribution of wealth. . . . But this need imply no constraint . . . they are free to give the fullest expression to any conclusions or convictions to which their inquiries may carry them. That they are able to do so is a fortunate circumstance, due to the fact that their intellectual horizon is bounded by the same limits of commonplace insight and preconceptions as are the prevailing opinions of the conservative middle class. . . . The volume of work done is large and of substantial value, but it runs chiefly on compilation of details and on the scrutiny and interpretation of these details with a view to their conformity with the approved generalizations of the day before yesterday. . . . The influence of this academie science, both in its discipline and its tenets, appears to be wholly salutary; it conduces, on the whole, to a safe and sane, if not an enthusiastic, acceptance of things as they are, without an undue curiosity as to why they are such.

We perceive that stating the direct causal relationship between class and delinquency would be both a theoretical analysis of a social problem and a contribution to a realistic and dynamic sociological theory. By helping to deflect attention from the relationship, the canon of orthodoxy perpetuates the existing gap between social theory and social problems.

There are deep resistances to analyzing social problems from the standpoint of an organic theory of society. In most people's minds, deviant or "bad" behavior is sharply and completely separated from conforming or "good" behavior. The canon of orthodoxy is an academic counterpart and buttress of that popular lay belief. So strong are the habits making for the compartmentation of "good" and "evil" that they have profoundly affected the scientific study of social problems – witness the "vicious circle" approach, the myth that "evil causes evil." A less extreme version of this view is that "science cannot solve social problems," which was developed some years ago by Richard C. Fuller in a very influential series of papers.[20]

Yet if the burdens of delinquency and mental illness are to be rationally lightened, they must first be seen in their entirety, as integral parts of our society. We may grant that the statement of the organic relationship between our class system and delinquency is "ideological" – i.e., that it implies a need for some significant changes in social policy and social structure. Nonetheless it is also scientific, although the exact degree of the relationship is yet to be worked out. Some propositions, then, are both scientific and ideological. We believe that directly or indirectly a considerable proportion, perhaps a majority, of scientific statements in social science have an ideological aspect, either in what they say or fail to say.

The canon of orthodoxy, on the other hand, is a protective device for contemporary academic social science, just as the popular compartmentation of "good" and "evil" contributes to the stability of the existing social order. Scientists have no independent power status such as corporations and labor unions have. Most of them are hired employees of educational, medical, commercial, and governmental organizations ultimately controlled by the dominant business class and its allies. The expediency of the orthodox canon is therefore obvious, at least for social scientists. For the latter, far more than the natural and biological scientists, deal with intrinsically controversial data—though we must not overlook such bitter and protracted controversies as that centering on vaccination.[21] Yet the latter was probably generated at least as much, if not more, by its implications for social, rather than for strictly medical, change. Hence it seems valid to say there is fairly general agreement that, within the limits of the existing institutional order, scientific knowledge and control of nature and of health should be extended. But with respect to society there is no such consensus.

It is not by chance that the development of social science lags well behind that of natural and biological science. Social phenomena, much more than natural phenomena, are objects of people's moral sentiments, which are often outraged by—and therefore tend to block or even to punish—comprehensive scientific analysis and impersonal manipulation of moral values and social institutions.

(But if the natural scientists do not meet this *noli me tangere* directly in their subject matter, they often confront it with respect to the social consequences of their scientific discoveries. Here we may mention the machine-smashing tendencies of British workers in the early nineteenth century, the popular talk of a holiday on scientific inventions during the depression of the 1930's, and current sentiment against H-bomb experiments. Nor is such pressure always from below. The government security program, underscored by occasional punitive measures against individual scientists (as in the Oppenheimer case), inculcates conformity to official government policies—"Enthuse, don't think," as one cartoonist captioned the matter. That the result, if not the aim, of the security program is thought control has been cogently argued.[22])

The canon of orthodoxy, then, in academic social science tends on the one hand to preserve scientists from the pitfalls of political partisanship, and on the other hand to perpetuate the mutually stultifying gap between the fields of social theory and social problems. It affects academic philosophy as well as social science. In a provocative book, *Psychoanalysis and Ethics*,[23] L. S. Feuer states: "Contemporary philosophers have contrived an academic analysis which culminates in a devaluation of values; they achieve a self-destructive consummation in asserting they have nothing to say." And elsewhere: "Academic ethics, preoccupied with linguistic devices, resists the suggestion that ethical inquiry is related to great social issues . . . [But] the great innovators and contributors to scientific ethical philosophy were men . . . who regarded their analyses as part of a work of social reconstruction."

Another contemporary philosopher, more honorable than honored, has this to say: "When the heats and hunts are on, therefore, thinkers tend to escape into language. . . . In an age of Analysis (for so our present time describes itself) there is a natural tendency toward such extremes. Analysis likes to explain everything away, and one of the things she has lately explained away is ethics. . . . Now, ethical theory is the effort at explaining the nature of values, of things worthy to be desired and done. It deals with the precise point at which theory joins practice. To say, then, that ethics cannot be elucidated is to say that the union of theory and practice must remain obscure and even unknown."[24]

In academic philosophy, therefore, as in social science, an artificial separation of theory from practice is to be found, with similar resultant tendencies toward self-negation in both fields, and with the same orthodox premise that ethical and social analysis are mutually exclusive.

An Alternative Philosophical Premise for Social Science

In place of the orthodox premises of "ethical neutrality" and "nonideological science," we suggest that social science and philosophy adopt a premise of change as a central focus for its theoretical-empirical studies, and a further premise recognizing that such an approach has frankly ideological implications to be faced rather than avoided.

Earlier we defined an ideological statement as one that directly or indirectly recognized a need (real or imaginary) for a fundamental change in social policy and social structure. But the orthodox academic view that social science and ideology are mutually exclusive is usually interpreted in academic circles to mean that science avoids all political orientation whatever. This is fallacious. In fact, the premises of ethical neutrality and nonideological science directly or indirectly support the political orientation that affirms the existing social order and policies with no more than minor reservations. They buttress the established order by exempting its basic mores and institutions from critical and

dynamic analysis–that would be ideological!–and by deflecting scientific attention into harmless areas–such as abstruse theory or a surface view of social problems–that may or may not serve the vested interests, but at least do not challenge them. On scrutiny, then, the canon
of orthodoxy turns out to be something of a myth. The premises of ethical neutrality and nonideological social science are, perhaps more often
than not, neither neutral nor nonideological.

It is well to recognize that probably much research now under way
would be relatively unaffected by the changes here proposed. The issue
is one of comparative emphasis on overlapping patterns rather than of
mutually exclusive polar opposites. We are discussing the differences,
however, not the continuities.

Does not the fact that ours is a revolutionary age have implications
for rethinking academic conventions, in many areas of scholarly endeav-
or? Let us consider for a moment. As the key social process of the recent
past has been the Industrial Revolution and the rise of Western Capitalism, so the central event of the present and foreseeable future may be
the continuing Industrial Revolution in the form of Eurasian socialism.
In that perspective, does not the rebirth of China–normally a leader of
civilization for the last three or four millennia, except during occasional
interims like the past century or so–have implications for revising the
orthodox Western world-view? The latter characteristically conceives of
world history as a three-phase movement–ancient, medieval, modern–
centered on western Europe and its offshoot societies, with a few other
continents like Asia, Africa, and South America vaguely in the background. Events should have warned us some time ago that this view is
obsolete. Yet it still patterns the teaching and the studying of history in
the majority of our educational institutions.

Or consider the present hothouse departmentalization of academic
social sciences, notwithstanding the great gains made by cross-discipline
work in late years. Segregated from many basic aspects of social life, the
social sciences of the universities, it appears, tend to become static and
compartmentalized. Cross-discipline cooperation in such circumstances
produces complex models which, though less departmentalized, are
more static, like the Parsonian theory of action discussed above. What
these disciplines need, however, in addition to and perhaps even more
than contact with each other, is direct and comprehensive association
with everyday social life and problem situations. Should not graduate
study in sociology deal less with academic classrooms and laboratories
and more with practitioners of social relations like public health officials
and labor organizers? For the latter must deal concretely with community processes as dynamic wholes, and with a blend of theory and prac-

tice. One of the most insightful community studies of this generation, *Street Corner Society* by W. F. Whyte, was a product of active participation in a working-class slum.[25] The new edition of that book shows that the author won his understanding of Cornerville organization by transcending his middle-class background sufficiently to take an active—not merely observant—role, and a sincere role, in Cornerville life, from "repeater" voting to marching on City Hall. "I suppose no one goes to live in a slum district for three and a half years unless he is concerned about the problems facing the people there. . . . One time I gave in to the urge to do something. I tried to tell myself that I was simply testing out some of the things I had learned about the structure of corner gangs, but I knew really that this was not the main purpose."[26]

Medical science advanced just when theory was most fully combined with practice, as Farrington has indicated, and it declined when they became separated.[27] There is nothing new in pointing out the relevance of this fact for academic social science. What is novel, perhaps, is our belief that social science will not attain full maturity until it is joined with social planning and administration in a socialist-type society, engaged in solving some of our common social problems. Science, that is, must become more frankly ideological, although one may debate how far, and how fast. Such seems to be the drift of the times. This does not mean that scientists should set social policy, but only that they should orient their work more explicitly toward the evolutionary development of society and its major issues and conflicts, and that they should transcend some of their middle-class preconceptions—enough at any rate to recognize (where relevant) the implications of their work for social reform. It also means that academic social science must come to terms with, by ending the present unofficial boycott of, the Marxian tradition, just as the capitalist societies eventually got around to recognizing the Soviet Union, and now seem to be coming round to recognize China. Is it unreasonable to anticipate that political coexistence will, after the customary lag, conduce to intellectual rapprochement?

This is not to overlook the risk involved. The social scientist who centers his work on a premise of change may invite an annihilating charge of heresy. But science must study the world as it is, and as it is becoming, not as it is wishfully imagined to be. Bridging the gap between social theory and social problems by means of an organic theory of change in modern industrial society should make for a more realistic and useful scientific discipline. Theory should become more practical, and practice more theoretical, if the interests of society and of science are both to be served.

Let us sketch a sample dynamic approach in the field of social prob-

lems, not to press specific hypotheses but to illuminate the general direction in which a realistic theoretical approach to social problems may
take us. Testing of the following hypotheses appears to be warranted by
knowledge now available to us: (1) that certain social problems, such as
mental disease, are to a considerable degree inherent in our institutional
order, particularly in its class system; (2) that many of these problems
are becoming more rather than less acute; (3) that in the present social
order there is no basic solution, but only fringe repairs, for those problems, because the same institutional conditions that produce the problems also block fundamental reforms; (4) that in the long run only a society comprehensively planning for peace and welfare can attack those
problems with any realistic expectation of reducing them to manageable
proportions. We have reason to believe that some or all of these hypotheses may prove relevant to such diverse issues as crime, the municipal-
finance crisis, slums and housing, and juvenile delinquency. Be that as
it may, this suffices to show that the analysis of social problems, if it is
to be both theoretical and realistic, is not a cloistered pursuit. Only such
truth, wrote Thomas Hobbes, "as opposeth no man's profit, nor principle, is to all men welcome."

It is of course essential not to view social planning as a panacea. It
is neither a "solution" nor a specific institutional order, but simply a
method. That a socialist phase of social evolution will succeed the capitalist phase seems clear. But specific institutional patterns will vary with
local conditions which can hardly be anticipated, and concerning the
phases of civilization that lie beyond socialism we cannot even speculate.

Some Implications of, and for, the Social Control of Science

Every society cuts its science to its particular institutional pattern, for
a fair degree of institutional integration is necessary for the effective
functioning of any social system. American science is controlled partly
by the governmental, commercial, and university organizations sponsoring it, partly by such informal ethical premises as we have discussed.
A science free of some sort of institutional controls is not a thing of
this world. Hence it becomes a question, To what controls and ends
should science be harnessed?

In 1952 roughly 90 percent of all American research expenditure went
for military and commercial purposes, with the Federal Government paying for nearly 60 percent of the total.[28] The recent trend toward expanding government control of scientific enterprises has occasioned some
uneasiness in various circles, though without concerted dissent. But government control of science need not necessarily be a hardship either

for science or for the society it serves. Most continental European scholars and scientists are State employees, directly or indirectly. The Soviet
Union doubtless exercises a more thorough control of science than does
any other government—not always with happy results, to be sure. Yet
its science by and large is probably second to none, despite some notorious failings.

It is possible, of course, that certain aspects of scientific creativity and
bureaucracy are mutually incompatible, and that where science functions in a bureaucratic setting a fraction of the potential fruits of science
are therefore destined always to be wasted in order that the remainder
may be garnered. But beyond that uncertain point bureaucracies can
serve different purposes, and they can be efficient therein or not. It
would seem, then, that the basic issue in the relations of government
and science is not simply government control, but government control
for what ends? and by what means?

These are matters of the most fundamental social policy and social
philosophy, to be decided by all the citizens. But since World War II it
has become increasingly difficult to debate such questions in America.
At present, the bulk of current scientific work is bent to special military
and commercial ends. Secondarily there is, mostly in the universities,
a tendency toward "Science for science's sake," which comes to much
the same thing, and which reflects the ivory-tower quarantine of such
science as has not been drawn into business or military projects. If this
pattern of scientific effort is to be changed, modifications in the other
social and economic institutions controlling science will be necessary.
Simply wishing that science could serve open and non-invidious social
aims instead of security-ridden commercial and military undertakings
will not make it so. In the last analysis, the quest for a better science
is inevitably part of the drive for a better society.

In the long run the goal of social science, like that of natural science,
is greater knowledge and control of phenomena for human welfare. Comprehensive social planning appears to be as implicit in the advance of
science as it is in the growing economic and political centralization we
have come to know since the inception of the industrial revolution. The
very progress of science, therefore, tends to raise such basically political
questions as, Planning for whom and by whom? For what ends and by
what means? "Knowledge for what?" asked Robert Lynd in a too-little-
heeded book.[29] These are questions the citizenry will answer—are
answering continuously—either directly or by default. Social scientists
are sure to confront them, too, the more they address themselves to realistic and dynamic analyses of social change and social problems.

Veblen often pointed out that knowledge is a collective product of the community, as if to ask why its fruits should not also be collectively appropriated. Is not the humanistic justification of science the disinterested, utilitarian services it renders to people everywhere, without exploitation?

It seems important to recognize, in conclusion, that no society—whatever its type—fails to present major obstacles to critical self-analysis. Does not every social order have its canon of orthodoxy? It is utopian to suppose that resolving a current problem-situation will bring us into a problem-less state. At best the matter is probably one of degree. When the major institutions of a particular society are functioning harmoniously and efficiently—when the innate needs and learned expectations, in other words, of the membership are being effectively met by their social organization—then science (like other institutions) can operate smoothly, with little concern for its basic premises. But when institutions become markedly more maladjusted than usual, as they seem to do every few generations, then science and learning meet with corresponding dilemmas. Social science faces that sort of conflict today. The philosophical premises which now define and express its relation to the social order tend to prevent science from realizing its most fundamental aim—the realistic analysis of social phenomena.

If our hypothesis that institutional disharmonies are intensifying is valid, conflicting pressures in science will be increasingly evident. In due course, new philosophical premises for social science may be worked out if necessary, which is to say that the institutions that mold and underlie philosophical principles can be changed. This is not a light undertaking, nor one likely to be welcomed in all quarters. Nonetheless, says Barrows Dunham, "the thinker has the power of knowing and asserting what really is the case . . . the power of describing both the course of events and the means by which human beings may control that course. He may, indeed, not prevail with that power, but no one without that power can prevail."[30]

Notes

* For assistance in preparing Sections I and II of this paper, I acknowledge with appreciation my indebtedness to the University of Vermont for a Faculty Research grant-in-aid.

1 "The Aims of the Society for the Study of Social Problems," *Social Problems*, Vol. I (June, 1953), p. 2.

2 For example: the first systematic and dynamic analysis of the phenomenon of McCarthyism known to the present writer appeared in the *Monthly Review* ("The Roots and Prospects of McCarthyism," by Leo Huberman and Paul

Sweezy, January, 1954); this general approach was elaborated in *The Nation* ("Crisis in the G.O.P.," by Carey McWilliams, March 20, 1954), and further developed in *The American Socialist* (April, May and July, 1954); doubtless there were similar analyses in other such publications. By the following year—an unusually short time lag—the professional academicians were publishing their views on the same topic. Their views were in general less comprehensive, less dynamic, less clearly expressed, and less original. Cf. Daniel Bell, ed., *The New American Right* (New York: Criterion Press, November, 1955).

3 *The Religion of China* (Glencoe: The Free Press, 1951), ch. 5.

4 Reprinted in his *Essays on Sociology and Social Psychology* (New York: Oxford University Press, 1953), pp. 185–194.

5 The core of this theoretical orientation is stated in Parsons and Shils, *Toward a General Theory of Action* (Cambridge: Harvard University Press, 1951); Parsons, *The Social System* (Glencoe: The Free Press, 1952), and *Essays in Sociological Theory* (Glencoe: The Free Press, 2nd ed., 1954); Parsons, Bales, and Shils, *Working Papers in the Theory of Action* (Glencoe: The Free Press, 1953).

6 Cf. Parsons, Bales, and Shils, *op. cit.*; and Parsons, Bales, et al., *Family Socialization and Interaction Process* (Glencoe: The Free Press, 1955).

7 Cf. Parsons, *Essays* . . . (1954), chs. 6, 7, 13, and 14, dealing with Germany, Japan, and aggression in Western Society; also "McCarthyism and American Social Tension," *Yale Review* (Winter, 1955).

8 *The Place of Science in Modern Civilization* (New York: Huebsch, 1919), pp. 409–456; *Imperial Germany* (New York: Macmillan, 1915); *The Theory of Business Enterprise* (New York: Scribners, 1904). Cf. A. K. Davis, "Thorstein Veblen Reconsidered," *Science and Society*, Winter, 1957, 52–85.

9 See, in part, Parsons, *The Structure of Social Action* (New York: McGraw-Hill, 1937). Professor Parsons is, of course, well aware of the problem of social change and of the alleged "static bias" of the structural-functional theory of action. For cogent statements of the applicability of his conceptual approach to social change, see his *Toward a General Theory of Action*, pp. 230–233, and *The Social System*, ch. XI. Another good defense of the same viewpoint is B. Barber's "Structural Functional Analysis," *American Sociological Review*, Vol. 21 (1956), pp. 133–135.

10 Some of the students of Parsons have gone even farther in this direction than has Parsons himself—e.g., M. J. Levy, *The Structure of Society* (Princeton University Press, 1952). In the light of such results, it would seem that R. K. Merton's plea for "theories of the middle range," in contrast to Parsons' more comprehensive approach, was well conceived—cf. "The Position of Sociological Theory—Discussion by R. K. Merton," *American Sociological Review*, Vol. 13 (1949), pp. 164–168. A middle-range focus—empirical analysis in a limited conceptual setting—appears to assure more securely the necessary continuous contact with empirical variables. That a theoretical approach may effectively be comprehensive, involving a whole society or system of societies, provided it is also dynamic and historical, is suggested by the success of Owen Lattimore's classic work, *The Inner Asian Frontiers of China* (New York: Oxford Press, 1951).

11 In W. F. Whyte, ed., *Industry and Society* (New York: McGraw-Hill, 1946), ch 3.

12 *The Fabric of Chinese Society* (New York: Praeger, 1953). Much the same might be said concerning other recent Chinese community studies by the Western-trained anthropologists Hsiao-tung Fei, M. C. Yang, and F. L. K. Hsu.

13 E.g., F. E. Merrill et al., *Social Problems* (New York: Knopf, 1950); H. Bloch, *Social Disorganization* (New York: Knopf, 1952).

14 E.g., Cuber and Harper, *Problems of American Society* (New York: Henry Holt, 1951); Horton and Leslie, *Sociology of Social Problems* (New York: Appleton-Century-Crofts, 1955); T. L. Smith et al., *Social Problems* (New York: Crowell, 1955).

15 M. L. Barron, *The Juvenile in Delinquent Society* (New York: Knopf, 1954); Albert K. Cohen, *Delinquent Boys* (Glencoe: The Free Press, 1955).

16 "The Social Sciences in the United States," *Zeitschrift für Sozialforschung*, Vol. IV (1935), pp. 63–65.

17 *The Place of Science in Modern Civilization*, pp. 56–179.

18 "The Functions of Small-Group Research," *Social Problems*, Vol. III (1955), pp. 5–6.

19 *The Higher Learning in America* (New York: Huebsch, 1918), pp. 186–190.

20 Especially his "Sociological Theory and Social Problems," *Social Forces*, Vol. XV (1937), pp. 496–502.

21 Bernhard J. Stern, *Shall We Be Vaccinated?* (New York: Harpers, 1927).

22 *Monthly Review*, July, 1955; cf. also *Bulletin of the Atomic Scientists* for April, 1955.

23 (Springfield, Illinois, Thomas, 1955.) The citations are from pages 121 and 36. The reference "preoccupied with linguistic devices" is to C. L. Stevenson, *Ethics and Language* (New Haven: Yale University Press, 1944).

24 Barrows Dunham, "Thinkers and Treasurers," *Monthly Review*, December, 1955, pp. 327–329. Also printed separately.

25 (Chicago: University of Chicago Press, 2nd edition, 1955.)

26 *Ibid*, p. 337.

27 Benjamin Farrington, *Head and Hand in Ancient Greece* (London: Watts & Co., 1946), chs. I–II.

28 Derived from Bernhard J. Stern, "Freedom of Research in American Social Science," *Science and Society*, Vol. XVIII (Spring, 1954), pp. 106–110.

29 R. S. Lynd, *Knowledge for What?* (Princeton University Press, 1939).

30 "Thinkers and Treasurers," *Monthly Review (October*, 1955), pp. 208–209.

Editor's Note

The preceding article, *Social Theory and Social Problems*, received a short favorable notice in *The Fundamentals of Marxist-Leninist Philosophy*, Academy of Sciences of the USSR, Progress Publishers, Moscow, revised Russian edition, chapter 23, "Contemporary Bourgeois Sociology." The following excerpt is from pages 656–658.

The problems of group life figure prominently in bourgeois sociology. Bourgeois sociologists refer to the fact that all human life is group life; everywhere people live in association with other people. But instead of revealing the causes that compel people to live in groups, instead of singling out among all the manifold human relations the decisive relations of production, bourgeois sociologists confine themselves to describing various aspects of group life. The problem of small groups of people (who have direct relations with one another) is studied by sociometry. The founder of this discipline was J. L Moreno, who expounded his conception in the book *Sociometry*. He formulates his programme as follows: "Instead of analysing social classes composed of millions of people, we are making painstaking analyses of small groups of persons. It is a retreat from the social universe to its atomic structure." (J. L. Moreno, *Sociometry. Experimental Method and the Science of Society*, Beacon, N.Y., 1951, p. 25.) Sociometry is an example of the unsuccessful attempts of bourgeois sociologists to "overcome" the class conflicts of capitalist society by improving psychological relations within small groups and transposing this microclimate of people who are "sympathetic" to one another, to society as a whole.

Bourgeois empirical studies have certain general features.

First, they are extremely narrow and limited in character because they usually rely on the polling of small groups.

Second, as a rule they are superficial, lacking any power of penetration into the essence of things. Description instead of explanation is a characteristic feature of research in specialised fields of sociology. The American sociologist Arthur Davis rightly observes: "From the professional literature on social problems, then, we can readily learn how Jack Doe happened to become a delinquent in his youth, but we will learn much less about the deeper relations of juvenile delinquency to the social structure as a whole. Why does delinquency persist in our society, what interests does it serve, what frustrations does it relieve? Such questions tend to be avoided in academic treatments of social problems. . . ." (Arthur K. Davis, "Social Theory and Social Problems." In: *Philosophy and Phenomenological Research*, December, 1957, Vol. 18, No. 2, p. 197.)

Empirical studies are frequently highly subjective. On the one hand, they see the ultimate explanation of the facts under consideration in man's social behaviour, in socio-psychological phenomena. On the other, any interpretations, including "economic" interpretations, are mostly based on the opinions derived from polling.

The narrow empiricism of concrete studies in bourgeois sociology, the minute splitting up of their research targets, the superficial factual description, etc., have been sharply criticised even by bourgeois theoretical sociologists, such as Pitirim Sorokin, Robert Merton, Paul Lazarsfeld, and others. Speaking at the 4th International Sociological Congress, Robert Merton stated: "Sociologists are busily engaged in studying trivial problems while everything that concerns the really significant issues of human society is left unstudied. . . . Despite the fact that wars and exploitation, poverty, injustice and uncertainty poison people's lives and that of society or threaten their every existence, many sociologists devote themselves to problems that are so far removed from these catastrophic phenomena as to be irresponsibly petty." (Translated from the Russian, as quoted in an article by P. Fedoseyev and Y. Frantsev, "Bourgeois Sociology at a Dead-End," *Kommunist*, No. 17, 1959, p. 96.)

But the appeal for a scientific sociology organically synthesising theory and empirical analysis and therefore capable of presenting a true picture of social life, its main stages and prospects of development cannot be realised because of the class position of bourgeois sociology, its limited methodological approach.

Bourgeois sociology, both theoretical and empirical, is in no condition to provide an integrated scientific picture of society and its development, or consistent scientific analysis of the individual aspects of capitalist reality. In present-day conditions the crisis of bourgeois sociology is also expressed in the fact that it is compelled to reflect in various forms the adaptation of capitalism to the new situation, to employ social demagogy and preach the ideas of "modernisation," "growth," and "development."

But the intricate problems of modern times cannot be solved without precise scientific knowledge of society and social development. Such knowledge is provided by Marxist-Leninist philosophy and sociology.

At the same time Marxist sociologists do not ignore the wealth of factual material gathered by bourgeois empirical sociology in studying separate aspects and phenomena of capitalist society; rather they take it into consideration, and make use of its carefully elaborated techniques and methods.

Lenin wrote that when it is a matter of a general theory of political economy one must not believe a single word of what is written by bourgeois economists, but that when he is concerned with the factual side of the economic life of the capitalist countries the Marxist cannot do without the studies of bourgeois economists. These words of Lenin's apply equally well to the attitude to be adopted by Marxist sociologists towards bourgeois sociology and its results.

The development of concrete social studies on the basis of the theory and method of historical materialism constitute one of the essential tasks facing Marxist sociologists. It is the function of these concrete social (and also sociological) researches to enrich Marxist sociology and historical materialism and by their conclusions help in the practical construction of communist society.

Thorstein Veblen

T HORSTEIN BUNDE VEBLEN (1857–1929), American sociologist and social critic, was born in Cato, Wisconsin, and brought up on subsistence farms in Wisconsin and Minnesota. His parents had migrated to the United States in 1847 from rural Norway; Veblen was the sixth of 12 children.

In that newly settled frontier region the Norwegian immigrants were divided from the Yankee upper class by religious, linguistic, and other cultural barriers. The first-generation immigrants held tenaciously to their ancestral peasant ways. Veblen's father, for example, did not learn English. Even in college, Veblen and his brother Andrew–the first members of the family to attain higher education–were handicapped by lingering difficulties with English, their second language. Their generation tended to be "marginal"–oriented partly to the Yankee and partly to the Norwegian way of life and skeptical of both. In later years Veblen looked upon this kind of skeptical marginality as a stimulus to intellectual creativity, especially among Jews (*Essays in Our Changing Order*, p. 219). Veblen's own alienation was reinforced by early encounters with the mutual hostility of townspeople and farmers.

In 1880 Veblen graduated from Carleton College, Minnesota. After one term at Johns Hopkins, he took his PH.D. in philosophy at Yale in 1884. Failing to find a job because of his agnosticism, he returned to the Minnesota countryside for seven years of reading and rustication. Finally, in 1891, wearing a coonskin cap, he enrolled as a graduate student in economics at Cornell, under J. Laurence Laughlin, who took Veblen with him when he moved to the University of Chicago the following year.

Reprinted with permission of Macmillan Publishing Company, a Division of Macmillan, Inc., from *International Encyclopedia of the Social Sciences*, David L. Sills, Editor. Vol. XVI, pp. 303–308. Copyright © 1968 by Crowell Collier and Macmillan, Inc.

Fourteen years on the Chicago faculty were followed by three at Stanford, from 1906 to 1909. He was unemployed in 1910–1911 and then went to the University of Missouri for seven years. In 1918, he left the academic profession – his tenure therein had always been somewhat precarious because of his unorthodox classroom performance and his domestic difficulties – for a brief period of wartime government service, occasional teaching at the New School for Social Research, in New York, and writing. He retired to a California cabin in 1926 and died there three years later in obscurity and poverty.

The American Midwest, during Veblen's youth, was the scene of repeated agrarian revolts and urban labor struggles. Many people were receptive to the reformist ideas of Henry George and Edward Bellamy, and scathing attacks on the great corporations by social critics like Henry Lloyd and Upton Sinclair were widely applauded. It was an age of head-on confrontations. But enthusiasm for Populism, radical unionism, Debs's brand of socialism, and for other left-leaning movements was, in Veblen's adult years, gradually eclipsed by increasing support for business and imperialist values. The outcome, which marked a major turning point in American history, was largely settled by 1920, at the expense of the radical protest movements; and Veblen, who was keenly interested in and sympathetic toward these movements, perceived far more clearly than most of his contemporaries the decisiveness of the triumph of business civilization. The study of that great development and of some responses to it became Veblen's life work. This is not to say that Veblen thought that the nature of change was reducible to the clash of business values with protest movements. Instead, he believed it hinged on the long-run, indirect, and often "opaque" interactions of both business values and various institutional norms with the "machine process" (which included, among other key elements, technology).

Veblen took no direct part in any social movement. Although basically critical of modern capitalist institutions and culture, he claimed to be a detached observer, above the battle. His ironic wit did not spare his friends; if he did not chastise them as much as he did his foes, he did so enough to support plausibly his claim to objectivity. His general orientation, of course, was unmistakably leftward, and his career is a minor chapter in the history of American radicalism.

Main Intellectual Influences

Although Veblen's major works in the social sciences were produced over four decades and cover a wide variety of concrete topics, their central ideas show a high degree of consistency. This unity derives from the fact that three important intellectual strands run through all of Veblen's work: Darwinian evolutionism, utopian anarchism, and Marxism, each of which Veblen developed in an original way.

The element in Darwinism that especially influenced Veblen was its implication that individuals have little or no control over the forces of change. His focus on this aspect of historical development helped to correct the overemphasis of the classical economists and of Marx on the role of rational decisions in social life. However, unlike many social scientists of the time, including William Graham Sumner, his own teacher at Yale, Veblen implicitly denied the relevance for social science of such other key Darwinian concepts as natural selection, the struggle for existence, and the survival of the fittest. Social Darwinism, he believed, tended only to reinforce capitalist values.

Somewhat more important in Veblen's work than evolutionism was the strand of utopian anarchism. His vague picture of the prehistoric "savage state," in effect a primeval golden age, was based on the conjectural evolutionary theories of the anthropologist L. H. Morgan and on Veblen's own interpretation of anthropological and archeological reports. This idyllic era was characterized by the absence of class hierarchies, states, and organized warfare. By implication Veblen judged social institutions to be "evil" and human instincts to be "good." (More will be said below about his conception of instincts.) Veblen's own ideal, never openly professed, seems to have been the irreverent "masterless man," living frugally but independently in small rural communities too poor to support any overlords.

Certain of Veblen's core ideas are strikingly similar to those of Marx, not in terminology but in content. The principal similarities are an emphasis on class and on economic and property institutions as keys to historical change, and the relegation of ideological elements to secondary importance; a belief in the proposition that crises of overproduction are inherent in capitalist economies; a conception of class structure as resting primarily on two mutually antagonistic groups of occupations (in Veblen's case, these two groups consisted of business owners and industrial producers); a view of the modern state as "an executive committee for businessmen"; and a conviction that states are bound to become involved in militarism and war. Unlike the Marxists, Veblen made little use of such concepts as surplus value, capital accumulation as a stimulus to imperialism, and the inevitability of socialism. Finally, he usually relied on vaguely defined sociological and psychological mechanisms to explain major social changes, rather than on the kind of tightly reasoned economic analyses used by Marx.

Analytical Categories

Veblen analyzed human behavior primarily in terms of instincts and habits, and social processes in terms of culture lag.

He distinguished three "instincts," all of which he considered benevolent and all of which, in fact, he used as norms: the parental bent, a benevolent feeling toward kin and fellowman; the instinct or sense of workmanship, a desire to maximize production of goods and services and to do a job well for its own sake; and idle curiosity, the most difficult of the three to define. Two interpretations of idle curiosity seem possible. The usual one is that it refers to the norm of disinterested pursuit of scientific knowledge, i.e., the pursuit of such knowledge for its own sake. But it may also be argued that Veblen was aware of the extent to which socioeconomic institutions mold knowledge and ideologies and that he anticipated–however awkwardly–our latter-day sociology of knowledge (Davis 1957).

The greater part of human behavior was attributed by Veblen to habit. The more persistent among the patterns of "use and wont" he designated loosely as social institutions. Veblen never classified institutions systematically. Rather, he characterized them broadly by such terms as "patterns of pecuniary emulation" or "patterns of conspicuous consumption" (which we would now call status competition) or, again, as "patterns for the maintenance of national integrity" (i.e., nationalism) or "patterns for the maintenance of the price system" (capitalism). Habits or institutions, unlike instincts, were according to Veblen far from benevolent. Indeed, he maintained that all social institutions have three properties in common: they are predatory; they are wasteful; and they are survivals from earlier historical epochs. Briefly, they are obstacles to utopia.

The concept of culture lag, which Veblen used to analyze social processes, has been widely used by American sociologists to account both for social change and social problems. Change stems mainly from science and technology, and problems are due to the failure of institutions and organizations to keep pace. For example, factories were introduced in Western nations several decades before the institutional arrangements–safety rules, child-labor laws, and retirement pensions–needed to round out the industrialization process were established. On a broader scale, Veblen often contrasted the still-surviving eighteenth-century institutional framework of private property and national sovereignty with the twentieth-century "machine process" of industrial production, which was severely restricted, he argued, by its archaic eighteenth-century institutional context. In his later, more outspoken writings Veblen frequently spoke of the "triumph of imbecile institutions."

The culture-lag approach has been one of the master concepts of modern social analysis. The realization that technologies may sometimes change faster than the organizational patterns and institutional norms which control their application is a germinal insight. However, Veblen did not adequately recognize that the concept of culture lag may give undue weight to factors of ignorance and drift, at the expense of vested-interest rationality, or that technology may not always change first. Thus, in his books on Germany (1915) and peace (1917) Veblen could readily show the waste created by the chauvinism and colonialism of the Great Powers, but he could not as clearly depict the organic relationship between capitalism, imperialism, and war; hence his interpretation of World War I as a clash between Germany's obsolete yet still potent feudal dynasticism and England's "free institutions," instead of as an inevitable collision between two inherently expanding capitalistic imperialisms.

Veblen did not originate the important yet one-sided culture-lag approach; the ideal is central in Marx and in the emphasis on "survivals" evident in the Darwinian and other evolutionary traditions in social science. However, Veblen's work did give considerable impetus to a culture-lag perspective, although it was left to W. F. Ogburn and others to develop the concept explicitly.

Social and Economic Analysis

Veblen's primary interest was in the analysis of latter-day industrial society, but characteristically he took a long historical view. Thus, in his *Instinct of Workmanship* (1914) he attempted a social-evolutionary analysis of stages preceding the emergence of modern society.

He divided social evolution into two great phases: the prehistoric "savage state" and the "predatory society." Except for the unduly idyllic description of the former phase, Veblen's outlines of social evolution roughly parallel those of such later authorities as V. Gordon Childe and Leslie White. He saw the snail-like advance of technology ultimately producing, in the hunting-and-gathering economy of the savage state, an economic surplus, which was decisively enlarged by the appearance of agriculture. Society then took on a modern cast, with the development of property, classes, the state, priesthoods, and war. Predatory society, or historic times, has had two main subdivisions, according to Veblen: barbarism, wherein coercion was exercised directly by military and priestly agencies; and pecuniary times, the postmedieval age, wherein exploitation was effected by roundabout, semipeaceable methods. In turn, pecuniary society may be subdivided into the handicraft era (early modern

Western times) and the machine age (the last two centuries). Veblen emphasized the wasteful nature of pecuniary institutions and their intrinsic bent toward crisis and change.

Veblen modified the Marxist analysis of machine-age society, stressing the key importance of the conflict between "business" (profit-seeking ownership) and "industry" (maximum production of goods and services). He described production as a seamless web of specialized technological processes. The conflict between business and industry arises because, although the "industrial arts" have been developed over centuries by the whole community and are its proper heritage, they have come to be controlled by a few owners, in whose interest it is to restrict output in order to maximize profit. Welfare, to Veblen, meant maximum output at lowest cost—such is the spirit of industry. The spirit of business, on the other hand, he defined as sabotage and salesmanship, "charging what the traffic will bear."

It is business management, according to Veblen, that is responsible for depressions. These are inherent in the profit-oriented control of competitive industrial enterprises, because new and more efficient firms (that is, efficient in profit making) force the liquidation of older ones. Moreover, the efforts of profit-oriented business to counteract depressions can only have undesirable consequences. Veblen predicted such consequences as increased mergers, the expansion of salesmanship, and "wasteful" consumption by the government and by the "kept classes."

The dominance of business values, said Veblen, extends over many areas of American life, including higher education. His *Higher Learning in America* (1918) was a searing analysis of the effects of pecuniary canons upon university organization, administration, teaching, and research. In general, however, Veblen's main focus throughout his life was on the development of American social and economic institutions in their international setting. Most of his major works have that sweeping outlook: two on the American economy (1904; 1923); the books on Germany (1915) and on peace (1917); and many of the essays in his collected papers (see *Essays in Our Changing Order* and *The Place of Science in Modern Civilization*). These two volumes also include his occasional forays into technical economic theory. But Veblen was much more interested in the social milieu and the consequences of economic factors in modern industrial society than in abstract economic analysis. Perhaps the best short introduction to his leading ideas on social change, business versus industry, nationalism, and other modern developments is the small book called *The Vested Interests and the Common Man* (1919a).

---

* Posthumously published, 1934.

By far the best known of Veblen's work is his first book, *The Theory of the Leisure Class* (1899)–the only one that became popular during his lifetime. This treatise is essentially an analysis of the latent functions of "conspicuous consumption" and "conspicuous waste" as symbols of upper-class status and as competitive methods of enhancing individual prestige. Veblen's term "conspicuous consumption" has become part of everyday language. Although most relevant to the gilded age in which he wrote the book, the work is also based on many examples from leisure-class behavior in barbarian and feudal times. Most of the key concepts of Veblen's thought are either present or clearly foreshadowed in *The Theory of the Leisure Class*–for example, his distinction between industrial and pecuniary pursuits; his concept of evolutionary stages; his definition of certain cultural traits as survivals, with consequent implications for the importance of culture lag; his nostalgic bias for the simple, preindustrial life. Although some of his evolutionary history and anthropology was conjectural and although racial theorizing was a recurrent vein in his earlier works, Veblen's chief method was strikingly modern. He practiced, without so naming it, the analysis of latent or unintended functions of social phenomena. Veblen was never a methodologist; he was always concerned with substantive theories about empirical groups, structures, and processes. That is why commentators see his works both as exposés and as objective expositions.

Veblen believed that although business had acquired a dominant position in society since the eighteenth century, in the long run the incompatibility of business and industry would undermine that position. The real threat to profit-oriented business (based on eighteenth-century canons of mutual right) came not from the business cycle but from the impersonal, skeptical, matter-of-fact habits of thought engendered by the twentieth-century machine process. These would eventually erode the institutions necessary to business, such as nationalism, religious observance, and private ownership. The very tendency of the machine technology toward ever greater productivity seemed to Veblen increasingly likely to shatter the eighteenth-century institutional bonds that restricted output and bent it to wasteful nationalistic and class ends.

What then? Two inconsistent answers were advanced by Veblen. The more optimistic one, which he stressed less, but which occurred more prominently in his earlier work, was that the machine process, through its promise of unlimited abundance for all, might triumph over the obstacles to welfare created by profit-oriented business. The other answer, stressed more heavily, especially in his later writings (and also stressed in Dorfman's classic biography, 1934) was the likelihood of a reversion to predatory, coercive barbarism. In what is perhaps his greatest book,

Absentee Ownership (1923), he concluded that the forces of business-as-usual and of national integrity were steadily coalescing "by night and cloud" and that the continued supremacy of business nationalism would probably lead to a renewal of the servile despotism characteristic of earlier epochs. As he grew older, Veblen became increasingly doubtful that the "underlying population" could shake off its conventional faith in "business principles" and nationalism and come through "alive and fit to live." The social consequences in America of World War I only served to confirm Veblen's pessimism. The influence of the Machiavellian press, controlled as it was by vested interests, was being reinforced, he believed, by the influential weight of traditional values and by the unplanned drift of large social forces, "And the common man pays the cost and swells with pride" (1919a, p. 137).

Influence

Veblen founded no school. He influenced many scholars and public officials (often former students), but nearly always they differed from him more than they resembled him. Even so, those whose work in some respect touched his constituted a large portion of the intellectual leaders of two generations.

Among academic economists may be mentioned such diverse personalities as H. J. Davenport, Joseph Dorfman, and Walter Stewart. W. C. Mitchell, a pioneer in the field of business-cycle history and theory, often acknowledged his indebtedness to Veblen, his onetime teacher at Chicago. (In 1920 Mitchell founded the National Bureau of Economic Research; Stewart later created the Federal Reserve index of industrial production.) In labor economics Robert Hoxie, a former student, and Carleton Parker were both strongly influenced by Veblen. Some writers have grouped Veblen, Mitchell, and J. R. Commons together as "institutional economists," along with Clarence Ayres, Sumner Slichter, and a handful of others. A view of these men as members of a school, however, would be difficult to defend.

When the New School for Social Research was founded in 1919, Veblen was one of the "big four"–along with Dewey, Robinson, and Mitchell–who lectured there intermittently for two or three years. Early workers in consumer economics (Hazel Kyrk, Theresa McMahon) owed something to Veblen. A stronger Veblen impress is discernible in the writings of Robert Brady, A. A. Berle, and R. A. Gordon on modern corporate development. At least one minor social movement was a direct heir of certain of Veblen's ideas, although Veblen carefully avoided participation in that enterprise. This was technocracy, a movement founded about 1920 with the aim of maximizing engineering (i.e., productive) efficiency in modern society.

Veblen's influence has been less pervasive among sociologists than among economists, although Ogburn developed the concept of culture lag in *Social Change* in 1922. During the 1930s Veblen's germinal views on waste and lag reached a wide public through the popular books of Stuart Chase. About the same time, several leading legal and academic minds reflected Veblenian themes—especially Thurman Arnold, Felix Frankfurter, and J. Laurence Laughlin. The same can be said of a number of New Deal public administrators—Henry Wallace, R. G. Tugwell, Isador Lubin, and others. Several younger academics, like Max Lerner and David Riesman, have learned from Veblen. In the era after World War II it seems to have been C. Wright Mills who spoke the loudest in Veblen's accents, although Mills was far more outspoken as a social critic than Veblen.

While most of the aforementioned persons disagreed with Veblen more often than they agreed with him, all of them had a penchant for a long, broad view of their several fields and for a more or less skeptical attitude toward "establishments." In these respects, rather than in specific thought systems, they were spiritual followers of Veblen.

Someone once said that Veblen was the last man who knew everything. His interest ranged over several disciplines and long periods of time. Several writers have compared him to Keynes and Schumpeter. He was one of the few Americans who sensed that victory in World War I might prove to be an adverse turning point in American history. American intervention, wrote Veblen bitterly in 1922, had saved the war system. Indeed, his essays on international relations in the early 1920s are still meaningful for the years following World War II. He remains a source of astonishingly relevant insights, of ironic humor, of saving skepticism, and of a chilling presentiment of the present as tragedy.

[*For the historical context of Veblen's work, see* ECONOMIC THOUGHT, *article on the* INSTITUTIONAL SCHOOL; *and the biographies of* DARWIN; GEORGE; MARX; MORGAN, LEWIS HENRY; SUMNER. *For discussion of the subsequent development of Veblen's ideas, see* ECONOMY AND SOCIETY; EDUCATION, *article on* EDUCATIONAL ORGANIZATION; FASHION; MARXIST SOCIOLOGY; *and the biographies of* COMMONS; DAVENPORT; MILLS; MITCHELL; OGBURN.]

Works by Veblen

(1899) 1953 *The Theory of the Leisure Class: An Economic Study of Institutions.* Rev. ed. New York: New American Library. A paperback edition was published in 1959.

1904 *The Theory of Business Enterprise.* New York: Scribner.
1914 *The Instinct of Workmanship and the State of the Industrial Arts.* New York: Macmillan.
(1915) 1964 *Imperial Germany and the Industrial Revolution.* New York: Kelley.
(1917) 1964 *An Inquiry Into the Nature of Peace and the Terms of Its Perpetuation.* New York: Kelley.
(1918) 1957 *The Higher Learning in America: A Memorandum on the Conduct of Universities by Business Men.* New York: Sagamore.
(1919a) 1964 *The Vested Interests and the Common Man: The Modern Point of View and the New Order.* New York: Kelley. First published as *The Vested Interests and the State of Industrial Art.*
(1919b) 1921 *The Engineers and the Price System.* New York: Huebsch. A series of papers reprinted from *Dial.* A paperback edition was published in 1963 by Harcourt.
(1923) 1945 *Absentee Ownership and Business Enterprise in Recent Time: The Case of America.* New York: Viking.
1925 VEBLEN, THORSTEIN (translator) *The Laxdœla Saga.* Translated from Icelandic, with an introduction by Thorstein Veblen. New York: Huebsch.
Essays in Our Changing Order. Edited by Leon Ardzrooni. New York: Viking, 1934. Contains some essays first published between 1892 and 1925 and some previously unpublished.
The Place of Science in Modern Civilisation, and Other Essays. New York: Huebsch, 1919. Contains essays first published between 1891 and 1913.

Supplementary Bibliography

DAUGERT, STANLEY M. 1950 *The Philosophy of Thorstein Veblen.* New York: King's Crown.
DAVIS, ARTHUR K. 1957 Thorstein Veblen Reconsidered. *Science and Society* 21: 52–85.
DORFMAN, JOSEPH (1934) 1961 *Thornstein Veblen and His America.* New York: Kelley.
DOWD, DOUGLAS F. (editor) 1958 *Thornstein Veblen: A Critical Reappraisal.* Ithaca, N.Y.: Cornell Univ. Press. Contains an extensive bibliography of Veblen's writings.
DUFFUS, ROBERT L. 1944 *The Innocents at Cedro: A Memoir of Thorstein Veblen and Others.* New York: Macmillan.
HOBSON, JOHN A. (1936) 1937 *Veblen.* New York: Wiley.
HOMAN, PAUL T. 1928 *Contemporary Economic Thought.* New York: Harper. See especially Chapter 2.
INNIS, H. A. 1956 *Essays in Canadian Economic History.* Univ. of Toronto Press. See especially pages 17–26.
Institutional Economics; Veblen, Commons, and Mitchell Reconsidered: A Series of Lectures. 1963 Berkeley: Univ. of California Press. By Joseph Dorfman, C. E. Ayres, and others.

JOHNSON, ALVIN 1935 Veblen, Thorstein Bunde. Volume 15, pages 234–235 in *Encyclopaedia of the Social Sciences*. New York: Macmillan.

PARRINGTON, VERNON L. 1930 *Main Currents in American Thought: An Interpretation of American Literature From the Beginnings to 1920*. Volume 3: The Beginnings of Critical Realism in America, 1860–1920. New York: Harcourt.

RIESMAN, DAVID 1953 *Thorstein Veblen: A Critical Interpretation*. New York: Scribner.

ROLL, ERICH (1938) 1963 *A History of Economic Thought*. 3d ed., rev. & enl. Englewood Cliffs, N.J.: Prentice-Hall. See especially pages 439–454, "Veblen."

Thorstein Bunde Veblen, 1857–1957. 1957 *Monthly Review* 9:65–122.

A New Look at Chinese History

I.

REVOLUTIONS bring profound changes in a social order. One of their secondary effects is to stimulate new perspectives on the history of the revolutionary society.

The triumphant emergence of new powers and of revolutionary socialism in Asia has already rendered obsolete the traditionally bigoted Western view of world history. Spacewise, this view encompasses little more than the end of the European peninsula plus North America, with a few vaguely conceived hinterlands like Asia, Africa, South America, and Eastern Europe in the background. Chronologically, it is usually divided into three periods: Ancient, Medieval, and Modern. Despite its present unreality, this scheme still controls the teaching of history in American schools and colleges.

Yet most of the human race has always lived in Asia. India, the Near East, and China all achieved urban civilization several centuries before Western Europe did. The West's supremacy over the rest of the world is a recent development of the last three hundred years. Moreover it is a transitory phenomenon. That the Western-led and capitalist phase of modern industrial civilization is rapidly giving way to an Eastern-led and socialist phase seems clear, now that China has turned to socialism and has re-emerged as a great power.

Few Westerners realize that major-power status was China's normal place in history for 2000 years. Most of us would be astonished to learn that during the greater part of recorded history the main flow of scientific and technological discoveries has been from China to the West. As late as three centuries ago, China's productive technology was still superior to that of England.

In the nineteenth century, however, the many-sided impact of European capitalist industrialism combined with China's internal decay to crumble her agrarian and handicraft economy. An agonizing century and a quarter of civil strife and foreign exploitation followed. From this abnormal period, the West acquired its stereotype of China as a backward nation of heathen coolies.

The restabilization of China required the regaining of economic and political independence and the establishment of socialist industrialism. The West's Kuomintang collaborators having been expelled and the Communist regime consolidated, China has her five-generation crisis well in hand.

Happily, some glimmer of these truths has willy-nilly begun to penetrate Western consciousness, not only in ruling circles (so rudely disillusioned and drubbed in Asia during the past decade) but also in learned circles. History, of course, is made primarily by great social processes, not by books about them. The West's learning the facts of life about Asia doubtless owes more to the shocks of political and military defeats than to explanatory treatises. But books can help. We don't *always* have to learn by banging our heads against stone walls.

The recent publication of two scholarly works about China is a significant step toward a new Western perspective on Chinese history. The first is Joseph Needham's *Science and Civilization in China*, Volume 1 (Cambridge University Press, 1954). The second is Thomas T. Meadows' *The Chinese and their Rebellions*, originally published in 1856 (London and Bombay) and lately reprinted by Academic Reprints (Stanford, N.D.). We should also mention the Australian C. P. Fitzgerald's *Chinese Revolution* (New York, 1952), perhaps the best analytical volume on its subject in English. Among the few good journalistic reports on contemporary China, our preference is for Anna Louise Strong's stirring *The Chinese Conquer China* (New York, 1949). We shall return to Needham and Meadows later.

Our aim in these papers is to help crystallize a new Western perspective on China, one that avoids capitalism's past parochialism and its present hostility. The recent victory of Chinese socialism is surely to this generation what the triumph of Russian socialism was to the last: the pivotal event of the age. To understand the China of today, we need to know something about its antecedents, especially the Feudal Bureaucratic Empire which existed more than 2000 years till the mid-19th century, and the Foreign Imperialist Interregnum extending roughly from the 1840s to the 1940s.

The Span of Chinese Civilization

We may divide the span of human society in China into five broad stages:

1. Neolithic prehistory, including several cultures scattered about China, and lasting perhaps until the middle of the second millennium B.C. Being relatively isolated and existing in different locales, these neolithic communities varied considerably, but in general they seem to have been characterized by such typical neolithic traits as stationary or nomadic agriculture and domesticated animals, pottery manufacture, weaving, housebuilding, and the beginnings of trade, population growth, and war.

2. The Bronze or Shang Age, a five-century development in North China showing feudal trends and forming a cultural bridge from stage 1 to stage 3.

3. Regional Feudalism or the Warring Feudal States, sometimes called the Chou Era (10th–3rd centuries B.C.), during which an intensive agrarian economy, segmented into self-sufficient districts and ruled by hereditary military nobles, began to spread from the northwest loess hills* to the great river valleys.

4. Imperial Feudalism or the Feudal Bureaucratic Empire (3rd century B.C.–19th century A.D.), wherein the same intensive agrarian economy was developed from a regional to an inter-regional basis, a confederation of walled-town-and-rural-hinterland units loosely linked in stable periods by an imperial dynasty and its bureaucratic staff of mandarin civil servants, but falling apart into its regional and district components in unstable times.

5. Socialist Industrialism and centrally planned economy, a great new historical epoch just now opening.

In Regional Feudalism, the state of the productive arts was such as to support a society of no more than local extent—a river valley or a natural basin. The ruling class consisted mainly of soldier landowners. In Imperial Feudalism, the organization of production developed sufficiently to make a degree of inter-regional exploitation more profitable than purely regional production—given conditions of relative social stability. The social organization of production remained basically feudal, but the larger scale of exploitation required an elite corps of literate administrative officials instead of military leaders. Hence in imperial times the ruling class came to consist of scholar landowners.

Imperial Feudalism, compared to Regional Feudalism, entailed a somewhat greater development of economic specialization, such as com-

---

* Loess in northwest China is brownish-yellow, fine windblown soil, very fertile when watered.

merce and handicrafts, and hence of urbanism. It also involved a slow advance in the productive arts and sciences, and a trend–often reversed–toward geographic expansion of the Chinese realm. The Han Dynasty at the beginning of the imperial era ruled only a portion of the area owing suzerainty to the Ching Dynasty at the end.

Although China's two feudal epochs deserve to be distinguished from each other, it is important not to overemphasize their differences, as such Western writers as Wittfogel, Max Weber, and, to a lesser extent, Owen Lattimore have tended to do. Their picture of Imperial China as a society rather highly centralized and bureaucratized by the influence of the great public water works is a partial distortion. Actually, the pre-industrial economy never freed itself from the limitations of local self-sufficiency, even in the prosperous times of national unity and dynastic stability. Nor did the class system ever deviate notably from its basically feudal character of landlord domination of peasant and craftsman. Loose integrations of villages constituted a walled-town district; similar confederations of districts comprised the region; and of the regions, the nation. In times of strife, village and town and region alike necessarily fell back on increased self-sufficiency, and the central power virtually disappeared, sometimes for centuries. Mao Tse-tung, writing of the contrasts between present-day China and pre-industrial China, characterizes the latter as essentially feudal for the 3000 years prior to the mid-19th century. That he makes no distinction between Regional and Imperial Feudalism in contrasting feudal with post-feudal China is in itself significant (*Selected Works*, International Publishers, New York, Vol. III, pp. 72–101).

Further study of Chinese and other feudalisms should greatly increase our knowledge of the laws of social evolution. Indeed, the new perspectives on social change entailed by the Chinese Revolution, shattering, as it does, many of our outworn and imprisoning Western preconceptions of social life, should prove to be among the great landmarks of contemporary social science.

As we look back over the five stages of Chinese civilization we have somewhat arbitrarily marked off, we may observe that kinship groups (like family and clan) become less prominent, while specialized occupational and economic roles become more important. This is just another way of expressing the long-run trend toward economic centralization. As Engels wrote in 1884:

> The social organization under which the people of a particular historical epoch and a particular country live is determined by . . . the development of labor and of the family. The lower the development of labor and the more limited the amount of its products and the wealth of the society, the more the social order is found to be dominated by kinship

groups. . . . As the productivity of labor develops, and with it private property, differences of wealth . . . and hence the basis of class antagonisms
. . . the old society founded on kinship groups is broken up; in its place
appears a new society, with its control centered in the State. . . . (*Origin
of the Family*, New York, 1942, pp. 5–6.)

To the five primary stages outlined above we should add transition
or interregnum periods. These may, perhaps arbitrarily, be divided into
two types: those that fall *between* the primary stages, and those that
occur *within* them. Both are periods of social upheaval. The former we
may appropriately call revolutions, because the social order emerging
after the conflict differs substantially from that which existed before.
The latter we shall call rebellions, since the reconstructed order that
grew out of the period of disorder was a variation of the same basic type
existing before the interregnum. For this distinction, we are indebted
to T. T. Meadows.

The Feudal Bureaucratic Empire had a well-defined cycle of relative
stability and collapse. Even during its comparatively stable periods, local
peasant uprisings were not uncommon. But especially between the powerful dynasties there intervened long stretches of civil strife and partition. "The gigantic scale of such peasant uprisings and peasant wars in
Chinese history is without parallel in the world." (Mao Tse-tung, *ibid*,
p. 76.) Yet until the 19th century it was fundamentally the same feudal
type of society that was always reconstructed, with some adjustment to
changed conditions and with a new dynasty in control. Reform and several generations of uneasy stability would follow, and then another
phase of decline. These interregna are examples of rebellions.

But the interregna before and after the Feudal Bureaucratic Empire
marked off Regional from Imperial Feudalism, and Imperial Feudalism
from Socialism. Since they demarcate different social systems, we may
view them as genuine social revolutions. We shall call the last revolutionary interim (1840s–1940s) the "Foreign Imperialist Interregnum." More on
this later.

Considered as a living and effectively functioning social system, the
type of society which had prevailed in China for 2000 years ended in the
mid-19th century. The domestic cycle of dynastic and internal decline
coincided with European capitalist expansion, and was accentuated by
it, especially after the 18th century. A crescendo of regional uprisings
and famines culminated in the Taiping holocaust, 1850–1865. The relative
importance of foreign and domestic causes of this debacle is not clear,
nor does it greatly matter. Mao Tse-tung holds that Chinese feudalism
was slowly developing a market economy which would in time have
brought forth an indigenous capitalism, and that the intrusion of foreign

capitalism merely speeded up this process (*ibid*, p. 77). Certainly, the pulverizing impact of an aggressive and technologically superior industrial society made forever impossible the hitherto "normal" restoration of the feudal bureaucracy. Of course, important elements of that social order survived for another century, but only as subordinate parts of what Mao calls a "semi-colonial and semi-feudal society" (pp. 76–82). Unable to stand on its own feet after the Taiping appeared, the feudal ruling class of scholar gentry, in return for preserving a portion of their old privileges, sold out the rest to foreign (and later domestic) capitalist interests. The tension between feudalism and capitalism (foreign and domestic), though great, was usually less than that between feudal landlord and rebellious peasant. But however the feudal elements contrived to stave off the final reckoning, their contingent and partial survival after the 1850s cannot be considered as simply the same old feudalism. The moribund Manchu Dynasty, for instance, was rescued from the Taiping revolution by the Western powers, after they had extorted from it all sorts of political and economic concessions. As their exploitive tool, it nominally reigned until 1911.

Like most such summaries, our system of stages and interregna is oversimplified. Historical eras, even revolutionary ones, merge into each other. This must be understood of all our chronological divisions. For example, there were feudal elements in Chinese society both before and after the "feudal age," but they were unqualifiedly dominant only during that period. Another example: the impact of the industrial revolution,* most of which lies ahead, started with the advent of European maritime traders in the 17th century. It became a decisive force, via foreign imperialism, in the 19th century. But only today, domesticated in an unfolding socialist society, has the industrial revolution become a central feature of a major new historical era.

Having glanced at the general span of Chinese civilization, we now turn to the last two phases, the Feudal Bureaucratic Era and the Foreign Imperialist Interregnum, which are the important antecedents of contemporary China. To take a comprehensive and dynamic approach, let us consider the Imperial Feudal Era as thesis, the Foreign Imperialist Interregnum as antithesis, and the merging socialist order as synthesis. This dialectical frame of reference highlights the organic emergence of the present from the past. It helps us to set off the main phases of a society's history without sacrificing its continuity. It brings out both conflict and integration. It impels us to look at history in the long run

---

* Defined, not merely as technological inventions, but as a broad social transformation attending the introduction of a machine economy, and affecting all aspects of life.

as a process of change and to fit into that dynamic context the often extensive periods of relative stability. But we must remember that this three-phase scheme is simply an aid to understanding, a point of view, not a set of substantive concepts with fixed historical content. Any given period may be viewed in terms of thesis, antithesis, and synthesis—with the content depending on the problem in hand.

Thesis: The Feudal Bureaucratic Empire (3rd c. B.C.–19th c. A.D.)

The intensive agricultural economy that characterized this era origi-nated in the loess (wind-blown soil) region of northwest China. The key to its successful expansion was the control of water and manpower. For the great rivers of China pour from the central Asian highlands onto fertile lowlands, where they dump their heavy silt loads long before reach-ing the sea. The resulting instability of water courses prevented exten-sive human settlement without a vast system of flood control and irri-gation works. That problem was solved by the development, over many centuries and with many setbacks, of a state apparatus responsible for building public works, administering manpower and taxes, keeping rec-ords, and so on.

In the loess hills, single families or villages could manage the small-scale beginnings of irrigation techniques. Eventually the greater returns accruing from more intensive farming led to regional feudal kingdoms. For the same reason, the feudal empire ultimately supplanted regional feudalism. The colossal river systems could be harnessed more profitably by an imperial confederation than by provincial feudal units.

Wealth and power in feudal China ultimately depended on control of grain and manpower, chiefly in the form of rents, taxes, and labor levies. The economic and political demand for a dense and docile pop-ulation was expressed and reinforced by the Confucian ideology of filial piety and prolific families. Families and villages rather than individuals were the basic social units. Most peasants lived in compact villages, out-side of which lay their small and scattered patches of tillage. Wherever the land was fertile, the Chinese countryside was typically segmented into fairly self-sufficient and heavily populated districts, each consisting of a walled town and the surrounding villages within a score or two score miles.

If we overlook subdivisions and fringe groups, we find three main so-cial classes: peasantry, artisans, and gentry. Peasants and artisans were the producers; many owned their tiny plots of land. The gentry were landlords, usually on a small scale, for China had few large estates. Some-times they were also officials and merchants. The peasants were villag-

ers, living in one-family households. The gentry were town dwellers residing in the "Great Houses"–joint households with parents, married
sons, and servants under one roof and patriarchal authority but in separate apartments. Artisans were sometimes villagers, but more commonly townsmen, where they were often organized in kinship-oriented
gilds.

Now, the munificent gentry style of life could not long be maintained
by landed wealth alone, because of the large proportion of idle household members and because of the tendency to divide the land among
all the sons. In contrast to feudal Europe, primogeniture and entailed
estates were absent from China, where free trade in land was general.
Hence gentry families were under chronic pressure to acquire additional income, either mercantile or official, to supplement their rents.
Placing a son or a relative in the mandarin bureaucracy was the best
solution. It enabled a family to tap systematically the various public taxes
and levies–the prime available source of wealth, next to rent, in pre-
industrial China. For the mandarins farmed the taxes. They collected as
much as custom and local imposts permitted, but they passed on to the
imperial treasury only the legally fixed minimum.

Mandarins were civil officials appointed by the emperor and stationed in the cities and towns to administer the local engineering, police, fiscal, and other public functions. Admission to their bureaucratic
elite depended on passing a series of examinations in the Confucian classics. Nominally these tests were open to all comers. But because education was largely private and because mastery of the purposely intricate
Chinese script required years of leisure, the gentry cornered the plums.
Hence the gentry and the scholars constituted one class, the scholar gentry, feudal China's ruling elite.

While most peasant families lived close to a subsistence minimum,
the economy as a whole produced a surplus under normal conditions.
It was this surplus, appropriated by the gentry in the form of rent and
taxes, which made possible China's great public works, her central governing apparatus, her class system, the centuries of cultural achievement, and a degree of urbanization, modest perhaps by contemporary
Western standards, but unequaled by pre-industrial societies.

We can now understand the cycle of rebellions which was indigenous
to China. The gentry's role as landlord conflicted with its role as tax-
collector. The more rent, the less taxes. When the gentry diverted too
much of the national surplus to their private interests, the indispensable
public works were neglected. The economy suffered, floods and famines
fanned mass discontent, and in extreme cases general rebellions broke
out. The nation fell apart into its regional components. After a long

period of civil strife, a strong man arose to clean house and reunify the country under a new dynasty.

To domestic competition for the economic surplus was added the pressure of the northwest frontier for trade, subsidies, and resources for defense or offense. A symbiotic relationship prevailed between China and the nomadic steppe society of Mongolia and western Manchuria, ably analyzed in Owen Lattimore's classic *Inner Asian Frontiers of China* (New York, 1940). The two societies competed for control of the trade naturally developing between complementary economies, and for control of the border zone along the Great Wall between them. Neither could permanently master the other, however, without becoming like the other. Invasions by either were little more than plundering raids. If the nomads tried to stay in China, for instance, they had perforce to adopt Chinese social organization, since the Chinese realm—given its geography and the existing pre-industrial level of the productive arts—could be profitably exploited in no other way. Hence the proverbial saying, valid for pre-industrial times, that "China swallows her conquerors."

Only when imperial China was efficiently administered could she produce enough wealth to meet the demands of both the central realm and the northwest periphery. The drain of the frontier on Chinese resources reinforced the more basic domestic pressures toward extreme social atomization inherent in feudal China, where the fundamental tension was that between landlord and peasant. These centrifugal tendencies were clearly evident during the various interregna.

Imperial China went through several periods of decline and restoration. That the same basic type of society, with variations, was always rebuilt must not obscure the reality of social change, however slow. There were at least five stretches of relative stability: The Han dynasty (202 B.C.–220 A.D.), the Tang dynasty (618–907), the Sung dynasty (960–1280), the Ming dynasty (1366–1644), and the Sinified Manchu or Ching regime (effective span c.1660–c.1850). The framework of the imperial feudal confederation was first constructed by the Han in north and central China. Later times saw the Chinese realm extended far southward. The civil service examination system was mainly a Tang accomplishment. So was the development of printing, although further important contributions to printing came during the Sung. The crucially important Grand Canal, linking the lower Yangtze and Yellow rivers, was completed around 600 A.D. Great scientific and engineering advances, including the invention of gunpowder and the magnetic compass, were made in the Sung age. In that same period, the Confucian ideology, originally a product of the revolutionary transition from feudalism to the empire, was considerably refined. Imperial China was definitely not a static social order.

We must not limit our attention to economic, political, and class aspects of Chinese society, basic as those are. All phases of social life are more or less interrelated. Perhaps nowhere is this more evident than in Chinese history, the longest known span of social evolution. The appearance of an important book on the contributions of preindustrial China to science is therefore timely. Let us consider it briefly before we take up the foreign imperialist interregnum.

Science and Civilization in China

Professor Needham's book of this title is the first of a seven-volume work which has been called with considerable justification the West's most significant contribution to Sinology. It covers mainly the feudal and imperial eras.

An eminent biochemist and historian of science, Needham is one of several first-rank British scholars who have shown a humanist awareness of progressive world movements, and who have not feared to use Marxist ideas where relevant to their special fields. Unfortunately for American scholarship, this group has almost no counterpart in America, except beyond the academic pale.

This does not mean that Needham's work is Marxist. But it takes account of the social environment of Chinese science and its evolutionary development. This contrasts sharply with the current emphasis on ideal factors and static approaches in American social studies. Indeed, Needham's notable work probably could not have been written in the United States today, partly because of the inner bent of American social science, but even more because of the dominant institutional and class pressures against social changes that seem to threaten the primacy of monopoly capitalism.

Needham's first volume emphasizes three premises: a dynamic framework, the close relation between history and geography, and the mutual interdependence of economy, art, science, and religion. There are impressive summaries of Chinese history, foreign contacts, and geography. The geographic description is perhaps too detailed to be as revealing as the one in Fitzgerald's *Chinese Revolution*. Later volumes will deal with the history of physics, mathematics, chemistry, biology, and their related technologies. The philosophies of China are to be analyzed in terms of their social contexts in Volumes 2 and 7. This is as it should be. Social theory has little meaning apart from its institutional setting. All in all, few other recent works are as significant for so many different fields of learning.

It is equally valuable as a contribution to international understanding.

Its illumination of pre-industrial Chinese civilization will help to clear away obsolete Western stereotypes about China. To realize its potential impact, however, an inexpensive one-volume abridgement in simple language should be made available. A seven-volume work, somewhat expensive and including innumerable footnotes in both English and Chinese, is not very likely to have a mass appeal.

We can perhaps best convey the humanist spirit of Needham's work by citing his preface, page 9:

> For better or worse, the world is one. The citizen of the world has to live with his fellow-citizens. . . . He can only give them the understanding which they deserve if he knows the achievements and precursors of their culture as well as of his own. We are living at the dawn of a new universalism, which, if humanity survives the dangers attendant on control by irresponsible men of sources of power hitherto unimaginable, will unite the working people of all races in a community both catholic and cooperative. . . . Are not Europeans, viewing the effects of science, tempted too often to say to themselves that this began in Europe with Galileo and Vesalius, and to conclude that Wisdom was born with us? A salutary correction of perspective is necessary. There *was* a Chinese contribution to man's understanding of Nature, and his control over it, and it was a great one. . . . Their achievements should be mutually recognized and freely celebrated with the joined hands of universal brotherhood.

II.

OUR AIM in this paper is to outline a view of Chinese history that accords with the facts better than prevailing Western conception does. The latter stems from the limited experience of the past century, when China was weak, backward, and forcibly opened by and for Western exploitation. During most of history, however, China has been not only a great state, but a leader in science and civilization. With the recent consolidation of the Communist regime, China has resumed her normal Great Power status. We believe that this event, like the Russian Revolution, is a decisive turning point of world history. The two revolutions, really chapters of the same worldwide industrial revolution, indicate that the mainstream of man's social evolution has now entered irreversibly upon its socialist phase.

Perhaps human society will yet be wrecked by the suicidal schemes of irresponsible Western leaders. Barring that catastrophe, the next age of man is already unfolding in Eurasia. As we work toward socialism ourselves, we must study its origins and development elsewhere. In the first half of this article we suggested that this can be effectively done, in the case of China, by viewing the latest three epochs of Chinese history as *thesis* (the 2000-year Feudal Bureaucratic Empire), *antithesis* (the Foreign Imperialist Interregnum, mid-19th to mid-20th c.), and *synthesis* (Socialist Industrialism, mid-20th c. ff.). Having already discussed the first, let us proceed to the second.

Antithesis: The Foreign Imperialist Interregnum

We feel that this term best sums up the last century of Chinese history, from the Anglo-French opium wars of the 1840s and 1850s to the unsuccessful American intervention of the 1940s and 1950s. During that period, the dominant social process in China, which all others had to adjust to or take major account of, was surely the aggressive invasion of foreign capitalist civilization – not simply political and military but also technological and intellectual. That several foreign powers, including Japan and the United States as well as the European states, were active in this invasion at different times does not alter the general picture.

The broad result of the era was the crumbling of the agrarian feudal society and the introduction of new social elements. Of itself, it brought no stable reconstruction. It was a time of troubles, of chronic unrest and occasional upheaval – a revolutionary interim between major historical epochs.

The conventional view of Western bourgeois historians terminates the Chinese Empire and begins the Revolution in 1911, when the Manchu Dynasty finally gave way to Sun Yat-sen's Republic. It sees the culmination of the Chinese Revolution in the Nationalist uprising of the mid-1920s under Chiang Kai-shek. We disagree with this superficial view. It obscures the basic social processes, both Chinese and worldwide, instead of revealing them.

The essence of the Chinese Revolution is the replacement of the locally self-sufficient agrarian economy by a centrally planned, world-oriented industrial economy. This means the transformation of all aspects of social life. As a long stretch of ferment, beginning perhaps in the 17th century, preceded it, so an indefinite time of consolidation lies ahead. But the more violent upheavals attending this social revolution appear to have been concentrated, barring another world war, in the hundred years just passed. The industrial way of life first came to China by force from without. Independence was lost, and had to be regained.

In the 19th century, Western capitalism was aggressively expanding, and Chinese society was in one of its periodic phases of internal decay. The stage was set for foreign imperialism. Agrarian China could not cope with the superior economic, military, and political technologies of the West. British factory-made textiles, for instance, could undersell Chinese homespun in China. A major prop of the peasant economy—handicrafts—was thus badly damaged. Political and religious imperialism followed these economic inroads. Mao Tse-tung states that feudal China's slowly growing market economy "would have developed into a capitalist society even if there had been no influence of foreign capitalism. The penetration of foreign capitalism accelerated this development . . . because it destroyed the foundation of her self-sufficing natural economy and disrupted her handicraft industries in both the cities and peasant homes, and it accelerated the development of commodity economy in town and country." (*Selected Works*, Vol. III, p. 77.)

Later in the interregnum, two new processes emerged organically from world capitalist society: the intensification of international war, and socialism. These developments ultimately enabled China to escape from imperialist domination. Her captors cut each other down in two world wars. Japan finally expelled the European powers from China, and America defeated Japan. Meanwhile Russian socialism showed the way to rational mastery of the new economic techniques for the general welfare.

Settlement of China's century-long crisis required the regaining of independence and the carrying through of drastic reforms toward socialism. Slowly pressures toward these two ends grew, at first unsuccessfully, as in the 1900 Boxer outbreak, then inadequately in the Nationalist rising of the mid-1920s. Chiang Kai-shek's Kuomintang failed because it fought against reform and not against Japanese aggression, by far the worst of the entire interregnum period. Independence and reform proved to be inseparable. Rejecting one, Chiang lost both. China recovered herself only when the Communist movement united all classes in the 1940s for full independence and complete social reform.

During the interregnum China took on the typical features of economic colonialism: foreign domination of strategic economic sectors, such as modern industry and transport, banking and foreign trade; rural stagnation and overpopulation; a luxurious upper class and poverty-ridden masses; and a conspicuous lack of the diversified investment, mass education, and other assets necessary for general industrialization. Until the 1920s the Chinese tariff was set and managed by Westerners!

For a century, foreign powers dominated China, both indirectly through a series of weak native regimes and by occasional surges of direct action. In 1860, and again in 1900, Western forces seized Peking and dictated conqueror's terms. In the 1930s, Japan helped herself to several provinces. But in the late 1940s and 1950s, the intervention of the mightiest capitalist nation was decisively repelled. Though foreign imperialism may remain an important pressure in Chinese affairs, it can no longer dominate them. The interregnum has ended. A new historical epoch has begun. Antithesis has given way to synthesis.

The Taiping Revolution

The rest of this paper deals with a little-known phase of the early interregnum. The Taiping state is important because its impending victory in civil war led directly to hostile Western intervention, and because it was the first chapter of the modern Chinese revolution.

About 1850, revolt broke out near Canton. It was a peasant rising, a response to a half century of growing tyranny, economic disasters, famines, Manchu decadence, plunder, piracy, and foreign defeat. Disorder pervaded China. Not only was the outbreak a typical rebellion seeking to replace a hopelessly incompetent dynasty. It was a revolution looking toward major changes in the traditional social order. Its ideology included a vigorous homespun version of Protestant Christianity mixed with Confucian elements. This was the only occasion when anything resembling Christianity won a mass following in China, doubtless because it was a *native* prophetic movement.

Like the Communists of a later day, the Taipings developed superior military organization and tactics. Following a long march northward, they established the Taiping, or "Great Peace," kingdom with Nanking as its capital. At one time or another they controlled much of central and south China. The revolutionary State was not suppressed for fifteen years, and then only by foreign intervention. Estimates of all fatalities run as high as twenty million.

Clearly this was a social upheaval of the greatest magnitude. Yet most Occidentals have never even heard of this epic event. Could there be a more dramatic proof of Western insularity?

Bourgeois historians usually belittle the Taiping movement as foredoomed to failure by its own weaknesses. The *Encyclopedia Britannica* account by K. S. Latourette of Yale says, "[The Taipings] showed an utter lack of ability to organize their conquests."

But a fresh review of the matter suggests that this is a distorted verdict. Compared to their Manchu foe, whose degeneracy is attested by all concerned, the Taipings were a progressive force. They reduced taxes on the oppressed peasantry, redistributed land, notably improved the status of women, restored order, and vigorously combatted bribery and opium. They ended the use of legal torture in judicial proceedings, regularized the calendar, and introduced a colloquial literary style. Their fanatical assaults on Buddhist idolatry hit hard at religious superstition, a bulwark of mass docility (because of its other-worldly preoccupation) and therefore a mainstay of gentry class rule.

At least around Nanking, the Taipings practiced a form of theocratic socialism. Units of 25 families worked their land together and pooled their crops and handicrafts in a common treasury, distributed according to need, with the surplus belonging to the community. Pyramided like an army, these units carried out the major economic, civil, military, and religious functions. The military officers were also the civil and religious leaders. There were serious but sporadic efforts to determine leadership by merit. In their mass printing and study of the Bible, the Taipings showed tendencies toward popular education.

As they became more aware of the outside world, the chiefs reacted favorably to the idea of Western technology and trade, but only on the basis of equality, without extraterritoriality. In certain respects, especially where knowledge of alternatives was lacking, they manifested retrogressive feudal patterns—nepotism, royal pageantry, religious escapism, harsh punishments. They had no comprehensive awareness of their social situation, such as the industrial experience of the West was then making available in Marxism.

Yet their natural posture was indisputably forward leaning. A contemporary British traveler pictured the Taipings as "a clever, candid and martial people, rendered peculiarly attractive by the indescribable air of freedom which they possess." In the Manchu-ruled areas he noted "dull apathetic countenances, without expression or intelligence . . . their energies seem bound, their spirits crushed by oppression." (A. F. Lindley, *Ti-Ping Tien-Kwoh*, London, 1866, p. 67. Incidentally, the late General Stilwell was a great admirer of this book.)

Counter-revolution: Western Style

Several factors contributed to the Taiping defeat. Among them were failure to concentrate their forces against the Manchu capital, lack of a united front with other anti-Manchu but non-revolutionary rebelling groups, the divisive effects of surviving local and clan loyalties, and the tendency of religious fanaticism to obscure political realism. More important, probably, was the violent internal schism of 1856, which seems to have lopped off much of the radical and realistic wing. Little is known for certain, but nepotism and religious obscurantism seem to have been considerably strengthened after the purge. Yet the regime soon produced new and very able leaders who could again inflict great defeats on the Manchu forces. And Lindley's firsthand comparison of the Manchu and Taiping sections of the Yangtze valley in 1861 clearly shows the social and economic superiority of the latter. (*Ti-Ping Tien-Kwoh*, Vol. 1.)

The bourgeois theory that the Taipings fell because of their internal weaknesses does not carry much conviction in view of the even greater Manchu failings. Let us suggest instead that the productive and defensive and communicative techniques and social organization needed to stabilize the new order were not available to a pre-industrial and practically preliterate peasantry *surrounded by hostile and far more powerful industrial nations.*

For what really tipped the balance against the Taipings was the intervention of the British and French (especially after 1860) with their vastly superior military technology. What use were Taiping spears and matchlocks against Armstrong-Vickers cannon?

Why did the Western powers intervene? Because of their vested interest in a weak, corrupt, and opium-besotted China. Profits, power, and social reaction molded the coalition of Manchus, Chinese gentry, and Westerners against the revolutionary Taipings.

Western capitalists sought to expand their trade with the Chinese. By far the most profitable item was the smuggling of opium from India, where it was produced under government auspices, into China. Although imperial decrees forbade the import and use of opium, Chinese local officials were easily bribed. The opium trade became a prime source of the Indian government's revenue. Moreover, opium was the only product that could be sold in China on a wide enough scale to pay for Britain's purchases of Chinese tea. The tea trade was another huge vested interest, both in terms of profit to English importers and in terms of revenue to the British Crown. After the 1830s opium smuggling into China by Western merchants became so extensive that it caused a large drain of Chinese silver to India and a disastrous inflation in south China. This greatly intensified revolutionary conditions, as Marx pointed out in one of his brilliant New York *Tribune* articles in 1853. (*Marx on China*, London, 1951, Ch. 1.)

Although pre-industrial China's trade was well developed, it operated within local, clan, and traditional controls, dominated by the provincial and district mandarins. There was no nationwide standardized tax system, market, legal code, or coinage. The West's depersonalized capitalism, confined to one or two ports, therefore met with innumerable "squeezes" and restrictions. So the British, seeking new trade outlets, picked a suitable occasion in the early 1840s for a short and successful war. They repeated the performance again in the late 1850s with French aid. Western armies seized Peking, razed the priceless Summer Palace as an object lesson, and dictated terms which legalized the opium trade, broadened extraterritorial concessions, imposed an indemnity, and set up a Western-staffed tariff system wholly favorable to the West.

"No right-thinking foreigner now wished to support the Taiping cause," as the scholarly S. F. Wright, a former Commissioner of the China Customs Service, so candidly puts it. (*Hart and the Chinese Customs*, 1950, p. 147.)

Having plucked these choice plums from the helpless Manchu regime, the Europeans then intervened against the Taipings. British and French warships and troops went into action; Manchu armies were transported on the Yangtze; supplies and arms were issued; militia forces were imported from the Philippines; contingents of Chinese soldiers were trained and led by white officers. Among the latter were Frederick Ward, an American freebooter, and Charles Gordon, an English artillery major. European cannon beat down Taiping city walls, and Manchu soldiers butchered civilians by the thousands.

Familiar pattern, isn't it?

Even the handful of Christian missionaries, with a few exceptions, tacitly joined the counter-revolution against the Taipings. More than one Protestant parson acted as intelligence agent, and a Catholic priest was killed in action while leading a Filipino militia detachment. At first very sympathetic to the Taipings, most missionaries were alienated when they discovered that the new movement insisted on its own prophetic inspiration and interpretation. The Taipings welcomed exchanges with missionaries, but refused their leadership. That the Chinese should deal directly with God, and vice versa, was inconceivable to the Westerners. So the religious imperialists, somewhat reluctantly, climbed on the interventionist bandwagon.

This uneasy alliance of native reaction and foreign imperialism was in effect a united front against the Chinese people. It stifled China's first modern revolution and made possible the gradual partitioning of her empire. Within a generation or so of the Taiping defeat in 1865, Britain annexed Burma, France seized Indo-China, Japan took Formosa and Korea, Germany began on Shantung, and Russia on Manchuria. And let us not forget that America's allegedly altruistic "open door" policy in China was simply an imperialist version of "me too."

Let us observe also the demonstrated futility of seeking social reforms within China's traditional social structure. From Tseng Kuo-fan (leader against the Taipings) to his ardent admirer Chiang Kai-shek, "reform within the existing framework" has been a professed aim of many native and foreign opponents of China's various revolutionary movements. It is still American policy in Southeast Asia and in the Point Four idea. But it is a contradiction in terms. A viable industrial order cannot be grafted onto a pre-industrial class and political structure.

An English Civil Servant on Chinese Rebellions

In 1856, an able analysis of the Taiping uprising was published by a British Civil Service interpreter stationed in China. This was Thomas Meadows' *The Chinese and their Rebellions*, recently reprinted by Academic Reprints (Stanford, N.D.). Besides being a noteworthy contribution to historical scholarship, this work influenced the development of the British Civil Service and was an important stimulus to Tolstoy's profound interest in China during his later years. Meadows had a rare ability to discern deeper historical trends beneath surface events. His book was written, first, to lay bare some basic social forces in Chinese history; and second, to warn the Western powers, in the light of his analysis, against intervening in China's internal affairs. It succeeded in the first aim but failed in the second. Let us quote some key passages, abridged from Chapters 2 and 20:

> *The Nature of Dynastic Authority.* "The successor to the throne is not considered by himself or by others the [legitimate ruler] unless he gives peace and plenty to the empire. The disasters of war, pestilence and famine are but ways by which Heaven declares that the occupant of the throne is not its chosen representative, or that he has ceased to be such. All nature animate and inanimate is based on the principle, the "way of Heaven." So long as the occupant of the throne rules with the rectitude and goodness which are the chief features of this law, both man and nature gladly submit, and peace and plenty prevail. When he violates this law, the passions of man and the powers of the elements alike break loose. Rebellion is the legitimate means of stopping vicious legislation and administration." [Formosa and the China Lobby, please copy!]

That Meadows was basically correct in his understanding of pre-industrial China's rebellion cycle and in his perception of the corrupt Manchu Dynasty's imminent collapse is clear. But he did not realize that the Western impact would preclude restoration of the traditional order, nor that the Taipings were challengers rather than rebuilders of the old empire.

> *Meadow's Advice to the Western Powers.* "Disinterested interference of one nation with another has never yet taken place. But we are being summoned to interference with the Chinese in the cause of humanity and civilization. All interference is bad; unsuccessful interference is the least bad. When put an end to by the final success of the party which it opposed, an internally very strong government is the certain result. If the interference is successful, the certain result is a weak government – a cowardly, vicious and cruel government. In this volume it has been shown that periodic dynastic rebellions are necessary to the well-being of China; that the nation is well aware of the political functions of its

rebellions; and that it respects successful rebellions as executions of the
Will of Heaven, operating for its peace and prosperity. Will not the
reader freely pardon me, if I have been unable to repress a somewhat
bitter expression of the feelings I entertain for all attempts to urge or
entrap the maritime powers of the Occident into a coarse physical repression of the Taiping rebellion?"

Surely this is one of the most perceptive passages in all political literature. Did not the successful Western interference of the 1860s produce a weak and vicious Chinese government? And did not the unsuccessful American intervention in the 1940s and 1950s facilitate the
emergence of a strong Chinese regime?

Judging by present-day American parallels, we might expect Meadows to have been sacked—or worse—for telling his government some
unpalatable truths. Not so, however. Imperialism a century ago was expansive and self-confident; today it is neither. Meadows was promoted
to Consul and stationed at Shanghai; by 1864, he was at Newchwang in
south Manchuria. This transfer to the far provinces seems to have been
the extent of his punishment. He continued to refute the official slan-
ders against the Taipings and to criticize European interference even
after intervention was well under way. Small wonder that his imperialist-
minded colleagues considered him "impracticable and mischievous."
(*Hart and the Chinese Customs*, p. 214.)

Compare the cases of Service, Vincent, and Davies, recently hounded
out of the American Foreign Service. Or consider Owen Lattimore, a
target of official persecutions for several years. No one familiar with
Marxism would classify these men as Marxists. But they could recognize
that the Kuomintang was bankrupt and on its way out. Their basic crime
was an ability to face this fact. In 1944, J. P. Davies wrote to the State
Department from Chungking: "The Communists are in China to stay.
And China's destiny is not Chiang's but theirs." (*United States Relations
with China*, Department of State, 1949, p. 573.)

Should Americans become generally aware that Chinese Communism grew out of native resources and old-regime corruption, that it has
unified China into a great power, and that the Foreign Imperialist Interregnum is therefore ended, the ground would be cut from under the
present United States policy of intervention against the revolutions in
Asia by whatever means our own people and our allies can be persuaded
to accept. To protect that policy and the murky interests it serves, people
like Lattimore, who tell much truth about China, are sealed off from
public opinion by governmental smears and official persecutions.

Imperialist aggression against China, by force and by alliance with
weak native reactionaries, has seldom been due to *official* ignorance.

From the beginning to end of the Foreign Imperialist Interregnum, the aggressor nations have had at their disposal excellent analyses of Chinese affairs. *Popular* ignorance about China, carefully fostered by official propaganda and by indirect ruling-class control of communication and education, has always been an essential condition of Western imperialism. Certain elements in our ruling circles, it seems, do not trust their interests to an enlightened democracy. How else, except in terms of a conflict between the interests of ruling capitalist groups and the interests of the common man, can we explain the glaring discrepancy between the facts about China which our government receives (or could receive if it had not deliberately fired all its competent Far East experts) and the parochial tripe concerning China which it hands out?

Imperialist aggression against China could not be ended until the Chinese were strong enough to repel it by force. No amount of window dressing can obscure that historical fact. We therefore face the disastrous prospect of continued imperialist activity by American capitalism until all other colonial areas are similarly closed. But is there no alternative policy? There is indeed. Not Point Four: the impossibility of grafting an industrial economy onto a pre-industrial social order has been demonstrated more than once in this magazine. The sole practical alternative is for Americans to reorganize their society along socialist lines. "Socialism is the only answer."

Town and Countryside vs. Metropolis:

The Canadian Scene from Moose Jaw, Saskatchewan October 19, 1970*

Introduction

M R. CHAIRMAN, fellow citizens of Saskatchewan, ladies and gentle-men: When I first came to Saskatchewan a dozen years ago, Tommy Douglas was Premier. Tommy must have been one of North America's greatest orators, at least while he stayed in Saskatchewan. He could roll up an audience in the hollow of his hand, even when it was initially skeptical or hostile. How he could do this was one of the things about Saskatchewan that puzzled me for some years. It could hardly have been his jokes. He always began with a few good stories, but in time we could almost always tell which one was coming next. Like the one about the husband-wife argument over who was boss. As the husband put the mat-ter, *she* decided how the family budget was spent; *she* decided where they should live, and where they should go for holidays. But–and this was the punch line–*he* decided all the really important questions in the household–what should be done about Communist China in the United Nations; what should be done about Cuba; and how race relations in the United States ought to be handled. So the husband concluded, he was boss. And with that climatic line, Tommy Douglas' audiences would rock with laughter–sometimes even before he finished telling the joke.

Reprinted by permission of the University of Saskatchewan. From *Plain Talk*, 1970/71. A Series of Public Lectures on the Theme–Survival. Sponsored by the Regina Campus. Transcribed from the tape.
* The War Measures Act was proclaimed on October 16, 1970.

After observing Saskatchewan for a while (I lived here six years, 1958–64, before moving to Alberta), it occurred to me that perhaps the reason for the popularity of such jokes in the Saskatchewan hinterland was their theme of conflict. The Tommy Douglas story I just recounted includes several types of conflict themes: the universal one of marital argument, and several political conflicts that might affect Saskatchewan in important ways, but about which for the most part Saskatchewan people could do little or nothing to decide their own future.

The history of Saskatchewan has been full of struggles – struggles against the natural elements of an adverse climate, struggles against the exploitation of Eastern corporate interests and their local henchmen. From pioneering times, the people of Saskatchewan towns and farms found themselves involved willy-nilly in one confrontation after another. By touching on these realities, instinctively recognized by his audiences, Tommy Douglas hit upon a central fact of prairie life. The humour lay in the slightly incongruous presentation of some very deep realities.

Social Erosion of the Hinterlands by Metropolis

Let us now turn to another aspect of conflict. Much is being said nowadays about the erosion of the Saskatchewan environment and indeed of the Canadian environment. The worsening impact of air pollution, water pollution and land pollution needs no emphasis from me. There are those who talk about the possibility that man may be sealing his own fate unless strong countermeasures are taken soon on a large scaie. A later meeting in this series will deal in detail with "Survival and the Pollution Problem." What I wish to suggest tonight is that environmental erosion, or pollution, is best seen in a much larger perspective, and one that is already familiar to Prairie people. This perspective is that of hinterland against metropolis.

Ordinary pollution is a by-product of the erosion of the social environment. It is an aspect of the on-going exploitation of hinterland people and resources by metropolitan corporate and political interests. If there is a solution to this problem; if we hope to preserve any substantial part of our present community and social values, we must change those particular corporate principles and practices which threaten us. In other words, the answer to air and water pollution is not merely repairing the obvious physical damage – we need to do that too, of course – the answer lies in a drastic change in Canadian values and Canadian organizational structures, and in Canadian public policy.

Our biggest problem is social erosion, not air or water erosion. And in line with my conflict view of Canadian history and Canadian regions,

I believe that we must approach any salvage program in terms of hinterland against metropolis. The hinterlands of Canada must unite to reconquer metropolis, just as the hinterlands of the world must either pull down the American metropolis, or else perish from the earth.

Here may I backtrack, to explain some of my terms. *Metropolis* refers to centres or groups exercising political and economic control of large enterprises, usually headquartered in big cities. For example, this could mean decision-making urban elites, corporation managers, political party bosses, the military leaders, university boards of governors, heads of the big churches, and so on. *Hinterland* includes any comparatively underdeveloped rural or colonial area which—like the Prairies—exports grain, beef, potash, oil and gas, or other raw or semi-processed extractive goods. Hinterlands also export people to metropolitan regions—people who migrate to seek better opportunities in the cities. Indeed, the hinterlands include several pools of under-employed reserve labour, like small farmers in Saskatchewan, young people in small towns, and some persons living on Indian reserves or in Metis hamlets in the isolated countryside. These potential labour reserves are available as resources for metropolitan employers—whenever it may become profitable for the corporate managers to hire them. Meanwhile, they subsist on minimum incomes or on welfare allowances until their superiors need them. This is what I mean by "underemployment."

But here we meet a new dimension. There are positive values in small-town life, on the farms, and on the Indian reserves. So we are told at any rate, by some people that ought to know—those who live there. One witness is Harold Cardinal, President of the Indian Association of Alberta, and author of a best-selling paperbook, *The Unjust Society.* Here is what he says:

> The new Indian policy promulgated by Trudeau in 1969 is a thinly disguised program of extermination through assimilation . . . a program which offers nothing better than cultural genocide. . . . Indians have aspirations, hopes and dreams, but becoming brown white men is not one of them. (pp. 1, 3)

Some younger Indians of Canada, then, are emphatically rejecting the middle-class suburban style of life. Yet: it is this style that is upheld, propagated, propagandized, and even subsidized at times by the metropolitan bosses, because this provides them with something they cannot live without—a rising multitude of docile, faceless suburban consumers. Let me read you a few lines from Stokely Carmichael's book, *Black Power,* published in 1967.

The goal of black people (in the USA) must not be to assimilate into middle-class America, for that class—as a whole—is without a visible conscience as regards humanity. The values of the middle class permit the perpetuation of the ravages of the black community. The values of that class are based on material aggrandizement, not on the expansion of humanity. The values of that class ultimately support cloistered little closed societies tucked away neatly in tree-lined suburbia. (p. 40)

The hippies and many young people are saying similar things. They may not know just what they want in place of the middle-class metropolitan values they are rejecting. But they seem to be very sure that they do not want any great part of the values and norms upon which North American capitalist society has been built.

The movement for Quebec independence leans in the same direction. It will repay us western Canadians to ponder every phrase of the following quotation from Rene Levesque's 1968 book, *An Option for Quebec.*

We are Quebecois. What this means first and foremost . . . is that we are attached to this one corner of the earth where we have the unmistakable feeling that "here we can really be at home." Being ourselves is essentially a matter of keeping and developing a personality that survived for three and a half centuries. . . . We are heirs to the group obstinacy which has kept alive that portion of French America we call Quebec. . . . This is how we differ from other men and especially from other North Americans. (pp. 14–15)

Quebec, like the western Prairies, has been a hinterland of English Canada ever since the conquest of 1760. More of this later. Here I must emphasize a key point concerning the meanings of *metropolis* and *hinterland*. Do not confuse these terms with geographic referents. *Metropolis* can equally well refer to any over-class group; *hinterland* is likewise synonymous with any urban or rural underclass. In Saskatchewan today, organized labour and the teachers federation are hinterland or underclass groups, and so too is the Farmers Union. Others could be named, but the point should be clear.

The Social Costs of Profit-Oriented Corporate Expansionism

A generation ago on these Canadian prairies, life looked a lot more simple than it does today. Things were tough enough even then. But the visible horizon was familiar; the hostile corporate interests lived just a few miles down the line, or in Regina, or in Winnipeg, or above all in Toronto, Ottawa and English Montreal. Now all that is changed. The Anglo Establishment in Ottawa, having exploited the Prairie hinterland since 1870, and the Quebec hinterland since 1760, has bought into—or sold out to—the American Empire.

It is a fact of life that metropolis exploits hinterland; over-class exploits under-class. Even more significant is the fact that hinterland eventually fights back against metropolis. Underclasses and hinterlands seek to improve their status in the chain of exploitation. They buy into the system, and by so doing, they force the system to be even more exploitive at the expense of outlanders, foreign "investment frontiers," the coloured nations of the world. There is a direct connection between Main Street, USA, and the cutting edge of the military meat-grinder in Vietnam.

Because of the increasing complexity of our contemporary world, it seem relevant to take a new look. At the same time, this is something of an old look. Now as before, the basic rationale of metropolitan domination of Canadian hinterlands and underclasses is the logic of economic centralization, rationalization, and maximization of corporate profits. This entails the squeezing out of the small producers. Nowhere is this better exemplified than in the farm industry.

Last December, 1969, the Federal Task Force on Agriculture published a report called, *Canadian Agriculture in the Seventies*. This report was written by four big-business-oriented economists and by a chartered accountant. A more capitalistic-minded group would be hard to imagine. The essence of their "1990 model," sketched on page 9, is the immense rationalization and expansion of business. The farming population in 1990 would be reduced to perhaps 3 or 4 percent of the total population; many of these huge farms would be corporate enterprises rather than family farms; costs would be progressively reduced and farm agencies would become steadily larger. Vertical integration would expand. In short, the same trends that characterize corporate monopoly in steel, oil, food marketing and so on would come to predominate in farming with the blessing of the present Ottawa regime.

It hardly seems necessary to spell out the social costs of this mindless Ottawa policy of economic streamlining in the interest of capital owned by fewer and fewer monopolists. Small farms, villages, small towns and the smaller cities would all decline; a few larger metropolitan centres would continue to grow. What would become of the small farmers who like to live on the land and who would continue to do so, if only a more reasonable return could be assured? What would become of the workmen, the teachers, the small-business firms in the middle-sized towns? Is it not obvious that the same logic of mergers-and-squeeze-out can be applied to nearly every other business besides agriculture?

Still on that notorious page 9 of the Task Force report, the authors admit that there will be a need for more welfare and guaranteed annual incomes, in connection with the progressive corporatizing of farming.

I translate this to mean that while the few will merge and prosper, the many will be put on thinly disguised relief, at a minimum level. In other words, history seems about to repeat itself in Canada. As the Indians were shoved onto reservations a century ago, with microscopic "payments" of $5 a year per person, plus some vaguely spelled out welfare, educational and medical benefits—so now the farmers are to be pensioned off and moved out.

By this logic, the same prospect confronts every other occupational group in Canada. A few will get richer; most of us will get poorer.

Yet this is not all. Perhaps the most important cost of centralization has still to be estimated. So far, we have been talking about economic costs. This is one very important side of the matter. But another side—the social side—cannot be estimated in economic terms. The logic of corporate rationalization which governs the Agriculture Task Force Report makes no allowance whatever for the destruction of local communities that would attend the economic rationalization of corporate agriculture. It makes no allowance for the social costs of annihilating the countryside and its little communities. Indeed, how could this be done? There is no way to translate the values of social communities into cash terms.

Four or five years ago, Professor McCrorie made a study of some of the social costs of eliminating Biggar, Saskatchewan, as a railway diversion point, or place where trains change their crews. He showed conclusively that the social costs to the train crews, the unions, and the community could not be measured in cash terms, whatever might be the economic benefits to the railroad managers and owners. Much the same can be said of the closure of branch-line railroads. No means of translating the social death of small communities into the economic values of corporate centralization has yet been found. I think they never will be found.

I am not arguing that economic or technological "progress" should be ignored. It seems clear that both farms and railroads were overbuilt on the Prairies, so to say. Some cutbacks have taken place, quite rightly, and further adjustments in both industries may be in order. What I am saying is that the criteria for making these adjustments must cease to be exclusively the profits yardstick of the giant corporations. When the labour unions fight for "job security," and when the farmers union stakes its future on the family farm, these grass-roots organizations are defending the social values of underclass and hinterland, as well as their own particular economic interests.

A few minutes ago, I said that the hinterland-vs.-metropolis confrontations today are much more large-scale than they were two generations

ago. To understand Prairie settlement up to World War II, and the attendant social movements and political conflicts, we could look at the
National Policy set up a century ago to create a new "investment frontier" in the West for eastern business and financial interests. Then we
would look at the local and regional responses to those eastern policies.
Now, however, we in the West must also understand the hinterland role
of Canada in the metropolitan American empire. Finally we must add
in some conception of Quebec, that tortured nation, as another hinterland long exploited by the Anglo-Canadian Establishment, and now re-
volting against that exploitation. Let us turn briefly to each case.

The Crisis and Impending Fall of the American Metropolis

Later in this PLAIN TALK series, Walter Gordon will discuss Canadian survival and foreign investment in detail. My present point is a different
one. It is this: as we look back over the ebb and flow of American history,
it seems apparent that ever since World War I the United States has been
becoming increasingly rigid and out of touch with the rest of the world—
so much so that it may well have lost the capacity to adjust peacefully
to the new socialist nations arising in eastern Europe, Asia, Cuba, and
probably in other underdeveloped nations in the near future. I suggest
that the main reason for American rigidity and isolation is the fabulous
over-success of American capitalism. There is no massive, well organized opposition with a different program or a distinctive social philosophy. Nearly everyone buys the "American way of life." There are dissent
and splinter groups, but none that is massive and well organized. Student dissent in the United States, and the various Black Power groups
are small, scattered, and—as I read them—negative in tone. They may
know what they do not want, but as yet they have not agreed on what
they do want. Of course that may change. Theoretically, the Black Panthers, who have apparently rejected capitalism and opted for socialism,
might just save the United States provided they could win the necessary
white support. At this time, however, such groups are neither massive
nor well organized. And throughout the twentieth century, such opposition movements as threatened to become massive have been co-opted
and taken into the feast. The radical labour movements of the late 19th
century by the 1920s became "business unionism;" the radical farmers
settled for generous subsidies.

I am assuming, with some reason I believe, that substantial social and
economic change in a modern society stems in large part from the confrontation of oppositions. Hence my pessimism about the United States.
There is and always has been plenty of conflict in our neighbour to the

south, but it has generally been conflict over who is going to get the largest piece of the "American way of life"–who is going to get a bigger share of the pie. Not for two or three generations has there been any serious debate–on a massive scale–about the way that pie is baked. Meanwhile all sorts of problems are piling up, unresolved and I suspect unresolvable, in the American cities and countryside. This is important for us Canadians concerned with survival. The Ottawa Establishment, especially since World War II, has systematically furthered and encouraged the drift of Canada into a branch-plant status of the American economic empire–with a few honourable exceptions. And no better friend of "continentalism" (the economists' term for going along with the plans of the American multi-national corporations)–no better friend or servant of continentalism exists in Canada than Pierre Trudeau, Prime Minister of Canada.

If we are really being drawn into the orbit of a metropolitan empire that is likely to beat itself and the rest of us to pieces, we had better start operating on some other course.

Quebec as Hinterland against the Anglo Metropolis

Almost overnight, the agony of Quebec has become the agony of Canada. Who would have supposed that political kidnappings and assassinations could have happened here? Such dismal events may be expected from "unstable" countries in Latin American and Middle East. But here they are happening in Canada. For myself as well as all of you, the shock has been severe, even traumatic. Never again will the Canadian social and political landscape look quite the same. We have turned an historic corner.

But however we deplore the outbreak of political violence in Montreal, it is all-important to try to sense what is happening, and what may happen, and why this affliction has been visited upon us. Praise and blame are beside the point. We need a new social map, if we are to achieve any sort of objective understanding. Let us try to transform our common shock into a "shock of recognition." For the new situation that confronts us is not entirely new; it is a further stage of historic forces deeply rooted in our past.

Confederation in 1867 and the "National Policy" of western settlement was basically a competitive response by English Canadian business to the immense American industrial and westward economic expansion that burst forth in the 1850s. Somewhat later, another "investment frontier" was opened up in conquered Quebec. English-speaking people manned most of the managerial positions, while French-Canadians

made up most of the working class. In our own day, populist counter-
attacks have appeared in the Raoul Caouette Creditiste movement,
based on the support of "colonials" in northern Quebec and on other
small producers around the Province. Another counter-attack has been
the so-called "quiet revolution" of the Quebec middle class. More recently, this movement has been spearheaded by the drive for an independent Quebec. There are numerous factions in this general development, and I have greatly over-simplified the picture in order to high-light
the broad drift of affairs.

The confrontation in Quebec between the francophone independence movements and the anglophone corporate establishment has now
gone so far that overt violence has broken out. To understand this event,
we may turn for partial insight to a book called *The Wretched of the Earth*,
by Frantz Fanon. Fanon was a black West Indian psychiatrist who practiced in Algeria during the 1950s, when Algerians were waging civil war
against France for independence. It was a dirty war, with all sorts of
atrocities and tortures on both sides. Quebec is not like Algeria–at least
not yet. But Fanon has a valid insight for the world we live in. Here is
what he says, and I summarize. The decolonizing process now going on
in Africa, East Asia and Latin America is an inherently violent process.
The slave or the exploited colonial underclass man, after generations
of brainwashed inferiority, is less than a man. The act of violence against
his exploiter frees the rebel, both from himself and from his former
master, by one stroke.

In support of Fanon's interpretation, we may point out that for three
or four centuries, Europeans and later North Americans conquered and
at times enslaved the world. Now the worm has turned, and liberation
is the new order. It is not surprising that, at times–in Africa, Cuba,
China, India, Southeast Asia–liberation entails violence.

Let us remember that Quebec since 1760 has been a conquered nation. If the plunder of Quebec was far less extreme than was the British
plunder of India (conquered about the same time)–it is only because
there was much less boodle in Quebec. In both Quebec and India, British imperial policy was–divide, rule, and exploit the colonials.

As the Bilingual and Bicultural Royal Commission has shown, the average French-Canadian income in Quebec is the third lowest. Only the
Indians and the Italians are lower. There is a long history of insults and
contempt and coercion against French Canadians. Now all that accumulation of suspicion, misunderstanding and exploitation has come home
to roost. The piper must now be paid. And this I say in sorrow rather
than in anger.

I do not know how far this agony in Quebec will go. Hopefully, we shall escape those more extreme seizures of violence that broke out in Africa during the present generation. From another view, this cup may not pass us by. In my opinion the Ottawa Establishment and its francophone lieutenants in Quebec have seriously misjudged the Canadian situation. They have panicked. They have over-reacted by using massive force, by taking a hard line. They are inviting—perhaps even assuring—more violence from FLQ-type extremists. They are making a bad situation worse. And what is the firm evidence for the Establishment claims of massive plots and dark enterprises? Is it not likely that the vested interests in Ottawa, Quebec City and Montreal City are using the FLQ excesses not simply to suppress the FLQ, but to short circuit the legitimate and obviously flourishing left-wing trend toward a new social order in Quebec?

More than a year ago, I came to feel that, in the long run, the movement for Quebec independence was promising and good, not only for Quebec, but for the rest of Canada. Why? Because the movement for an independent Quebec (not be confused with the FLQ) does have a promising side. For if Quebec goes independent in the next few years, as seem likely, it will also be forced at the same time to move decisively toward socialism—toward the harnessing of its resources and the planning of whatever new life-patterns it may choose to seek. It will have to face up to the key question of our times—how do we want to live? This means rejecting the roles of faceless consumers and docile employees and pensioners of multi-national corporations. And however dicey the gamble, perhaps the agony and the example of Quebec may stimulate Anglo-Canada to face up to these same issues.

The appalling events of the last fortnight made me re-think my analysis. The price clearly is much higher than I had expected or hoped. But I have found no reason to alter my basic perspective. I have little doubt that Ottawa's blind over-reaction has assured that Quebec will in our time become an independent nation.

Conclusion: Looking Back and Looking Ahead

Ladies and gentlemen, tonight we have come a long way in a short time. We began by showing the social erosion of town and countryside by metropolitan corporate interests, which are governed by the logic of economic centralization in order to maximize the profits of a few. This corporate expansionism is steadily eroding our local communities; it threatens to put more and more of us on the shelf. A few corporation farms can feed the nation; a few huge and vertically integrated oil companies can and do dominate the oil and gas industry with machines and computers that need only a handful of operators to run them. How far is all this centralization going to be allowed to proceed? What is happening to the social quality of our lives?

Man is a social animal, said Aristotle, more than 2000 years ago. He needs to live much of his life in small groups, in communities. But big cities tend to reduce the quality of social contacts, even if they increase the quantity. In a recent TV documentary on the Peace River country in Alberta, a local resident put the matter this way. "How are we able to keep up with the best in the world, and use the best we see?" No learned academic has put the issue quite so well as did this plaintalking man in Peace River.

In my opinion, only the underclass and hinterland groups of Canada (and of the world) can answer this challenge. Most of the professors who should offer us socially relevant advice are too busy pursuing their esoteric and over-specialized, jargonized, irrelevant monologues that no one listens to. But in our own Prairie history and experience, there are guidelines for action. The prairies have long been the scene of underclass and hinterland groups that slowly realized their precarious position, and gradually organized economic and political counter-offensives against their metropolitan masters. So it must be again. Only this time the theatre is much larger—indeed, it is the whole of North America, if not the world. It may be too late for Canada to shake loose from the American empire and its satellite regime in Ottawa. Perhaps the prospects for a hinterland victory over metropolis are more promising in Latin America or southeast Asia. But we never know until we try.

Survival today means confrontation against metropolitan overclasses committed to the logic of economic centralization and maximal profits. Without confrontation, we face annihilation in the wake of the American empire, apparently bent on suicide. A decade ago, I wrote that the United States would probably not make it into the twenty-first century, alive and fit to live. Now more than ever, I think that hunch was true.

But all over Canada there are signs of stirring and arousal. If Quebec is further along this road, smaller-scale confrontations have recently happened on the prairies. Last year an arrogant Prime Minister was showered with verbal abuse by angry farmers in Regina and Saskatoon. Many Indians and Metis are fed up with their encapsulation in a racist strait jacket. Organized labour in Saskatchewan, and teachers, are threatened with Bill 2, another kind of strait jacket that aligns the power of the Regina government on the side of the employer.

There are still other stirrings on the Prairie scene, among women's groups, students, people on welfare, Indians and Metis. Although un-co-ordinated and often quite diverse in their programs, they seem to agree on one important point: they do not like some aspect or other of the society we now have, and they want some role or a share of power in changing it. I think it is clear that if we want to change our society, we have got to organize from the grass-roots, because we are not going to get what we want from the top elites of corporate business and the present governments that serve those elites. This means organization. It means confrontations. Consensus or compromise politics will not suffice, because it plays into the hands of the existing power elites.

I have no blueprint for survival, and I doubt if anyone else has. Three guidelines, however, seem evident. *First*, we must dismantle the present corporate economic structure based on centralization and private profit, and we must replace this with social property organized for public benefits. This doubtless means expropriation of many of the giant Canadian and American corporations. Why not? Why should the 6 percent of the world's population that lives in the USA own 55 or 60 percent of the world's wealth? In 1963 in Quebec, Rene Levesque as provincial minister of natural resources expropriated Quebec Hydro, an American-controlled corporation. To pay the compensation, he borrowed the money from the Americans. We should all reflect carefully upon this precedent. The Americans might be persuaded to finance Canadian independence, especially if they are bogged down in foreign and domestic troubles of their own. And we could always hope to scale down the interest payments in due time.

The *second* guideline is this: the economic question, though important, is not by itself enough to assure survival. We still have to decide — what kinds of communities do we want to live in? Then we have to build those communities. Harold Cardinal, the Alberta Indian leader, put this matter very clearly. Speaking at Banff last December, he said:

> People in my generation are no longer Indian, because for generations our people have been brainwashed. The real Indianness among us is very small. We had the missionaries who were the front-runners, we had the residential schools that taught that brainwashing. In order to create a new society, we must combine our skills, protect whatever economic power we can acquire, and create in a contemporary way a new meaning to Indianness. . . . No White man can tell us what Indianness means. It is something we ourselves have to discover, and it is something we ourselves have to create.

Cardinal is saying to us that economics is not enough; there is also the social question — how do we want to live? The white community faces precisely the same problem. Who are we? How should we live?

The *third* and final guideline for survival, ladies and gentlemen, is the necessity for action. Inaction means non-survival in a situation where as today, we are drifting toward catastrophes of pollution, catastrophes of social erosion, and catastrophes of military annihilation. Roy Atkinson of Saskatoon, president of the National Farmers Union, put the matter like this last December at Banff.

> If we as a society haven't the intelligence to cut through the ritual and the barbaric behaviour, and civilize this society, it won't be only the native people who become militant. There will be whole sections of the population. In a recent publication in the USA, Milton Eisenhower predicts that people will have to fortify themselves in castles to protect their possessions. . . . Once before in the history of mankind, a similar situation developed—the fall of the Roman Empire. Then they walled themselves into that ancient city, modern beyond belief, and perished, while the academics and the intellectuals and the people in power sat round and talked about what to do. And they finally concluded, the hell with it, we will do nothing, because those fellows outside don't know what it's all about.

There are still people around the Canadian prairies, around Quebec, and in other underclass and hinterland groups, who do know what it is all about. They can be found in the labour movement, in the farmers union, indeed almost anywhere that grass-roots people gather together to think about and do something about the things that trouble us. Survival means conflict and confrontation. If that fact seems to you to be unfortunate, all I can answer is, I believe it is still a fact. Thank you.

Selected References

J. N. McCrorie, *In Union is Strength* (Saskatoon, 1965).

Vernon Fowke, *The National Policy and the Wheat Economy* (University of Toronto, 1957).

Harold Cardinal, *The Unjust Society* (Edmonton: Hurtig, 1969).

Rene Levesque, *An Option for Quebec* (Toronto, 1968).

Andre G. Frank, *Capitalism and Underdevelopment in Latin America* (N.Y. Monthly Review Press, 1967).

I. Lumsden, Ed., *Close the 49th Parallel* (Univ. of Toronto, 1970).

J. F. C. Wright, *The Louise Lucas Story* (Montreal: Harvest House, 1966).

S. Lipset et al., *Agrarian Socialism* (new ed., N.Y. Doubleday, 1968).

William A. Williams, *The Roots of the Modern American Empire* (N.Y. Random 1969).

A. K. Davis, "Decline and Fall," *Monthly Review*, vol. 12 (1960).

A. K. Davis "Canadian Society and History as Hinterland vs. Metropolis." In R. Ossenberg, Ed., *Canadian Confrontations* (Scarborough: Prentice Hall, 1971).

Philip Loehr, *Exploiting the Western Farmer* (Muenster, Saskatchewan, 1968, 44 pp.).

Canadian Society and History
as Hinterland Versus Metropolis

Thrust and Drift in Canadian History:
Looking Back from 1967

THE CENTENNIAL OF 1967, on the surface, was a year of efferves-
cence and affirmation for Canada. This was especially true in
English Canada. But two of the most significant events of that year occurred in Quebec. One was the fabulous Expo 67 at Montreal. Here
were the pavilions of the ascending metropolitan Great Powers, the Soviet Union and the United States; and those of such descending metropolitan empires as Great Britain and France. And here also were the exhibition buildings of hinterland communities—some of them on the
upswing—like Cuba, Czechoslovakia, Mexico, the Arab Nations, Africa
Place, Quebec, and the Indians of Canada. The metropoles of the world
confronted the hinterlands of the world at Expo 67, and all made their
declarations.

The second of the two significant events was the thunderous shout
of Charles De Gaulle, President of France, somewhere in Quebec along
the lower St. Lawrence River: "Vive le Québec libre." This slogan rattled
the tea cups in Ottawa; indeed, it evoked screams of rage—a sign of insecurity on the part of the screamers, no doubt. One interpretation of
the incident is that it may owe something to the sense of frivolity on
the part of some of the University of Montreal students who helped to
arrange the General's tour. Yet it can also be argued that De Gaulle's
real target was the rival imperium at Washington, rather than
Washington's Ottawa satellite. This points up to a central concern of this

Reprinted by permission. R. Ossenberg, Editor, *Canadian Society*, Scarborough, Ontario, Canada.
Prentice-Hall, 1971. Chapter 1.

article: the history, present stance, and future of the North American hinterlands vis-à-vis the United States empire. The South American hinterlands, beginning with Mexico, can be examined in a similar manner.[1] But these answers must wait.

Four themes emerge from our review of Canadian history since Confederation. One is the development of the western wheat economy, stemming from the "National Policy" that shaped up from Confederation. The second is the continuity of the French community in Quebec, despite–and even because of–its subordination to English Canada ever since the conquest of 1760. The third is the key importance of foreign imperialism throughout the entire development of Canadian society– mostly British but more recently American. The fourth is urbanization and the rise of urban industries in a capitalist context. The urban population of Canada first exceeded the rural population during the 1920s, and by 1966, about three Canadians out of four lived in urban centres. All these themes seem to be best viewed in terms of a metropolis-versus-hinterland frame of reference.

Looking back in 1967 over the English Canadian historical record, the milestones of change during the past two or three centuries were there for all to see and read. From a straggling line of colonial settlements along the St. Lawrence valley and the maritime region, a new nation–or perhaps a collection of regional communities–had emerged, built on fur-trading posts, fishing outports, timber exports, wheat exports, and oil and gas exports.[2] The pattern of export staples is still important, but manufacturing surpassed primary industries (agriculture, fisheries, forestry, mining) in the 1920s, and has continued to forge ahead.[3]

From the standpoint of English Canada in 1967, the century of Confederation had been a pronounced success. The national policy of western settlement as a new "investment frontier" for Ontario and Montreal business and financial interests–a competitive Canadian reaction to the immense American industrial and agrarian expansion after the mid-nineteenth century–had achieved a great deal, not all of it intended. By 1885, the heavily subsidized all-Canadian railroad link between the maritimes and the Pacific had been forged, despite the thousand-mile barrier of rocky bushland north of the Great Lakes and in spite of the 600 miles of far-western mountain ranges. To make way for agricultural settlement on the prairies, the Indians had been shunted aside onto isolated reservations, and the rebellious Métis had been defeated at Batoche, Saskatchewan. The ill-advised hanging of the Métis leader Louis Riel at Regina in 1885 doubtlessly reinforced the resentment as well as the sense of subordination of both the French and the Indian underclass communities to the Anglo metropolitan elites of Toronto and Montreal.[4]

Another key aspect of the national policy–too little recognized–was the federal program of agricultural research to adapt techniques imported from the humid East to the semi-arid conditions of the western high plains.[5] Above all, low cost land settlement policies in the western reaches were backed by strong government and business encouragement of massive immigration from Europe, Eastern Canada, and the United States. The Canadian achievement, seen in historical perspective, is truly of epic proportions. For eastern manufacturing interests, the high-tariff policy instituted in the 1870s was of prime importance.

By 1930, however, the wheat economy was over-established in the prairie provinces; the exodus of farmers from the Palliser dry triangle in southwestern Saskatchewan and southeastern Alberta to the forested fringe north of Prince Albert, Saskatchewan, and to the Peace River country in Alberta had begun during the 1920s. Indeed, although the number of farms in Saskatchewan reached a peak in 1936 and thereafter declined, the percentage of farms having 200 acres or less began declining in 1901 and continued to decline thereafter except for a slight increase during the depressed 1930s.[6]

There were other unplanned reactions to the national policy. The western hinterlands, settled by persons many of whom shared the acquisitive motivation of the eastern capitalists, displayed from the turn of the century a chronic and insolent tendency to fight back against the railroads, the elevator companies, the old-line political parties and other eastern-oriented agencies and interests that exploited the western colonials.[7] But with some concessions, the eastern establishments usually prevailed. The West made no headway against the tariff.

In brief, the Canadian national policy for Rupertsland or (from 1870) for Western Canada turned aside, at least for the time, the threat of American political absorption of the western region. For example, the decision to run the Canadian Pacific rail line parallel and close to the American border, straight across the Palliser dry triangle and over the Kicking Horse Pass of the Rockies instead of further north over the more fertile and profitable crescent and the more gradual Yellowhead route, was basically a political rather than an economic decision. The national policy came along in the second half of the nineteenth century just in time to nourish enough Canadian nationalism and Canadian socio-economic power to stave off the burgeoning American western and industrial expansion–a defensive role played earlier in the nineteenth century by British imperial might. After the mid-nineteenth century, however, Great Britain became increasingly pre-occupied by challenges from other rising metropolitan empires–European, Japanese, and ultimately American. In the twentieth century, Britain was so decisively drained and undercut by two world wars, by the surging communist revolutions in eastern Europe and China, and by the successful nationalist drive for independence in India, that she sank to the status of an American satellite. Canada, accordingly, had to face up to the American colossus without outside aid, and without adequate internal development of national self-consciousness and self-confidence.

If the national policy, developed in Canada mainly during the third quarter of the nineteenth century, had its most obvious successes in western development during the century of Confederation ending in 1967, no less significant—and perhaps more so, in the long run—was its impact on Quebec after the turn of the twentieth century. The rising importance of urbanization, manufactures, and the service industries (including public administration and defence) in Canada has been previously indicated. These have steadily surpassed primary industries; small towns and country life have consequently been subjected to increasingly frustrating, backward conditions—with diminishing chances of catching up—barring drastic institutional changes in Canadian society.[8]

Yet Quebec, like the western prairies, presented itself to the Anglo-Canadian business and political establishments as a promising hinterland for economic and political exploitation.[9] Quebec was rural, Catholic, politically stable, guided by conservative and anti-labor ecclesiastical and provincial regimes, and afflicted with a large surplus rural population—only part of which could be drained off to the factory towns of Ontario and New England. Consequently, the pattern of Anglo management and French-Canadian labour soon became established in Quebec industries, and still continues. Industrialization proceeded apace. The local French municipal and provincial political and professional elites were not seriously threatened by these developments. They simply did business with Anglo entrepreneurs as middlemen; and as time went by, the entrepreneurs became Americans. The Duplessis regime in Quebec (1940s and 1950s) sold economic concessions, like good middlemen, to the Anglo-American exploiters.

The retaliative reaction of the prairie hinterlands, as manifested most overtly but by no means exclusively in the populist movements of the Saskatchewan Co-operative Commonwealth Federation (CCF, 1930s ff.) and Alberta's Social Credit (1930s ff.), has emerged with compound force in Quebec during the 1960s. Perhaps the first manifestation was the Creditiste movement of Raoul Caouette, based on the small-producer, petit-bourgeois entrepreneurs and farmers of northern Quebec and to a degree on the urban working class. The second and probably more decisive manifestation is *Le Parti Quebecois* led by René Lévesque, aiming at complete independence for Quebec. Today it is Lévesque who is surely the real "leader of the opposition" in Canada.

Looking back in 1967, therefore, there was – for English Canada – a centennial record of epic achievement, at least in the short-run. Cities, farms, railroad lines, airlines, universities – in a word, an advanced civilization – had been built against immense odds of geography and climate. More important, all this had been done on the dangerous edge of American expansion. But for Quebec, the same could not be said. French Canada remained economically, politically, and psychologically inferior to Anglo Canada. And the Quebec question lent much ambiguity to the Canadian self-image in that summer of 1967. Many people spoke rhetorically and wishfully of "national unity," but few tried to spell it out.

Looking ahead, therefore, the grounds for Canadian optimism and self-congratulation in 1967 seemed dubious and shadowy. Despite the great national development achieved during the preceding century, there was no clear and common purpose or direction for the Canadian people in 1967. The old national policy had obviously run out of gas years ago. Nothing had emerged to replace it. Indeed, as Peter Newman put it:

> It was a time of distemper . . . a time when many Canadians were left with the feeling that much of what was happening had no meaning. . . . We were only dimly aware that we were enduring the pains of passage from the safety of the past to we knew not what. The politics of the period (1963–68) was essentially a politics of transition.[10]

It seemed to be an era of issues rather than of resolutions – of questions rather than answers. How could Canadian political independence survive in the face of the soft undermining lure of the on-going American economic and communications take-over? What about those still festering injustices long ago inflicted upon Canada's native Indians and Eskimos? What about the perennial and well documented grievances of various agrarian, urban and regional underclasses? Perhaps the most potent – and in our view the most hopeful – of the unresolved issues was the smouldering ferment of independence in Quebec. In brief, it appeared in 1967 that the challenges ahead could easily outweigh the accomplishments of the past.

Two minor indicators may be cited here to point up the irresolutions of our time. One was the series of five graduate seminars on Canadian society given during the Calgary summer session of 1967. This program brought nearly a score of leading academics and writers to the foothills campus for short visits at different times. The essays in this volume, though incomplete, convey a fair cross-section of the ideas and insights that glinted in the bright western sunlight of that landmark summer. Yet many questions went unanswered. Doubts remained. No consensus on the nature or course of Canadian society emerged.

The other indicator of the unfocused and uncertain nature of the national self-image was the present writer's auto trip from Calgary to Montreal in early June, 1967, for a visit to Expo 67. Speeding eastward over the endless prairies along the Trans-Canada Highway, we passed hikers with packs and signs on their back reading: "Expo 67. No Rides Please." Somewhere north of Lake Superior, we passed a train of mule wagons marked Expo 67. Newspapers we read on the way carried stories about canoes heading for Expo from the edge of the Rocky Mountains. But the most impressive of all these happenings were the dozens of yellow school buses we passed. They were loaded with school kids headed for Expo. On the sides of those buses were big banners stating their origin and destination—Expo. Some, like ourselves, had started from the far West. Everyone was headed for Expo. By the time we reached Expo, something had happened to us. Expo was a transcending experience. And I think something happened to Canada during that centennial summer of 1967, just because of Expo. Like the primitive, rock-bottom Australian corroboree, Expo was in some part a national and multi-national and international affirmation.

But an affirmation of what no one could say.

Notes on Method

Why have academic sociologists, both Canadian and American, found it so difficult to produce and convey a live and realistic conception of Canadian society? This question warrants further discussion. In our view, it is impossible to conceptualize a holistic view of Canadian society apart from American society. This means that the minimal frame of reference for Canada is North American society. Such a perspective has been well established in the works of such Canadian economic historians as Innis, Fowke, Aitken, and others.[11] Even North America as a frame of reference is not enough. The perspective must ultimately include Latin America and all the other satellite hinterlands of the American metropolis that are scattered around the world.

Most Canadian and American-trained Anglophone sociologists do not understand either Canadian or American society mainly because they have been trained in the prevailing static, abstract, ideal-typical, structural-functional, ahistorical tradition. Structural-functionalism affords important insights, both segmental and holistic, but it lacks a time dimension and must therefore be supplemented by a historical perspective. Further, this historical dimension must include a dialectical aspect: the viewing of the evolution of a society as a series of oppositions.

The premise of thesis-antithesis-synthesis may at some times and in some places be relevant and applicable. But for the historical review of Canadian and North American society presently in hand, we prefer a metropolis-hinterland perspective. Metropolis continuously dominates and exploits hinterland whether in regional, national, class, or ethnic terms. But the forms and terms of domination change as a result of confrontations. Spontaneous and massive social movements in regional hinterlands or urban underclasses may force their way toward an improved status for the colonials within the going system. On the other hand, metropolis-hinterland conflict may be latent for long stretches of time rather than overt. It may be outweighed by conditions of prosperity or by temporary alliances in the face of larger confrontations.

Hinterland means, in the first instance, relatively underdeveloped colonial areas which export for the most part semi-processed extractive materials—including people who migrate from the country to the city for better educational and work opportunities. Hinterland may also usefully denote urban under-classes as well as rural peasantries and rural proletariats. *Metropolis* signifies the centres of economic and political control located in the larger cities. Further, the term may denote urban upper-class elites, or regional and national power structures of one sort or another.

Moreover, we must recognize hierarchies of metropolis-hinterland relationships. As northern Saskatchewan in certain respects may be seen as an economic and political hinterland of southern Saskatchewan, so Saskatchewan, itself, is in large part a hinterland of eastern Canada; and Canada, of the United States. Needless to say, the United States likewise includes a complex network of hinterland or under-class groups, regions, marginal colonials, and so on.

The symbiotic *metropolis-hinterland* model assumes (1) conflict of interests between metropolis and hinterland; and (2) a tendency on the part of hinterland groups and interests to fight back eventually against their metropolitan exploiters in order to gain a larger place in the regional or national or international sun. In fact, we really need to think of inherent "surges and down-swings" of specific metropolitan-hinterland conflicts—to borrow J. N. McCrorie's terminology.[12]

The metropolitan-hinterland perspective is obviously a variation of the dialectical approach stemming from the Marxian tradition of social thought. The dialectical premise is that major long-run changes in the socio-economic structure of a society result from oppositions. In the limiting case of major revolutions, as analyzed by the historian Crane Brinton,[13] a collision of incompatible interests eventually produces a new institutional pattern which is not wholly like either of the original opposing complexes, but which includes significant elements from each—doubtless in unequal proportions—the mix depending on the particular case.

Brinton's dialectical approach to four major revolutions probably owes more to Marx than to Pareto, his official mentor. It would apply also to the mid-nineteenth century American Civil War, which finalized the transfer of economic and political power from the southern plantation capitalists to the northern industrial capitalists allied with the western agrarians. But for Canada, where political change has been less extreme at least since 1760, and also for American society since 1865, a modified dialectical model seems more appropriate. The metropolis-hinterland perspective lends itself to a wide variety of conflicting situations, both latent and overt. It also lends itself to the analysis of cases wherein hinterland successfully wins successive concessions from metropolis, particularly under conditions of increasing affluence or under conditions where the concessions to hinterland interests can be compensated by greater exactions or revenues from new or other external hinterlands.

In a nutshell, for analyzing such cases of modern development as Canadian western settlement, Quebec-in-Canada, Canada-in-North America, and United States-in-the-world during the last century of Canadian history, as well as American domestic evolution, a comparatively short-run metropolis-hinterland variation of the long-run dialectic seems preferable. We need a frame of reference somewhere between the timeless, static and usually non-holistic structural-functional model on the one hand, and the holistic, dynamic, long-run limiting case of the Marxian dialectic on the other hand. It should be essentially dialectical, holistic, and historical, but capable of illuminating those regional and national confrontations which do not evolve into full-fledged structural revolutions. Instead, these colonials seek to improve their status within a modified existing order rather than in a drastically and perhaps violently re-structured system. However modified, the metropolis-hinterland hierarchical and exploitive pattern remains. This might not necessarily be true for a full-fledged thesis-antithesis-synthesis sequence.

For example, as historian W. A. Williams has shown, in 1900 the American population was still rural by a three-to-two ratio. (In 1870 the ratio had been three-to-one.) It was the agrarian majority (including flour millers, meat processors, and farm machinery manufacturers) that first opted in the 1870s for market expansionism abroad, in order to help sell agricultural surpluses. They saw themselves as domestic colonials of the northeastern United States metropolis; only in the 1890s did those north-eastern industrial leaders adopt a similar attitude toward economic expansion abroad, as the price of avoiding even more radical agrarian and western populist movements.[14] In this way, the American colonials improved their position within the system that was exploiting them, not by decisively altering the system, but by shunting part of the exploitation stress abroad—by intensifying the American thrust toward foreign imperialism.

Another example is the radical American labour unionism of the 1870s to the early 1900s which evolved into "business unionism" by the 1920s. The skilled craft unions, and later the big industrial unions in the 1930s, forced their way to a better place at the head table of the American establishment. But the "victory" turned organized labour into one of the strongest supporters of reactionary and aggressive American foreign imperialism after World War II.[15]

A parallel case of regional mass movements making their way into the national establishment is documented in J. N. McCrorie's history of the Saskatchewan farmer's movement since 1900.[16] Another Canadian example is the slow drift of the Canadian economy vis-à-vis the United States during the last generation from a competitive to a branch-plant status.[17]

Throughout all these changes, however, metropolis-hinterland patterns appear to persist, whatever the alterations in the degree, scope, intensity, and terms of the stressful relationship. Thus, in drifting into the American empire, Canada has acquired a share or stake in the American metropolitan domination of Latin America, Vietnam, and other such hinterlands. For instance, Canadian industries produce armament materials for sale to the United States and use in Vietnam.

The aridity of the prevailing structural-functional interpretations of Canadian society is easily illustrated. They are authored by sociologists born and/or trained for the most part in the United States. Their views run approximately as follows. Canadian values stand somewhere between those of the United States and Great Britain: "We are not American, and we are not British." Ordinarily, such an argument ends with a perfunctory nod to the presence in Canada of a French-speaking minority. A typical example is the late K. Naegele's "Canadian Society: Some Reflections" and "Further Reflections."[18] Because thousands of Canadian university sociology students have been nourished on this volume of readings during the past decade (the first edition was published in 1961), the message of this package deserves our careful attention. In essence, the abstractions of the German sociologist Max Weber are the model for Naegele's essay. That Weber's life ended in 1920, and that he wrote nothing about Canada seems not to have worried his North American disciples one whit. Two generations later, they can come up with nothing better than a watered-down application of Weber's sociological analysis.[19]

True, the latest (1968) edition of *Canadian Society* wisely retitles Naegele's opening essay as "Modern National Societies," but with no gain in insight into the Canadian situation. In place of Naegele's "Further Reflections," there appears a much more informative paper by Vallee and Whyte. After summarizing a number of key population, economic and social trends, Vallee and Whyte remark upon the difficulty, the scarcity, and (we might add) the relative barrenness of efforts by Anglo-Canadian sociologists to see Canadian society as a whole. In our opinion, the real obstacle to a holistic view of Canada is the inherently static and piecemeal structural-functional approach from which Vallee and Whyte do not entirely escape.

Further to the present argument, static and abstract structural-functional exercise is displayed by S. Lipset in another widely used Canadian university sociology textbook.[20] Lipset is the author of a significant albeit mistitled book on the Saskatchewan Co-operative Commonwealth Federation.[21] But in his 1964 paper, he merely applies the well-known Parsonian pattern-variables to Canadian society. The scheme runs like this. All societies may be ranged according to Lipset somewhere on the following continua: (1) achievement-ascription, (2) universalism-particularism, (3) self-orientation–collectivity-orientation, (4) equalitarian-elitism. Lipset concludes that the United States shapes up nearer the left-hand edge of these continua than does Canadian society.[22] He further argues that in contrast to the United States, Canada has a counter-revolutionary bent.

We believe that both of these claims by Lipset are largely erroneous, insofar as they are applied to the past century. First, the conception of the United States as a universalistic, achievement-oriented, equalitarian society–a conception so deeply rooted in three centuries of ideological expressions and verbal ritual that a majority of American social scientists automatically affirm it–needs severe revision. Judged by the evidence of historical fact rather than by the liberal rhetoric, the United States is a hierarchical, racist society–contrary to the long-nourished American middle-class, "liberal" self-image. At least, it makes far more sense to attach the necessary qualifications to the latter statement than to the former. Second, Canada as a hinterland society vis-à-vis France (until 1759), then Great Britain, and (in recent decades) the United States should have considerably more revolutionary potential than the United States simply because of the metropolis-hinterland relation between them, and the greater intensity of internal metropolis-hinterland confrontations within Canada during recent decades. Sooner or later, hinterlands fight back against the metropolitan interests that exploit them.

The Lipset concept of American society and Canadian society based on diluted Max Weber is so laced with invalid claims and ideological blind spots that it is a waste of time to refute it. For example: "The existing Canadian national identity is in large part a reaction against a long-term supposed threat to its independence and traditions, against absorption into the American republic."[23] Supposed? The threat was and is real. It has been amply documented by such writers as Vernon Fowke, Charles Beard, George Grant, and Melville Watkins. John A. Macdonald, the first Prime Minister of Canada (1867–73; 1878–91), knew very well that the main threat to Canada came from the south. Far more important, the threat of the United States has been a guiding light of Canadian foreign policy until the recent fad for "continentalism," a euphemism for buying (or selling) into the American economic empire.

When Robin Mathews argues that the threat to Canada's identity is a consequence of too many Americans in Canadian universities, he misses a main point.[24] Perhaps a better target would be, not the nationality of professors, but the relative merits and demerits of professorial ideas. Canadian social scientists are by no means exempt from the charge that their emphasis on structural-functional approaches – usually mediocre piecemeal studies of short-run situations and of a very limited number of empirical variables – has obscured their view of the forest because of their focus upon specific trees. Wrote the late C. Wright Mills:

> Classic social analysis . . . is the concern with historical social structures; . . . its problems are of direct relevance to urgent public issues and insistent human troubles . . .[25] Of late the conception of social science I hold has not been ascendant. My conception stands opposed to social science as a set of bureaucratic techniques which inhibit social inquiry by 'methodological' pretensions, which congest such work by obscurantist conceptions, or which trivialize it by concern with minor problems unconnected with publicly relevant issues. . . .[26] Neither the life of an individual nor the history of a society can be understood without understanding both. Yet men do not usually define the troubles they endure in terms of historical change and institutional contradiction. . . .[27] The sociological imagination enables us to grasp history and biography and the relations between the two within society. That is its task and its promise. To recognize this task and this promise is the mark of the classic social analyst.[28]

It is time to emphasize the historical, holistic and comparative approach of classic social analysis in our studies of Canadian society. In no way would this detract from the significant and indeed indispensable contributions of orthodox structural-functional analysis to an understanding of Canada in the modern world.[29]

We can learn certain valuable lessons from orthodox structural-functional analysis. First, social systems change unevenly; but they change as wholes. In the short-run, one sector of the system may lead at one time, another sector at another time. In the long-run, of course, the system as a whole changes in one direction, until confronted by a major opposition. For example, changes in one institutional area may induce changes in another. One effect of the post-World War II extension of education and family allowances in far Northern Saskatchewan was to tie the formerly semi-nomadic Métis and Indian trapping families more closely to village settlements.

In other words, social systems share a property common to systems in general – some degree of interdependence of parts. This also means, in some measure, cohesiveness of the whole, however loose. Hence follows the limited capacity of each component part of the system to continue short-run change that is not paralleled by complementary changes in other components. Thus during the late 1940s and early 1950s, the Saskatchewan CCF Government built a modern elementary school system in the far northern reaches of the province. This well-meaning education effort declined by the middle 1950s, because it was not acccompanied by such other changes as greater job opportunities, wider experience, and acceptance by Métis and Indians of modern standards of living or migration to the south.

Finally, while we suggest that major changes in social structure result from oppositions, this does not mean that all structural changes are explainable in this way. At least one other leading mode of structural change must be considered. That is the impersonal, unplanned evolution of large social processes.[30] As illustrations of this category of change, we may point to the cumulative development of science and technology, of voluntary migrations, and the movement in advanced economies toward large-scale corporate organizations in business and the modern State. This type of change seems to consist of the realization of potentialities inherent in a system; of the unfolding of immanent tendencies as facilitated or modified by external, local, or otherwise varying conditions. Max Weber's concept of "rationalization" appears to convey what we mean. Equally relevant is Sorokin's concept of immanent change.

Let us affirm above all, however, that Weberian rationalization, Sorokinian immanence, Marxian dialectical oppositions, and our own metropolis-hinterland modification of the Marxian dialectic (by no means original with us) are not mutually exclusive concepts and processes. Our sense of the present as on-going history may be illuminated by all of these and indeed by other conceptualizations.

Canadian Society in the North American Empire: Looking Back and Looking Ahead

Since the seventeenth century, Canadian history has been in large part a reaction to the activities of foreign empires. Until 1760, it was the French impact that was pre-eminent; then came the British impact for over a century and a half. After the first World War, the Americans quickly displaced Britain as the primary influence on Canadian society—a trend that was reinforced by the rapid decline of Britain itself to a satellite status within the American orbit. So far had the American fact developed in Canada by the 1960s that George Grant felt constrained to write his well-known essay on the demise of Canadian nationalism.[31] Yet the American influence on Canada began long before the 1920s. Its origins go back at least to the war of independence of the American colonies, 1776–83. And when we review the origins of the national policy during the third quarter of the nineteenth century, it is not too much to say that Canadian history and socio-economic development during the century of Confederation just ended have been a secondary reaction to the initiative of American events. It has indeed, been a pale reflection of American stratagems and American drift.

The stirrings toward nationalism and independence in Quebec today may, however, open the way to an alternative to "continentalism," which means the continued drift into an affluent but second-class status within the burgeoning American empire; for the price of affluent continentalism includes not only second-class status, but also "homogenization"— the eroding of particularistic communities like the French-speaking Canadians, the Indians of Canada, the Eskimos, and many other presently unique groups in Canada.

Meanwhile, the most important perspective for Canadians—both in and outside Quebec—to grasp is the present situation of American society. The prospect appears grim. Let us consider the surge and downswing of oppositions within American society. In our view, this pattern is a key to contemporary Canadian alternatives.

Nearly a decade ago, the present writer argued that decisive structural change comes from oppositions, and that there had been no major oppositions in American society since approximately the time of World War I.[32] It is too early to assess the opposition role of the American Black revolt; this may yet prove to be America's best hope. In the meantime, we may review the two major confrontations in the United States during the history of that Republic.

The first was that leading to the American Civil War, 1861–65. It consisted of the competitive clash between two increasingly divergent societies—North and South—both based on capitalistic economies which had to expand or perish. By mid-century, the outcome of the contest was no longer doubtful. The northern coalition of commercial and industrial interests, linked with the western farmers, steadily forged ahead in wealth and power. In 1860, with the election of Lincoln, the control of the national government passed to the new order. It only remained to win the Civil War and make the victory official. As usual, the old regime preferred to initiate a desperate counter-revolutionary war rather than to acquiesce in its own displacement. We quote from historians Charles and Mary Beard.

> Viewed under the light of universal history, the fighting was a fleeting incident; the social revolution was the essential portentous outcome. . . . The capitalists, labourers and farmers of the North and West drove from power in the national government the planting aristocracy of the South. . . . The physical combat merely hastened the inevitable. As was remarked at the time, the South was fighting against the census returns that told of accumulating industrial capital, multiplying captains of industry, expanding railway systems, widening acres tilled by free farmers. Once the planting and the commercial states, as the Fathers with faithful accuracy described them, had been evenly balanced; by 1860 the balance was gone. . . . Viewed in the large, the supreme outcome of the civil strife was the destruction of the planting aristocracy which, with the aid of northern farmers and mechanics had practically ruled the United States for a generation.[33]

No other war in American history, before or since, ever made such an indelible impression on the minds, the memories, and the traditions of the American people and their descendants—both North and South.[34]

The second great opposition in recent American history began to take shape soon after the end of the Civil War. As the immense expansion of post-war American industrialism got under way, nurtured by the new protective tariff, by public subsidies to transcontinental railroads, and by the fabulous resources of the West, rumblings of discontent and revolt appeared among workers, miners, farmers, and various other colonials. Frustrated farmers, excluded from the feast for one reason or another, organized to raise hell instead of corn. Strikers fought pitched battles with police and militiamen across the country. Socialist splinter groups sprang up here and there, and numerous other strange counsels and cults alarmed the ruling burghers. By 1900, a fledgling indigenous Socialist movement led by Gene Debs was under way. In 1912, the various

Socialist groups together received 6.3 percent of the popular vote for the presidency. But since then, the combined Socialist percentage of the American presidential vote has steadily declined. It was seven-hundredths of 1 percent in 1956.

What happened? Why did the emerging opposition collapse? Why did the opposition to capitalism, generated by capitalism as predicted by Karl Marx, collapse immanently in the United States – where the lack of non-capitalistic alternatives and the absence of anti-capitalistic traditions should theoretically have made for a classic case of socialist displacement of capitalism? The basic reason seems to have been the over-success of American capitalism.

The fantastic resources of the American heartland; the absence of any competing traditions of rival aristocracy; a vast domestic market protected by a high tariff; an endless supply of cheap immigrant labor; friendly politicians in control of the national government (which owned more than half of all land in the nation in 1860) who were eager to help and to share; these are the factors pointed out by the historians Charles and Mary Beard in their *Rise of American Civilization* as the key elements in the "triumph of business enterprise."

We explain American economic and social development, then, in terms of capitalism evolving under unique domestic, geographic, and international conditions – a perspective applicable to any other capitalist society with appropriate modifications in the components. This approach has not prevailed among the majority of American historians and intellectuals. The more common focus has been upon the development of the western frontier. In a famous essay in 1893, "The Significance of the Frontier in American History," F. J. Turner portrayed the westward movement as perennial rebirth, as a movement away from European influence and toward American uniqueness, and as the basis of democracy and prosperity.[35] Despite its genuine insights, this viewpoint obscures at least as much as it reveals. It embodies a large element of nationalistic parochialism. Set in our larger and more realistic frame of reference, however, the Turner thesis helps to bring out the central fact that throughout its course, the American republic has resorted to expansion in order to escape its domestic contradictions and tensions. And when the western frontier was essentially closed in about 1890, expansionism had to continue abroad. If the historians missed this key point, the more perceptive business and political leaders of the United States from the earliest days of independence were in no doubt where their interests lay.

And when, much as Marx had predicted, capitalism began to generate the resisting forces of labour organizations and populist agrarian revolts toward the end of the nineteenth century, those thrusts in the case of the United States were turned aside by a combination of sharing the goodies at home and imperialistic expansion abroad. The crisis of the 1890s threatened by the closing of the frontier was resolved in part by extending the necessary economic expansion and investment frontier beyond the national boundaries. Indeed, as William A. Williams, another American historian, has shown, it was the rural colonials–farmers and small town processers in the American hinterland–who pressed most strongly for market expansion abroad. Some of the disappointed colonials moved to the Canadian prairies for a second try.

In other words, interest groups that feel deprived often strive first and foremost to improve their position in the going economic system. With a few adjustments, the system then carries on with some new faces at the head table. A parallel conclusion was reached by McCrorie in his recent study of the Saskatchewan farmers' movement in the twentieth century.[36] The American farmers got markets; later they received subsidies. American labour turned to "business unionism." The real process was much more complex, naturally.

The foreign expansion of business was decisively and irreversibly reinforced by the effects of two relatively cheap world wars that brought still further American economic growth, and which wrecked the rival British, French, German, and Japanese capitalistic empires. But these same world wars, in destroying America's rivals, also cleared the way for the communist and nationalistic revolutions in Russia and China, thus closing off vast regions of the world to American business expansion, and forecasting an ultimate confrontation between the American empire and the rising new socialist world.

On another level, the domestic Keynesian and social security reforms have likewise bolstered the fairy tale American version of capitalism since the 1930's. In our own generation, the military and space budgets, which Thorstein Veblen would have called waste, have operated as additional investment frontiers. In truth, the limitless sky has become the limit. It all adds up to the most fantastic success story in human history. It staggers the imagination.

My central concern, however, is not the dynamics and contours of American history, but certain consequences that appear to follow from them, in the light of our dialectical premise. Since the first World War, there has been an absence of great oppositions in American society. Competition has been sharp, often nasty, sometimes violent. In our own day, assassination has become a standard political response; consider the cases of Malcolm X, Martin Luther King, the Kennedy brothers, and the hunting down of the Black Panthers. But no new philosophy, with organizational resources and potentially decisive mass support, has arisen to challenge seriously the prevailing pattern of corporate structures and middle class style of life. The hippies have opted out for their own encapsulated thing; some student groups may drop out, turn on, or even sit in,[37] the Blacks–so far–simply riot; the old left is largely defunct; the new left–at least in the foreseeable future–has far less organizational and mass support than has George Wallace's reassertion of traditional White racism. Practically everyone that matters, power-wise, in the United States accepts the traditional American middle class way of life. The protests seem negative; none of them sounds positive–with the possible exception of certain stirrings among the Blacks.

At the moment, the best hope for a great change in American life seems to be in the emerging non-racist socialist humanism of such Black leaders as the late Malcolm X and Eldridge Cleaver. Whether these types can secure the necessary mass support among both Blacks and Whites is still a question mark. Surely no country in the world, for its own interest, has greater need for a social revolution than the United States. And the interest of the rest of the world in a new American revolution is equally compelling. In estimating the American future, therefore, we should reserve judgment on the potential of the Black revolt.

Meanwhile, the present absence of major internal oppositions acts as a block to the necessary structural changes that might adapt the United States to the modern world. The investment frontiers abroad are successively being closed out by the rising revolutionary tides of nationalism and communism. The Soviet Revolution of 1917, the Chinese upheaval of 1949 have slammed the door on American expansion in those vast and heavily populated heartland regions. Latin America could follow suit any day, any year. Yet, in this mounting crisis, there is as yet– apart from the aforementioned murmurings–no dialogue, no positive opposition in American society. On the contrary, there is rigidity and nativistic revivalism. In this perspective, the decline of American society may have set in two or three generations ago. It is interesting to note that Toynbee, in his study of civilizations, puts very early in his grand cycle the shift from a creative to a dominant (i.e., uncreative) minority, even though a long period of increasing national power and glory may follow.

The oppositions to American society and to the American ethos are today external rather than internal. This further impedes meaningful dialogue between Establishment and Opposition, by virtue of the emotional barriers of patriotism, nationalism, and racism. Yet without such a dialogue, without massive and positive oppositions, the United States may well become increasingly obsolete, like the dinosaurs that in a long ago age failed to meet the challenge of their own time. Unfortunately, the United States still bestrides the world like a muscle-bound and inflexibly programmed colossus. It holds the fate of all of us in a finger tip poised above a nuclear push button.

The problem of the United States in 1970 is not primarily Vietnam. "Uncle Sam" could get out of Vietnam tomorrow without fundamentally altering his underlying dilemma. Indeed, the real problem of American society is not even the ghetto-encapsulated Blacks. The crisis, the failure of nerve, the Achilles heel of American civilization surely lies in the colossal, almost indescribable failure – and need – to face up to itself.

> The central issue of the mid-twentieth century is how to sustain democracy and prosperity without imperial expansion and the conflicts it engenders. . . . The way to transcend tragedy is to reconcile the truths which define the tragedy. . . . To transcend tragedy requires the nerve to fail. . . . For the nerve to fail has nothing at all to do with blustering and self-righteous crusades up to or past the edge of violence. . . . For Americans, the nerve to fail is in a real sense the nerve to say that we no longer need what Turner calls "the gate of escape" provided by the frontier. . . . The traditional effort to sustain democracy by expansion will lead to the destruction of democracy.[38]

So wrote William A. Williams in 1962. Using different terminologies, a number of writers have come to similar verdicts – Veblen, Sorokin, Walter Lippman, Paul Sweezy – to name but a few.

"Over-success as failure" – this is the tragic verdict on the American republic, seen from afar by the present writer in 1970. In all the checkered course of human history, no other national rise has been more brilliant or more meteoric. No nation's fall could be more cataclysmic. It might well engulf not only Canada, but most of the world.

> Once there was a way to get back homeward,
> Once there was a way to get back home . . .[39]

Once upon a time it was not too late to retreat. But not any more.

The dreadful impasse in the United States, the mindless rigidity of American societal development during the last three or four generations – especially since World War I – this is what Canadian society has bought (or sold) into, and is now confronting. That the American Blacks in alliance with other underclass and dissident groups may break through the reigning conservative orthodoxy that pervades the American Establishment (including both major political parties) – is not impossible. But it seems uncertain. Is the consequent drag upon Canadian society inevitably fatal?

Let us first consider the objective pessimism of George Grant, a perceptive Anglo thinker, a dissenting product of the Tory establishment of eastern Canada, and chairman of the McMaster University Department of Religion. He argues that in Vietnam the American empire is destroying an entire nation in order to preserve its domination, and that Canada is an integral and subordinate part of the United States order.[40]

In the light of our dialectical premise, we think there may be something more to be said. Regional and class oppositions have been more prominent in Canadian society during the half-century since the first World War than in the United States. And the half overt, half latent opposition between Canada and the United States still lives.

Today the prime confrontation within Canada, combining partly overlapping regional, ethnic, linguistic, and class oppositions, is that between Anglo Canada and French Quebec. It is wholly possible that Quebec may yet be the salvation of Canadian society, especially if Quebec opts for independence – as seems increasingly likely. And in our dialectical perspective, this domestic confrontation – particularly if Quebec moved decisively toward socialism (as she would almost certainly be compelled to do, in order to manage successfully her natural and human resources for national French-Canadian survival) – might awake unforeseen reactions and resources in English Canada. To be sure, these reactions might produce either a collapse into the American camp or a spine-stiffening resolution to remain different.

There are only two basic alternatives for Canadian society in the foreseeable future. One is a continued drift toward continentalism which means further absorption into the American capitalist empire. This policy since World War II has been pursued largely without public debate by most elements of the Canadian elites – the policy makers in the private, public, and governmental corporations – anti-national and therefore anti-Canadian. The other alternative is a Canadian Castro. This means socialism: expropriation of selected foreign and domestic major corporations, closer control of certain other key industries, and the overall planning of the use of our major resources for national purposes and public services.

But there may also be intermediate possibilities, such as the watered-down socialism of René Lévesque. According to certain lines of contemporary economic thinking, it is apparently desirable to leave a fairly large private sector in the economy, perhaps along Scandinavian lines, particularly in "small business," but also in a few large scale industries. In principle, however, the choice lies between American imperialism and Canadian socialism.

Compensation for expropriation? In principle, yes. But unforeseeable circumstances would doubtlessly control the amount. At one end of the range of possibilities is a minimal token compensation, based on the argument that past profits should be weighted off against present value. At the other end of the range is full compensation for present value. The pattern could vary for different industries. Here we may revert to a remarkable occurrence in Quebec. Some years back, the Province of Quebec nationalized an American-owned corporation—Quebec Hydro— and borrowed the money from the Americans to pay for the take-over. We should all reflect at length upon this significant event. We might just possibly make it financially worthwhile for the Americans (who know a good business deal when they see one) to finance Canadian independence. And we could always hope to scale down the interest rate in due time. In any case, there are other sources in the world for borrowing capital for investment and for compensation. The Americans understand competition—or so they say. Let them compete with France, the Soviet Union, Japan, and so on for the financing of Canadian independence.

Still thinking in terms of metropolis-hinterland oppositions as a core concept in the history and the future of Canadian national development, we may suggest that the coming confrontation between Quebec and English Canada may be the best promise for both parties to that great dialogue. In Quebec's drift and thrust toward independence, it is secondary that a subjected and exploited nationality may some day soon recover its freedom. That would be no more than poetic justice for past wrongs. What really matters is what Quebec may do to stimulate the revival of independent nationalism in the rest of Canada. And even more important, perhaps, is what such socialist and nationalist development in the form of two independent nations north of the American border might do for the United States. That may be too optimistic, of course. Yet the fate of homo sapiens may well rest upon the issue: Can the United States recover—or more accurately, achieve—a national identity and national policy that is compatible with the emerging revolutionary mainstream of the rest of the world? Consider the words of W. A. Williams, American historian in the classic tradition of Charles Beard:

> For the rest of the world, be it presently industrial or merely beginning to industrialize, is very clearly moving toward some version of a society modeled on the ideal of a true human community based far more on social property than upon private property. That is what the editors of *The Wall Street Journal* meant in 1958 when they candidly admitted that the United States was on "the wrong side of a social revolution." The socialist reassertion of the ancient ideal of a Christian commonwealth is a viable utopia. It was so when the Levellers asserted it in the middle of the 17th century, and it remains so in the middle of the 20th century. It holds very simply and clearly that the only meaningful frontier lies within

individual men (and women) and in their relationships with each other. It agrees with Frederick Jackson Turner that the American frontier has been a "gate of escape" from those central responsibilities and opportunities. The socialist merely says that it is time to stop running away from life.[41]

All this may seem speculative, of course, but it is not entirely so, given the dialectical promise herein adopted. It is one task of the sociologist to clarify alternatives, regardless of how improbable they may appear in the light of current professional and political orthodoxies. Having said that, it may be well at this point to emphasize the importance of contingencies in social affairs. We may plan our futures, yet much depends on the larger trends of the times. For example, the National Policy that constituted and guided Canadian Confederation over most of the past century was "planned" only in a limited sense. Fowke has put the matter in this way:

> . . . The National Policy was not by itself sufficient to make Western development possible on the scale eventually attained. The establishment of the prairie wheat economy, which may be regarded as its first major economic triumph, was accompanied by tremendous economic expansion throughout the entire Canadian economy, and was an integral part of a complex of dynamic forces which pervaded the western world. Professor Mackintosh has spoken of the "conjuncture of favourable circumstances" which marked the transition from the nineteenth to the twentieth century and which gave to Canada three decades of unprecedented expansion. This conjuncture of world circumstances created the opportunity for Canadian expansion, but a half-century of foundation work along the lines of national policy has prepared Canada for the opportunity.[42]

R. Heilbroner points up the same argument in even stronger terms:

> For the common attribute of contemporary events is not their responsiveness to our designs, but their indifference to them. . . . History less and less presents itself as something we find or make, and more and more as something we find made for us.[43]

Yet part of this deepening impasse may be due to the fact that the United States, like King Canute forbidding the tide, is attempting to stand against and to turn back the rising swell of anti-colonial and communist revolutions that are sweeping much of the world in the twentieth century.

This brings us to our final issue. By contrast with the United States, Canadian society has been characterized as "pluralistic." This means that ethnic and regional differences for example have been more generally accepted, more legitimized than they have been in our southern neighbour. There has not been as much pressure in Canada for "assimilation" as there has been in the United States–though it is easy to exaggerate the importance of the American "melting pot" ideology (in the case of the Negro, and the southwestern Mexican-American, for instance)–just as one may readily over estimate Canadian tolerance for ethnic differences. Canadians seem to prefer Indians and Blacks to keep their distance. Yet the Hutterite communities unquestionably are granted more autonomy in Canada than in the United States. Likewise, the Indians of Canada, however rudely they were shunted onto reservations when the fur trade no longer needed their labour and the eastern Anglo Establishment wanted their land for white settlement, were seldom treated with such overt coercion as were the American Indians. Above all, the English and the French, despite the conquest and subordination of the latter, had to arrive at a *modus vivendi* that involved mutual compromise and autonomy as well as exploitation.

Another way of describing and perhaps of partially explaining Canadian pluralism is to observe the fact that capitalism never developed to such extremes in Canada as it did in the United States. The American colonies broke their ties early with England, and the philosophy of laissez-faire Manchesterism could run wild until the rise of new internal oppositions late in the nineteenth century. Even then, as we have seen, the competitive challenges of the labour and the agrarian movements were blunted by taking the rebels into the feast and paying for this by means of foreign economic expansion. In England, on the other hand, elements of pre-industrial classes and values survived industrialization. The first reforms in the nineteenth century were sparked, not by the "new men of Manchester," but by Tories from the old landed classes motivated by feudal norms like *noblesse oblige*. Something of these restraining values seem to have carried over into English Canada. And French Canada has embodied still other and different traditions.

Now, however, all Canadian particularisms are threatened by what George Grant calls the "homogenizing and universalising power of technology."[44] What kinds of community do the various segments of Canadian society want? This is one of the key questions posed by the Alberta Indian leader, Harold Cardinal:

> The new Indian policy promulgated by Prime Minister Pierre Elliot Trudeau's government . . . in June of 1969 is a thinly disguised programme which offers nothing better than cultural genocide. . . . Indians have aspirations, hopes and dreams, but becoming white men is not one of them.[45]

The Indians, according to Cardinal, want a respected place in Canadian society, but they also insist at least in some degree on remaining Indians.

A similar theme is voiced by René Lévesque, leader of the Quebec independence movement:

> We are Quebecois. What this means first and foremost . . . is that we are attached to this one corner of the earth where we can be completely ourselves: this Quebec, the only place where we have the unmistakable feeling that "here we can be really at home." Being ourselves is essentially a matter of keeping and developing a personality that has survived for three and a half centuries. At the core of this personality is the fact that we speak French. . . . We are heirs to the group obstinacy which has kept alive that portion of French America we call Quebec. . . . This is how we differ from other men and especially from other North Americans . . . [46]

In calling for an independent Quebec, Lévesque is striking out for the survival of a major Canadian particularism. He is arguing that only in their own sovereign state can French-speaking Canadians develop their own special style of life and shape their own institutions. Unlike the Indians of Canada, the independence movement in Quebec has such assets as numbers, concentration of population, organizations of all types, important natural resources, well developed economic enterprises, and so on. The Indians are scattered, divided into over 500 bands on more than 2200 reservations, further separated into 11 language groups, and for the most part poverty-ridden.

In affirming that the survival of various nationalisms in Canada requires (among other things) a shift to a socialist economy, we must refer to the thesis of André G. Frank concerning "underdevelopment." Although Frank based his analysis on Latin American studies, his conclusions seem equally applicable to Canada:

> Underdevelopment is not due to the survival of archaic institutions and the existence of capital shortage in regions that have remained isolated from the stream of world history. On the contrary, underdevelopment was and still is generated by the very same historical process which also generated economic development: the development of capitalism itself.[47]

The history of the fur trade in Canada is a classic illustration of this thesis. The development of the fur trade tied the Indians to a world market as colonialized workers managed by others. When the fur industry declined, capital migrated to other sectors of the economy, and the Indians were left stranded and by-passed in a world they did not make. Now the Indians are beginning to knock on the door of the modern world. They no longer wish to be a poverty-ridden rural proletariat, they are not content to move into urban slum ghettos. Nor do they wish to be merely "brown white men." They want to be different it seems: they want to be Indian.

The Frank thesis can be applied also to Quebec. Modern economic development came relatively late to Quebec, compared to Ontario, and it came mainly for the benefit of Anglos. Now Quebec is catching up, but Quebeckers, too, wish both to retain their cultural differences and to have more of the economic goodies.

If this approach is valid, it greatly reinforces the argument that the salvaging of Canadian pluralisms requires a socialist economic base. The economic aspect of the issue is essential, but it is clearly not the only essence. There is also among many Indians, the Quebeckers, and perhaps among many other groups such as students and young people as well, a quest for community. Socialism by itself does not guarantee community. There is still the problem of large scale bureaucracy. Much experimentation in making bureaucratic organization more responsive to the control and needs of its members and clients is still needed. But a regime of social property rather than private property seems one obvious prerequisite of the next great phase of North American society. If that society has a future – a big "if" – the American empire must be decolonialized. What Quebec and the Indians of Canada appear to be seeking to escape from is their dependent and colonial status. English Canada's branch-plant condition relative to the United States economic empire is objectively parallel in certain respects to the hinterland status of the Indians and French vis-à-vis the Anglos in Canada. But English Canadians have not yet awakened to their dependency and fate in the homogenizing and expanding American empire.

The coming confrontation between English and French Canada – if it does occur – may help to change all that. Lévesque's insight seems valid, in the light of our dialectical frame of reference.

> As for the other Canadian majority, it will also find our solution [independence for Quebec] to its advantage, for it will be set free at once from the constraints imposed on it by our presence: it will be at liberty in its own way to rebuild to its heart's desire the political institutions of English Canada and to prove to itself, whether or not it really wants to maintain and develop on this continent, an English-speaking society distinct from the United States.[48]

Looking back and looking ahead, the Canadian Centennial of 1967 may well prove to be a watershed in Canadian history, an interlude between eras. This is the view suggested by our conception of Canadian history and society as a dynamic sequence of oppositions, irregularly and alternately latent and overt between overlapping hierarchies – regional, class, ethnic, urban-rural – of metropolis-hinterland relationships within North American society. Does this schema have any predictive value? If it does, then it could inform policy.

In the present writer's judgment this modified dialectical approach seems to "fit" the Canadian and North American past reasonably well. Whether it will continue to offer a realistic interpretation in the future, only time will tell. Life is full of surprises. Somewhere in his postscript to *War and Peace*, Tolstoy remarks that some interpretations of modern history are like "a deaf man answering questions which no one has asked."

The mythical scientific analyst must assume a completely deterministic premise: If he knew all the factors in a situation and their relative weights and vectors – currently an impossible "if" – he could predict the resultant outcome of that situation. The actor, however, cannot know all the factors in his action situation; therefore he has "choices." Hence we suggest no more than this: A dialectical approach illuminates the past and perhaps also clarifies the future alternatives of Canadian societal development. In other words, it fulfills what C. Wright Mills called the interpretive task of classical social analysis (see p. 123). All we are certain of, at this point, is that for such a purpose the dialectical frame of reference is superior to the orthodox structural-functionalism of academic sociology.

Is it unrealistic to take into account this dialectical perspective as one factor in making policy decisions in various interest-groups in Canadian society? For example, is it reasonable to suppose that Quebec or Canada can "confront" the American colossus and still survive? The answer seems obvious. Why not? We never know until we try. And if nothing is attempted, then the drift into the American empire will simply continue. What the fate and value of American society will be is presently indicated in the obscenities now proceeding in Vietnam. American policy in Vietnam – and potentially in Latin America – is like the Assyrian armies that flayed alive thousands of their opponents, only it is mechanized and on a vastly greater and more "efficient" scale. If the heart of American society is Main Street, its cutting edge is in Vietnam, and there is an organic link between the two aspects. This is barbarism, not civilization.

Many turning points of history appear to be a chancy process of "slipping successfully between the icebergs." The collection of puny American colonies was able to achieve its independence from the superior might of the British empire because Britain was pre-occupied by a major war with France. The Bolshevik revolution in Russia succeeded because the hostile western powers, exhausted by a world war, could not muster sufficient force to smother it. Castro led a successful revolution in Cuba, right under the nose of the United States, partly because of American involvements in Asia and Europe and partly because the Americans assumed they could do business as usual with the new leader as they had always done with previous rebels in Cuba and Latin America. When the Americans finally woke up, it was too late.

Contrary to George Grant, therefore, we believe that nationalism in Quebec and in English Canada is not necessarily defeated. But it will require a socialist transformation to salvage and rebuild what remains and even that may not be enough.

Earlier in this paper (see endnote 1) it was suggested that "North America" may in certain respects be too small a framework for analyzing Canadian society. The American empire is not merely a hemisphere but a global operation. It seems appropriate for students of Canadian society to take into account so far as possible key developments all over the world.

Looking at that larger picture, the chances for a successful confrontation with the United States may well be better in Mexico or elsewhere in Latin America than in Canada. A "successful confrontation" may be defined as one that leaves the people of the world both alive and fit to live. Mexico has vitality, great numbers, longer and deeper roots in distinctive Indian and Catholic cultures, a revolutionary tradition, and so on. On an even larger canvas, as Sorokin suggested during his last years, the best hope for a viable and humane stabilizing of the world may lie with Oriental societies–Japan, China, and India–especially the latter two. These societies have already made extensive progress in adapting such western patterns as science and technology to their own ancient cultural heritages, and in "kicking out the White man."[49] Indeed, during most of world history the leadership of civilization has rested with the river-valley imperial societies of the near East, India and China. Perhaps the meteoric rise and evident decline of Western Europe during the last few centuries is but a passing episode.

This massive transition, however, could well be cut short by nuclear war, precipitated by the terminal convulsions of the American juggernaut in the face of rising domestic and external oppositions. That would be the end of all of us. Meanwhile, we may offer one final thought. If a new Gene Debs appears to lead a revolutionary transformation in the United States, he may perchance be a Black. In Canada, he will probably be a French Canadian or a western farmer. He–or she or they–will come from, or be identified with, one or more of the underclass and regional hinterlands of North American society.

Notes

1 Visits to Mexico and to India in 1969 by the present writer persuaded him that the concept of North American society should be broadened to include Mexico as well as Canada, and that even such a vast canvas as the New World American empire may be too small in an economic and political sense, if we want to understand the modern world. Conspicuous in both Mexico City and New Delhi were neon signs, branch plants, and subsidiaries of American multinational corporations.

2 The "staples theory of Canadian economic development" deserves our special attention. Cf. H. A. Innis, *The Fur Trade in Canada* (Toronto: University of Toronto Press, 1956); H. A. Innis, ed., *Essays in Canadian Economic History* (Toronto: University of Toronto Press, 1956); W. Easterbrook and H. Aitken, *Canadian Economic History* (Toronto: Macmillan, 1958); Deutsch, et al., *The Canadian Economy* (Toronto: Macmillan, 1962); W. Easterbrook and M. Watkins, *Approaches to Canadian Economic History* (Toronto: McClelland and Stewart, 1967).

3 The contribution of manufacturers to gross national product was 105 percent of all four primary industries for 1926–29; it was 205 percent for 1953–56. Within the primary sector, mining (including oil) had risen to constitute about one-third of all primary production by the mid-1950s. See R. Leach, ed., *Contemporary Canada* (Toronto: University of Toronto Press, 1968), Chap. iv, esp. p. 84; figures cited from M. Urquhart and K. Buckley, *Historical Statistics of Canada* (Toronto: University of Toronto Press, 1956), pp. 133, 141.

Other parameters substantiate the rising importance of manufacturing and the service industries relative to primary industries. The following is the percent distribution of the employed labour force for 1946 and 1967.

	1946	1967
Agriculture and other primary industries	29.4%	10.6%
Manufacturing	26.0	23.8
Service (incl. public admin. & defense)	16.8	29.5
Trade	12.3	16.6
Transportation, Utilities	8.1	8.9
Construction	4.8	6.4
Financial, Insurance, Real Estate	2.7	4.2
TOTAL	100.1	100.0

Further, the net income of farm operators from farm production in 1966 was 5.1 percent of net national income at factor cost—although farmers made up 7.6 percent of the 1966 labour force. (*Canada Year Book*, 1968, pp. 759 and 1064).

4 Even so, pacification of the Indians was accomplished in Canada with much less violence than in the United States. We say this in full awareness of the near-deliberate extermination of the Beothuk-speaking Indians in Newfoundland by 1820. See D. Jenness, *Indians of Canada* (4th ed.) (Ottawa: National Museum of Canada, 1958), p. 266.

5 The first of the Dominion Experimental Farms on the prairies was established in 1886. Over the next two or three generations, these research stations resolved a series of key problems, culminating perhaps in the salvaging of the semi-arid Palliser triangle in southeastern Alberta and southwestern Saskatchewan during the 1930s. James Gray writes: "The conquest of the desert in the Palliser triangle is the greatest success story since the completion of the Canadian Pacific Railway. . . . Canada could not have existed without the settling and farming of the Palliser triangle. . . . Canada could not have survived economically or politically if the vast area had been permitted to go back to wheat-covered wasteland and short grass cattle range." *Men Against the Desert* (Saskatoon: Modern Press, 1967).

6 Census of Canada. Cited in Saskatchewan Royal Commission on Agriculture and Rural Life, Report No. 7, *Movement of Farm People* (Regina: Queen's Printer, 1956), p. 86.

7 See J. N. McCrorie, *In Union Is Strength* (Saskatoon: Saskatchewan Farmers Union, 1964); J. Irving, *The Social Credit Movement in Alberta* (Toronto: University of Toronto Press, 1959), and sources therein cited.

8 "Drastic" here means such institutional changes as a guaranteed annual income issued without regard to work or residence; or a policy of central planning for, and massive investment in, economically depressed communities and/or regions.

9 Hubert Guindon, "Two Cultures," in *Contemporary Canada*, ed. R. Leach (Toronto: University of Toronto Press, 1968), Chap. ii; also M. Chapin, *Quebec Now* (New York: Oxford Press, 1955), Chap iii in particular.

10 *The Distemper of Our Times* (Toronto: McClelland and Stewart, 1968), p. xii.

11 See H. Aitken, J. Deutsch, W. Mackintosh, et al., *The American Economic Impact on Canada* (London: Cambridge University Press, 1959).

12 McCrorie, *In Union Is Strength*, 1965.

13 *The Anatomy of Revolution* (Englewood Cliffs, N.J.: Prentice-Hall, 1952). This work analyzes four modern revolutions: the English Revolution of the mid-seventeenth century; the American Revolution of 1776; the French Revolution of 1789; and the Russian Revolution of 1917. Brinton would have done better to include in his four cases the second American revolution (1861) rather than the first (1776).

14 W. A. Williams, *The Roots of the Modern American Empire* (New York: Random House, 1969).

15 See Bert Cochran, Ed., *American Labor in Mid-Passage* (New York: Monthly Review Press, 1959), pp. 29–30: "American labour history has been one of the most violent of the whole world. Goaded beyond endurance, workers would rise up every fifteen to twenty years. But the system was never in danger. The variegated composition of the American people ensured that the uprising affected but a segment of the nation. The growth of the middle classes stunted the numerous labour parties that repeatedly dotted the landscape. The extreme expansion of American capitalism, thwarted by no feudalistic obstructions, and with a virgin

continent to ravage, permitted the doling out of material privileges. The mass movement, in defeat or victory, would inevitably lapse into acquiescence." See also C. and M. Beard, "The Labour Movement," in *The Rise of American Civilization* (New York: Macmillan, 1930), Chap. xxi.

16 McCrorie, *In Union is Strength*, 1965.

17 George Grant, *Lament for a Nation* (Toronto: McClelland and Stewart, 1965); M. Watkins, et al., *Foreign Ownership and the Structure of Canadian Industry* (Ottawa: Privy Council Office, 1968).

18 B. Blishen, Jones, Naegele, and Porter, *Canadian Society: Sociological Perspectives* (2nd ed.) (Toronto: Macmillan, 1964), pp. 1–19, 497–522.

19 They do not even do justice to Max Weber, who was not merely a sociologist, but also a first-class economic historian. The North American disciples of Weber have latched onto Weber's timeless abstractions while ignoring for the most part his deep-rooted historical context. Here we refer, of course, to T. Parsons and his followers.

20 W. Mann, ed., *Canada: A Sociological Profile* (Toronto: Copp Clark, 1968), pp. 488–498. The Lipset paper originally appeared in the *Canadian Review of Sociology and Anthropology*, November 1964.

21 *Agrarian Socialism* (Berkeley: University of California, 1950). Lipset in this early volume of the CCF movement collected much information and many insights, but he erred fundamentally in mistaking this primarily rural, petty-bourgeois populist surge for a transplanted urban socialism. Fortunately, Lipset's blunder is corrected in the new edition of *Agrarian Socialism* (New York: Doubleday Anchor, 1968) not by Lipset (his 1950 text is purposely unchanged) but by the new non-Lipset material in Part II, especially the essays by anthropologist John Bennett and economist John Richards. See also A. K. Davis, "The Saskatchewan CCF: The Unfinished Battle for the Shire," *Our Generation*, VI, No. 4 (1969), 48–62.

22 See Mann, *Canada: Sociological Profile*, for explanation of these concepts.

23 Mann, *Canada: Sociological Profile*, p. 497.

24 R. Matthews and J. Steele, *The Struggle for Canadian Universities* (Toronto: New Press, 1969), especially pp. 1–11.

25 *The Sociological Imagination* (New York: Oxford University Press, 1959), p. 21.

26 *Ibid.*, p. 20.

27 *Ibid.*, p. 3.

28 *Ibid.*, p. 6.

29 The interesting point is that a great deal of work has already been published along historical and holistic lines in Canada. No student of Canadian society should be ignorant of the previously mentioned "staples theory" of Canadian development. The same may be said of Harold Innis' classic study of *The Fur Trade in Canada* (Toronto: University of Toronto Press, 1956) and his *Essays in Canadian Economic History* (New Haven: Yale University Press, 1930). The series edited by S. D. Clark, *Social Credit in Alberta* (10 vols.) (Toronto: University of Toronto Press, 1950–59), and an earlier series edited by W. Mackintosh and W. Joerg, *Canadian Frontiers of Settlement* (Toronto: Macmillan, 1930's), are likewise

indispensable. Yet it must be said that some of the keenest insights into modern Canadian and North American social development are to be found in non-sociologist sources like George Grant, Peter Newman, Pete Seeger, Joni Mitchell, Buffy St. Marie, and so on. The academic sociologists are making very few contributions to national self-understanding.

30 Unplanned as a whole, that is, however rationally the component actions of the larger process may be planned and carried out.

31 *Lament for a Nation* (Toronto, McClelland and Stewart, 97 pp., 1965).

32 "Decline and Fall," *Monthly Review*, XII (1960), 334–344.

33 *The Rise of American Civilization*, (New York: Macmillan, 1927), XI, 54, 99.

34 When the death of latter-day American hero-presidents like Franklin Roosevelt and John Kennedy were memorialized and publicly solemnized, the poem invariably recited was Walt Whitman's great elegy to President Lincoln: "When Lilacs last in the Dooryard Bloomed." The greatest American national crisis evoked the greatest national poem. Subsequent American crises, because they have been lesser, have merely echoed the greatness of that earlier day.

35 *The Frontier in American History* (New York: Henry Holt, 1921), Chap. i, xii *et passim.*

36 All that my friend Roy Atkinson, President of the Saskatchewan Farmers Union, is trying to do by organizing a National Farmers Union is to give farmers an effective trade association such as most other categories of capitalistic entrepreneurs have long enjoyed. A more conservative, truly capitalistic goal could hardly be imagined.

37 The student strikes and the march on Washington in Spring 1970 provoked by the Kent State University killings and Nixon's move into Cambodia may have been a step toward organization and mass support on campus, however fleeting.

38 *The Tragedy of American Diplomacy* (New York: Dell, 1962), pp. 303, 307–309.

39 The Beatles, *Abbey Road*, 1969.

40 *Technology and Empire* (Toronto: House of Anansi, 1969), pp. 63, 65.

41 *Contours of American History* (Cleveland: World Publishing Co., 1961), p. 487. Copyright © 1961 by William Appleman Williams.

42 *The National Policy and the Wheat Economy* (Toronto: University of Toronto Press, 1957), p. 70.

43 *The Future as History* (New York: Harper, 1959) (1968 Torchbook paper edition).

44 *Technology and Empire* (Toronto: House of Anansi, 1969), p. 69.

45 *The Unjust Society* (Edmonton: Hurtig, 1969), pp. 1, 3.

46 *An Option for Quebec* (Toronto: McClelland and Stewart, 1968), pp. 14–15.

47 "The Development of Underdevelopment," *Monthly Review*, No. 18 (September, 1966), p. 23. See also A. G. Frank, *Capitalism and Under-development in Latin America* (New York: Monthly Review Press, 1967).

48 *An Option for Quebec*, p. 28.

49 P. A. Sorokin, *Basic Trends of Our Time* (New Haven: College and University Press, 1964), p. 64, and Chap. ii *passim*.

A New Sociology:
Metropolis/Overclass
Hinterland/Underclass

E VER SINCE the early civilizations of Greece, India and China, the
social thinkers and teachers of the world's societies have had something relevant to say about their times.

Unfortunately much of the teaching and research by anglophone academic sociologists in Canada has presented an abstract, bland, and static
picture of Canadian society. Canadian social scientists see the world
through a middle-class lens: conflict is underestimated. Few of them deal
with Canadian society as a whole. For the most part, academic sociologists appear to be talking to each other about esoteric topics, although
most of them are paid—fairly well—by Canadian public funds. For the
average person (who pays the shot), Ann Landers is usually more relevant.

Whatever qualifications and exceptions may be cited, the prevailing
tone is one of equilibrium, timelessness, value integration, natural harmony of interests. Deviance and conflict tend to be defined as short-term
sub-cultures. In turn sub-cultures usually appear as, and remain, deviant; their potential progression into large-scale structural changes is seldom seriously contemplated.

The concept of *deviance* itself implies a dominant and more or less
stable order. This assumed order is the North American middle-class pattern. Measured thereby, other patterns such as hippies, peaceniks, draft-
evaders, ghetto gangs, et al, come to be defined as sub-cultures. On the
other hand, in a dialectical, conflict-oriented perspective these "deviations" become "oppositions" or alternatives, any of which might turn
out to be sources of key structural changes.

Reprinted by permission. *Canadian Dimension.* Winnipeg, Manitoba, Canada. Vol. 8, 1972.

The second reason for the aridity of anglophone sociology in Canada is the general identification of sociologists with the Anglo-Canadian bourgeois Establishment and/or with the latter's country-cousin status as a branch plant of the American capitalist empire. Even if the majority of our sociologists are indifferent to or unaware of Canada's subordination to the United States, they can be said to support it by default. Surprisingly little attention is given to historical overviews, to regional studies or to the potentially massive conflicts creeping up both inside and outside Canadian society.

On occasion, to be sure, the so-called structural-functional approach has attained a relatively complete view of Canadian society: John Porter's work contains much information and some useful historical data. But to find out what is really going on in Canadian society today, one would be better advised to turn to philosopher George Grant; to economist Mel Watkins; to journalist Peter Newman; and to the documentaries of the Canadian Broadcasting Corporation (CBC) and the National Film Board. For relevant reading on Canadian society, one should probably pass over at least half of the *Canadian Review of Sociology and Anthropology* in favour of *Canadian Dimension* and *The Last Post*. The best study of poverty in Canada is by journalist Ian Adams. Lipset's well-known study seriously misinterpreted the Saskatchewan Co-operative Commonwealth Federation (CCF) movement as a transplanted offshoot of urban socialism, when it was mainly an indigenous manifestation of western petty-bourgeois populism fighting against eastern metropolitan domination. In the new updated edition of this book, the record has been set straight, not by Lipset or by some other sociologist, but by anthropologist John Bennett and economist John Richards.

If I were a CBC official responsible for staffing a documentary radio or television program on what is going on in Canadian society, I would pass over most of the anglophone sociologists and present the ideas of people like René Lévesque, Harold Cardinal, certain journalists, a handful of academics (mostly non-sociologists), and of the more sensitive and intelligent folk-singers like Buffy Sainte-Marie. They could do the job.

Our francophone colleagues have not been contaminated by over-concern with structural-functionalism to the same extent as the anglophones. Living close to the central conflict in contemporary Canadian society—the question of independence for Quebec—they are more conscious of conflict and change than are most of the rest of us.

Another really sad fact is that the majority of anglophone sociologists do not know what their francophone counterparts are doing, because they do not speak or read French. In my judgment, even our western Canadian universities within a few years will have to give priority to appointing fluently bilingual professors to their faculties to correct this. I believe that the Canadian Sociology and Anthropology Association should re-establish communication with Quebec social scientists by pressuring anglophone members to take total-immersion courses in the French language.

Roughly speaking, the dialectical premise is that major changes in the institutional structure of a particular society stem from internal and external oppositions in that society and its milieu. These oppositions or confrontations of interests and values eventually work into a new institutional pattern not like either of the original opposing complexes but usually including important elements of each. A good example is historian Crane Brinton's study of four major revolutions (1952). In the Canadian context, the dialectical approach may be seen in the conflict of interests between metropolis and hinterland and in the inherent tendency of hinterlands to fight back—though these conflicts at different times may be hidden or counteracted by other factors, as conditions vary.

Metropolis refers to centres of economic and political control, usually in the larger cities. *Hinterland* means any comparatively underdeveloped or colonial area which exports for the most part raw or semi-processed materials—including people migrating to better opportunities elsewhere. In the broad sense, it seems convenient to use *metropolis* and *overclass* interchangeably, likewise *hinterland* and *underclass*.

Obviously hierarchies of metropolis-hinterland relationships overlap. Northern Manitoba may be viewed as a hinterland of Winnipeg—or in certain respects as a hinterland of Ottawa. Manitoba may be seen as something of a hinterland to industrial and commercial eastern Canada, and Canada itself is in the same relation to the United States economic and political empire. Needless to say, the metropolis-hinterland schema does not include all the relationships that may exist between or among these entities. Rather, it highlights the conflict and exploitive aspects of such relationships in Canadian and North American society in a way that takes account of unique local and historical conditions and sheds light on future developments.

There is nothing really new in these remarks. In fact, a good deal of work has been done along these lines by Canadian scholars, especially by such economic historians as Innis and Fowke. A number of sociologists have made consistent use of historical materials and perspectives—among them S. D. Clark, B. Y. Card, R. Ossenberg, S. Ryerson, Hubert Guindon—to name no others. But the contributions of such writers seem outweighed, at least in volume, by work that leans toward the structural-functional tradition. Consider, for example, the array of textbooks commonly used in anglophone introductory sociology courses in Canadian universities. The majority of them impress me as useless "mickey mouse" exercises imported (for a good price) from the United States, or produced by Canadian branch plants of American publishers. What they tell us about North American society is too often less important that what they leave out.

For nearly a decade the Blishen reader has been a mainstay of anglophone Canadian university undergraduate sociology courses. First published in 1961, it must have been used by thousands of students. It has probably widened the gap between Anglo and French Canada—willy-nilly—because it takes little account of conflict-oriented, dialectical views of Canadian society. Further, it has contributed to the obscuring of the one issue that can over-ride the Anglo-French issue: the stance of Canada vis-à-vis the American empire. In other words, the Blishen reader is—ideologically and doubtless unintentionally—a prime indirect supporter of the present middle-class Anglo-Canadian Establishment. Much the same could be said of the Laskin reader and likewise the Mann reader.

It is regrettable that anglophone Canadian sociologists have not critically debated the relevance of the currently fashionable concepts of United States bourgeois sociology for analysis of Canadian society. Occasionally, along with a tendency to transplant those concepts, Canadian academics have displayed an almost supine attitude toward their American opposite numbers. Consider the following Foreword by Dr. Murray Ross, a well-known writer on community organization and formerly president of York University, Toronto, for the W. Mann (1968) reader:

> The popular view is that sociological analysis and study in Canada has lagged far behind similar work in the United States. . . . Unfortunately the popular view is correct . . . Canada has not yet produced original sociological theorists comparable to Talcott Parsons, Robert K. Merton, and C. Wright Mills.

Ross is looking in the wrong place. The original theorists about Canadian society are not to be found in orthodox academic esoterica, but in such sources as Lumsden's *Close The 49th Parallel*, *Canadian Dimension*, *Mysterious East*, Harold Innis and Vern Fowke.

Not the least unhappy aspect of this deference to prevailing American intellectual concepts is that it is unwitting, stemming from class- and culture-bound blindspots.

But sociologists are not alone in being culture-bound. As the following Toronto *Globe and Mail* account of Prime Minister Trudeau's visit to President Nixon in Washington in March, 1969, indicates, the deferential attitude of the Prime Minister of Canada parallels that of the President of York University toward things American.

> Responding to the President's words about a commonality of back-
> ground, Mr. Trudeau said this extended to "a common outlook on the
> world. We have the same values and we tend to face the issues in a com-
> mon way." Because of that he was looking forward to the discussion . . .
> "to listening to your views on world problems, on the information and
> the wisdom you will want to impart upon me in your talks."
>   Some observers who have travelled extensively with Mr. Trudeau said
> that he had not sounded so humbled, or looked so shy, since just before he
> decided to run for the Liberal Party leadership more than 13 months ago.

Robin Mathews of Carleton University justifiably attacks the "Americanization of Canadian universities." His solution is more Canadians –
trained in Canada – on Canadian faculties. This is scarcely adequate. As
long as Canadian sociologists (for example) continue to be trained in
such obfuscating orthodoxies as structural-functionalism and symbolic
interaction, they will remain junior lieutenants in the intellectual empire of the American Establishment.

Conceptual orientation rather than nationality would be a more appropriate target for Mathews. No one wants or needs universities dominated by a particular viewpoint, any more than we want professional
appointments to university faculties to rest heavily on non-professional
criteria such as citizenship. Either outcome would make for parochialism – the very opposite of what a university ought to be.

Canadian society and history may be viewed as a series of hinterland
reactions to foreign metropolitan imperialisms. First came the French
and, soon afterward, the English. This European intrusion tied the native
Indians to the capitalistic European fur trade. In the eighteenth and nineteenth centuries, the native Indians were bent to colonial status: the Eskimo followed approximately a century later.

The conquest of French Canada by a British army in 1760 paved the
way for the Anglo primacy in Canada. But Confederation was basically
a response to the mid-century American industrial and westward expansion. The "National Policy" that emerged by the 1870s and included western settlement as a new investment frontier for eastern business, a transcontinental railroad, a protective tariff, shunting the Indians to
reservations, etc., had some unintended consequences. From the beginning of western settlement, the hinterland residents struggled to improve their status within the system of capitalist expansion and exploitation. The Metis and some Indians kicked up in 1885. From the early
1900s, western farmers entered one skirmish after another against the
railroads, the grain exchange, elevator corporations and finally against
the eastern-dominated political parties. Populist movements eventually
came to power in the form of Social Credit and the CCF. In effect, the

broad course of events in Canada, as industrialization progressed, has followed the pattern anticipated by Marx in the *Manifesto* (1848), at least up to the beginning of a socialist movement. Later I talk about why socialism so far has been stillborn.

A similar metropolis-hinterland framework may be applied to Quebec, as another investment frontier for business interests that were predominantly Anglo, later American. In our own day, populist counter-attacks have appeared in the Caouette movement, speaking primarily for the northern Quebec colonials, and in the bourgeois "quiet revolution" more recently spearheaded by the drive for an independent Quebec.

In my view, this "metropolis-vs-hinterland" dialectic is more realistic and more revealing as an interpretation of Canadian society. It also implies a more openly political role for the social sciences to redefine the nature and transitory status of current institutional patterns in Canada. An excellent application of dialectical analysis of Canadian society by Danny Drache appears in *Close The 49th Parallel*.

Exploited colonials in the North American hinterlands have in the past battled to improve their status in the economic order, as shown for Canada by Fowke and James McCrorie; and for the United States by historian William A. Williams. The American empire has so far been able to carry the cost of concessions to its internal underclasses by expanding its business interests into foreign "hinterlands." But there are signs that the "Open Door" abroad is rapidly closing, so that a major crisis impends in American society, just when its monolithic rigidity and its lack of critically articulate and organized internal oppositions render it incapable of adjusting to the new orders emerging in other parts of the world. It is doubtful, in my view, whether the United States will make it into the 21st century, alive and/or fit to live. If this is valid, then Canada is directly involved, for Canada has become in large part an informal annex of the American empire.

Obviously, not all Canadians will want to be absorbed when they understand what is afoot. For if my analysis is even half valid, the American imperium is coasting toward disaster both at home and abroad. It has not been able to do anything significant about urban and rural poverty, the ghettoized Blacks, the disaffected students, the multiple hard-core problems in the cities. It is bogged down in a military morass in Asia, and its economy appears headed for a serious recession. Assassination of leaders and shooting civilians have become standard political responses in the United States. The savage aspect of American society is revealed in southeast Asia for all to see. The link between Main Street and Vietnam is direct and organic. Other such cases may arise any day in Latin America. If continentalism continues to prevail as Canadian national policy Canada can expect to be dragged down in the American wake.

Veblen Once More:
A View from 1979

To re-read one's PhD thesis nearly four decades after it was written is no light task. There are some rewards: an opportunity for stock-taking and for second thoughts. There are also a few agonies, as the sophomoric gaffes sink into one's mind. What a chastening experience, to realize that those youthful cocksure judgments are spread on the record for anyone to see and read! Consider this summary judgment of Sumner and Veblen: "Sumner, however, was doubtless the greater scientist." (p. 190) Even worse is the following bray: "Thus, from the standpoint of systematic analytical social theory, Marx today is only of historical interest." (p. 371) Q.E.D.

What my advisory committee thought about such over-extended judgments is not recorded. It was a distinguished committee. Parsons chaired it. Sorokin, Zimmerman, Merton, Taylor—they were the others. I have since come round to believe that I learned more from Sorokin than from Parsons—and that is indeed ironic. Sorokin was an idealist, in philosophical terms. A few years after I left Harvard with my PhD, I became a Marxist materialist. But Sorokin was the universal scholar. There was no one else like him. It was Merton who directed my attention to Veblen. I had read one or two of Veblen's books: *The Leisure Class*, and *The Place of Science in Modern Civilization*. Merton told me to read the rest of Veblen's books when I was a graduate student looking around for a thesis topic. He said there was a job needing to be done. Merton was right. I do not think I ever did a definitive job on Veblen. No one can do that,

Reprinted by permission. Arthur K. Davis, *Thorstein Veblen's Social Theory*. New York, Arno Press, 1980. XV and 449. (Cf. Ayer Co. Publications, Salem, N.H. 03079.)

because times and evaluations change. But Veblen has been the subject of several of my re-thinkings. Over the years and decades, I have published perhaps a half-dozen papers revising my ideas about the great iconoclast.[1] Yet there is still more to say.

Readers of this dissertation may notice my pre-occupation with the dichotomy, "scientific" vs. "non-scientific," most prominent in chapter II but not limited to that chapter. That sophomoric distinction now appears superficial and misleading. Every cosmology, including science, rests on non-scientific or, better put, on arbitrary philosophical premises—that is to say—every cosmology rests on faith. Sorokin tried to teach me that elementary insight long ago, but I did not listen. It disturbs me that I took so long to learn.

Marxian Movements

I find little to change in my assessment of Veblen's theory of social evolution, except to emphasize more strongly its Marxian character. Indeed, that emergent evaluation is probably my central re-interpretation, over the decades, of Thorstein Veblen. He belongs in the Marxian tradition, not in the positivistic tradition as I argued in the dissertation.

Let me say here that "tradition" is the wrong word. That concept implies stability, persistence of the existing order. But stability and persistence in the long run are not the prime characteristics of Societies and Establishments, if we properly define their general life-span in terms of decades and generations instead of years. Let us speak of the Marxian movement, or of the movement toward socialism in its various forms— for each socialist country is in some considerable degree unique, for a combination of historical, geographic, cultural, economic and other socio-political reasons. In this sense, Marxian movements include a "knowledge" aspect—the ideas, ideologies, definitions of the situation— with a number of more or less common concepts and premises. Among the latter would be history defined as process, a dialectical view of totality (e.g., a nation, a nation-State, a society) comprising a number of interacting oppositions or contradictions which conduce to basic institutional change; class struggle; other nationality and ethnic and regional groupings; an immanent conception of change; recognition of the inherently aggressive and expansionist nature of modern capitalisms (note the plural) in order to escape or postpone the terminal cancer of over-production and over-accumulation of surplus capital; and last but not least, a recognition of the inevitability of some form of socialism. One has to think of socialisms, of course—once again, note the plural.

In short, Marxian movements are on-going and developing organizational developments, with intrinsic spin-offs in the form of hortatory and analytical and condemnatory verbalizations. One must say as follows: a writer is Marxian to the extent that he or she takes into account some or even all of the above listed concepts.[2] And other concepts might be included, as well. Rigid orthodoxy must be avoided; new national developments must be allowed for.

Marx and Engels clearly understood European feudalism (especially in central and western Europe), early competitive capitalism, the transition from the first to the second, and the immanent press toward socialism. As one's attention moves away from Europe, in both time and place, Marx and Engels become increasingly less reliable guides. After all, they did their work a century and more ago. They were bound, as we all are, by inherent ethnocentrisms and blind spots. Marx on India achieved a few brilliant insights, yet he did not really understand India. He still viewed British imperialism in India as a necessary and progressive phase, however motivated by greed and pillage. And on China, Marx was positively ignorant of the character and inner dynamics of Chinese history.

For the analyses of late capitalism, we have to turn to Lenin, who understood imperialism better; and to Baran and Sweezy; and to Frank with special reference to Latin America; to Samir Amin and Rodney* with reference to Africa. Doubtless the most significant developments have emerged in China, where one must begin with Mao Tse-tung thought. Veblen, shortly before his death in 1929, recognized albeit dimly the promise of the on-going Chinese revolution, though he did not perceive the temporary nature of the defeats of 1927. To some extent, every national and socialist revolution stands on the shoulders of earlier revolutions. Chairman Mao recognized that class struggle continues under socialism. Lenin said it, too. However, it was Mao who implemented the insight decisively in the Great Proletarian Cultural Revolution of 1966–68, which sought to minimize the new emergence of hierarchy and privileged life-styles based on higher education and high party and State offices. Since then, zigs and zags have appeared at the top of the Chinese power structure, and these will doubtless continue, with uncertain and possibly remote effects on the evolving Chinese socialist society.[3] Remote, that is, in terms of Western China-watchers' overbaked (better still–half-baked) pre-occupation with speculations and gossip about goings-on at the top levels of the Chinese power hierarchy. Such emanations express the ahistorical and unrealistic concern of Western individualism with the Great Man theory of history.

We cannot end this sketchy and inadequate discussion of Marxian socialist movements without mentioning, at least in passing, Tanzania and

Cuba. The *Ujamaa* village concept in Tanzania seeks to combine elements of socialism with traditional African extended-family and rural
values.[4] Fidel Castro's Cuba has emerged from the contradictions of
North American capitalism and imperialism. It owes much to the parochialism of the United States and to the presence on the world stage
of the Union of Soviet Socialist Republics. It is a classic case of sliding
between the icebergs of history. So, indeed, was the United States: it may
be seen as a spin-off of the great European wars between England and
France during the middle and later decades of the eighteenth century.
France intervened on the side of the American rebels at a critical point
by sending money, supplies, a fleet and trained soldiers. At the final battle of Yorktown in 1783, the French forces were almost as numerous as
the Americans. "Very great weight" must be attached to the French intervention against England, wrote the leading American historian Charles
Beard.[5]

Marxian movements in the United States of America have been unexpectedly weak. Here was a vibrant nation-state, blessed with fabulous
continental resources (stolen in large part from the Indians and the Mexicans, to be sure—but is not piracy and pillage a major element in the
building of any nation?). There were practically no significant historical
remnants of earlier powerful social orders such as feudalism was, in
Europe. The aboriginals were either exterminated or shoved onto reservations that no one else wanted at the time. In Canada, the same end-
result was achieved, but with much less violence and fewer massacres.
In brief, the United States became the most unqualified capitalist country in the history of the world. Here was where the proletarian revolution leading to socialism should have occurred, according to the formulations and prognostications of Marx and Engels in the 1848 *Manifesto.*
For Marx and Engels looked toward the more advanced industrialized
countries for the first socialist revolutions. More specifically, Marx and
Engels looked toward western Europe. But the United States became
even more likely within a few decades to become, hypothetically, a leading candidate for socialism. Yet this did not occur. The first socialist revolutions took place in the less industrialized and still predominantly peasant economies, Russia and China.

The reason for this "lapse" is readily explainable in terms of the development of Marxian theory after the time of Karl Marx. In a word—
imperialism, combined with the fabulous over-success of American
business enterprise—given its vast natural resources, large domestic markets, new industries, relative isolation from major wars, and the propen-
sity of its chief capitalist rivals to decimate themselves in suicidal world
wars. On the one hand, imperialism facilitated the expansion of Amer-

ican capitalism abroad, especially after the closing of the domestic frontier in the 1890s. On the other hand, imperialism by all the world capitalist powers evoked from its victims (Russia, China, et. al.) overwhelming
nationalist reactions.

In the short run, however, measured in decades from the end of the
American civil war (1865) – socialist movements in the United States were
bound to be relatively attenuated, even more than in the advanced countries of western Europe. Yet there was a crescendo of social and economic conflicts between 1865 and 1914. I quote from a 1960 paper of mine:

> The second massive opposition in the history of the American Republic
> began to develop with the industrial boom after the Civil War. As indus-
> trial capitalism triumphantly spanned the continent, class conflicts sharp-
> ened. Epic labor battles broke out. Agrarian revolts flared. The first seeds
> of modern socialism took root. By the end of the century, elements of
> various farm, labor and other groups were taking up socialist positions.
>
> The beginnings of a mass socialist movement were unmistakable. A so-
> cialist newspaper, *The Appeal to Reason*, reached a circulation of 600,000,
> with special issues in the millions (U.S. population, 1900, nearly
> 78 millions); Socialists were elected to local offices; Gene Debs running
> for President in 1912 got 6.2 percent of the popular vote – the best showing
> a professing socialist has ever made in an American presidential election.
>
> Until World War I, the American economy was running generally true
> to the course that Marx, a half-century earlier, had forseen as normal for
> capitalism. Capitalist conditions of production, he had said, would pro-
> duce a disciplined and eventually anti-capitalistic labor force, which
> would be driven to reject capitalism and adopt socialism. (*Monthly Review*,
> 12, Oct. 1960, 339)

By the 1890s, the more perceptive American business and political
leaders felt that they were looking into the abyss of all-out class war.
But the nation, in the net, shifted slowly to a policy of imperialism, with
the strongest support coming from the rural hinterlands.[6] From 1912,
the socialist vote in U.S. presidential elections steadily dropped by 1956
to .07 percent. The Communist vote began at .12 percent of the popular
vote for president in 1924, rose to .26 percent in 1932, fell to .10 percent
in 1940, and thereafter disappears in the percentages. Reformist social-
democratic eruptions appear several times, but at a decreasing rate ever
since 1912. In that year, the T. Roosevelt Progressives got 27.5 percent of
the popular vote for president. In 1924, the La Follette movement received only 16.7 percent. By 1948, when Henry Wallace led another "progressive" third party, the share of the vote fell to 2 percent. These "progressive" movements were never socialist; they sought mild reforms
within the existing capitalist order.

Is it surprising, then, that Veblen should play down or camouflage his Marxian ideas, given the enormous preponderance of American capitalism in his day? He used such euphemisms as "the price system" and "business enterprise" instead of referring specifically to "capitalism." He spoke of "getting something for nothing" rather than of class struggle and surplus value. Until he retired from academia, his style of writing remained cloudy and indirect–suitably academic, perhaps–but un-Marxian in terminology, however Marxian in meaning. The tiny Marxian splinter groups had ties with European transplants, some of whom corresponded with Marx and Engels. These writers, and such others as De Leon, used the explicitly Marxian concepts. Veblen's first and best-known book, *The Theory of the Leisure Class* (1899), was reviewed by the well known American novelist William Dean Howells as a work of literary satire!

Veblen Today

As already indicated, since writing my dissertation I have concluded that Veblen's Marxian content deserves much more emphasis than I originally gave to it. But there are also some other changes to report. Looking back, it now appears that imperialism and colonialism were not as central to Veblen's analysis as they would be, had he been writing a generation later. This is hardly a reason to fault Veblen. Rather, world historical processes have moved along since Veblen's day. So, too, has the Marxian analysis of the roles of the State in various capitalist societies.

It must also be said that the dissertation probably underestimates the elements of racism in Veblen's thought. His frequent references to "dolicho-blonds" can scarcely be overlooked or written off. Let us recall that there were prominent manifestations of European ethnocentrism in Marx. For example, he had no illusions about the greed for plunder that motivated British rule in India, yet he regarded Europeanization however bourgeois a net step forward for India, if only as a necessary stage to be endured as an escape from the old order–stagnating Asiatic mode of production. Concerning China, Marx was even less perceptive. Indeed, he was quite ignorant of the historical dynamics of mandarin China. The flashes of brilliant insight into India, written during the 1850s, have no counterpart in his fragments on China. Far better was the contemporary book by the British bourgeois civil servant, Thomas T. Meadows–*The Chinese and their Rebellions* (London, 1856).

If Veblen struck out on China, his compatriots of the same and later generations have done even worse. By and large, China has been viewed by the prevailing sectors of American opinion as "backward" until Liberation (1949) but until then very deserving of American aid—on American terms, of course. And for a very good price, payable to the American multi-national corporations. The basic tenet of United States foreign policy for more than a century has been the expansion of American business. China appeared to be a prospectively immense market, and a large source of raw materials at low cost, and of crafted products in great variety at bargain-basement prices. Exploitation, almost unlimited. Fortunately for human civilization—the short-run calculations of special interests often prove counter-productive. The leadership of civilization for millennia has rested with the riverine civilizations of the Nile, the Tigris-Euphrates, the Indus, the Yellow River. Temporarily, that leadership passed to the Mediterranean and to western Europe and its colonial offshoots, especially North America. Clearly, it is in our day returning to Asia. And after that, Africa? South America?

Another major change in my original evaluation of Veblen must be recorded. Veblen charged the neoclassical economic theory with having a static, abstract and unrealistic character. That is to say, orthodox economic theory was unable to explain everyday economic phenomena. In the dissertation, I defended the orthodox economic schema. It was an analytical abstraction, not meant to explain concrete economic events.

That defense is still valid, of course. But it is not relevant, unless one accepts the premises of timeless, ahistorical normal equilibria—instead of immediate understandable insights into short-run and long-run processes. Today, I would defend Veblen's criticism of the orthodox economics. What he said about neo-classical economics is just what I have been saying for 25 years about Parsonian structural-functional sociology. The latter is an interesting logical system—existing in an academic vacuum. It has, on occasion, useful investigative functions. But it has very little significance for understanding the real world of social action, in which we all have to live, make adjustments, and make choices where possible. For a comprehensive and in-depth understanding of the real world, both short-run and long-run, a dialectical perspective is far superior. It should be basically neo-Marxian, but Georg Lukacs has shown that a dose of Hegelian idealism is an asset.

Next to self-conscious dialectics, applied creatively and flexibly, the best understanding of what is afoot in a society comes from the journalists. The most able of the journalists "put it all together"—or try. This is bound to fall short of the neo-Marxian concept of totality. Yet the two approaches are sometimes on similar wave-lengths, even if they differ in sophistication. For years, I have been telling my students that one good investigative journalist is worth several academics. The orthodox university division into "departments" of economics, of political science, of sociology—has long been counter-productive. The academics slice social reality into arbitrary and increasingly meaningless abstractions. What use is this ivy-tower exercise to ordinary people?

C. Wright Mills wrote that classical social science addresses itself to the basic issues of the times.[7] The prevailing structural-functional academic orthodoxy certainly does not so address itself. It has been corrupted by the successes, monetary grants, advisory positions on public commissions, survey commissions, and the like.

Fortunately, in both the United States and Canada, new responses have arisen. These are often in the Marxian tradition—suitably updated, and flexibly adjusted to the local, regional or national scene. In Canada, the social-science scene is vigorously recovering from the American inundation of the 1960s and early 1970s, with its bent for quantitative gymnastics at the cost of understanding in depth and in totality. There was a firm foundation laid by such scholars as Harold Innis and Donald Creighton—to name no others. Younger Canadian scholars are building on that foundation—but they are redefining totality and its constituent oppositions in class, national, and dependency terms.

Veblen, therefore, was right, and I was wrong. Academic economic theory is largely useless, bound to the support of a decaying capitalist imperium. Similar charges apply to academic sociological theory, and to all other social sciences. I spent four years on the Social Science Research Council of Canada (SSRCC), in the mid- and later 1970s, attempting to persuade the Canadian academic community to undertake a substantial critical review of university organization in anglophone Canada. I wasted my time. The SSRCC approved the study, but the bureaucracy put it on an unlit back-burner. (The SSRCC is an umbrella academic organization.)

What was Veblen's best work—most insightful—on a lasting basis? In the dissertation, I nominated *Imperial Germany* and *The Nature of Peace*, 1915 and 1917 respectively. I now believe that this judgment was erroneous. *Imperial Germany* still stands as a work to be seriously considered, at least with respect to Germany. But Veblen's greatest work surely has to be *Absentee Ownership*. And just as important is the collection of posthumous essays, *Essays in our Changing Order*. Why? Because they are still pregnant with insights into the terminal disease of the United States of America. The name of that disease? DEMENTIA PRAECOX.

This 1922 essay still carries much valid insight. Let us consider it. Veblen argued that the belated American intervention in World War I saved the "war" system: every great Power needs something really or allegedly dangerous to lean against. For the German menace was substituted the Bolshevik menace. Part of the price, however, was saddling America with dementia praecox—hysterical fears of treason, repression of civil rights, officially sponsored witch hunts, with "the Secret Service kept faithfully on the job of making two suspicions grow where one grew before."[8] And in another paper:

> So long as the underlying populations . . . are taken up with patriotic blare and national jealousy the division of interest within these nations, between those who own more than they can use and those who have urgent use for more than they own, will be held in abeyance; a symphony of national hatred and suspicion will be heard in the land, and absentee ownership will be secure. . . . America is taking war by the forelock—with very decently voluble disclaimers of course.[9]

One could not ask for a more prophetic statement.

> Commenting on Veblen today calls for more emphasis on *The Higher Learning in America* (1918) than I accorded it in my dissertation. What little I said seems still relevant, but more ought to have been made of Veblen's caustic remarks on academic social science. Its "intellectual horizon is bounded by the same limits of . . . commonplace insight and preconceptions as are the prevailing opinions of the conservative middle class. That is to say, a large and aggressive mediocrity is the prime qualification for a leader of science . . ."[10]

This view has doubtless appealed widely to the younger North American social scientists associated with the movements of critical sociology. Another aspect of Veblen's thought that may have attracted new readers is his vein of utopian anarchism. Given today's renewed interest in decentralization and regionalism, and in generally humanizing large bureaucracies—Veblen's penchant for idealizing the "masterless man" and the natural affinity of certain peoples for the "live and let live" of the "Savage State" would find new echoes. It is appropriate to refer to the re-discovery of the early papers of Marx, as well. And the leading American Marxist historian, William A. Williams, in his 1976 book, *America Confronts a Revolutionary World, 1776–1976*, calls for a return to the relatively decentralized Articles of Confederation in place of the present centralized and business-oriented constitution of 1789.

Four decades ago, it was not easy to find many of Veblen's ten books except in the second-hand bookshops and the largest libraries. The *Leisure Class* has always been in print, and *Business Enterprise*—the latter in the Harvard Square bookshops. (It was used as a textbook in certain classes of the Harvard Business School—of all places!) A few of Veblen's books were reprinted in the depression-ridden 1930s. In the 1950s and later, a number of his books were reissued in paperback format.

C. Wright Mills said it best, in his Introduction to the 1953 Mentor edition of *The Theory of the Leisure Class.* "There is no better set of books written by a single individual about American society."

Beyond Veblen

I do not wish to leave the impression that Veblen speaks to us today just as he always did. It is not true that "the more things change, the more they are the same." Some things do change–significantly. Others persist.

One of the big changes since Veblen's era is the "End Game" syndrome. Is high-technology industrialism and urbanization–especially under capitalism–viable? All signs suggest that it is not. But is it viable under socialism? Severe doubts arise, however modified by socialist planning for environmental and resource protection.

Marx and Veblen both assumed that industrialism was the wave of the future. In part, this is a manifestation of European ethnocentrism, with racist overtones. With the re-birth of the People's Republic of China, this parochialism is no longer acceptable. It seems impossible– and most undesirable–to automobilize the world.

The dilemma of industrialization may well be settled by World War III–nuclear. It seems likely that, with the emergence of China, we have entered the pre-war phase, leaving the inter-war phase. Here, I borrow from Quincy Wright's *Study of War.* Wright showed that no modern arms race has failed to end in war. Does anyone believe that the present arms race will not follow the same pattern?

It is the third-world nations that have the best prospect of surviving the crisis of over-urbanization and over-industrialization, which feed upon uneven development and exploitation of majorities by privileged minorities. Whether the high-technology societies destroy each other by nuclear war or by collapse from internal contradictions as described in John Brunner's *The Sheep Look Up*–is yet to be seen. Either way, the American imperium seems a temporary one. Two decades ago, I suggested that the United States might well be "over the hill" because of its relative lack of internal oppositions and its consequent rigidity.[11] Despite fierce competitions and conflicts, no massive popular group since World War I ever challenged the "American way of life"–that is to say–bourgeois capitalism. Cheap and successful wars, fought abroad, and imperialism headed off the indigenous socialist beginnings that were taking shape around the turn of the century. A similar pattern emerged in three wars: the Cuban-Spanish war, and the two world wars. The United States came in at the late stages of all three, and picked up most of the booty–the empires of the exhausted combatants.

Dialectical philosophy sees basic change as a resultant of immanent oppositions. But the main oppositions to the American capitalist empire are now external; meaningful dialogues are minimized by the parochial fires of nationalism. Even the massive resistance to the Vietnam war by many Americans seems not to have shaken seriously the present American Establishment. Once again, the Cold War is warming up. Military aggression is being readied against popular anti-colonial movements abroad. The resilience of American capitalism is remarkable.

Veblen remains relevant, chiefly for that very reason. He was a perceptive critic of the capitalism of his day—major aspects of which still persist. But he is not the prophetic analyst of the post-capitalist epoch—if indeed such an era emerges with people "alive and fit to live."

Notes

1 Chiefly the following: "Thorstein Veblen Reconsidered," *Science and Society*, 21, pp. 52–85 (1957); "The Postwar Essays," *Monthly Review*, 9, pp. 91–98 (1957); "Thorstein Veblen and the Culture of Capitalism," ch. 15 of H. Goldberg, ed., *American Radicals*, Monthly Review Press, 1957; "Thorstein Veblen," *International Encyclopedia of the Social Sciences*, 1968.

2 Georg Lukács, *History and Class Consciousness* (Livingston trans.), M.I.T. Press, Cambridge, Massachusetts, USA, 1971; Damir Mirković, *Dialectic and Sociological Thought*, Diliton Publications Inc., St. Catherines, Ontario, Canada L2R 7J8, 1979.

3 Dr. Don Willmott, *Canadian Far Eastern News Letter*, March, 1979, Toronto.

4 J. Nyerere, *Ujamaa: Essays on Socialism*, Oxford University Press, Nairobi, 1968.

5 Charles Beard, *Rise of American Civilization*, Macmillan, New York, 1930, p. 279.

6 W. A. Williams, *The Roots of the Modern American Empire*, Random House, New York, 1969, *passim*.

7 *The Sociological Imagination*, New York, 1959, chapter I and *passim*.

8 "Dementia Praecox," *Essays in our Changing Order*, Viking, New York, 1934, p. 432.

9 "Between Bolshevism and War," *ibid*, pp. 445–446.

10 *The Higher Learning in America*, New York, 1918, p. 186.

11 "Decline and Fall," *Monthly Review*, 12 (1960), pp. 334–344.

* Walter Rodney (1942–1980) born in Guyana and trained at the University of the West Indies and the University of London, became Professor of African History at the University of Dar es Salaam, Tanzania, 1967–74. In 1974 he returned to the University of Guyana, but the Government negated his appointment. However, he remained politically active. Rodney in our schema practiced holistic social science. He closely linked academic research with practical politics on behalf of the have-not classes. Hence he was a rare credit to his profession. On June 13, 1980, Professor Rodney was assassinated by a car bomb in Georgetown.

Another Look at
Ibn Khaldun (1332–1406)

I WOULD LIKE to begin by explaining how I happened to get interested in Ibn Khaldun. My awareness of him started some forty years ago. He was brought to my attention by P. A. Sorokin at Harvard University. Sorokin was one of my greatest teachers.

I first read something by Ibn Khaldun in the *Systematic Source Book in Rural Sociology*, which is in three volumes edited by Sorokin (Univ. of Minnesota Press, 1930). In volume 1, there are some fifteen pages of excerpts from the *Prolegomena* of Ibn Khaldun. This was about the only thing then available in English. It was translated from the French, "Prolégomènes historiques," by Ibn Khaldun, in *Notices et extraits des manuscrits de la Bibliothèque Imperial*, vols. 19 and 20, Paris, 1862.

In 1930 Nathanial Schmidt had published his little book, 60–70 pages: *Ibn Khaldun: Historian, Sociologist and Philosopher*, re-issued in 1967. However, this volume was about, rather than by, Ibn Khaldun. There was one other early work in English about Ibn Khaldun, by Mohammed Enan, a Pakistani lawyer who published in Lahore in 1941 a small book called *Ibn Khaldun: His Life and Work*.

A complete translation of the *Prolegomena* into English did not appear until 1958, translated from the Arabic by Franz Rosenthal in three volumes: (*The Muqaddimah; An Introduction to History*, by Ibn Khaldun, London: Routledge and Kegan Paul.)

Still more recently, we should be aware of work done by Walter Fischel, at Berkeley, on Ibn Khaldun. Fischel published many articles

Religious Studies Public Lecture Series, March 16, 1983. Sponsored by the Department of Religious Studies, University of Alberta, Edmonton, Canada. The original lecture was taped, then revised, by the author.

and two important books—*Ibn Khaldun in Egypt, 1382–1406* (Berkeley, 1967) which we have in our University of Alberta library; and *Ibn Khaldun and Tamerlane: Their Historic Meeting in Damascus, A.D. 1401* (Berkeley, 1952), which our library does not have.

In 1950 there was published in London a book edited by Professor Charles Issawi called *An Arab Philosophy of History*. It contained a larger series of excerpts from the *Prolegomena*. A more extensive work was that by Muhsin Madhi—a book called *Ibn Khaldun's Philosophy of History*, published in London, 1957, and issued again in paperback at the University of Chicago in 1964. A new book has just been published in Boston, by Baali and Wardi: *Ibn Khaldun and Islamic Thought Styles* (1981).

European thinkers in general, and those in Western Europe in particular, did not begin to rediscover Khaldun until the 18th century. In the 19th century there were several translations of the *Prolegomena* into French.

Besides this bibliographical preliminary, I can also refer to my personal visits to Islamic Soviet Southwest Asia in 1980, when I visited Samarkand, the capital of Tamerlane, whom Ibn Khaldun met in Damascus in 1401. I had some earlier contact with Islam on my 1977 trip through Yugoslavia. During the 1970's, I took a bus safari from India through Pakistan, Afghanistan, Iran, Iraq, Syria and Turkey.

So my Islamic contacts have been with what Ibn Khaldun would have called Eastern Islam. But it was Western Islam which produced Ibn Khaldun—meaning North Africa and southern Spain. I have had no contact with Western Islam.

I am dividing this discussion into three parts: Ibn Khaldun's life, his social milieu, and his work. The epilogue deals with Ibn Khaldun today.

Life

The key facts about Ibn Khaldun can be summed up very simply: he was an Arab, and further he was a Moslem.

His dates were 1332–1406. He was born at Tunis in 1332, and died in Cairo, Egypt, in 1406.

His life had three phases. One was the early phase: for 20 years of his adult life he was involved very much in politics and public administration in Western Islam, a hinterland of eastern Islam.

Then he withdrew for about five years to write the *Prolegomena*, with which I shall deal shortly.

The *Prolegomena*, or *Muqaddimah*—*Introduction to Universal History*, was written about 1374 to 1379, in a castle near Oran, in northwestern

Algeria. In the 1390s, he re-entered active political life: administration, law, and so on, this time in Egypt. That was a very different kind of place from what he had experienced in the first twenty years of his working life. Ibn Khaldun came from a prominent family – prominent for several centuries. The origin of the family, as far back as we know, was South Arabia. From the 9th to the 13th centuries, the family was based in Seville, southern Spain. The Khalduns were one of the few elite patrician families – active both in public administration and in the military. They left Spain in 1248, since there was pressure from the North – coming from the Christians, then in the process of recovering Spain.

Ibn Khaldun's grandfather was Minister of Finance in Tunis. His father was an administrator, a soldier and a scholar who died in the black plague of 1349.

As for Ibn Khaldun's education, he first learned the Koran by heart. Then he studied grammar and poetry.

At age 20, he became secretary to the Sultan of Fez in what is now Morocco. This was a "time of troubles" in British historian Arnold Toynbee's language, a time of civil strife, a time of wars among the petty local dynasties, and of uprisings within these local dynasties. It was a dicey mode of existence. Khaldun himself was jailed for two years, 1357–1359. He fared considerably better than his brother, however, because his brother somewhere along these times was executed.

In 1362, at the age of thirty, he returned to southern Spain to enter the service of the Sultan of Granada. He soon went back to North Africa to places that today are in Morocco and Algeria. Ibn Khaldun led several military ventures against the nomadic Berber tribes in the mountains of southern Algeria. He lived with the Bedouin Nomads.

Ibn Khaldun wrote his *Prolegomena*, or *Introduction to Universal History*, on a fief or estate near Oran. It took four years. His age during this period was 43–47. Once again, this is an example of Toynbee's idea of *withdrawal and return*. He withdrew from active political life to sift his ideas and analytical interpretations of his life experiences and his studies of history.

A look at geographic distances is instructive. Oran is roughly 300 statute miles east of Gibraltar, as the crow flies. Tunis is another 600 miles, eastward. Seville is about 100 miles north of Gibraltar. This was Ibn Khaldun's main theatre of operations during the first 25 years of his adult life.

South of the North African towns just named was a region of nomads and oases, in chronic conflicts with the sedentary town populations along the coast.

After the writing of the *Prolegomena* Ibn Khaldun's career moved eastward. In Tunis again during the early 1380's, Ibn Khaldun resumed his public career. His lectures earned him a notable reputation as a learned man.

His next base was to be Cairo, 1400 statute miles east of Tunis, as the crow flies. In 1382, Ibn Khaldun left for Egypt, en route to Mecca on a pilgrimage. He intended to pass through Cairo, the largest city he had ever seen. However, his fame held him: the Sultan of Egypt offered him a university lectureship. Later he was appointed Chief Justice of Egypt.

In 1384, Ibn Khaldun sent for his family to come from Tunis to Egypt by sea. On the way, they were lost. The ship sank. His wife and all his children were drowned. It was a very serious, personal blow. How can we grasp this fearful tragedy?

In 1387, he completed his pilgrimage to Mecca. Ibn Khaldun then retired to periods of quiet life in Cairo. He wrote his autobiography in 1394. Subsequently this work was occasionally updated. We have his autobiography almost to the last month of his life.

Ibn Khaldun was taken to Damascus, 400 miles northeast of Cairo, by the Sultan of Egypt in 1400–1401. There was a threat of invasion by the emperor Tamerlane, based on Samarkand, 1800 miles east of Damascus.

The leading question was, how to head off an invasion of Egypt. Ibn Khaldun had several conferences with Tamerlane outside Damascus. Ibn Khaldun advised the Sultan of Egypt and the Damascus authorities to accept the terms offered by Tamerlane—essentially a very large ransom. The city authorities, however, were divided. Tamerlane with his army of Mongolians outside the city eventually sacked the city in 1401.

It appears, however, that Ibn Khaldun managed to get some of the prominent Damascus citizens out of the massacre. At that time, Ibn Khaldun was aged 69.

Returning to Egypt, he once again became Chief Justice, a post which he held until his death. He was something of a reformer. He attempted to clean out the widespread corruption that existed in those courts at that time, and as a result, he made enemies. His grave is in a Sufi cemetery outside Bab el Nasr, where he died in March, 1406. As I speak in March, 1983, he would be nearly 651 years old.

His life, then, was one of great pragmatic activity, alternating with periods of contemplation. The kind of life he led as a diplomat involved a great deal of intrigue and risk. Yet he was good at this game. He survived, although he could not keep out of jail.

In 1362, Ibn Khaldun was offered a post by Pedro the Cruel, a Christian king in Northern Spain who was impressed by Ibn Khaldun's qualifications. Ibn Khaldun was also offered a post by Tamerlane in 1401. According to the books I've been looking over, he "skillfully" declined both offers. Had he accepted Tamerlane's offer, he might have wound up as the Prime Minister in Samarkand.

Social Milieu

The social milieu was a "time of troubles" in Western Islam – North Africa west of Egypt, and southern Spain. Much of that region was semi-arid. It was an era of intrigues, unrest, and uprisings. Political instability was chronic.

In central Islam were two great river systems – the Nile and the Tigris-Euphrates. In eastern Islam, semi-arid plains and mountains prevailed. Even today, around Samarkand and Bukhara and Tashkent, in spite of the immense irrigation that has taken place under the contemporary Soviet power, much of this region is still semi-arid or arid.

In other words, Ibn Khaldun experienced a wide variety of geographic and social milieu. His was a life of mobility. He ranged from Seville in Spain to Damascus in what is now Syria. He was a man of great energy, needless to say. He acquired a perspective which allowed him to sift and interpret the essential elements of what was going on around him.

To borrow a phrase from Georg Lukacs, Ibn Khaldun could see "the present as history." The rise and fall of local dynasties was a symbiotic process. It has to be understood in a dialectical context. Ibn Khaldun comprehended the dialectical relation between the rural nomads, on the one hand, and the urban communities, on the other. The rural nomads, bound together by strong kinship ties, came first. Eventually they were to attack the towns. They would in due time succumb to the towns they conquered, in the sense that their tough kinship-oriented social organization would become weakened. Perhaps a generation or two later, they would be conquered by another wave of nomads.

The example I shall take is that of Tamerlane himself, who was a nomad from the barren steppes of Mongolia. Moving southwest to base himself on Samarkand, Tamerlane gathered a vast empire in a very short period of time. He is the ruler, the conqueror who had the interesting habit of constructing pyramids with the skulls of his victims. He was a "toughie."

By contrast, Tamerlane's grandson, Uleg-Beg, became famous as an astronomer. He could measure the solar year with an error of less than one minute. For that he was known throughout Europe. Today near Samarkand there is once again an astronomy observatory named after Uleg-Beg.

In the course of his reign as emperor, Uleg-Beg ran into trouble with the orthodox Islamic clergy. The learned humanist was forced out of power by the clerics. His abdication didn't get him off the hook, however. A secret clerical court had Uleg-Beg assassinated. This took place in the 15th century.

So we have that dynastic cycle from Tamerlane to his grandson. It illustrates the kind of cycle that Ibn Khaldun was portraying in the observations recorded in his *Prolegomena*. It involved a mixture of Islamic religion, political violence, and a certain amount of statesmanship. On a deeper level, it was an immanent development of dialectical impersonal historical forces and interacting oppositions. Action always generates reaction. The Establishment eventually produces its nemesis — which becomes a new Establishment — which nurtures another nemesis . . . until some great new process from within or without brings on a decisively new historical epoch. An example of the latter is the intrusion of European/Japanese/American imperialism upon Mandarin China's 2000-plus years of its native internal cycle of stability and rebellion. (cf. T. T. Meadows, *The Chinese and their Rebellions* (London, 1856; reprinted Stanford, 1956); and A. K. Davis, "A New Look at Chinese History," *Monthly Review*, Feb. and March, 1956; reprinted in this volume, p. 8off.)

Alexander the Great passed through Samarkand about 330 B.C. on his way to India. He destroyed the town, as did Genghis Khan some 1500 years later. It was Tamerlane, however, who made Samarkand an imperial capital.

Franz Köhler, an East German who visited Samarkand in the mid-1970s, writes as follows:

> Here Tamerlane ruled, Timur the Lame, the man who made the universe tremble with unexampled ferocity . . . yet he conferred upon his new kingdom a state structure and laws which presented a great contrast with those barbarities which the Tartar hordes committed at his orders.
>
> However, it is Tamerlane's grandson, the scholar and ruler, astronomer and state figure, humanist and sultan Uleg-Beg, who holds a more vital place in the memories of today's men and women. The man whom Laplace called "the greatest observer in the history of astronomy" is regarded as the Galileo of Asia. His catalogue lists 1018 stars and his astronomical tables are more accurate than those of Tycho Brahe. . . . As a ruler it was his duty to do everything he could to preserve the existing order, but as a scholar he found fresh proof every day that the existing order needed to be changed — and ultimately this insoluble contradiction defeated him. . . . The problem of the social function of the scholar in an exploitive society remained. (*Across the Soviet Union*, Progress Publishers, Moscow, 1979, pp. 182–183. Trans. from the original German edition, Leipzig, 1975.)

Today the Soviet state has restored a number of Islamic monuments in Samarkand, including the tomb of Tamerlane and the observatory of Uleg-Beg. Another prominent Islamic figure whose fame spread far beyond Islam, also originated in this region. He was Avicenna (980–1037), a physician and philosopher. His brooding statue stands in a pleasant garden near the central square of Bukhara. In 1980 when I visited that small city, the 1000th anniversary of Avicenna's birth was being celebrated.

The Sociology of Ibn Khaldun

Ibn Khaldun wanted to write a history of the Western Islam that had not been done before, or at least not very well done. His problem came to be–what facts can I collect, and how shall I know that these are accurate facts? To resolve such questions, he said, one must understand the nature and the causes of history. In other words, he had to formulate a new science of culture–one which he believed would also contribute in pragmatic ways to the art of ruling.

The key concept of Ibn Khaldun's sociology was *asabia* (pronounced assa *bee* ya). It means group collectivity or solidarity, or esprit de corps. It is like the *conscience collective* of Durkheim. Rosenthal translates *asabia* as "group feeling."

In Ibn Khaldun's use of *asabia*, kinship was often the most important component. Solidarity, he said, the sense of the primacy of the group, is strongest amongst the nomads who have ties to each other rather than to the land. In towns, however, group feeling weakens, because wealth is accumulated from crafts and commerce; strife rises over who is going to get how much of the wealth and luxuries. Consequently cycles of conquest and decline emerge. The nomads conquer the town; they take on its character, its stresses. They become decadent, and in turn, are conquered by later nomads.

Let us clarify Ibn Khaldun's concept of "group feeling" by citing some lines from the *Prolegomena*, vol. I, ch. II (Rosenthal trans., London, 1958).

> For those who make a living through the cultivation of grain and through agriculture, it is better to be stationary than to travel around. Such, therefore, are the inhabitants of small communities, villages. . . . Those who make their living from animals requiring pasturage, such as sheep and cattle usually travel around to find pasture and water. . . . They do not go deep into the desert, because they would not find good pastures there. . . . Those who make their living by raising camels move around more. They wander deeper into the desert. In the desert sands, camels can find places to give birth to their young ones. Of all animals, camels have the hardest delivery and the greatest need for warmth in connection with

it. Camel nomads are therefore forced to make excursions deep into the desert. Frequently, too, they are driven by the militia, and they penetrate farther into the desert because they do not want the militia to punish them for their hostile acts. As a result, they are the most savage human beings that exist. Compared with sedentary people, they are on a level with wild, untamable animals. . . . Such people are the Arabs. In the west, the nomadic Berbers are their counterparts, and in the East, the Kurds, the Turkomens. . . .

Bedouins (desert nomads) are prior to sedentary people. The desert is the basis and reservoir of civilization and cities. . . . Bedouins are closer to being good than sedentary people. . . . The Bedouins live separate from the community. They are alone in the country and remote from militias. They have no walls and gates. Therefore, they provide their own defense. . . . They always carry weapons. They watch carefully all sides of the road. They take hurried naps only when they are together in company or when they are in the saddle. They pay attention to every faint barking and noise. They go alone into the desert, guided by their fortitude, putting their trust in themselves. . . .

The reliance of sedentary people upon laws destroys their fortitude and power of resistance. . . .

Only tribes held together by group feeling can live in the desert. . . . Group feeling results only from blood relationship or something corresponding to it. . . . One feels shame when one's relatives are treated unjustly or attacked and one wishes to intervene. . . . Leadership over people cannot be vested in those not of the same descent. This is because leadership exists only through superiority, and superiority only through group feeling. Leadership over people, therefore, must derive from a group feeling that is superior to each individual feeling. . . . Prestige lasts at best four generations in one lineage. . . . Savage nations are better able to achieve superiority than others. . . .

Group feeling produces the ability to defend oneself, to offer opposition, and to press one's claims. Whoever loses his group feeling is too weak to do any of these things.

Luxury wears out the royal authority and overthrows it. . . . A nation that has been defeated and comes under the rule of another nation will quickly perish. . . . The group that has lost control of its own affairs continues to weaken until it perishes. Duration belongs to God alone. . . .

In the foregoing citations from the *Prolegomena*, however sketchy, we can derive a sense of the panoramic sweep of Ibn Khaldun's dialectical vision of history and societies in Islamic North Africa and the Middle East during his own time and the preceding centuries. It is a cyclical view of history, as well as dialectical: Ibn Khaldun perceived the symbiotic, self-generating repetitious sequences stemming from the interaction of nomads and townspeople. Let us cite another description of nomadic life. Ivan Yefremov (1907–1972) was a distinguished Soviet scientist, university professor, and paleontologist, whose work took him into the deserts and steppes of Soviet Asia. He was also a leading writer of science fiction. His *Andromeda: A Space-Age Tale* was first published in 1956. The following passage is quoted from the 3rd printing of 1980, Progress Publishers, Moscow (trans. by George Hanna), p. 130. Obviously drawing upon his own observations, the author has this to say about the steppe nomads.

> Try to understand these people. The great expanse of the steppe was to them really boundless, with horses, camels and oxen as the only means of transport at their disposal. These great spaces were inhabited by little groups of nomad herdsmen that not only had nothing to unite them but who were, on the contrary, living in constant enmity with one another. Insults and animosity accumulated from generation to generation, every stranger was an enemy, every other tribe was legitimate prey that promised herds and slaves, that is, people who were forced to work under the whip, like cattle. . . . Such a system of society brought about, on the one hand, greater liberty for the individual in his petty passions and desires than we know and, dialectically, on the other, excessive limitation in relations between people, a terrible narrow-mindedness. If a nation or a tribe consisted of a small number of people capable of feeding themselves by hunting and the gathering of fruits, even as free nomads they lived in constant fear of enslavement or annihilation by their militant neighbours. In cases when the country was isolated and had a big population capable of setting up a powerful military force the people paid for their safety from warlike raids by the loss of their liberty, since despotism and tyranny always developed in such powerful states. This was the case with ancient Egypt, Assyria and Babylonia.
>
> Women, especially if they were beautiful, were the prey and playthings of the strong. They could not exist without the protection of a man and were completely in his power.

Before leaving Yefremov, I wish to record my surprise at the optimism of his world-view as expressed in *Andromeda*. He pictures mankind as prosperous and united, not only on earth, but with other worlds and intelligent beings in outer space. The conflicts of the Era of Disunity during the last stages of capitalism have been transcended. By contrast, I view my contemporary world with the profoundest pessimism. I offer two reasons: the first is Quincy Wright's careful conclusion that every single arms race in modern times has ended in war, (*A Study of War*, Chicago, 1964). The second reason is the fact that the United States has a history of cheap and profitable wars (e.g.; 1898, 1917–18, 1941–45); it has entered these wars during their late stages, with relatively light losses, and during periods of domestic economic depression. Today, the United States government has apparently sold itself the illusion that it can win a nuclear war by a pre-emptive first-strike. Hopefully, history may prove me wrong.

Let us now return to Ibn Khaldun. We can better appreciate the wisdom of his advice to the Damascus authorities to pay the ransom demanded by Tamerlane in 1401. Ibn Khaldun well understood the savage nature of the besieging Mongolian nomad army. He knew that the army had to live by plundering the people wherever it went. His judgment that the city could not withstand such an army proved to be correct.

Another historical parallel presents itself at the opposite end of Asia: the interaction between the agrarian Chinese and the Mongolian nomads northwest of China. The nomads erupted from beyond the Great Wall, built in the third century B.C., which roughly marks the cultural boundary between the nomads and the agricultural Chinese. If the nomads stayed in China, they had to adopt Chinese ways. They had to learn to write and to administer. They had to operate the state waterworks, for irrigation and flood-control. They had to learn to live in towns.

Chinese history is marked by very clear, built-in cycles of stability and instability. During the periods of instability, the recurrent times of troubles, China broke up into its component regions. Strife verged on wars of each against all. That is very well discussed in Owen Lattimore's book, *The Inner Asian Frontiers of China*, published in the United States about 1940. Lattimore, however, does not mention Ibn Khaldun.

Ibn Khaldun perceived the basic similarities of nomads everywhere. He grasped the geographic, economic and political components or factors in that uniformity. He achieved, in effect, a dialectical sociology—a blend of sociology and history. I do not think it matters whether you call it historical sociology or sociological history. It was, in any case, a dynamic perspective, oriented to change.

As another example of that, let me cite Volume 1 of the *Prolegomena*, page 249 of the 1958 English translation. "It should be known that differences of condition among people are the result of the different ways in which they make their living. Social organization enables them to co-operate toward that end and to start with the simple necessities of life before they get to conveniences and luxuries." That proposition, I suggest, could have come right out of Karl Marx. Ibn Khaldun says, earlier on, "Human social organization is something necessary." The philosophers expressed this fact by saying "man is political by nature," that is, he cannot do without the social organization for which the philosophers used the technical term "town" or "polis." The term *polis* appears to be an echo of Aristotle.

Every once in a while, Ibn Khaldun had to keep in mind the Islamic orthodoxies of his day. He had the habit of ending his sections and subsections with a phrase like this: "God gives success and guidance." Such a usage may remind us of Lucretius, Roman poet and philosopher of the first century B.C. In his long poem, *Nature of the Universe*, Lucretius had to do something with the Gods. He put them way, way out in the last (seventh) sphere. They were in his picture of the universe, but they had little or no significance for men. Yet the device allowed Lucretius to cope with the orthodoxy of his day. So it seems to have been with Ibn Khaldun, as well. In both writers we find recurring statements to the effect that God has power to do what he wishes.

Ibn Khaldun saw history as a series of impersonal social forces. Yet, like Plato, he himself was actively involved in history. He could stand aside from it occasionally, he could analyze it. He had what C. Wright Mills calls the "sociological imagination." According to Mills, "the sociological imagination enables us to grasp history and biography and the relations between the two within a society. To recognize this task and this promise is the mark of the classical social analyst" (*Sociological Imagination*, Oxford University Press, New York, 1959, p. 6).

We can also recognize Ibn Khaldun as a "marginal man." Everett Stonequist, an American sociologist, wrote a book called *The Marginal Man* some 46 years ago. He pointed out that the marginal man has an in-between situation—he becomes an acute and able critic of the dominant group and his culture. This is because he combines the knowledge and insight of the insider with the critical attitudes of the outsider. His analysis is not necessarily objective; there is often much emotional tension. But the marginal man is skillful in noting the contradictions and hypocrisies in the dominant culture. He can spot the gap between the moral pretensions and the actual achievement of the Establishment.

Very much the same point was made by Thorstein Veblen in an essay published in 1919, "The Intellectual Pre-Eminence of the Jews in Modern Europe." He portrays the Jews as people with a foot in two different but partly overlapping cultures. With a foot in Jewish culture and one in Gentile culture, Jews are able to develop this skeptical insight, this analytical insight which allows them to make great contributions in the arts and sciences of their times. Veblen wrote: "the first requisite for constructive work in modern science and indeed, for any work or inquiry that shall bring enduring results is a skeptical frame of mind. The enterprising skeptic alone can be counted on to further the increase of knowledge in any substantial fashion."

This is highly debatable, let us note. History is made by true believers rather than by skeptics—when all is said and done. What I am arguing is that Ibn Khaldun qualifies as a great and perceptive thinker. Historian Arnold Toynbee, who lived much later, said, in assessing Ibn Khaldun: "In the *Prolegomena* to his universal history Ibn Khaldun has conceived and formulated a philosophy of history which is undoubtedly the greatest work of its kind that has ever yet been created by any mind in any time or place." (*A Study of History*, vol. III, London, 1935, p. 322). Perhaps that is a bit sweeping, but that is what Toynbee wrote. And surely Toynbee was a great historian.

In 1980 I visited Dushanbe–capital city of the Tadzhik Soviet Socialist Republic, which lies north of Afghanistan, over the high Parmir mountains. Our tourist group was taken to a historical museum. To me, the interesting thing about that museum was that it showed a lot of things about the old times and many exhibits of the present, but it did not show the transition from old to new–except for one painting. In that picture you really could feel the transition of feudal Islam to modern socialist industrialism. The picture shows four elderly male Moslems in their robes and turbans smoking under a tree. They are glaring at two young women in the foreground who are on their way to school carrying armfuls of books. The girls are frightened, particularly the younger one who is looking up at the older girl for psychological support. They are hurrying past the hostile men. They are not veiled, and they are headed for school–two major departures from Islamic traditionalism. In my mind, I gave that painting a caption: The Agony of the Transition. It is a powerful work of art. Unfortunately the museum at the time of my visit had no handbook or reproductions for sale.

This concludes my brief look at Ibn Khaldun. Perhaps for the next few minutes we can have a discussion.

Epilogue

What can Ibn Khaldun say to Canadians today?

Spin-offs from the Discussion

Across the six centuries since the writing of the *Prolegomena* near Oran in 1374–78, what is the significance of that great work for us in the 1980s? Is the *Prolegomena* simply an esoteric, archival exercise to be read by a few ivy-tower scholars? Or does the study of the *Prolegomena* illuminate in varying degrees some of our pressing Canadian domestic and inter-national problems? I opt for the latter.

The *Prolegomena* offers us two leading lessons. One has to do mainly with method. The other deals with content: the importance of *group feeling* (*asabia*–pron. *asaa bee ya*).

As for method, the *Prolegomena* is comparative and historical. It is also holistic, cross-cultural and cross-disciplinary. Ibn Khaldun takes ac-count of geography, climate, economy, kinship and other aspects of the social systems with which he deals. Thereby he sets us an example. He helps us to transcend the narrowly specialized and increasingly archaic compartments into which contemporary academic social science has drifted, thus isolating itself from many pragmatic concerns of Cana-dians. He fits into the compensatory trend toward inter-disciplinary studies in Canadian universities today.*

Ibn Khaldun gives us a holistic view of a major world region – the semi-arid and desert nomad belt across North Africa, the Middle East and Asia. Though he wrote a long time ago, he is still relevant for an under-standing of the historical and cultural background of that distinctive life-pattern, important aspects of which still survive in certain places.

A study of Ibn Khaldun contributes to the transcending of our natural parochialisms. Every person's upbringing, or socialization, is necessarily and decisively molded by familial, class, ethnic, regional and other ele-ments of his or her social milieux. (Please note that I said "molded;" I did not say "determined.")

We can go even further. Today, for the sake of human survival, some mixture of study, travel and practical experience is necessary to over-come our parochialisms. Our educational and mass-media institutions, for the most part, are not doing an effective job in this respect.

---

* For further discussion, see A. K. Davis, "Failings of American Import Sociology in Anglophone Canada," in R. Nelsen and D. Nock, eds., *Reading, Writing, and Riches*, Between the Lines Press, Toronto, 1978, pp. 212–230. Reprinted here, Vol. I, Part II, pp. 349–367.

The urgency cannot be overstated. In this interdependent modern world, each super-power can completely destroy the other in a 30-minute nuclear exchange, and the rest of the world would in very large part succumb to radioactive fallout shortly thereafter. There is no possible defense against a major nuclear war—and every war involving local nuclear weapons would instantly escalate to total nuclear war.

That cross-cultural or comparative perspectives in various media are necessary for human survival does not mean they are sufficient. In a powerful documentary film, *End Game*, produced by the CTV network in Toronto, 1973—Stanford biologist Paul Ehrlich said, "The trouble is, we have to solve the war problem, the race problem, the poverty problem, the population explosion, the technological explosion, pollution and the shortages of non-renewable resources—and we have to solve them all at once. This causes some of us to be very pessimistic." (The quotation is inexact, but it truly conveys the gist of the message of this notable film, obtainable from the University of Alberta Extension Film Library. The chief commentator is Dr. Donald Chant, University of Toronto biologist).

Ibn Khaldun's *Prolegomena* is not the only route toward intercultural understanding. It is historically and dialectically oriented; it conveys major insights into Islam, one of the world's great religions, often grossly misunderstood by non-Islamic policy-makers. Yet Ibn Khaldun lived and worked in a pre-industrial economy. His day is not ours. He speaks to us from an earlier phase of social evolution.

Besides, there is an even more important point to be made. Cross-cultural understanding is not enough to ensure human survival. Someone else has said this better than I can. "The philosophers have only *interpreted* the world in various ways; the point is to *change* it." That was written in the spring of 1845 by the young Karl Marx, the centennial anniversary of whose death in 1883 we are observing this year.*

Now for the second lesson from Ibn Khaldun: the primacy of *group feeling* in social evolution. This concept is especially important today to North Americans. *Group feeling* refers to the superiority of the collectivity over the individual in certain times and societies. North America along with the rest of the capitalist world is suffering from a major economic depression. This is a severe challenge to the ideology of individualism, which invites either atomization or radical transformation to its opposite—coercive centralization. In fact, the mythology of individualism/free enterprise is a camouflage for corporate capitalism.

---

* Theses on Feuerbach, *Collected Works of Marx and Engels*, Vol. 5, p. 5; jointly published by Lawrence & Wishart, London, International Publishers, New York, and Progress Publishers, Moscow—1976. The citation is engraved on the gravestone of Marx in Highgate cemetery, North London, England.

English Canada in my view has a deficiency of *group feeling*, compared to francophone Quebec—which has the benefit of two centuries of English oppression since the 1759 conquest. But certain ethnic minorities in English Canada seem to have a considerable degree of *group feeling*. I will suggest such ethnic communities as the following, among others: Ukrainians, Italians, Poles, Chinese, Jews and some native groups. The latter are experiencing a renaissance of *group feeling*—especially the Dene in the Mackenzie River valley. Let us note that all these ethnic communities in Canada have a history of discrimination in varying degrees.

I will limit my comments on nations to a few of those I have visited. *Group feeling* is readily apparent in Iceland. The population is less than a quarter-million. Yet it has twice produced a world-class literature: the medieval sagas and Halldor Laxness, who won the Nobel prize for literature in 1955. Icelanders take great pride in showing visitors Thingvellir, the rocky lakeshore site where the oldest parliament in the world met in June starting in 980 A.D. The Lutheran church architecture is impressive, and so likewise is the public sculpture and statuary in Reykjavik, the capital city.

Cuba's intense *group feeling* seems to be rooted in the long struggles against Spain in the later 19th century and against United States domination in the 20th century. The Ten Year War (1868–78) was a stalemate, but it brought the end of slavery in 1880. The second uprising (1895–98) was organized by José Marti, a poet and writer of world stature. The Cubans were robbed of their victory by American intervention in 1898. Not till the Castro uprising (1956–59) was the indirect control by absentee United States interests cut off. From that century of struggle came a long list of heroes and martyrs—Maceo, a black guerilla general never defeated by the Spaniards, killed in battle, like Marti, early in the Second War for independence. In front of every school in Cuba today is a white bust of Marti.

Group feeling is strong in the People's Republic of China, where Mao's revolution was the culmination of a long series of peasant upheavals and the expulsion of European, American and Japanese intruders. The strength of the Chinese extended family is still evident, whatever the changes in the power structure and property relations of the postrevolutionary kinship system. In China the individual exists to serve the family and such larger collectivities as the army, party, and nation.

In Russian-Soviet history, too, a multitude of wars, invasions and resistances have contributed to strong *group feeling*. On my first visit to the USSR in the late summer of 1980, the Soviets were observing the 600th anniversary of the battle of Kulikovo Field, where a poorly armed

mass of 150,000 foot soldiers defeated a militarily superior Mongolian
army of mounted archers – the Golden Horde. The Russians suffered 90
percent fatalities. Poltava was a similar case: Peter the Great defeated
a superior Swedish invading army in 1709.

In two World Wars and in the bitter Civil War of 1918–21, Russian
Soviet military and industrial inferiority (on paper) was very serious. Fourteen nations (including Canada) sent armies into the Soviet Union during the Civil War. An American demographer has estimated a population
deficit between the Russian/Soviet census of 1897 and that of 1926 of
nearly 30 millions, mostly attributable to the Civil War and its attendant
famines and epidemics. (Frank Lorimer, *The Population of the Soviet
Union: History and Prospects*, Geneva, League of Nations, 1946, ch. 3.) Soviet fatalities during World War II are estimated at 21 million, including
7 million military deaths. By contrast, United States fatalities during
World War II were less than a half-million, none on US soil.

Group feeling as Ibn Khaldun conceived it, is oriented toward group
survival, although the cost of survival may be immensely high. For *group
feeling* is often generated by war, and war by *group feeling*. In Ibn
Khaldun's day, technology was at a much lower level than now. Nations
might perish, but most of the human race survived. In this nuclear age,
no such assumption can be made, certainly not for the northern hemisphere. A basic change has happened. War is suicide in a nuclear age.
How does this affect the two super-powers?

Both the USSR and the USA have strong *group feeling*. But there are
strong differences with respect to their recent war experiences. The
Soviets have suffered beyond measure, as sketched above. The USA, by
contrast, has not experienced a great war on its home soil since the Civil
War of 1861–65. In that conflagration, an agrarian plantation elite was
displaced by an industrialist elite. Both were capitalistic. Subsequent
wars, however, have weighed lightly upon the USA. The pattern has
been – enter late, bear few casualties, and grab most of the loot. This
applies to the Cuban-Spanish-American War of 1898; it applies to the first
World War; and to the second World War. None of these three wars was
fought on US territory. Compared to the rest of the industrial world,
both capitalist and socialist, the USA has an atypical and unrealistic
awareness of the present global reality.

Hence the United States, accustomed for two generations to relatively cheap wars abroad as a way out of economic depression at home,
is a very dangerous threat to world peace today.

I have stressed the importance of *group feeling* in this epilogue. Its
limitations must also be kept in mind, especially in this nuclear age.

Attention to business-cycle theory has recently revived. The late Sen-

ator Maurice Lamontagne, a Harvard-trained graduate economist, published an update of cycle theory applied to Canada (*Quest*, Sept.–Oct.,
1981). It owes much to Harvard economist Joseph Schumpeter (*Business
Cycles*, 2 vols. N.Y., 1939; see the summary in the last chapter). In turn,
Schumpeter confirmed independently the long-cycle theory of Kondra-
tieff, a Russian economist who published his work in the early 1920s.
Schumpeter predicted in 1939 a long-run net upswing for capitalist economies for the following three decades. This is roughly what has happened. In the mid-70s, the capitalist world (three worlds or complexes,
really – Japan, West Germany and North America) seems to have entered
a long-term downswing. Schumpeter also distinguished short-term (in-
ventory) cycles of four years (three expansive and one contracting), and
intermediate (investment-construction) cycles of eight to ten years (four
or five up, and three or four down). Lamontagne makes the serious point
that in the early to middle 1980s, all three cycles coincide downward.
He concludes:

> If this pessimistic scenario does develop and if no strategy has been pre-
> pared for it, the Western World, including Canada, will be in great
> difficulty. Some of us remember the social, political and military conse-
> quences of the unexpected 1930s. A repetition of this tragedy in the more
> or less immediate future might have even more serious consequences.
> (*Ibid*, p. 24).

Mary Kaldor, a British scholar, issued a similar warning. (*The Disin-
tegrating West*, Pelican, 1979). More recently, anti-Semitism has resurfaced in rural Alberta, and hate literature against Blacks and Asiatics
has been dumped into Alberta from Toronto and the United States. In
1977, I spent a grim afternoon visiting Auschwitz, a former Nazi death
factory, now a museum in southern Poland. For those unable to see it,
I refer to Walter Laqueur, *The Terrible Secret* (Penguin, 1982), and to Leo
Kuper, *Genocide* (Penguin, 1981). After reading Kuper, who deals with several other genocidal cases as well as with the German effort to exter-
minate the European Jews, one can hardly escape wondering whether
the human race does not deserve its apparently impending extinction
by nuclear holocaust.

Social life was more simple in Ibn Khaldun's day. In the 14th century,
cities and towns were sacked, but not hemispheres. Though times have
greatly changed, however, the *Prolegomena* in my view remains germinal,
both as to method and content.

Fireworks in Eastern Europe, 1989–1990: Tragedy or Farce?

KARL MARX is our springboard. In his *Eighteenth Brumaire*, 1852, he penned those famous lines. "Hegel remarks somewhere that all great world-historical facts and personages occur, as it were, twice. He has forgotten to add: the first time as tragedy, the second as farce. . . . Men make their own history, but they do not make it just as they please; they do not make it under circumstances chosen by themselves, but under circumstances directly found, given and transmitted from the past. The tradition of all the dead generations weighs like a nightmare on the brain of the living . . ."

Those lines, of course, constitute one of the great germinal statements of Marxism. By directing our attention to the influences inherited from history, they set our eyes upon the longer views – the factors that contributed to the molding of our past and present. But in the 1989–1991 political clashes in central and eastern Europe, we may find more detailed insights in the short-run theoretical tracts of C. Malaparte (1898–1957) and Roberto Michels (1876–1936). Respectively, their books are entitled *Coup d'Etat* (French original, 1931, English translation, 1932), and *Political Parties: A Sociological Study of the Oligarchic Tendencies of Modern Democracy* (1915). Both writers were Italian in background.

On June 14, 1977, in Prague, our party of travellers hosted a half-dozen Czech professional-intelligentsia for our farewell supper. Our guests were educated and English-speaking. One of the key points that came out of that meeting reads as follows (I quote from my field notes):

> The brief invasion in August, 1968, by the USSR and its allies came up. "Not a good thing, but necessary"–was the message. . . . Alexander Dubcek tried to go too far and too fast. . . . (as a liberalizing reformer)

Soviet–U.S. relations at the time were coloured by acute Cold-War antagonisms, born in 1917.

The Propaganda Veil in the Western Media.   This also dates from 1917. It has been a constant element on the international scene ever since. Occasionally it was obscured by other historical forces: the wartime alliance of World War II, for example. But even then the underlying hostility showed up. The Soviets read the two-year delay of a second front in Western Europe as a deliberate stall. Some American elite circles (including Harry Truman, U.S. Vice-President and later President when Roosevelt died in 1945) let it be known that they favored a hands-off stance in the European war while the German Nazis and the Soviets bled each other to death. After the war, there was a succession of thaws and freezes in Soviet-American relationships. That basic condition has continued to this day.

The veil is only partly a conscious construct. It may consist largely of inherited stereotypes, traditions and myths. The veil, however, is reflective of the interests and preconceptions in the societies wherein the veil originates. It obscures what is really going on in those east European States. But, if spotted and properly interpreted by a clued-in analyst, it tells us something about the originating society or its ruling circles. Let us look at an example.

The Case of China, 1989.   On June 4, 1989, a demonstration took place in Tiananmen Plaza in Beijing. The western media reported that students were prominent among the participants, and that "democracy" was their goal. Analysts have their first clue here: *democracy* is a vague term, and it is a plus-word in western capitalist countries, though in China it may well have a different connotation. A military force cleared the square, with casualties not yet precisely known. There were enough, however, to arouse a negative response in western capitalist countries. This is not because those countries object to massacres of people they dislike (including their own), but because the June 4 incident was a convenient propaganda club with which racist westerners could whack the socialist Chinese.

On the day after the clash, the anti-socialist-China wave of propaganda began in the western media. Clearly the propaganda apparatus was previously in place. Among the several hundred American-Chinese studying in China are certainly a number sending back intelligence reports to the various listening posts of the American C.I.A. in Hong Kong and Taiwan and elsewhere. And some of the student victims of the June 4 crackdown were persons returned from several years of study in capitalist countries.

The important point is that China has a very long history of settling key political decisions, especially the perennial problem of succession, by coercive means. In the days immediately following the June 4 riot, two University of Alberta academics confirmed this fact (*Edmonton Journal*, June 8 and June 10, 1989). They pointed to similar riots in Tiananmen Plaza in 1976 and 1966, the former prompted by the power struggle over the succession to Chairman Mao; the latter by issues arising from the Cultural Revolution of 1964–66, when Mao's measures to cut down bureaucratic elitism in China got out of hand. My own letter (*Edmonton Journal*, June 14, 1989; reprinted on page 423 of *Farewell to Earth*) pointed out that settling major policy issues by force is a tradition going back at least 2000 years. The naive students on June 4 sealed their fate as "un-Chinese elements" by setting up a replica of the American Statue of Liberty as their symbolic totem pole. Appropriately, a Chinese tank ran over it.

Eastern Europe, Autumn of 1989. The Rivers Run Uphill. According to the propaganda veil, the target of the coup d'etats in eastern Europe was the rejection of socialism/communism. This is the view of the capitalist West, motivated by subjective wishful thinking and the long-standing ancient greed for control of eastern markets and resources. On an objective level, however, the following statements seem more realistic.

- The political overturns were limited *coups* affecting the top echelons of the Governments involved. They were not sweeping comprehensive changes affecting all aspects of the societies: for such far-reaching and in-depth changes we reserve the term *revolution*, not applicable here.

- The motivation of the coups was anti-bureaucratic rather than anti-socialist. Unfortunately, a bureaucratic type of social organization (meaning a hierarchy of specialized roles fitted together more or less harmoniously to achieve the goals of the organization) is necessary to realize the aims of long-range concerted activities of large numbers of people. What, then, did the anti-government elements want? I suggest – "socialism with a human face" – not faceless, less impersonal and less remote. In brief, the slogan of the 1968 Prague Spring has revived. Was it ever really dormant?

- The international context has changed since 1968. The Americans were defeated in Vietnam by 1975 and ignominiously withdrew, but they learned little or nothing. In central America they are now flexing their inflexible armour: they have revived the "gunboat diplomacy" of former President Theodore Roosevelt, who used his "big stick" to carve out Panama from Colombia in order to set the stage for the Panama Canal and the unofficial colony now known as Panama. That was back in 1903. The United States, in other words, consistently walks backward into the future.

—The Soviets, by contrast, went reluctantly into Afghanistan in late 1979, and withdrew a decade later. To the astonishment of Western Capitalist countries, the Afghanistan Marxist regime, expected to collapse, has more than held its own.

—New faces have appeared in the top echelons of Eastern Europe, but no new social class.

—Corruption has become evident. This is customary in times of unexpected change; it arouses widespread resentment and envy.

—Perhaps more important, neglect of the environment seems to have been acute. This might be better classified as bad planning. The necessity of good planning remains stronger than ever.

—As always in periods of rapid change, opportunism intensifies. Even the exiled King of Romania, dumped in 1947, has offered to return from the dustbin of history to resume the leadership of his former realm. Likewise the Albanian pretender, now based in apartheid South Africa.

Only once in recent months did I see in the news reports from Eastern Europe any mention of "coercive rates of rural modernization" (in the *Globe and Mail*, mid-December, 1989, regarding Romania). One would expect more: the basic process in Eastern Europe has been from a rural to an urban-industrial way of life (which includes of course the mechanization of agriculture). Moreover, when rapid, this process is very stressful. Let us now look at some comparative indices of urbanization.

The table on the next page shows how urbanization falls off as one moves from western to eastern Europe and from north to south. Infant mortality varies inversely with urbanization. Here we should recall that western Europe began urbanizing three or four centuries ago; the socialist countries have been industrializing mainly since World War II, when the big push for industrialization by central planning was underway. The table also shows how we use infant mortality as a rough but sensitive index of health and social conditions in a society. For comparison we have included three cases of low urbanization: Africa, Asia without China, and the USSR in 1926, a census year in the latter nation before the big push for industrialization began in the 1930s.

The Population Growth Cycle in Capitalist States.   In pre-industrial societies, the economy is at or near subsistence levels. High birth rates are roughly balanced by high death rates, setting aside for the moment the effects of migration. As health and medical services improve—that is, as urbanization and industrialization trends develop—the mortality rate falls first. Decades later, birth rates also decline. The time lag allows for very large population growth. The table on the next page invites com-

European Urbanization and Infant Mortality, By Regions, with Comparisons

	Percent Urban Population	Infant Mortality: (deaths under 1 year per 1000 live births)
Northern Europe (Scandinavia, U.K.)	84	8
Western Europe (incl. Austria, FRG)	83	8
Southern Europe (Mediterranean)	68	15
Eastern Europe (socialist bloc except Albania, USSR and Yugoslavia)	63	17
USSR, 1988	66	15 (1987)
North America	74	10
Africa	30	113
Asia (except China)	33	90
USSR, 1926, pop. 147m (total Soviet territory)*	18	187 (European USSR only)

Source: Population Reference Bureau, Washington, 1989, as re-issued by the Population Research Laboratory, Department of Sociology, University of Alberta, September, 1989. Except where indicated, data applies to the late 1980s. Also used: *Encyclopedia Britannica*, 1989 Book of the Year.
* Statistics for the USSR in 1926 are based on data taken from Frank Lorimer, *Population of the Soviet Union*, Geneva, League of Nations, 1946, p. 80.

parison of the Soviet Union rising urbanization and falling infant mortality in the era between 1926 and 1984.

The Growth Cycle in Socialist States. Additional factors come into play under socialist regimes. These can be classified as consequences— planned and unplanned (or unforeseen)—of central planning in the varying historical and geographic settings of the respective States. An holistic approach is necessary. What are the costs and benefits, economic and non-economic, short-run and long-run—of megaprojects? What insurance measures can be built into planning systems (seen as a policy-making process) to offset costs? Benefits without costs are utopian, as are costs without benefits. But where in the intervening ground can more or less workable policies be made and implemented? In this realm of "social calculus," national survival is still a bottom line.

The February 1990 *National Geographic* (Washington) published an article on the Aral Sea in southwest Soviet Asia: "A Soviet Sea Lies Dying." This paper presents aspects of the problem, but not in an holistic context. Without the latter, the article scores as a heavily propagandist exercise in the veil that clouds the world-view of American capitalist society like an impenetrable cocoon. This case comes to my mind because I have seen more than once an airliner view of the Aral Sea.

Tragedy or Farce? We return briefly to the question that opened this paper, "Fireworks in Eastern Europe, 1989–1990: Tragedy or Farce?" The answer: there are elements of both. The tragedy perhaps is concentrated in eastern Europe; the farce, in the Western capitalist media and their self-made propaganda veil. "We have won the Cold War," the media have been telling us since the Tiananmen riot on June 4, 1989.

Systematically analyzed, however, the farce becomes another tragedy. Consider the data for European Socialist States on population, life expectancy, education, health, GNP per person, and related indices. These are not holistic pictures. But they are what is available in statistical form. GNP data, for example, does not take into account income-in-kind (gardens, dooryard animals and chicken flocks); GNP relies mainly on cash income. Our information covers aspects of nine socialist countries and three capitalist nations. The table indicates that socialist societies in the last one or two generations have moved well into an urban-industrial way of life, to the point where they press upon and occasionally exceed capitalist achievement levels, which took several centuries to accomplish.

But "tragedy or farce" is not the most relevant level of analysis. We must transcend partisanship as much as possible—recognizing that we cannot escape responsibility for offering conclusions as holistic as possible, however imperfect they must be.

The relationship between consumer-price and monthly-earning indices is important to check out. The table on the next page is not ideal, but it is the best data available. It shows the following, for approximately 6 to 8 years starting in 1980.

- —one socialist country had no data (Albania).
- —two socialist countries suffered runaway inflation (Yugoslavia, Poland).
- —of the remaining six socialist States,
  2 showed very low inflation rates (Czechoslovakia, Romania);
  4 showed earnings rising distinctly faster than prices (Bulgaria, Hungary, GDR, USSR).
- —two of the three capitalist States had very low inflation rates (Sweden, USA).
- —one had an earning rate rising distinctly faster than its price index (FRG).

Since we do not know the exact scopes or definitions, we can say nothing more: we cannot compare one country with another, for instance. What we have is the direction of the consumer-price index and the monthly-earnings index for eleven individual States. We can make the tentative conclusions outlined in the preceding paragraph. But these

Consumer-Price and Monthly-Earnings Indices, 1980s
(1980 = 100)

	Price Index		Earnings Index	
Albania	n.a.		n.a.	
Bulgaria 1988	108.3		123	
Czechoslovakia 1985	120.9		118	
GDR	100.3	(1986)	107.1	(1984)
Hungary 1987	163		172	
Poland 1987	577		476	
Romania 1986	126		123	
Yugoslavia	5909	(1988)	2077	(1987)
USSR 1985	105		109	
Sweden	167	(1987)	165	(1986)
FRG 1988	123		133	
USA 1988	143		139	

Source: *Encyclopedia Britannica 1989 Yearbook.*

are better than the wild speculations and blanket assaults now being emitted by the Propaganda Veil of the Western media.

A reminder is in order: socialism does not call for equality of incomes. It presses for relatively more equality than characterizes capitalist economies. And not just incomes: there is an important new category in socialist States—social consumption. We have referred to this latter concept in Vol. II of *Farewell to Earth*—field notes I took in socialist societies. The proper slogan for socialism is: From each according to his abilities; to each according to his work. If we buy the slogan put forth by Marx in the *Communist Manifesto* (1848)—namely, from each according to his abilities; to each according to his needs—we would be invoking Utopia. In this imperfect world, Utopia is nowhere.

Yet this is too abstract, however theoretically true. In practice, we learn our needs from our social experience. People need food, clothing, decent shelter, adequate and nutritious food, work to provide for those needs (full employment)—all those things spelled out in the United Nations Human Rights Declaration of 1948—give or take a few modifications, such as allowance for cultural differences.

Ethnicity and Religion. Now let us look at *ethnicity* and *religious affiliation* in the dozen societies under our consideration. These are important because they are persistent norms and criteria of social identification; they change but slowly. They are also sources of major social cleavages—actual or potential. Our source is the 1989 Yearbook of *Encyclopedia Britannica.*

Ethnicity and Religious Affiliation
Nine Socialist and Three Capitalist States, 1980
(in percent; columns total 100% unless otherwise noted)

Albania

Ethnicity, 1983		Religious Affiliation, 1980	
Albanian	97%	Muslim	21%
Greek	2	Atheist	19
Romanian	0.5	Christian	5
Other	0.5	None	55

Bulgaria

Ethnicity, 1986		Religious Affiliation, 1982	
Bulgarian	85%	Atheism	64.5%
Turkish	9	E. Orthodox	26.7
Gypsy	3	Muslim	7.5
Other	3	Protestant	0.7
		Roman Catholic	0.5
		Other	0.1

Czechoslovakia

Ethnicity, 1986		Religious Affiliation, 1980	
Czech	63.2%	Roman Catholic	65.6%
Slovak	31.5	Atheist	20.1
Hungarian	3.8	Czech-Slov. Church (Hussite)	4.4
Polish	0.5	Evangelist Czech Brethren	1.4
German	0.4	Other	8.5
Ukrainian	0.3		
Other	0.3		

German Democratic Republic

Ethnicity, 1986		Religious Affiliation, 1986	
German	99.7%	Protestant	47.0%
Other	0.3	Roman Catholic	7.0
		Unaffiliated and other	46.0

Federal Republic of Germany

Ethnicity, 1987		Religious Affiliation, 1980	
German	92.6%	Protestant	47.3%
Turk	2.3	Roman Catholic	43.8
Yugoslav	1.0	Non-Roman Catholic	0.6
Italian	0.9	Orthodox	1.0
Greek	0.5	Other Christian	0.1
Spanish	0.3	Muslim	2.4
Austrian	0.3	Atheist and non-religious	4.6
Dutch	0.2	Jewish	0.1
Other	1.9	Other	0.1

Hungary

Ethnicity, 1987		Religious Affiliation, 1980	
Magyar	96.6%	Roman Catholic	53.9%
German	1.6	Protestant	21.6
Slovak	1.1	Jewish	0.9
Other	0.7	Atheist	7.2
		Non-religious	8.7
		Other	7.7

Poland

Ethnicity, 1986		Religious Affiliation, 1986	
Polish	98.7%	Roman Catholic	94.2%
Ukrainian	0.6	Other	5.8
Other	0.7		

Romania

Ethnicity, 1983		Religious Affiliation, 1980	
Romanian	88.4%	Romanian Orthodox	70.0%
Hungarian	7.7	Greek Orthodox	10.0
Other	3.9	Muslim	1.0
		Atheist	7.0
		Other	3.0
		None	9.0

Yugoslavia

Ethnicity, 1981		Religious Affiliation, 1980	
Serbian	36.3%	Serbian Orthodox	34.6%
Croatian	19.7	Roman Catholic	26.0
Bosnian Muslim	8.9	Crypto-Christian	11.3
Slovenian	7.8	Muslim	10.4
Albanian	7.7	Other	17.7
Macedonian	6.0		
Montnegran	2.6		
Other	11.0		

Sweden

Ethnicity, 1987		Religious Affiliation, 1986	
Swedish	91.0%	Church of Sweden	
Finnish	3.1	(30% non-practicing)	89.6%
Other	5.9	Roman Catholic	1.4
		Pentacostal	1.2
		Other	7.8

USSR

Ethnicity, *1983*		Religious Affiliation, *1987*	
Russian	51.9%	Orthodox	31.5%
Ukrainian	15.8	Protestant	3.1
Uzbek	5.1	Roman Catholic	1.8
Belorussian	3.6	Muslim	11.2
Kazakh	2.6	Jewish	1.1
Tatar	2.4	Atheist	21.4
Azerbaijani	2.2	Non-religious	29.7
Armenian	1.7	Other	0.2
Georgian	1.4		
Tadzhik	1.2		
Moldavian	1.1		
Lithuanian	1.1		
Other	9.9		

USA

Ethnicity, *1987*		Religious Affiliation, *1987*	
White	84.5%	Protestant	55.1%
Black	12.3	Roman Catholic	29.7
Other	3.2	Jewish	3.2
		Eastern Orthodox	2.3
		Muslim	1.9
		Hindu	0.2
		Non-religious and atheist	6.8
		Other	0.8

Canada

Ethnicity, *1981*		Religious Affiliation, *1981*	
British	40.2%	Roman Catholic	46.5%
French	26.7	Protestant	41.2
German	4.1	Eastern Orthodox	1.5
Italian	3.1	Jewish	1.2
Ukrainian	2.2	Muslim	0.4
Dutch	1.7	Hindu	0.3
Other European	8.5	Sikh	0.3
Asiatic	2.1	Nonreligious	7.4
Indian & Inuit	1.7	Other	1.2
Other	9.7		

Cuba

Ethnicity, *1981*		Religious Affiliation, *1980*	
White	66.0%	Nonreligious	48.7%
Mulatto	21.9	Roman Catholic	39.6
Black	12.0	Atheist	6.4
	99.9	Protestant	3.3
		Afro-American Spiritist	1.6
		Other	0.4

| | 1989 | |
	Canada	Cuba
Population (millions)	26.3	10.5
Life expectancy at birth (yrs)	76	74
Percent urban	77%	72%
MDs/persons ratio	1/491	1/399
Per capita GNP (in U.S. dollars)	$14,100	$2,690
Infant mortality rate		
per 1000 live births	7.9	13.3

Ethnicity and Religion as Cleavage Lines. These have limited value, except perhaps to indicate real or potential trouble spots. Looking at the preceding 14 countries in the light of ethnicity and religion, we find only four in eastern Europe that show any substantial (well over 2 percent) minorities that are *both* national and religious.

- Bulgaria has a 9 percent Turkish minority that is largely Muslim, and concentrated near its southern (Turkish) border.

- Czechoslovakia contains a 3.8 percent Hungarian minority.

- Romania has a 7.7 percent Hungarian ethnic minority.

- Yugoslavia has numerous ethnic minorities and substantial religious minorities. Muslim Albanians and Bosnians have figured in the 1989–1990 agitations in the southern and central portions of the country. In part, the latter reflect the Turkish incursions of past centuries.

However, one must not oversimplify. Each country has unique aspects. The USSR, for example, has an 11.2 percent Muslim minority scattered over southwest Soviet Asia and southern European Russia. Canada has a large mainly French and Roman Catholic community in Quebec, which in many respects has the makings of a separate nation-state. By popular vote, Norway established its full political independence from Sweden (it already had considerable autonomy) in 1905, without serious conflict. However, both countries are heavily Lutheran in religious background. Their differences were limited to ethnic (nationality) aspects, including linguistic contrasts.

"Pilot Error." This term covers corruption, misuse of public funds and resources, maladministration, and the like, by States and State agencies. There are many allegations and considerable truth therein, judging by the flow of "news" reaching us in the West as sifted by the Western "propaganda veil."

The term pilot error also involves faulty planning, including failure

to keep up with the intensifying issues raised by the environmental movement in the more economically and technologically advanced nations.

Obviously the hard facts are not clear. They will likely be sorted out
with arbitrary decisions by the States of Eastern Europe, the main parties
and interests on the scene. Meanwhile the onlooker States at a distance
will be guided chiefly by their own domestic considerations and preconceptions.

Efforts at relatively disinterested analysis can start with historical dimensions, but the closer to the present they come, the more speculative
and tentative they must necessarily appear. The present effort is no
exception.

Summary and Conclusions
for the Buffer Socialist States West of the USSR

1. Events in the socialist bloc of Eastern Europe in late 1989 and early
1990 add up to coup d'etats—a change of the top echelons—not to full-
blown revolutions that affect all aspects of a society.

2. The closest element to observers in Western countries is the Propaganda Veil either organized or allowed to evolve by leading circles whose
interests the Veil mainly expresses and serves. The Veil consists of
socialist-bashing by the western media. Example: (*Globe and Mail*, Jan.
31, 1990, p. A5)

> "Bulgaria's economy is in a perilous state, with a foreign debt of nearly
> 10 billions . . . and an inflation rate believed to be 20 percent." My sources
> show a foreign debt of $1.3 billions (1986), and an inflation rate of minus
> 15 (1980–88), when consumer prices rose 8 percent, and wages rose 23
> percent.

3. The revolts in Eastern Europe were basically anti-bureaucratic, not
anti-socialist. As the reform President of Bulgaria put it on Jan. 31: "Some
people want us to renounce socialism and impose private capitalism, but
this would do away with the progress the party made in the past and
would cause social cataclysm in society." The speaker was Mr. Mladenov,
who replaced the long-time former leader, Mr. Zhivkov.

By contrast, Poland under the leadership of Solidarity recently removed price controls; food prices immediately shot upward, leaving the
Poles in the cities considerably worse off than they were before. Privatization of factories has brought unemployment and disillusionment.

4. Realistic grievances against bureaucracies include secrecy, the corruption of many bureaucrats (the extent of corruption has yet to be documented), and the monopoly of older bureaucrats in top posts which
restricts career opportunities of younger people.

5. Another realistic grievance is poor planning with respect to environmental damage. This point is widely accepted in eastern Europe. It is part of a worldwide tardiness in reacting to the damages of industrialism to the natural environment.

6. The basic on-going social processes are urbanization and industrialization: the latter includes the mechanization of agriculture. These are stressful processes, especially when rapid. There are many superficial eddies classifiable as incidental or opportunistic. These must be identified and evaluated in a holistic perspective. A headline today may be irrelevant in a short time.

7. The socialist mode of centrally planned development (Industrialization and Urbanization) has been generally successful, but not evenly so, either among the several socialist States, or within them. There is a law of uneven development under socialism as well as under capitalism.

8. Successes, however, generate rising public expectations, which in turn develop utopianism – or unrealistic hopes and thinking. On the one hand, utopian hope may be necessary to fuel the motivation to undertake change in any social movement. On the other hand, it easily overreaches itself and turns into frustration. This is a built-in contradiction. Some writers prefer to call it "action and reaction," but the meaning is the same.

9. Temporarily, perhaps, a "loss of nerve" may have appeared in some leading elements of the East European block. Did they misjudge their situations? Adjust too fast or too slowly?

10. Have we witnessed an example of the resilience of capitalism in the form of the Propaganda Veil? Hardly. If the expected crash in capitalist economies, predicted in the Kondratief-Schumpeter-Lamontagne long-cycle theory, appears in 1990 & ff.–the worldviews in the international arena will soon experience a drastic change.

11. The table on the next page summarizes some basic living conditions of nine Socialist and three Capitalist States. Industrialism began in the capitalist West three or more centuries ago. Socialist industrialism has a history only four to seven decades long. A success story? Of course. Indeed, it is, despite all the obstacles, one of the greatest chapters in civilized human achievement.

12. One extreme threat to world peace and human survival has been intensified by the fireworks in Eastern Europe, 1989–90: German reunification. The first two World Wars in the long view were generated by capitalist imperialism, but in a short-run perspective they were precipitated by Germany. Germany reunified would be 78 million people, 72 percent from the right-wing FRG (West Germany). Already the reformist GDR Interior Ministry has warned that the 1000 organized neo-Nazis

Assorted Data for European Socialist States, with Comparisons
(late 1980s, except Alba. education 1979)

	ALBA.	BULG.	CZ-SL	GDR	HUN.	POL.	ROM.	YUGOSL.	USSR	SWED.	FRG	USA
Population (millions)	3.3	9.0	15.7	16.4	10.6	35.1	23.3	23.4	290.1	8.5	62.6	251.4
Life expectancy at birth												
Males	69.4	68.2	67.4	69.8	66.2	67.2	66.3	66.1	64.8	74.2	72.1	72 W: 66 Bk.
Females	74.9	74.4	75.4	75.9	74.0	75.7	72.3	73.6	73.6	80	78.7	77 W: 74 Bk.
% urban	36	67	75	77	60	61	54	46	66	83	94	77
Education (percent)												
Literacy over 15 yrs	100	95.5	100	100	98.9	98.7	82.6	89.6	99	100	100	95.5
Primary, second'y												
(some or all)	95.6	n.a.	93.8	100	92.6	91.5	95.4	94.4	n.a.	91	100	n.a.
Post-secondary	4.4	7.5	5	9	6.1	5.7	4.6	5.6	n.a.	15.4	8.9	n.a.
Health												
Infant death rate	28.2	14.4	11.9	7.6	15.8	16.1	26.9	24.3	22.3	5.8	8.3	9.4
MDs/persons ratio	1/574	1/319	1/312	1/424	1/342	1/480	1/551	1/534	1/229	1/320	1/351	1/404
Hosp. beds/persons	1/176	1/103	1/99	1/98	1/104	1/174	1/108	1/164	1/80	1/148	1/92	1/192
Daily calories/person	3060	3650	3540	3855	3540	3434	3327	3570	3403	3031	3528	3644
% FAO/UN norm	127	146	143	147	130	131	126	141	132	113	132	138
GNP per cap. (US $/yr)	880	6766	7870	11180	7890	4560	3445	2490	8700	19150	20750	21100
Radios per person	1/14	1/4.6	1/3.3	1/2.5	1/1.8	1/3.6	1/7.1	1/5	1/1.5	1/2	1/2.4	1/0.5
TV sets per person	1/59	1/5.3	1/3.3	1/2.7	1/2.5	1/3.9	1/5.8	1/5.8	1/3.2	1/2.6	1/2.6	1/1.2
Telephones per person	n.a.	1/3.6	1/3.9	1/4.4	1/6.3	1/8.2	1/9	1/5.6	1/6.4	1/1.1	1/1.5	1/2

Sources: *Encyclopedia Britannica 1990 Yearbook; 1990 World Population Data Sheet,* Population Reference Bureau, Washington, as issued by the Population Research Laboratory, University of Alberta, 1990. Most data are at least one or two years old.

have multiplied several times since early 1988, not counting "hordes of supporters." (*Globe and Mail*, December 29, 1989). Clearly, German reunification is suicidal.

Fireworks in Eastern Europe: Soviet Perspectives

Mikhail Gorbachev: A Capsule Biography. In March, 1985, Mr. Gorbachev, then 54, was elected by the All-Union Central Committee of the Communist Party to the most powerful post in the USSR–Secretary of the Party Central Committee. In 1988 he became, as well, President and Chairman of the Supreme Soviet, an important but less powerful office.

After taking a law degree in 1955 at Moscow State University (the "Oxbridge" of the USSR), Gorbachev's career developed in the Party apparatus and the field of agriculture. His father was a peasant and World War II veteran. Mikhail was born in Privolnoye village, Stavropol Territory, north of the Caucasus Mountains.

His wife, Raisa, a former school teacher, is now a Senior Lecturer in Philosophy at Moscow State University.

Mikhail Gorbachev has emerged as a charismatic leader, skillful administrator, and a person of wide interests and ideas. The key concepts associated with his name are *perestroika* (restructuring of the economy) and *glasnost* (open-ness). A book of his selected speeches, *A Time for Peace*, was published in the United States in 1985 by Richardson and Steirman, New York. The present writer reviewed a 1985 biography of Gorbachev by Thomas Butson, a New Zealander on the *N. Y. Times* staff and a specialist on Soviet affairs. That review, published in the *Edmonton Journal* on May 25, 1985, is reprinted in the present work, Volume II.

The Russian Revolution: a New Conceptualization.
PHASE I: 1905–06. Following the humiliating defeat by Japan, seeking in 1904–05 to block Russian imperialist expansion into northeast Asia, uprisings in 1905 by several bourgeois and working-class interest-groups forced the Czarist Autocracy to move toward a constitutional monarchy. Nationalist uprisings in non-Russian territories (the Baltic provinces, Poland, Georgia, Siberia) pressed in the same direction. An elected advisory Duma (Assembly) was promised. These concessions defused enough of the anti-Autocracy sentiments to allow the suppression of the workers' Soviets (Councils) in the cities and the nationalistic movements around the frontiers. Phase 1 may be called the bourgeois stage of the Russian Revolution.

PHASE II: 1917–21. Proletarian Russia. The Czarist Autocracy crumbled in the face of massive defeats by Germany and its allies during

World War I. Efforts to keep Russia in the war under the short-lived bourgeois Kerensky regime, supported by the Western capitalist powers, soon failed in 1917. Peasants began spontaneous desertions from the Army and widespread seizures of the estates of the feudal nobility. The suppressed non-Russian ethnic nationalities around the Russian borders rose again. Government inefficiency and corruption were painfully evident. Power passed to the workers' Soviets in Petrograd and Moscow, by nearly bloodless default. The Bolshevik program of "Peace, Land and Bread" carried the day.

But the 1918–21 Civil War which followed was ferocious. Fourteen Capitalist States invaded Russia; even colonial Canada sent 5000 badly-trained recruits at British behest. A Polish invasion captured Kiev in 1920; the Soviet counterattack got as far west as Warsaw, where it was defeated with French help. In the net, the Civil War left much of Russia in ruins, and cost the Soviets a 200-mile strip along their western border. They recovered that strip in 1939. That is a good example of the "armed and bended bow"– in this case aimed westward. Finally it went off.

PHASE III: The Industrialization Drive, 1930s and After. This was the real Russian Revolution: its culmination, heart and soul. All that went before in Phases I and II, necessary as they were, merely led up to the climaxes of Phase III, the Stalin Revolution, still unfolding, global in its many impacts, extending later even into outer space.

The essence of Phase III was the transformation of "backward Russia" into a centrally planned modern urban-industrial social order, based on socialism, science and a Marxian key. The latter offered insights, not blueprints. Unquestionably the costs in stress, coercion and miscalculations were immense. Only by looking at selected aspects and subphases can we even begin to comprehend the outlines of what happened. Nothing more is attempted here.

The 1920s: the "New Economic Policy" (NEP) Era. In this period came a "strategic retreat" from the centralization and egalitarian aspects of Civil War Communism. Growth occurred in State and private capitalism among small industries, but the "commanding heights" of large-scale industry, transport, utilities, finance and natural resources remained socialized. By the mid-1920s pre-war levels of production had been recovered.

Earlier expectations of socialist revolutions in the advanced European nations had proven utopian. A new definition of the world situation emerged: "Socialism in One Country." This became a new worldview and national goal, honed in bitter intra-Party strife centering first on the issue of succession to the ailing Lenin (d. 1924), and leading to the great purges of the 1930s. Inexorably the Russian people edged toward forced or rapid industrialization led by Stalin and his supporters. In 1922 began the coalescence of the component republics into the Union of Soviet Socialist Republics. The four initiators of 1922 numbered 11 in 1936 and 15 in 1990. Control, however, usually lay with the Party.

The Five-Year Plans. The first Plan began in October, 1928, backdated from April, 1929. It ran in fact only four years and three months. The second Plan ran a full five years, January, 1933 to January, 1938. Planning had begun in the early 1920s. Inherently the Plans made for increased centralization. As well, they brought uneven development—contrary to original intentions: heavy industry was emphasized (and became a bureaucratized vested interest), while agriculture and consumer goods lagged. Agriculture in particular proved refractory.

The essence of the Plans were simple and logical. Giant power stations were to be built, to supply surrounding circles of new industries. Peasant farms were to be mechanized and the surplus population moved to the new factories in the new towns and cities. Farm machinery was to be centralized into Machine Tractor Stations (MTS depots) serving large farm areas and servicing the machines. Total production would rise and thus generate new investment capital, new social services and an overall higher living standard.

History, however, is refractory. The international situation turned, or rather remained hostile. In Phase II of the Russian Revolution, the peasantry sided with the Revolution because the peasants got the land from the nobility. But in Phase III the larger and middle peasants resisted collectivization and mechanization. Resolution was by intensification of class struggle and coercion in the countryside. Abroad, the rise of fascism in Germany, stemming from capitalist imperialist rivalries, shifted Soviet production toward armaments and a garrison State in self-defense. Let us illustrate.

Stalin in February, 1931, addressed a council of businessmen who had asked him to slow down the tempo of industrialization. His reply is even more pertinent in 1990 than in 1931.

> No, comrades, the pace must not be slackened. . . . We do not want to be beaten. . . . Old Russia was beaten ceaselessly . . . by the Mongol Khans, the Turkish Beys, Swedish feudal lords, Polish-Lithuanian *Pans*, Anglo-French capitalists, Japanese barons—beaten for her backwardness—military, cultural, political, industrial, agricultural. She was beaten because to beat her was profitable and went unpunished. . . . We are fifty or a hundred years behind the advanced countries. We must make good this lag in ten years. Either we do it or they crush us. (Cited in I. Deutscher, *Stalin*, Oxford, 1949, p. 328)

Nonetheless, Stalin did slacken the tempo of industrialization, if only from necessity. A peasant population which never before handled machines simply could not become wage-paid mechanics overnight. The timing and co-ordination of complementary aspects of industrialization were often far from perfect. Peasants hid their grain allotments due to the State as taxes. Collections became coercive. Many displaced or rebellious peasants landed in labor camps where they were used on huge public works. Before bowing to the horror stories, readers should remember the "Propaganda Veil." War is horrible, too. But those things happen nonetheless.

The bottom line is—*National Survival.* It is irrelevant to judge by any other measure.

As the Hitler menace loomed abroad, the USSR sought alliances wherever possible. In the mid-thirties, "popular fronts" were urged. The rightwing rising by the fascists led by General Franco in Spain became a testing ground for weapons and tactics, for example. In response to the Nazi threat, promoted to maximum priority by the 1938 Franco-British decision to give Hitler a free hand in the East, the USSR undertook the 1939 "Winter War" against Finland in order to improve the defenses of Leningrad, and the 1939 pact with Hitler, whereby the USSR was able to recover most of the 200-mile strip lost in March, 1918, by the treaty of Brest-Litovsk.

In 1940 Hitler crushed France and England in western Europe and occupied Norway and Denmark in northern Europe. The attack on the USSR began on June 22, 1941.

The Great Patriotic War. There is no doubt that the USSR carried the main burden of the war against fascism. Most of the fighting was on the Soviet-German front, where the victory was won over the Nazis. Twenty million lives were lost by the Soviets; the Nazis destroyed 1710 Soviet towns, 70,000 villages, 32,000 factories, 98,000 collective farms— the details are spelled out in the official war history (*Great Patriotic War of the Soviet Union*, Progress Publishers, Moscow, 1974; English trans. same year). In a word, the Soviets out-fought and out-produced the Nazis.

It is therefore distressing to hear even Mr. Gorbachev echoing criticism of the "crimes of Stalin." The buffer States in Eastern Europe have discarded all or parts of their postwar regimes: the armed and drawn bows, pointed eastward since the Soviet 1945 victory, have been discharged, with results as yet unforeseeable. "Ambivalence" seems to be the most suitable term for their current state of mind. The great issue, of course, is the unseemly rush to re-unite the two Germanys, supported by the USA Government and most of the other capitalist States in the West.

The New "Drang Nach Osten"–Drive to the East. It may be too early to evaluate the full results of the events of 1989–90–the *fireworks*, as we have called them in this paper. But some indications have appeared, and they are mostly very disquieting.

At first West Germany refused, then agreed to "guarantee" the present Polish borders. Such ephemeral words are meaningless. The new Czech President, Mr. Havel, has spoken to the American Congress of the need for American help by aiding the USSR "on its irreversible but immensely complicated road to democracy." But what is meant by "democracy"? We have raised that question before in this paper, but a firm answer cannot be given to such a vague term. (*Edmonton Journal*, February 22, 1990) The Americans have just published a book, *Targets of Rage*, by A. M. de Zayas (University of Nebraska Press) reviewed in the *Globe and Mail*, February 24, 1990. This author estimates that Allied policies of exposure and starvation caused two million German deaths, 1945–47. Neo-Nazi fascist skinheads are voicing anti-Semitic and anti-Communist sentiments in East Germany–as in Alberta and Idaho.

Is the new Germany hopelessly diseased by the relics of Hitler's era? Are we being prepared for a new crusade to make over the USSR?

The Intrinsic Long Cycle of Capitalism: One Generation of Expansion, One Generation of Contraction. The USSR in the 20th century has come through the greatest revolution in history. New potential threats from western capitalism may be gathering, partly in the form of a reunified Germany, and partly in the inherent instability of capitalism itself. (See "Dangers of the mid-Eighties" by M. Lamontagne, *Quest*, Sept.–Oct. 1981, on the Kondratief-Schumpeter-Lamontagne long cycle of capitalist downswing, which still has a decade or more to run. Or see Joseph Schumpeter, *Business Cycles*, New York, 1939, 2 vols.)

Looming Imperialist War in the Middle East. The American State apparatus is especially dangerous during a serious economic downswing. For more than a century wars in American experience have been economically beneficial. Except for the skirmish-conflicts with native Indians, wars have been fought abroad, with light casualties and plenty of loot.

Wrote *Maclean's Magazine* (November 19, 1990): "Polls (in early November) indicated that U.S. voters' two greatest concerns were a recession and a war in the Middle East. . . . Bush resorted to campaigning against Iraqi Saddam Hussein . . . He aggressively announced that he was switching to an offensive posture in the Middle East, increasing American troop strength (already 230,000) by at least another 150,000. . . . A White House report shows a sharp deterioration in the U.S. economy, worsened by the combined Gulf and energy crises."

Democracy. We may define this as "one person, one vote, for policy-making posts." It does not fit easily (if at all) into a complex urban-industrial society undergoing rapid change and attendant stresses. One great obstacle is bureaucracies: large hierarchical structures of specialized skills or roles indispensable for the existence of urban-industrialism. Another obstacle is the impossibility of an adequately educated citizenry: no one can know everything. Moreover, knowledge must be not only comprehensive but critical of both ultimate ends and instrumental means thereto. But bureaucracies are vested interests; universities themselves are cast in a bureaucratic framework, and as Thorstein Veblen showed (*The Higher Learning in America*, New York, 1918), they effectively limit critical analysis so as to protect the prevailing institutional order. In brief, social life itself generates conflicts and built-in struggles for survival by both individuals and groups. In the longer run, self-destruction is inherent in social life, and inevitable in highly complex societies like urban-industrial States.

Hence democracy appears suitable only in relatively stable, self-contained and slowly changing social settings wherein the differences among competing interests (including those most basic categories of age and sex) are distinctly less important than the similarities.

Conversely, for situations of rapid and inherently stressful innovation, the "vanguard" type of leadership with a coherent – and partly utopian – vision and the necessary political will to realize at least portions of that vision is essential. There will always be unintended consequences; not all elements of a utopian vision can be achieved. Witness the endless flow of books on the corruption of American Democracy and on the failure of Soviet Socialism. The Propaganda Veil, remember, is not simply a rational construct; it contains in great part inherited notions, traditions, biases; it is a lens through which a society, or more likely parts of a society, view the world, or portions thereof. Failure to recognize these basic truths has led to the undoing (perhaps temporary) of Ortega in Nicaragua, where American threats, interventions and money have brought about a Socialist defeat despite the Socialist victory in the civil war. Stalin's forced industrialization saved the USSR and the rest of the western world from fascism. If he had had to face a popular referendum in 1936, where would he (and the rest of us today) have wound up?

The Third World. We must not lose sight of wider and more weighty matters: poverty and the Third World; and the population explosion now underway in the poorer countries of the world.

What has the USA to offer the Third World? Misleading rhetoric and more neocolonialism to harness third-world resources and markets to capitalist exploitation.

What has the USSR to offer to the Third World? Guidelines for planning (both good and bad) which the Third World nations can adapt to their own conditions, or mistakes they can avoid; and perhaps limited grants for pump-priming; arms for defense against Western colonial powers or their local agents. However, the economic flexibility of Socialist central planning may be less than that of capitalism; if so—and the issue is debatable—limited decentralization may be useful. But we cannot generalize from single cases: their history, geography and national character are unique.

Ethnicity, Language and Religion as Cleavage Lines in the USSR. Half of the population in the Soviet Union is ethnically non-Russian. There are over 100 nationalities, ethnically and linguistically defined. School is taught in 52 languages; in the non-Russian areas, Russian is taught as a second language and the language of instruction is the local language. In other words, every non-Russian language group of any substantial size has the right to be educated in its own native tongue. The Russian second language thus becomes an avenue for job mobility and job opportunities outside one's native district—for those who so wish.

Gone are the days of scapegoating pogroms (riots) usually against Jews in the late 19th and early 20th centuries. While the Czarist Autocracy did not itself organize such mob attacks, its anti-Semitic and crude Russification policies indirectly fostered a favorable climate for grassroots violence. The concentration of Jews in middleman mercantile petty-bourgeois storekeeping and trading occupations, seen by the peasants as exploitive, was the major objective source of anti-Semitism. Religious and linguistic differences reinforced the basic economic cleavage. In the Jewish ghettos in the towns and in the shtetls (Jewish villages) of eastern Europe and European Russia, Yiddish was the spoken language. Its written form used the Hebrew alphabet.

Though anti-Semitic attitudes still exist here and there in the Soviet population, they cannot be expressed in overt discrimination without becoming an object of legal punishment in the court system. The head of Pamyat, an ultra-nationalist Soviet organization, was convicted of anti-Semitic behaviour in 1990. On the other hand, Nazi swastikas and other anti-Semitic slogans have been recently painted on a Jewish restaurant in Moscow. "Affirmative action" programs undertaken by the authorities on behalf of minorities and women have not always been widely popular. An excellent analysis of these problems is a readable yet authoritative book, *Soviet but not Russian: The "Other" Peoples of the Soviet Union,* by William Mandel, jointly published in 1985 by the University of Alberta Press (Edmonton) and Ramparts Press (Palo Alto).

The Union of Soviet Socialist Republics (USSR)—founded in 1922 with four Republics—is now 15 in number. A republic is basically an ethnic nationality. With two exceptions, a majority of the population belongs to the Republic to which it has given its name. The two exceptions, both in Soviet southwest Asia, are the Kazakh (15 million) and the Kirgiz (3.6 million). In their respective Republics, the Kazakhs and the Kirgiz form a plurality rather than a majority. By far the largest ethnic Republic is the Russian (139 million, or 48 percent of the total, 1990). It stretches from the western border Republics—the Baltics and White Russia— eastward across the rest of European Russia and across Siberia to Vladivostock on the Pacific Ocean. This stretch of the earth covers 11 time zones. By contrast, Canada crosses four time zones.

The next four largest Republics are the Ukrainian (50 million), the Uzbek (16 million), the Kazakh (15 million), and the White or Belorussian (9.7 million).

Scattered within the 15 full Republics are 20 Autonomous Soviet Socialist Republics; 16 lie within the huge Russian SSR. ASSRs are all inside 4 million population. Many are named for minorities within their borders; they constitute pluralities. But the top Party and Government posts are reserved for them.

Smaller administrative subdivisions are the 8 Autonomous Regions (oblasts); 10 Autonomous Areas (okrugs), and 128 Districts and Territories (krays). The highly centralized Communist Party ties together all these various subdivisions. Perhaps, however, a multi-party system may emerge from the present ongoing "fireworks" in Eastern Europe.

Seven alphabets are used in the USSR: Cyrillic (the largest), Latin, Armenian, Georgian, Hebrew, Arabic and Korean.

The "National Question" in the 20th Century. The worldwide expansion of European and American imperialist capitalism was based in large part on the premise of racial superiority. The basic motivations were economic aggrandizement; the supporting ideological rationalizations involved a large element of racism. There were dissident ideas, but significant change had to await the emergence of Soviet socialism after the turn of the present century.

Lenin led the way, starting about the turn of the century, by pressing the Russian Social Democratic Party, especially its socialist wing, toward a dual goal: equal rights for all citizens in the old Russian Empire and later the USSR irrespective of sex, race, religion or nationality. That was the first general goal; it appealed to dispersed minorities. The second goal was aimed at oppressed geographic nations: self-determination including the right of secession. Finland and Poland both broke away from the Russian Empire during the upheavals of 1917 and the ensuing civil war. For the period between World Wars I and II, Poland held Vilnius and southern Lithuania, and the Lvov region of the western Ukraine. When the Solidarity movement in Poland, which attained State power in mid-1989, voiced a claim to the Lvov region, Soviet Ukrainians were distinctly turned off.

The Revolution of 1917 greatly extended the public and private use of non-Russian languages in the non-Russian Republics, where Russian was relegated to second-language status. In the net, the Soviet policy on the nationality question was of key importance in building the new Soviet Union. It did not entirely eradicate "Great Russian chauvinism," of course, but it was indisputably a major leap forward in Soviet development, and widely popular. Foot-dragging surfaced at times in ethnic Russian groups, drawing critical attention from *Pravda* (the Party newspaper) and from the All-Union Politburo (executive organ of the Supreme Soviet). Let us keep in mind the fact that the Supreme Soviet includes two chambers: the Council of the Union and the Council of Nationalities. Each consists of 271 elected members.

Ethnic Russian Migration to Non-Russian Areas.   New industries and service organizations have drawn migrants in considerable numbers from the ethnic-Russian population to the non-Russian cities and towns. Estonia, for example, the only Protestant Republic (it is Lutheran, with a small population of 1.5 million) is one-third ethnic Russian; the capital city, Tallinn, is half ethnic Russian. In part this is because the three Baltic Republics started their industrial development well before the 1917 Revolution; hence they enjoy a higher standard of living than do most other parts of the USSR. Soviet citizens can live where they choose; economic considerations in the USSR, as elsewhere in the world, are the major factors in most migrations.

Toward a Mixed Economy?   The USSR has always had a mixed economy. In addition, "co-operatives" have appeared in recent years. These are private-sector enterprises; quality of retail goods is often better than in the State stores, but prices are higher. Shortages in consumer goods may be partly, if not largely, due to hoarding; this pattern is usually handled by means of rationing of the more essential items and by police crackdown. Rationing is not new in Soviet history. The stress on imminent disaster in the USSR, circulated in the Western media, also reflects the Western propaganda Veil that has been operating with varying emphasis since 1917. At the worst, famines swept large parts of old and new Russia before World War II. Nothing like that seems to be imminent, despite the scare headlines in North American newspapers and news telecasts.

Perchance in the next few years we may observe in the Soviet economy a greater share of efforts and emphasis upon the private sector. But the stresses of such a change of direction can be seen in Poland and in the other East European nations. A few get rich; unemployment and bankruptcies are re-born; prices spiral upward as inflation spreads. The securities of the planning economy with its built-in social nets rapidly erode. Privatization is not the road to utopia.

Soviet Foreign Policy: Peaceful Co-Existence. This policy so far has been a great success. Since World War II, a major war between the Socialist and the Capitalist super-powers has been averted. Confrontations, yes; war, no. This success has been won in spite of the encirclement of the USSR by American bases. Even worse, the USA does not accept the idea of living as an equal alongside different social systems; it feels that it must establish superiority. The USA has fueled the arms race in the hope of breaking the Soviet financial resources. This has not worked: now neither super-power can afford the arms race, and each can destroy the other in an hour of nuclear exchange.

Meanwhile the United States has lost colonial battles in Cuba, Vietnam, China and Afghanistan. The Soviets went into Afghanistan in response to repeated requests from the Afghan Government, which was confronted with an American-financed input of arms through Pakistan to feudal factions attempting to upset the Government. A decade later the Soviets withdrew; the Afghan Government still stands, but now on its own feet.

In the long run, however, little has changed. Co-existence still lives, but not securely. American capitalism still has the inner necessity toward expansion. Socialism still survives. The Cold War, whatever the Western clamor, also survives. It lurks like a giant shark a short distance beneath the deceptively calm ocean surface, perhaps a little deeper than usual, but still cruising on its predatory quest.

The Cold War between capitalism and socialism can hardly end definitely until the internal dynamics of capitalism usher an American version of socialism into the USA. Alternatively, of course, the American imperium may perish in the course of events, turning first to fascism. No one can see beyond that. There may be nothing to see.

Soviet Domestic Policy: Central Planning, but in Limited Sectors. As a largely pre-industrial country when the USSR began its industrializing Five-Year Plans in 1929, the Soviet Government necessarily emphasized heavy industry, steel and coal. Those trusts became vested interests; they injected elements of inflexibility into the economy. Military production was also stressed, especially when Hitler's Germany appeared on the European scene in 1933. Russian primacy in artillery dates back into the 18th century. Space technology came to the fore in the 1950s: the first "Sputnik" went into orbit in October, 1957. Then living in Burlington, Vermont, I still remember that electrifying *New York Times* headline: SOVIETS LAUNCH FIRST SPACE SATELLITE: IT IS CIRCLING THE EARTH AT 18,000 MILES PER HOUR.

Priorities for certain goods and services meant shortages and delay for others—many consumer goods, retailing organization, for examples. What they emphasized, therein they excelled. Other fields had to wait.

An American writer estimates that the Soviets have already accomplished one-third to one-half of the prerequisite technological studies for placing people on Mars.

> Scientific method is an important part of Marxist philosophy . . . one activity where they have succeeded better than anyone else. Why go to Mars? Mars is the most earth-like terrestrial world in the solar system. . . . Water-concentrated ores are possible. . . . It has more-or-less accessible water under the surface. . . .
>
> The Soviets plan their future . . . It is space where any future resources must be found once Earth is eventually, inevitably exhausted of whatever resource you care to name. The Soviet Union's leaders know this. They may be planning that far ahead. We in the West are not. ("Mars: The Soviet March," by D. F. Robertson, *Analog: Science Fiction/Science Fact*, 1989).

It may be argued that what the USSR needs is not less social planning, but more. Sectors with low priority—like consumer goods—should be given more systematic attention and investment. With the return of the occupying armies from the former buffer States in Eastern Europe, retraining is in order, and they can be fed into new housing and other consumer production. Soviet troops in East Germany number 375,000.

Let us remind ourselves of certain key objective trends in the USSR.

- the population has approximately doubled since 1926. The Census of 1926 counted about 147 million people; the estimated 1990 population was 289 million. (Population Reference Bureau, Washington)

- In 1926 only 18 percent of the population was urban; in 1990, 66 percent.

- Obviously there has been a great increase in the educational level.

- We may safely infer a rising level of expectations.

- War-linked population and material losses, along with the costly arms race, have seriously undercut realization of those expectations.
- Classical Marxism held that socialism could emerge only after and through capitalism. But Lenin showed that there can be a great leap from pre-capitalism or pre-industrial peasant feudalism to socialism.
- Classical Marxism also taught that the emergence of socialism in Europe would require a socialist revolution in all the advanced capitalist industrial States of Europe. Stalin pointed the way toward "Socialism in One Country."
- If and when the Soviet leadership decides on internal reform policies today, the tempo of change will rise, and so will the stress level. This will foster "vanguard leadership," doubtless not democratic. After all, the USSR has no tradition of democracy. Yet in an educated population, some sort of public consultation and rotation of higher offices, plus sharp curtailment of special privileges for higher posts—all those will be essential in some significant degree. Coercion would increase, even so.

And so we come back to the need for a temporary period of self-criticism and stock-taking—a New Economic Policy (NEP) re-grouping—leading into an era of community-building and nation-building. Help from Western Capitalism? Food handouts, yes. During the Civil War and the first NEP Herbert Hoover organized a large-scale relief program from the United States. But what capitalism demands is a docile category of faceless consumers—now more than ever—because the American economy is sliding into another phase of contraction inherent in the nature of capitalism—the long business cycle in its downward spiral. The United States is on the brink of generating a war of aggression in the Middle East that is bound to entail unforeseen and disastrous consequences.

The USSR can hardly hope to find itself in a short time. Its salvation surely does not lie in building a consumers' paradise, copying western models as they are imagined to be. Something nearer the ground is more likely to pay off. The Soviets still have a powerful army to defend their homelands from the western vultures.

When the West talks about democracy, it really means capitalist society. This is not for export: it grew out of a unique history and social evolution. Abroad, it seeks neo-colonial client States. It struggles to wipe out rival independent types of evolutionary development. States like the USSR, China, India and others will have to stay on their guard to protect their own heritages. Some day, perhaps, the American people will restructure their own society. They may finally realize that peaceful co-existence or detente is the only viable *modus vivendi* for Earth Nations to build themselves viable social orders. The Soviets have already grasped this leading principle. The North American Governments have not, although some of their citizens have seen the light.

» «

About the middle of the 19th century, Alexander Herzen, a Russian noble living in voluntary exile in Western Europe, wrote a number of essays published in a small book, *From the Other Shore*. In the Introduction he strongly urged his son to cross the bridge to modernity. "Do not, I beg, remain on this shore. . . . Better to perish with the revolution than to seek refuge in the almshouse of reaction." (1855)

Earlier, in Paris in 1848, he had written–"The future of socialism is not an enviable one. It will remain an eternal hope." (*Vixerunt!*)

That was some five generations ago. Herzen still speaks to us, but there is some updating to be added. When will that new Russian voice be heard? Or will it be a Soviet voice?

Krushchev was First Secretary of the Communist Party, 1953–64. This made him the top leader of the USSR. In 1959 he visited America for the first time, with the following reaction: "The main thing I noticed about the capitalist West–it's not the man that counts but the dollar. Everyone thinks of how to get more dollars. . . . Profits and not people are the center of attention." (*Krushchev Remembers*, Boston, 1970, p. 513)

Krushchev sought two main goals: peaceful co-existence, and improving the life-conditions of the Soviet people. "We must make sure that we don't allow ourselves to get involved in a lot of senseless competition with the West over military spending. . . . We will be exhausting our material resources without raising the living standard of our people." (*ibid*, p. 518)

Nikita Krushchev, son of a poor peasant like so many other Soviet personalities, remains an attractive figure. He was something of a boat-rocker–enough to prevent his burial in the elitist little cemetery behind Lenin's tomb in Red Square, Moscow, when he died in 1971 after a few years of quiet retirement. He rests in the grounds of the Novodevichy Convent amidst the memorials to many artistic and literary figures. It is interesting to note that many Americans took a liking to Krushchev during his 1959 visit. He came across as sharp, spontaneous, brash perhaps, and out-going. He shot from the hip, as Americans say, and he was colorful at times. Americans can identify with such characters.

Years may pass before the Soviets sort out their future. In 1990 the leading issue seems to be–what sort of socialism do we want? I believe that no conversion to capitalism is a realistic option, despite the populist noises thrown up by certain factions. The essence of the Soviet domestic problem is a crackdown on hoarding, and temporary rationing of key consumption items.

In the rest of Eastern Europe the prospect is quite different. The buffer States have experienced roughly half the exposure to socialism compared to the USSR—and that was associated with Soviet military occupation or the threat thereof. Much suffering has suddenly appeared in the 1980s. Old feuds and nationalisms have revived. Especially in Poland and East Germany, where privatization has meant economic disaster, unemployment is rampant, along with inflation and bankruptcies. Roman Catholic majorities exist in Hungary, Czechoslovakia and Poland—a belt across central Europe from the Baltic Sea to the Adriatic. The present Pope is Polish. The Roman Church is both ultra-conservative and aggressive in secular affairs. Its views on political morality and women's roles are pre-industrial, that is to say—feudal. The prospect is grim. But is that not more or less normal for central Europe over the centuries?

» «

END NOTE

Lithuania over Seven Centuries

On March 11, 1990, the small Lithuanian Soviet Socialist Republic, bordering on the Baltic Sea, and one of the 15 members of the Union of Soviet Socialist Republics (USSR) declared its independence from the USSR. A month later the all-union Soviet Government in Moscow cut off essential gas and key foodstuff shipments into Lithuania. When Lithuania agreed to freeze its declaration of independence pending negotiations, the Soviet bans were lifted.

As the hostile socialist-bashing Western capitalist media have endlessly repeated, Lithuania was independent from 1920 to 1940, when it was seized by the USSR. This is true, but it is a very small part of the whole relevant truth. Ignored is the historical evolution of Lithuania both before and after the 1920–1940 period. In this End Note we shall sketch a more holistic overview of Lithuanian history.

The Lithuanian Empire, 14th–16th century. Lying between Poland and Russia, the Grand Duchy of Lithuania by 1400 extended from the Baltic Sea southeastward to the Black Sea. It included large parts of what is today the western Ukraine, western Russia and eastern Poland. It withstood pressures from the domains of the Teutonic Knights to the west and to the north of Lithuania.

But Poland grew more powerful than Lithuania in the 15th and 16th centuries. In 1569 came the Lublin Union of Poland and Lithuania at a dynastic level. However, the largely self-sufficient peasantry retained its Lithuanian language and folk culture.

Boundary Changes, 16th–18th century. It is not necessary here to chronicle the multiplicity of boundary changes during these two centuries. Interested readers may consult the *Historical Atlas of Poland*, 1st English edition 1981, printing of 1986, Department of State Cartographical Publishers, Wroclaw, Poland. Suffice it to say that as a result of the many 18th-century wars involving the European Powers from England to Russia inclusive, by 1795, the opening of the Napoleonic era, Poland was partitioned out of existence. The Grand Duchy of Lithuania, greatly reduced in size, passed to the Russian Czar. Indeed, by 1795 all the Baltic lands were under Russian rule, and they remained so until 1920.

World War I: German Defeat of Russia; the Russian Socialist Revolution. The defeat of Russia by Germany, followed by the Bolshevik Revolution, cost the new socialist regime a 200-mile strip along its western border. Along the northern part of that strip the three Baltic provinces (Estonia, Latvia and Lithuania, reading from north to south) became temporarily independent. Fourteen capitalist States sent troops to intervene in the 1918–21 Russian Civil War against the Bolshevik State. The invaders were defeated, however. These events and their main consequences have been outlined earlier in this paper.

The Coming of World War II. By the 1930s the Soviets were well into their planned industrialization and urbanization, building socialism in one vast country. Central Europe, however, never recovered from World War I; it went fascist and set up extreme right-wing and racist dictatorships bent on revenge and domination. By 1938 the popular-front movements in western Europe had failed; Spain had gone fascist; the capitalist interests running England and France gave Hitler a free hand in eastern Europe. In the Pacific, Japan switched sides, invading China, driving out the Europeans and later the Americans. The victors in China would be the peasant revolution led by Marxist Mao Tse-tung, but not till the late 1940s. America was a mixture of isolationism and a major capitalist depression.

The Soviet Responses. 1939–1941. As war approached, the USSR was caught up in the general frenzy of unstable alliances and machinations— an Hobbesian "war of each against all." The Soviet-German Non-Aggression Pact of August 23, 1939, contained secret clauses restoring much of the Soviet western border-strip lost in 1920, from Finland south to Bessarabia and eastern Poland. By mid-1940, those areas were largely occupied by the Red Army.

Finland proved recalcitrant, however. This led to the Soviet-Finnish "Winter War" of November, 1939–March, 1940. It stalled at first, but later achieved its purpose: adjustments in the Soviet-Finnish border near Leningrad to improve the defensibility of Leningrad. However, the war aroused hostility against the USSR in Western countries, which had poor understanding of the basic trends in world politics. The war also further encouraged Hitler to take the Red Army lightly.

More successful for the USSR was the Soviet-Japanese Neutrality Pact of April, 1941. This succeeded because it suited Japanese interests as well as Soviet concerns. Japan was then pre-occupied with its expansionism in China and southeast Asia, where the plunder was far more profitable than in the grasslands of northern Manchuria.

Lithuania as Nazi Collaborator in the Holocaust. Lithuania had only the briefest experience of Soviet socialism—less than one year in 1939–1940. It was a buffer State like the other East European States west of the USSR after World War II. Lithuania was basically Roman Catholic—the only such Republic in the USSR. (Estonia was Lutheran; Latvia was mixed.)

When Nazi Germany marched into the USSR on July 22, 1941, Lithuania began three and one-half years of racist Nazi discipline and organized destruction of Lithuanian Jews. Let us consider this aspect of Lithuanian history—never mentioned these days in the Western capitalist media. We cite *The Holocaust*, by Martin Gilbert, Fellow of Merton College, Oxford University, official biographer of Winston Churchill, author of many historical atlases and historical studies. *The Holocaust* was published by Fontana, London, 1987, pp. 959.

> Operation Barbarossa, the German invasion of the Soviet Union launched on 22 June, 1941, marked a tragic turning point in German policy towards the Jews. In the twenty-one months before Barbarossa, as many as thirty thousand Jews had perished. . . . But in no Jewish community had more than two or three percent been murdered. . . . From the first hours of Barbarossa, however, throughout what had once been eastern Poland, Latvia, Lithuania and Estonia, as well as in the Ukraine, White Russia and the western regions of the Russian Republic, a new policy was carried out, the systematic destruction of entire Jewish communities. These were the regions in which the Jew had been most isolated and cursed for more than two centuries, the regions where Catholic, Russian Orthodox, Ethnic Germans and Jews had been most marked in their distinctive ways of life, in which language differences had been a barrier, social divisions a source of isolation, and religious contrasts a cause of hatred. The Ger-

man invaders knew this well and exploited it to the full. In advance of the invasion of Russia, the SS leaders had prepared special killing squads, which set about finding and organizing local collaborators, Lithuanians and Ukrainians, into murder gangs, and were confident that the anti-Jewish hatreds which existed in the East could be turned easily to mass murder. In this they were right. (p. 154)

In Kovno, Lithuania, on June 26, hundreds of Jews were seized in their homes, taken to one of the fortifications which surrounded the city, and murdered. . . . (p. 157)

The ferocity of hatred was directed not only against Jews. Russian prisoners-of-war were also murdered in cold blood by the occupying forces. . . . by the end of the war two and a half million Russian prisoners-of-war had been murdered." (p. 159)

From among the local populace, especially in Lithuania and the Ukraine, hundreds could be found not only to round up Jews, but to kill them. (p. 172) . . . Within five weeks of the German invasion, the number of Jews killed exceeded the total number killed in the previous eight years of Nazi rule. . . . The first five-figure massacre ended on July 31, in Kishinev, Bessarabia, after 14 days' uninterrupted slaughter, in which ten thousand Jews were murdered. . . . (p. 175)

In summary, we must see Lithuania in full-length historical terms, and in the light of its geopolitical situation. If this small nation of 3.8 million people were located far away in the North Atlantic like Iceland, "independence" might make sense. But such a goal is nonsense, unrealistic in the extreme, given its location in the crowded northwest corner of the USSR, surrounded by neighbours of many contrasts.

Utopian Thinking in the Lithuanian Independence Movement. In a world rapidly industrializing and urbanizing, old-fashioned notions of absolute national sovereignty are obsolete. The economically advanced nations may be heading toward some version of "sovereignty-association," to apply a concept that is becoming familiar in Canada with respect to the debates on the future of francophone Quebec and anglophone Canada. This means a modification of sovereignty by an economic union, to be negotiated between or among otherwise sovereign parties. The concept clearly implies a limitation of any type of absolute sovereign powers of national States.

The Lithuanian "independence" leaders, however, appear to be thinking in more traditional terms. Yet the benefits of socialist planning are obvious. The northwest Baltic corner of the USSR has income levels higher than most if not all of the other Soviet republics. Industrialization has older roots among the Baltic towns than in other Russian cities, with few exceptions. Sending their leaders to the United States soon after they declared independence from Moscow was surely a major political blunder. Did they hope to tap those legendary "streets of gold" that have lured so many millions of migrants from Europe to the New World during the past century? Alas, Utopia is nowhere. Calling in support from abroad affronts domestic nationalisms. Such efforts boomeranged in favor of the Bolshevik forces during the 1918–1921 civil war. So likewise did the pro-Nazi collaborationist movements by Soviet dissidents during World War II and the holocaust against Jews and captured Soviet soldiers.

Of course it is necessary to transcend old-fashioned absolute nationalism by such legitimate measures as the European Community and the Nordic Council. There are numerous such political institutions that may be classified as trans-national corporations. Further development thereof is overdue, in order to cope with the private trans-national corporations which are taking over the global economy, with little regard for meeting human needs.*

The Soviet Union itself is a notable step toward the linking together of diverse nationalities in a unified political structure.

NOVEMBER 27, 1990

---

* On this point I am indebted to Professor Barbara Kasinska, Memorial University of Newfoundland, Department of Political Science.

Selected Public Letters
1948–1990

Social Status and Fertility

Low Birth Rate in College Graduates' Families
Not a Sign of Biological Deterioration

To the Editor:

In your June 13 news columns is summarized a study of college graduates' birth rates by the Population Reference Bureau. The bureau grimly announces that college graduates are not reproducing themselves, whereas people with four years' schooling average more than twice as many offspring.

Discussions of this matter are commonly loaded with much loose thinking, which this latest study will unfortunately encourage. The inverse relation between social status and fertility is well known. But it does not follow that the country is faced with biological deterioration. There is simply no scientific evidence, or even acceptable objective criteria, of either biological decay or improvement.

That there is a reservoir of unused talent in the lower brackets the Population Reference Bureau blithely ignores. Indeed, low upper-class fertility directly contributes to the American tradition of individualism by providing a vacuum into which able persons can rise. The real problem is to extend educational opportunity downward.

The larger issue here is the recruiting of personnel to man the social system. Some societies do this by making social position hereditary. Ours seeks instead to rely on individual achievement. Already our social mobility appears to be declining, mainly for economic reasons. Greater upper-class fertility would further impede mobility. Moreover, there is some evidence that the current inverse relationship between social status and fertility may disappear. This makes it all the more urgent to broaden educational opportunity, so that the better occupational statuses may be recruited from all social levels on the basis of ability.

The alternative is the sharpening of class lines and class conflict. Hereditary social classes do not jibe with democracy.

These matters are well known to competent sociologists and demographers. There is no excuse today for failing to place population facts in their proper perspective. What is the Population Reference Bureau trying to sell us?

On my desk are the published fertility data of two colleges included in the bureau's survey. The details are summarized in a widely circulated pictograph showing the decreasing descendants of college graduates and the multiplying descendants of the less educated. The drawing of the uncouth giant in overalls towering over a pee-wee college graduate fifty years hence is sensational! Which of the two is the birdbrain isn't specified, but we may infer that the purpose of the pictograph is to convey the imminent triumph of mediocrity. Oh, horrible fate!!

Closer scrutiny reveals the propaganda behind the "scientific" facade. The incompletely labeled graphs are impossible to interpret precisely. Citing intelligence tests as valid measures of hereditary abilities is an ancient wheeze. The Eugenics Line is "science" only to the gullible. Its misuse would be amusing except for the possibility that it may serve to soften us up for racism of a much more vicious brand.

What is really biting the eugenists is status anxiety. Many of them are upper-middle-class Anglo-Saxons who are frightened out of their skins by the prospect of competition from the great unwashed. Eugenics rationalizes those fears and nicely bolsters their threatened self-esteem.

New York *Herald-Tribune*
June 20, 1948

To Deal With Gambling

Legalization and Regulation Are Urged to Eliminate Abuses

To THE EDITOR:

The Kefauver hearings have cast a healthy beam into some dark corners. Popular reaction seems to be: Punish the rascals, tighten up the laws! This cuts at symptoms, but leaves intact the underlying conditions causing the corruption.

Mass demand makes gambling a big business. Most participants do not make their living by gambling. They are "customers" to whom gambling is a sport, an occasion for conviviality plus a long shot at a big purse. To most participants gambling is commercial amusement. Gambling is not a biological instinct, but it is rooted in psychosocial motives almost as universal.

ODDS AGAINST WINNING

Few participants are full-time professionals. Of these the great majority are probably purveyors of gambling services. Neither of the customers nor of the purveyors can we say that "gambling is getting something for nothing." The customer gets what he pays for: an interesting pastime. He usually knows the odds are against his winning. The seller works hard—sometimes too hard—to supply the demand for gambling opportunities.

Only a minority of the professionals seem to make their living simply from successful wagering. We may dismiss them as inconsequential, because the large capital needed for such gaming sharply limits their number. Their activity in any case is indistinguishable from stock market or real estate speculation.

What is the answer to the gambling problem? Clearly it is the legalizing and public regulating of gambling, at least of its mass forms like off-the-tracks horse betting and the numbers pool. We suffer from the abuses of gambling, not from gambling itself. The abuses are rooted mainly in the gap between the anti-gambling laws and present-day morals.

LIMITS OF LAW

The function of law is to reflect existing attitudes or to reconcile those that conflict, not to create attitudes. We cannot legislate morals. Whoever opposes gambling may freely do so by persuasion. It is against the public interest to do so by law. Have we learned nothing from Prohibition?

By legalizing and regulating organized gambling, we will greatly reduce bribery, stop making hypocrites of our public officials, and remove a major source of popular contempt for law. We will reduce fraud in gambling, which needs customer education and safeguards like any other enterprise. We will gain large tax revenues. We will bring more rational uniformity into our laws. Above all, we will remove a serious class discrimination. The numbers pool is the poor man's stock market.

Gambling does not flourish because of the frailty of a few public officials or the conspiracy of an underworld czar. It thrives because of the demand of countless ordinary people, especially working-class people. In so far as they gamble for gain, they are simply seeking the great American goal of wealth, which lack of opportunity prevents their attaining by other means. There is no reliable evidence to support the myth that gambling tends to become a ruinous and impoverishing obsession.

To be useful, the Kefauver hearings should result in something more than taking a few sacrificial scalps, or enacting additional unenforceable laws. Legalized and regulated gambling would not eradicate all the evils associated with gambling, but it would decisively diminish them. When will we gain the insight and courage to recognize this?

The New York Times
March 28, 1951

Death Penalty Seen Too Great for Rosenbergs' Offense

To the Editor:

I believe that most Americans, once fully informed on a controversy, will make a just decision. Hence I offer some comments on the Rosenberg case.

First, some facts. The Rosenbergs are charged with conspiracy to commit espionage, not with espionage or treason. Never before in our history has a civil court imposed a death sentence for espionage. Even for the much more serious crime of overt wartime treason, on behalf of enemy nations, Axis Sally and Tokyo Rose got only 10 years. The Rosenbergs' espionage conspiracy involved a wartime ally: the date of their alleged conspiracy was 1944.

The espionage law does not distinguish between ally and enemy. But the moral distinction will not down. Espionage for Russia in 1950 would show a clear intent to injure the United States. The same act in 1944 shows no such intent. And intent is of major importance in weighing guilt.

So much for the facts. Three issues make this case controversial.

First is the issue of guilt. The Rosenbergs were convicted on the testimony of one principle witness, Greenglass, himself under indictment on the same charge of espionage conspiracy. Greenglass later got off with 15 years. The sole corroborator of his testimony was his wife, who was also under the same indictment. She was never brought to trial.

Second is the issue of the death sentence. Even if the Rosenbergs are guilty, do they deserve such a severe sentence?

Third is the trial atmosphere. In stirring up prejudice and hysteria the prosecutor's conduct was "wholly reprehensible," to quote the U.S. Circuit Court of Appeals. In pronouncing sentence the judge accused the defendants of treason, responsibility for the Korean War and for Soviet atomic power. Yet nothing of the sort was ever legally charged or proven.

Justice has not been served. We may differ on the issue of guilt; we must surely agree that the death sentence is too severe. Only the President can change that sentence now. Letters to Eisenhower may help to commute a sentence that is stirring up anti-American feeling all over the world.

Barre, Vt. *Times*
January 22, 1953

Nobody Owns the Office

To the Editor:

Mr. Aiken's refusal to debate the farm problem with his opponent Bernard O'Shea on the ground that "there is no sense shooting at sparrows" will tickle confirmed Republicans. It is less likely to impress "Joe Smith," the independent voter. Joe may well object, not to the refusal to debate, but to the reason for refusing. This is not said in defense of Mr. O'Shea, who can evidently look after himself, but in the interest of "Joe Smith." Mr. Aiken's crack about sparrows is funny—at first. But the shaft, though aimed at Mr. O'Shea, really hits "Joe Smith." It implies that the voters can be satisfied or diverted by a wisecrack.

There is nothing new about "Joe Smith" getting the shaft. Most of us have few illusions about our political influence. But we would like to have the candidates at least go through the motions of submitting their views on current questions to the electorate in good faith. Resorting to personalities merely befogs the real issues. Perhaps our campaigns are full of sham, but do we have to admit it openly?

Mr. Aiken is a United States Senator and a superior one. In the present campaign, however, his status is exactly the same as Mr. O'Shea's: both are candidates for public office. Nobody owns the office. That presumably belongs to the people, not to the politicians or to a party.

Whatever the merits and demerits of the Democratic and Republican positions on the farm problem, it seems clear that there is a farm problem, and that personal disparagement doesn't clarify it. As the candidate of a long-dormant party, Mr. Aiken should be leaning over backward to disprove Democratic charges of bureaucratic smugness, instead of illustrating them.

Burlington Free Press, Vt.
Sept. 25, 1956

An Arena for Ferment

To the Editor:

Your March 29 Novikoff editorial says university trustees assume full power to hire and fire faculty members. That is the way the steel barons talked before the advent of the CIO unions.

If the trustees could decide tenure questions with complete objectivity, and if there were no conflicts of interest involved, their claim might have merit. But another condition is present.

First, a teacher is too often retained or dismissed by administrative whim. In the elite universities, professional competence is more likely to be decisive. In average and inferior institutions, factors unrelated to competence—politics, conformity, prejudice—become more important.

Second, employer and employee interests clash in universities no less than in industry. Such conflicts must be compromised.

This requires an organization of employees strong enough to contend on equal terms with administrators, and able to present its case to the public.

What little headway has lately been made in academic tenure and freedom owes much to the national AAUP. But the AAUP deals mainly with senior faculty having "permanent" tenure. My work last year on the academic freedom committee of the Eastern Sociological Society, which studied 40 Novikoff-type cases, convinced me that a union of all university employees is essential. No one ever hears about the lowly instructors who are annually turned out with or without cause. Seldom do we learn of the sacking of minor administrative employees, like Leader.

It is unnecessary to agree with Novikoff's alleged ideas. It is only necessary to defend a teacher's right to be nonconformist. The

Novikoff case is a symptom of the anti-intellectual drift of American life, the stagnation of education, and the low status of teachers.

Any professor who voices opinions out of line with those of his superiors knows he is risking his neck. He can expect to have his motives attacked, his character blackened, his competence questioned. Likely as not, the chief hatchet man will be his own president.

Universities are supposed to provide an arena for the ferment and competition of different ideas. Especially in these times of mounting foreign and domestic tensions,

this function is essential to our national security, perhaps to our survival. Cases like Novikoff, and many other incidents, show that our universities are producing conformity instead of ferment. The groups that govern our universities, and the top officers who administer them, are therefore failing in their duty. It is time for them to move over and to share their responsibilities with other groups in the community, including the teachers.

Burlington Free Press, Vt.
April 1, 1958

Sociology in Anglophone Canada

To the Editor:

A survey of sociology in Canada and France has been undertaken by the Organization for Economic Co-operation and Development (OECD), Paris. In charge of it is Professor Henri Mendras, University of Paris–Nanterre. In October 1973, Professor Mendras, headquartered at the Ottawa offices of the Secretary of State for Science, spent one day each at the University of British Columbia and the University of Alberta, then returned to central Canada, and shortly thereafter to Paris.

To supplement the brevity of Professor Mendras' visit, the following brief (somewhat condensed here) was submitted to him.

1 The writer notes with concern that Professor Mendras' visit was unduly short. Further, it is sponsored by OECD, a civilian arm of NATO, which is dominated by the American metropolis. To offset these handicaps, we urge that Professor Mendras' draft report be submitted for feedback to the Anglophone and Francophone members of the profession. Arrangements should be worked out by OECD and the Canadian Sociology & Anthropology Association, with such additional professional and regional associations in Quebec and the West as can be involved.

2 In Quebec, the spreading independence

movement requires special consideration by Professor Mendras, because a number of Quebec social scientists are involved in that movement and because the social milieu in Quebec differs from that in Anglophone Canada. Quebec is doubly colonized: since the 1760 conquest, it has been an internal colony of English Canada; and since World War II, English Canada has become a colonial annex of the United States–which dominates NATO. It is hoped that Professor Mendras will sort out these factors in such a way that his report is credible to the satellite publics in Quebec and in Anglophone Canada.

3 The colonized status of Anglophone sociology in Canada is underlined by the presence of an unduly large proportion of American imports in Canadian universities. Some have identified with the movement for Canadian liberation from American economic and cultural domination. The majority have not. The latter may claim some Canadian experience, but most are still exponents (more often than not) of American cultural and economic imperialism, however unwittingly. This is because they adhere to a-historical, consensus, micro-system, ultra-positivistic studies that do not illuminate– let alone challenge–the local, regional or national Establishments. This sociology of

the trivial serves the American imperium and its Canadian annex, willy-nilly. Anglophone sociology in Canada, more than Francophone sociology, services the private and public corporate apparatuses more than the people.

4 Canadian universities need a variety of viewpoints. Under-represented are third-world countries; over-represented, the USA. Our prime problem is to disentangle ourselves from the over-presence of Americans, which is to say we face the problem of freeing ourselves from the economic and political primacy of American capitalism, in order to attain a free dialogue of ideas. But it is not enough to exchange the American urban-industrial complex for a Canadian urban-industrial complex. For Ottawa's policy has been continentalist, centralist, and urbanizing: witness Ottawa's Indian policy and its farm policy.

5 A major problem of Canadian Anglophone sociology, therefore, is to clue in on what is going on, and to get involved in a resistance. This means, among other things, strengthening our regional institutions, and our rural communities, by reversing the centralist trends that sap our vitality.

6 A major problem of Anglophone sociology in Canada is the fostering of multi-disciplinary research, over extended periods of time. This calls for regional institutes, financed for six to eight years, with enough grants from several governments to assure critical independence; and it calls for a severe limitation of contract research for private or public agencies, lest this tail wag the dog. One-province institutes are not good enough. This limited financing eventually doomed the Saskatchewan Center for Community Studies (1957–65), and the Alberta Human Resources Council (1967–72). There were other factors in each case.

7 Most of the work of regional research institutes would need to be policy-oriented and problem-oriented to justify federal and provincial grants. There should be minimal whimsical research by ivy-tower academics. But exploratory work on a limited basis should be underwritten, even though policy implications seem remote.

8 Canadian social sciences are divided into obsolete analytical disciplines or departments. It is very difficult to set up cross-discipline research. This is another strong reason for regional research institutes.

Further, research institutes, besides fostering cross-discipline studies, offer a good chance to reduce the present over-emphasis in Anglophone Canada on abstract, a-historical 'systems' types of analysis, such as US functional-structuralism and micro-economics. Though these claim to be modelled on the physical and mathematical sciences, in fact they are based on a misunderstanding of the logic and nature of physical science. They make for purely formal theoretical exercises that cannot explain the real social world, and that are not amenable to empirical verification, practical application, or prediction relevant to everyday affairs.

By contrast, research institutes might find it possible to encourage historical, dialectical, and problem-oriented studies. The latter do relate to, and explain, the real world of society; they are subject to empirical verification; and they lend themselves to predictive forecasts, however rough.

Little is done in Canadian Anglophone sociology to encourage critical dialectical studies. It is difficult to publish such studies: editorial boards are dominated by orthodox positivists and structural-functional technocrats who do not understand dialectics.

9 Yet dialectical and critical studies, particularly those oriented to Canadian nationalism, will become increasingly relevant and essential as Canadian people become aware that Canada's emerging role in the American empire is de-industrialization, and downgrading to the level of a colony supplying the American metropolis with raw materials. The American policy is to concentrate manufacturing jobs within its own borders, and to avail itself more fully of the resources and raw materials in countries outside its borders, at bargain-basement rates. Can a NATO survey of Canadian sociology, sponsored by an arm of the American empire, adequately serve Canadian national interests?

10 My fifteen-year experience in Canada as researcher and professor strongly sug-

gests that neither universities nor governments in Anglophone Canada want independent and critical research institutes. Governments, both federal and provincial, seem to prefer innocuous, in-house research, confined to refining their instrumental procedures, but scrupulously avoiding critical reviews of governmental end-goals. To avoid this co-optation, regional research institute governing boards should be dominated by representatives of popular organizations (farm, labour, ethnic, consumer, etc). Criticism must be deepened; responsibility broadened. Though lower-income people pay a disproportionately high share of the taxes that support the Canadian post-secondary education system, they derive relatively little benefit so long as the university system serves primarily the corporate apparatuses, public and private, which in turn serve the American imperium.

11 Many layman and practitioner audiences await whatever sociologists can offer toward individual and public services. Education sociologists in Canada have done considerable in this respect. But other sociologists have lagged. Feedback procedures involving practitioners are not adequate. Specialists and laymen must learn from each other: one-way education from the experts is not enough, according to Paulo Freire. But Anglophone academic sociology in Canada still is wedded to the old practices of 'education by narration.' This *élitist* pattern serves neither the advancement of knowledge nor the public well-being.

Science Forum
Vol. 7, February, 1974

Every Arms Race Ends in War

To the Editor:

Your opening section on the nuclear crisis is most impressive (*Journal*, Nov. 3).

A supportive approach is worth noting. In 1942, the University of Chicago Press published a two-volume Study of War, by Quincy Wright. The upshot of this careful study of arms races is clear. Every arms race in history has ended in war. In early modern times, those races were first local, then regional. Now they are global.

Recently, the 1972 British Broadcasting film, War and Peace, based on Leo Tolstoy's great novel, was re-run on local television. In the war between France and Russia, 1812–14, Napoleon and Kutozov lacked the power to destroy the world. They could only destroy each other.

Today, nuclear technology assures global destruction. The Americans seem bent on a preventive strike. Will the Soviets jump in first? Does it matter? The outcome will be the same: mutually assured self-destruction.

Perhaps in some other galaxy, eons hence, a more viable form of life may develop. Our human race, however, has flunked out. It is not viable. It does not deserve to survive.

Consider the slave trade, the imperialist rape of the world, mainly by European powers, and all the other outrages.

Has the exploited Third World, itself scarred by intensifying assaults, learned anything? Not at all. The emerging nations wish to emulate their exploiters. They seek to urbanize and increase their material wealth, especially for their own selfish elites. Greed prevails.

An obscure Canadian poet, Archibald Lampman, published a poem in 1899: "The City of the End of Things." He said it all.

Edmonton *Journal*
November 23, 1986

Quebec: An Example to Other Regions

To the Editor:

I recently read the Quebec white paper *Quebec-Canada: A New Deal*. What appals me is the completely negative stonewalling reactions by Anglo politicians and publicists.

I think the white paper is sensible. Certainly, its proposals are negotiable. Indeed, many of the things Quebec is doing should be done by the other regions of Canada. Confederation has primarily benefited southern Ontario. Within a generation, the Maritimes were deindustrialized by the golden horseshoe of southern Ontario and English Montreal. The Maritimes have been stagnating since the turn of this century.

Western agricultural settlement and the transcontinental railroads were likewise designed for the business interests of southern Ontario and English Montreal. The "national policy" of Sir John A. Macdonald worked well – for central Canada – until the 1930s, when it ran out of steam.

Look at Canada today. Its one industrial sector, southern Ontario, has been stagnating for a decade. All the other regions depend mainly on resource extraction and export. And two-thirds of Canadian manufacturing is under foreign control, chiefly American.

Several studies by the Science Council of Canada point with alarm to the loss of research and development (R & D) capacity to the U.S., as the big multinationals concentrate their R & D south of the border. No manufacturing sector can survive without a large R & D effort to develop new products and markets. How many Canadians know that Canada developed the four-engine jet commercial aircraft first? And competitive military aircraft? We blew it all to the U.S. in the 1950s.

Why is Quebec moving to take over the asbestos industry? There are about 5,000 jobs in that industry in Quebec, mostly in mining. There are 25,000 jobs in asbestos processing, where the well paying jobs are concentrated. But those jobs are in the U.S.

Quebec has higher unemployment than does Ontario, though the Maritimes rates are higher. Much of Quebec's industry is obsolete and small-scale. Massive R & D and technological renovation will be needed in the next few years.

But, all that is equally true of the other regions of Canada – including fat-cat southern Ontario. If we want to overcome regional disparity, rising unemployment, and inflation, then we need massive R & D to diversify our resource economies, to channel public and private investment into new industries. The R & D will have to be done by federal and provincial governments and by universities, loosely co-ordinated. We can only finance this by recovering control of our natural resources, province by province, from foreign domination.

We cannot even dream of these measures until we get Canada back from the American corporations. Yet, no political party is saying this. The Liberals and the Progressive Conservatives are both serving the foreign corporate elites. The federal New Democratic Party is unduly influenced by the big American-headquartered unions.

Quebec is at least moving towards taking greater control of its own destiny. I wish it well. I think the other regions of Canada should do likewise. A regional association in Canada is viable. Confederation is not. Those politicians who say they will not negotiate with Quebec and that sovereignty-association won't work are like ostriches burying their heads in the sand. Are they inviting a diversionary civil war? We can't afford that.

The coming referendum in Quebec is probably not very important. Whatever the results, they will satisfy no one. I give Quebec between five and 25 years to go independent. In fact, Quebec is already halfway out of Confederation. There have been earlier surges towards greater autonomy and independence in Quebec. There will be others. If Claude Ryan becomes premier of Quebec, he will be forced to tilt in the same direction as Rene Levesque.

Let us take a longer view. Historian Herbert Bolton pointed out in 1932 that a hemispheric view of history is necessary. In that perspective, every major New World colony has shaken off its subordination to European colonizers – except Quebec and Puerto Rico. Their turn will come.

Edmonton *Journal*
Dec. 4, 1979

Guaranteed Annual Income Best Solution

To the Editor:

Unemployment and poverty are among the worst afflictions we bear. Yet we live in one of the richest societies in the world.

The occasional sharing with those less fortunate than ourselves is not enough. I'm sure that the food bank and other private volunteer enterprises are necessary in these times of harsh provincial welfare policies – but they fall short.

There is a better solution – a guaranteed annual income. This is not a new idea, but it's an idea whose time has come. It means a partial or, in some cases, entire income adequate for every man, woman and child in Canada to achieve a decent livelihood.

To finance a guaranteed annual income, most present social allowances should be phased out over time.

This is not an argument for income equality which no nation in the world possesses or seeks. It's an argument for less inequality than we currently have. Dire poverty in the midst of plenty can shatter any society by generating intolerable social strife.

A half century ago unemployment insurance in North America was a new idea. Its critics forecast all sorts of horrid results.

Unfortunately it's designed for short-term layoffs, not for protracted unemployment. After the unemployment insurance runs out, there's only welfare – inadequate, demoralizing and destructive to the morale of the recipients.

Private charity, like the food bank, is a subsidy for low wages. It's no accident that Alberta has the lowest minimum wage in Canada – thanks to a harsh provincial government. Yet no political party has taken a stand for a guaranteed annual income. Shame on them.

Edmonton *Journal*
December 18, 1987

Separate From Quebec

To the Editor:

English Canada should separate from Quebec. The link between them, originally based on military conquest (1760) and now on unhealthy political ploys, has become an obsession.

All three federal political parties have anglophone leaders. The Tories and Liberals take turns swapping Quebec votes for sleazy handouts. The NDP is frozen out of Quebec, partly because it is an anglophone outfit and partly because its social democratic program (reforms within capitalism) has been pre-empted by the provincial Parti Quebecois.

Fluency in French does not make a Quebecer. In Quebec eyes, the Prime Minister of the day is Father Christmas, however competent in French.

The midnight Meech Lake deal called Quebec a "distinct society." What does that mean? No one can say for sure. It means what any person or interest group says it means. Hence it is ambiguous, ephemeral, already dying on the vine. Meech Lake was a desperate effort to paper over the cracks in that Blarney Stone of Canadian politics – national unity.

But national unity is largely mythical. The realities of Canada are regional differences and inequities.

Both English Canada and Quebec have much nation-building to do. Together, they exasperate and cripple each other. Bilingualism will not fly. Multiculturalism, however, should work for both English Canada and Quebec, once they separate.

Toronto *Globe and Mail*
November 29, 1989

Quebec Will Go its Own Way
Apart from Death of Meech

To the Editor:

The *Journal's* June 19 lead editorial (Harper rolls the dice) sharply attacked the long-standing injustices toward native peoples. Right on.

Then you said that Manitoba MLA Harper's blocking of the Meech Lake deal would intensify Quebec separatism, thereby worsening our national conflicts. Right, again.

But you viewed this latter trend as dreadful. Dead wrong. For Quebec will go its own way despite the demise of the hocus-pocus called Meech Lake. This leaves anglophone Canada to face up to itself – a soft nation, a collection of conflicting regional interests, an economic colony of the American empire.

We shall have to face up to ourselves; that is the real crisis today. It is an Anglo crisis, not a Quebec crisis.

Ever since the conquest of 1760 by a minority British army, Quebec has been pounded and pressured into a hardened nation. Force has been applied several times by ill-advised Anglo authorities against the anti-conscription riots in both world wars, and against the "apprehended insurrection" of October 1970.

Like Meech Lake, the October crisis was phoney, whipped up by top-level federal policy-makers, a whiff of grapeshot meant to frighten the independence movement of that day. Was it rigged, or simply allowed to happen?

Quebec has responded since Confederation by trading votes for political handouts. The record is coated with sleaze, whether Liberals or Tories ruled in Ottawa. Yet structural changes can reduce such stresses. Both Quebec and anglophone Canada must move decisively toward sovereignty-association.

The Quebec 1979 white paper, *Quebec-Canada: A New Deal*, analyses the past and points toward the future. It is the most significant document in Canadian political history since Confederation. It should be reprinted with an updating epilogue.

We Anglos, today, must learn from Quebec, however galling that may be. Quebec the long dominated has become Quebec the teacher, for the moment.

The Parti Quebecois has an able leadership, planning, as *Journal* news columns for June 1990 have documented. No longer is that leadership drawn mainly from the intelligentsia and the young people. A major landslip has occurred. Important segments of the business community have joined the independence movement.

PQ leaders are planning for negotiations with Anglo Canada about division of federal assets and debts in Quebec, customs, duties, defence, currency.

By contrast, Anglo Canada has no united leadership. It rides blindly into the future, sitting backwards on a donkey. It does not initiate, it merely reacts. It has no common vision. It lives by its shopping malls and imported American TV soap operas. About the rest of the world, Anglo Canada is almost as ignorant as the U.S.

Edmonton *Journal*
June 26, 1990

PART II

From Western Canada:
Toward Cross-Disciplinary Holistic Analysis
Cases and Disciplines of Change

Book Reviews

I N THESE REVIEWS, it is not enough to consider the intellectual content by itself. Rather, I try to place that intellectual work in an historical context, changing and conflict-ridden. For example, it is not enough to study Plato's philosophy without placing it in the setting of his conservative, elitist landlord class of Athens; and considering also the place of Athens in the Mediterranean world.

For another example, in our own day the context may be the emergence of capitalism from feudalism, the emergence of socialism from capitalism, the development of pre-industrial Third-World nations toward "modernization"–never forgetting that all three of these categories contain numerous variations and internal differentiations, and several kinds of interactive patterns with each other. Last but perhaps not least, all these collectivities today must operate in situations none of them made; hence the stress-generating elements of risk and uncertainty are inherent and often acute.

ANNALS OF THE AMERICAN ACADEMY OF POLITICAL & SOCIAL SCIENCE

Vol. 292 (March, 1954), pp. 188–189

DINO BIGONGIARI (Ed.). *The Political Ideas of St. Thomas Aquinas.* New York: Hafner Publishing Company, 1953. Pp. xxxviii, 217.

The social sciences have long needed a one-volume edition of St. Thomas' writing on man and society. For political science, at least, this book will fill the gap. The text is mostly from the *Summa Theologica*, Part II, with a few pages from *On Kingship*.

More excerpts would have made the book more useful for the other social sciences. Perhaps a later edition may include more of the early chapters of *Kingship*, some of the commentaries, and additional "questions" on law and ethics, especially those on heresy, war, equity, and precepts of justice (*S.T.*, II-II). Even for political science the present selection is a bare minimum. The editor's excellent preface, however, rounds out a full picture of St. Thomas' political thought. But no effort is made to relate Aquinas either to the history of social theory or to the society that produced him.

St. Thomas (d. 1274) was the master theologian and philosopher of western Europe's later middle ages. The isolated rural community, the social basis of early medieval culture, was being transformed by the renewed rise of town life and commerce. The transition from Greco-Roman urban society to early medieval rural society had involved the triumph of other-worldly over worldly values. As Augustine epitomizes the world-outlook or ideology of that earlier era, so Thomas expresses the spirit of the later.

The eleventh-century rebirth of urbanizing trends meant on the ideological side a revival of secular values and a rediscovery of classical philosophy, especially Aristotle's. Thirteenth-century western Europe was something of a balance of rural and urban elements, and so was its philosophy. In reconciling the rival Augustinian and Aristotelian dogmas, Thomas combined two great traditions of thought: Christian supernaturalism and Greek rationalism. The framework of his cosmology is Christian; its political content, chiefly Aristotelian. Yet his work is an organic synthesis, a whole greater than its parts.

That the West in this era of revolution and reaction should show renewed interest in Thomist orthodoxy is not surprising. At least four one-volume excerpts have been published in English since 1948. The Modern Library and Everyman editions are mainly theological in content. The Blackwell selection has the best coverage of Aquinas' political thought, but it prints only the conclusions of the "Questions." This Hafner version, fortunately, includes the arguments as well as the conclusions. Its text is the official Dominican translation revised and clarified by the editor.

No single book can convey adequately the structure of St. Thomas' immense work–the *Summa Theologica* alone runs to a score of volumes. The present edition, despite its brevity, is the best short introduction to the political theory of Thomas Aquinas now available in English.

University of Pennsylvania

SCIENCE AND SOCIETY

                                              Vol. XXIII, Summer, 1959

FERDINAND TÖNNIES. *Community and Society: Gemeinschaft und Gesellschaft.* Translated and edited by Charles P. Loomis. East Lansing, Michigan: Michigan State University Press, 1957. Pp. xii, 298.

Loomis' out-of-print 1940 translation of Tönnies' *Gemeinschaft und Gesellschaft*, first published in the United States as *Fundamental Concepts of Sociology*, has now been reprinted in a re-arranged edition, with a new preface by R. Heberle and a partly new introduction by the editor. The foreword is by P. A. Sorokin. In format and readability, the new volume is a considerable improvement over the 1940 version. We are greatly indebted to Professor Loomis for making available once again this minor classic of modern sociological thought.

Gemeinschaft und Gesellschaft was originally published in 1887, when the author was in the early years of his long academic career (ended by the Nazis in 1933) at the University of Kiel. Tönnies (1855–1936) came from a prosperous peasant family, with ties to the commercial bourgeoisie. He grew up where he could observe the emergence of urban capitalistic enterprise from the relatively self-sufficient agrarian peasant economy. His intellectual orientation, and indirectly his subject matter, was drawn from the great social transition in western Europe, variously described by other writers as a movement from feudalism to capitalism (Marx), from status to contract (Maine), and from the simple to the complex (Spencer).

Tönnies' attitude toward this great transformation of European civilization was, on the one hand, analytical. The best known of his analytical concepts are *Gemeinschaft* and *Gesellschaft*, commonly translated as "community" and "society." These are polarized models – theoretical constructs rather than empirical phenomena. The social organization of a given group may be classified as *Gemeinschaft*-like to the degree that it includes such elements as family relationships, traditional folk customs, close-knit neighborhood ties, and face-to-face contacts. It may be classed as *Gesellschaft*-like to the extent that it involves such elements as rationality, formalized conventions, and limited-purpose contractual relationships. Any social organization must include both types of relationships. Neither type, Tönnies emphasized, constitutes by itself a viable social entity.

On the other hand, Tönnies' attitude toward the modern industrial revolution in Europe contained an element of romantic nostalgia for the *Gemeinschaft* sort of social relationship. Like Tolstoy and Gandhi, Tönnies seems to have reacted to modern industrialism with a certain antipathy toward the new urbanism, and with a backward-glancing yearning for the simpler life of an over-idealized earlier age. This reaction, however, was a minor aspect of his thought. Tönnies' main interest was the application of social science to the "social question" of the present.

How useful are Tönnies' two key concepts today? That they have attained considerable vogue, especially in American sociology, is evident. Certain aspects of the transition from peasant agrarian societies – or from nonliterate hunting and gathering societies – to urban-industrialism can be described, roughly, as a shift from a relative prevalence of *Gemeinschaft*-like relationships toward a pattern wherein *Gesellschaft*-like relations become increasingly prominent. But the *Gemeinschaft-Gesellschaft* approach does not include all the relevant social processes and relationships. And those it does include are arbitrarily abstracted from their concrete historical and geographic setting. Useful and discerning when employed as an auxiliary method, the *Gemeinschaft-Gesellschaft* typology by itself is transhistorical. In other words, it describes social change in such broad terms that it loses the greater part of what should be the heart of social science – analysis of the structure, functioning, and above all the evolution of concrete personalities, institutions, communities, and societies.

Let us illustrate. There is probably no society in the world today which is not characterized in some degree by a trend from *Gemeinschaft* to *Gesellschaft*. This statement can be applied to African tribes, American farming communities, villages in India, the Chinese nation, Russia, and so on. But what of the differences among these societies? What of their origins, development, and mutual interactions? Obviously, a generalization which indiscriminately links such disparate entities is of limited practical value for a realistic and historically based social science.

Tönnies himself, of course, never made any such generalization. The preceding paragraph merely epitomizes the characteristically wooden analyses of social change found in most American textbooks of introductory sociology. Those analyses often borrow heavily from Tönnies' terminology, but ever so lightly from his insight.

Perhaps our real problem is to explain why modern sociology, especially American sociology, has paid so much attention to the concepts of *Gemeinschaft* and *Gesellschaft*, and so little to the other phases of Tönnies' work.

Tönnies learned a great deal from Hobbes, and probably even more from Marx. He accepted Marx's historical materialism while firmly opposing revolution. His 1926 work on progress and social evolution shows a clear sense of the movement of modern capitalism toward socialism. It shows, too, an awareness of the significance of class strife, and of the increasing destructiveness of modern war under capitalism. Here we may observe in Tönnies a vein of pessimism (or should we say, realism?) similar to that which crops out occasionally in the writings of Thorstein Veblen. Tönnies surmised that centuries of dissolution might attend and follow the impending death of European culture, before the latter could be succeeded by a "universal culture of humanity."

It is regrettable that *Community and Society* is the only book by Tönnies available in English. Interested readers can find a fragment of his 1926 *Fortschritt und Soziale Entwicklung* translated in the American journal, *Social Forces*, Vol. XIX, 1940.

Posterity may yet decide that Tönnies' chief contribution was to applied rather than to theoretical sociology. Such a verdict would reverse the prevailing American estimate of Tönnies. But it would probably accord with Tönnies' own belief, and practice, that the prime responsibility of the social scientist is to come to grips with the basic problems of his time.

Although there are many useful and subtle insights scattered throughout the book, *Community and Society* seems destined to be set down as a work primarily of interest to professional historians of social thought. Its numerous short chapters hang together but loosely, and they contain a great variety of economic, philosophical, legal, artistic, and other material. Indeed, it is a considerable achievement on the part of the editor and translator that we now have at our disposal such a readable and well annotated version of this work.

Saskatoon, Canada

SCIENCE AND SOCIETY
Vol. XXVII, Fall, 1963

FERDINAND TÖNNIES. *Custom: An Essay on Social Codes.* Translated by A. Farrell Borenstein. Glencoe: The Free Press, 1961. Pp. 151.

First published in Germany in 1909, this essay is an extension of Tönnies' leading work, *Gemeinschaft und Gesellschaft* (1887). An American translation of that earlier book was published as *Community and Society* in 1940 and 1957, and was reviewed in these pages in 1959.

It is important to recognize that *Gemeinschaft* and *Gesellschaft* are analytical concepts or "ideal types" of social relationship. They do not refer to actual groups or societies, but only to analytical elements of social organization. A group may be characterized as *Gemeinschaft*-like to the extent that its internal social relationships are face-to-face, intimate, long-lived, and based on family, neighborhood, or tradition. Its social relationships may be defined as *Gesellschaft*-like to the extent that they are limited, formalized, impersonal, contractual. Both types of relationship, Tönnies held, are essential to every concrete group; neither type by itself constitutes a viable social entity.

Like Maine, Gierke, Spencer, Marx and Weber, among others, Tönnies sought to illuminate nothing less than the great social transition of modern Europe—from rural peasantry to urban industrialism. This transition, and its attendant social problems and tensions, formed the background of Tönnies' particular studies. Unfortunately, his two sociological books thus far translated into English do not adequately convey the breadth of his interests.

Aimed at educated general readers rather than at academic specialists, *Custom* was written near the middle of the author's long career at Kiel. (He was dismissed by the Nazis in 1933.) That the text is broken only by asterisks every few pages may make it difficult for some readers to grasp the "parts and whole" of this essay.

Tönnies viewed "custom" as a key characteristic of social orders that are predominantly *Gemeinschaft*-like. He distinguished three meanings of custom: a factual regularity of behavior, a self-imposed norm, and a "willed" behavior-pattern rooted in the collective sentiment or "natural will" of the folk. The book deals with the third meaning.

Following the introductory definitions is a long section (pp. 41–67) relating custom to tradition. Here Tönnies discusses customary reverential attitudes of young people toward their elders, of subjects toward rulers, of the living toward the dead. He next takes up customs regarding women's roles, rights, and dress. "Custom has a pronounced partiality for women" (p. 68). The author was considerably influenced here by Bachofen, whose matriarchal theories, however, have not weathered subsequent criticism. Various other domestic customs are described (pp. 86–103)—family holidays, marriage and reproduction, birthday gifts, drinking, and the like. The views of Spencer and Jhering are criticized (pp. 103–118), followed by a fifteen-page discussion of dress, fashion, and etiquette. Although much use is made of examples, these are typically abstract and drawn from literature, rather than presented in the context of a specific historical society.

The emotional overtones of Tönnies' treatment of custom are worth noting. "As a rule, custom gives preference to supporting the preserving and peaceful instincts and in the course of human development, so far as this allows the *humane* to grow in men, does so more and more. . . . Custom is ever directed toward fraternal fellowship, cooperation and mutual aid . . . the dignity and honor of labor, as in the earlier times the custom of the guilds" (pp. 101, 103).

In the final section (pp. 133–146), Tönnies draws a series of contrasts between *Gemeinschaft*-like and *Gesellschaft*-like social orders. As an interpretive summing-up, this is one of the great passages in modern social science. Balanced insights, contrasts, and the quietly phrased personal hopes for the future course of social evolution–all these mark the hand of a master artist.

Tönnies' main theme is the inevitable advance of urban-industrial society at the expense of the stable and integrated rural community. His mildly romantic attachment for *Gemeinschaft* sharpened his feeling for the inherent tragedy of "progress," yet never outweighed his basic realism. "The state serves progress, the development of independent personalities, but always," he noted sadly, "at the expense of the folk and their *gemeinschaftlich* cooperative life. It is futile to lament this. The more one understands the inner necessity of the process, the more his lament will be silenced. But he does not need to suppress a sense of the tragic in the course of things. . . ." (pp. 137–138). The shortcomings of *Gesellschaft* could be transcended, he felt, by major economic reforms along co-operative lines, and by the growth of rational planning and ethics.

The translator's work has been well done, and Heberle's introduction is very helpful. Even though it is not one of Tönnies' major works, it was well worth translating. We may hope that other books by Tönnies will be published in English before long–particularly his *Kritik der öffentlichen Meinung* (1922), *Fortschritt und soziale Entwicklung* (1926), and *Geist der Neuzeit* (1935).

Saskatoon, Canada

THE ANNALS OF THE AMERICAN ACADEMY OF POLITICAL AND SOCIAL SCIENCE

January, 1960

W. LLOYD WARNER. *The Living and the Dead: A Study of the Symbolic Life of Americans.* (Yankee City Series, Vol. 5.) New Haven, Conn.: Yale University Press, 1959. Pp. xii, 528.

Nearly twenty years separate the publishing of the initial and this final volume of the Yankee City Series. Surely no other community study of this generation has had so much influence on sociologists in particular and on intellectuals in general as has this analysis of a small city on the North Shore of Massachusetts–Newburyport.

Part I of this book deals with the colorful career of Yankee City Mayor "Biggy" Muldoon. His successes and defeats are described in terms of kinship, class, and other symbols.

Part II is a study of the city's 1930 tercentenary celebration. This is perhaps the best part of the book. A great number of ceremonies, historical reconstructions, and other activities comprising the festival are analyzed with reference to the status and myths of the participating groups. In the symbolic representations of the past are indirectly expressed the social organization, aspirations, and anxieties of the present.

Part III turns to the symbolic meanings of Memorial Day, Abraham Lincoln, funeral rites, and the cult of the dead. In Part IV are discussed both sympathetically and analytically the symbols of Protestant and Catholic Christianity–its buildings, ceremonies, and social organization.

The last section on methods of studying social symbolism will appeal mainly to specialists. The other parts, although they seem unduly long and not always clearly organized, should interest not only social scientists but also many laymen.

Such limitations in the Yankee City study stem largely from the one-place, one-time approach characteristic of American community studies. In a modern industrial society, however, many if not most of the decisive forces in a locality are manifestations or local variations of the structure and processes of the national society.

For the theoretical framework of his study of symbolism, Warner relies mainly on the generalizing, nonhistorical approach of such writers as Frazer, Durkheim, Robertson, Smith, Radcliffe-Brown, and Freud. "The influence of the moral order on the creation and maintenance of symbol systems [is emphasized], the influence of the human species as an (organic) animal organization is also stressed. . . . Most religious beliefs are fundamentally based on the simple realities and on the relations of family deities" (pp. 447, 506). In practice, however, Warner devotes much attention to class and economic factors as well as to moral and familial elements.

This book is a fitting conclusion to a monumental community study.

Center for Community Studies
University of Saskatchewan

SCIENCE AND SOCIETY

Vol. XXIV, Summer, 1960

M. HALBWACHS. *The Psychology of Social Class.* Translated by C. Delavenay. Glencoe: The Free Press, 1958. Pp. xvii, 142.

Maurice Halbwachs (1877–1945) was probably the leading sociologist of France, and therefore an eminent figure in European social science, between the wars. Strongly influenced by his early teacher, Bergson, under whose influence he wrote a monograph on Leibnitz, Halbwachs later moved into the fields of sociology and social psychology. Here his chief mentor was Durkheim, who died in 1917. Among the one-time students or associates of Durkheim were such well-known names as Mauss, Hubert, Maunier, Bouglé, Fauconnet, and Granet. Halbwachs may perhaps be considered as the chief second-generation exponent—by no means an uncritical one—of the Durkheimian approach to sociology. He taught for many years at Strasbourg, and later at the Sorbonne. Arrested by the Nazis in 1944, Halbwachs' tragic death occurred six months later at Buchenwald.

Halbwachs' early writings in social science appeared in *L'Année sociologique*, a serial edited mainly by Durkheim during the dozen or so years before World War I. This publication printed a few well-known original monographs and a great number of long reviews of scholarly works in every field of social science. Indeed, merely to glance over the tables of contents of these volumes is to look at a synopsis of European and North American intellectual life at the turn of the present century. Beginning in 1903, Halbwachs' reviews appeared chiefly in the sections devoted to economics, statistics, population, and social structure, the editorial responsibility for which was often shared by Durkheim, Halbwachs, and the economist, Simiand, among others.

The first important sociological work by Halbwachs was *La classe ouvrière et les niveaux de vie* (1913). This study was updated and expanded in scope in his *L'évolution des besoins dans les classes ouvrières* (1933). He published several works on statistical methods – in fact, Halbwachs is considered by some writers to be the leading statistician among the French sociologists of his time. But the book for which he is best known is undoubtedly *Les causes du suicide* (Paris, 1930). This classic study was originally intended simply to bring up to date the pioneering work of Durkheim in 1897. But the increases of data and the advances in statistical methods since Durkheim's day demanded a new work. Halbwachs broadened his analysis to include countries and factors not available to Durkheim. He modified considerably the conceptual apparatus used by his great predecessor. The result was that this 520-page monograph, along with Dublin's statistical *To Be or Not To Be* (1933), stands today as the leading sociological analysis of suicide. The only major development in the study of suicide since Halbwachs' work has been in the area of individual psychology and psychoanalysis. That area has so far proven to be the only significant gap in Halbwachs' treatment.

The Psychology of Social Class, although translated only recently, dates from the late 1930s. We may wonder why this book was chosen for translation, for in more ways than one, it is a very thin work.

Since the last war a considerable vogue for translation of sociological works, mainly French and German, has been evident in the United States. Most of the translations were published in their original languages one or two generations ago. In part, this tendency represents a welcome broadening of perspective on the part of American scholars. It may also mark a step in the legitimation of American sociology, a relative newcomer on the American academic scene. An intellectual pedigree for a new discipline may be as important as an ancestral tree for a family "on the make." And what pedigree could be more respectable than one including the names of Durkheim and Max Weber? It would be ungracious to suggest that the vogue for translations reflects any lack of linguistic facility on the part of American social scientists.

Yet one other aspect of the penchant for translations may deserve our notice. That is the political aspect. While the Left is represented among the translations – some of Kautsky's works, for instance, have lately been reprinted – books with rightist implications of affinities are far more numerous. Surely the American cult of Weber and Durkheim is partly nourished by indigenous conditions in American society – conditions which foster idealist, psychological tendencies in intellectual life.

Perhaps, then, Halbwachs' *Psychology of Social Classes* offered itself as an appropriate translating and publishing undertaking – only 142 pages long, linked to an eminently respectable school, written by a highly respected author, and appealing to a ready-made market. Of course, we welcome its appearance in English. Yet we may nonetheless regret that the work of a scholar so eminent as Halbwachs is represented in translation by one of his relatively minor productions, while such incontestably major works as his monographs on suicide and levels of living remain untranslated.

Four essays, each dealing with a major social class, make up the greater part of *The Psychology of Social Class*. Most of the empirical data are drawn from modern France. Yet the book does not convey a clear impression of the life circum-

stances of any of the classes. One feels baffled by the desultory nature of
Halbwachs' descriptions. The few statistics are poorly presented—an astonish-
ing performance for a statistician of his stature. The author's experience with
the social life he writes about seems slight—as if his four classes were viewed
from an armchair in an ivory tower.

Halbwachs discusses first the peasant class. His next essay, on the entrepreneurs, contrasts the early-modern bourgeoisie—preoccupied with security and
tradition—with the latter-day capitalist, bent on unlimited profit and innovation.
The author leans heavily on Sombart and Weber, who idealistically attribute that
great change to shifts in moral and religious attitudes. That Halbwachs found
a contemporary trend toward social conscience among big industrialists (p. 65)
suggests how little he understood the social forces which finally engulfed him.

The third class described is the working class, seen from afar. The final essay
deals with such "intermediary" groups as the artisans and small traders, the
clerks, and the lower ranks of the civil service.

Indeed, the book as a whole is little more than a commentary upon the work
of other writers, the validity of whose viewpoints is often highly debatable. It
contains no original ideas and no new material. Let us hope that the main works
of Maurice Halbwachs will soon appear in English, in order that we may see
the achievement of this scholar in true perspective.

Saskatoon, Canada

SCIENCE AND SOCIETY

Vol. XXVI, Spring, 1962

MAURICE HALBWACHS. *Population and Society: Introduction to Social Morphology.*
Translated by O. D. Duncan and H. W. Pfautz. Glencoe: The Free Press, 1960.
Pp. 207.

Halbwachs' brief essay was first published as *Morphologie sociale* in Paris in
1938. This study in the Durkheim tradition of French social science is probably
the leading work on the relations between social organization and population.

As Halbwachs uses the term, morphology refers to the structure of society,
including the spatial distribution of its population in different geographic
milieux, its age and sex composition, migrations, birth and death rates, and so
on. The author sees these material facts as the physical forms—manifestations,
we might almost say—of collective values and social institutions. "If we fix our
attention on the physical forms of social life, it is in order to discover something
of the collective psychology lying behind them" (p. 41).

In brief, Halbwachs resorts to an interdisciplinary approach, using the sciences of human geography and population to illuminate the study of sociology.
To him as to his mentor Durkheim, the heart of sociological reality is "collective
representations," which we may define as social institutions or common-value
systems.

Because of the prominence of ecological and demographic studies in American social science, Halbwachs' book may well attract numerous readers. Its brevity should commend it. Moreover, the translators' preface reviews some French

and English forerunners of the interwar Chicago ecologists and their postwar successors. This intellectual perspective should usefully temper the short-run empiricism prevailing in most North American studies of social ecology and demography.

Of course, the main interest of this publication is the translation itself. Halbwachs begins with a short introduction on the nature of social morphology. The rest of the work is divided into two parts.

Part I deals with some effects of geographic and demographic factors upon religious, political and economic organization.

> The number of the faithful, the space occupied by their groups, their more or less compact formations, the cohesion of the ecclesiastical organization—all these give an initial and already sufficiently expressive insight into religious activity. The same characteristics observed in the political body show us its cohesion, at what point the rights and duties of the citizens are recognized, affirmed, and imposed throughout this body, and what common spirit circulates throughout all its territory, animating and supporting the great public functions. Finally, in economic life, by observing the size of the enterprises and the extent, the numerical importance, and the distribution of social classes, we will know how the production and distribution of wealth is organized within the society. In each particular domain social activity thus builds structures on which it leans as on a system of well coordinated customs. These forms of society well express its spirit. They result from its attitudes, from the reflection of its legislators, and from its experiences as well. It is in them that the meaning of its activity is most clearly perceived (pp. 75 f.).

The essentially idealist nature of the Durkheim tradition is clearly apparent in this passage. So, too, is the cursory nature of Halbwachs' work. Nowhere does the author apply systematically the analytical methods he recommends.

Part II, nearly two-thirds of the book, deals with demography. First, some of the more static aspects of population, by continents, from 1650 to 1929 are summarized. Cities are compared in terms of types—administrative, commercial, producing, residential.

Next is taken up the more dynamic elements of population, such as migration, crude birth and death rates, gross and net reproductive rates. Throughout, Halbwachs' procedure is to emphasize concepts rooted in abstract logic, with a sprinkling of empirical data to illustrate his definitions, an interesting anticipation of Parsonianism.

The theoretical keynote of Halbwachs' treatment of these topics is the social conditioning of demographic and biological phenomena. For example: "The restriction of births is certainly a collective phenomenon. It appears to us that it must be explained primarily by the development of great cities" (p. 137). If the author's general orientation seems correct by today's standards of professional knowledge, his detailed theses do not fare equally well. The following statement would hardly meet with unqualified support from contemporary demographers and sociologists. "Jostling against one another in these new and large compact cities, men began to feel that they could remain in them only on the condition that they not multiply too rapidly—a feeling that was, perhaps, in part economically motivated, but that in itself was only an instinctive reaction to a new population structure" (p. 139). This type of criticism could be aimed at many of Halbwachs' specific propositions.

What is the value of this book for readers today? It lies partly, of course, in its historical interest, for it illustrates a certain phase of intellectual development in French social thought. It has value, too, for its cross-disciplinary treatment of sociological and demographic phenomena. Scholars may derive from this sketchy essay of Halbwachs a clearer over-view of certain phases of a sociology of population than they can get from (let us say) T. L. Smith, although the latter is far superior to Halbwachs' in empirical analysis. Let us add that we need to master the viewpoints of both Halbwachs and Smith.

But we must also recognize the limitations of a Halbwachs. That an essay written a generation ago should seem worth translating – an essay which is much less important than the author's still untranslated greatest work – is suggestive. It suggests an affinity between the static idealism of Durkheim and Halbwachs and the drift of contemporary American academic social science. As the translators say, Halbwachs' book on population is sketchy. We think it is not only sketchy, but also definitive. By this we mean that its abstract, qualitative, non-historical approach to social phenomena can be developed no further. Demographic phenomena are most meaningful when interpreted in the context of specific historical societies in particular regions at a particular stage of their evolution. The course started by Halbwachs does not lead in that direction.

Center for Community Studies
University of Saskatchewan

ANNALS OF THE AMERICAN ACADEMY OF POLITICAL AND SOCIAL SCIENCE

July, 1963

BRIAN JACKSON and DENNIS MARSDEN. *Education and the Working Class: Some General Themes Raised by a Study of 88 Working-Class Children in a Northern Industrial City.* New York: Monthly Review Press, 1962. Pp. ix, 268.

In "Marburton," a small and prosperous industrial city in northern England, roughly three-quarters of the 1951 labor force was working-class. Yet working-class families supplied only one-third of the students successfully graduating from the city's best academic high schools. For most British young people, those State-supported high schools – called "grammar schools" in England – are the main avenue to universities and the professions. Despite the 1944 abolition of fees for grammar school, the middle-class character of those schools has evidently not been greatly altered. Why do so few working-class students get through the academic high schools? To cast light on this problem, the authors undertook an intensive study of 10 middle-class and 88 working-class graduates of Marburton grammar schools. They chose their cases from the lists of those graduating around 1950, to permit follow-up of their subjects' higher education and job careers. Lengthy interviews were conducted separately with the graduates and their parents.

Middle-class families, the authors found, have educational traditions and resources to pass on to their children "in a host of small but telling ways" (p. 42).

Usually working with the school, but sometimes against it if necessary, these parents could steer their children through many a threatening social and educational crisis. They would endow their offspring, not with money, but with "social capital," in the form of ability to use the educational apparatus as an avenue to middle-class jobs and status.

What were the parental families of the 88 working-class students like? In general they were smaller families, from mixed residential districts permitting contacts with middle-class children or families. A few were "sunken middle-class," re-establishing themselves by State education of their children. More often, they were upper working-class—for example, foremen. Sometimes one parent had been to grammar school. Another index—the parents were often leaders in local voluntary organizations. In brief, the successful working-class children had important family pressures behind them. The educational success of these 88 children moved them from working-class to middle-class status. What this upward social mobility—symbolized by new manners, new accents, new friends, new values—meant for relations with parents, with the home neighborhood, with the Labour Party—these complex problems are traced by the authors with profound and sensitive insight. "Most wish to forget" (p. 193).

This book is notable for its concern with practical public policy, as well as for its keen analytical insights. This is in keeping with the orientation of the sponsoring organization, the London Institute of Community Studies. Part II of the study offers socially useful suggestions on school and record-keeping, giving more information on schools and careers to parents, extending student leadership and responsibility downward a year or two from the senior year, and so on. Above all, say the authors, let us accept working-class life as part of the broad "culture" which Matthew Arnold saw as "the best knowledge and thought of the time." Let the school be less exclusively a screening and indoctrinating device for narrowly middle-class values.

So, we say again, this is a notable book. It deals, though on a small scale, with a great issue. It introduces the reader to key British studies on that issue—for instance, the Crowther and Floud Studies. The questions it confronts, and perhaps some of the answers, are relevant to North American experience, and it is a clear, simply written book.

Center for Community Studies
University of Saskatchewan

CANADIAN JOURNAL OF AGRICULTURAL ECONOMICS

October, 1963

A. R. DESAI. *Rural Sociology in India.* Bombay: The Indian Society of Agricultural Economics, 3rd Edition, 1961. Pp. xxix, 730.

This book seeks the social reconstruction of India through rural sociology. In the first 140-page section, the author, strongly influenced by Sorokin and Zimmerman, maps out the main aspects of Indian society. These are not described; often they are not defined. But the importance of studying them is emphasized as the best way to evolve "a scientific programme of the reconstruction of the rural society" (p. 133).

The rest of the book consists of readings on Indian society by various Indian and Western scholars. Demographic and geographic analyses of India are followed by an historical section. The readings from some of the authors—Kosambi, for example—seem too brief to convey adequately their thought. More attention is naturally given to rural villages, tribes and stratification. Here again one could wish for longer excerpts. Chatterji's paper on agricultural labor and contemporary land reforms is a happy exception.

Nearly half of Dr. Desai's book deals with problems of contemporary agrarian change. The author's masterful analysis (pp. 546–560) of India's Community Development projects is relevant far beyond India. There are similarly incisive reviews by Thorner, Gadgil, Shah and others, of efforts for voluntary ethical reform from above—the Bhoodan (land-gift) and Sampittidan (profit-sharing) movements. The last section, Rural Society in Transition, is especially valuable.

Government and other reform "measures have failed because they only benefit those farmers who are in a sound economic position. . . . The co-operative societies only favor the clever farmers. . . . The upper classes tend to circumvent all the protective measures devised by the Government to help the [rural] working classes, or to turn these same measures to their own profit." (pp. 719–720).

The earlier sections on India before independence could well be made more concrete by adding selections on caste by such writers as Gait, Max Weber, Senart, and Hutton. An historical and sociological over-view of the last two centuries would also help the Western reader, whose understanding of colonialism cannot be taken for granted. Goshal or the early Nehru come to mind as possible sources.

This book is a major work. It should be widely read in Canada, not only as an authoritative book on contemporary India, but as an important contribution to the comparative study of rural change. In the latter context, this book is relevant for Canadian problems of rural development.

Centre for Community Studies
Saskatoon, Canada

ANNALS OF THE AMERICAN ACADEMY OF POLITICAL AND SOCIAL SCIENCE

Vol. 359, May, 1965

IRVING LOUIS HOROWITZ (Ed.). *The New Sociology: Essays in Social Science and Social Theory in Honor of C. Wright Mills.* New York: Oxford University Press, 1964. Pp. xv, 512.

In recent years, symposia like *Sociology Today* have been published as authoritative summaries of current thinking and research in the various fields of sociology. Without detracting from the usefulness of such works, it can still be said that they seldom deal directly with what sociology is not, yet might be. In brief, they are orthodox rather than critical. The present volume is a good companion piece to set beside the official symposia, because it injects into the picture some searching criticisms of current trends in social science. It is also in its own right a good summary of research on certain highly significant social problems.

The introductory paper by the editor develops several of Mills' ideas on the shortcomings of "grand theory" and "abstract empiricism." In the best tradition of Veblen, it sketches the recruitment and training of sociologists, and it similarly criticizes "middle-range" theory and research–hitherto a popular escape from the dilemma posed by the Parsonian Scylla and the International Business Machine (IBM) Charybdis. In general, the contributors to this volume agree that the master problems of sociology are the changing forms of capitalism and socialism, the rise of new nations, automation, racism, anomie and alienation, war and peace, and the like. They also believe that sociology should be a critic, rather than a tool of social policy.

Ten contributions deal with various aspects of Mills' work as a social scientist. Dowd's comparison of Mills and Veblen will interest many. Other colleagues and one-time students of Mills give us firsthand glimpses into his ways of tackling such problems as class, power, trends in labor, Cuba, World War III, his use of the "outrageous question," his contempt for the "trivialization" of social science. This section is occasionally repetitious; it is also exciting.

The greater part of the volume is a collection of eighteen papers on a variety of subjects. Gouldner's iconoclastic analysis of Weber and the myth of a value-free sociology will probably rattle a few china closets. Scott and Mizruchi trace some sources of alienation in modern society, and McCord considers similar trends in the cities of the new nations. Miller's paper on race and poverty conveys a sense of the urgency of political change in the United States. Two well-known British scholars, Bottomore and Worsley, scrutinize incisively the bureaucratic elite in France and colonialism in northern Saskatchewan.

This book is a fitting tribute to Mills, because it exemplifies the historically oriented, humanistic social science for which Mills worked–a science that focuses critically yet with commitment upon the great issues of our era.

University of Calgary
Calgary, Canada

CHOICE (AMERICAN LIBRARY ASSOCIATION)
_____

December, 1968

T. B. BOTTOMORE. *Critics of Society: Radical Thought in North America.* Pantheon, 1968. Pp. 150.

Few books of 150 pages contain as much information and arresting interpretative insights as does this one. Its 139 pages of text (plus a select bibliography and index) brilliantly summarize a century of North American social dissent. Its key feature is continual reference of new ideas to changing economic and social realities presented as the source and context of ideologies. Like Myrdal a generation ago, Bottomore doubtless owes to his foreign origin many of his fresh insights about the American experience. The main scope is the last century of American social evolution. A chapter is devoted to recent Canadian dis-

sent: chiefly Social Credit, the Co-operative Commonwealth Federation, and nationalism in French Canada. Canada seems inadequately comprehended, almost
an afterthought. Neither Innis, Fowke, nor Grant is mentioned. With respect
to the U.S., Bottomore's treatment before World War II is both original and detached. But it is less successful for the last generation, i.e., there is no reference
to W. A. Williams or to the *Monthly Review.* Nonetheless, few other works so
successfully convey to the general reader a clear sense of "the present as history." Favorable comparison with R. Hofstadter's intellectual histories is immediately suggested. A generous expansion of the book might well put it in the
same class with such standard treatises as those of Parrington (*Main Currents
in American Thought,* 1958), Edmund Wilson (*To the Finland Station,* 1953), and
F. O. Matthiesson (*American Renaissance,* 1941). Even as it now stands, it distills
the spirit and main movements of a great historical epoch.

CHOICE (AMERICAN LIBRARY ASSOCIATION)

October, 1974

A. M. SHAH. *The Household Dimension of the Family in India: A Field Study in
a Gujarat Village and a Review of Other Studies.* California, 1974. Pp. 281.

This is the best work to appear yet on the organization of the Indian family.
It is particularly valuable as a corrective to simplistic notions about the decline
of the extended family in urban environments. There is also a noteworthy discussion of the pitfalls in using statistical data from such macro studies as the
census of India. Useful too is the discussion of the different developmental sequences a given family may pass through over time. Advanced students, for
whom the book is primarily intended, will welcome the extensively annotated
bibliography. This volume should be a part of any specialized India collection.

CHOICE (AMERICAN LIBRARY ASSOCIATION)

November, 1970

JOHN C. McKINNEY and EDWARD A. TIRYAKIAN (EDS.). *Theoretical Sociology; Perspectives and Developments.* Appleton-Century-Crofts, 1970. Pp. 538.

This symposium is the latest and easily the most authoritative reference volume on the present state of sociological theory in anglophone North America.
Twenty well-known writers contribute papers on nearly every major viewpoint
in academic sociology, except the dialectical—a glaring but standard omission.
The older orthodoxies, such as structural-functionalism and the Parsonian four-
function paradigm, are restated in somewhat refined forms. More interesting,
perhaps, are indications of shifting emphases and new directions. Comparative
analysis, systems theory, conflict and change come in for more attention than
would have been the case a decade ago. Ethnomethodology, one of the newest
developments, is given a substantial exposition, and so is "futurology," which
has attracted a few sociologists during the last five years. The Douglas paper
on "deviance and order" is one of the best: it effectively criticizes the unsatis-

factory nature of traditional approaches to deviance. Finally, there are papers relating sociology to neighboring disciplines—history, social psychology, social anthropology, and economics. The book is important for advanced students and professional scholars. Much of the language is necessarily technical, but within these limits the style is clear. Likely to overshadow but not displace such earlier symposia as R. Merton's *Sociology Today* (1959). It does for today what *Sociology today* did for the field a decade ago.

CANADIAN STUDIES IN POPULATION

Vol. 1, 1974

JOSEPH HANSEN. *The "Population Explosion": How Socialists View It.* New York: Pathfinder Press, 1970. Pp. 47.

First published in 1960, this bulletin appears to be a second printing rather than a second or revised edition. The political orientation is Trotskyite. The style is "salty" and non-technical.

That the work was written in the late 1950s is reflected in its argument. In brief, the heart of the so-called "population problem" is not the overproduction of people, but the maldistribution of available wealth. The imperialism of capitalist countries is at the bottom of all ills. The main reliance for a solution is placed on technology: food production can be indefinitely increased, once we get rid of capitalism and its shackles—that is, inequitable distribution and artificial scarcity. Socialism is the only answer.

A much emphasized point is, American food productivity has increased faster than population. The differing socio-economic and demographic conditions of the non-industrialized colonial world are not adequately recognized.

The author is obviously familiar with R. Meek's *Marx and Engels on Malthus* (London, 1953). This is good. However, Marx and Engels wrote in the light of conditions prevailing a century ago. In that earlier day, the promise of technological productivity, once freed from its capitalist chains, seemed much brighter than it does today.

The reason is that the heavy impact of waste, pollution, and exhaustion of non-renewable resources is a phenomenon of our own day.

However, the fundamental insights of an updated Marxian perspective should not be obscured by the shortcomings of this bulletin. In a dialectical view, it is necessary to look at the totality of a social system, and it is essential to mutually adjust theory and practice. The experience of the People's Republic of China shows that both an increase of productivity and a decrease of births are complementary imperatives.

Initially, the Chinese Communist Party adhered to a view roughly similar to that expounded by Hansen. By the late 1950s, however, the inherited theory was adapted to reality. The latest reports show that, alone among the peasant societies of East and Southeast Asia (excluding industrialized capitalist Japan)— China has succeeded in decisively reducing its rate of net natural increase, and at the same time increasing its productivity so as to feed its 800 millions. (See Sidel and Sidel, "Delivery of Medical Care in China," *Scientific American*, April, 1974.)

We must go further. Not only are productivity increases and reproduction decreases complementary; they are best achieved under a socialist regime. In 1881, Engels foresaw this great truth. Writing to Kautsky, he said that a socialist society could best achieve a regulated reproduction policy, as well as a planned production program.

Piecemeal projects, such as the two decades of family planning program in India, have had little or no effect on rural birth rates. This is mainly because the total structure of values, life-prospects, and class-caste realities have changed but little (Mamdani, *Myth of Population Control*, New York, 1972). By contrast, in China there has occurred a comprehensive socio-economic and political transformation. This statement does not deny the large elements of continuity between old and new China.

Interested readers may find an updated presentation of official Chinese views on the "population problem" in the *Peking Review* for August 30, 1974. Here is the speech of the head of the Chinese delegation at the United Nations World Population Conference at Bucharest in August, 1974. Like the Hansen pamphlet, the Chinese analysis stressed the effect of imperialism on Third-World poverty, the promise of technological abundance once clear of capitalist restrictions, and the importance of maldistribution of such wealth as is now available in the world. Unlike Hansen, however, the Chinese argument recognized the need for, and implementation of, a policy of reduced birth rates in a socialist context.

If the Hansen essay seems one-sided, even utopian, in its emphasis on the promise of technological abundance, it correctly draws our attention to the necessity of viewing population problems and policies in a total institutional context, both capitalist and socialist. It also shows the inherent racism and colonialism of much Western thinking about the "population explosion." The non-White nations should reduce their birth rates, but not reform their institutions.

The University of Alberta
Edmonton, Alberta, Canada

CANADIAN STUDIES IN POPULATION

Vol. 2, 1975

RICHARD L. CLINTON, WILLIAM S. FLASH and R. KENNETH GODWIN. *Political Science in Population Studies.* Toronto: Lexington Books, D. C. Heath and Company, 1972. Pp. xviii, 156.

It is becoming increasingly apparent that the rigidly compartmentalized social science and life science disciplines in North American universities are not competent to deal with such cross-discipline problems as urban congestion, high-technology pollution, the symbiotic relationship between wealth and poverty both within and among nations, and alternative types of development. This organizational condition tends to cripple the application of university resources to the great tasks of public understanding, participation, and policy-formulation in those and other key crises of our time.

Population factors or "demographic phenomena" are components of most of the aforementioned world problems. It is therefore good news that a few academics, mainly political scientists, are tackling the interface relationships between political science and population. These eight essays stem from a 1971 Political Science/Population workshop at the University of North Carolina.

Bachrach's discussion of how scholars can relate more effectively to public policy-formulation raises many questions and alternative proposals about population and political policy in various countries, without offering conclusions. Saunders' paper explores some implications of seven demogenic phenomena: rapid population growth, population size, dependency ratios, uneven population distribution, the tight balance between food and population, the dampening effect of population parameters on development, and the environmental aspects of over-urbanization and rapid industrialization.

For a comparative account of population policy in India and Pakistan, at the government levels, with speculative comments on political contexts, we may turn to the paper by Finkle. His treatment is neither systematic nor in-depth, but it gets us into Asia.

The absurdities to which quantification has reduced political science in its post-war II behavioural phase are illustrated in the paper by Organski et al. Though admitting the "tenuous" character of their efforts to define "effective population," "national power," and "security," they, nonetheless, advance several indicators and national rankings based on GNP, voting participation, and the ratio of employed non-agricultural workers to total population. They are perplexed (p. 80) by the fact that the United States, a super-power, cannot defeat North (sic!) Vietnam. Perhaps it is too much to expect from Americans, historical understanding of the force of anti-colonial revolutions.

A more hopeful note is struck by Lipsitz, who recalls us to the mainstream tradition of political philosophy. He reviews, too briefly, the ideas of Plato, Aristotle, the modern western liberals, and the Marxists regarding the nature of community, the good life, development and rapid social change. Classic social analysis, wrote C. Wright Mills, has been concerned over the centuries with historical social structures, and has been "of direct relevance to urgent public issues and insistent human troubles" (*Sociological Imagination*, Oxford University Press, 1967, p. 21). Lipsitz verges upon a rediscovery of that classical tradition.

The final paper by Clinton and Godwin recognizes some of the organizational handicaps afflicting North American universities mentioned at the start of this review. Clinton and Godwin do not go far enough. The dry rot of bureaucracy now overlies many universities. Inter-disciplinary research institutes offer one countervailing and promising response. Symposia like this one are further omens of rebirth, whatever their inevitable shortcomings.

What did this particular workshop overlook? There was no adequate input regarding the experience of the People's Republic of China. There was no real comprehension of a dialectical perspective in general, nor of the developing Marxist intellectual tradition in particular. There is an overdose of American ethnocentrism and parochialism.

What was achieved? A dialogue between two major streams of scholarly work was initiated: population experts and political scientists established a small breakthrough, with promise of more to come.

The University of Alberta
Edmonton, Alberta, Canada

CHOICE (AMERICAN LIBRARY ASSOCIATION)

April, 1984

DAVID GEORGE PEARSON and DAVID C. THORNS. *Eclipse of Equality: Social Stratification in New Zealand.* Allen & Unwin, 1983. Pp. 287.

A definitive work on the emerging social and economic structure of New Zealand. It reflects the theoretical orientations of Durkheim, Marx, and Max Weber. All three are critically viewed, hence the book is given a creative and original character. A historical perspective prevails. New Zealand went through its colonial phase, roughly 1840–90. A pastoral economy prevailed between 1890 and 1935, followed by the development of a welfare state. In 1967, New Zealand moved into the global capitalist system. Large-scale organizations and foreign investment became important, displacing the small-town individually owned enterprises. Competition with the cheaper-labor enterprises in Southeast Asia sharpened. Regional disparities are analyzed; the main differences center upon the growing wealth and power of the North Island over the South Island in recent decades. Factors of gender and race are also considered. The status of women is carefully reviewed as well as the status of the native Maori. Both these groups are minorities with respect to social and economic power, although compared to treatment of minorities in North America and most European states, New Zealand's policy regarding the Maori has been exemplary. Tensions between emerging centralism and inherited ideology of localism, always a central theme of New Zealand history, still continue. The style of the book is clear despite its immense detail. For college, university, and public libraries.

CHOICE (AMERICAN LIBRARY ASSOCIATION)

April, 1985

ROKURŌ HIDAKA. *The Price of Affluence.* Kodansha International (dist. by Harper & Row), 1984. Pp. 176.

Though this penetrating book deals only with modern Japan, it has lessons for all other advanced industrial societies. The last quarter-century has seen the rise of Japan to relative affluence as a capitalist giant. But affluence has also brought sharp dilemmas: environmental pollution, corruption, exploitive relations with many Third World nations, and a "controlled" domestic society. Such control is effected by material benefits and a philosophy of comforts rather than by coercion. Japanese education, says Hidaka, produces conformist rather than truly self-reliant adults. Of course, large pockets of poor nonunion workers still remain. Emergent Japan is, however, mainly an economic colossus, expanding overseas and poisoning its environment. Hidaka argues for decentralization, shifting money from the threatening world arms race to poor Third World populations, and cleaning up the environment. One chapter deals with the dreaded Minamata disease—mercury poisoning of animals, fish, and people. Originally published in Japanese in 1980, this 1984 translation is eminently concise and successful. The book is easy to read and to understand. Hidaka makes a large humanistic input that is both imaginative and analytical. For academic libraries, secondary school upward, and public libraries.

University of Alberta

CHOICE (AMERICAN LIBRARY ASSOCIATION)

September, 1984

MANUEL CARBALLO and MARY JO BANE (Eds.). *The State and The Poor in the 1980s.* Auburn House, 1984. Pp. 328.

These 11 essays focus on poverty trends and policies in Massachusetts during the last 15 years. Comparisons with U.S. national data are often made. Most of the authors are staff of the Kennedy School of Government, Harvard. Despite its detail, the book successfully achieves a clear overview of key developments. Its wide scope makes it relevant not only for American readers but also for people in the other English-speaking nations. In 1980 about 10 percent of the Massachusetts population was poor. The rate rose slowly during the 1970s. Seniors, singles, racial minorities (smaller in Massachusetts than in the U.S. as a whole), and female-headed (FH) families with children are overrepresented among the Massachusetts poor. The latter category looms as the largest and the most seriously affected group. Part 1 (three essays) analyzes policies for pre- venting poverty in terms of health, employment, and education. Most of the poor (elders, the disabled, FH families with children) cannot be expected to work. Part 2 (four essays) looks at policies to ameliorate poverty. Income trans- fers work well for short-term poverty. State housing programs, transportation services, and crime patterns are all discussed with reference to the poor. Part 3 (two essays) deals with taxation policies and program planning for coping with poverty. This book is a landmark study. For college, university, and public libraries.

University of Alberta

CHOICE (AMERICAN LIBRARY ASSOCIATION)

June, 1985

GERRY RODGERS. *Poverty and Population: Approaches and Evidence.* International Labour Office, Geneva, 1984. Pp. 213.

Rodgers's book is essentially a review of the relevant literature on relations between poverty and population. It is also a clarification of public policy options. It is a sophisticated and heavily quantitative overview of this wide field. Fertility, mortality, and migration are considered. The author also draws upon other variables such as landholding patterns, natural resources, capital, nutri- tion, occupational patterns, and education. A few conclusions may be cited, not all of them new. For example, higher parental education tends toward re- duced fertility; the poor have lower fertility if nutrition is deficient; lower fer- tility tends to reduce inequality and poverty, but only by a little; lower migration tends to worsen inequality; unwanted children have higher mortality rates. A

socialist model is introduced. "Inequality is less in Eastern Europe, and population growth is also low" (p. 132). In peasant societies, high fertility can benefit
the poor; high mortality favors excessive childbearing. The book suggests that
reductions in poverty and inequality will not much reduce population growth,
but it pays insufficient attention to age structure. An extensive and excellent
bibliography. For every large public and university library.

University of Alberta

CHOICE (AMERICAN LIBRARY ASSOCIATION)

March, 1986

TOM JOE and CHERYL ROGERS. *By the Few for the Few: The Reagan Welfare Legacy.*
Lexington Books, D. C. Heath, 1985. Pp. 163, index.

This condensed book deals with the rising pressures on such hard-core poverty groups as American Blacks, other inner-city groups, female-headed families, farmers. It traces the roots of public policy toward poor people to the 16th-
century Poor Laws of England. The 19th–20th centuries saw a retreat from those
harsh policies. By the 1930s massive federal intervention was necessary: the key
was the 1935 Social Security Act. By the 1950s–60s, public policy moved into
prevention and rehabilitation. These efforts focused on Aid to Families with
Dependent Children. Programs included medical care for the aged and for
welfare clients, food stamps to reduce food costs, housing subsidies. Public costs
rose.

The Reagan administration changed all this. In 1981, benefits and clients of
social programs were heavily cut, in the face of big defense increases, large cuts
in corporate taxes, and the Reagan refusal to consider a tax increase. The book
looks at the effects of the Reagan changes on 10 States and on several localities,
in terms of cases.

The book is clearly written: statistics do not obscure the main arguments.
13.6 million children in the USA are growing up in poverty. Neither the private
sector nor States or localities can cope with this intensifying problem. The
authors conclude that the federal role must be re-expanded, "if democracy is
to prevail over government by the few for the few" (p. 157). They understate their
case.

University of Alberta

CHOICE (AMERICAN LIBRARY ASSOCIATION)

1987

MICHAEL B. KATZ. *In the Shadow of the Poorhouse: a Social History of Welfare in
America.* Basic Books, 1986. Pp. 338, index.

This detailed work puts the American semi-welfare State under a micro-
scope. Two main categories are used. Public assistance is means-tested, stig-
matized and aimed at the very poor. Social insurance is not means-tested; it
includes old-age and disability pensions, and cuts across class lines. Public funds
have always served more people than private funds have.

Part I deals with the poorhouse era, roughly the 19th century. Inherited from early modern England, the poorhouse was meant to limit outdoor or home relief. Yet outdoor relief could not be dispensed with: it was cheaper than institutions. Public opinion came round to keep families together by home relief.

Part II outlines new concepts of childhood, public health and other city reforms emerging in the later 19th century and the pre-New Deal period, as the growth of urban industry brought critical changes in American life.

In Part III is sketched the war on poverty, 1950s–70s, and the attack on welfare in the 1980s. It is a grim prospect. Cuts in public assistance coincided with a deepening depression. The middle class, however, successfully defended social insurance. The author concludes that women and youth still suffer, while the elderly have gained from their pensions. The book is well organized; its many facts make for slow reading.

University of Alberta

CHOICE (AMERICAN LIBRARY ASSOCIATION)

November, 1986

SHELDON H. DANZIGER and DANIEL H. WEINBERG (Eds.). *Fighting Poverty: What Works and What Doesn't.* Harvard, 1986. Pp. 418, index.

A stock-taking volume by social workers, administrators, academics, and other experts, this collection is a critical and condensed review of US approaches to poverty from the 1930s into the 1980s. It surveys a maze of federal, regional, state, and local initiatives and compromises against a background of key social trends. Until the early 20th century, most black and white low-income families lived in two-parent households. By 1940, rates of divorce, female-headed families, and out-of-wedlock births were all rising. Governments reacted partly with bureaucratized policies from above, not always well joined. Among the measures enacted were cash relief, work relief, educational upgrading, food stamps, health services, subsidized housing, student loans, and special programs for youth and the disabled. These essays show that certain categories of the poor have benefited: the aged, the disabled, women with dependent children, and others. Yet poverty in the US has not been overcome or even contained. Jobs now shrink as automation and the arms race expand. Women still face insecurity. Both the business cycle and affirmative action need more attention in a work like this. Too often, as these authors show, ambivalence and backlashes have limited progress in the war on poverty. A distinguished volume for both general and academic readers.

University of Alberta

CANADIAN STUDIES IN POPULATION

Vol. 13 (1), 1986

S. A. SHAH (Ed.). *India: Degradation and Development.* Secunderabad, India: M. Venkatarangaiya Foundation, 1983. Pp. xvi and vii, 609 (2 vols.).

These 23 essays convey a critical but not unanimous overview of basic social and economic trends in India, mainly since World War II. The author is a consulting economist with the United Nations, with long experience in Canadian and American academia.

A keynote paper by the editor outlines two views on the Indian economy. The first is that significant and all-round gains in material productivity and social well-being have occurred. The second is that most of these gains have been limited to the affluent sectors of the rural and urban populations. The editor tilts toward the second viewpoint and the majority of the papers support this perspective.

Certain large realities need to be kept in mind regarding India. A comparative approach is invaluable. According to the Population Reference Bureau 1984 world summary, the mid-1984 population of India is estimated at 746 million. This is the second largest population in the world. The crude birth rate is 34 – in the high range. For China the corresponding rate is 21; for Canada, 15.

Dr. Shah's first volume is devoted primarily to general surveys of contemporary India. D. D. Kosambi's well-known "Notes on the Class Structure of India" (mid-1950s) heads the collection. Kosambi traces the crumbling of Indian feudalism in the 18th and 19th centuries before the onslaught of British imperialism. Now the Indian bourgeoisie rules India. However, a later essay in this volume by P. H. Prasod, "The Rising Middle Peasantry in North India" (late 1970s) calls attention to "semi-feudal blocks" to economic development.

N. K. Chandra writes that a new international economic order means reducing the power of trans-national corporations, new terms of trade between North and South, and greater technical and economic assistance. Few will disagree. He hopefully believes that such measures would speed up third-world economic development. We remain skeptical. The first world is still ruled by corporate greed. If old-fashioned direct imperialism is in full retreat, indirect imperialism or neo-colonialism remains. Indeed, Chandra admits that the mid-1970s breakthrough by O.P.E.C. oil-producing third world countries changed existing realities but little. Oil profits rose for O.P.E.C. nations, but much of the money went for arms, luxury imports for native elites resisting modernization; the Trans-national corporation passed their higher costs to their consumers. The O.P.E.C. masses gained little.

Two regional papers conclude the first volume. S. K. Baruah deals with the impacts of the great migrations of Moslems and Hindus into Assam in India's far northeast corner. K. C. Alexander analyzes the emergence of peasant organizations in Kerala and Tamil Nadu in south India. The most effective organizer was the Communist Party (Marxist) which has a Maoist tilt. The older and more elitist Communist Party of India, Soviet oriented, proved less successful. The Congress Party, India's ruling party since the 1947 independence, refused to organize agricultural tenants and labourers.

Vol. II is divided into two sections: Agrarian development and degradation, and industrial development and degradation. Ashok Rudra's 1978 paper, "Class Relations in Indian Agriculture," bears mention. In capitalist agriculture a surplus is extracted from free sellers of labour-power in a process of commodity production and exchange. The surplus is re-invested. By contrast, in pre-capitalist or feudal agriculture a surplus is extracted through the non-economic coercion of unfree labour, and is dissipated in luxury consumption and unproductive investment. Rudra sees the elite class in Indian agriculture as a mix of feudalism and capitalism.

The agrarian section includes several regional and community studies of land reforms in Harayana, Kerala, West Bengal and Tamil Nadu. The industrial section is keynoted by the all too brief paper by Daniel Thorner: "Economic Realities and the Future of Indian Business" (1977). Among his basic concepts are the close ties between Indian business and the Congress Party, the smallness of the internal market because of low worker and peasant incomes, and the universal desire of business firms for State handouts. Both agricultural and industrial outputs have increased in recent years, but not by much. Land reforms have been largely circumvented. Businessmen, according to Thorner, lack self-confidence and corruption is taken for granted. Labour is limited in its right to strike. Caste, communal and language lines remain strong.

This grim picture is reinforced by Deepak Nayyar, "Industrial Development in India: Reflections on Growth and Stagnation." From 1950 to 1975, industrial production quadrupled, but growth slacked off in the late 1960s. Why this sluggishness, asks Nayyar? He finds his answer in the narrow base of consumer demand, and in the inequitable distribution of income. In both the rural and urban sectors in 1964–65, the richest tenth consumed about a third of industrial production; the bottom half received about a fifth.

The two volumes edited by Dr. Shah convey much information, yet there is a basic unity. India is in mounting trouble. This reviewer notes that in 1945 China and India were both large impoverished peasant societies with high birth rates and low productivity. There were differences, of course – India was the more fractioned of the two, by caste and communalism. But China took itself in hand by means of a mutually consistent package of reforms. India resisted its internal pressures by coercive and repressive measures, especially in the last decade. Utopia is nowhere, to be sure, but the prospects for a harmonious stability in India are not reassuring. Meanwhile we are indebted to Shah for making available to us this insightful collection of papers.

University of Alberta
Edmonton, Alberta, Canada

UNPUBLISHED MANUSCRIPT
April, 1986

Jack Ondrack. *Big Game Hunting in Alberta.* Edmonton: Wildlife Publishing, Ltd., 1985. Pp. 346.

This is a finely crafted book, thoroughly Albertan. It is the first systematic treatise on Alberta big game hunting. Not only is it well written, it is also a notable physical production printed on good paper with a handsome eye-catching cover.

Above all this is an interesting book to read, whether or not the reader happens to be a hunter. Numerous true stories are included about contests between people and animals: the balance sheet is less one-sided than we might expect.

The author grew up in Alberta. He attended university in Edmonton and at Harvard, and now lives in Edmonton. He pursued a highly successful career in private business company management in Canada. He has hunted for several decades in North America and Europe, from the age of six. Hence he is able to offer us comparative insights on public policy and game management in Europe and Canada. He points out, however, that Alberta has the greatest variety of game and environments in North America.

Ondrack has divided most of his book into chapters devoted to a dozen large animals: mountain sheep, goats, black bears and grizzlies, whitetail and mule deer, elk, moose, cats and wolves. Also included is a backward glance at yesterday's hunting of buffalo and caribou.

The basic pattern of these chapters consists of a sub-section on the life cycle of the animal, then sub-sections on the distribution of the animal in Alberta, the history of public policy regarding the animal and the hunting of it. Of course there are variations in details as needed.

The first chapter is a condensed history of hunting and related public policy in Alberta, set against a background of prairie settlement. The development of hide exports is traced. As the white population increased in the later 19th century, and as farming and ranching became established, game populations necessarily receded. Then as now, regulation of hunting by Indians remained an especially difficult problem due in part to its cross-cultural nature.

Along with human settlement and population increase over the past century, technology marked a decisive turning point in the balance between people and game animals. Technology does not refer simply to firearms, but also to the cutting up of animal ranges by roads, rails and fences. Naturally game laws and management become ever more complex.

Especially vivid is Ondrack's chapter on bighorn sheep. To hunt sheep, one must climb high mountains. Just to spot a sheep may take days of grinding effort. Ondrack discusses the merits of hiring outfitters to allow the hunter more time for concentration on hunting. No game is more prestigious than a ram with full-curl horns. That fact, plus the immensely agonizing activity of chasing a magnificent old ram, sometimes invite poaching by wealthy trophy seekers, often from outside Alberta. Demand, money and short supply set the stage for black-market operations.

Hunting mountain goats is also physically demanding. They stay year-round above the tree-line. Inaccessibility is their chief defense against predators. Ondrack conveys clearly the mystique of hunting as well as the technology and logistics.

The book reproduces about two dozen old photographs of hunting scenes and personalities, both Indian and White, of two or three generations ago. Other enhancements are the occasional short poems and black-and-white drawings by the author.

Doubtless the most intriguing chapter in this book is the last one, dealing with the philosophy, psychology and sociology of hunting. The meanings of trophies are further discussed in terms of those fields. Ondrack draws lightly on Freud's Oedipus complex to understand in part the symbolism of horned trophies. He draws more heavily on such factors as social class, supply and demand; he contrasts European with Albertan game management; he mentions the predominance of male and rural hunters; he sketches the organization of the Alberta Fish and Game Association, and its several educational and environmental functions.

In simpler societies, and among certain classes in our own, hunting is food-gathering. It may also be something more: achievement against great odds, coping with the element of uncertainty, seeking a scapegoat, escaping from boredom, macho self-assertion. A man of many talents, Ondrack has given us a creative and germinal book.

University of Alberta

CHOICE (AMERICAN LIBRARY ASSOCIATION)

1987

ROBERT COLQUHOUN. *Raymond Aron.* Sage, 1986. v. 1: *The Philosopher in History, 1905–1955.* Pp. 540. v. 2: *The Sociologist in Society, 1955–1983.* Pp. 680.

Philosopher, sociologist and journalist, Aron (1905–83) was one of the three or four leading intellectuals of France for two generations. He produced an extraordinary flow of articles and books, some translated into eight or nine languages. He defended his doctoral thesis in 1938 at the Sorbonne, where he was Professor of Sociology 1955–68.

A formidable undertaking, Colquhoun's work is mainly an intellectual biography of Aron. As well, it is a condensed political history of France. Aron was ever a moderate westerner and a moderate anti-communist. In the 1930s he studied several years in Germany. He admired England where he spent World War II editing a Free French magazine. To a lesser extent he admired the United States; on one of his trips there, he was a Visiting Researcher at Harvard.

Aron regretted the erosion of the French colonial empire, though he took a pro-Algerian stance when Algeria rebelled. He travelled widely about the world. Yet his insights into the USSR and Cuba remained cloudy. The list of his visiting lectureships and honorary degrees is a long one.

Colquhoun's clearly written book deals effectively with a distinguished personality, a "committed observer." Chronological tables, extensive notes and indices are included in each volume.

University of Alberta

CONTEMPORARY SOCIOLOGY: A JOURNAL OF REVIEWS

Duke University, Durham, N.C., October, 1988

MARLENE SWAY. *Familiar Strangers: Gypsy Life in America.* Champaign: University of Illinois Press, 1988. Pp. xi, 155.

This condensed yet comprehensive study of American Gypsies as a "middleman minority" has several major aspects. It includes comparative and historical dimensions, effectively combined with life-history and community frames of reference. The non-Gypsy author has a lifetime of insightful contacts with Gypsy families and communities culminating in nine years of systematic field work mainly in California and Virginia, with brief sojourns in southern England and Yugoslavia. The monograph is relevant to socialization and the life course, community studies, social control, and comparative and historical sociology.

The present reviewer has visited Gypsy caravans in southern England, eastern Europe and Yugoslavia. Much of Dr. Sway's report can apply to Gypsy life in both socialist and capitalist nations. There are differences, of course.

Gypsies originated in the Untouchable Dom sub-caste of northern India. The traditional occupations of the Dom were metal-working and entertaining. Some 1200 years ago, offshoots of the Dom began a series of migrations north-westward into Persia and beyond. By the 14th century they were nomadic communities in North Africa and southeastern Europe; a century later, in western Europe and Scandinavia. A number of Gypsy wanderers were deported from Europe to the American colonies in the 17th and 18th centuries. More came in the later 19th century with the great migrations from central and eastern Europe.

Dr. Sway estimates the present world population of Gypsies at 8 to 10 millions living in 40 countries, with perhaps a million in the United States. She believes that about half of the latter are urban residents. During World War II around one million Gypsies died in the Nazi death camps. Some of these figures are higher than those found in other sources.

The author's main focus is the internal organization of American gypsy life: kinship, community, social control and values, and economic patterns. Gypsies live in close-knit extended-family networks. Their economic base is small-business, especially the fortune-telling parlor, supplemented by such activities as junk-collection, short-term harvest contracts, welfare when they can get it, and occasional pilfering and begging (usually by children). They move around to take advantage of seasonal opportunities. They avoid settling down and individual wage labor, preferring to work as family groups with the aged and the children participating where they can. Their primary ethos is not work- or education-oriented; it is the survival of traditional Gypsy values and customs. Hence they have a very high illiteracy rate, and they avoid assimilation. Their relations with the host society are therefore uneasy and mutually suspicious.

Some Gypsy activities like crafts, music and folk-dancing are acceptable to the mainstream society; certain other pursuits are "nuisances." Yet Gypsy groups survive despite the absence of written history and a written language. There is an unknown but apparently low rate of defection to which the author alludes but does not analyze in detail.

Dr. Sway reports that Gypsy marriages are patrilocal and arranged by older family members. Economic considerations take priority. Weddings may last three or four days, financed by the groom's extended family along with the bride-price ($5,000 to $30,000). No State license is involved. Female virginity is an absolute; couple dating is taboo. Gypsies socialize at *pomanas*—informal gatherings in a hired hall where interested persons can "look over the field." Married couples use family planning to limit family size. Divorce in the early years of marriage is common; the main contentions are bride-price refund (if the wife is judged at fault) and child custody.

Besides kinship, territoriality is a major principle of Gypsy social organization. The location of fortune-telling parlors is carefully planned to minimize competitive overlapping. The *kumpania* is a territorial group of extended families led by a prestigious chief, ordinarily male. Minor offensives are controlled by such informal sanctions as gossip. For major disputes a *kris* is set up: a public tribunal of two to five prominent males, perhaps with a member from another *kumpania*. The party found guilty must finance the food and liquor for the two- or three-day hearing. Far worse is a judgment of *marime*–impurity due to violation of basic Gypsy norms. This entails social ostracism by other Gypsies–a lasting blot upon a family.

This fascinating study, clearly written, is a fine example of classical social science, with minimal jargon and without verbosity.

University of Alberta

AMERICAN SOCIOLOGICAL REVIEW

1958

MIRIAM CHAPIN. *Quebec Now.* New York: Oxford University Press, 1955. Pp. 185.
——. *Atlantic Canada.* New York: Oxford University Press, 1956. Pp. 179.

Quebec Now should not be neglected by sociologists for several reasons. French Canada is a living laboratory of the modern industrial revolution, with a unique variety of social patterns ranging from feudal and peasant remnants to metropolitan cities. It is also the prime center of Canadian resistance–such as it is–to the growing American domination of Canada. Americans ought to study Quebec, not to manipulate it better for their own ends, but to find alternatives to those ends.

Quebec communities have been analyzed by sociologists, notably Hughes and Miner. Mrs. Chapin's book differs from theirs in that it is a full-length portrait of the province. It is probably the best social analysis of Quebec yet produced. Why a writer who is not a professional sociologist can beat us at our own game is something for us to ponder. This book has implications for basic social theory and methodology.

Among its topics are interest groups, classes and political parties, women's roles, the Catholic Church, urban and rural problems, minorities, the arts, and literature, both English and French. We see Quebec as a changing whole. Perhaps that is the secret of its insight and its realism. It does not try to compress a dynamic social reality into the static categories of orthodox structural-functional sociology.

Atlantic Canada is a lesser work, probably because the maritime provinces are less distinctive communities than Quebec, and perhaps because the author has lived and worked in them much less than in Quebec. A general essay on the region is followed by chapters on each of the four provinces. In its interweaving of economic, political and other aspects of maritime social life, this book is another fine example of reporting in depth.

These works are relevant for such fields as regional culture, social change, classes, minorities, and conflict. Their simple but salty style makes them especially suitable for undergraduate reading. They show us that, with a dynamic and realistic approach, competent social analysis can be written for both specialists and laymen at once, without resorting to professional jargon that often obscures more than it reveals, and without condescendingly writing down to the supposed level of the nonprofessional reader.

That the publisher permitted these books to be issued without maps and without indices is hard to understand.

University of Vermont

PHILOSOPHY AND PHENOMENOLOGICAL RESEARCH

Vol. XXI, March, 1961

JOHN A. IRVING. *The Social Credit Movement in Alberta.* Toronto: The University of Toronto Press, 1959. Pp. xi, 369.

Social Credit first came to power in Alberta during the great depression. It still rules unchallenged. The forces maintaining it differ considerably from those which produced it. This book describes the origin and triumph (1932–35) of this social movement, one of the most interesting in North America.

Among the author's key analytical categories are the Social Credit ideology, the personality of Aberhart, and the organizing tactics used by that magnetic leader. Irving also takes account of the historical environment–the decay of the United Farmers regime, the religious fundamentalism of Alberta, and the catastrophic depression of the hungry thirties.

Social Credit was a mass movement for monetary reform. It became an expression of western agrarian and small-town protest against eastern big business and against the two parties (Tory and Liberal) which spoke for eastern business interests. But Social Credit was never anticapitalistic. It attacked only certain alleged abuses of capitalism, especially its financial plutocracy and its monetary system. Here it spoke for the petty bourgeois farmers and small traders who bulked large in the Albertan electorate.

If Irving's well-written book lacks the analytical brilliance of C. Macpherson's *Democracy in Alberta*, it is a very capable social history and psychological study indispensable to our understanding of modern western Canada. We particularly recommend it to American readers, that they may partly offset their parochial ignorance of Canadian affairs.

Centre for Community Studies
University of Saskatchewan

ANNALS OF THE AMERICAN ACADEMY OF POLITICAL AND SOCIAL SCIENCE

March, 1968

ROBIN F. BADGLEY and SAMUEL WOLFE. *Doctors' Strike: Medical Care and Conflict in Saskatchewan.* New York: Atherton Press, 1967. Pp. xiii, 201.

In 1962 organized medicine in Saskatchewan staged an unsuccessful twenty-three day strike against the new medicare program of a reformist Canadian Provincial government, which had been re-elected in 1960 in a campaign fought specifically on the medicare issue. The authors in Part I present an historical account of that epic confrontation. While attention is focused on the 1960s, the social background of Saskatchewan and the history of its medical services are also outlined. Some hitherto undisclosed aspects of the 1962 strike are revealed.

In Part II, the Saskatchewan experience is placed in an international perspective. British, American, and Canadian health-service developments over the last three generations are described and critically evaluated in very broad terms. These comparisons could well have been enlarged, and other countries might have been included. Finally, in the light of this overview, the authors attempt to estimate both the achievements and the deficiencies of Saskatchewan medicare.

Few recent professional publications have so effectively combined academically acceptable analysis with historical clarity and dramatic momentum. One author was a medical sociologist at the University of Saskatchewan; the other was a practicing doctor of medicine and public health, who supported the government medicare program. Although they are not neutral, they are objective. If that judgment seems paradoxical, let us remember that many of the best social analyses have dealt with large contemporary issues in both an evaluative and an insightful way.

Many weighty and disturbing problems are discussed in this book. Why has the technically admirable and socially prestigious North American medical profession become a social isolate? What is wrong with modern medical education? Why do social-reform movements like the Saskatchewan Co-operative Commonwealth Federation fall victim in their later phases to "hardening of the arteries?" How does the prevailing oligarchical and entrepreneurial organization of medical practice in North America militate against top-quality health services? Why did the Provincial university, long supported with pride by the people of Saskatchewan, so dismally fail in 1962 to provide disinterested leadership and counsel?

Some of these leading questions are tentatively answered in this book. The work is not definitive, but it is of lasting value: whatever it may lack in detail it makes up for by its sense of historical depth. To this reviewer, an eyewitness of the 1962 drama, *Doctors' Strike* so far as it goes is a true and moving record.

University of Calgary

AMERICAN SOCIOLOGICAL REVIEW

December, 1971

MARK NAGLER. *Indians in the City: A Study of the Urbanization of Indians in Toronto.* Ottawa, Canada: The Canadian Research Centre for Anthropology, 1970. Pp. 107.

This study, focused upon social and economic adjustment to urban life, is based on 150 interviews taken in 1964–66 with adult Indians residing mainly in Toronto. The interviews covered reasons for migrating to the city; education and vocational training; employment; and such problems of social adjustment as welfare, drinking and criminality, organizational participation, and attitudes toward Indian ancestry. No systematic sampling was possible, but Nagler interviewed representatives of all six of the categories into which he classified his respondents: *white-collar workers* (a small minority), *blue-collar workers, transitionals* (seeking to enter urban life but still often returning to the home reservation), and three classifications of short-term urban residents: *urban "users"* (coming for supplies, a "bust," or medicare), *seasonal workers,* and *vagabonds.*

According to official figures, the registered Indians of Canada are slightly over 1% (probably an underestimation) of the total Canadian population. They are divided into 558 bands on 2274 reserves mostly scattered in isolated rural areas. With some exceptions, these reserves are economically inadequate to support their inhabitants: several other studies have estimated the annual per capita cash income of Indians as not more than one-third as high as that of the average Canadian. Yet the Indians are increasing faster than any other ethnic category in Canada except the Eskimo and the Hutterites. Since World War II extended government services, private economic development in the hinterlands, and the mass media have brought closer contacts between whites and Indians, and rising aspirations among many Indians.

Despite the mounting economic pressure on the reserves, Indian migration to Canadian cities has been slow. Few studies of urban Indians have been made: one in Winnipeg (field-work in 1957), another in Saskatchewan (early 1960's), and now Nagler's in Toronto. Other relevant professional studies are limited for the most part to a few graduate theses and unpublished papers.

The Toronto respondents came to the city as most migrants do, primarily for jobs, education, and excitement. The few white-collar Indians who have made it into the middle class work and live much like their white counterparts; they appear to be assimilated rather thoroughly. The blue-collar and other categories, however, have little education, scarcely any organizational contacts, much unemployment, rely often on welfare, and frequently retreat to the home reservation. Indians from reserves near a city seemed to adjust better to urban life than Indians from remote places. That Indians do not create urban ghettos is attributed to the variety of their original local backgrounds and to the ease with which they can retreat to the reserves. Hence most of them live scattered throughout downtown working-class Toronto. The same diversity of background makes it difficult for Indians to form their own ethnic organizations. Their main loyalties still lie strongly with their bands and their kin.

Other contributions of this book include good critiques of the federal vocational training programs and of the work of the Indian-Eskimo Association, a white-led voluntary organization. The results of interviews with 30 employers about their experiences with Indian employees are also reported.

One may question whether a white interviewer can obtain maximum rapport with Indian respondents. One may likewise query the author's premise that assimilation is desirable. Many younger Indians are rejecting the idea of integration into either middle-class suburbia or working-class urban slums. However, militancy and pan-Indian tendencies began to emerge among Canadian Indians chiefly after Nagler did his field work.

University of Alberta, Canada

CONTEMPORARY SOCIOLOGY: A JOURNAL OF REVIEWS

1973–74

MURRAY L. WAX. *Indian Americans: Unity and Diversity.* Englewood, New Jersey: Prentice-Hall, 1971. 236 pp.

This is a very condensed volume on American Indians, their history, demography, selected present-day communities, urban Indians, and a typology of Indian-white relations. There are perfunctory references to Mexico and Canada.

Part I, Historical and Comparative, includes brief accounts of the Yaquis of northwestern Mexico, the Iroquois League, and the Dakota horse archers. Often attacked, first by the Spaniards and later by the Mexicans, the Yaquis were never completely conquered. They worked out a blend of Yaqui and European beliefs and practices. Another example: In the late 18th century, Iroquois leaders were received at the British court. British and Iroquois elites intermarried. A unique cultural blend seemed to be emerging. Perhaps the most conspicuous example was that of the Cherokee Nation, which adapted to white technology, developed its own courts and legislature – until it was destroyed by the American Congress in 1906, by means of displacing Cherokee collective land ownership in favor of individual titles, mostly given to whites. Today, the remnants of the Cherokee Nation live in rural slums in northeastern Oklahoma.

This volume is not an orthodox ethnographic report on Indians. It places Indian communities in their larger context of American colonialism. If this perspective is unclear in the text, the data are there, and the reader can draw his own conclusions. A realistic effort is made to show how the Indians have been ripped off by Americans. For example, between 1887 and 1934, American Indians – by various devices – were parted from 62 percent of their original 138 million reservation acres. And from 1948 to 1957, another 2.6 million acres were lost (p. 54).

Part I also includes a demographic review of Indian populations in Central and Northern America, and a few pages on the intrusive roles of traders, missionaries, and government administrators.

What almost but never quite emerges is a clear typology of Indian-white relationships in North America over the last three or four centuries. In a minority of instances, extermination was the pattern: Whites in the United States, Canada and Mexico hunted and killed Indians for sport. At the other end, parallel structures emerged: Indian and European collectivities met as equals, mutual cultural borrowing took place, and unique blends appeared. But the great majority of Indian-white relationships fall into two categories: proletarianization of the Indians, and isolation of Indians on hinterland reservations, both in the United States and Canada.

These two major patterns are interrelated. The Indians became the part-time or seasonal laborers in the North American fur trade. To get European metalware, trinkets, muskets and booze, Indians had to over-trap for furs. When agricultural settlement by Whites displaced the Indian hunting and gathering economy, the Indians were shunted onto rural reserves, with minimal subsistence allowances. The reservation system has indeed been a bargain-basement welfare scheme. Reservation Indians are available as a part-time labor force, mostly unskilled. A few Indians, of course, have assimilated to white, urban cultural standards, middle class in character. This development cannot be measured. It is primarily an urban phenomenon.

Part II reviews contemporary United States Indian communities. Wax presents one chapter on Plains reservations and one chapter on the Oklahoma Cherokee. This represents over one-fourth of this book, and it reports the author's own research for the most part. This is a very rewarding and insightful section. If it is not very well integrated with the other parts of this work, it tells us much, and thus justifies itself.

Wax first reviews the historical development and legal status of Indian treaties and Indian people. He quickly zeros in on the essential poverty and lack of economic potential on most reservations, located as they usually are far from agricultural, mineral and urban resources. Moreover, the imposition of federal-government administrators and programs, and the impact of various church missions, traders and anthropologists—have made the once homogeneous Indian communities into highly diverse factions.

The author's division of contemporary Indians into "country" and "town" types seems realistic. Most country Indians pay no rent, and receive certain key services—health, education, surplus commodities—at little or no cost to themselves. Hence, as Wax shows, they often spend such little cash as they get, on "luxuries." These non-bourgeois consumption patterns tend to distress and even shock white administrators, police, and welfare workers. Indian sharing practices also run counter to white middle class individualism.

A number of bureaucratic public agencies service the country Indians. The main beneficiaries seem to have been the white professionals and officials who staff these agencies—for a good price. Even universities in some cases now administer large service and research programs in which, of course, they have a strong vested interest. Despite all these white pressures, or perhaps partly because of them, the country Indians have successfully resisted assimilation into the American mainstream. For the prevailing assumption of American Indian policy has been to encourage Indians to become like middle-class whites.

It is good to report that Wax neatly demolishes the tacit white premise that education is *the* solution to the "Indian problem." His criticisms could well be extended to the wider American delusion that education is the key to "development" of underdeveloped societies.

The chapter on the Oklahoma Cherokee research during the 1960s by Wax and his associates succeeds in bridging the cultural gap between whites and Cherokee at least to the extent that the researchers make the life situations of the Cherokee come alive. That the researchers did not describe the gap as merely "cultural" is to their credit. What they explicitly show is the economic, political and educational exploitation of the Cherokee by whites, buttressed by their "Uncle Tomahawk" Indian retainers.

Part III deals with Indian reactions to the American expansion and disruption. One chapter reviews the religion of Handsome Lake among the Iroquois, the Ghost Dance among the Sioux, the Native American Church, recent pan-Indian nationalism, and alcoholic pathology. Another summarizes one Eskimo and three Indian urban communities: in Minneapolis, Rapid City, Barrow (Alaska), and the high-steel Caughnawagas in Brooklyn. Only the last group has achieved a viable blend of Indian and white ways.

The final chapter of the book deals with various modes of white-Indian relationships: genocide, melting pot, cultural pluralism. Though insightful, this chapter is oriented to adjustments within the prevailing American racist and capitalist society. Little explicit analysis is given to class-struggle perspectives on the Indian efforts for survival. Yet such perspectives have fruitfully emerged in the "radical caucuses" of social scientists and in the much more relevant Chicano liberation movements, not to overlook the numerous popular risings in such places as the Portuguese colonies and elsewhere in Africa and Latin America. Even Canadians (especially French Canadians) are now resorting to Marxist interpretations of U.S. economic expansion and cultural homogenization of Canadian life.

The appendix includes data on bibliographies, Indian population, Indian health and education, and federal expenditures on Indian affairs. There is a good index. The style is clear. Wax has come up with a fine book. Though probably intended for university readers, it is above all a work for the general reader.

University of Alberta

Foreword to
Sociology and Dialectic *

THIS SCHOLARLY WORK by Professor Mirković is another witness to the ongoing North American revival of interest in dialectic, especially Marxian dialectic. To explain why the revival is occurring now, one must analyze the changing social context – chiefly the constricting world situation of North American monopoly capitalism. Before we look at that problem, however, let us anticipate in brief certain key points much more fully developed by Mirković in Part I of the present volume.

Dialectic, he says, is a way of looking at the world, of understanding it, and above all of changing it. It is an older and broader philosophical tradition than its latter-day and best known variant, Marxism. Among the ancient Greeks, dialectic was an influential school – more important than some historians have told us, as the works of Benjamin Farrington and A. D. Winspear show.

Even earlier, among the Chinese, dialectical schools flourished. Indeed, it is not too much to say that dialectic has consistently been a basic theme in Chinese philosophy and social thought. Here, for example, we may refer to the *yin-yang* dualism, and the periodic cycles of rebellion inherent in gentry-peasant class relations over the twenty-odd centuries of the feudal or mandarin Chinese empire. In our own time, the late Chairman Mao Tse-tung combined in a creative way the dialectic of Marx and Lenin with the traditional bent for dialectic intrinsic to Chinese civilization.

Significant elements of dialectic, then, have appeared in many writers

---

* Damir Mirković, *Sociology & Dialectic*. Diliton Publications, P. O. Box 1351, St. Catharines, Ontario 1978.

255

and in several societies. Perhaps the most important has been the development of dialectic in modern Europe. The great names, of course, are Hegel, whose dialectic was idealist in character; and Marx, whose dialectical materialism evolved from the Hegelian school. Professor Mirković handles this great development with admirable clarity. It seems necessary to repeat here but a single point: that any dialectical tradition—the Marxian tradition in particular—is emergent. It evolves both as a system of ideas and as an aspect of an emerging historical society or societies.

By "tradition" we mean a group of thinkers using similar but not identical concepts, with new concepts and shifting emphases in response to changing historical milieux. A social and intellectual tradition is dynamic, not static. A good example is Parsons' study of the utilitarian tradition in the English classical and neo-classical economics.[1]

To restate: Marx did most of his writing between the mid-1840s and the early 1880s. He thoroughly understood late European feudalism, the early modern transition to capitalism, and the basic laws of European capitalism of his time. Given his grasp of the dynamic and crisis-generated self-transformation of capitalism into socialism, Marx had some key insights to offer concerning the outlines of a generalized socialist society. But here the touch of genius begins to shade off into speculation, even error. The further we move, in time and place, from Marx's west-European mid-19th-century base, the less dependable Marx becomes. Despite his flashes of insight concerning the India of his day, Marx did not fully understand that complex sub-continent, and he comprehended China even less. Having no illusions about the motives of greed and plunder that underlay British rule in India, he yet saw the embourgoisement of the world as a necessary preliminary to proletarian socialism.

Such Eurocentrism or ethnocentrism was common in Marx's era. It constitutes a reification, however, of Marxian dialectic—the mistaking of a concrete case for an abstract theoretical proposition. The application of dialectic must vary in time and place. For example, the main analysis of capitalist imperialism came with Lenin and others, after Marx's time. Conditions have changed since Marx wrote his landmark studies. They have changed in Europe and in the entire world. Every country is more or less unique with respect to its history, its culture, its demography, its internal geography, and its external geopolitical relations. Already there are several socialist societies, each one partly different from every other. The questions posed by "socialism in one country," between the first two wars, no longer are the most pressing ones that confront us. (But some powers, lagging behind developments, seem not to have recognized this salient fact.)

Rather, we see the rise of "Eurocommunism" in west-European capitalist societies—Italy, Spain, Portugal, and France. Is this merely a repetition of Bernstein revisionism of the 1890s in Germany? This seems unlikely: too much has changed in Europe during the last three generations. More likely, in the very long run we obviously confront before the triumph of socialism, Eurocommunism is one of several halfway houses—a status it may share with the Soviet Union, no less. No doubt whatever: Eurocommunism is a prime phenomenon of our time. It deserves the most careful study, in a dialectical perspective.

It is equally essential to recognize the differentiations within the socialist bloc. My study tour of eastern Europe last year (1977), along with prior and subsequent study, made it clear to me that Eurocommunism in western Europe has rough counterparts in eastern Europe. Poland, for example, invaded and partitioned three times by Russia and central-European empires during recent centuries, obviously feels highly ambivalent about the USSR; but it hates even more the German Nazi death machine that crucified Poland during the course of World War II. (Go to visit Auschwitz in southern Poland, west of Krakov. It is now a museum. The Museum handbook estimates 4 million executions in that death camp, and 10 million in all Nazi camps.)[2] Polish foreign policy follows closely that of the USSR, but its domestic policies differ significantly—agriculture in Poland, for example, socialized after World War II, was desocialized in large part during the 1950s, and in 1973 about three-quarters of agricultural land was in private holdings.

Romania, by contrast, patterns its domestic economy, both industrial and agricultural, roughly according to Soviet models. But its foreign policy is quite different from the Russian. The Socialist Republic of Romania fosters cordial relations with both the United States and the People's Republic of China. Indeed, the Romanian Government played an important role in arranging the first visit of U.S. President Nixon to Peking in 1972. In 1964, Romania declared that every Communist State has the right to develop its own national economic plans. It was the first state in the "Eastern Bloc" to implement a détente with the Federal Republic of Germany, now its second leading trading partner. Romania belongs to several U.S.-dominated international institutions—the International Monetary Fund, for example, and it received Most-favoured-nation trading status from the United States in 1974. In the larger Bucharest stores today, it is often possible to discourse in French. Romanian ties to western Europe do not stem merely from early-twentieth-century capitalist imperialism, but go back to Roman times.

Clearly, it is impossible to view East European socialist countries as miniature replicas of the Soviet Union. This underscores our earlier point—that each country and situation studied in a dialectical perspective must be seen as in considerable degree unique in the light of its history, culture, demography, internal geography, and external geopolitical relations. Moreover, Marxian dialectical analysis is an historically evolving tradition.

Above all, one must avoid reification—the mistaking of a concrete case for the abstract analytical schema.

In the present volume, Professor Mirković runs no risk of reification. In Part I, he works out his definition of dialectic. An analysis is dialectic, he says, to the extent that it uses a dialectic concept of totality, a dialectical concept of contradictions or oppositions that constitute the given totality, the ongoing interactions among contradictions which ensure transformation of the totality; and to the degree that the analysis is praxis—that is—the analysis must be closely involved in interaction with its object, so that theory and practice mutually modify each other, intertwined, and produce a new emergent.

In Part II, the author measures selected writers against his concept of dialectic. The writers include Simmel, Gurvitch, the Chicago School (especially Small and Park), and three historical sociologists—Sorokin, B. Moore and E. H. Carr. Carr should probably be described as a sociological historian.

This is a vast oversimplification of the Mirković work. But it is enough to show that the author addresses himself to some of the largest and most basic issues of modern western social science. He is dealing with dialectic as method, not with specific applications except as illustrations. He draws heavily on Hegel and Marx, of course, and particularly on Georg Lukács, but on numerous others as well—Althusser, Kosik, Meszaros, Mao and so on.

All this is worked out in the text, and need not be repeated here. Dialectic is a sophisticated method. It is easily subject to misuse and over-simplifications—perhaps vulgarization is a better description. What, in any given object of study, is the relevant totality? What are the operative contradictions therein, and how can they be evaluated and seen in an historical or dynamic context of change? Looking back, what were the roots and main evolutionary developments? Looking ahead, what are the chief options? There is no simple mechanical way to answer such questions. Even the greatest dialecticians have their limitations. Reference was made earlier in this Foreword to the boundaries of time and place that (in my opinion) ought to be applied or recognized for Marx's analyses. Mirković in parallel vein speaks of some well-known rigidities regarding dialectical schema developed in the later work of Engels, and carried on in Soviet "Dia-Mat." There are social reasons, understandable in a dialectical perspective, for such rigidities, of course. For example, the rigidities in Soviet Diamat doubtless reflect the pressures within and upon the USSR generated by going first into socialism in a hostile capitalist world. The "penalties of going first" is a dialectical concept of great penetrating power. It was used in a different context by Thorstein Veblen, who did not fully recognize its potentiality.[3]

It is well to stress that Mirković describes the simplistic reduction of dialectic to "thesis-antithesis-synthesis" as unacceptable. We must agree in principle, except perhaps in the most critical turning points of history. In the transition from feudalism to capitalism, for instance, the late-18th-century French revolution may be viewed as just such a critical conjunction of world history. Things afterward were never the same, nor could they be. Yet even in this case, there were numerous fluctuations—zigs and zags—two steps backwards and one step forward—during the subsequent two centuries of French history.

Another critical conjunction of world history was the Soviet revolution of 1917—although this specific date means even less than 1789 for France. Nonetheless, Russia went forward first into socialism. This entailed all sorts of handicaps and limitations, which we have somewhat arbitrarily grouped under the "penalties of going first." And there have been zigs and zags in Russian history ever since 1917, and these are sure to continue.

As the British and the French (with the United States on their coattails) won World War I, the Russians won World War II (again with the United States in a coat-tail position). With or without U.S. intervention in World War II, the outcome would have been the same, however delayed. The USSR saved the world, at a frightful price, still being paid.

But a qualitative change materialized in world history in our day, with the emergence of the Chinese Revolution. The Chinese are not so bound by the penalties of going first; they have a much older continuity in world history than any other nation; they have already rejected urbanization; they find dialectical thinking and acting to be in accord with earlier Chinese world-views, though needing re-interpretation. In the People's Republic of China, past and future meet in the present. But now, we suggest, there are two steps forward for every step backward, at least in China. Also interesting in a dialectical context are recent developments in Tanzania, Cuba, Algeria, Yugoslavia, Bulgaria, and Vietnam—to mention no others.[4]

Because social phenomena are basically dialectical in nature, dialectical methods offer the best modes of analysis, comprehension, predictability and planned control of changing societies. In all these respects, dialectical modes are far more powerful than the structural-functional and systems models—variants of extreme positivism—which tend to prevail in bourgeois capitalist social orders.

Training in dialectics is inherently cross-disciplinary, with strong foundations in philosophy and history and comparative institutions. Professor Mirković's European university education (including a degree in law at Zagreb) combined with further degrees in sociology at two North American graduate schools has stood him in good stead. It must be said that graduate training in most anglophone Canadian universities still leans one-sidedly toward narrowly specialized ultra-positivistic studies. Such training turns out technicians rather than well-rounded professionals.

Why have dialectical studies revived in North America in late years? In part, this reflects the slowly intensifying crisis of North American monopoly capitalism, increasingly constricted by the rival capitalist complexes in western Europe and Japan, by the successful development of old and new socialist economies, and by its own deepening internal contradictions. The post-war expansion seems to be over; Europe has been rebuilt. With both inflation and unemployment worsening, the era of "austerity capitalism" is upon us. The neo-colonial dependencies in Latin America and Africa are either opting out of the American orbit or are held down by harsh police-state regimes trained in or subsidized by the United States. Dependent capitalist states like the OPEC countries, though they are client-nations heavily oriented to the capitalist complexes which are their markets, have learned how to exact pounds of flesh. Even a docile appendage like Canada, a dependent capitalist state of another type, is showing disturbing signs of unrest and anti-American nationalism.

More specific to the Canadian scene, the failure of ultra-positivistic structural-functionalism to explain Canadian society is a prime cause of the rise of dialectic studies. Dialectic conveys a far more realistic and comprehensive analysis of Canada than does the imported bourgeois American positivism. For example, anglophone positivist sociology has consistently described Québec as just another of Canada's many ethnic minorities. This reflects the mythology of the dominant anglophone capitalist Establishment in Canada, which would very much like to sustain its dominance over Québec, first conquered over two centuries ago, and dutifully supported today by the francophone *vendus* who represent in Ottawa the public-sector interests of the U.S. and other multi-nationals.

In fact, a dialectical perspective on Canadian society reveals at once that "Canada" is a bi-national state. Québec is a nation, not "just another province." Whether anglophone Canada is also a nation may be debatable. Nations are created out of dialectical struggle. The struggle for an independent anglophone Canada, freed of its compradors (agents for foreign interests) both anglophone and francophone, lies even more in the future than does the struggle of Québec for an independent destiny. For Québec has already won two-thirds of its battle. For anglophone Canada, two-thirds of its independence struggle lies immediately ahead.

Let us look at a readily available dialectical view of the hemispheric history of the New World, developed by American historian Herbert E. Bolton (d. 1953) and his students. Our narrowly trained positivistic, structural-functionalist sociologists, unfortunately, have probably never heard of Bolton, a Berkeley professor for many years between the wars.

In 1893, historian Frederick Jackson Turner gave a famous address to the American Historical Association. It was entitled, "The Frontier in American History," often celebrated and reprinted.[5]

Some four decades later, Bolton made his presidential address to the American Historical Association at Toronto in 1932. It was entitled, "The Epic of Greater America." It was a far more insightful paper than that of Turner. Taking a parochial one-nation perspective, Turner depicted the United States as an increasingly unique development, a "perennial rebirth" on the westward-moving frontier, steadily diverging from Europe and its bondage to the past. Bolton, however, recognized that a one-nation view is never enough. In his hemispheric overview, he highlights the key historical patterns common to the Americas: the centuries of European colonization, the wars among the colonizers, genocide of natives, the slave trade from Africa, the struggles for political independence (mostly 1776–1826), continued dependence on European capital, immigration, and resource development.[6]

John Harbron, a University of Toronto historian trained in the Bolton tradition, has applied the Bolton theses to Québec, the last great Latin colony in the New World.[7] Recognizing the inevitable "self-determination of colonial peoples," Harbron discusses the historical parallels among Québec, Mexico, and Venezuela; sketches probable political, economic, cultural and diplomatic policies for an independent Québec, and possible reorientation of English Canada toward closer association with Québec and other Latin nations surrounding the United States. The work is a dialectical analysis, though not Marxist. Yet Harbron's analysis with respect to immanently generated pressures toward colonial liberation is distinctly parallel to A. G. Frank's studies (in Latin America) of the necessary causal ties between capitalist metropolitan over-development and colonial underdevelopment. Like dialectic, Bolton and Harbron are critical of existing institutional arrangements (because they write about immanent change) and creatively productive of options for emerging restructuralizations.

The revival of dialectic in Canada clearly is a promising trend. Professor Mirković's volume merely opens the door. It could well start a new movement in the study and development of social theory. Many other social theorists deserve the sort of analysis used by Mirković. Indeed, in a larger view, the orthodox schools of academic social theory—including functionalism, ethnomethodology, symbolic interactionism and similarly much touted "new" ploys—work out basically as small variations on sterile ultra-positivism. In the pages that follow, however, the questing reader may find a key to something new, yet not new; simple but profound; a returning that is also a going ahead; a theoretical perspective that is also praxis. To define dialectic as the same as "conflict theory" is misleading, superficial and erroneous. But let the reader turn these pages and see for himself or herself.

Edmonton, Alberta
July 26, 1978 (Cuba Day)

Notes

1 Talcott Parsons, *The Structure of Social Action*. New York: McGraw-Hill, 1937.

2 Kazimierz Smoleń, *Auschwitz, 1940–1945: Guidebook Through the Museum*. Państwowe Muzeum w Oświęcimiu, 6th edition, 1976, p. 19.

3 Thorstein Veblen, *Imperial Germany and the Industrial Revolution*. New York, Macmillan, 1915; reprinted by the Viking Press, New York, 1939. See page 132 and *passim* of the latter edition.

4 On Tanzania, see *The Silent Class Struggle*. Dar Es Salaam: Tanzania Publishing House, 1973. Also I. G. Shivji, ed., *Tourism and Socialist Development*. Dar Es Salaam: Tanzania Publishing House, 1973. On Vietnam, see Kathleen Gough, *Ten Times More Beautiful: The Rebuilding of Vietnam*. Vancouver: New Star Books, 1978. On Bulgaria, see two manuscripts by Dr. Eleanor Smollett, Dept. of Anthropology, University of Regina, Saskatchewan: "Implications of the Multi-Community Co-operative for Rural Life in Bulgaria," 1978; and (with Dr. Peter Smollett) "The Ninth Comes to the Village of Kirilovo," 1976. The present writer has visited Bulgaria, Cuba and Yugoslavia one or two times each. For Algerian insights I am indebted to Mr. Mohamed H. Abucar, whose field work in Algeria, 1976–77, is now materializing into his Ph.D. thesis at the University of Alberta. English-language sources on Cuba, Yugoslavia and Tanzania (in addition to those mentioned above) are readily available in any large library.

5 F. J. Turner, *The Frontier in American History*. New York: Holt, 1921.

6 H. E. Bolton, *Wider Horizons of American History*. New York: D. Appleton-Century, 1939.

7 John D. Harbron, *Canada Without Québec*. Don Mills: General Publishing Co. 1977.

Sociology without Clothes
in North America

THE STERILITY of much American academic social science, especially sociology, has been evident for some time to a few observers and practitioners. Yet the numbers, publications, salaries, and prestige of sociologists have been increasing. Because of this swelling chorus of success, it has been easy to ignore the critics.

But the prosperity of sociology is like the prosperity of the United States—lush on the surface, unsubstantial underneath. And now comes a famous sociologist, C. Wright Mills—author of *White Collar*, *The Power Elite*, *The Causes of World War III*, and other major works, and a professor at Columbia University—to proclaim in rolling periods that the emperor has no clothes. It will be hard for sociologists to ignore Mills' new book and even harder to face up to it.*

This book exposes the failure of American sociology to identify and clarify the basic historical processes and social problems of our time. We shall discuss this argument first. On a broader canvas, the book may be interpreted as a symptom of a much greater failure—the apparent incapacity of American society to assess and adapt to changing world conditions. For social scientists and intellectuals are part of their society. May not their common disabilities be similarly linked? This question we shall take up later.

Spilling the Beans about American Sociology

Many look with awe at the Scientist with a capital S, whose unintelligible language and esoteric techniques serve to confirm his superior knowl-

---

* *The Sociological Imagination*, Oxford University Press, New York, 1959.

Copyright © 1959 by *Monthly Review, Inc.* Reprinted by permission of the Monthly Review Foundation, New York.

edge and achievements. These trusting souls will be distinctly shocked to learn from Mills that much of the work now afoot in American social science is just what it appears to be and nothing more—unintelligible and esoteric. When an insider of Mills' stature spills the beans, the results are likely to be sensational. Probably Mills will never make the grade as president of his national professional association. Neither did Thorstein Veblen.

What is the "sociological imagination?" To Mills, it means the ability to relate parts to wholes, to see individual roles and problems in terms of institutional movements and contradictions. It means viewing "the present as history." It characterizes the work of Comte, Spencer, Marx, Veblen, and the other great analysts of society. And it is precisely what is absent from most of the current work in American sociology.

> Nowadays men often feel that their private lives are a series of traps. They sense that within their everyday lives they cannot overcome their troubles . . . their visions and their powers are limited to the close-up scenes of job, family, neighborhood; in other milieux, they move vicariously and remain spectators. . . . Underlying this sense of being trapped are seemingly impersonal changes in the very structure of continent-wide societies. The facts of contemporary history are also facts about the success and failure of individual men and women. . . . Neither the life of an individual nor the history of a society can be understood without understanding both. Yet men do not usually define the troubles they endure in terms of historical change and institutional contradiction. . . . Ordinary men do not usually . . . possess the quality of mind essential to grasp the interplay of man and society. . . . They cannot cope with their personal troubles in such ways as to control the structural transformations that usually lie behind them. (*The Sociological Imagination*, pp. 3–4)

Artists, novelists, preachers, journalists—indeed anyone, says Mills, can exercise the sociological imagination to reveal the links between individual experiences and historical processes, and thereby help people to understand and guide their social destinies.

More than half of Mills' book is a devastating criticism of two types of sociological effort: theoretical analysis and factual studies.

The sociological theory which draws Mills' fire is the kind produced by Harvard's Professor Talcott Parsons and his disciples. During the last fifteen years Parsonian books and papers have multiplied, and Parsons-trained Ph.D.s have come to flourish in most of the leading universities.

Parsons' theoretical system stems from English neo-classical economics and from such continental writers as Max Weber, Durkheim, Pareto, and Freud. Like orthodox economic theory, Parsons' "theory of action" is premised on stability, harmonious equilibrium of interests, and on universality. The model is presumed to be applicable to any social system.

From Parsons' work has grown the American cult of Max Weber. Now Weber, who wrote in Germany two generations ago, represented a bourgeois counteroffensive against Marx. He tried hard to prove that ethical ideas rather than material and economic factors are the dominant forces in social change. But Weber was never able firmly to establish his case. His propositions on the leading role of ideas in India, China, and modern Europe were always stated in the subjunctive mode – as possibilities rather than as proven truths. He was too competent an historian to go beyond his facts, despite his idealist predilections. Parsons, however, takes from Weber chiefly the idealistic elements. He does not have Weber's saving sense of historical movement. And Parsons' students are even further removed from reality.

Mills demolishes Parsonian "Grand Theory" with a characteristic Millsian grand salvo. Grand Theory is a "fetishism of concept." Its chief weakness is neither its cloudy verbiage nor its bad English, but its lack of contact with social life. How can a dynamic society be encompassed by an abstract, static, and non-historical theory? Mills concludes that Grand Theory is fifty percent verbiage, forty percent conventional textbook sociology, and ten percent conservative ideology.

Far more prominent than Grand Theory in number of practitioners, budget resources, and practical application is "Abstracted Empiricism"– Mills' term for the quantitative school of social science based on statistical analysis of questionnaires and interviews. Here are the public opinion, attitude, and advertising surveys sponsored by business and governmental agencies. Such studies are usually narrow in their focus but elaborately refined in their techniques. They are also expensive: naturally they gravitate into the orbit of well-heeled sponsors. Finally, they are very useful for sharpening up commercial, administrative, and financial policies.

Hence sociologists, and probably even more psychologists, have won subordinate but acknowledged places on the staffs of the great business and military bureaucracies during the last two decades. This has brought them good salaries and vicarious prestige. But it has also entailed, says Mills, the harnessing of social science to corporate ends and the reduction of social scientists to hired technicians. The new bureaucratic social science is characterized by teams of highly specialized personnel who, willy-nilly, are helping to bend other men and women to ends not their own. "Its use has been mainly in and for non-democratic areas of society – a military establishment, a corporation, an advertising agency, an administrative division of government." (p. 114)

If social scientists are to serve the public interest responsibly, writes Mills, they must control their own means of research "in some collective way." (p. 106.) But he does not follow out the implications of this delayed-action blockbuster. Let us try to do so. First, it is scarcely conceivable that scientists could control, even indirectly, their own means of production except in a socialist society. Second, even though bureaucratic social science has great intrinsic limitations, as Mills makes exceedingly plain, this does not preclude its having socially useful roles within those limitations—provided that the bureaucracies it serves are democratically run for genuinely humanitarian purposes. There is the real rub. Science, both natural and social, is increasingly twisted in our latter-day capitalist society to anti-social ends, chiefly commercial and military. Does it not follow that scientists who would best serve their professional fields should join some progressive political movement to revise those anti-social policies and the institutions responsible for them?

If Mills' political follow-through is weak, his critique of Abstracted Empiricism is pulverizing. Grand Theory is trans-historical—a fetishism of concept; Abstracted Empiricism is subhistorical—a fetishism of method. Neither can deal with the basic problems of our time, because both are incapable—for different reasons—of grasping the structural and historical realities that govern our destinies.

Studies in the style of Abstracted Empiricism are confined to small milieux from which data are collected by sampling and interview techniques and then processed by a statistical ritual. The results, of course, are no better than the original data. Even carefully designed interviews usually cannot get at the larger historical factors, nor can they get very deep into an interviewee's personality. "The details, no matter how numerous, do not convince us of anything worth having convictions about." (p. 55)

Studies of voting, for example, correlate political preference with the voter's occupation, religion, education, and so on. This is interesting. But it ignores most of the key American political institutions: party machines, class, and faction, the dynamics of which mold election campaigns. Similarly, studies of factory workers' cliques and attitudes turn up all sorts of details while overlooking the broad alignments and conflicts of power that frame our industrial system.

Mills' final broadside at Grand Theory and Abstracted Empiricism is squarely on target. "They may be understood as insuring that we do not learn too much about men and society—the first by formal and cloudy obscurantism, the second by formal and empty ingenuity." (p. 75)

Is it not astounding to hear such things from an American college professor?

Is the American Experiment Failing?

Mills' book accurately characterizes many salient features of American sociology. It would have been a better book if it had discussed more fully those studies successfully applying the "sociological imagination"–for there are a few such works, even in the United States. The book would also have been better had it devoted a chapter to the ossification and promise of the Marxian tradition in social science. Such a critique is needed both by Marxists and by bourgeois academicians. Although obviously holding his nose at times, Mills regrettably continues the stifling academic convention of boycotting Marxian ideas officially, while using them to good advantage in practice. Indeed, it may be said of Mills, as of Veblen, that the superiority of his insight stems primarily from the influence of the Marxian tradition, creatively and critically applied by an independent mind.

Now let us interpret *The Sociological Imagination* against the larger canvas of American society today. Let us bring into play our own sociological imagination.

The world is moving unevenly and painfully out of one historical era and into another. The significance of this overwhelming process is not even remotely apparent to the American people. True, there is incessant propaganda on behalf of the cold war, free enterprise, and other vested interests of American ruling circles. But the prevailing American ideology does not accurately portray American reality. Nor does it convey a valid picture of what is going on elsewhere in the world. Worst of all, it has no competition–no significant faction has challenged the official ideology or offered a different one. Hence, the United States is, in effect, an isolated nation, like a victim of schizophrenia walled off from the real world by an impenetrable veil of delusions and fantasies.

This is just another way of saying that American society has a false consciousness–a severe misconception of its own nature and of its place in world history–which is to say, a misconception of world history as a whole.

Why?

Because American intellectuals and social scientists have failed to exercise the sociological imagination? Because they have flunked out on their responsibility to clarify to their fellow citizens the basic problems and trends of their own and other societies? That is the answer which Mills' book suggests to me.

Undeniably American intellectuals, especially the sociologists, have failed–wretchedly and colossally. There have been some honorable exceptions, but Mills' scathing indictment will stick to most of them:

> Intellectuals, artists, ministers, scholars, and scientists are fighting a
> cold war in which they echo and elaborate the confusions of officialdom.
> . . . They do not try to put responsible content into the politics of the
> United States; they help to empty politics and keep it empty. (p. 183)

This abdication of the intellectuals, however, needs to be explained.
For ideological elements are ordinarily subordinate parts of a society—
more moved than moving. What Mills has documented in *The Sociological Imagination*, it seems to me, is really the failure of American society.

American progressives have optimistically assumed that a new leap
forward is simply a matter of time. But it appears more likely that the
United States lacks sufficient internal creativity to get itself out of the
political and social ruts in which it is now mired. For social progress
depends on oppositions, and in the States today there is no real internal
opposition to official national and foreign policies. The decisive oppositions seem to lie, not within the United States, but between American
and other societies, with the States representing the reactionary thesis.
Decisive oppositions exist also within a number of societies abroad. Present indications suggest that the leadership of world civilization, held by
Western nations during the last two or three centuries, is returning to
the East—where indeed it has generally resided during most of history.

Why is there no significant opposition in the United States? Perhaps
because capitalism has overdeveloped. There was no important pre-
capitalist social order to be overcome—no anti-capitalist traditions surviving into the present—as has been the case in Europe. Great oppositions have emerged only twice in American history since independence.
The first, the slave-owning agrarian capitalism of the South, was dissolved in civil war, a conflict between rival capitalisms. The second, the
turn-of-the-century farm and labor movements and the beginnings of a
mass socialist drift, has been stifled or bought off by the prosperity of
two cheap world wars.

As Marx foresaw, capitalism does tend to generate its working-class
rival, and this labor movement eventually tends to become socialistic
in character. That has been the general course of events in most Western
societies. But in the case of the United States these inherent tendencies
of capitalism seem to have been offset (not removed) by unique historical
and geographic conditions. If this is true, the outlook for American society is, at best, stagnation; otherwise, regression.

Prosperity sustained by wars, government spending, and Madison-
Avenue fakeroo has been enough to preoccupy most Americans and to
maintain their false consciousness. Instead of a realistic awareness of the
world social revolution and a rational assessment of its possible mean-

ings for the United States, the American public's departures from conformity have chiefly been vague anxieties and widespread apathy.

It is the task of the sociological imagination, says Mills, to reassert
the principles of reality and reason in American public life. But this
would be possible only if there were close ties between intellectuals exercising the sociological imagination and segments of American society
most likely to be motivated to large-scale political action, i.e., the labor
movement. Between the academic section of the intellectuals and the
labor movement, no such tie exists, as Mills clearly shows.

> American social scientists have seldom, if ever, been politically engaged
> in any large way. . . . One often encounters journalists who are more
> politically alert and knowledgeable than sociologists, economists, and
> especially, I am sorry to say, political scientists. The American university
> system seldom if ever provides political education. . . . Most social sci-
> entists have had little or no sustained contact with such sections of the
> community as have been insurgent; there is no left-wing press. . . . The
> academic community has few if any roots in labor circles. (p. 99)

The social bankruptcy of the academic community does not rule out
the development of intellectual leadership from other segments of the
population, of course. At the moment, however, the prospect is not reassuring. Labor leaders as a group, for example, seem far more unimagi-
native and anti-intellectual than the right-wingers of Big Business.

If we cannot settle these issues here, we can surely agree that *The
Sociological Imagination* is a most significant book. It is written with fiery
conviction, full of striking phrases—"The history that now affects every
man is world history." (p. 4) If the work is smaller in scope than *White
Collar*, it equals the latter in quality and insight. Unquestionably its
author is now the leading American sociologist. Posterity may yet record
that the mantle of Thorstein Veblen, America's greatest social scientist,
fell upon Wright Mills.

Lessons from Sorokin

MORE THAN TWENTY YEARS AGO I enrolled as an undergraduate in Professor Sorokin's best-known course, Principles of Sociology, officially catalogued as Sociology A, but commonly called Sorokin A by the irreverent Harvard *Crimson's Confidential Guide*. My Saturday section man was R. K. Merton, who taught me a thing or two one day when he dispassionately atomized a juvenile term paper of mine. When in the course of events I became an instructor, one of my assignments would be to act as a section assistant in this same course. That association with Sorokin and Sociology A would last for several years, just before and just after the second world war. All that lay ahead, however.

Another well-known course I took that first year was Social Dynamics. Here the professor gave a preview of his *magnum opus, Social and Cultural Dynamics,* the first three volumes of which were to be published the following year (1937). In later years there were other Sorokin courses, and then graduate seminars, notably in social theory and social mobility. The professor had already published standard works in both of these fields.

These three or four courses, I think, carried the essence of Sorokin's formal teaching. In any case, they are the ones I best remember.

Now a time has come to consider, reflectively, just what were the lessons we learned from Sorokin. On such a matter each of us must speak for himself. My own feeling is that the majority of my graduate-school generation did not learn much from Sorokin, and that because of this fact North American sociology is the poorer.

In this age of deep and chronic crisis, formal education is likely to

From *Sociological Theory, Values and Sociological Change.* Edward A. Tiryakian, Editor. Copyright © 1963 by The Free Press, a division of Macmillan, Inc. Reprinted by permission of the publisher.

become somewhat divorced from contemporary realities. This seems to be especially true in American society. A stiff dose of academic training, such as we unquestionably got at Harvard, is likely to require an inordinate amount of sifting and seasoning over the years before it can be satisfactorily adjusted to the realities of a fast-changing world. One gets his education, and then, as it were, one must get over it.

Too many of us in my university generation have not yet gotten over our academic educations.

If we had, certain key elements of Sorokin's teaching would be considerably more prominent in North American sociology than is now the case. Five of those elements are: an emphasis upon social change as the primary frame of reference; the corollary that change is inherent or immanent in social systems; the premise that social conflict and social problems are basically organic aspects of a society rather than external accidents; the revolutionary nature of our time; and the necessity of taking a universal view of social life and social thought, both ancient and modern, rather than a perspective limited to modern Western societies.

These ideas did not, of course, originate with Sorokin, nor do they include all the facets of his thought. Some awareness of most of them can doubtless be found in most contemporary social scientists. But these propositions are central elements of Sorokin's system, whereas they tend to be relatively peripheral with many other writers. Only brief comment on each of the five points seems desirable here.

Elsewhere[1] I have discussed the high degree of unrealism that naturally results from attempting to analyze a dynamic society like our own in terms of an essentially static social theory. A conspicuous example of this is the theory of action. We must freely acknowledge the significance of Professor Parsons' work for systematic interdisciplinary theory, analytical sophistication, small-group and family studies, and for many brilliant insights into special situations too numerous to mention. Yet when all is said and done, this approach remains basically static and a priori, logical rather than empirical, transhistorical rather than historical, structural rather than dynamic. It owes much to the concept of "normal equilibrium," borrowed mainly from neoclassical economic theory.[2]

Similar comments can be made about the closely related but more general and more widely known structural-functional approach in sociology and anthropology. The development of functionalism has doubtless been one of the major phases of social science in the last twenty-five years. But its implicitly static frame of reference more or less obscures our awareness of concrete historical processes operating in specific social and geographic settings.[3] With some exceptions, this seems particularly true of community studies in both literate and nonliterate societies.

Developing a functional type of social analysis has been a notable achievement, notwithstanding its shortcomings in certain areas. As a matter of record, Sorokin has made significant contributions to this chapter of modern social science. Some of his early works, first published in Russia, place him in the vanguard of this movement. But the main drift of his thought has not been in that direction.

The second key premise of Sorokin's sociology is that social change is inherent in social systems. In the equilibrium frame of reference characteristic of much theorizing in economics and sociology, change necessarily appears as external or accidental force. Sorokin's emphasis on the immanence of change is most clearly set forth in his *Social and Cultural Dynamics.*

The third premise views social problems primarily as organic aspects of society, and only secondarily as external factors or accidents. The prevailing emphasis in North American social science has tended to reverse the relative position of these two points of view. No doubt this oversimplifies the general picture, but hardly to the point of serious distortion. For example, Sorokin sees war, crime, and rising divorce rates as phenomena inherent in an excessively sensate and materialistic culture. One may debate Sorokin's application of this premise. I would say that concrete material institutions, especially those centering around economy, class, and property, are usually the key elements of social life and social evolution. But concerning the validity of the basic premise itself, serious doubts can scarcely be entertained, for the alternative is confusion in social science and social policy. Explaining depressions by "accidents" like wars, or wars by depressions, or juvenile delinquency by slums or broken families, is neither scientifically accurate nor conducive to realistic remedial policy. It seems likely that juvenile delinquency and slums are both more or less directly linked to the social-class system. Modern war probably stems in considerable part from the institutional complex of capitalism and absolute nationalism, and from the movement of hitherto dependent nations toward socialism and independence. If these propositions are true, the conventional remedial measures we now rely upon for relief from delinquency and war are bound to be inadequate. Effective policies can be based only on insightful knowledge. Minor repairs will hardly suffice where major surgery is called for.

Another key teaching of Sorokin is the revolutionary nature of our time. This view has become accepted—more or less—even in North America as a result of the impact of assorted wars, revolutions, and depressions during the past generation. But general acceptance of this disturbing prospect has come reluctantly, especially among those governments and social classes having vested interests in the old order. As yet the depth and pervasiveness of the revolutionary currents are incompletely realized in the relatively prosperous sections of the Western world. For twenty-five years Sorokin has been one of the few voices to warn us of the true situation. If his analysis has underestimated some of the specific historical factors and overestimated the role of ideas, at least he has consistently recognized that we are passing painfully over one of the great watersheds of world history.

The last major lesson is the importance of a universal view of social life, Oriental as well as Western, ancient as well as modern. Modern Western social thought has naturally tended to concentrate upon the institutions and internal problems of Western societies. An unfortunate feature of this emphasis has been a relative neglect of the social evolution and thought of Near- and Far-Eastern civilizations. For several decades the outlook of Western scholarship and education has been little short of provincial in this respect. History, for example, is still taught in American schools and colleges in terms of the narrow categories *ancient*, *medieval*, and *modern*. Much the same is true of philosophy.

This preoccupation with the West European peninsula and its cultural extensions in North America and elsewhere means that the greater part of the world and its peoples has either been arbitrarily relegated to the background or else ignored. Yet most of the human race has always lived in Asia, and still does. The first urban civilizations emerged in India and Southwest Asia. China represents perhaps the longest span of social evolution. Although Western Europe was the first to reach the urban-industrial stage, thereby attaining a worldwide technical and political supremacy, other regions of the world with larger populations and potentially greater resources are now becoming industrialized. Already it seems possible to distinguish two partly overlapping subphases of urban-industrial development—Atlantic capitalism and Eurasian socialism. In the long-run view, the political and cultural hegemony of Western Europe and North America appears to be a temporary and receding tide.

No doubt the reasons for these deficiencies in Western-world outlooks are numerous and complex. But one practical result is that we of the West find ourselves confronting a major crisis without the intellectual concepts needed to understand it. American social science and education suffer from a relative unawareness of the deep historical currents of the times. In Sorokin's works, however, we are continually reminded of the importance of studying Eastern history and social thought.

Thus far we have mentioned only a few aspects of Sorokin's thought. These surely belong among the basic premises of a mature and realistic social science. Had we learned these lessons from Sorokin better than we did, North American sociology might be considerably more advanced than it is. With certain other features of his approach, to be sure, I would differ profoundly. Nonetheless, in recent years it has become clear to me that there are more fundamentals of sociology to be learned from Sorokin than from almost any other academic social scientist today.

Why is this? Chiefly because Sorokin has usually—with now and then a lapse—addressed himself to the basic problems of the age without being sidetracked by the current cult of "objectivity." According to the latter view, which seems to prevail among sociologists of some leading North American universities, a social scientist should religiously avoid making value judgments in his scientific work—as if this were really possible! May not such antisepsis in science invite sterility rather than progress?

Writers who do not adhere to the canon of objectivity are likely to be looked upon by orthodox social scientists as "philosophers" rather than "scientists"—and in this context, "philosopher" is hardly a complimentary term. The orthodox are inclined somewhat to look askance at these deviant characters, among whom are commonly included Sorokin, Toynbee, the Marxians, Charles Beard, Veblen, and others. A distinguished list of sinners, indeed!

The great social thinkers of all times have dealt with the leading social and ethical issues of their day. In so doing they have necessarily made value judgments. Perhaps facing up to the leading ethical questions of the day is by itself not a sufficient condition of greatness—one must come up with some relevant answers, too. But it is surely a necessary condition of greatness.

One more point remains to be made, concerning the scholar's integrity in his public role. At a time when the great majority of American scholars were climbing onto the cold-war bandwagon and accepting uncritically the official Washington line, Sorokin was one of a few who now and then spoke out for peace. The members of the Harvard faculty who took this risky and unpopular stand probably numbered less than half a dozen, if my memory is correct.

Is not the scholar, like any other citizen, duty-bound to speak out on public issues wherein he has both special insight and deep convictions? Then where were our academics during the cold-war buildup, the heats of the loyalty-security purges, the insanities of the Truman-Eisenhower Far Eastern policy? In an age of spreading conformity, Sorokin was one of the exceptions who continued to exemplify the best tradition of the independent scholar. A man of extraordinarily wide interests and long views, he remained relatively unmoved by passing political tempests, just as he has been generally unaffected by most of the short-term enthusiasms in social science.[4]

Once, during my college days, I volunteered with some other students to hand out organizing leaflets for an embattled CIO union in a Boston suburb. This trifling incident brought some of us before a local magistrate for allegedly infringing a long-forgotten local ordinance. The Court in his wisdom sent us back to our studies unscathed. Afterward, one of my professors warned me that the affair might jeopardize my scholarship. But when the matter (so I was told) came up in a Department meeting, Sorokin – then Chairman – turned the question aside with the humorous comment that he himself had been arrested six times – three times by the Czar of Russia and three times by the Bolsheviks.

In small things as well as in great ones, Sorokin is a teacher to remember. Of what he offered us, and what he stood for, we learned too little.

Notes

1 "Social Theory and Social Problems," *Philosophy and Phenomenological Research*, XVIII (December 1957), 190–208.

2 Neoclassical economic theory, it must be noted, has developed its abstract and analytical apparatus at the cost of losing contact, to a considerable extent, with concrete historical processes. And "normal equilibrium" has become one of the major frames of reference in North American social science. A generation ago Charles Beard wrote: "What schemes of organization and valuation have generally prevailed among American scholars in the social sciences? In the main the system of British Manchesterism has prevailed, with modifications in detail." *Zeitschrift für Sozialforschung*, IV (1935), 63–65.

3 Another example of the inherent incapacity of academic social science to deal effectively with problems of social change can be found in the introductory texts in sociology and anthropology. Usually the topic of change is reserved for the last section, and a pretty lame treatment it ordinarily is.

4 Sorokin's recent volume, *Fads and Foibles in Contemporary Sociology and Related Social Sciences* (Chicago: Henry Regnery, 1956), is too cutting to be a popular book, but it deserves more attention than it has received. One may say of this work that it is erroneous in many of its details but accurate in most of its basic propositions.

The Protestant Ethic and Change: Max Weber as Ideologist

THE MAIN CONTENTIONS of this paper are:

I that Max Weber's protestant-ethic theory of western capitalist development seriously misrepresents how modern capitalism actually evolved.

II that Weber's one-sided model has heavily reinforced the ideological preconceptions of such writers as Lipset, Hagen, and McClelland, as to how economic development in present-day underdeveloped nations ought to take place.

III that the main reasons for both the foregoing tendencies are ideological: they suit the prevailing economic and political interests of western capitalist societies – chiefly the USA.

Directly or indirectly, every social-science perspective has ideological aspects. For example, some orthodox neo-classical economists in the 1930s stubbornly refused to recognize the great depression then racking western Europe and North America. A partial reason for this blind spot was the inherited, dead-hand weight of Say's Law, an early 19th-century dogma that demand always equals supply. Except for short-run, self-correcting disturbances of the economic equilibrium, therefore, no major depression was possible. Not until J. M. Keynes published his *General Theory* in 1936 was that dogma displaced. Keynes, it seems, was one of the few academics of his time who, at least occasionally, looked out the window of his ivy tower and tried to relate the real world to the scholar's shadowy reflection of reality in Plato's cave.

Presented at the 13th annual meetings, Western Association of Sociology and Anthropology, Calgary, Canada, December 28–30, 1971.

Still another example of blindspots due to ideological distortion was the general inability of most American structural-functional sociologists in the 1960s to predict or even explain the urban ghetto riots in the United States. The inherited, white middle-class liberal dogma of inevitable, gradual "progress" toward racial integration and toward equality of racial opportunity obscured the truth: that integration is impossible in the United States under the institutional patterns now prevailing.

If university-trained specialists in social science were unable to tape that situation, a number of Black-Power leaders have had no such difficulty. The latter have bluntly rejected integration as not only impossible, but undesirable. That significant insight and development owes nothing whatever to academic social scientists.

Natural scientists, too, are sometimes prevented from properly assessing phenomena by ideological blindspots stemming from their vested professional interests. At these W.A.S.A. (Western Association of Sociology and Anthropology) meetings two years ago (1969), Jack W. Ondrack argued that senior academic zoologists are among the chief scoffers at the sasquatch phenomena. He suggested this is due to their strong vested interest in the 18th-century classification of primates by Linnaeus. After all, the academic zoologists are the professional experts, aren't they? This orthodox taxonomy might require considerable modification if the sasquatch phenomena should ever be verified.[1]

I.

Weber's theory of capitalist development claims a key facilitating role for the "Protestant ethic" of hard work, ascetic thrift, and systematic maximization of profit-making (and work) as an end in itself. Other essential elements of modern western capitalism, according to Weber, were the ownership of the means of production by private business firms, an extensive and open market, a mechanized technology, bookkeeping, a stable legal system to enforce and regulate contracts, and a propertyless labour force under compulsion of hunger to hire out to private entrepreneurs. In these respects, Weber does not differ essentially from Marx or Schumpeter—to name no others. Where he does differ is in the key role assigned to the ethical attitude toward economic activity fostered by Protestant religious zeal.

True, this model or ideal type of capitalist development was presented by Weber as an abstraction—i.e.—to the extent that these characteristics or elements were empirically realized in a particular economy, that economy was capitalistic. Weber's analytical sophistication cannot be faulted, at least on a formal level. But in practice, and in halo effects, ideal types are notoriously prone to reification—taking the abstract model for empirical reality. Weber's model is no exception. For there is a widespread tendency among orthodox middle-class sociologists and economists to accept this abstraction as a fairly accurate picture of capitalist reality, and to accept the Protestant ethic as a decisive factor in the origin and development of capitalism. Indeed, Weber himself is open to the same charge of unrealistic reification.

What is underestimated or omitted by some writers (including Weber) with respect to this idealized ideal type of capitalism is the role of force, fraud, waste, and government subsidies (direct and indirect) to the more powerful capitalistic interests. Let me cite some examples for each of these four categories.

Force includes war, piracy, the slave trade, conquest and plunder of weaker nations and tribes, and so on. *Fraud* covers such phenomena as indirect colonial rule, divide-and-rule policies by major western powers (especially Britain), stock watering and misrepresentation by corporations, land speculation, and so on. *Waste* refers to much advertising, planned obsolescence, government procurement of military hardware, uneconomic methods of production and distribution perpetuated by pre-existing vested interests, and in general all those methods and techniques that make for charging what the traffic will bear. *Public subsidies to private interests* include the tariff, tax favoritism to corporate and upper-class interests, public grants to such middle-class pre-emptions as universities, symphony orchestras, bargain-basement allowances for welfare recipients and the aged and the Indians, generous piece-rates paid to fat-cat medical doctors through fee-simple medicare programs, expense-account allowances for business and professional types, and so on. (Of minor importance is the Canadian practice of exemption of income tax for two years to American professors who come to Canada. But isn't this rather like paying a bonus to cultural imperialists from abroad?)

These four categories overlap. We need a more analytical typology of exploitation. Here is a worthy Ph.D. topic for some inspired student.

What is the documentation for these four categories of force, fraud, waste, and public subsidies to private interests? It is the record of history, the history of European imperialism, the history of the slave trade, the opium trade, the ruthless extermination of Middle-American and African and Asiatic societies by European powers, the on-going raids on the public treasury and public resources by private interests, and the like. Space precludes an adequate catalogue. Thorstein Veblen, a contemporary of Max Weber, was much the more aware of the role of force, fraud and waste in modern capitalism. Even Veblen, however, far underestimated the role of waste, public subsidies, and global military programs (not to mention space programs). Since his day, these kinds of phenomena have greatly multiplied. On another level, the importance of corporate crime has been amply substantiated by the studies of "white-collar crime" that followed E. Sutherland's landmark study of 1942. Much support for my counter-view of capitalist society rests on public documents of North American government agencies, or on analyses of these documents.[2]

But let us return to Weber. What account did he take of the role of force and fraud in the development of capitalism? His answer is given in ch. 26 of his *General Economic History*. There, he speaks of the profits of imperialism, slavery and related forms of exploitation.

> It is true that the colonial trade made possible the accumulation of wealth to an enormous extent, but this did not further the specifically occidental form of the organization of labor, since colonial trade itself rested on the principle of exploitation and not that of securing an income through market operations. (London: Allen and Urwin, F. H. Knight, trans., 1927, 300)

Is there a difference between exploitation and market operations? Contrary to Weber, we suggest that these two levels are closely related. Weber's distinction between colonial exploitation and ideal-typical capitalist operations is a non-sequitur. He merely asserts that they are unrelated, without presenting evidence. Further, he belittles contrary evidence. He writes off the loot from Bengal as insignificant, and likewise the contribution of slavery to capitalism – though on the next pages (*ibid*, 301) he admits that five million Africans were carried from Africa to the New-World English colonies between 1807 and 1847. Moreover, in Weber's day ample documentation of slave-trade profits was readily available.

It is time to listen to another voice. Writing in a British prison in India in 1944, Jawaharlal Nehru concluded:

> . . . Bengal, once so rich and flourishing, after 187 years . . . of British rule . . . is a miserable mass of poverty-stricken, starving and dying people. Bengal had the first full experience of British rule in India. That rule began with outright plunder . . . It was pure loot . . . the most terrible famines ravaged Bengal . . . And this lasted for generations . . . The corruption, venality, nepotism, violence, and greed of money of these early generations of British rule in India is something which passes comprehension. (*Discovery of India*, London, fourth edition, 1956, 295–296)

Nehru then cites the American writer Brooks Adams, whose *Law of Civilisation and Decay* first appeared in 1897.

> Very soon after Plassey (1757), the Bengal plunder began to arrive in London, and the effect appears to have been instantaneous . . . for all authorities agree that the industrial revolution began in 1770 . . . Inventions are passive . . . waiting for a sufficient store of force accumulated to set them in motion . . . Before the influx of Indian treasure, and the expansion of credit which followed, no force sufficient for this purpose existed . . . Possibly since the world began, no investment has ever yielded the profit reaped from the Indian plunder . . . (B. Adams, cited in Nehru, *ibid*, 296–297)

My conclusion is that Weber had a large blindspot. He had a poor grasp of the nature and impact of western imperialism and colonialism. He was out of touch with a major facet of the modern world.

II.

Despite its one-sided ideological, pro-capitalist leanings – or perhaps because of them – Weber's view of "modernization" has provided an influential model for American thinking about and advice to the pre-industrial nations on how to get themselves industrialized. Like Weber, such writers as Lipset and McClelland divide the world into "traditional" and "modern" societies. Weber saw the chief obstacle to modern capitalism as "traditionalism": the desire to live as one's ancestors did, rather than to gain more. (*Protestant Ethic*, 1939, ch. 2)

Let us consider the implications of this dichotomy. "Traditionalism," obviously, is a residual category. It includes all societies other than those chosen few who are the elect societies of the western world – indeed of the whole world. The inferiority of traditionalist societies is clearly implied. There is a second implication that all such societies are alike. Neither implication is justified. Both betray an arrogant, holier-than-thou world-view. Weber's parochialism is underscored by the fact that he wrote mostly before World War I. The world has greatly changed since that time, yet many North American "scholars" still cling to Weber's work as the foundation of their own world-view.

A longer view is at hand. Civilization (the discovery of agriculture and the rise of town life and nation-states) originated in four river-valley complexes: the Nile, the Tigris-Euphrates, the Indus, and the Yellow River. A fifth indigenous pattern arose in Middle and South America. The irruption of Europe during the last three or four centuries now looks like an afterthought, a backwash of history – indeed – a bad dream. Europe and its New World offshoots may better be seen as a negative contrast-conception, a special case, not a general model. All sorts of new perspectives are opening up in Russia, Yugoslavia, China, Scandinavia, Mexico, Cuba, Iceland. Who can say where the clouds of time may unfold tomorrow to reveal still other unanticipated vistas?

Considered as a whole, in its particular historical and geographic setting, every society is unique, whatever common elements it may share with other societies. Analytical comparison of institutions and societies such as Weber attempted in his work on India and China, is an important field, but it runs into difficulties stemming from the interrelationships of parts and wholes. Marx did not fall into this error. His concept of social class, for instance, is stated in generalized terms in the *Communist Manifesto*, a highly abstract, long-run view of history. In dealing with concrete situations, however, like the coup of Napoleon III in France or the American civil war, Marx uses additional concepts: factions, interest-groups, occupational groups, geography, personality, and so on. His analysis is dynamic, holistic and realistic. His academic critics miss the boat when they accuse him of not clarifying his concept of social class. The static and timeless abstraction they are seeking is irrelevant in dynamic Marxian analysis.

In comparing the economic ethics of India and China with that of modern western Europe, Weber became parochial and culture-bound. His latter-day followers do not escape from the same trap. Here are the main points advanced by such American sociologists as Lipset, Hagen, McClelland, Parsons, et al. To rise above "traditionalism" and to attain "modernism," a society must, they say:

- latch onto some sort of achievement-motivation or Protestant ethic;
- make changes gradually;
- go through the same stages as the USA (after Rostow).

But history does not conform to this idealistic, culture-bound dogma. Weber published his work on China in 1915; on India in 1916–17. He found that neither Hinduism nor Confucianism was likely to foster appropriate attitudes for economic development. Notwithstanding Weber, China today is well on the way to her own version of modernism. And it seems probable that the Weberian view of India will prove equally unrealistic.

David McClelland finds that "it is values, motives or psychological forces that determine ultimately the rate of economic and social development" (*The Achieving Society*, Princeton, N.J.: Van Nostrand, 1961, 238). He argues that plans for economic growth in underdeveloped countries should "mobilize more effectively the high need-achievement resources to select and work directly with the scarcer high need-achievement resources in underdeveloped countries" (*ibid*, 391).

What does this academic jargon mean? I suggest it tells us little about the needs of underdeveloped countries. It may tell us something about the incapacity of North American academics to explain what the contemporary world is all about. Last spring I lived for several months in Amritsar, a city in northwest India. Having been in close contact with local business and professional circles there, I believe there is no lack of entrepreneurial talent in India, nor is there any scarcity of motivation for material gain and upward mobility. The trouble lies rather in the institutional and structural obstacles, such as class, caste and communalism. This is confirmed by S. A. Shah's book, *Structural Obstacles to Economic Development* (New Delhi, 1967).

Seymour Lipset in *The First New Nation* (New York: Basic Books, 1963) has made one clear change in Weber's model of economic development. He has substituted as a model for underdeveloped countries the USA in place of western Europe. Perhaps this is progress. But it merely exchanges one ethnocentrism for another, with little or no gain in comparative or historical or futuristic insight. Zero plus zero still equals zero.

III.

What explains the parochialism, the one-sided conception of capitalism and its evolution, that we find in Weber and his many followers in North American sociology? From a sociology-of-knowledge viewpoint, the congruence between the political interests of western capitalist societies and the intellectual productions of the Weberians is obvious. As public-relations men, Weber and his successors are experts. They tend to portray capitalism in idealized terms. They play down the seamier aspects of its development. They encourage underdeveloped nations to adopt a world-view and a theory of history congenial to the ideological and political interests of western imperialism.

Doubtless these are important services. But they are political and ideological rather than sociological. They do not convey a realistic history or a dynamic analysis of the modern world. They neglect the insights afforded by a dialectical perspective. Hence they fail to meet one of the prime professional responsibilities of the sociologist—cultivating the "sociological imagination" of ordinary people. By the same token, they also fail to meet another major responsibility—making available realistic pictures of the modern world and its alternatives, as a resource for informing public and social policies. If policymakers choose not to use such insights, that is their own responsibility.

C. Wright Mills put the matter this way:

> Classic social analysis . . . is the concern with historical and social struc-
> ture; . . . its problems are of direct relevance to urgent public issues and
> insistent human troubles. (*Sociological Imagination*, New York: Oxford
> University Press, 1959, 21)

Every sociological perspective has ideological implications. It is a question of recognizing such implications, and assessing them all, and not
avoiding them. Some perspectives are more realistic and insightful than
others. Weber's error was not that he was ideological, but that his particular ideological orientation was hidden, parochial, unrealistic, and
not conducive to a holistic, dynamic view of the modern world. It is
therefore time to cut Weber down to size.

Notes

1 J. W. Ondrack, "The Sasquatch Phenomenon in Alberta," in A. K. Davis, editor, *Canadian Confrontations* (University of Alberta, 1970), pp. 51–59.

2 P. M. Sweezy and Paul Baran, *Monopoly Capital*, N.Y., 1966. H. Magdoff, *The
Age of Imperialism*, N.Y., 1969. R. Rhodes, *Imperialism and Underdevelopment: A
Reader*, N.Y., 1970.

India's Looming Destiny: Revolution*

T HE DECISIVE 20th-century revolutions (so far) have been those in
Russia, China, and Cuba. Two produced a Great Power, economically and politically. By contrast, India in 1947 gained only political independence. She has not yet won the battle for economic independence
and economic productivity, despite her immense resources in population, historical traditions, unused minerals. In many ways, the structure
of exploitation inherited from the British has simply been Indianized
and even intensified. But events on the great Indian sub-continent may
be entering a new phase.

Indian Politics Since 1947

The Congress Party has ruled India since independence was won from
Britain after a generation of intense struggle, non-violent on the part
of India but not of Britain. That epic mass surge was led by Gandhi,
Nehru, Bose¹ and many others, including numerous Moslems. Indepen-
dence began with partition of the sub-continent into India and Pakistan –
Britain's last official act, or imposition.

Non-violence meant that the Indian leaders undertook civil disobe-
dience: they put themselves and their followers in positions inviting British violence which the Indians endured passively as best they could.
Upon such a moral base was built one of the greatest mass movements
in world history. It shook the British empire to its foundations, and restored India to sovereign self-rule.

The new India, like Pakistan, began independence with an economic
and social structure stunted and impoverished by two centuries of Brit-

* 1972 unpublished manuscript, with 1989 afterthoughts.

ish rule. Partition was another complication, from which both India and Pakistan suffered, whatever each may have gained. The reform problems confronting India were overwhelming, and progress in resolving them has been desperately slow. India has 14 major languages and perhaps 3000 sub-castes. The latter are hereditary occupational, regional and ethnic groups, rooted in the dim past and changing only slowly. Religious or communal divisions are still significant. The Hindu majority is not politically united; there is a 10 percent Moslem minority; and there are still other small religious communities like the Sikhs and Parsees. India is a fractionated society. Changes, including the growth of national unity, have been creeping.

Yet some progress in economic, political and educational affairs has taken place. However, no great dent has been made in the abysmal poverty, and rapid population growth has tended to wipe out the small gains in productivity and literacy.

Like most Indian parties, the Congress Party has been divided, vacillating and too often corrupt. Its large landlord element has retarded needed land reforms. Its urban business minority, a source of limited innovation, has successfully enlarged the capitalistic sector of the economy. Party policy has also supported a sizable public sector. Nonetheless, State-assisted capitalism has not yet got the new nation off the ground. The gap between rich and poor seems to be widening. At the same time, mass aspirations for a better level of living are rising. This will intensify pressures for reforms.

Another thread in Indian politics is socialism. This has stemmed from a small group of intellectuals, formerly led by Nehru (1889–1964), one of the greatest of modern world leaders. The real roots of socialism in India lie in the exploitation of British colonial rule, and in the examples of Soviet and Chinese achievements.

As Prime Minister, 1947–64, Nehru managed to hold together the diverse elements of the Congress Party. After his death, rifts widened. By 1967, when Nehru's daughter Indira Gandhi had emerged as Prime Minister, the Party split into a moderately progressive majority led by Mrs. Gandhi, and a large right-wing minority. That paralyzing split was finalized during my first visit to India in late 1969.

The March, 1971, election ended this impasse. Mrs. Gandhi won a sweeping victory on a platform of social justice, rising productivity and ending poverty. While I was in India that spring, even the decimated rightists talked glibly of social justice and socialism—these being the popular slogans. As usual, most of this was talk. Politicians are talkers the world over, but in India they seemed to me to talk more than usual, yet say less. This included the Communists.

Even under peaceful conditions, Mrs. Gandhi would have had to work miracles to achieve a small part of the promised reforms and pro-ductivity gains. Not the least of her obstacles would be the apathy and corruption in her own party. The Bangladesh crisis, however, jeopar-dized any prospect of productivity gains. Eight or 10 million refugees fled or were shoved into impoverished northeast India in the spring of 1971, when West Pakistan troops were unleashed upon the people of East Paki-stan. The economic and social cost of supporting those refugees in India threatened the delicate balance between stagnation and progress for years. The popular mandate for a new deal in India could give way to factional extremism. That could mean suicide for the Indian Congress regime. War, preferably limited, appeared to India as the lesser evil.

Let us be clear. The first aggressive move in the 1971 war was made by Pakistan, shovelling refugees into India. The reply has been the counter-invasion by India.

The Spectre on the Left

The other reason for the Indian military reply was the threat of a Com-munist Bengal republic, possibly including 120 million people–about 70 million in Bangladesh and the rest in India's West Bengal. Talk of West Bengal separatism during my 1971 stay in India was speculative–as in Quebec–but there is an underlying substance. Like Quebec, the Bengalis have their own language, culture and a viable economic base. The great poet Tagore was a Bengali. West Bengal includes India's largest city Calcutta (7 million), a big industrial development, and a rural proletariat.

Once-wealthy Bengal was plundered by the British in the late 18th cen-tury. In our own day, West Bengal has been exploited by India, and East Bengal (now Bangladesh) by Pakistan. For example, India compensated 1947 refugees from West Pakistan with land left by Moslems fleeing north-west India. But 1947 refugees from East Pakistan–about 4 million–were not compensated. On the other side: in the mid-1950s West Pakistanis held over 90 percent of the top civil service posts in Pakistan, and over 70 percent of the top military posts (95 percent of the officers, by another source).

Bengal has a radical tradition. It is a suppressed nation, like Quebec, only more so. Nowhere in India is poverty more intense. In March, 1971, the Communist vote across India was about 10 percent, split between the Moscow-oriented Communist Party of India (CPI), and the China-oriented Communist Party of India Marxist (CPIM). But in West Bengal the vote was 45 percent Communist: 35 percent for CPIM and 10 percent for CPI. Mrs. Gandhi's all-India vote, incidentally, was 43 percent, though this was enough to win 68 percent of the Lok Sabha (House of Commons) seats.

West Bengal is a police state. Its 1971 State government, formed without the State's largest party, the CPIM, was dismissed in July, 1971, by the New Delhi federal government, and replaced by "President's rule." This step, previously invoked several times, and in accord with India's centralized constitution, shows the basic dilemma of the Congress regime. The Congress government has been unable to produce the necessary reforms; yet it owes its mandate to the rising mass aspirations it has stimulated in order to win votes and stay in power.

The Indian Left is highly fractionated, like the rest of Indian and Pakistani society. The CPI may be written off as "Establishment." It is led by old-elite, upper-class types, with many middle-class followers. In June, 1971, I visited its New Delhi headquarters, an imposing mansion. Asking for party literature, I was politely put off: the functionary in charge of handing out literature was out having tea. The CPIM is another matter. It is well organized and radical. A third radical faction waits in the wings. This is the Communist Party of India Marxist-Leninist (CPIML). They are usually called Naxalites, after a district they once seized. They do not bother to run electoral candidates or print programs. They operate by direct violent action. They capture districts in the countryside, redistribute land, shoot or expel landlords and other Establishment types, and function out of the barrels of their rifles. During my stay in India, the CPIM and the Naxalites in northeast India seemed to be shooting mainly each other.

We have next to explore the internal pressures that have impelled Pakistan toward war with India, and the complex international aspects of the 1971 India-Pakistan war.

In the India-Pakistan crisis, past and future meet in a confrontation that may be the first phase of great changes in the Indian sub-continent. More important than the opposing claims of both governments over the secondary question of who first attacked whom—are such underlying realities as traditional Hindu-Moslem enmities, internal tensions in both India and Pakistan, the baleful heritage of British rule and British partition, and the self-interested machinations of foreign Great Powers, the USA, the USSR and China. In a situation so complicated as this one, it is safe to say only that many calculations of the five governments will prove erroneous. Indeed, unforeseen consequences may be the rule rather than the exception.

Pakistan Since 1947

Both India and Pakistan began their independence with economies twisted and stagnated by two centuries of British rule. The British treated India as a colony. Indian manufacturers, flourishing in the early 18th century, were deliberately stifled. India was reserved as a market for British manufactured exports, and a source of raw materials for British factories. The opium foisted on China in the 19th century was grown largely on British-managed plantations in India. The balance of crafts and farms in the pre-British Indian village was broken. Driven out of crafts, the Indian population piled up on the land, creating that imbalance, that overdependence on agriculture which still survives in both India and Pakistan. By 1921 the rural population had grown to 89 percent of the total; it eased only a little to 82 percent by 1961. In contrast, about three-fourths of the Canadian population was classed as urban in 1966.

Before British rule, Indian farms were larger, and there were exports of Indian steel and textiles. After the battle of Plessey in 1757, direct plunder, especially in Bengal, became a major source of capital for Britain's industrial revolution. Indeed, one reason why Quebec, conquered about the same time, got better terms than Bengal was that the loot was far less in Quebec. In both Quebec and India, however, a divide-and-rule policy prevailed; the conquered populations were crowded onto the land, while urban industry and commerce were reserved for the British.

The 1947 partition left Pakistan with roughly one-fourth of the sub-continental population (including a 20 percent Hindu minority in East Pakistan) and by far the smaller part of the land, mineral resources, trained administrators, universities, and popular leaders.

After partition, Pakistan was less successful than India in consolidating the nation and improving the lot of the common people. Pakistan has been more dominated by reactionary landlords and narrow elites, civilian and military. For a decade, the civil bureaucracy ran the show. Since 1958, an even more reactionary military regime has been in power. Its failure to resolve the worsening social and economic problems led to the ousting of the dictator in 1968, after some bloody strikes by workers, students and peasants. But another general took his place.

East Pakistan, treated as a colony by West Pakistan, is now wholly alienated. Even in West Pakistan, large ethnic and civilian groups feel left out. A limited war is therefore welcome to the West Pakistan military clique, to put down its civilian rivals and to justify its budget claims (over 80 percent according to the New Statesman, compared to about 40 percent in India). If they could win Kashmir in place of Bangladesh, the West Pakistan generals would hope for a reprieve for their tottering regime.

Internal pressures, therefore, seen as dire threats to survival of the two regimes, have impelled India and Pakistan to resort to war as the lesser of the evils.

Pakistan as a Non-Nation

In historical retrospect, the venture of establishing Pakistan as a Moslem nation seems to have failed. Religion alone as a basis of national unity is not enough. (Israel is further proof.) Class, regional, ethnic and linguistic differences were not adequately taken into account. A reading of G. Myrdal's *Asian Drama* and other sources leaves the inescapable impression that the chief basis of Pakistan has been its Moslem-oriented hostility to Hindu India. This is a negative foundation. Nations need a positive basis of coherence: a history of past struggles and achievements, and widely shared aspirations and participation in realistic future progress. India has moved in that direction, however inadequately. Pakistan has accomplished less. India has the past traditions of civilizational achievement, dating back some 5000 years; it has the present resources to become a Great Power, if it can wield the iron broom as China has done. But Pakistan can never be a Great Power.

Even Kashmir, where I spent May, 1971, might think twice before it adhered to Pakistan. Kashmir has a Moslem majority, but a Hindu ruling minority. Nehru came from Kashmir's upper-class Brahmin aristocracy. But what does Pakistan offer Kashmir? Some 20 families in West Pakistan control two-thirds of the industry, four-fifths of the banking, and nearly all the insurance. By UN data, the Pakistan masses were consuming fewer calories in 1960–61 than they were a decade earlier. The gap between rich and poor has been widening in Pakistan, as indeed all over the world. My own brief visit to West Pakistan in June, 1971, gave me a keen impression of the early 19th-century Sikh kingdom based on Lahore, but a very blah sense of present-day Pakistan. The military regime today is reactionary and brutal.

This does not mean that West Pakistan cannot make it as a small nation. I believe it can. But it must work out its positive ethos, its own program of social and economic uplift that will do something for the ethnic minorities and the common people of Pakistan. Hitherto, West Pakistan has had its own colony of East Pakistan to exploit. The best jobs, both civil and military, have gone to West Pakistanis; East Pakistan produce (jute, tea, rice, etc.) has been exported for the prime benefit of West

Pakistan. UN and Harvard studies clearly establish the exploited status of East Pakistan in relation to West Pakistan. Now all that is over.

In the West, we have neglected the significance of small nations as viable entities of modern community living. We have paid too much attention to the super-powers. My 1971 visits to Iran, Yugoslavia and Iceland (to mention only three) strongly suggested to me the importance of our learning to think in terms of smaller, more decentralized national units. The point is directly relevant to the case of Quebec in Canada.

What accounts for the unstable stance of Pakistan since 1947? Here we must turn to the complicated web of international meddling on the Indian sub-continent in our time.

Foreign Complications

Britain engineered the India-Pakistan partition in 1947 as a divide-and-rule device. No Great Power wants to see a new Great Power on the Indian sub-continent. But if Britain was responsible for the decrepit condition of colonial India, the USA perpetuated that dependency by supporting Pakistan as an outpost of American encirclement of Russia and China. Early in the 1950s, Pakistan became an ally of the USA, with appropriate financial and military grants. This has served to perpetuate the myth and deluded self-image of Pakistan as a major military power on a par with India.

By contrast, India under Nehru pursued a policy of non-alignment with either Cold-war bloc. Nonetheless, in practice India leaned toward the USSR, although it vigorously worked both sides of the street. Today, India gets the greater part of her military hardware from the Soviet Union.

But India and the USA can agree on a middle-class, Awami-type regime for Bangladesh, and on the suppression of Maoist-type peasant revolutions in Bengal.

What about China? In the early 1960s, Pakistan and China effected a rapprochement. The spectacle of communist China in bed with fascist Pakistan is something to think about. One obvious explanation is the alignment between USSR and India: China would automatically take the other side because of China's quarrels with the USSR. Yet this is not wholly satisfactory. In Bangladesh and its embattled peasantry, we see a close parallel to China's own struggle against imperialism. My hunch is that China may change its position: already there are signs of that shift. But China will not likely support a middle-class regime in Bangladesh that would be under the influence of India and the USA. A radical grass-roots regime in Bangladesh could be another matter.

A Tentative Summing Up

For different internal reasons, both India and Pakistan find a limited war the least of the evils. But the war may not be limited. The revolutionary movements both countries fear may not be contained indefinitely. The roles of foreign powers may change on short notice. The aspirations of the masses seem to be rising in both warring countries, but the gap between rich and poor is also increasing. War will not solve the long-run problems of either India or Pakistan, nor will it ease them. War can only defer or intensify their internal dilemmas. Hence it may catalyze some events not foreseen or not desired by the harried Establishments in New

Assorted Data for India, Pakistan and Bangladesh

	India	Pakistan	Bangladesh
1990 Population (millions)	853	123	113
Life expectancy (years)			
Males	58	59	56
Females	59	61	56
Infant death rate			
(deaths/1000 live births, first year)	91	113	98
Percent urban	28	32	24
Crude birth rate per 1000 persons	32	43	33
Crude death rate	11	10	11
Total fertility rate (live births per 1000 women 15–49 assuming no mortality or change in current fertility patterns)	3.9	6.4	4.2
Annual per capita Gross National Product (GNP) (in U.S. dollars)	$350	$370	$180
Literacy (people over 15 yrs)	44%	26%	33%
Post-secondary education	n.a.	1.9%	1.3%
M.D.s per person	1/2471	1/2081	1/6166
Hospital beds/person	1/1130	1/1783	1/3233
Daily calories per capita	2104	2167	1925
Percent U.N./FAO food norm*	95%	94%	83%
Radios per person	1/15	1/11	1/25
TV sets per person	1/42	1/73	1/315
Telephones per person	1/189	1/152	1/572

* FAO—Food and Agriculture Organization.
Source: *Encyclopedia Britannica 1991 Yearbook* (most data are at least one or two years old).

Delhi, Islamabad, Washington, and Moscow. Peking, on the other hand, appears to have some flexibility in its options.

When I first went to India in 1969, I was convinced that India would never make it into the modern world because of the staggering burdens of poverty, illiteracy, apathy and reactionary vested interests. I changed my mind. India could cope, if she stopped postponing social and economic reforms, and if she rid herself of the large remnants of colonialism inherited from the British.

An Indian renaissance might be important for the rest of the world, too. Science and technology as used in western societies have resulted in destructive life-ways. Harnessed to a different and more co-operative social framework, science might become part of a humane civilization. If such a civilization is to emerge on this planet, seemingly bent on self-destruction, the best chances appear to lie with the Oriental societies – Japan, China and India.

» «

1989 Afterthoughts

WHILE ATTENDING a 1969 conference in mid-November on Third World Development, meeting in New Delhi, I remembered that the late Jawaharlal Nehru's birthday, November 14, is widely observed as Children's Day. Doubtless there would be ceremonies at the Nehru Palace, now a State Museum within easy walking distance of my posh hotel, the Asoka. So, early in the evening I joined a throng of visitors in the magnificent Palace grounds. Nehru came from a very wealthy Brahmin family in Kashmir, far northwest India. There were folding chairs for 2000 on the great lawn. Several hundred seats for officials and special visitors were roped off, front and center. To my astonishment I was steered into the reserved section, simply because I was a Caucasian, and a Sikh friend with me was also admitted – because he was with me! How ironic and revealing, I thought to myself: a white foreigner was given precedence over a native son.

Prime Minister Indira Gandhi (1917–84), Nehru's daughter, soon arrived and was seated in the front row. Her bodyguards – two soldiers – promptly wandered over to a nearby wall and fell asleep on the ground. We were then entertained with a Sight and Sound show on the history of India.

The political career of Indira Gandhi over the years was stormy, to say the least. She was Prime Minister, precariously at times, 1966–77 and 1980–84. There were chronic confrontations driven by unrealized reformist promises, mass poverty, separatist tendencies and clashing vested interests fed by feudal landlords, religious intolerance and expanding capitalism—not to mention India's imperialist ventures northward inherited from British days.

In June, 1984, Mrs. Gandhi committed a colossal blunder by sending the Army to attack the most sacred of Sikh shrines, the Golden Temple at Amritsar. I visited there many times in 1971. Nearly 500 Sikhs perished in that siege. Mrs. Gandhi thereby signed her own death warrant. Five months after the attack she was assassinated by members of her Sikh bodyguard.

In 1971, I returned to India for a sabbatical leave, based on Amritsar, the Sikh cultural and historical center in Punjab, a constituent state in the northwest of the Republic of India. As in 1969, my mentor was Dr. Gurbachan Singh Paul, friend and fellow scholar. My sojourns in India were lessons in holistic insights and dialectical perspectives.

Note

1 Subhas Chandra Bose (1897–1945) was an important Hindu leader for India's independence movement, 1920s to 1940s; occasional associate of Gandhi, but also an advocate of industrial and military action, both contrary to Gandhi's philosophy. In World War II Bose led an army of 30,000 Indian and Southeast Asian volunteers. With limited German and Japanese aid he invaded northeast India in late 1943, but was narrowly defeated in 1944, in Imphal.

Research as a Resource for
Community Development

I N NEARLY EVERY FIELD of human activity today, both public and private, there is a growing awareness of the prime importance of research. Research means nothing more than the scientific collection of facts, and the refinement of verifiable theories, more or less relevant to some field of effort. Social research means finding out as much as possible, in a systematic way, about the characteristics and development of some segment of social life.

Sometimes social research is mistakenly confused with policy-making. Research, if it is competently done, increases our knowledge about social processes. Such knowledge may serve as a resource for policy-making in various groups and communities. But knowledge is only one of several factors that enter into policy-making. Traditions, emotions, vested interests and sheer inertia are other factors. Moreover, the people who decide and administer social policy are usually completely distinct from those who carry on social research. As a publicly financed agency, the Centre for Community Studies makes its research results freely available to all interested persons who wish to use, check, criticize, or merely read its reports. The Center does not make policy for communities or for any other social groups.

Why Community Research is Essential

Research becomes the more necessary as enterprises become socially more complex and technically more advanced. The physical and biological sciences are a cornerstone of our advanced industrial machine-age

Research orientation of the Saskatchewan Center for Community Studies, Saskatoon, Canada, 1958.

society, and of our high standard of living. Support for social research, however, has lagged far behind. Yet our institutions and communities have long been highly specialized. They are becoming more complex, and more subject to change. The welfare of people and communities, both urban and rural, depends increasingly on events and decisions made elsewhere. Clearly, social foresight and systematic knowledge about social groups are indispensable to public well-being.

But only in recent years has social research been encouraged on even a small scale by various universities, governments, and private corporations. This is a perilously tardy response to an overwhelming need.

Sixty years ago, when Saskatchewan communities were still fairly self-sufficient and isolated, perhaps they could well afford to go their own ways. Now that agriculture and trade centers are specializing, that early saga of the independent farmer and the idyllic country town is fast ending. Few communities today, if they wish to preserve−or regain−something of their former initiative and self-reliance, can afford to be ignorant of the social and economic forces that mold their existence.

Prospects of the Small Community

In recent decades, centralizing tendencies have become a growing force. The modern nations of the world have become dominated by metropolitan and regional cities. In the cities are the highest standards of living. There the key decisions on a nation's economic and social policy are usually made. Meanwhile a many-sided crisis of the cities is intensifying, especially in the older and larger cities of North America. Far-reaching changes will be necessary to resolve such urban problems as antiquated administration, taxation, housing and blight, transportation, and so on. Although our main interest at the moment is the smaller communities of Saskatchewan, all of us−city and country people alike−need to be aware of these urban crises, because we all have a stake in their successful resolution.

Urban trends and influences, after all, are among the more basic causes of the Saskatchewan social changes. Already it seems possible to divide Saskatchewan communities of all sizes into two distinct types: those which are growing and those which are declining. Does this mean that the small community has no future?

A long-run view suggests a more favorable prospect. The development of automation and of decentralized atomic power plants, along with certain other technical advances, may enable our smaller centers eventually to attract the skills and to enjoy the amenities now concentrated in the cities. This assumes, of course, the achievement of a stable peace and full employment, which can be worked out only on the inter-national and national levels. The social changes now underway in the modern world and in Saskatchewan irresistibly demand adjustments in our smaller communities. But these adjustments have a hopeful side as well as a painful one. And there is room for reinforcing the more de-sirable adjustments, and for easing the painful ones, by means of com-munity self-study, foresight, and self-development.

The Changing Concept of Community

Enough has been said to underscore the diverse meanings of "commu-nity." In early Saskatchewan the term was much less ambiguous. It usu-ally meant a fairly well defined hamlet or small town. Now it may mean any social group from a neighborhood to the whole world. Smaller cen-ters look up to larger ones for certain specialized services and look down to their own satellite neighborhoods. School and hospital districts along with numerous other divisions complicate the picture. Even regional cities like Regina and Saskatoon are in no sense self-sufficient. They are simply more complex nuclei in the national social system.

What then is a community? Let us think of it as a nucleus, partly ter-ritorial, plus an indefinite number of extensions upward toward the prov-ince, nation, and beyond; outward to other centers; and downward toward subordinate groupings. Thus for certain legal purposes the rele-vant community may be the incorporated town of Davidson; for edu-cational purposes the community is the enlarged unit school district, plus certain relationships to the Provincial Government; for trade pur-poses the relevant community may be Davidson plus the nearby sur-rounding towns—although for certain specialized services Davidson may be part of the Saskatoon trade area. In still another context, the signifi-cant community may be a neighborhood within Davidson town.

Finally, communities tie into and overlap each other in numerous ways.

In brief, the concept of community is a flexible and dynamic one, vary-ing with the situation in hand. Learning to think of themselves in these terms may be an important skill for people in communities to acquire.

Contributions of Research to Communities

If properly done on a sufficient scale, social research should give us a reliable sense of the over-all drift of the times, and an index of the rela-tive importance of the basic changes underway in Saskatchewan commu-nities. This means, in part, further analysis of some of the general Saskatchewan trends already identified by the Royal Commission on Rural Life. We need to know more about leadership changes, for example, and about the social effects of in- and out-migration upon communities. We need to know more about the pre-conditions and the effects of industrial development upon communities, since this seems to be a matter of growing importance. What are the chief interest groups in various types of communities, and how do they interact in political, educational and leisure activities? Are there discernible uniformities in community self-development and problem-solving?

Social research gives the community a clearer self-image. It identifies those elements in the social environment to which a community must adapt, and those other elements which an active community may hope to modify by its own actions. Research can help to define more precisely what are the problems facing a community. It can analyze the experiences of other communities in similar circumstances. It can highlight the assets and liabilities associated with alternative courses of action. In short, research can make for more realistic and self-controlled communities.

The Limitations of Research

Research, like community self-development of which it is a part, is no panacea. Research reveals the hard facts of reality; it does not change them. Community policy is probably determined more often by emotional considerations, vested interests and inertia than by rational considerations buttressed by systematic research. As societies become more industrialized, however, the areas of rational planning by public and private groups tend in the long run to widen. In any case, what use is made of research findings depends on a community's policy-making forces – its legal agencies, voluntary organizations, informal factions and inherited traditions.

Another limitation on research is scarcity of resources. In this imperfect world it is necessary to establish priorities on projects, and invariably it turns out that only a few of even the most essential studies can be made.

The Center's Research Premises

Though we cannot for some time to come spell out the Center's research program, we can sketch some of the principles that will guide us. I think the five premises about to be listed are all related to each other.

The first of these is clarity of communication. We think that competent social analysis can be presented to both the man in the street and the specialist, without resorting to professional jargon that often obscures more than it reveals, and without writing down to the supposed level of the non-professional reader. Since the Center is a publicly financed agency, we feel a special responsibility for clear reporting to the people of Saskatchewan.

The second is an action frame of reference. Much of modern social science has been developed as a static system, especially on the theoretical side. It hardly seems realistic to analyze an obviously dynamic society like ours in terms of a static social theory. Yet a surprising number of social scientists have leaned in that direction. They have analyzed communities as stationary rather than as evolving groups. The study of social change has been one of the weakest areas in modern social science. Granted—this is an oversimplification—just lately, for instance—in the last five years—there has been a revival of scientific interest in social change. But it seems not far wrong to say that in the past generation the majority of community studies have focused on social structure rather than on social change.

While structural approaches will be useful to us, they will be subordinated to dynamic approaches. In other words, we are more interested in communities viewed in transition from yesterday to tomorrow than in communities viewed as if they were standing at a fixed point.

Our third premise is that, by using a dynamic frame of reference, we may help to bridge the conspicuous gap between theoretical and applied social science. Theory without concrete application tends to be useless; practice without theoretical insight tends to be superficial. We have a great number of statistical studies and case histories on crime, juvenile delinquency, and mental illness. But when it comes to adequate theories for interpreting this wealth of factual data, we are poverty-stricken. Public policy on crime, delinquency, and mental illness therefore continues to flounder in half-measures that are generally both inconsistent and ineffective.

A fourth premise is viewing communities as wholes, keeping all their aspects in sight, social as well as economic, ceremonial as well as political, informal as well as formal.

A fifth premise is that foresight and planning, in our increasingly complex society, are becoming more and more essential to our well-being, perhaps to our very survival. The future of local democracy and self-determination may well lie, not in the avoidance of planning, but in more planning—and more effective implementation of planning—by the local community. As a distinguished British scientist recently said, "We can steer our community only if we combine a general knowledge of where we are bound with a specific will of where we want to go."

Community Development: Science or Ideology?
A Prairie "Dust Devil;"[1]
The Rise and Decline of
a Research Institute

IN 1963 THE ADMINISTRATIVE HEAD of a Canadian social science research institute prohibited the private circulation and the independent publication of several research reports produced by permanent and
part-time members of the staff. The Institute was located on a university
campus, but it was not an integral part of the university. It was chartered
and financed mainly by a provincial government. Several years earlier,
the establishment of this Institute had been greeted with national and
international acclaim. By mid-1962, however, the enterprise was obviously declining without ever having realized its promise. The size and
quality of the research staff had begun to decrease. The prohibitions of
1963 were actually symptoms rather than causes, although they accentuated the downgrading. Less than a year later, the Province cut off its annual grant to the Institute. Within the next year, the Institute was being
eased off campus by the host university, and its basic (i.e., Ph.D.) scientists had left.

How can these events be interpreted? How can the auspicious beginning be reconciled with the dismal ending? These questions provide the
main focus of the present paper, which assays a dynamic analysis of the
life-history of an organization, by the person who was Chief Research
Officer and Senior Research Sociologist at the Institute from 1958 to
1964. A second and perhaps more important focus is the relation be-

Reprinted by permission of the Society for Applied Anthropology from *Human Organization*,
Vol. 27, No. 1, 1968.

tween the social organization of a research agency and the type of research produced by that agency. This case seems particularly relevant for illuminating such perennial problems as: (1) the internal administration of social research institutes on university campuses, especially the relations between bureaucratic administrators and professional specialists; (2) the relation of social science research institutes to university administrations, faculties and norms, particularly the norms of academic freedom; and to external clients and publics. I offer no definitive solutions to any of these dilemmas. Indeed, I believe there are no real solutions. There are only *ad hoc* compromises. But the alternatives can perhaps be clarified, and this limited gain seems worthwhile.

In the present paper, therefore, I describe a case of social research activity that had neither a purely university nor a purely governmental setting. It was a unique and, as it turned out, unstable combination of both.

At the risk of oversimplifying, a rough continuum of organizational contexts for social research may be set up. At one end would be the bureaucratic, action-oriented agency, such as a private Madison Avenue market research firm, a Project Camelot, or a public governmental department. In such a setting, the researcher is primarily a technician seeking more efficient means for realizing the given ends of his agency or its clients. At the other end of the continuum is the university where a social researcher may analyze not only the means but also the ends of action.[2] Our conceptions of "technician" and "professional" are almost identical with P. Baran's definitions of "intellect worker" and "intellectual."[3]

I imply no ethical judgments as to the relative social value of technicians and professionals. Indeed, none is possible on scientific grounds. Both types are obviously needed in modern society. Still, there is a certain antipathy between the two. Technicians readily stereotype professionals as aloof, alienated, and overly sceptical. Professionals easily view technicians as "brainwashed." My aim is not to judge but to clarify these two roles. There is a social cost attached to both role-types. The professional research-scientist may have to sacrifice popularity and perhaps also some material gains. The technician may struggle for a professional status that is largely denied him. After all, what the great universities profess to train is the independent and critical Ph.D. scholar—the professional. "Classic social analysis," said C. Wright Mills, "traditionally deals with whole situations."

"Scepticism is the beginning of science," wrote Veblen. Yet participation and involvement—for individuals, not for agencies—may likewise be a source of sociological insight.[4] Perhaps the academic social scientist, to practice his profession as a professional, needs to combine Olympian detachment with participation, so as to achieve an often personally frustrating "sceptical involvement." But he also requires an appropriate organizational context in which to operate.

Considering the problems inherent in scientist and technician roles, the following hypotheses may be stated:

1. To the extent that the research organization is dominated by political or bureaucratic elements committed to serving directly or indirectly the real or imagined interests of a non-university action group or agency, to that extent the social researcher is pressed toward a technician role by the research organization.

2. Conversely, to the extent that the research agency is controlled by university norms of disinterested teaching and research, the social scientist may operate as a professional who critically analyzes both the means and the ends of the action situations he studies.

The Organizational Development and Structural Tensions of the Research Institute

The institute involved in the present case study was created in 1957 by an Order-in-Council of the cabinet of a Canadian province. It was located on the campus of the provincial university, which agreed to act at least informally as a "co-sponsor." Financing came from an annual provincial grant of approximately $135,000 until this was cut off in 1964. Within a few years, additional income, mainly from contract research for provincial government agencies and occasionally from federal and cooperative corporations, raised the annual budget to about $200,000. At its 1962 peak, there were some thirty permanent and temporary employees. Roughly half were of professional or semiprofessional status; the rest were clerical and secretarial.

Half of the Institute's Board of Governors were nominated by the university's Board of Governors. The other half were nominated by the provincial cabinet, which made all board appointments. The chairman of the Institute Board was for some years the Provincial Minister of Education, who was dependent on and responsible to the provincial legislature. Appointed in 1957 to direct the Institute was the former head of a provincial public commission. Essentially a promoter, he held a Bachelor of Science degree in agriculture, and had served briefly as an assistant professor and director of the university's two-year vocational school of agriculture. The hiring of the professional staff began in 1958.

Salary scales and tenure policies in the Institute paralleled those of the host university, except that the Institute's professional staff were on an eleven-month schedule and usually got salary increments a year late. By an Institute Board minute, the administrator of the Institute was rated as a dean, salarywise. The professional staff of the Institute were rated and paid on the basis of their academic qualifications. Division heads, for example, held Ph.D.'s and usually had considerable postdoctoral experience; they were classified as Professors or Associate Professors with tenure. They were not, however, eligible for membership in the Canadian Association of University Teachers. Nor were they members of the faculty-staff association or the faculty council. At best, the Institute had a step-child status in the university community.

Three main reasons may be suggested for these facts: (1) the predominantly governmental sponsorship of the Institute, in terms of financing, client, and board composition; (2) the non-academic image of the Institute head; and (3) the conflicts between the internal organizational aims of the Institute, and traditional university functions. To the last of these topics I now turn.

The Fatal Organizational Flaw

Officially, the Institute had three parallel divisions for research, training, and consultations; each was responsible to the administrative head. In fact, this tripartite structure obscured the operating realities. It therefore seems best to look beyond the formal blueprint to the dualism that actually controlled the work of the Institute's staff. Throughout its existence, the Institute had two *de facto* wings: (1) *social research* and (2) *community development*. The latter was an action program, albeit vaguely and mildly conceived. Both wings were primarily interested in the smaller towns and rural areas, although the research wing had some urban projects.

The prime concern of the research wing, at least during the Institute's ascending years, was objective analysis, let the chips fall where they may. The chief interest of the extension and consulting divisions on the other hand, was "local community development"[5] – a confusing combination of adult education and local developmental goals seeking limited and harmonious change in small communities. Moreover, the ethos of the two action or program divisions was basically the same. Most of their professional staff held Ph.D.'s in the closely allied fields of adult education or extension. Hence it is realistic to speak of the two non-research divisions as a single "extension-and-action" wing of the Institute.

In a nutshell, the great flaw in the organization of the Institute was the ill-conceived combination of research and action programs in a single structure operating (however marginally) from a university campus.

It would appear, first, that an independent and university-oriented research program cannot be harmoniously coordinated with an action program, except on the basis of autonomy for each wing. That autonomy was achieved and with some difficulty maintained during the early years of the Institute, but it was lost during the years of decline that followed. Second, social-action projects, with their unavoidable political implications, run counter to the non-political tradition of modern universities. The only two legitimized corporate functions of a university, regardless of its sources of financial support, are education and research. In this case, the political program was eventually scrapped, nominally by the Institute itself in 1962, then effectively in 1965 by the university, which moved to edge the Institute off the campus. These events merely underline the incompatibility of the research and extension-and-action programs which prevented the Institute from ever acquiring a clear public image.

Let us now consider in more detail the built-in organizational tension between the two wings of the Institute. Throughout the Institute's history, the extension-and-action wing was numerically and hierarchically dominant at the all-important senior staff level. The administrator of the Institute and two of the three division heads were "community developers"—the first by emotional inclination, the others by training. This made the head researcher a permanent minority of one on the Institute Executive Committee. By contrast, at the junior level, the researchers outnumbered the extension-and-action personnel by two or three to one. Moreover, roughly two-thirds of the Institute's budget was devoted to research. In brief, the power structure did not adequately reflect the functional importance of research activity in the Institute.

In practice, this internal political imbalance enabled the extension-and-action wing to mount periodic attempts to harness the research wing to its own program. The original planning of the Institute, indeed, called for involvement of research personnel in the study and implementation of the Institute's action program, and this view persisted in the minds of the director and other senior persons in the extension-and-action wing. This approach might have been workable, if the Institute had not been located on a university campus, and if the research wing had not been staffed with graduate Ph.D.'s, broadly trained for independent research in terms of whole situations—let the chips fall where they may.

Research people of this caliber were attracted to the Institute because of its university location and its personnel policies parallel to those of the host university. The Institute planners placed great emphasis upon employing fully qualified (Ph.D.) staff, so as to attain so far as possible a university image. Except for a few marginal juniors, the Institute recruited scientists from leading universities of three Western nations. Such persons could hardly collaborate with people more concerned with politically acceptable programs.

In short, the action-and-extension wings, if associated with "technical" instead of basic "professional" research, would doubtless have functioned well as part of a government department. But given an academically-oriented research staff in a university setting, assigned to analyze an action program carried on by their own Institute—such research could not have been independent and comprehensive, by the prevailing standards of their scientific disciplines. To cite only one example: research was conducted in 1961 in a town where the action-and-extension wing had for some years operated a local "community council." The latter had played an important partisan role in local affairs; omitting it meant a serious gap in the research report. But to include it would have meant something of an "exposé," an attack on the extension-and-action wing, on its public integrity, and on its self-esteem. For a comprehensive review of the community council would have had to include both its intended and its unintended consequences. Hence the data on the council, although collected, was largely omitted from the research report, which thereby acquired to some extent a "house-organ" aura. A few years later, after the project director had left the Institute, a paper based on the omitted data was presented at a meeting of a professional association.[6]

Organizational reasons, then, explain this built-in inhibition of professional research in the Institute. The only viable compromise was complete autonomy for each of the Institute's two wings, with limited areas of free collaboration.

During the early years, that autonomy was successfully fought for and maintained by the research wing, partly because the other wing was preoccupied by its own projects, and partly because the chief administrator, by spending much time away, left a benevolent vacuum in the home office. Nonetheless, the internal imbalance manifested itself in sporadic efforts by the extension-and-action wing to "get the divisions together," by which they meant tying the researchers to the Institute's action projects. Much costly staff time was wasted in these abortive campaigns, in the form of innumerable committee meetings which critically delayed the basic research programs. This in turn adversely affected the Institute's image on campus. When the application of the Institute to join the university was turned down in 1961, only one research project had been completed, a "classified" study that could not be shown to the reviewing faculty committee. Numerous documents from the extension-and-action wing, including the speeches of the administrator, had if anything a negative effect on the committee.

Actually, a policy statement that the Institute would do no "classified" research was drafted by the researchers and passed verbatim by the Institute Board in 1959. It became a dead letter within a year. This critical lapse was as much the fault of the researchers as of the administration. In retrospect, it seems clear that university-oriented social research institutes should not undertake classified research. In this case the first work was done for Co-operatives. Once opened, the gate could not be closed. The stage was set for eventual conflict between basic research desired by the senior researchers, and technician-type research sought by the Institute administration and clients. The struggle over contract projects, perhaps more than anything else, eventually led to the Institute's professional decline.

This does not mean that the Institute failed completely. Considerable work was accomplished by both wings. The research wing produced studies of various regional social movements, problems and organizations. The extension-and-action wing carried out several stimulating adult education projects. The services of the consulting division were especially in demand by rural communities and provincial voluntary organizations.[7] All in all, there was an air of élan, optimism and expansiveness about the Institute during its early years.

Institute–University Relations

Ambivalence was the prevailing tone. That the Institute's community-action program entailed involvement in local politics clashed directly with the traditionally non-political character of a university.

The political overtones of several action projects befogged the Institute's image, both on and off campus. The annual attacks on the Institute by Opposition politicians in the provincial legislature at budget time reinforced the impression that the Institute carried on activities unsuited to its academic environment. The attacks were invariably stereotyped barrages rather than informed critiques, but so were the Government party's defense. Neither the Opposition nor the Government party really knew much about the Institute's purpose or activities. In the ivy tower of academia, however, it was enough that political controversy was focused upon the Institute, and, by association, on the host university.

Although some Institute staff members, as individuals, formed fruitful professional relationships with university professors, there was little or no organizational rapport. The university representatives on the Institute Board were mainly natural scientists and administrators, rather than professors, with little grasp of the problems of social research or community development. They were letterhead legitimizers, not policy-makers or counselors.

Originally, the Institute, after a trial run, was to be considered for incorporation into the university. An application by the Institute was duly filed in 1961. The outcome was so crucial to the Institute's fate that it deserves special consideration.

The Turning Point, 1962

With its rejection by the university early in 1962, the Institute reached a point of no return. Paradoxically, the seven-member faculty committee appointed to evaluate the Institute was heavily weighted with friends of the Institute. At least five were favorably disposed; another, a campus power figure, was neutral. Yet the committee unanimously advised against admitting the Institute "at this time." That recommendation was accepted by the faculty council without a dissenting voice. How could this happen?

Some of the main factors have already been mentioned. They include (1) the Institute's internal dualism, which introduced a political element foreign to university traditions, and tensions which had delayed the research program, and had blocked the emergence of a clear Institute public image; (2) the professionally uncertain character of the numerous documents and speeches submitted by the extension-and-action wing to the faculty committee in support of the Institute's application; few or none of these would have been publishable in academic journals; and (3) the non-academic image of the administrator, which inhibited the general confidence of the academic community.

A secondary cause of rejection was doubtless the last-minute proposal of the administrator that the Institute should enter the university, not as part of the faculty responsible to the faculty council and the academic dean, but as an autonomous unit directly responsible to the university president. To most members of the reviewing committee, this looked like a move to put the Institute's director in a vice-presidential position within the university.

The full consequences of the university's decision were not apparent for several months. On the surface, the summer of 1962 marked the zenith of the Institute with respect to research activities and size of staff. By September, however, there were decisive signs of decline. Several of the most qualified researchers, both permanent and temporary appointees, departed and were never replaced. A strategic, grass-roots study of the 1962 Saskatchewan medicare crisis was cancelled on political grounds by the Institute administration over the unanimous opposition of the research wing—a symptomatic failure of leadership nerve. Probably the main result of the university's rejection of the Institute, however, was a reorganization of the Institute's internal structure by the director in late 1962.

Demoralization

On the surface, the new order seemed to scrap the extension-and-action program. But the extension-and-action people all remained on the Institute's staff. They were simply reassigned to going research projects, although none of them had any demonstrated competence in research. Restated: a majority of the Institute's senior staff (including the head) suddenly found themselves functionless in their fields of professional competence in extension and community action. They were forced to seek desperately for new roles to justify their positions.

The reorganization, which was meant to extricate the Institute from its problems by dropping the politically "hot" and academically unacceptable community action program, thus had the actual effect of intensifying internal stresses. Assigning the extension-and-action people (still numerically superior at the senior level) to research[8] meant a massive interference with certain of the research projects under way. Those projects so affected were converted from broad-gauged professional-type projects to technician-type exercises in program planning—the supplying of more efficient means to the contract clients' pre-existing organizational ends.

For example, a survey of Métis communities in the wilderness hinterlands north of the Canadian prairies had started out as a comprehensive and critical review, not only of the instrumental provincial programs in that region, but also of the ends of public policy. After the Institute reorganization, the "official" report of this project confined its attention to the problem of how to improve the implementation of existing policies of the provincial government (which was paying for the survey). The aims and premises of current policies were tacitly endorsed, with no assessment of their practicality. This was Madison Avenue soapselling, not university research.

There is, of course, nothing wrong about program-planning, technician-type research *per se*, so long as it is properly labelled and not passed off as something else, and provided it is carried on outside a university context. Neither proviso was realized in this case. In effect, the Institute was assuming a partisan role (for a good price) in the organizational politics of its clients, while appearing (by virtue of its university location and campus ties) to provide objective and neutral analyses.

Another major consequence of reorganization was a great prolifer-ation of bureaucratic rules, committees, and paper work. This was par-ticularly true of the administrator's bailiwick. In due time, a detailed Institute Manual worthy of a large and ancient military bureaucracy was produced after endless staff conferences, just when such a handbook was least needed. A more magnificent example of Parkinson's Law would be hard to find. "Paperwork expands so as to occupy all the time and staff available."[9] During the ascending years of the Institute, when the two wings were each engrossed in their respective concerns, few rules were necessary because people were too busy. But in the period of contrac-tion and decline, more staff time was available for make-work activities.

The change from professional to technician-type was only one out-come of reorganization. Another result was the suppression by the In-stitute administration of research reports, the authors of which could not be pressured into conformity with the new dispensation. Still an-other effect was a decline in the number and quality of the research staff. These developments were interrelated in the following way.

First, senior extension-and-action personnel were given responsibility for some of the final research reports. Some junior researchers were read-ily won over, perhaps because they were given write-up and authorship credits, promotions, et cetera, beyond their normal expectations. In gen-eral, these people did not share the ethical norms governing university-oriented research. Second, a series of "consultations" were held between research clients whose agencies were financing certain Institute studies and the Institute's extension-and-action and junior (usually B.A. level) research staff. Institute research drafts were discussed in those meetings and gradually brought more into line with the clients' pre-existing spe-cial organizational interests. This process of reaching consensus was in-formal. Indeed, it was a latent function of such meetings.

The Final Phases

Rejection of the Institute by the university in 1961 posed the question of the Institute's future in acute form. There was talk of incorporation by a legislative enactment that would give the Institute a stronger legal base.[10] Incorporating legislation was drafted, but the Cabinet in January 1963 decided not to proceed. The reasons are not entirely clear, although the 1962 reorganization had reduced government representation on the Board and increased university membership. Government officials also were generally aware of the Institute's organizational and public rela-tions difficulties, and governments usually shy away from hot potatoes. Whatever the reasons, the government's decision to postpone incorporation was repeated in January 1964, although financial support from the government was unchanged.

A few months later, however, the Opposition won a provincial election, and promptly ended provincial subsidy to the Institute. By then, however, staff departures had so reduced the Institute's budget that it could survive for a considerable time on the proceeds of its federal contracts. To outsiders, the fall of the provincial government appeared to be the death blow of the Institute. That view is erroneous. The political overturn was no more than the proverbial last straw. The Institute's internal difficulties, including its leadership problems, suggest a verdict of suicide.

Regarding relations with the university, the 1961 rejection of the Institute had paradoxical results. On the one hand, it brought the Institute into closer touch with the university (on paper) than ever before. University representation on the Institute Board of Governors was increased, while government representation decreased. Above all, the official work program of the Institute was now almost entirely labelled research.

Operationally, however, very little had changed. The Institute's two wings were still there, but no longer autonomous: the extension-and-action wing had won a Pyrrhic victory over the research wing. Government financing and government research contracts still paid most of the shot. Most significant was the steady shift away from research guided by a broad university orientation, toward a technical service for government, Co-operatives, and other organizations. In historical perspective, this was a return to the original plans of the Institute, whereby research was to serve the political action program. Fundamentally, this intensified the negative attraction between the policy-oriented Institute and the traditionally non-political university.

Left at the altar by the government in 1963 and 1964, the Institute had no choice but to court the university once again. For example, a dozen fat fellowships for university scholars were offered. More important, the Institute made its second application for admission to the university in early 1965, under quite different circumstances from the 1961 overture. With its professional staff severely depleted and its pipeline to provincial coffers severed, the Institute offered itself on almost any terms. It agreed in advance to give the university a veto power over Institute policy. A faculty reviewing committee offered two alternatives: (1) that the university should not widen existing relations with the Institute (this was passed by the faculty council); (2) that the university should end existing relations with the Institute. The latter did not pass, but the effect was the same as if it had passed. For the Institute could hardly re-staff with competent professional (i.e., Ph.D.) researchers without full university membership. Only by offering joint appointments and university tenure could it hope to attract fully qualified personnel. Such university membership was denied. Opposition to the Institute centered in the social science faculty members; support came mainly from natural scientists, who could see only that the Institute might "bring in research money." Soon afterward, the removal of the Institute from the university campus was announced by its administrator. Whatever its ultimate fate, a chapter in the history of Canadian social science had ended. Another prairie "dust devil" had subsided.

Conclusions

Toynbee and other historians have argued that civilizations do not usually fall victim to assault from without; they first decay from within. A similar verdict seems applicable here: death by suicide, not murder.

Looking back at the original ambitions of the Institute, it seems evident that the whole emphasis on hiring Ph.D. researchers had "unintended consequences" that spelled disaster. Likewise, locating a technician-and-action-oriented agency upon a university campus had unforeseen disturbing results. The Institute's penchant for Madison Avenue slickness in its public relations was unimportant by itself. But it was symptomatic, in academic eyes, of an underlying disregard for university and professional norms. Such nonconformity on the part of the Institute was a significant source of organizational difficulty.

Three modes of adjustment would have greatly reduced the organizational tensions. The Institute would probably have functioned well as a government department or as a private agency off campus, provided it did not try to include a university-oriented research wing. To prove viable in the university, it would have had to drop very early its action program and to substitute an academic leadership for its promoter-type administration.

However, the lasting interest of this case study lies in its implications for understanding the relationship between the type of social research and the nature of the organizational framework in which it is carried out. A single case, of course, does not permit definitive judgments. But the evidence suggests that a research organization committed to the service of non-university agencies or interests tends to limit or reduce its researchers to technicians bent only on improving the means to the client's given ends. Conversely, a research organization oriented to university norms can more readily undertake comprehensive or professional kinds of study that include the analysis of the ends as well as the means of action.

Both researchers and graduate students need to recognize the implications of different organizational contexts of social research—not only for such obvious things as salary, working conditions and career potential, but also for the very character and quality of their research reports. Comprehensive social analyses are ordinarily undertaken most effectively from a university base. The chief exception would probably be "radical" studies too controversial to find a haven in university settings. These are often of great importance, but they are outside the interests of this paper. In government departments and private agencies, there is a risk of "cooking the results" by bureaucratic pressures or financial concerns over future contracts. Both kinds of pressure occurred in the present case. Other cases may offer divergent evidence.

The tentative conclusion is that university social research institutes should not undertake "classified" projects.[1] Indeed, the technician-type of social research has no place in a university setting because it implies an unethical camouflaging role for the traditionally disinterested university. Whether this statement ought to apply also to the natural sciences would be an interesting question. Finally, I suggest that university-based or university-oriented social research agencies should be directed by academic personnel who have the confidence of the academic community.

The matter of administrating university research centers is, of course, far more complex than has been indicated in the present paper. It is inevitably, in part, a bureaucratic and collectivistic enterprise. There are large problems of mustering financial, library and personnel resources, especially in projects which cut across traditional disciplinary lines. Communications with scholars and projects elsewhere must be established. Above all, the administrator must, in my opinion, be a practising scholar; otherwise, he risks the disrespect of the scholarly community and a consequent loss of the moral authority prerequisite to successful administration. Moreover, assigning a scholar to administration incurs a loss of scarce scholarly potential since administration has a way of becoming a full-time task. Perhaps the solution (which has been suggested by others) is to have two administrators, so that each may remain a part-time scholar. Such a pattern would doubtless present its own special problems, but at the moment no better solutions come to mind.

Notes

1 Dust Devil: a short-lived dust column raised by spinning hot air.

2 That there are limitations on freedom of research, even in universities, was long ago recognized by Thorstein Veblen, *The Higher Learning in America*, Huebsch, New York, 1918.

3 P. Baran. "The Commitment of the Intellectual," *Monthly Review*, Vol. 13, 1961, pp. 8–18.

4 Consider, e.g., the appendix of William Whyte's *Street Corner Society*, University of Chicago Press, Chicago, 1953.

5 The Institute never achieved a consensus on the meaning of "community development." United Nations agencies apply the term to technical assistance programs aimed at helping underdeveloped communities to help themselves. Under favorable conditions, those small-scale projects have achieved varying degrees of success. On the other hand, the concept of community development, especially in North American social policy, has become a euphemism for "doing little things in little places" i.e., for talking about social change in rural hinterlands without actually doing much about it. To be significant, social change must be structural: it must entail relatively lasting revisions in economic, political and social role patterns. This in turn requires not only the involvement of the people who are supposed to change, but also among other things – the investment of real money. Too often, North American programs of community development (whether in the New World or the Old) have been strong on grass-roots involvement but weak on investment. They appeal to politicians, naturally enough, because they cost little more than a few staff salaries for field workers. Such programs also attract many other well-intentioned people, because "community self-development" conjures up the magic aura of grass-roots democracy and the sacred myth of gradualism, so dear to the hearts of "liberals." This sort of mystique pervaded the extension-and-action wing of the Institute. It was difficult for the Institute's community developers to face up to the fact that substantial local development would mean large scale investment – inevitably from outside sources – either in the area's underdeveloped resources, or else in the relocation and rehabilitation of underemployed local populations.

6 D. E. Willmott, "The Role of a Community Council in a Developing Prairie Community," unpublished manuscript, University of Toronto, n.d.

7 Institute extension-and-action personnel usually operated in terms of manifest functions: they took their "small-communities-are-good-and-they-ought-to-be-saved" ideology largely at face value. In practice, however, their effective functions seem to have been latent. In the smaller communities without an economic future, the latent function of the action program of the Institute was mortuary – presiding at the wake and facilitating the transition to new horizons. In the larger centers that had an economic and therefore a social potential, the Institute's community councils provided a channel and sounding board for the competitive emergence of new local elites. Both types of cases inevitably involved the Institute in highly emotional, local issues. The facts of social conflict, unfortunately, tended to be obscured from the consciousness of the extension-and-action wing by a mythology of "consensus through talking and conferencing."

8 The leading adult educator was not assigned to research, but to "research utilization." When this proved part-time and relatively menial, he shifted his

focus to outside agencies. He thus retained a professional role in his own field. However, it had little to do with the Institute's official program.

9 C. N. Parkinson, *Parkinson's Law,* New York, Ballantine Books, 1964, p. 15.

10 Its existence had hitherto rested upon a provincial Order-in-Council – that is, an executive decree. It could be rescinded by a cabinet vote, should the government fall to an opposition party. Changing a legislative act would be more difficult.

11 I. Horowitz, "Michigan State and the CIA: A Dilemma for Social Science," *Bulletin of the Atomic Sciences,* September 1966, pp. 26–29.

» «

A Note on
The Community Development Movement

SOME HARD LOOKS at the ideological mystique and the objective roots of the community development movement are long overdue; Professor Erasmus' paper is a large contribution toward meeting that need.

Where the modernizing of rural communities is associated with successful revolutionary mass movements (as in China) or with large-scale investment (as with new mines or oilfields in the Canadian prairie hinterlands), we can perhaps talk realistically about community development. By community development I mean the movement of a population toward higher material levels of living and toward the institutional patterns associated with urban-industrial society, whether of the capitalist or the communist variation. Such planned change as accompanies this complex process is probably best viewed as an embroidery on much larger, unplanned economic and social trends. But where "planned change" becomes a program of governmental agencies without such a context of massive investment or a mass movement, community development is mainly an ideology of change without the substance of structural change. Indeed, it often functions as a defense against structural change. In such cases, its proponents and practitioners are in the position of those who take their own propaganda at face value without recognizing the real score.

My limited observations of community development projects in Canada would reinforce the analysis by Erasmus. Two supplementary comments seem relevant. I think the distinction between growth-generating investment in mines, manufacturing, etc., and auxiliary investment in roads, schools, and similar social services is a useful concept that we can borrow from the economists. The late Paul Baran, for example, holds that no amount of auxiliary investment by itself can generate economic growth. Since governments are mainly responsible for this type of investment in most Western nations (the other type being in private hands), and since the same governments usually undertake community development programs, the limitations of government-sponsored community development projects are further compounded in the light of this distinction.

My second comment concerns the *encogido* syndrome. I agree with Erasmus' description of the tendency of many community development projects to establish or to reinforce patron-client dependency relationships. But to what extent is this dependency a "front" used by the local community to exploit their superiors for whatever tangible and intangible benefits may hereby be gained? A forthcoming paper by P. T. Spaulding indicates that in certain isolated Métis and Indian settlements in Northern Saskatchewan the conning of white administrators and other unaware middle class types is a well-developed art.* This "fun and games" aspect may not be a general property of community development programs, but its presence or absence deserves further checking.

---

* In A. K. Davis (ed.), *A Northern Dilemma: Reference Studies*, Western Washington State College, Bellingham, Washington, April 1967. Two volumes.

Urban Indians in Western Canada: Implications for Social Theory and Social Policy

I N THE ADVANCE 1968 PROGRAM of the Royal Society of Canada, the topic of this paper was announced as "Indians of the Plains." This conveniently unspecific title permits me now to narrow the focus to urban Indians in western Canada's Prairie Provinces–the subject of my own empirical researches, in recent years, in Saskatchewan and Alberta. It is not enough to present facts and figures about Indians living in towns.[1] It is also necessary to think about the facts, and to conceptualize them. Above all, it is indispensable to relate the facts to contemporary alternatives of national and local social and political policies. That a cleavage between theory and practice can be devastating to both practice and theory has been demonstrated by Benjamin Farrington in his papers on ancient Greek science and medicine.[2] Nonetheless, we still do not know how to relate–systematically and fruitfully–theory and practice in the social sphere. This remains very much an *ad hoc* compromise, at best. The vested interests of academia and public bureaucracy defensively confront each other, like the two towers in Tolkien's fantasy, *The Lord of the Rings*. Which one you define as the dark tower depends on where you happen to sit.

Broadening Concepts and Lengthening Historical Perspectives

My general contention is that to understand the phenomenon of the urban-dwelling Indian in western Canada, we must draw upon all the social sciences, including history in particular; and upon both the ortho-

Reprinted by permission. *Transactions of the Royal Society of Canada*, Vol. VI, Series IV, June 1968. Sec. II.

dox and the Marxian intellectual traditions of social philosophy and political economy.

Two or three generations ago, the anthropologist could pitch his tent on the outskirts of a tribal village in Polynesia or in Africa or Canada, and then take his field notes on the attitudes and behaviour of the local inhabitants, confident in his faith that he was reporting a unique way of life. Today this is much less possible; indeed, it is becoming increasingly rare. In some quarters, perhaps, the term "Indians of the Plains" may still conjure up an image of pre-industrial and pre-reservation life in the nomadic camps of the old West, before the white ranchers, farmers, and miners elbowed the Indians on to their restricted reservation backwashes. A host of writings by travellers and anthropologists is available for the reconstruction of that way of life as it was yesterday and the day before yesterday. But the effective frame of reference in terms of which we now view the Indian has drastically changed.

Social scientists now look upon these small Indian communities, which in Canada's prairie provinces exist for the most part in rural areas, as integral parts of our complex, large-scale national society. They are linked to that larger society partly by an historical background of colonial relationships and colonial exploitation going back to the fur trade, the classic account of which was written by the economic historian Harold Innis.[3] The Indian communities are also linked to the national society by the kinds of administrative relationships that have developed between Indians and government. While these involve relationships of power and dependency, they may also be conceived as a process of "encapsulation"[4] progressively imprisoning both the Indians and the administrators in a comparatively inflexible, self-maintaining bureaucratic system. The federal Indian Affairs Branch is a prime example of encapsulated system-maintenance, but similar phenomena are to be found in certain provincial agencies and programs in Saskatchewan and Alberta.

Finally, Indian communities are related to the national society by informal patterns of apartheid perhaps best understood in terms of the sociological concept of social class. For apartheid in Canada, as in the United States and in South Africa, is not based on race, but on differential access to the complexes of property, wealth, organizational skills, and technology that form the essential institutional structure of modern urban industrial societies, both capitalistic and communistic. In other words, apartheid is only superficially a matter of inherited biological differences and geographic separateness. Such physical differences, which the physical anthropologists categorize as stocks, races, and breeds of *homo sapiens*, have indeed become symbols of class status, but they are not otherwise casually or essentially significant. In plain language, Indians behave differently (in certain respects though not in all) and live apart from middle-class whites chiefly because they are poor. With few exceptions, they have not been substantially drawn into the middle or upper reaches of that complex of economic and political patterns which is the distinguishing institutional feature of North American society. They exist—or subsist—in its lower echelons. They are not apart; they are way down below.[5]

In this sense of social class, apartheid is an integral aspect of Canadian social structure, just as much as (if not more than) in the United States. It is simply less visible, because that particular segment of the Canadian under-class which is demarcated by racial as well as by economic and social criteria is proportionately smaller than its counterpart south of the border. Indians and Métis may constitute three or four per cent of Canada's population, compared with the twelve per cent of the American people who are black. Moreover, the latter are concentrated in urban centres; this is not yet the case with Canadian Indians.

As is probably evident by now, the term Indian is used in this paper to mean all those persons living in Canada who perceive themselves, and who are defined by others, as people of Indian ancestry. This is not to argue that the differences between the legal concept of "Treaty Indian," the kinship category "Métis," and the term "non-Treaty Indian"—not to mention other minor classifications—are not important in certain relations. But I have not found them to be of any great significance for describing the "Indian way of life" in the isolated, impoverished rural enclaves which comprise most of the Indian reserves and the Métis hamlets in Saskatchewan. Similarly, Treaty Indians and Métis living in towns face basically the same range of problems, life prospects, and living conditions.

As mentioned earlier, the general frame of reference for analysing both rural and urban Indians in Canada has come to be the national society, especially since World War II. The works of anthropologists Hawthorn, Belshaw, and Dunning, among many others, may be mentioned as examples of the prevailing tendency to see these small, and still to some extent culturally unique, Indian communities as parts of the national whole. In addition, we need a comparative view of institutional structures and social systems. Here sociologists as well as anthropologists[6] have much to contribute. Sociological studies of ethnic group relations and of rural-urban comparisons are of major importance for illuminating White-Indian relationships in Canada. And for understanding numerous aspects of the urban migration of Indians, sociological and historical analyses of European and Negro immigration to American cities during the nineteenth and twentieth centuries are indispensable.

Thus far, we have singled out as essential analytical aids for the scientific study of contemporary Indians in western Canada a broader frame of reference and a comparative approach. It now remains to stress the importance of an historical overview. The germinal work of Innis on the fur trade in Canada has already been cited. If anything, this may underestimate the significance of the historical legacy in latter-day Indian-White relationships. In this context, I do not refer solely to the intensifying sense of inherited grievances against the White man voiced today in crescendo style by the youthful Indian advocates of "Red Power." Attention should also be called to the work done by neo-Marxian writers on the subject of the exploitive relationships prevailing between advanced industrial nations and under-developed countries, or (as I prefer to put it) between metropolis and hinterland. The basic idea that metropolitan elites exploit their hinterland retainers is, of course, not new; indeed it is widely accepted among both orthodox and Marxian analysts. Adam Smith was in no doubt about the heart of the matter when he wrote in *The Wealth of Nations* that advanced or manufacturing countries characteristically secure a great share of the "rude produce" of underdeveloped economies in exchange for a very small part of their own manufactured goods. What needs to be emphasized today, it would seem, is the point that the metropolis not only exploits its hinterlands, it creates them, and perpetuates as long as possible their economic, social, and political dependence.

Here we may refer to the work of the contemporary economic historian, Andre G. Frank. Though he specializes in Latin-American case studies, his key ideas apply to the circumstances of Indians in Canada.[7]

> Historical research demonstrates that contemporary underdevelopment is in large part the historical product of past and continuing economic and other relations between the satellite underdeveloped and the now developed metropolitan countries. Furthermore, these relations are an essential part of the structure and development of the capitalist system on a world scale as a whole. A largely erroneous view is that the development of these underdeveloped countries will be stimulated by diffusing capital, institutions, values, etc., to them from the international and national capitalist metropoles. Historical perspective suggests that on the contrary in the underdeveloped countries economic development can now occur only independently of most of these relations of diffusion. (p.18)

Two key points, applicable to the Indian under-class of Canada, follow from this model. First, Canadian Indians since the beginning of the fur trade in the seventeenth century have been systematically harnessed to the world capitalist market. To obtain such desirable European products as metalware, trinkets, fire-arms, fire-water, Indians were compelled to harvest and export furs, on an increasing scale, at prices set in the markets of the advanced countries (England and France, originally). Later, structural changes in world markets brought forth new forms of economic development and a relative decline in the fur trade. Following Canadian federation in 1867, agricultural settlement, transcontinental railroads, immigration, and the build-up of commercial towns in western Canada became keystone elements in the new "National Policy." This necessitated shunting the Indians onto out-of-the-way, federally administered reserves, where most of their descendants still remain—the cast-offs of an earlier, by-passed phase of modern capitalism.

Second, in order to free themselves from their historical legacy of encapsulation in a strait-jacket of subordinating relationships, Indians must fight back. The recent appearance of militant Indians agitating for concessions and talking of "Red Power" points to new phases in White-Indian relationships. Whatever may or may not result, the general point is the immanent tendency of hinterland groups, sooner or later, to rebel against their metropolitan exploiters, and to try to improve their position within the larger national economy. Their first move is to seek an improved status in the going system, rather than to reject that system and substitute another.[8] That was the upshot of all the main phases of the farmers' movement on the Canadian prairies during the twentieth century. It is also the core, thus far, of the message now being sent by Black Power advocates in the United States and by the spokesmen of Canada's embryonic Red Power movement. Despite their apparently radical goals, they are really seeking a better position within the existing capitalistic social system. Moreover, they are not even presenting a new theme in North American society. Rather, they are reiterating one of the oldest value and behavioural patterns in the New World. Historically, newly arrived immigrant groups in Canada and the United States have always made their place in the sun by sticking together, by organizing into ethnic pressure groups. So it was with the Germans, the Italians, the Jews, and the others. Here is an example from Winnipeg in the early 1930s. James Gray describes the efforts of ethnic minorities to catch up with the dominant Anglo-Saxons under conditions of economic scarcity in the following words: "The North End filled up with home-based contractors. When a Ukrainian went into the construction business, he trailed a small army of other Ukrainians behind him—a Ukrainian excavator, a Ukrainian concrete-mixer, a Ukrainian plumber, a Ukrainian carpenter, a Ukrainian painter, a Ukrainian plasterer. It was the same with the Germans." (*The Winter Years* [Toronto, Macmillan, 1966], p. 133)

Thus far I have argued that a traditional, locally oriented ethnological approach to Indians of the Plains has long been obsolete; that Indian and Métis communities must now be viewed in terms of Canada's national urban-industrial society; and that historical comparisons with minority patterns elsewhere are indispensable, and especially with social movements arising in under-class and hinterland groups seeking to improve their status vis-à-vis exploiting metropolitan elites. Let us now turn briefly to some facts and figures about urban Indians in Saskatchewan towns. As these results have been reported in detail in a research report published last year by Western Washington State College, only a few of the major findings need to be mentioned here.[9]

Urban Indians in Saskatchewan: Some Research Findings

This study of about 160 Métis and Indian households living in Prince Albert, North Battleford, and Meadow Lake, Saskatchewan, was conducted in the early 1960s. The report is entitled "Edging Into Mainstream."[10]

The chief interviewer, a Métis from La Ronge, Saskatchewan, resided in the two larger towns during two successive winters for a total of nearly six months in each, and a somewhat shorter time in Meadow Lake. Supervisory visits were carried out by myself on weekends. Anthropologist P. M. Worsley, now at the University of Manchester, played an important role in the early stages of the project.

By and large, the Métis and Indian households in our three survey communities were not recent arrivals. The average length of time our respondents had spent in their present (at the time of our survey) place of residence was about a dozen years. Yet we found much longer terms of mean residence in other Saskatchewan towns, such as Esterhazy, Biggar, and Melfort; and much shorter residencies were reported in the 1957–8 Greater Winnipeg study of Indians by W. and J. Boek.[11] A majority of our informants were born within fifty miles of their current residence. Before they arrived, most of them moved short distances to other rural places, perhaps three or four times, staying roughly eight years in each place. Over the years, they had come to town slowly and steadily, rather than by spurts. But here we must say that household surveys can tell us nothing about over-all in-migration and out-migration patterns; they inform us only about those survivors of migration currently resident in the community at the time of survey, not about those who, having in-migrated, have since died or moved away.[12] .

Our figures suggest that Métis-Indian migratory and residential behaviour conforms roughly to the pattern of urban-rural differences established by many other studies. In general, the geographic mobility of residents tends to vary directly with the size of the community—the larger the town or city, the shorter the terms of residence.

Our migrants came "on their own" to the city, mainly for better jobs and better public services—including among the latter social assistance and schools. They moved into unskilled and semi-skilled jobs, and experienced frequent terms of unemployment and dependency on government welfare payments. Despite the hardships they met, a majority of our respondents intended to stay in town. A minority would like to move elsewhere, to other towns and cities (large urban centres in Alberta and British Columbia were most often mentioned), wherever work could be found. Hardly anyone seriously intended to retreat to the bush or the reserve. Ninety percent identified as "home" the place in which they then resided. In other words, home was the place in which the pay cheque—or the relief cheque—was cashed.

But there was a large undercurrent of ambivalence among these urban migrants. For many of them, the rural Indian reserve or the back-country Métis hamlet was still a second home—"the place, where when you have to go there, they have to take you in," so wrote the poet Robert Frost. Yet they could size up their life prospects with much realism. "Stay here? I guess I'll have to stay here. No other place to go." This entry in our field notes came from a Prince Albert man in his late forties, after fifteen years in the city with intermittent semi-skilled employment. Said another female respondent, "Staying here? Yes, it is the only place that will look after me. I have no home on the Indian reserve, and they won't give me enough to live there." This elderly widow had moved to Prince Albert two years before our study, because the city seemed to offer a better living—even on relief—than did the reserve. A North Battleford man, chronically unemployed and willing to move anywhere for a job, weighed his prospects this way: "I would be better off in the country if I had a job, but I would be worse off in the country with no school and no job." This informant had four children in school.

On the other hand, a young ten-year resident of North Battleford reacted this way to his chronic unemployment and to some other frustrations of town life: "Well, in town you just spend your money and you haven't got anything anyway. When you live in town you owe so many bills. You see something. You want to buy and they give it to you if you put something down. If you live in the Reserve there is nothing there you want to buy. This way in town you want to buy everything."

What were some of our other findings? Métis-Indian households were almost half again as large as their white counterparts in the same communities. Extra persons in the home were invariably relatives, whereas in white households, according to contemporary census data, they were more likely to be non-relative boarders. The educational level of our Métis-Indian respondents was approximately one-half as high as that of the white residents in the same town. Though the younger immigrants were distinctly better educated than their older co-migrants, considerable numbers of the latter are still being attracted to the prairie cities. Obviously, this presents a problem for the communities of in-migration.

"What nationality are you?" In answer to this question, about half of our respondents defined themselves either as some sort of half-breed or as "Indian." Another third saw themselves as "French." Only 5 percent said they were "Canadian"; these were mostly older people with fifteen or more years of city residence. In other words, ethnic identifications, which normally fade rapidly in cities as compared with rural areas, tend to persist longer among Indians than among most other Canadian groups.

Diverse and uncertain self-images are to be expected among people experiencing drastic social change. And migration from rural reserves to urban centres often entails culture shock. Confusion and self-rejection were common themes among our informants. "I guess I'm just a plain old breed." Rare indeed was the affirmation, "I'm a Canadian Indian." The over-all direction of change toward assimilation, however, was unmistakable. A young Métis householder summed it up better than he knew. Two or three years before our survey, he had moved into Prince Albert from the fringe agricultural belt north of that city. "My sister talks Ukrainian and can even sing it. Even Ukrainians are marrying Indian girls. The thing is, now everybody is so badly mixed up, they are all Canadian." This may yet prove to be one of the best definitions of a Canadian.

The economic facts concerning Indians are too well known to warrant much attention here. In relation to the population it had to support, the Métis-Indian labour force in our sample was about half as large, proportionately, as was the labour force in the three towns we studied. Moreover, Métis and Indian workers were overconcentrated in the lowest paid and least skilled jobs; they were also overrepresented among the unemployed. Incomes of course were low, about one-third as high as the corresponding figure for Saskatchewan in 1960, on a per capita basis. Nearly half of the total household, family, or per capita incomes came from transfer payments, although only one-sixth of the total income of all Saskatchewan families came from that source.

Did it pay to work? Yes, indeed. Métis-Indian households with employed heads had notably higher average and per capita incomes than did households with unemployed heads. Our findings contradict the popular notion that welfare payments to Indians are higher than earned family incomes, and thus an incentive not to work. In Saskatchewan during the early 1960s, at least, welfare payments and family allowances were no Santa Claus for Métis-Indians.

In our study, we paid special attention to housing and household amenities. Needless to say, the problem of substandard housing is both acute and widespread among Métis and Indian people living in or on the edges of Saskatchewan towns. We believe, however, that this is not primarily a Métis-Indian difficulty. It is a manifestation of the perennial problem of housing in urban centres. There is an acute need for good-quality houses and for rental housing which low-income families can afford. At present, the biggest and poorest families tend to be squeezed into the smallest and most substandard dwellings. A disproportionate number of these families are Métis-Indian.

A few specific findings may be worth citing. We found more doubled-up families proportionately among our Métis-Indian sample than were reported by the 1961 census for the three towns we studied. The number of rooms in Indian houses averaged about three-quarters that in all houses in those same towns, even though Métis-Indian households were half again as large as average households in these towns. Persons-per-room ratios for our Métis-Indian dwellings averaged about twice those for the whole community in the three urban centres and in Saskatchewan as a whole. We have devised what we think is a better measure of overcrowding than the commonly used persons-per-room ratio. Room-deficits per household were calculated by relating the age and sex composition of the household to the number of rooms in the dwelling unit, on the basis of standards set by the American Public Health Association, which in turn relies in part on British housing norms. In general, we concluded that Métis-Indian dwelling-units should have had half again as many rooms as they actually had, assuming a conservative standard of two non-sleeping rooms per household.[13]

What stands out among all these empirical findings is this: badly off as are these Métis-Indian households, in regard to both income and housing, they are vastly better off than their cousins on Indian reserves in northern Saskatchewan and around the Lesser Slave Lake in northern Alberta. Cash incomes were higher by one-third than they probably would have been "back home" on the reserve or in the isolated Métis hamlets. For example, a doubled-up, two-family household, despite its thirteen people crowded into six rooms, saw its ancient North Battleford domicile as a step up. They could look back on worse. "It's an old house, but it's in good condition. It's a damsight better than we ever had before." (Quoted from field notes)

We must now report on the participation of our Métis-Indian respondents in formal organizations, their use of the mass media, and their informal leisure activities. Membership in associations ran notably below the levels that characterize other working-class and lower-middle-class groups in various Saskatchewan and other North American communities. About three-quarters of our informants reported that they had no membership whatever. In Biggar, Saskatchewan, only 40 percent of the unskilled and clerical respondents were without memberships.[14]

Use of the mass media by our respondents was common, at least the radio. Ninety percent of the households had radios, and these were turned on most of the time. Chiefly favoured programs were western and popular music.[15] Two-thirds claimed to read at least one newspaper or magazine, usually the local daily or weekly paper. Book-reading, on the other hand, appeared to be light, and concentrated mostly on confessions, mysteries, and westerns. Little use was made of public libraries, which are associated with middle-class behaviour standards and with a certain level of procedural know-how. Most of our respondents were indifferent to movies. Only 40 percent had television sets, as compared with a figure of 70 percent for all Saskatchewan households in 1962. For newscasts, radio was the main reliance, even in homes with television.

The most commonly reported informal leisure activities were visiting friends and relatives, staying around home, or just hanging around downtown. The leading forms of commercial entertainment were visiting pubs and poolrooms, and playing bingo. Few said they watched or participated in sports, and not many reported that they liked to go fishing or hunting. Their leisure activities were much like those of low-income city people almost anywhere in North America.

Only one other major area of investigation remains to be summarized: Métis-Indian aspirations and their view of what special problems they face. On the latter topic, most responses were fairly realistic: they referred to the need for jobs, higher incomes, better health and housing. A minority (about 20 percent) thought they had no problems. From the standpoint of urban middle-class society, they appear to be either apathetic or unperceptive. Only 8 percent of the responses showed tendencies toward scapegoating—blaming others for their difficulties. In such cases, the usual scapegoats were other low-status groups like displaced persons.

Much to our surprise, only one-fifth of our respondents said they had personally experienced ethnic prejudice in their present communities. We had expected a much higher incidence. It may be suggested that the low incidence of prejudice reported in our survey was due to the fact that these Métis-Indians were not striving aggressively to improve their status and were not seriously competing with their white neighbours for better jobs and housing. Hence they did not perceive the treatment they received in these towns as discriminatory. We think that ethnic conflict is bound to increase in the future, as the Métis-Indians become more numerous in urban centres, more aggressive, and better able to compete for scarce jobs, housing, and public services.

Some Implications For Social Policy and Social Theory

The first implication for social policy may be summed up as the need to foster migration, especially of younger Métis and Indians, out of the rural hamlets and into the cities. Here we must remember the very rapid increase of population that now characterizes those Indian communities; remember also their substandard economic potential (with a few exceptions). Above all, Indian aspirations are rising: they want the material amenities of modern life. Hence there is a potentially irresistible push off the reserves. Yet so far the flow of migrants to urban areas has been slow. It has been retarded by a mistaken and ill-conceived public policy of subsidizing these unviable rural communities, and by the natural reluctance of many Indians to accept the white man's "rat race" as a way of life. The reserve or the rural hamlet is still their home, their basic source of security, however inhospitable in certain respects. Of necessity or preference, many Métis and Indians, especially the older generations, will remain in their ancestral countryside retreats. But this should not prevent us from recognizing those reserves which are economically inadequate to support their rising populations at modern levels of living for what they really are—outdoor custodial institutions and rural slums. I believe that public subsidies to these economically unpromising country slums should be tapered off; that the money should instead be spent on relocation, housing, anti-discrimination, educational and job-expansion programs on behalf of cities receiving Indian migrants; that the Indian treaties should speedily be renegotiated; that birth control clinics should be made available at once to Indians so desiring (and to whites, too); and that the encapsulating federal Indian Affairs Branch should be phased out of the picture. Here I am criticizing the bureaucratic system rather than the undeniable skills and good intentions of the officials; surely these people would be useful, perhaps indispensable, in another organizational context.

The second implication for social policy is the need for general programs aimed—in a non-ethnic perspective—at such national Canadian problems as housing, low incomes, unemployment and underemployment and undereducation. The most promising principle seems to be "general programmes, with special liaisons" to reinforce the appeal for participation by specially handicapped groups. Those politicians who are advocating merely limited, special programs aimed at "problem pockets" in Canadian society appear to us to be operating on a mistaken premise.

Social reforms on the scale here envisaged do not arise because professors write papers like this one; even less do they materialize from bureaucratic programs laid on from the upper reaches of public or private establishments. A comparative view of other societies suggests that a wide social movement aimed at modifying the fundamental structure of Canadian society appears to be the only way to transcend the basic problem of poverty. The latter, rather than the "Indian problem," should be our third and major target. In line with our theorizing about the metropolis as creator of dependent hinterlands, we believe that it is the economic and institutional order of urban-industrial Canada which produces and perpetuates the Other Canada—the culture of poverty which includes not only Métis and Indians, but also many small farmers, older people, the automated unemployed, and so on.

Even greater issues will then confront us. Indeed, they are upon us now. Here are the perennial questions of social class, poverty, social revolutions abroad, the world population explosion, Canada's relation to big Yankee brother, and of course nuclear war. But these are problems we face, not as Indians and whites, but as Canadians.

Notes

1 This has appeared elsewhere. Cf. A. K. Davis (ed.), *A Northern Dilemma: Reference Papers*, vols. 1, 2 (Bellingham: Western Washington State College, Bureau of Faculty Research, 1967).

2 *Head and Hand in Ancient Greece* (London: Watts, Thinkers' Library, 1947) and *Greek Science* (Penguin, 1961).

3 *The Fur Trade in Canada* (Yale University Press, 1930).

4 A concept borrowed from anthropologist Peter Carstens, University of Toronto. Much relevant insight into the situations of Indians in Canadian society may be derived from Carstens' study of a South African Cape Coloured reservation: *The Social Structure of a Cape Coloured Reserve* (Oxford University Press, 1966).

5 The primacy of social class over race is recognized even by laymen. In the course of a community study I am currently conducting near an Alberta Indian reserve, I was repeatedly informed by local white community leaders that the so-called "Indian problem" is a question of class, not race. Many members of the white rank-and-file still talk in terms of the older racial stereotypes, but the conversion of the local elite to more realistic analytical categories is surely noteworthy—and likely of course to filter down to the general populace as time passes.

6   As the modern world moves into regional and ideological variations of a generalized urban-industrial social system, which sooner or later irresistibly absorbs
and appropriates the rapidly dwindling handful of culturally unique, pre-
industrial "islands," the traditional academic distinctions between sociology and
social anthropology become largely meaningless. Looking back, these inherited
departmentalisms seem irrelevant, and even diversionary. Above all, they obstruct the development of a sociology capable of transcending its present sterile
preoccupation with timeless, structural-functional, discrete analyses and with
Weberian-Parsonian deductive pronouncements on social theory. If ever we are
to achieve a social science which explains what contemporary societies are like,
and how they got the way they are, we appear most likely to realize such a goal
by a selective combination of archaeology, comparative institutions, and history.
Such a development, focusing on social evolution, might bring us closer to a
predictive social science than we are now.

7   See A. G. Frank, *Capitalism and Underdevelopment in Latin America* (New
York: Monthly Review Press, 1967); also his paper, "The Development of Underdevelopment," *Monthly Review*, September 1966.

8   W. A. Williams, "Sodbusters, Share-Croppers and the American Empire," unpublished ms., 1967; also J. N. McCrorie, "In Union Is Strength" (bulletin; Saskatchewan Farmers Union, Saskatoon, 1964).

9   See "Edging into Mainstream," in *A Northern Dilemma: Reference Papers*, vol.
2, pp. 338–577.

10   Two other relevant supplementary studies are now underway in Alberta:
an exploration of kinship factors in attracting Indians to Calgary, by Phyllis At-
well, an M.A. candidate at the University of Calgary; and a community study
near an Alberta Indian reserve. My field assistant in the latter project, supported
by a Canada Council grant, is Mr. Lorne Mullen of Calgary.

   No researcher works alone. I should like to acknowledge my great indebtedness to my field workers, especially to my chief interviewer in the Saskatchewan survey, Mr. James P. Brady. I first met Jim Brady, a fabulous character of
Sioux extraction, at Lac la Ronge in northern Saskatchewan, where he had a
cabin full of books. Early in June, 1967, he mysteriously disappeared while on
a prospecting mission in the northern Saskatchewan bush. Intensive searches
throughout the summer failed to locate him. This seems an appropriate occasion to record the meticulous care and the penetrating insight of his work as
a field researcher. My association with Jim Brady was one of the highlights of
my recent years.

11   Jean Lagasse, ed., *The People of Indian Ancestry in Manitoba* (Winnipeg:
Queen's Printer, 1959), vol. II, p. 20.

12   Cf. S. Goldstein, *Patterns of Mobility, 1910–1950* (University of Pennsylvania
Press, 1958), for a discussion of these considerations. I would like to acknowledge my debt to the Norristown, Pa., survey.

13   Our calculations took no account of variations in room size, future changes
in family size, a family's special interests, the presence of invalids, or children's

needs for special play or study space. Compared with the room-deficit per house-hold, the one advantage of a persons-per-room ratio as a partial measure of hous-ing adequacy is its readier availability in published statistics. Yet a room-deficit per household is almost as easy to figure, given the necessary data on age-sex composition and on the number of rooms in the dwelling. It can be quickly adjusted to any desired standard of sleeping and non-sleeping room arrange-ments. Finally, this procedure lends itself to a concept of household room-surplus as well as one of room-deficit.

14 R. Laskin, *Voluntary Organizations in a Saskatchewan Town* (Saskatoon, 1963).

15 In 1960 at La Ronge, when asked to sing Cree songs into a tape recorder, older Crees would respond with genuine native traditional chants. The teen-agers, by contrast, would come up with "Home on the Range" sung in Cree. Such is the rate of cultural assimilation.

The Saskatchewan CCF

The Unfinished Battle for the Shire

IN MORE WAYS THAN ONE, the story of the Saskatchewan Cooperative Commonwealth Federation (CCF) is like the epic journey of the hobbits through the shadow land of Mordor, so dramatically described in J. R. R. Tolkien's saga, *The Lord of the Rings*. The hobbits were little people who lived in a sunny out-of-the-way place called the Shire. They were unheroic country folk, petty burghers with a sharp eye for bargains, property values, and good food and drink. However, put to a test they did not seek, these diminutive rustics overcame armies of brutal orcs, underground goblins, giant cave trolls, the Nine Dark Riders of the Enemy, and all sorts of other evil forces. At critical points, to be sure, the hobbits were helped by countervailing supernatural powers ranged on the side of justice and the civilizing arts. The battles were fierce, and often lost, yet the hobbits somehow found the resources to come back and win the next round.

> The road goes ever on and on
> > Down from the door where it began.
> Now far ahead the Road has gone,
> > And I must follow, if I can,
> Pursuing it with eager feet,
> > Until it joins some larger way
> Where many paths and errands meet.
> > And whither then? I cannot say.
>
> (Tolkien, *Fellowship of the Ring*, 62)

Reprinted by permission from *Our Generation*, Volume 6, Number 4, June 1969.

Organized in the depressed, drought-ridden 1930s, the CCF came to power in Saskatchewan, the Wheat Province of Canada, in 1944. For twenty years the only professedly socialist regime ever to rule a middle-level government (that is, State or Provincial) in North America presided over one of the most rural, backward, underdeveloped and ill-favoured regions on the whole continent. Ill-favoured it was, indeed, by an extreme climate, by distance from wheat markets, by lack of capital, and by shortages of trained skills. Yet this latter-day frontier backwash on the northern high plains under rarely favourable conditions could produce the best hard wheat in the world. Even more important, the Saskatchewan CCF pioneered in a long list of progressive social reforms. These included expanding and publicly financed health services, larger and therefore up-graded school units, a generously supported provincial university, inexpensive and compulsory government auto insurance, encouragement of co-operatives, and modern labour legislation that was possibly the best in North American jurisdictions. The CCF reforms also included low-cost public utilities and inter-urban bus transportation by means of crown corporations, and the bringing of modern amenities (like electrical power) to the countryside and the small towns – no small achievements for a sparsely populated, poor province. In the impoverished far northern Metis and Indian settlements, for the first time new schools were built, all weather roads were constructed, a government-operated air service was set up, and a chain of government trading posts was established to break the Hudson Bay Company monopoly. Such were the high-priority goals of the Saskatchewan CCF government, 1944–1964.

In 1962 Came Medicare

Saskatchewan medicare meant universal, compulsory, tax-financed, pre-paid health insurance. Compared with other health plans over the previous three generations in North America, the Saskatchewan plan – though conservative when contrasted with European programmes – was a tremendous break-through. It was a fitting climax to nearly two decades of health-service pioneering. Universal, compulsory hospital insurance in Saskatchewan dated from 1947 – after two generations of accumulating experience limited in local and provincial medical health efforts. And in the summer of 1962, medicare came to stay in Saskatchewan, despite an unsuccessful, last-ditch stand by a doctors' strike that created an international uproar.

Almost everywhere else in North America after World War II, conservative and at times reactionary governments prevailed, with a few exceptions. Yet the Saskatchewan CCF after its landslide victory in 1944 won four more general elections. Then in 1964 it lost a hair-breadth contest to the Liberal Opposition, which conspicuously lacked both positive ideas of its own and well-founded criticisms of the CCF. Indeed, the immediate cause of the overturn had little to do with either the CCF or the Liberals. The immediately critical factor seems to have been the collapse of the provincial Social Credit party: the Liberals inherited enough Socred votes to win. The CCF defeat was confirmed in 1967 by a somewhat wider margin than in 1964, but with no significant change in the peevish character of Premier Thatcher's Liberal government.

How can we explain these paradoxes? Is the CCF era in Saskatchewan an example of the modern tendency of socialism to emerge in backward rural economies, like Czarist Russia and Mandarin China instead of in the advanced industrial countries of western Europe as originally predicted by Karl Marx? Or is it a unique phenomenon that baffles comparative analysis? Is the CCF finished in Saskatchewan, or merely dormant? Something can be said for each of these interpretations. But a different view will be offered here. We shall argue that the CCF in Saskatchewan was populist or petty-bourgeois, never socialist; that it was simply a new phase of "the farmers' movement" which has loomed large in the province ever since the turn of the century; that its similarities to Social Credit in Alberta outweigh differences; and that the farmers' movement–though subject to alternating phases of ebb and flow–is deeply rooted in persisting economic and social relationships on the Canadian high plains.

Let us look first at the voting results of the nine provincial general elections in which the CCF has participated. For our purpose the popular vote is more revealing than the legislative standings, which we will ignore. It is important to note, however, that in Saskatchewan as everywhere else in North America the rural population is over-represented in the Legislature.

How extraordinary the voting participation in Saskatchewan Provincial elections has been may be seen by looking at the extreme right-hand column in Table 1. Jupp found, for eight Saskatchewan elections between 1929 and 1960, inclusive, an average voting turnout of 83 percent of the eligible voters. For Alberta's nine provincial elections, 1930–1963 inclusive, the corresponding figure was only 67 percent–a significantly lower turnout (ibid, p. 12). Indeed, only once in the past generation have Alberta voters attained a Saskatchewan level of participation. That was in the landmark 1935 election when Aberhart's Social Crediters first swept to power. We should also note that after the peak medicare election of 1960, voter participation in Saskatchewan has moved slowly but steadily

Table 1

Saskatchewan Provincial Elections:
Popular Vote by Parties, 1934–1967
(in Percent)

	CCF	Lib.	Socred	Conserv.	Other	Total	% Eligible Voters Who Voted
1934	24.4	48.5	–	27.1	–	100.0	84.9
1938	18.3	45.5	16.0	12.3	7.9	100.0	83.8
1944	53.6	32.5	–	11.2	–	100.0	80.3
1948	47.6	31.2	8.1	7.6	5.5	100.0	83.4
1952	54.0	39.3	3.9	2.3	.5	100.0	82.9
1956	45.2	30.3	21.5	2.0	1.0	100.0	83.9
1960	40.8	32.7	12.3	14.0	.2	100.0	84.1
1964	40.3	40.4	.4	18.9	–	100.0	81.6
1967	44.4	45.5	.3	9.8	–	100.0	77.8

Sources: Chief Electoral Officer, Govt. of Saskatchewan and G. A. Jupp, "Implications of Political Participation for Social Change," unpub. ms., 1967.

downward from about 84 to 78 percent. Even so, the latter figure is well above the national norm. F. Engelmann and M. Schwartz show an average voter turnout of 71 percent for provincial elections in seven provinces from the 1920's to the early 1960's: Saskatchewan led with 83 percent, while Alberta lagged at 67 percent, and Manitoba trailed with 63 percent. (*Political Parties and Canadian Social Structure*, Prentice-Hall, 1967, p. 40.)

Looking now at the left-hand columns of the table, the record shows that the CCF achieved two peaks, 1944 and 1952, the only two occasions during this period when any party won a majority (over 50 percent) of the votes cast. Government in Saskatchewan since 1930 has typically been established by plurality decisions in multi-party elections. During the generation we are discussing the CCF and the Liberals have been the major contestants, year in and year out; the Conservatives and the Socreds have functioned as minor parties. But the latter have been important nonetheless.

In 1938 the protest vote was more or less evenly divided between Social Credit and the CCF. Differences between these two groups were still not clearly defined; joint candidates were run in four constituencies. However, the Social Credit tide which swept Alberta in 1935 had not produced the promised monetary reforms or the monthly cash dividends, and voter discontent in Saskatchewan began to coalesce in favour of the CCF. The 1944 CCF landslide followed. But Social Credit resurfaced in

Saskatchewan in 1948, when the CCF, the Liberals and the Progressive Conservatives all experienced losses. The Socreds picked up two-thirds of these losses. About one-third went to four independent candidates (usually Liberal–Conservative coalitions) and one Labour-Progressive (Communist) in the heavily ethnic (non-Anglo) far northern and eastside rural constituencies, and in Moose Jaw city. Table 2 shows the net gains and losses of each party in percentage points, comparing 1948 with 1944. For example, the table shows that the difference between the 1944 CCF popular vote (53.6%) and the 1948 share of the vote (47.7%) was 6.0 percentage points.

If we consider percent change instead of arithmetic percentage-point shifts, a similar but sharper picture emerges. The CCF loss of 6.0 percentage points in 1948 compared to 1944 was 11.2 percent of the 1944 CCF share of the popular vote (53.6%). The corresponding Liberal Figure was 11.4 percent; the PC figure, 32.2 percent. From this standpoint, the two major parties (the CCF and the Liberals) suffered small and equal losses, while the PC's took a much heavier set-back. But if we add most of the "other" vote to the Liberals and the PC's (say 3 and 2 percentage points, respectively) then it appears that the CCF and PC losses in 1948 compared to 1944 were approximately equal (about 11 percent of the 1944 share of the popular vote), while the corresponding Liberal loss was only two-thirds as much.

The main Socred surge came in 1956. In that year Social Credit won over one-fifth of the province-wide vote, concentrated in the far northern and northern fringe-of-settlement, east-central and southwestern constituencies. In those areas live relatively larger proportions of small farmers, many village pensioners and certain ethnic groups like the German Mennonites. The Socreds exceeded their province-wide share of the popular vote (21.5%) in 21 of 46 rural constituencies. As in 1948, the Socreds hurt the Liberals much more than the CCF. (See Table 3.)

The other minority party, the Progressive Conservatives (PCs), went

Table 2

Party Gains and Losses (%), Elections of 1948 and 1944

Losses (1948/1944)		Gains (1948/1944)	
CCF	6.0	Socreds	8.1
Libs	4.0	Others	5.5
PCs	3.6	Total	13.6
Total	13.6		

Source: calculated from Table 1.

Table 3

Province-wide Voting Changes, 1952–1956

	CCF	Lib	PC	Socred	Other
1. Change in % points	−8.8	−9.0	−0.3	+17.6	+0.5
2. Line 1 as % of share of popular vote in 1952	−16.3	−22.9	−13.0	+450.	+100.0

Source: Calculated from Table 1.

through a surge in 1960 that peaked in 1964, mainly at the net expense of the Socreds. In 1964 the Liberals were also surging, and they continued to show gains in their share of the popular vote in 1967, though at a much lower rate. The CCF gained almost as much in 1967 as the Liberals. Minor-party activity, then, has been very significant in the electoral fate of the two Saskatchewan major parties.

Let us look more closely at percentage-point gains and losses, 1958–1967. The figures in Table 4 show these changes for six provincial elections, each compared with the preceding. Thus, for example, the CCF in 1948 dropped 6 percentage points below its 1944 share of the popular vote, and the Liberals lost 4 percentage points.

Some interesting facts emerge from this table. In four of these six elections (excepting only 1960 and 1964) the CCF and the Liberals gained or lost shares of the popular vote in concert. That is, they both went up or they both went down, although not equally. And in the same elections, the combined minor-party vote, of course, moved in the opposite direction: when both major parties gained, the combined minor-party

Table 4

Percentage-Point Changes in Share of Popular Vote, Six Provincial Elections, by Parties, 1948–1967

	CCF	Lib.	Combined SC/PC
1948	−6.0	−4.0	+4.5
1952	+6.4	+8.1	+9.5
1956	−9.2	−9.0	+17.3
1960	−4.4	+2.4	+2.8
1964	−0.5	+7.7	−7.0
1967	+4.1	+5.1	−9.2

Source: Derived from Table 1.

share of the vote decreased, and vice versa. However, a temporary aberration seems to have occurred in the 1960 and 1964 elections. In those contests, the major parties moved in opposite directions, while the minor-party vote fell sharply. Finally over these two decades, combined minor-party gains seem to have cut into the CCF more than into the Liberal vote. Conversely, combined minor-party losses have tended to favour the Liberals, especially in 1964.

More specifically, the big CCF drop in percentage points occurred in 1956, when the combined minor-party vote leaped from 6.2 to 23.6 percent of the popular tally. Yet the Liberals lost almost as much. That year the minor-party combination drew about equally from each major party. In 1960 the CCF experienced another loss in percentage points, but only half as much as in 1956. The Liberals gained slightly (2.4 percentage points), and the minor-party vote peaked at 26.3 of the total votes cast. Yet the CCF won substantial victories in terms of Legislature seats in both 1956 and 1960. In 1964, however, the minor-party share fell sharply, mainly to the Liberals, who took over the government. An even greater minor-party decrease in 1967 was translated into almost equal gains for each major party. Judging by the last two elections, the Liberal rate of gain has slacked off, while the CCF is still rising.

Who Voted For Whom

Let us now consider what kinds of people voted for which party in Saskatchewan provincial elections. Our main source is Lipset, *Agrarian Socialism*, Berkeley, 1968, and Silverstein, ch. 5 of Part II, *Agrarian Socialism: Twenty Years Later* plus certain studies and impressions of my own. The hard data is sketchy: strong on the side of survey and quantitative census and voting studies, but weak in terms of personal and depth interviews properly sampled.

The record clearly suggests that the CCF from 1944 and ever since has stood on two power bases: the upper-middle and middle-income farmers (especially the grain farmers, less so the mixed grain-and-dairy-or-cattle farmers), and the urban blue-collar workers. The Liberals have relied upon three bases of social power: the mercantile and professional oligarchies in the villages and small towns and cities; the city white-collar groups; and the Roman Catholics in town and country. (These three categories overlap in part.) The poorer farmers have been ambivalent: some have opted for the CCF, more have gone for the PCs, the Socreds, and the Liberals.

Secondary to class divisions are those based on religion and ethnicity.

Overlapping again is significant. The CCF in rural Saskatchewan was primarily a WASP movement: United Church members, with their emphasis on applied Christian ethics, have consistently been over-represented among CCF voters. Anglicans and Lutherans, the next largest Protestant denominations, have leaned toward the rightist PCs-Socreds-Liberals. The Ukrainians (Greek Catholics and Greek Orthodox) have been divided between anti-Soviet and pro-Soviet viewpoints, reflected in pro-CCF and pro-Liberal voting behavior, with lesser deviations toward Social Credit. Roman Catholics have bent heavily toward the Liberals.

In ethnic terms, the predominant British-origin group has split between CCF and PC. The small French enclaves have voted Liberal; the Dutch and Germans (especially Mennonites) have gone Socred first, and Liberal second. Speaking generally, the Scandinavians are CCF; the Indians, initially CCF, have switched to the Liberals. (Nothing much having changed since the Liberal victory of 1964, the Indians and Metis could switch again in the near future. But they are important only in two Northern constituencies.)

What about urbanization? This is a key process in Saskatchewan. Paradoxically, although rooted mainly in rural populism, the CCF has always run higher in the two largest urban areas (Saskatoon and Regina: 1966 population 116,000 and 131,000 respectively) than in most of the rural constituencies. From 1946 to 1966, the province's urban population practically doubled from 25 percent to 49 percent of the total; the farm population fell from 53 to 29 percent; and the rural non-farm sector (small towns and villages below 1000 people) remained constant at about 22 percent. The flow of people toward the cities might help the CCF in its union labour support, but this does not necessarily detract from its farmer appeal. The village mercantile oligarchies have always been prone to vote Liberal (with large PC and Socred minorities) mainly, I suspect, because of latent resentment against the local social supremacy of the larger farmers rather than because of Liberal ideological ranting. This is not likely to change. Neither is the ranting, however wasted.

Another key long-run trend is age: the population is showing an increasing proportion of younger people. A study of voting in Saskatoon in the 1964 election by Courtney and Smith indicated that the CCF lost out to the Liberals among the younger adult voters. (Silverstein, *op. cit.*, 469.) This is a potentially serious trend for the CCF. On the other hand, the current revolt among students and young people could more than offset this development, provided the CCF takes a turn or two for youth. It is no longer possible in Canada to assume that younger voters have been captured by affluence for the conservative parties, as appeared to be the case in the early 1960s.

CCF Ideology

A realistic theoretical view of the Saskatchewan CCF is indispensable both for understanding what happened and for guiding future political action in the Shire. While the Shire now means mainly Saskatchewan, the trends in the North American economy are such that Canada itself is becoming another shire. As George Grant has shown, the national business elite in eastern Canada since World War II has—without public debate—opted for inclusion in the affluent American economic empire. Branch-plant capitalism has operated politically through the Canadian Liberal party; it has recently recaptured the Progressive-Conservative party after a decade of Diefenbaker's renegade populism. (See Grant, *Lament for a Nation*, Toronto, 1965) What really happened in Saskatchewan during the CCF era? The answer may provide a clue as to how the hobbits of North America may deal with the cave trolls that rule the Dark Tower in Washington.

In previous studies, two views of the CCF have predominated. One has emphasized indigenous agrarian unrest; the other, the impact of leaders and ideas imported to the rural hinterlands from urban labour and other metropolitan radical sources outside the high plains. Examples of the first are P. Sharp's *Agrarian Revolt in Western Canada* (Minneapolis, 1948) and D. McHenry's *Third Force in Canada* (Berkeley, 1950). The second approach is best represented by S. Lipset's well known *Agrarian Socialism* (Berkeley, 1950; expanded Anchor edition, 1968). Similarly oriented is L. Zakuta's *A Protest Movement Becalmed* (Toronto, 1964). But the latter study is limited to the CCF in Ontario, where urban labour groups and middle-class intellectuals have always dominated the party.

In our judgment the first perspective is much nearer the truth, for the region west of Winnipeg. In the 1968 edition of *Agrarian Socialism*, the insightful papers of John Bennett and John Richards support this view.

A wider frame of reference is required to include both the rural and the urban CCF movements. We suggest "metropolis versus hinterland." In essence, metropolis dominates its hinterlands politically, and exploits them economically. Hinterlands are sooner or later impelled to fight back: the initial dominance of metropolis is inherently unstable. In North America the main goal of exploited groups has typically been to improve their relative position within the prevailing system. And they usually succeeded—there has been enough affluence since World War I to substitute business unionism for radical unionism, and to subsidize the discontented commercial farmers—more clearly so in the United States than in Canada.

Examples of metropolis-hinterland relationship? For one, the small town and its surrounding market areas in the nearby countryside, so well described by Thorstein Veblen in "The Country Town" (*Absentee Ownership*, 1923, ch. 7). For another, the relationship now prevailing between southern Canada and its far north. Or between eastern industrial Ontario and the less developed Prairies and Maritime hinterlands. Perhaps most significant of all is the metropolitan-hinterland symbiosis which has emerged since World War II between the American empire and Canada.

However, *metropolis* and *hinterland* must not be confused with territorial referents. Every metropolis contains within its boundaries large exploited groups. *Upper-class* and *under-class* are interchangeable terms with *metropolis* and *hinterland*, respectively. In brief, the modern world can be viewed as a hierarchy of overlapping metropolis-hinterland, or upper-class and under-class relationships. The core of the upper class consists of the larger entrepreneurs and corporation managers, along with upper-level government policy-makers and a wide fringe of professionals – advisory lawyers, chartered accountants, and so on. The heart of the under-class is the wage-labour category, especially if organized into unions; together with a fringe of lower-level white-collar employees and of small entrepreneurs. The latter would ordinarily orient toward big business, provided they could make it into that club. When they find themselves excluded, they are sometimes available for anti-establishment stances.

From this standpoint, the CCF in Ontario was an urban under-class movement appealing mostly to trade unions and a few middle-class nonconformists. On the prairies, supporters of the CCF were overwhelmingly the middle and upper-middle farmers uneasily allied with a few trade unions and a handful of professional and middle-class reformers motivated mainly by the "social gospel" – applied Christianity.

Though we shall come back to the "social gospel" later in this paper, let us acknowledge here its prime importance in the Western populist, hinterland reaction against the impact of unbridled laissez-faire capitalism. This reaction was rooted in fraternal and egalitarian sentiments harking back to primitive Christianity, generated by similar conditions of rural scarcity vis-à-vis urban plenty – by the New Testament rather than by the Communist Manifesto of 1848.

> The social gospel of Christianity is difficult to define . . . Its central purpose was to work for "the Kingdom" in this world. It laid heavy emphasis upon the doctrine of love and proclaimed the principle of co-operation as opposed to that of competition . . . All across the Canadian West these men helped prepare a fertile ground for the progressive movement, the

Social Credit party, and the Co-operative Commonwealth Federation. (K. McNaught, *A Prophet in Politics: a Biography of J. S. Woodsworth:* Univ. of Toronto Press, 1959, pp. 48–50, and Ch. IV)

But there were other, more important socio-economic developments. They had started earlier, and they stayed later.

A century ago in Canada, the "National Policy" was emerging. Confederation and western agricultural settlement was a competitive response by Montréal and Toronto business interests to the immense industrial expansion of the United States that began in the 1850s and was greatly stimulated by the American civil war, 1861–65. Though absorbed by domestic hinterlands till the end of the 19th century, American economic expansion was potentially a major threat to Canadian enterprise, for all capitalist complexes require expansion in order to survive. As finally crystallized, Canadian National Policy focussed on settlement of the West as the new hinterland cushion for eastern business and finance. Public capital would be made available for private business expansion by means of a heavily subsidized transcontinental railroad (the CPR, completed in 1885), a low-cost homesteading land policy, encouragement of immigration to the West, federally financed research farms to adapt farming technology to the semi-arid western plains, replacement of the Hudson's Bay Co. imperium in Rupertsland by public government (accomplished in 1870), and above all a protective tariff to reserve this vast developmental undertaking for British and Canadian capital against the Americans. (See V. C. Fowke, *The National Policy and the Wheat Economy*, Toronto, 1957; also Ch. 3 *The South Saskatchewan River Project*, Report of the Royal Commission, Ottawa, 1952; and C. Schwartz, *The Search for Stability*, Toronto, 1959.) Fowke neglected to mention another essential policy: shunting Indians onto reserves.

But eastern metropolitan expansion into western Canada by means of the National Policy contained the built-in seeds of a counterattack. Prairie settlement in large part (excepting mainly certain religiously-motivated colonies from central and eastern Europe) was a migration of profit-minded petty-bourgeois Anglos from Ontario, England and the U.S.A.–bent on realizing some fast bucks. These settlers brought with them a cultural heritage of achievement-motivation, of representative government, and of self-help through voluntary organizations. They moved into an isolated region and an unbelievable climate. No words can convey to unbelieving outlanders the extremes of the Saskatchewan landscape and seasons. For a recreation of the epic of prairie settlement, turn to the writings of W. Mitchell, S. Ross, E. McCourt, Jim Wright,

R. Stead, F. Grove, Kerry Wood and James Gray—among others; or see the National Film Board's "Drylanders" and "A Lake for the Prairies."* So what happened?

Populism, not Socialism

From the beginning of agricultural settlement in the late 19th century, prairie farmers were caught in a cost-price squeeze. They sold their grain in distant world markets at fluctuating prices outside their control. And they initially sold as individual producers, at the mercy of indispensable rail, storage and middleman costs. But they bought machinery from high-cost monopolies which charged what the traffic would bear. Central marketing under the federal Grain Commissioners has since modified that situation in some degree. Yet the underlying dilemma persists, intensified by the growth of monopoly among the industrial and financial corporations with which farmers must deal. This brings us to the central core of the Saskatchewan CCF: the "farmers' movement."

Since the turn of the century, prairie farmers have been involved in one campaign after another to improve their economic position. First came the establishment of the Grain Growers' Association and the clash with the Canadian Pacific Railroad over terms of grain shipment, culminating in the Sintaluta trial of 1902. A few years later came the drive for co-operative elevator companies, financed partly by public capital; and in the 1920s the battle for producer-owned wheat pools. An extensive development of other producer and consumer co-ops began in the 1930s. Provincial governments were responsive but only up to a point: in those early days the Conservative and Liberal Parties were viewed in the West as extensions of eastern business interests.

Independent political action by prairie farmers marked a new phase of the farmers' movement. It began in the 1920s with the short-lived Progressive upsurge in federal politics. At the same time, Alberta in 1921 elected a United Farmers government, which held power until swept out in 1935 by Social Credit, another small-producers' government. The simmering ferment was reflected in Saskatchewan by the brief appearance of the Ku Klux Klan during the 1920s. Its anti-Catholic and anti-Semitic overtones were echoed later in the Social Credit movement. Somewhat earlier, the Non-Partisan League had sprung up in the wheat-growing areas of the Dakotas, northwestern Minnesota and eastern Montana. During World War I, the League captured the state government of North

---

* For a historical background see "The Progressive Tradition" by Lorne Brown in this issue of *Our Generation*.

Dakota, and quickly spilled over into Saskatchewan and Alberta. The heart of all these movements was the high-plains region and the wheat economy, so vulnerable to weather and market fluctuations.

Last but not least came the Saskatchewan CCF. If it came late, it came to stay a while.

Three things need to be said about the farmer's movement. First, it proceeds by alternate periods of surge and downswings, depending on the intensity of rural unrest, as J. N. McCrorie has shown. (His study, *In Union is Strength*, Saskatchewan Farmers Union, Saskatoon, 1964, is the best recent over-view of the movement.) Second, the organizations that emerge out of the movement from time to time tend naturally to acquire vested interests in the social order they originally set out to change. For example, the Wheat Pool organized in 1924, now owns hundreds of elevators, stores grain (for a good price), employs a sizable staff at substantial salaries, and is unquestionably an important segment of the Saskatchewan Establishment. Third, the farmers' movement is essentially petty-bourgeois, aiming to improve the farmers' position within the capitalist system. This is equally true of the co-operatives, the CCF party and the CCF government. An alliance with the province's small labour movement has been an acceptable expedient, however uneasy and ambivalent.

The last point states the inner dynamics of the Saskatchewan CCF. Prairie farmers, even the larger ones, are small entrepreneurs. They cannot control in any close measure—on an industry-wide basis—their costs, their quality or quantity of production, or their selling prices. By contrast, the giant industrial and financial corporations achieve much control over these variables. In short, the Prairie farmer, though he owns income-producing property, cannot possibly move up into big business. He can merely modify the forces which determine his economic fate—if he is lucky. Co-operatives and public marketing boards, for example, or public regulation or railroad rates, in no way alter the key fact of the agricultural economy: the commanding heights of the national economy are securely in the hands of other interest groups. (Indeed, co-ops bolster capitalism by spreading the fringe benefits.) Hence the farmer is chronically frustrated. Though the larger operators may increase their gross income, other occupations and other industries gain faster in net income and in social power. The small farmers are completely outside the feast. If occasional crusts fall to the larger operators, not even crumbs accrue to subsistence farmers. The latter are readily available for pie-in-the-sky appeals.

The best analytical study of the small-farmer situation is by C. B. Macpherson (*Democracy in Alberta*, Toronto, 1953, ch. 8). His analysis is as applicable to Saskatchewan as to Alberta. His central point is that the hall-mark of big business is the ability to employ and profit from large amounts of labour. This the family farm cannot do. We need only add that the trend toward mechanization (Marx's "fixed capital") does not help: the machinery is in effect "rented" from the giant oligopolies.

Despite this adverse stacking of the cards, farmers retain an illusion of independence—like all small producers, rural and urban, artisan and independent professional. All of these retain some degree of choice over their working hours and everyday programs. Some live comfortably. More can steer their children into city white-collar occupations or to university, the gateway to the professional and upper-middle classes. In the net, the petty bourgeoisie—the farms, the small entrepreneurs and the artisans—have enough upward mobility and short-run occasional success to make them safe for capitalism. There is no risk that they will turn to Marxian socialism. Indeed, they cannot. The small producers must harry and irritate the big corporations; yet they cannot seriously threaten the big bourgeoisie. For they are property owners themselves, with a stake (however illusory) in the established order. Periodically, how-ever, they must fight the system from which they cannot escape, because their status in it is so marginal, and yet so beckoning.

The heart of the petty bourgeois order in rural Canada is the family farm. Only the minuscule Hutterite religious colonies have transcended it. These alone dispose of relatively large amounts of labour, as farms go. Other big corporate farms in Western Canada characteristically rent or share-crop their extra land. It is interesting to ask whether the chronic prairie antagonism to these Hutterite communal farms is due to competition for scarce land, resentment over non-participation in local businesses and other community activities, or to a vague sense that Hutterite colonies may be a superior breed of community.

Canadian historians have not sufficiently emphasized that the Na-tional Policy of the past century was based directly on the family farm. While the hinterlands were thus organized and fragmented, metropolis was impregnable. No matter that most of these farms produce and con-sume but little. They usually keep off relief, and they (or their children) form a labour pool for other occupations and industries, as needed. Above all, they do not reject the system which exploits them—occasional slogans to the contrary notwithstanding. They do not understand the sys-tem, by and large. Rather, they see it as a potential Santa Claus—if they can just find the magic formula. They deal with the immediate, concrete—but misleading—experiences of rural life. Like Indians on iso-lated reserves, farmers on family farms are encapsulated in a paradoxical combination of "security" (based on traditional ties to place, kin and

community) and "frustration" (rooted in a sense of deprivation generated by the gap between present reality and past tradition – in the case
of Indians – and between present circumstances and future aspirations,
in the case of Whites). The net outcome is that farmers seek to improve
their standing in the going system, but not at the expense of rejecting
the system.

Farmer resort to co-operatives and government actions is much like
the reactions of other industries to the pressures of extreme competition. By means of mergers and public subsidies, the non-agricultural industries have (in varying degree) made it to big-business status. This outcome has been denied to agriculture, partly because of its dispersed
location, its multiplicity of farms (their operators immobilized to a significant extent by ties of kin and local community,) and partly because
of the family farm's viability even when it is a business failure. Someone
can still carry it on as a subsistence farm. Or, if farmers quit farming,
as they have been doing for nearly two generations in western Canada,
the relative position of those that remain, vis-à-vis other industries and
power elites, changes scarcely at all. Even the most successful farmers
remain nothing more than small entrepreneurs.

What the western agricultural and small-business economy generates
is populism, not socialism. Populism means a belief in free enterprise –
for the little guy. It means hostility toward big business and toward eastern "vested interests" and their two national parties, the Liberals and
the PC's. In Alberta, populism came early, first in the UFA government,
later in the form of Social Credit, a more radical version. In Saskatchewan the movement took on ideological overtones of socialism, but this
was always superficial. McCrorie's 1961 study of the Biggar district (the
home riding of M. J. Coldwell, Woodrow Lloyd and of many Co-op and
other farm leaders for two generations) asked a random sample of farmers how they saw the CCF compared with other parties. Twenty percent
replied that the CCF was a socialist party; the rest said it was a farmers'
party – "that it stood for western rather than eastern industries interests;
that it had built roads, hospitals, etc. for the rural population." (*In Union
is Strength*, p. 42)

Lipset errs in describing the Saskatchewan CCF as "agrarian socialism."
Nor was it an offshoot of the great depression of the 1930s; at best the
incredible ordeal of the "dirty thirties" was an accentuating factor. It was
an integral part of the "farmers' movement," generated by the regional
conditions of family-farm production in a comparatively homogeneous
hinterland fighting back against two or three generations of metropolitan
exploitation. Its chief ideological orientation was not Marxism, nor even
Fabian socialism, but the "social gospel" of Protestant Christianity.

The social gospel movement, though never sharply defined, generally held that what counted in religious life was not only Sunday theological ritual but everyday ethical practice as well. The Industrial Revolution brought great riches for a few, especially in the mushrooming towns and cities. But not everyone accepted the laissez-faire philosophy of the survival of the fittest: that the rich were rich because they deserved to be, and that the poor would prosper likewise if they would just stop drinking, work hard and save their money. The growing contrast between upper-class luxury and mass poverty, and the links established by the muckrakers in the United States between big business and municipal corruption—such tendencies convinced many religious leaders that the gap between pristine Christian values and modern life was becoming uncomfortably wide.

Primitive Christianity, like the Jewish prophets of still earlier times, emerged from an economy of chronic and often acute scarcity. Underclass small farmers, shepherds and artisans necessarily inclined toward sentiments of egalitarianism, brotherhood and self-help through mutual sharing. Were things going badly for the little man because of pressures from rich property owners and urban merchants? Then drive the money changers from the temple. This situation has repeated itself many times. On the Canadian prairies the secular version was, chase the eastern monopolists and their political henchmen from the seats of government; make democratic government work for the common people. Most of the key leaders of Social Credit and the CCF on the prairies were originally preachers in Methodist, Baptist or other evangelical denominations: J. S. Woodsworth, T. C. Douglas, W. Aberhart, and E. Manning—to name but a few.

Calls to build the New Jerusalem in the western hinterlands were numerous and inherent in the regional order of small entrepreneurs. The CCF slogan of "Humanity First" was just another example. There will doubtless be others.

Decline of CCF and After

In this final section, we face two questions. Why did the CCF lose in 1964? What is likely to happen? Our answers are speculative, like the other attempts to answer this type of question. So far, the best effort is that of John Richards (in Lipset, 1968). However, this needs systematic checking.

The usual explanation of why the CCF lost in 1964 focuses on urbanization and the resulting increase of white-collar occupations, the decrease in the number of farms, the medicare battle in 1962, and the bureaucratization of the CCF government and party–successful protest movements become fat and conservative. These are not satisfactory, although not irrelevant. They largely ignore the voting shifts in the province, and the upsurge of CCF voting in 1967.

We suggest that the Liberal core of power in the upper and middle white-collar classes is likely to grow. Its village core, on the contrary, is likely to be undercut by the urban drift of population, and this sector is vulnerable to right-wing populist appeals by Social Credit and the PCs. The CCF should retain the middle-sized farmers, whose numerical decline may be offset by the growth of labour unions as the new potash and other industries are unionized. The spreading revolt of youth–a new factor–should damage the conservative parties considerably more than the CCF. A link-up between (moderately) radical youth and university types, as an idea group, and labour and farm grass-roots could ring the starting bell, provided the university types learn to do their organization homework and to get rid of some of their middle-class blinders. The provincial Liberals should suffer increasingly from their association with a federal administration increasingly identifiable with big-business, pro-American and elitist policies.

The central political fact on the high prairies is still populism. However relative, deprivation persists among the urban and rural underclasses of the western hinterlands. There are still acute housing shortages, a tightening cost-price squeeze for farmers and other small producers, and rising costs for all services, especially education and health. And the gravest questions about the worth of quality of middle-class life are being raised by youth. Radical appeals to the common man should become more potent, not less.

The persistency of western populism has been obscured by party labels. That Alberta and Saskatchewan voters supported Socred or CCF in provincial elections and PC in federal contests, during the last decade, is only superficially paradoxical. Diefenbaker, the prairie lawyer, was a populist through and through. He captured the PC party on the wave of nationwide under-class revolt against the arrogance of eastern metropolitan elites led by the Liberal Party. When the eastern big business interests ousted Diefenbaker as PC party leader in 1967, Saskatchewan swung back to its local populists, electing six of eleven CCF MPs in June, 1968.

Did the spreading affluence of the last decade undercut the CCF? Did the CCF, by bringing services to the countryside, preside over its own demise? We think not. True, the strongest impression of my first tour of the province in late 1958 was one of "embourgeoisement." The larger towns were seeking and getting all sorts of new services, from dry-cleaning firms and paved streets, to new schools and dentists. Farmers were installing indoor plumbing. Cocktail lounges and mixed drinking places came next year. But affluence is relative—and not all that widespread. The smaller farmers and the urban underclass were not involved.

Was the 1962 medicare ruckus an issue in 1964? I doubt this. The 1960 election was fought specifically on the medicare issue and won by the CCF. By the 1964 election, the 1962 doctors' strike had been long lost by the rash and out-of-touch medical leadership. Medicare was not an issue in 1964. Indeed, the Liberals promised to extend its benefits.

Did the CCF succumb to Michel's "Iron law of oligarchy"? No doubt there was a certain hardening of the arteries in the government—and the party—but probably no more—less rather—than in other parties. Richards indicates that in the CCF provincial council of 80 members— mostly non-politicians—the party had a built-in defence against bureaucratization, at least to some extent.

My own hunch is that what hurt the Saskatchewan CCF in the early 1960s was the party's federal alliance with organized labour. The farmer entrepreneurs can team up with labour unions in the province mainly because farmers and workers are not directly linked in common economic enterprises. Where labour strikes or costs affect farmers, as in railroads or in grain terminals, sharp conflicts of interest appear. From field experience in the Saskatchewan countryside I obtained a vivid impression of the latent antagonism of CCF farmers toward labour unions. This explains why I have used *CCF* rather than *NDP* as a label in this paper.

The role of the middle-class intellectuals and professionals in the CCF has been ambivalent. On the one hand, they supply the indispensable ideas and social analysis. On the other, they tend to be out of touch with the populist rank-and-file. Leadership by university people in Saskatoon in the early 1960s "put off" many lower-class activists. No grey-flannel image can win. Neither can a straight labour man. Least of all, an Easterner who can be tagged as a Labour henchman or a city slicker with creased pants and polished shoes.

In short, the Saskatchewan CCF, unless it is seduced by "consensus politics" seems certain to rise again. Its main hope lies in polarizing (within limits) the political spectrum, not in offering something for everybody.

But now let us consider a wider perspective. Canada has willynilly become an annex of the American empire. The Shire is national, as well as maritime or western. How can the hobbits recapture their domain? How can they link up with the underclass hobbits in the United States heartland? Perhaps even more important, how can they relate to the underclass hinterlands abroad—in Latin America and Africa and southeast Asia? To answer these questions, the homework has not been done. The essential workings of the economic and political systems have not been sufficiently researched, let alone made plain.

A generation ago, the CCF and Social Credit surged to power in the western high plains by means of local study groups, rooted in a social movement from below, and led by alienated middle-class professionals (mainly preachers and teachers) and by middle and upper-middle farmers. In both cases, a world-view was successfully established. The similarities and differences–behavioral and ideological–between these two social movements have yet to be spelled out. It is my hunch that the similarities significantly outweigh the differences. Why did Saskatchewan go CCF while Alberta went Socred? This key question I still cannot answer. Meanwhile, the world has changed during the past fifteen years. New study groups and study kits are needed. *Above all, a new people's movement.* The latent popular basis is already there. But social movements are not generated by professional papers like this one. They come from the people and from people-rooted leaders.

This raises the leadership question. As in Alberta, the people's movement in Saskatchewan was led by a charismatic leader. When preaching the social gospel on the high plains, Tommy Douglas could roll up his audiences with his vision of the New Jerusalem. He was doubtless the greatest orator in North America–given the context of the prairie farmers movement. Greatness is a result of a special empathy between the leader and the led.

Douglas' successor, Woodrow Lloyd (a former teacher and officer of the Saskatchewan Teachers Federation, and CCF Minister of Education for a decade and a half in the Douglas cabinet)–became Premier of Saskatchewan in November, 1961, when Douglas resigned to become national leader of the new-born New Democratic Party. It was a bad time to leave, and there were critical waverings in the Saskatchewan CCF government. But the medicare crisis of 1962, precipitated by the blind refusal of the Saskatchewan College of Physicians and Surgeons to accept the people's 1960 election verdict in favour of prepaid, universal and compulsory health insurance–this crisis resulted in a resounding defeat of the medical dinosaurs. The doctors' strike in the summer of 1962 was a dead loss. Lloyd's government stood like a rock. Yet it refused to take off the gloves with the misguided doctors, despite immense provocation. Perhaps this was a mistake. The doctors, who make a very fat living from other people's misery, were sitting ducks for an all-out attack on "bloodsuckers and leeches." Mistakenly or not, Lloyd took a conservative line. He saved the doctors' collective face, not in their interest but in the public interest.

Despite two lost elections (1964 and 1967) Lloyd has grown in stature in Saskatchewan. As much as Tommy Douglas, he is like Gandalf the ageless wizard in Tolkien's saga. There is no one in sight to challenge his party leadership. Urban business and professional types wearing polished shoes? A Madison-Avenue image in Saskatchewan is doomed. Alienated young people? The over-30 and under-30 cleavage is a misleading split, though not entirely irrelevant.

Such categories are insufficient. Douglas and Lloyd were only parts of the people's movement in Saskatchewan. The movement generates leaders; leaders mold the movement. In a period of downswing, someone from the rank and file may jump up and say, "Let's go." And a new surge starts. It's as simple as that—and as unpredictable. (For a good example, see J. McCrorie, *In Union is Strength*, pp. 48–49, on the 1948 meeting in Saskatoon, which saw a rebirth of the Saskatchewan Farmers' Union.)

After a lost battle, calls inevitably arise for new strategies, new leaders, new tactics, new images. This is understandable, but not necessarily valid. Looking back on prairie development, and viewing it in a national and continental context, much has changed—yet (after allowing for counter-actions) much remains the same. Prairie farmers and prairie labour unions and working people are still relatively deprived categories. Young people have greatly changed. Hinterland still confronts metropolis. This means that some of the old answers are still good. Especially the official CCF slogan, raised a generation ago: "Humanity First." Indeed, was not the best showing, in terms of facing the objective issues in the June, 1968, national election, made by Tommy Douglas rather than by Stanfield or Trudeau? Osculation may have won that election; it will not likely win the next one.

Estimates of past and present trends cannot predict future events. All we are sure of is this: the battles for the provincial and national shires are far from over.

> *The road goes ever on and on . . .*
> *Until it joins some larger way . . .*
> *Where many paths and errands meet . . .*
>   (Tolkien)

Failings of Anglophone
Import Sociology in Canada:

The Need for a Dialectical and Historical Perspective

The Failure of Structural-Functionalism to Comprehend
Canadian Society Holistically

Classic social analysis is . . . the concern with historical social structures;
its problems are of direct relevance to urgent public issues and insistent
human troubles . . .   (C. Wright Mills, *The Sociological Imagination.*
New York, Oxford University Press, 1959, p. 21)

BEGINNING WITH NEOLITHIC TIMES – the discovery of agriculture,
town life, writing, metallurgy, commerce, social classes, the bureaucratic State, and so on – the mainstream of social analysis has dealt
(among other things) with historical, holistic social communities. It has
done so in such a way as to be more or less relevant both to the major
public issues of the times and to the more widespread personal troubles
of ordinary people. The latter generally included such matters as livelihood, relations to authorities, kinship and spouse roles, relations to cos-
mic entities, neighbours, enemies, and so on. Ever since the early civ-
ilisations of Greece, India and China, the social thinkers and teachers
of the world's societies have had something relevant to say about their
times. Doubtless this has not always been the case. It is reasonable to
assume the co-existence of a category of irrelevant intellectual productions alongside the relevant.

In which of these two categories falls most of the teaching and research by anglophone academic sociologists in Canada is not a difficult

Reprinted by permission. R. W. Nelsen and D. A. Nock, eds., *Reading, Writing and Riches*, Between-
the-Lines Press, Toronto, Ontario, 1978.

question to answer. By and large, anglophone social scientists in Canadian universities have presented an abstract, bland, fragmental and static picture of Canadian society. Further, they see the world through a middle-class lens: conflict is underestimated, and regional studies are relatively neglected. Finally, few of them deal with Canadian society as a whole.

Looking over the back numbers of the *Canadian Review of Sociology and Anthropology* and the various "readers" on Canadian society indicates a primary focus on micro-empirical aspects of Canadian social organization, and a relative neglect of macrotrends—especially those concerning Canadian-American relations in an exploitive context. In fact, a goodly number of those papers are essentially timeless and placeless, in the sense that the main focus is on variables abstracted from time and place rather than upon the time and place from which they are "lifted." Not many have anything to say to ordinary people, even about limited specific and local problems. For the most part, anglophone academic sociologists appear to be talking to each other about esoteric topics, although most of them are paid—fairly well—by Canadian public funds. For the average person (who pays the shot), Ann Landers is usually more relevant.

That a roughly parallel critique of academic economics in Canada is made by M. H. Watkins[1] suggests that the points raised in this paper stem from a general condition of Canadian society and Canadian academia. Like orthodox economics, orthodox sociology is biased toward the dominant Anglo, capitalist Establishment.

There are at least two related reasons for the aridity of anglophone academic sociology in Canada. The first is the pre-occupation with structural-functionalism, a cultural import from the United States. Whatever qualifications and exceptions may be cited, the prevailing tone of structural-functional approaches to social analysis is one of equilibrium, timelessness, value integration, natural harmony of interests. Deviance and conflicts tend to be defined as fringe short-term sub-cultures that will (hopefully?) never amount to more than sub-cultures. Having been made before, these points scarcely need repetition here. The only one that deserves re-emphasis is this: in the typical structural-functional perspective, which is of course a middle-class perspective, sub-cultures usually appear as, and remain, merely deviant sub-cultures. Their potential progression into large-scale structural changes is seldom seriously contemplated.

Deviance, though a less negatively "loaded" term, and perhaps more sophisticated than the old-time category *social disorganization* in general use one and two generations ago, still implies a single dominant and more or less stable normative order. This assumed order is the North

American middle-class pattern. Measured thereby, other patterns such as hippies, peaceniks, draft-evaders, ghetto gangs, et al. come to be defined as sub-cultures (*sub* is short for subordinate in case the reader needs reminding), and hence as minor variations – probably? hopefully? – going nowhere. However, in a dialectical, conflict-oriented perspective these "deviations" become "oppositions." Any of them might turn out to be sources of key structural changes. To estimate their respective potentials, even remotely, would require an historical view in a dialectical tradition. A structural-functionalist analysis gets us nowhere.

For instance, here are some books that show rather conclusively how little our middle-class anglophone sociologists understand of the basic elements[2] involved in (1) the situation of the American ghetto Blacks vis-à-vis the White bourgeois order (L. Rainwater and L. Yancy, 1967, R. Abrahams, 1970);[3] (2) the refusal of the Canadian Indians and the French Quebecers to be assimilated into the dominant Anglo-Canadian pattern (Lévesque, 1968; Cardinal, 1969);[4] (3) the meaning of poverty, which by the most conservative measure afflicts at least one-third of the Canadian people (Ian Adams, 1970).[5] These are not mere deviances. They are not simply sub-cultures. They could prove to be decisive in the changing mainstream of tomorrow. In brief, structural-functionalism is culture-bound middle-class apologetics.

The second reason for the aridity of anglophone sociology in Canada is the general identification of middle-class anglophone sociologists with the Anglo-Canadian bourgeois Establishment, and/or with the latter's country-cousin status as a branch plant of the American capitalist empire. Even if the majority of our anglophone practitioners are indifferent to or unaware of Canada's hinterland subordination to the United States, still they can be said to support it by default. Many tacitly assume that Quebec separatism is wrong, that "federalism" is right, and that to make a big issue out of American economic and cultural imperialism in Canada is impolite, uneconomic and impolitic. Surprisingly little attention is given to historical overviews or to the potentially massive conflicts creeping up both inside and outside Canadian society. Regional studies have been seriously neglected in Canada, except by such persons as B. Y. Card (*Perspectives on Regions and Regionalism*, Edmonton, University of Alberta, 1969, Ed. B.Y. Card).

This is not to deny the value of limited specific insights and studies based on the structural-functional approach.[6] We have many such analyses in Canada. They are to be found in the collections of readings on Canadian society (Blishen, 1968; Mann, 1968; Laskin, 1964),[7] in the *Canadian Review of Sociology and Anthropology*, in Royal Commissions and other governmental reports, in special monographs and elsewhere.

Some of them are even published in American outlets. In the February, 1970, *American Sociological Review*, there appeared a study of the Saskatchewan Wheat Pool by John Craig and Edward Gross[8] – the latter is a famous name in American sociology. Only after reading one-fourth of the 13-page article does one realize that the topic is the Saskatchewan Wheat Pool, a large farmer-owned producer co-operative. Let me say that six years of rural and urban research in Saskatchewan made the present writer reasonably familiar with the Saskatchewan scene. In the 1920s the Wheat Pool was an innovating and slightly revolutionary hinterland movement of western grain farmers fighting back against eastern metropolitan financial and industrial interests. By the middle 1950s the Pool had become part of the Saskatchewan Establishment. Something of the epic quality of that conflict-ridden historical cycle is recaptured in J. McCrorie (1964), in J. F. C. Wright (1955a, 1955b),[9] to name but three accounts. But it was difficult for me to recognize a real-life organization in this analysis entitled, "The Forum Theory of Organizational Democracy: Structural Guarantees as Time-Related Variables." Though published in a prestige journal (so the trade opinion runs in North America), this paper in my opinion conveys little about either the contemporary grass-roots activities of the Wheat Pool or the historical role of the Pool in Saskatchewan. Indeed, there is more feeling and essential perspectives of Saskatchewan conveyed in Carlyle King's Saskatchewan literary anthology (1955).[10]

On occasion, to be sure, a structural-functional approach has attained a relatively holistic view of Canadian society: witness J. Porter,[11] 1965. This work contains much information and some useful historical data. But to find out what is really on-going in Canadian society today, one does not ordinarily resort to the writings of anglophone academic sociologists. One would be better advised to turn to philosopher George Grant (1965; 1969);[12] to economist Mel Watkins (1968);[13] to journalist Peter Newman (1963; 1968);[14] and to the documentaries of the Canadian Broadcasting Corporation (CBC) and the National Film Board. For relevant reading on Canadian society, one should probably pass over at least half of the *Canadian Review of Sociology and Anthropology* in favour of *Canadian Dimension* and *Canadian Forum*. Lipset's well-known study (1950) seriously misinterpreted the Saskatchewan Co-operative Commonwealth Federation (CCF) movement as a transplanted offshoot of urban socialism,[15] when it was mainly an indigenous manifestation of western petty-bourgeois populism fighting back against eastern metropolitan domination. In the new up-dated edition of this book (Lipset, 1968), the record was set straight, not by Lipset or by some other sociologist, but by anthropologist John Bennett and economist John Richards. Finally, the best study of poverty in Canada is by journalist Ian Adams (1970), or by novelist Gabrielle Roy (1947, 1958).[16]

In brief, then, concerning the contributions of anglophone middle-class sociologists to an understanding of Canadian society–with some exceptions–perhaps the less said, the better. If I were a CBC official responsible for staffing a documentary radio or television program on what is going on in Canadian society, I would pass over most of the anglophone sociologists. I believe it would serve the Canadian public better to present the ideas of people like René Lévesque, Harold Cardinal, certain journalists, a handful of academics (mostly non-sociologists), and of the more sensitive and intelligent folk-singers like Buffy Sainte-Marie. They could do the job.

The reader has doubtless noted that I have concerned myself only with anglophone sociologists in Canada. This does not mean that our francophone colleagues have not been contaminated by over-concern with structural-functionalism. I believe that they have, but not nearly to the same extent as the anglophones. This is doubtless because they live close to the central conflict in contemporary Canadian society–the question of independence for Quebec. Hence they are more conscious of conflict and change than are most of the rest of us.

Another really sad fact is that the majority of anglophone sociologists do not know what their francophone counterparts are doing, because they do not speak or read French. If we anglophones want a dialogue with francophone intellectuals, we must learn their language and culture, read their writings, and attend their meetings, and talk to them in French. I believe that it should be a prime concern of the Canadian Sociology and Anthropology Association to re-establish communication with Quebec social scientists by pressuring anglophone members to take total-immersion courses in the French language. Indeed, it seems entirely likely, in my judgment, that even our western Canadian universities within a few years may give priority to appointing fluently bilingual professors to their faculties. The assumption of North American anglophones–"if someone wants to talk to us, let them learn English"–is simply a linguistic reflection and reinforcement of Anglo imperialism in Canada. Though not yet over, that era is rapidly passing.

The Need for a Dialectical and Historical Perspective in Canadian Studies

Roughly speaking, the dialectical premise is that major long-run changes in the institutional structure of a particular society stem from internal and external oppositions that develop immanently in that society and its milieu. These oppositions or confrontations of incompatible interests and values eventually work into a new institutional pattern which is not like either of the original opposing complexes, but which usually includes important elements of each. A good example is historian Crane Brinton's study of four major revolutions (1952).[17] The process of revolution obviously lends itself admirably to a dialectical analysis. For less "extreme" confrontations, the present writer prefers a modified version of the dialectic applicable to Canada, where political change has characteristically been relatively moderate. The schema consists of a "metropolis-vs.-hinterland" frame of reference. It assumes a conflict of interests between metropolis and hinterland, and an inherent tendency of hinterlands to fight back—though these conflicts at different times may be overt or latent or counteracted by other factors, as conditions vary.

Metropolis refers to centres of economic and political control, usually in the larger cities. It may denote urban elites or regional or national or ethnic power structures. *Hinterland* means any comparatively underdeveloped or colonial area which exports for the most part raw or semi-processed extractive materials—including migrating people seeking better opportunities elsewhere. *Hinterland* may also refer to urban under-classes as well as to rural proletariats and peasantries. Indeed, it seems convenient to use *metropolis* and *overclass* interchangeably, and likewise *hinterland* and *underclass.*

Finally, there are hierarchies of overlapping metropolis-hinterland relationships. Northern Manitoba may be viewed as a hinterland of Winnipeg—or perhaps in certain respects also as a hinterland of Ottawa. Manitoba itself may be seen as something of a hinterland of industrial and commerical eastern Canada; and Canada, of the United States economic and political empire. Needless to say, the metropolis-hinterland schema does not include all the relationships that may exist between or among these entities. Rather, it highlights the conflict and exploitive aspects of such relationships. It is suggested here that the schema can be applied to Canadian and North American society with results that are insightful, dynamic, capable of taking account of unique local and historical conditions, and perhaps relevant for tentative prediction. By contrast, structural-functional analyses are practically useless for prediction.

There is nothing really new in these remarks.[18] In fact, a good deal of work has been done along these lines by Canadian scholars, especially by such economic historians as Innis and Fowke. A number of sociologists have made consistent use of historical materials and perspectives—among them S. D. Clark, B. Y. Card, R. Ossenberg, S. Ryerson (1960, 1965),[19] H. Guindon—to name no others. But the contributions of such writers seem greatly outweighed, at least in volume, by work that leans toward the structural-functional tradition. Consider, for example, the array of textbooks commonly used in anglophone introductory sociology courses in Canadian universities. The majority of them impress me as useless "mickey mouse" exercises imported (for a good price) from the United States, or produced by Canadian branch-plants of American publishers. What they tell us about North American society is too often less important than what they leave out.

Even the bare handful of readers on "Canadian Society" leave much to be desired. For nearly a decade the Blishen reader (1968) has been a mainstay of anglophone Canadian university undergraduate sociology courses. First published in 1961, it must have been used by thousands of students. It has probably widened the gap between Anglo and French Canada—willy-nilly—because it takes little account of conflict-oriented, dialectical views of Canadian society. Further, it has contributed to the obscuring of the one issue that can over-ride the Anglo-French issue: the stance of Canada vis à vis the American empire. In other words, the Blishen reader is—ideologically and doubtless unintentionally—a prime indirect supporter of the present middle-class Anglo-Canadian Establishment. The majority of the articles convey an Anglo, structural-functional orientation. There are perfunctory bows toward French-Canadian patterns, Ukrainian patterns, Eskimo patterns, and so on. Much the same could be said of the Laskin reader—except that it does a much better job on the Hutterites. And so likewise for the Mann reader.[20]

Here is the theme of two key papers, one by Naegele in Blishen (1961 and 1964 editions only) and the other by Lipset in Mann, 1968. In these two papers on Canadian society as a whole, a central idea is, "Canadians are not Americans, in terms of values, and they are not British; they are somewhere in between." Both writers rely mainly on the abstract, static, structural-functional Weber-Parsons concepts—an injustice to Weber, at least, because Weber had a keen sense of economic history.

Lipset's paper[21] in the Mann reader resorts to the well-known Parsonian pattern variables, and a more dismal exercise at explaining Canadian society I have never seen. It is not that Lipset is wrong; his approach is just irrelevant. What does it mean, for either American or Canadian society, when Lipset argues that the United States (and Canada only a little less so) is achievement-oriented rather than ascriptive with regard to status-assigment? That the United States pursues universalistic values over and above particularistic values? That it is self-oriented more than collectivity-oriented? Egalitarian rather than elitist?

Surely these jargonistic propositions do not capture the guts of American society or American history. Furthermore, they are not empirically

true without serious qualifications: they fail to take into adequate account the obvious hierarchical, racist, elitist and special-privilege aspects of American social structure. How can we analyze the evolution
of American and Canadian societies without central emphasis upon the
differential development of modern capitalism in the two nations? Finally, if it is claimed that a neo-Marxian, dialectical frame of reference
for sociological studies is bound up with ideological implications – and
so it is – then this claim is just as applicable to structural-functionalism,
Parsonianism, et. al. What could be more ideological than Lipset's one-
sided, special-pleading distortion of American social realities? If the
reader has doubts about this charge, let him re-read Lipset, a recognized
servant of the American Establishment, and then glance over the headlines of today's American newspapers. Lipset is listed as having received
$95,000 from the U.S. Air Force to study the "Implication of Compar-
ative National Development for Military Planning."[22]

It is regrettable that anglophone Canadian sociologists have not critically debated the relevance of the currently fashionable concepts of
United States bourgeois sociology for analysis of Canadian society. Instead, there has prevailed a tendency simply to transplant those concepts. Occasionally, Canadian academics have displayed an almost supine attitude toward their American opposite numbers. Consider the
following Foreword by Dr. Murray Ross for the W. Mann (1968) reader.
Ross is not only a well-known writer on community organization; he
is also the president of York University, Toronto.

> The popular view is that sociological analysis and study in Canada has
> lagged far behind similar work in the United States . . . Unfortunately
> the popular view is correct . . . Canada has not yet produced original
> sociological theorists comparable to Talcott Parsons, Robert K. Merton,
> and C. Wright Mills . . .[23]

Two of these eminent sociologists are structural-functionalists and
generally irrelevant for un-American Canadians. But mainly, Ross is looking in the wrong place. The original theorists about Canadian society
are not to be found in orthodox academic esoterica, but in such sources
as Lumsden (1970), *Canadian Dimension*, *Monthly Review*, Harold Innis
and Vern Fowke.

Not the least unhappy aspect of this deference to prevailing American
intellectual concepts is the fact that it is unwitting. Yet it is not merely
a function of ignorance. It is better described as stemming from class-
and culture-bound blindspots. How ironic that professional social scientists should display this shortcoming in their own professional field!

But sociologists are not alone in being culture-bound. Consider the following Toronto *Globe and Mail* account of Prime Minister Trudeau's visit to President Nixon in Washington in March, 1969. The deferential attitude of the Prime Minister of Canada parallels that of the President of York University toward things American. The scene is Trudeau's reception at the White House in Washington.

> Responding to the President's words about a commonality of background, Mr. Trudeau said this extended to "a common outlook on the world. We have the same values and we tend to face the issues in a common way." Because of that he was looking forward to the discussion . . . "to listening to your views on world problems, on the information and the wisdom you will want to impart upon me in your talks."
>
> Some observers who have travelled extensively with Mr. Trudeau said that he had not sounded so humble, or looked so shy, since just before he decided to run for the Liberal Party leadership more than 13 months ago.[24]

Is it necessary to say here that we are not arguing for a unique "Canadian sociology?" There is no such thing as a "national sociology." But there are alternative ways of viewing society and history. And every society is geographically and historically unique in some essential respects. Structural-functionalism does not adequately explain or convey a convincing image of these unique aspects—least of all in a realistic context of flux and change.

Another way to size up our present condition in Canada is the dialectical. Not only is this appropriate for analyzing a semi-colonial society like Canada. It is equally indispensable for understanding metropolitan imperial America.

Conversely, the structural-functional ideology obscures some key essentials of both Canada and the United States. Yet this is the prevailing school of sociology of North America. Its followers can fully understand neither Canadian society nor American society. The Canadian critic who complained that many American social scientists are not qualified to teach in Canada about Canadian institutions did not go far enough. Many Americans are not particularly competent to teach about the United States, either.

Robin Mathews of Carleton University justifiably attacks the "Americanization of Canadian universities."[25] His solution is more Canadians—trained in Canada—on Canadian faculties. This is scarcely adequate. What difference would it make, so long as Canadian sociologists (for example) continue to be trained in such obfuscating orthodoxies as structural-functionalism and symbolic interaction? They will still remain junior lieutenants in the intellectual empire of the Amercan Establishment.

Conceptual orientation rather than nationality would be a more ap-

propriate target for Mathews. No one wants or needs universities dominated by a particular viewpoint, any more than we want professional
appointments to university faculties to rest heavily on non-professional
criteria such as citizenship. Either outcome would make for parochialism – the very opposite of what a university ought to be. We should seek
for a variety of viewpoints and origins, and probably few people in the
North American academic professions would disagree in principle. What
I am contending is that, in practice, anglophone academic sociology in
Canada has become top-heavy in its leanings toward structural-functionalism and similar approaches, and that in consequence a dangerous
middle-class, continentalist parochialism has developed. Specifically neglected are the types of problems, conflicts and holistic perspectives best
treated in historical, comparative and dialectical terms. Let us now
sketch in tentative terms a dialectical view of Canadian and American
societies in a metropolis-vs.-hinterland frame of reference.

Canadian Society and History as Hinterland vs. Metropolis

Canadian society and history may be viewed as a series of hinterland
reactions to foreign metropolitan imperialisms. First came the French,
and soon afterward, the English. This European intrusion tied the native
Indians to the capitalistic European fur trade. In the eighteenth and nineteenth centuries, the native Indians were bent to a colonial status; the
Eskimo followed approximately a century later.

The conquest of French Canada by a British army in 1760 paved the
way for the Anglo primacy in Canada that still prevails today. But relations vis-à-vis the new American republic became increasingly important despite the predominantly British orientation during the nineteenth
century. Confederation was basically a response to the mid-century
American industrial and westward expansion. The "National Policy"
that emerged by the 1870s included western settlement as a new investment frontier for eastern business, a transcontinental railroad, a protective tariff, shunting the Indians onto reservations, and so on.

However, there were some unintended consequences. From the beginning of western settlement, the hinterland colonials carried on
chronic struggles to improve their status within the changing system of
capitalist expansion and exploitation. The Métis and some Indians
kicked up in 1885 (J. K. Howard, 1952). From the early 1900s, western farmers entered one skirmish after another against the railroads, grain exchange, elevator corporations, and finally against the eastern-dominated
political parties. Populist movements eventually came to power in the
form of Social Credit and the CCF. In effect, the broad course of events

in Canada, as industrialization progressed, has followed the pattern anticipated by Marx in the *Manifesto* (1848)–but only up to the beginning of a socialist movement. Why socialism has so far been stillborn will be discussed in the next section of this paper.

A similar metropolis-hinterland framework may be applied to Quebec. Quebec became another investment frontier for business interests that were predominantly Anglo, later American. In our own day, populist counter-attacks have appeared in the Caouette movement, speaking primarily for the northern Quebec colonials, and in the bourgeois "quiet revolution" more recently spearheaded by the drive for an independent Quebec. As "Canada" is colonized by the United States, Quebec is doubly colonized.

From a sociology-of-knowledge standpoint, structural-functionalism reflects and reinforces the interests of the Anglo Establishment–i.e., federalism in politics, capitalism in economic life. In my view, a conflict-oriented dialectic in the form of "metropolis-vs.-hinterland" is more realistic, and more revealing as an interpretation of Canadian society. It also implies a more openly political role for social sciences. Instead of tacitly supporting the institutional status quo, as most Anglophone social scientists do by default, a dialectical approach critically redefines the nature and transitory status of current institutional patterns of Canada. An excellent application of dialectical analysis of Canadian society by Drache appears in I. Lumsden (1970), pp. 3–27.[26]

Exploited colonials in the North American hinterlands have in the past battled to improve their status in the economic order, as shown for Canada by Fowke (1957)[27] and McCrorie (1965); and for the United States by historian William A. Williams (1969).[28] And the American empire has been able to carry the cost of concessions to its internal colonial underclasses by means of expanding its business interests into foreign hinterlands. But there are signs that the "Open Door" abroad is rapidly closing, so that a major crisis impends in American society, just when its monolithic rigidity and its lack of critically articulate and organized internal oppositions renders it incapable of adjusting to the new orders emerging in other parts of the world. It is doubtful, in my view, whether the United States will make it into the 21st century, alive and/or fit to live. This thought first occurred to me a decade ago (Davis, 1960).[29] It seems even more relevant today. More on this shortly. If this is valid, then Canada is directly involved, for Canada has become in large part an informal annex of the American empire. This sell-out to "continentalism" took place without debate in the Canadian Parliament or in any other large Canadian public forum.

In this perspective of impending catastrophe south of the border, any large confrontation in Canada may contribute to a Canadian-hinterland vs. American-metropolis showdown. For this reason alone, the most promising recent development in Canadian society may well be the movement for Quebec independence. If, as seems inevitable, Quebec goes independent, it will almost certainly be forced to move toward state socialism. Anglo Canada may then be compelled to face up to its own self and to its alternative absorption into the homogenizing American empire. The Anglo-Canadian Establishment has set its policy in favour of opting into the American empire as a junior partner, as George Grant and Mel Watkins have shown. Two-thirds of Canadian manufacturing is already under foreign control, according to the 1968 Watkins report. Certain large Canadian labour unions are controlled by American unions, which are very much an integral part of the American economic empire— also on a junior-partner basis. It seems too late for English Canadian society to preserve its shrinking uniqueness and vanishing independence by normal negotiations.

Quebec, however, may yet save Canada by going independent. And this sort of development in Canada may, in turn, stimulate the United States to face up to its real problem—its own character and its own social structure. Granted, this may be wishful thinking, yet just now it appears to be the most promising (i.e., the least costly) possibility. The alternative means might involve miliary defeat and conquest of the United States by rebellious hinterlands and rival metropolitan powers. But who would survive?

The francophone, Catholic character of Quebec may conceivably offer an adequate cultural and economic base for opting out of the American empire. The horrendous nature of that empire is now being revealed in Vietnam, in the black ghettos of American cities, and even on American university campuses. Let us turn to the nature of American society, into which the anglo-Canadian Establishment is so blithely taking us. It is contended here that only a dialectical perspective can realistically illuminate the character of American society.

American Society and History as Metropolis vs. Hinterland

Two major confrontations feature the last century and a half of American history. The first was that between southern agrarian capitalism and northern industrial capitalism linked with western farmers. Each had to expand in order to survive, and when expansion room ran out, civil war followed, 1861–65. The North won.

The second was the rising tide of agrarian and labour revolts that began to pile up against the burgeoning northern industrialism in the decades between the Civil War and first world war. Much as Marx had forecast, economic and political oppositions began to gather against triumphant business enterprise, and by 1900 a fledging native socialist movement led by Gene Debs was under way.

But after 1912, all socialist movements stagnated and declined; the agrarian colonials won concessions; militant labour for the most part became "business unionism"–safe for capitalism. Competition remained, of course, often nasty and bitter. Progressive reforms slowly materialized, especially in the 1930s. Yet after World War I, massive oppositions in America could hardly be said to exist. Everyone bought the prevailing American way of life–give or take a few modifications. Even the small civil rights movements marked by the National Association for the Advancement of Colored People and similar organizations accepted the bourgeois order. All they asked was–"Count us in."

What explains the collapse of the gathering, massive opposition to American capitalism? What explains the absence of any genuine "Left" on the American political scene after 1920? In theory, the absence of any important pre-capitalist order in America should have made for a classic example of the displacement of capitalism by socialism.

In a nutshell, what seems best to explain the absence of massive oppositions in the United States during the last half-century is the over-success of American capitalism. As historian Charles Beard (1927)[30] explained it, the triumph of business enterprise was due to fabulous resources, a protected domestic market, cheap immigrant labour, and a paternalistic national government that really looked after the business interests that controlled federal, state and local governments. Above all, two cheap world wars knocked off rival capitalist powers, and contributed immensely to American economic expansion abroad.

For what effectively smothered the gathering domestic crisis about the turn of the century, after the interior frontier was "closed," was the launching of the economy on renewed expansion abroad. The only variations in this policy have been the "hard-sell" vs the "soft-sell." When Washington stressed "good neighbour" policies in Latin America, for example, that was "soft-sell." When American troops landed in some banana republic, that was "hard-sell." No major American party or interest has opposed American economic expansion abroad as the keystone of United States foreign policy. Splinter oppositions of course do not count. There are other factors, too, in the American success story: the Keynesian reforms, military and space budgets, farm subsidies, social-security concessions, etc. It all adds up to the most spectacular success story in human history–in the short run.

But in the long-run disaster may be the consequence of this American over-success. If structural change depends on dialectical confrontations between massive oppositions in a society, then the USA must appear as a rigid monolith, incapable of adjusting to a changing world it cannot understand. Clearly, anti-colonial, national and communist revolutions in Europe, Asia and perhaps elsewhere have slammed the door on American expansion in many such areas. The massive oppositions to American society are now largely external, and a dialogue across national and racial lines seems unlikely because of the emotional blocks and the vested interests involved.

On a global basis, the existing tensions between the American metropolis and its foreign hinterlands must tend to increase, quite apart from whatever stresses or settlements may develop between the Communist empires and the United States. Hinterlands eventually are forced by their own internal conditions and inspirations to "fight back." If in the short run they—or their domestic "vendu" elites—gain a more favorable but still subordinate position within the metropolitan system, ultimately they cannot realize their aims for self-determination except by escaping entirely from capitalism, as China and Cuba have done.

Political economist André Frank has shown (1967)[31] that capitalist metropolis actively creates underdevelopment in its satellites. Underdevelopment, in other words, is immanent in the evolution of capitalism, and not an external or accidental separate system describable as "folk" or "traditional" or "pre-industrial" society. These terms may properly apply only to "undeveloped" societies, not to "underdeveloped" ones.

The latter are those which have been drawn into the world capitalist market and imperium, and then have been pushed aside into stagnation or confined to undiversified and even single-industry roles by new investment thrusts in other industries and other regions. In Canada, examples would be (in varying styles and degrees) the impoverished Indians, small farmers and an increasing proportion of middle-sized farm operators, large areas of the Maritimes and Newfoundland, francophone Quebec, and so on.[32]

The intensifying metropolis-vs.-hinterland syndrome, then, should make for mounting crisis in American society. There is still another factor making in the same direction. Why should the favored American six percent of the world's population enjoy more than 50 percent of the world's wealth and income? And this gap between rich and poor is widening, not only between advanced and "underdeveloped" nations, but within the advanced nations as well. (Williams, 1964, ch. 3).[33] Can anyone doubt that the economic progress of Canada's native peoples is not keeping pace with the economic development of the advanced sectors of our national economy? S. D. Clark says much the same thing about the gap between French-Canadian farmers and labourers in Northern Quebec and Northern Ontario company towns, compared with Anglo managerial groups in the same northern communities. (Ossenberg, ed., 1971.)[34]

But the economic aspect by itself is only part of the relevant picture. Probably most Canadians want more economic goodies. But how shall they use them? What sort of community life do they want? Do they want to be addicts of suburban consumerism like the Americans? Do they wish to be accessories of the American napalming of Asian peasants? That appears to be the end-result of "continentalism" – the on-going drift into the increasingly reactionary American empire fostered since World War II by the big-business Anglo-Canadian Establishment and its "vendu" francophone satellites who support Canadian "federalism."

However, not all Canadians may want to be thus homogenized when they understand what is afoot. For if our analysis is even half valid, the American imperium is coasting toward disaster both at home and abroad. It has not been able to do anything significant about urban and rural poverty, the ghettoized Blacks, the disaffected students, the multiple hard-core problems centering in the cities. It is bogged down in a military morass in Asia, and its economy appears headed for a serious recession. Assassination of leaders and shooting civilians have become standard political responses in the United States. If continentalism continues to prevail as Canadian national policy, Canada can expect to be dragged down in the American wake.

The opposite course would in some degree be anti-imperialist, anti-American, anti-capitalist, anti-continentalist and anti-Anglo Establishment. What evidence is there that hinterland and underclass groups in Canada are leaning in any of these directions? Outside of Quebec, the signs are scattered and weak. Let us cite statements by three different kinds of Canadians: Harold Cardinal, Alberta native Indian leader; René Lévesque, head of Le Parti Québecois; and George Grant, chairman of the Department of Religion at McMaster University. Each is raising basic issues of noneconomic cultural values – how we ought or ought not to live. In assessing the impact of these oppositions in a dialectical context, it is essential for us to remember that the noneconomic aspects are at least as important as the economic factors. For instance, if the economic problems of our Canadian Indians could be met, the conflict of values would still remain. Many Indians simply do not buy Anglo middle-class norms and life style.

> The new Indian policy promulgated by Prime Minister Pierre-Elliot Trudeau's government . . . in June of 1969 is a thinly disguised programe of ex-

termination through assimilation . . . a program which offers nothing better than cultural genocide . . . Indians have aspirations, hopes and dreams, but becoming white men is not one of them. (Cardinal, 1969 pp. 1, 3)[35]

There is no relief in our responsibility for creating, or utilizing the potential that exists in our communities. There is very little place for non-Indians, simply because it is we who have to do the job. The Honorable Minister can never tell us the true meaning of Indianess. The Federal government with its billions of dollars can never buy us the true meaning of Indianess. And no White man, no non-Indian in any profession can tell us what Indianess means." (Cardinal, speech to the Western Association of Sociology and Anthropology, Banff, Dec. 28, 1969)

We are Québecois. What this means first and foremost is that we are attached to this one corner of the earth where we can be completely ourselves, the only place where we have the unmistakable feeling that 'here we can be really at home.' Being ourselves is essentially a matter of keeping and developing a personality that has survived for three and a half centuries . . . We are heirs to the group obstinacy which has kept alive that portion of French America we call Quebec . . . This is how we differ from other men and especially from other North Americans. (Lévesque, 1968, 14, 15).[36]

What our fate is today becomes most evident in the light of Vietnam. It is clear that in that country the American empire has been demolishing a people, rather than allowing them to live outside the American orbit . . . The very substance of our lives is bound up with the western empire and its destiny, just at a time when that empire uses increasingly ferocious means to maintain its hegemony. (Grant, 1969, 63, 65)[37]

Though none of these writers spells out his alternatives, the upshot of all three suggests sharp disagreements with some of the key policies of the orthodox Canadian Establishment. But it requires an historical, conflict-oriented frame of reference to assess these dissents.

In this grim evaluation of American developments, the one great question mark is the Black-power movement, and secondarily, perhaps, the student disaffection. Black power may yet save the United States, as Quebec may salvage Canada. It is too early to say whether the Afro-Americans can come up with a mass-supported program of institutional reform along socialist lines.

Meanwhile, the savage aspect of American society is revealed in southeast Asia for all to see. The link between Main Street and Vietnam is direct and organic. Other such cases may arise any day in Latin America. Sooner or later, nuclear war seems likely, and that would be the end of all of us.

It is in the light of this urgent perspective that wider study and use of a dialectical, metropolis-vs.-hinterland frame of reference for anglophone Canadian social science seems essential, both for advancing social theory and for informing national policy and public opinion.

Notes

1 M. H. Watkins, "The dismal state of economics in Canada," *Close the 49th Parallel: The Americanization of Canada*, ed. Ian Lumsden, Toronto: University of Toronto Press, 1970, pp. 197–208.

2 *Reading, Writing, and Riches*, ed. by Randle W. Nelsen and David A. Nock, Toronto: Between-the-Lines Press, 1978.

3 See L. Rainwater and W. Yancey, *The Moynihan Report and the Politics of Controversy*, Cambridge: M.I.T. Press, 1967; and also R. O. Abrahams, *Positively Black*, Englewood Cliffs: Prentice Hall, 1970.

4 See René Lévesque, *An Option for Quebec*, Toronto: McClelland and Stewart, 1968, and also Harold Cardinal, *The Unjust Society*, Edmonton: Hurtig, 1969.

5 Ian Adams, *The Poverty Wall*, Toronto: McClelland and Stewart, 1970.

6 Symbolic interactionism merits some of the strictures here directed at structural–functionalism.

7 See B. Blishen, ed., *Canadian Society: Sociological Perspectives*, Toronto: Macmillan, 1968; also W. E. Mann, ed., *Canada: A Sociological Profile*, Toronto: Copp Clark, 1968; and also R. Laskin, *Social Problems: A Canadian Profile*, Toronto: McGraw Hill of Canada, 1964.

8 John Craig and Edward Gross, "The Forum Theory of Organizational Democracy: Structural Guarantees as Time-Related Variables," *American Sociological Review*, February 1970, 35:1, pp. 19–33.

9 See J. M. McCrorie, *In Union Is Strength*, Saskatoon, 1965; also J. F. C. Wright, *Saskatchewan: The History of a Province*, Toronto: McClelland and Stewart, 1955a; and *Prairie Progress: Consumer Co-operation in Saskatchewan*, Saskatoon: Modern Press, 1955b.

10 Carlyle King, ed., *Saskatchewan Harvest: A Literary Anthology*, Toronto: McClelland and Stewart, 1955. To go with the macro-historical and dialectical sociology for which I am arguing, we should foster an emphasis on realism in presentation of social data and social analysis. The leading questions should be of this sort: What was it really like (for example) in Saskatchewan in the 1950s, the 1960s, for the various occupational groups, classes, communities of various sizes and locations, age and sex groups, and for other categories of men and women? In answering this kind of query, the analyst, in my view, should deliberately include large subjective elements, descriptive materials, and emotional highlightings – including the analyst's own vantage point. In this way, we arrive at a micro-report that is somewhere between literature and conventional abstract sociology, as macro-dialectical historical lies between sociology and history. The common element is the confrontation theme. Examples would be cer-

tain works of W. F. Whyte and Oscar Lewis; R. Badgley and S. Wolfe, *Doctor's Strike: Medical Care and Conflict in Saskatchewan*, New York: Atherton Press, 1967; J. K. Howard, *Strange Empire: A Narrative of the Northwest*, New York: Morrow, 1952; William Hinton, *Fanshen: A Document of Revolution in a Chinese Village*, New York: Monthly Review Press, 1966; and numerous television, radio and film documentaries by the Canadian Broadcasting Corporation and the National Film Board.

11 John Porter, *The Vertical Mosaic: An Analysis of Social Class and Power in Canada*, Toronto: University of Toronto Press, 1965.

12 See George Grant, *Lament for a Nation*, Toronto: McClelland and Stewart, 1965; and *Technology and Empire*, Toronto: House of Anansi, 1969.

13 Melville Watkins, *Foreign Ownership and the Structure of Canadian Industry*, Ottawa: Privy Council Office, 1968.

14 Peter Newman, *Renegade in Power: The Diefenbaker Years*, Toronto: McClelland and Stewart, 1963; and *The Distemper of Our Times: Canadian Politics in Transition*, Toronto: McClelland and Stewart, 1968; and most recently, *The Canadian Establishment, Vol. I*, Toronto, McClelland and Stewart, 1975 (eds.).

15 S. M. Lipset, *Agrarian Socialism: The Co-operative Commonwealth in Saskatchewan*, Berkeley: University of California, 1950. See also the updated edition of the same book, Garden City: Doubleday Anchor Books, 1968.

16 Gabrielle Roy, *The Tin Flute*, Toronto: McClelland and Stewart, 1947 and 1958.

17 See Crane Brinton, *Anatomy of Revolution*, New York: Random House and Vintage Books, 1952.

18 They are amplified in the present writer's paper published in R. J. Ossenberg, ed., *Canadian Society: Pluralism, Change, and Conflict*, Scarborough: Prentice-Hall, 1971, pp. 6–32.

19 Stanley Ryerson, *The Founding of Canada: Beginnings to 1800*, Toronto: Progress Books, 1960; also *The Open Society: Paradox and Challenge*, New York: International, 1965.

20 However, note that Mann has heeded Davis' programmatic position since this paper was first delivered in 1970. In the third edition of Mann's reader (1976), Arthur K. Davis was invited to write the foreword. Also, papers by Davis' favourite authors, including Ian Adams, George Grant, Mel Watkins, etc. were published. Thus, since 1970 Davis has made an impact on the profession in Canada (eds.).

21 See S. M. Lipset, "Revolution and Counter Revolution: The United States and Canada," *Canada: A Sociological Profile*, ed. W. E. Mann, Toronto: Copp Clark, 1971, pp. 24–36.

22 See Ian Lumsden, "American imperialism and Canadian intellectuals" in Lumsden, ed., *Close the 49th Parallel*, Univ. of Toronto Press, 1970, p. 335.

23 Murray G. Ross, "Forward," Mann, ed., 1st edition (1968), p. vii.

24 Lumsden, ed., frontispiece.

25 See Robin Mathews and James Steele, *The Struggle for Canadian Universities*,

Toronto: New Press, 1969. Although Davis had certain reservations about Mathews, he has come to support a Canadianization hiring policy (eds.).

26 D. Drache, "The Canadian bourgeoisie and its national consciousness" in Lumsden, ed., pp. 3–26.

27 Vernon Fowke, *The National Policy and the Wheat Economy*, Toronto: University of Toronto Press, 1957.

28 See W. A. Williams, *The Roots of the Modern American Empire: A Study of the Growth and Shaping of Social Consciousness in a Market Place Society*, New York: Random House, 1969.

29 Arthur K. Davis, "Decline and Fall," *Monthly Review*, 1960, Vol. 12, pp. 334–344.

30 C. and M. Beard, *The Rise of American Civilization*, New York: Macmillan, 1927.

31 André G. Frank, *Capitalism and Underdevelopment in Latin America: Historical Studies of Chile and Brazil*, New York: Monthly Review Press, 1967.

32 Frank's work, based on a "metropolis-satellite" schema in a dialectical frame of reference, deserves to be better known among Canadian social scientists, because with little modification it is directly applicable to Canada – as a scanning of Harold Innis' work will easily demonstrate. For example, Canadian Indians and the reservation system today are to be understood primarily in terms of the relative decline of the fur trade (which originally reduced the Indians to the status of a rural, non-agricultural proletariat) and the shifting of capitalist development in the 19th century to new investment frontiers such as western agricultural settlement after confederation.

33 See W. A. Williams, *The Great Evasion: An Essay on the Contemporary Relevance of Karl Marx and on the Relevance of Admitting the Heretic into the Dialogue about America's Future*, Chicago: Quadrangle Books, 1964, chapter III.

34 S. D. Clark, "The Position of the French Speaking Population in the Northern Industrial Community," in Ossenberg, ed., pp. 62–85.

35 Cardinal, pp. 1, 3.

36 Lévesque, pp. 14–15.

37 Grant, *Technology and Empire*, pp. 63 and 65.

Canadian Underdevelopment: Toward a New Grassroots Social Movement

Reflections on Rural Study Groups, 1972

SOME FAMILIAR THEMES form the background of these remarks. The rich get richer, the poor get poorer. This is true, the world around. It is true within Canada, within the United States, and within India. And it is true when we compare these countries with each other. The gaps between the more advanced countries and the less developed nations are widening. For example, the American metropolis takes far more out of its Latin American hinterlands than it puts in, as Harry Magdoff has shown.[1] From 1950–65, direct U.S. investment in Latin America was $3.8 billions; the take-home on this capital was $11.3 billions, not counting profits retained abroad.

Poverty is relative. Though the real incomes of underclass groups in advanced societies and in such less developed nations as Mexico and India may be rising slightly, aspirations of underclasses and the real incomes of overclasses are rising even faster. Here is the rub.

Nor is this all. The theory has been widely advocated, especially in the advanced capitalistic powers, that the "backward" countries can catch up with the industrialized western States, given inputs of aid from major capitalistic powers and development of initiative on the part of the aspiring nations. This is a myth. The Americans, six percent of the world's population, control some 60 percent of the world's wealth. This

I am greatly indebted to the Regina campus, especially to Dr. J. N. McCrorie (Sociology Department chairman) and to Dr. J. Roberts (Political Science Department chairman), for sharing with me their common concern for building a university responsible to the people of Saskatchewan, who pay most of the cost of that university, but who get less than their share of the returns.

This unpublished paper on community development describes, in a broad setting, some events in Saskatchewan during the winter and spring of 1972. The rural study groups were co-sponsored by the University of Regina and the National Farmers Union. The writer was Visiting Professor at Regina, on leave from Alberta.

is not a static condition. The energy-hungry and resource-hungry American economy soaks up an ever-increasing proportion of the world's natural resources. There is simply not enough left for everyone else to catch up.

Moreover, "foreign aid" from the major western States–never adequate from the beginnings under the Marshall plan of 20 odd years ago–has steadily decreased during recent years, if we measure aid-giving as a percent of gross national product (GNP). "Though (16) developed countries in 1961 accepted the key goal that their net flow of resources to developing countries was to reach 1 percent of GNP in the First Development Decade, the actual figure in 1970 was 0.74 percent–as against 0.95 percent in 1961."[2] For Canada, the figure in 1970 was 0.50 percent of GNP; in 1970 for the United States, 0.33 percent.[3] Among the 16 contributing countries the United States ranked twelfth, but Canada ranked sixth. For the record, France was first; the Netherlands was second, and Australia and Belgium were third and fourth.

So what can people of good will in Canada do? Clearly, change must take place: basic change, and soon. The underclass hinterland groups must break the chains that bind them to metropolitan overclasses. But how? Should we raise the ancient cry of the Romans–*Carthago delenda est*? *Carthage must be destroyed?* This seems premature. The modern Carthaginians south of the Canadian border appear to be hell-bent on destroying themselves. Let us therefore concentrate upon our domestic situation.

Canadian scholars, from Harold Innis to George Grant, have taught us to see Canadian history as responses to a series of foreign imperialisms, first French and British, and now American. But to describe Canada as a branch plant of the United States is to oversimplify a great truth. There are also exploiting and exploited classes and sectors within Canada. Capitalist development inherently creates relative underdevelopment, as we know from Marx, Paul Baran and A. G. Frank.[4] In other words, metropolis creates and exploits its satellites or hinterlands. Further, there are hierarchies or chains of metropolis-satellite relationships. Melville Watkins put it this way.[5]

> We should take very seriously the point that Frank makes: wherever you happen to be, whatever country you study, whatever city–locate yourself within this chain that binds metropolis and satellite. Find out what your relationships are to those above you in the chain, and to those below . . . Perhaps the most interesting way to write the history of Canada is to write the history of Ontario. Look up the chain and you see New York. Then look down the chain and you see the Atlantic provinces, the prairie provinces, and further down–the Caribbean and Brazil.

Canadian history, then, may be viewed as a series of exploitations and resultant confrontations between metropolitan overclasses and hinterland underclasses. Various capitalist interest-complexes have succeeded one another, depending partly on which export industry has been dominant. First it was fur, then fish and timber. Later, paper, minerals and oil came to the fore. The high-tariff policy begun in 1879 set the stage for the branch-plant manufacturing economy that has emerged in central Canada during the last two or three generations.

As industries rise and fall, pools of underdevelopment are often left behind. For example, when the fur trade receded, the Indian labour force became largely redundant. Moreover, on the Prairies, Indian hunting ranges were needed for White agricultural settlement–a new "investment frontier" sponsored by and for eastern business interests. By 1880 or thereabouts, White hunters had exterminated the great buffalo herds upon which Plains Indians depended. Hence it was easy to brush aside the starving Indians onto reservations. The reserve system in effect was a bargain-basement welfare or pension scheme. It cost the White Establishment very little money. The Indians became a surplus pool of rural, largely non-agricultural proletarians, living cheaply by means of hunting and gathering, limited welfare, and poorly-paid casual labour.

In Western Canada, the wheat economy became a new investment frontier. The package included Confederation in 1867, a transcontinental railway completed by 1886, massive immigration, a cheap-land policy, scientific experimental farms to help adapt agricultural practices to the semi-arid plains, and so on. With respect to the West, Fowke has outlined very well the main contours (except for Indian affairs) of the "national policy."[6] Meanwhile, in Eastern Canada, Quebec became the other great investment frontier for the business interests of Toronto and English Montreal. Subsequently, in our own time, American multi-national corporations have moved into both Eastern and Western Canada.

Sooner or later hinterland groups learn to fight back against their exploiters. Saskatchewan and Alberta have a long history of agrarian, co-operative and political movements aimed at redressing the grievances of the farmers. Quebec likewise has brought forth a series of French underclass vs. English overclass struggles, of which the Creditistes and the Parti Québecois are only the latest vehicles.[7] The Indians, too, are becoming militant. Finally, vis-à-vis the United States there is a slowly rising tide of concerned Canadian nationalism, the main facets of which are economic, political, educational, military and cultural.

This is a theory of history, a world-view, dialectical in character. The established order generates conflicting oppositions which challenge the old regime. From that conflict emerges a modified new order. How modified, or how new—depends on the scale and depth of the clash (or clashes, more likely) between Establishment(s) and Opposition(s).

With this dialectical background in mind, let us now focus on the farmers of Western Canada.

The Prairies are witnessing today the decline of the wheat economy. This does not mean that wheat as a marketable commodity is becoming less important; quite the contrary. It is the farmers, not wheat, who are becoming redundant. A few huge farms, mostly corporations, can produce the wheat crop, with the aid of machines and a minimum of hired labour.

What is in store for Canadian farmers is clearly sketched in an official federal document, *Agriculture in the 1970s* (Ottawa, 1970). This report, written by a group of middle-class, urban types obviously oriented to big business and agri-business rather than to ordinary farmers, includes a preview of farming in the 1990s on pp. 8–9. Farms, marketing boards and processing firms will be much larger; the rural population (now 26 percent across Canada, by 1966 census figures) will fall to 3 or 4 percent of the total; professional management and data processing will grow in importance; the family farm will give way to corporation farms; vertical integration into the already massive food-processing industry will continue to expand, and control of farming will pass to the giant corporations.

What does all this mean in simple language? It shows three salient facts: the developments long evident in other capitalist industries are finally coming to dominate farming; the small town and village communities will disappear; and these trends have the firm support of the Canadian federal government. None of these facts is new; all have long roots in Canadian history and public policy.

Who will benefit? Capitalistic agri-business, mainly; certainly not the grassroots farmers who produce the food on which we all live. *Agribusiness* means processors, pools, meat packers, rural bankers, and so on; basically, they do not directly produce wealth, but only process it and act as middlemen—for a good price, of course. Agriculture will be "rationalized" in the interests of higher profits, less labour, an end of public subsidies, and much larger units—"not primarily for increased production efficiency, but to structure units that are large enough to afford better management." Besides the stockholders of agri-business, then, a small group of managers and attendant experts can expect to "share the melon" by means of high salaries and the fringe benefits that go to those who run the big corporations for the power elites. From the standpoint of the underclass farmers, it is just another rip-off at their expense. And from the viewpoint of all consumers, food becomes less pure and less healthful, as quality is sacrificed to the profits of the processors.

But this is not the full measure of the rip-off. What is to become of these redundant farmers forced off the land? The federal task force has that one figured out as follows: the ex-farmers will move to the cities to what are euphemistically styled "areas of alternate opportunities." The only trouble with that proposal is the fact that opportunities for re-training into *desirable* urban professions are in increasingly short supply. The task-force "experts" know this too. Hence the fall back on a vaguely phrased, back-up measure: "some form of guaranteed annual income will be taken for granted." As the two major parties up to now have discussed a guaranteed annual income, we may interpret this to mean the least costly, minimal welfare plan – not necessarily universal – that can "safely" be implemented. "Safely" here means avoiding costs large enough to disturb the current distribution of income, and averting any possibility of serious civil commotions by the expropriated underlying population.

Once more we may usefully turn to the position of Canada's native Indians. In June, 1969, the federal government issued an unexpectedly frank "White Paper," which proposed to phase out the special status of "treaty" Indians, the reserve system, and the Bureau of Indian Affairs – all within five years. A year later, the Alberta Indian Association, with wide support from other Indian groups across Canada, replied with its "Red Paper." The Indians totally rejected the proposed federal policy. They were prepared to re-negotiate the treaties with an eye to obtaining greater social equities in the one-sided treaties. Above all, they shunned the prospect of moving into the cities, of becoming absorbed in urban slums, and in the urban rat-race of White society. They particularly rejected the prospective destruction of their own communities on the reservations.

Allowing for minor differences in certain parameters (numbers, status differences, and so on) – the situation of Canadian Indians is roughly similar to that of Canadian farmers. Federal policy is exactly parallel in both cases: the basic capitalist policy of economic centralization and economic rationalization, as measured by maximization of efficiency in profit-making – must be furthered and fostered. The public coffers will bear the costs: from Ian Adams' *Real Poverty Report*[8] we know that the over-all tax system in Canada – federal, provincial and local viewed as a whole – is regressive. The benefits of economic centralization, however, will accrue mainly to the corporate elites of Canada and – increasingly – to the corporate elites of the United States. In brief, the underclasses of Canada are expected to pay the shot for their own exploitation and their own undoing.

Fortunately, there are signs of ferment among the Indians and the farmers of Canada. If these groups organize to resist the Establishment's policy of economic rationalization and centralization (including "continentalism"), why should not other underclass sectors of the population similarly mobilize themselves for basic structural change? The farmer's movement for rural redevelopment therefore demands our careful scrutiny.

In 1966, according to the Census of Canada, the rural population of Canada was one-fourth of the total. In Manitoba and Alberta, the corresponding figure was about one-third; in Saskatchewan, one half. Resident farmers constituted only part of the rural population. They were, in 1966, 10 percent of the total Canadian population. In Manitoba, they were 17 percent of the province's total population; in Saskatchewan, 29 percent; in Alberta, 19 percent. A generation ago, all these figures were much higher. Now three-quarters of Canada's people live in urban centres.[9] We are confronted with the social and economic erosion of town and countryside by metropolitan corporate interests, which threaten to put more and more of us on the shelf. A few big corporation farms can feed the nation; a few huge oil companies dominate the gas and oil industry with machines and computers that require only a handful of operators. How far is all this centralization going to be allowed to proceed? What is happening to the social quality of our lives? What is wrecking the physical quality of our lives? Are not both aspects being ruined by the capitalist logic of economic centralization in the interest of maximum profit rip-offs?

These are the questions already confronted by Canada's Indians and farmers. How do we go about finding the answers to those questions and ways of implementing the answers? In my dialectical perspective, only the underclass and hinterland groups of Canada and the world can meet the challenge. But where to start?

What Can Ordinary People Do?

This year, I had the opportunity to work as a "resource person" in a number of study groups sponsored in the Prairie Provinces by the National Farmers Union (NFU). From my experiences during the winter and spring of 1972, I believe I have learned some tactics suitable for Canada and perhaps for other advanced nations. There is no suggestion that these are the only possible tactics.

Two aspects of tactics against underdevelopment need to be worked out together: study groups and active demonstrations. The latter may range from local projects like the NFU tractor demonstrations aimed at impeding traffic on main highways while leaflets are passed out to

car drivers—to national enterprises like the NFU-sponsored Kraft boycott. In this paper, I am concerned only with the former aspect: study
groups. If successful, however, these two approaches together may lead
to much more ambitious undertakings, such as provincial expropriation
of the oil industry, now being informally discussed by various farm and
labour groups in Saskatchewan. The study groups were not conventional
"extension" education. The latter is oriented to up-grading middle-class
types in the existing bureaucratic and business apparatus. Our study
groups were in the spirit of the 1944 Saskatchewan Co-operative Commonwealth Federation (CCF) government. Its provincial Adult Education branch adopted the following goals: "to liquidate social scientific
and language illiteracy; to help clarify the thinking of citizens regarding
the fundamental issues of modern society; to promote responsible and
co-operative citizens' action; and to encourage integrated and creative
community life."[10]

Organization of Study Groups

Most of my groups had a locally elected chairman or chairwoman. In
a few cases, the chairing was done by an NFU head-office member. The
latter pattern seems undesirable, in retrospect, because the chief aim
of these study groups was to stimulate the formation of a network of
local groups, in contact with each other. This would enable the net to
undertake local and regional political and economic initiatives—loosely
co-ordinated with neighbouring groups—with and by regional and national leaders.

There may be another reason for minimizing the role of head-office
staff. (*Staff* means paid employees, as distinct from elected officials). Rank-
and-file members tend to have a skeptical attitude toward the expense
entailed by the operation of a head-office. The salary and expense-
allowance list inevitably seems rather high to grassroots people living
close to a subsistence level. One response of a leadership apparatus, as
we know from Michels' famous classic, *Political Parties* (1915), is to do all
it can to enhance its visibility and to convey a sense of its own indis-
pensability. There is no question that leadership structure is essential
to any organized social movement. It is equally clear that there is a
conflict of interest between leaders and the rank-and-file members over
the use of organizational resources. In this case, where the aim is to
build up local initiative, it seems best for the head-office roles to be
subordinated.

Study-group meetings usually opened with a plenary session. The
number present varied from 15 to 60 persons, drawn from a radius of

50–75 miles as the crow flies. Nearly all were active grain farmers, along with their teenage children, an occasional small businessman, public official, priest and pastor. The meetings were either once-a-week sessions for some six or eight weeks, or they were four-day conventions. All age-groups were well represented.

After the plenary session of one hour or less, the meetings would break up into small groups of five to eight persons each. These sub-groups would review, illustrate and criticize what had come out of the plenary session, usually from an NFU official or resource person. After an hour or more, the plenary would reconvene to hear the small-group reports, made by spokesmen elected in the small group. Any other member of that small group could then supplement what the "reporter" had presented. Discussion by the whole plenary would follow. This pattern ordinarily characterized each half-day session. The four-day conventions often held evening meetings as well as morning and afternoon programs.

The content for the next half-day would depend in large part on what materialized in the previous session. While an approximate program for a study group might be roughed out beforehand by the NFU head-office people and the resource people, this always had to be kept tentative. We learned this very early in our field work.

Many Prairie people are accustomed to this format of alternating plenary and small-group sessions. Audience participation is thus maximized. The principles of parliamentary debate are also widely understood and observed. A local person invariably kept minutes for later circulation and review. But our meetings were for the most part informal. Nearly everyone was interested in listening to what someone else had to say. Very few spoke out of turn, or too long – the chairman would see to that. Although some people were naturally more active than others, everyone spoke up sooner or later. This was a sign, I suggest, of successful group-formation. So likewise was the interested tolerance of each other that generally prevailed. People in a face-to-face community are interested in the idiosyncracies of their friends and neighbours. Urban people, accustomed to the impersonal, analytical, instrumental, exploitive relationships that dominate urban anonymity, may find this statement hard to understand. But this, in my view, was another indication of the existence and on-going character of group-formation. Indeed, it is this sense and living experience of "community" which farmers are fighting to preserve. This is what it's all about.

In no way were these meetings stiff and solemn affairs. Both in the plenaries and in the small groups, there were frequent and spontaneous witty sallies which produced gales of laughter. Much informal socializing took place. The coffee-breaks of the weekly meetings, and the "social evening" of the four-day convention, without exaggeration were indispensable factors in the process of group-formation.

Above all, we had to learn to trust each other. We had to become familiar with our associates—their idiosyncracies and their characters. This takes time. It requires various sorts of interaction in several kinds of situations. In this way, we changed—as individuals. We became different because we were involved in and committed to a new collective movement. We became more confident, stronger and happier. We were together. That is "group-formation." The occasion—study or action—is secondary. Building and linking groups oriented to basic change—that is primary. Without such group-formation, no social movement can arise.

The Role of the Resource Person

It is important to say, first, what this role is not. Most emphatically, it is not unilateral academic lecturing or authoritarian schoolroom teaching. Academics, teachers and university graduates have a "trained incapacity" to overcome, if they are to take part in this sort of group formation.

The role of the resource person is primarily learning and socializing, exactly like that of every other member of the study group. But his task in this respect is harder than that of most of the others, because he is an outsider, whereas many of the local participants already know each other. The common aim of the group is to reach a consensus on what the world is like, on how to change that world, and above all to become active in the change process. The key is group formation. Then the local groups must be linked into regional and national networks.

Group formation, in this context of a movement for basic change, in an advanced society like Canada, is not simply learning and socializing. It is un-learning and re-socializing. This can be an abrasive experience for everyone, especially for the resource person with a middle-class, unversity background. He must earn his group status as best he can. No formula can be offered, other than observing the usual social amenities of courtesy, mutual respect, and remaining aware of his initially marginal or trial status. Most of the time, the resource person should keep quiet. It was my impression that resource people and NFU head-office people in the 1972 study groups tended to talk too much.

As group members get to feel comfortable with the resource person, and he with them, he will more easily take part in group discussions and repartee. He will be free to make his mistakes, to get his ears pinned back by the group, and to offer whatever contributions he can. He will "find his own level." Every other member of the study group has the same task. They have to learn not to rely on outside experts, but to "use" them with critical discrimination for the aims of the group and the movement. Informal socializing is probably even more important than formal sessions in working out this process of stable group formation. In effect, that process involves counteracting to a considerable degree the isolating or "privatising" of our individual and family life-styles. The bourgeois capitalist social order, let us remember, emphasizes many such atomizing influences as consumerism, individual privacy, and competitive individual achievement at someone else's expense. All these influences have to be minimized.

Hitherto, we have talked about the general role of the resource person as just another group member. Like many other members, however, he also has a secondary, specialist role. Because of his special training—usually in the social sciences—he must also learn to function as a "group assistant." He makes available information sometimes on his own initiative and sometimes on request from others. His special responsibility, which he shares with other members, is to raise questions and help formulate alternatives. This is the "expert" aspect of his role. In essence, of course, the expert role is *advisory, not executive.* Both the resource person and the other group participants must come to an early recognition of this fact, as soon as possible in the process of group formation. It is always the group which either makes or consents to an executive or action decision.

How easily a resource person and the group as a whole can slip into the situation where the "expert" is expected to "give us the word"—is well known to all of us. For example, a resource person will often be asked to start off a meeting with a short statement, and end the session with a "wrap-up" or summary of what has been accomplished. Such requests may be viewed as both service and ritual functions. Sometimes this works out well enough. But it might better be done by the local chairman. Rural people, and no doubt many others, too, are inclined to be ambivalent about outside experts: on the one hand, the latter do have an indispensable role, albeit a subordinate one. On the other hand, they are outsiders. Underclass people know they are bombarded with an endless stream of advice, exhortation and propaganda. They tend to see it as biased and exploitive. Hence the resource person who unduly puts forward his own opinion runs a serious risk of jeopardizing his own credibility and of impeding the process of group formation. For a resource person to be told at the end of his series that he is the first person in forty years who didn't try to tell the farmers what to do—that is like getting a Ph.D. in group formation.

At the risk of unnecessary repetition, let me say again that the process of group formation requires, on the part of all concerned in and with that process, a clear advance understanding of the nature of group formation. This seems fully as important as an understanding of the world we are trying to change. This knowledge of group formation protects the members from being exploited by outside experts – resource persons and head-office officials. It also safeguards them from unnecessary fears of being manipulated.

Finally, any assumption that resource persons must be academics should be avoided. The resource role, in its expert aspect, involves looking up information, reviewing sources and alternatives. A number of local people can learn to contribute to this function. A university training facilitates the development of certain research and writing skills useful in group formation. But in our society, universities serve mainly the corporate apparatus we are seeking to change. They build up attitudes directly inimical to what radical grassroots movement must do. Only "retrained" academics can be resource people. Often, it may be both necessary and desirable that non-academic local members learn to carry out the resource function.

As a resource person, I learned much from my study groups. It was a Saskatchewan hog farmer who pointed out to me that the most sensible solution of the bilingual snarl in Canada is to let Quebec go independent. Then we can negotiate trade and other matters, and western Canadians would not be pressed to learn French. How simple is the truth! I also learned a lot about group formation that never was taught to me in my university classes and textbooks. And it was a Saskatchewan grain farmer who really straightened me out on how we are growing impure food, and how we can produce pure, healthful food.

Some Conclusions

Let us now return to our earlier question: how do we go about coping with Canadian poverty and underdevelopment in a substantial way?

First, a radical perspective is needed. Many farmers in the 1972 study groups began discussing their problems in very simple and immediate terms. Higher farm incomes would solve their economic dilemma. Okay, so how can we get higher farm incomes? Then we look at the distribution of incomes for Canada, and we discover that this has not changed significantly for a generation. Next, we examine the income-producing system, pricing policy, the ownership and control of corporations responsible for shaping our income structure. This uncovers the fundamentals of our capitalist economy. We consider the role of governments, we observe that they serve the corporate apparatus by making public resources generously available to large private interests, and by absorbing the costs of "infrastructures" of services that either underwrite private enterprises or patch up some of their damaging consequences. We see, further, that the tax system that pays for our public services rests on a regressive base: the poor pay more than their share.

Nearly every study group came to the conclusion that corporate capitalism must go. People must come before profits; communities must come before the logic of economic centralization; our resources must be returned to the people.

It does not matter where a study group begins. One started with the question, how can we produce pure food and get it to consumers? Another preferred to ask, how can we get more equitable incomes for farmers and other underdog groups? A third took on the large issue, can we redevelop rural Saskatchewan? Wherever we start, we soon find that we cannot avoid considering the entire social order, and changing it drastically, if we are to attain even the most immediate ends.

Second, the key to achieving the redevelopment of Canada in the common interest requires a process of grassroots group formation. We must go out and talk to our neighbours, and together work out a course of action. We must build a new power base. We must use such talents as we have – whatever our personal shortcomings. Given enough of such local groups, in contact with each other, basic change may be possible. We shall never know until we try.

Third, there are two central issues which cannot be separately treated. One is economic, the other is social. It is not enough to gain an adequate living for everyone. We also have to decide how we want to live. What sort of community do we seek? How shall we build it? It may well turn out that we best achieve "community" in the process of struggling for it, rather than in the end-product of that struggle. But some thought needs to be given to the end values and life-style for which we are striving. Material development and higher per capita real incomes are simply not enough by themselves to serve as ultimate goals.

Fourth, the study group memberships were not representative of all farmers. Those attracted to our study groups were already converted, or nearly so. The great majority of farmers were not there. They were out curling, watching television, doing chores on their farms. Here is a crucial problem, still unsolved. How can we break out? How do we enlist the unconverted? My own hunch is that we do this by combining study groups with action projects. We undertake demonstrations; we join with Indians and striking labour unions in their battles; we show our presence in any going contest on the side of the underdog classes. We raise a standed, so to say, to which others may flock. Starting a specific campaign – for example, expropriating the oil industry by provinces – may attract new people not hitherto involved.

Though few in numbers, the men and women who came to the study
groups are some of the grandest people in the world. They have an in-
satiable curiosity. I was confronted with questions about China, Australia and Chile, some of which I could not answer without spending
a few days in the university library. One farm wife, who had recently
read C. Wright Mills' *Power Elite*, wiped me out with her critique of that
book. Another group had a carton of paperback nonfiction books which
circulated freely about the district. It is an unforgettable experience to
see 35 heads around a big table in a village church, and to hear them
talk about our common problems of decent survival, and what sort of
a world we must get if we are to live in a humane social commonwealth.
In such moments we achieved both community and movement. Perhaps
the two are inseparable. This made it worthwhile for me to drive hundreds of miles across the endless prairies in sunshine or blowing snow,
night and day, to take part in these study groups and workshops.

Fifth, there were no voices raised on behalf of any of the four existing
national political parties. The study groups were moving toward political
action, but they recognized that to support any of the four meant buying
into, and compromising with, the Establishment which is skinning most
of us and destroying our communities. They came, sometimes very reluctantly, to the conclusion that confrontation politics must displace consensus politics. Only the Parti Québecois, a provincial party, today has
a promising and distinctive significance for the Canadian nation. Only
that party, should it come to power in Quebec, may make a decisive
difference for the people of all Canada.

Last but not least, the American presence must be taken into account. Any grassroots social movement that takes on the Canadian Establishment must also challenge the American colossus. That hard fact
should deter no one. The American empire is increasingly in dire straits.
Over a decade ago, I wrote that the United States likely would not make
it into the 21st century—either alive or fit to live.[11] Nothing since then
has changed my judgment. The decisive turning points of history have
been cases of "slipping between the icebergs." The American republic
came into being because England and France were at war. The Soviet
Union emerged out of the bitter war that exhausted the capitalist master-
powers of Europe. So it was with communist China. So it may be with
Canada.

The United States has never won a major war by itself. It has defeated
only Mexico, decrepit old Spain, and a large number of preindustrial
Indian tribes. (Some of the latter were not easy to beat.) Its other wars
have been won on the coat-tails of western Europe (World War I) and
Russia (World War II). Today the United States is losing in Vietnam. Yet,

Americans believe fervently in the myth that they have never been whipped in war. With their nuclear capacity, they are therefore very dangerous. They could push the nuclear buttons any day, any month, because they have no restraining conscious history of defeat. They can easily be stampeded and mobilized for mass genocide.

This is the nation to whose destructive, suicidal destiny the Canadian capitalist Establishment has committed us.[12] This is the new national policy defended by an elitist Prime Minister, and not seriously resisted by any other national Canadian party. Before we are swept over the brink, let us make our voices heard.

There probably is not much time.

The old CCF raised the magnificent slogan, "Humanity First." The motto of the Saskatchewan Farmers Union (now expanded to the NFU) was, "In Union is Strength." Now we can add something. In union is strength; from struggle comes community; in commitment lies freedom.

Notes

1 H. Magdoff, "Economic Aspects of U.S. Imperialism," *Monthly Review*, vol. 18 (Nov., 1960), p. 39. The original data are from official U.S. Department of Commerce figures for 1950–60. For 1962–65, the data are from *Survey of Current Business.* "Take-home" includes *repatriated* dividends, interest, and branch-plant profits after foreign taxes. It does not include profits retained abroad for re-investment.

2 *Survey of International Development*, Vol. IX (January, 1972), p. 5.

3 Ibid, p. 4.

4 P. Baran, *Political Economy of Growth* (N.Y., 1968); A. G. Frank, *Capitalism and Underdevelopment in Latin America.* (N.Y., 1967).

5 A. K. Davis, ed., *Canadian Confrontations: Hinterlands Against Metropolis* (University of Alberta, 1970), pp. 39–40.

6 Vernon Fowke, *The National Policy and the Wheat Economy*, (University of Toronto Press, 1957).

7 See J. McCrorie, *In Union is Strength* (Saskatoon, 1965); L. Bergeron, *History of Quebec* (Toronto, 1971); A. K. Davis, "Canadian Society and History vs. Hinterland Against Metropolis," Ch. 1 of R. Ossenberg, ed., *Canadian Society* (Prentice-Hall, 1971).

8 Ian Adams, et. al., *The Real Poverty Report* (Edmonton: Hurtig 1971), Ch. 5.

9 Census of Canada, 1961 and 1966.

10 Annual Report, Department of Education, Province of Saskatchewan, 1944–45, (Regina, 1945), p. 50.

11 A. K. Davis, "Decline and Fall," *Monthly Review*, vol. 12 (1960).

12 George Grant, *Lament for a Nation* (Toronto: McClelland & Stewart, 1966).

The On-Going Revival
of Dialectical Social Science:

Some Implications for "Alternative Values . . ."

IN OUR UPSIDE-DOWN CAPITALIST SOCIETY, it is only natural to find an upside-down social science. Most practitioners of this social science service some aspect of the Establishment, or at least they avoid challenging it, by operating under the guise of "value-free" technocratic studies of micro-systems or general systems.

But in some respects, changes are emerging. Unforeseen consequences sooner or later develop immanently from existing conditions. Social scientists oriented to an equilibrium model ordinarily must fail to predict such changes unless they are simple extrapolations of past trends. Very often, such changes are not extrapolations of past trends. Instead, they are negations thereof. They are comprehensible only in a dialectical framework. In an equilibrium perspective, they appear irrational.

Let me illustrate with a homely country story. Once upon a time, Little Red Riding Hood set out to take her ailing grandmother some home-cooked yummies. A wolf lurking in the nearby bushes overheard her plans. So he took a short-cut on his snowmobile to Granny's house, ate up Granny, and jumped into her bed with Granny's nightcap over his big, furry ears. When Red Riding Hood arrived, the wolf leaped out of bed and chased Red Riding Hood, who ran screaming out of the house. At this point, a nearby woodcutter, hearing the screams, rushed up and killed the wolf with a single blow of his sharp axe.

Now for the dialectics. At the inquest, new facts were brought out. The Civil Rights Association showed that the wolf was never advised of

Paper for the plenary session, 29 December, 1972, Western Association of Sociology & Anthropology (WASA), Calgary his rights; nor was he warned first by the woodchopper who dispatched him. The Association to Protect Wild Animals argued that the wolf was really just doing his thing. The local lunatic-fringe association claimed that Grandma was over 40, and that the wolf was trying to make love, not war. A few days later, the woodchopper's house mysteriously burned to the ground. Granny's cottage, where the tragedy had occurred, was established by the public authorities as an historical shrine to the wolf. The shrine was dedicated one year later, on the anniversary of the death of the wolf, before a big crowd. The memorial wreath was placed by none other than Little Red Riding Hood. And as she knelt to place the wreath, there was not a dry eye in the whole congregation. (For this story, I am totally indebted to Dr. A. Ditmar, of Saranac, N.Y.)

In all seriousness, ladies and gentlemen, I ask you—what equilibrium, structural-functionalist social scientist could have made any sense, even after the fact, of these events?

Let me cite another example closer to home. Ten years ago, studying Indians and Métis living in North Battleford and Prince Albert, Saskatchewan, we asked the question of our Indian-Métis informants: "Have you personally experienced any ethnic or racial prejudice in this community?" To my utter astonishment, 75 percent answered, *NO*. Mind you: we used a Métis interviewer who was far enough left-wing to ferret out any dissembling, and adept enough to explain the meaning of "prejudice" wherever necessary. We interpreted this finding as follows: Indians in 1961–62 were not going anywhere—they were still passive. They did not perceive obviously discriminatory treatment on the part of Whites as "discrimination" or "prejudice." Instead, our Indian informants defined such White behaviour as "normal." Nonetheless, we predicted an increase in Métis-Indian militancy within a few years, and sooner rather than later. That was before Howard Adams had become active among the Saskatchewan Métis, and before Harold Cardinal had appeared to become a spokesman for Alberta Indians. And we were right.

How did we arrive at this conclusion? Certainly not by extrapolating past trends toward militancy: among the Métis-Indian populations we studied, there were no such trends, at least in recent times. We made our prediction on the premise that, sooner or later, underclass or hinterland groups fight back against their oppressors. Our main reason was our awareness that this has demonstrably and chronically and immanently been the history of the Prairies.

Lest I be accused of blowing my own horn, let me say here that, in this same study, I fell into the major error of concluding that "assimilation" is the inevitable fate of our Indian-Métis populations in Canada. Some of my lines could have fitted directly into the June, 1969, Ottawa

White Paper, which proposed to phase out the special-status Indian treaties, the Indian reserves, and the Federal Bureau of Indian Affairs. Doubtless, the latter agency would never be missed. But dispensing with the
treaties and the reserves is an entirely different question.

Why did I so badly misjudge this issue? Chiefly, I submit, because I
forgot or underestimated the obvious dialectical guidelines. The central
drive of American multi-national capitalism, and of its Canadian satellite, is to standardize, urbanize, and thus to homogenize as docile consumers or as (where necessary) welfare recipients—the ethnic groups,
the farmers, the surplus fishermen, and so on. I now believe that this
"homogenization" (to use George Grant's term) is not necessary. Things
in Canada and even in the United States do not have to turn out this
way. But if we are to avoid the brave new world of 1984 which the corporate planners have in mind for us, we must join up with the underclass
groups of Canada and the USA, and cast our lot accordingly. This is not
in any sense a matter of our giving someone else the word as to where
things are likely to go. Rather, it is a question of casting in our lot, and
our joint efforts, to see where things may work out.

On a more abstract, epistemological level, let me call your attention
to a significant article by Robert Friedrichs, *British Journal of Sociology*,
September, 1972: "Dialectical Sociology: toward a resolution of the current crisis in Western sociology." Friedrichs points to a basic difference
between natural and social science. The discovery of stable uniformities
over time, abstracted from empirical events, is an object of natural
science, which has been most successful in developing engineering technologies based on such uniformities. Discovery, and knowledge, of those
uniformities does not affect their validity.

But discovery of social uniformities DOES affect those uniformities.
New knowledge is itself a dialectical factor. For example, confronted
with the facts about the exploitation of the resources and common
people of this continent, and of this world, by the multi-national corporations of American capitalism, and secondarily of Canadian capitalism—it is a natural tendency for ordinary people to revolt against this
rip-off which proceeds at their own expense. Hence, says Friedrichs, the
logic of the natural sciences is wholly different from that of the social
sciences. Those of us who were taught in North American graduate
schools to seek abstract uniformities valid over time—in other words,
those of us who were trained in the logic of positivism patterned after
the model of natural science—now find ourselves "sitting on a dry shoal
upstream." That probably includes most people in this room. For only
the dialectical paradigm can comprehend and encompass the dilemma
confronting us.

Feed-back phenomena in a general-systems perspective cannot meet this problem. Endless data-banks of information about the behaviour of people in similar situations do not help us. Given the available in-puts of information, the outcome of a conflict situation is literally unpredictable. For there is always the final reassessment by the actor and the group, and the ultimate decision – "We shall never know until we try." No computers can anticipate that type of decision. As Friedrichs says, "awareness of the patterned behaviour expected of them" gradually influences actors to "break out of the routines predicted." (BJS, xxiii, 271).

Both intellectually and socially, we face a revolutionary situation.

Intellectually: the search for stability, for laws of equilibrium (except in the short run) is futile. Further, "the traditional distinction between pure and action research is quite artificial." (Friedrichs, ibid., 267). Research, in other words, leads into action. Otherwise, something is wrong with research. Change is the main perspective, not stability.

Socially: underclass, hinterland and individual life-histories are full of cases of seemingly hopeless encapsulation in the chains of the *status quo*. Yet, many such cases led to break-outs. The dialectic, therefore, is a liberating force, vis-à-vis the determinism offered by the positivism based on the logic of the natural sciences.

What are the implications for WASA? As we look around, we see that the economists, the historians, the anthropologists – all have radical caucuses in full swing. Perhaps the sociologists may yet catch up. Terms like "imperialism," "exploitation," "genocide" by the Americans in Vietnam – terms which would have been rejected as "evaluative" even five years ago – are now commonplace in the learned professions. Last month at Toronto, I attended a three-day session at the American Anthropological Association annual meetings, on "Anthropology and Imperialism." In February, 1972, the *Saturday Review* carried a series of papers by six well-known American economists, severely criticizing the orthodox university Keynesian economics as both irrelevant and boring.

For the 1970s, then, the dialectic is "in." In this context, I can see several two-day WASA sessions, over the next few years. For example, the native peoples of the North vs. the pipelines; the farmers and small communities vs. the urbanization and homogenization of the Canadian and American countryside. But the greatest enemy of everyone in this room is the genocide of Vietnam by the American military machine. Its evil far exceeds anything perpetrated by Nazi Germany.

Reflections on the Decolonization
of Canada

NEXT to the several internal colonies of the United States, Canada is doubtless the biggest American patsy outside American borders. What saves Canadians–temporarily–is the fact that Canada has its own internal colonies–Quebec first and foremost. Then come the Western farmers, the Maritimers east of Quebec; and (last but not least) New-foundland. Canada has colonized clients in the Caribbean area and in Brazil. Canadian native Indians and Eskimo groups, although very few in numbers, are rock-bottom colonials in Canada.

How do we Canadians, with good will toward the entire human race, go about decolonizing ourselves? How do we align ourselves with the exploited majorities the world over? How do we get out from under the oppressions of the United States–by which I mean the capitalist oligarchy and the American capitalist power structure and power elite. I do not include ordinary working-class Americans–who are similarly exploited, like the rest of the world, but who benefit from the trickle-down fruits of American imperialism. Organized labour in America, for example, is officially one of the strongest supporters of the Imperialism of the American ruling class.

Obviously, what the world most needs is a socialist revolution in the United States. But manna does not fall from heaven. Only the American people can save themselves. More than a decade ago, I said that the United States would not make it into the 21st century, "alive and/or fit to live." (The phrase is borrowed from Thorstein Veblen.)

A paper for the Pacific Sociological Association, March, 1974

Since then, I have seen no reason to qualify my homely prophecy. Indeed, history seems bent on confirming this dismal prospect.

Perhaps this prospect is not all that dismal. Looking over various historical epochs, the Roman empire took several centuries to collapse. In our latter-day world, the British, German, Italian and Japanese empires went down in a matter of decades. This suggests progress. The tempo of technology and economy has immensely quickened.

» «

Let us return to the action problem facing us middle-level colonials in Canada. We look up to the American metropolis in the chain of exploitation. We look down to our internal colonies and our minor Latin-American and Caribbean satrapies – which we mind for the American overlords. How can we mobilize a Canadian liberation movement? How can we free ourselves from American imperialism, and at the same time free our internal colonies? Or rather, let them free themselves from us?

I do not have any blueprints to answer these leading issues. Ideas arise, however. Let me suggest:

- The Marxian tradition is a live and on-going social movement. This means that a succession of leaders, writers and regional or national movements think and act in a common tradition; but policies and theories vary, according to the current situation.

- In other words, every country, or internal colony therein, faces unique situations – imported dogmas and blueprints do not apply, though they may inform.

- Hangovers from the past survive beyond their logical "fit." That is, for example, Great-Power nationalisms survive from the 19th-century to influence contemporary socialist policies in the USSR and in China. *Item*: the USSR sold out the Greek communist movement just after World War II.

    Item: The People's Republic of China ignored the Bangladesh revolution of 1971–72, and sided with the fascist regime in West Pakistan.

    Such cases could be multiplied.

» «

Where does all this leave us aspiring colonials, seeking to free ourselves from the oppression of the American capitalist empire, and its subservient Canadian capitalist annex?

My conclusion is that much has to be left to local and regional underclasses. Professor Albert Szymanski's manuscript sets a relevant framework. There are two sets of factors, he says: *objective* (an oppressed class) and *subjective*—"the factors that produce class-consciousness in the oppressed class." (Szymanski, 1973, p. 16. The author is an editor of *The Insurgent Sociologist* published at the University of Oregon, Eugene, Oregon.)

This does not give us any action guides. Theory remains divorced from practice. Chairman Mao would hardly notice our tribulations, so long as they are confined to the academic ivy tower.

To go further: how do we break out? In an advanced capitalist society and technology, how do we move toward a socialist and an humane social order that offers us and everyone else in the world left alive, a way of life relatively free from exploitation?

» «

Clearly, the materialist, North American, capitalist social order is not viable. Nor is it exportable. It sucks up the resources of the entire globe. And the rate of suction increases, year by year. Already, the Americans— 6 percent of the world's population—absorb about 40 percent of the world's energy; they control about 60 percent of the world's wealth. Further, their energy and resource demands are ever rising. It is utterly impossible for the rest of the world to catch up, even if we could agree that the pattern of American civilization is worth perpetuating. I think it is not. The new nations of Africa and Asia have wisely rejected the models of Western Europe and North America. If the human race has a future—a doubtful proposition—it lies in the People's Republic of China, Tanzania, and in yet unheard-from countries.

This is not meant to discount the immense contributions of the USSR. It is fashionable these days in the western world and elsewhere, to write off the Soviet Union, Stalin, and so on. I do not share this view, although I recognize that the Russians paid the "penalty of going first." (Another phrase of Thorstein Veblen.) But for the Russians, and Stalin, many of us could be dead.

A generation hence, people may well be pointing up the shortcomings of the great Chinese revolution, just as the Chinese now attack the Russian regime as "revisionist."

» «

My experience in rural Saskatchewan as a "resource person" attached to "study groups" is relevant. It confirms Paulo Freire's approach, as stated in his *Pedagogy of the Oppressed* (Seabury Press, New York, N.Y., 1970). The time was the winter and spring of 1972.

Freire worked with non-literate groups in northeastern Brazil for some 17 years. My groups were literate farmers and small-town people.

Saskatchewan has a history of "fight-back" surges against their metropolitan exploiters. Let me summarize my experience.

First, the Saskatchewan groups, which numbered from 10 to 65 persons, were not really "study groups." They were cases of Group-formation and Group-consciousness-raising and Group-action.

Second, my job as a "resource person" was to keep still 98 percent of the time. I simply joined the group as best I could, as an "outsider." Once accepted, I felt free to put in my two cents worth, and to get my ears pinned back, like everyone else. It became evident that such a group does not need any experts or any resource persons. It can develop its own resource people, with a little effort.

Third, these local groups instinctively sought to fan out, by contacting other local groups, some of which were like-minded, others not.

This surge proved not to be going very far. But I think the model is valid for advanced nations. One has to start at the grass roots, join the local community, and go wherever that may lead.

This suggests that the "elite vanguard" approach is not appropriate. It is not enough, in other words, to scrutinize the records of other revolutions. One has to write one's own record. We may be informed by other records and other times. But we cannot copy. Every case is unique, to some extent.

Trotskyite groups, Marxist-Leninist groups, Stalinist groups—all of these (and others) seem to some degree to be "preparing for the last revolution." Not always, and not everywhere, to be sure. They usually appear to share an elitist premise: "We have the word."

To win the masses, one has to join the masses, and to go where they lead. The outcome is bound to be uncertain. It is not a question of instructing the illiterates. Since times change, and since places differ—innovations must be expected. The Marxian tradition—seen as a developing and live current of ideas-cum-actions—must inform us. But we have to come up with slightly new responses, everywhere. Such responses can hardly come from ivy-tower academics.

History records that the Russian influence on the world communist movement after the 1917 revolution—was heavily slanted in the direction of Russian national interests. Similar observations apply to China.

» «

Meanwhile, time is not on our side. We used to assume that socialism was inevitable. Now that we have added the environmental and pollution and shortages dimensions, it may prove that time is running out. Innovation seems necessary, more than ever. As usual, our necessity is to break out.

Corporations or Co-Operatives?

FRIENDS, FELLOW CANADIANS, FELLOW UNDERDOGS: My association with the farmers' movement now goes back some eighteen years.
I remember many bearpit discussions in Saskatchewan and Alberta at
workshops and meetings sponsored by the National Farmers Union.
One of the best features about those sessions has been that all of us,
myself included, have been both teachers and learners at the same time.
That is the best kind of education. That is why I think it is always an
honour to be invited back to meet again with the NFU.

Let me start with a story to get us into the right mood. Imagine that
medical science has reached a stage where brains can be transplanted.
A farmer in Vegreville has a serious accident, calling for a brain transplant. The surgeon takes the farmer's wife into the hospital storage
room, to show her the stock of brains available for her husband. First,
he shows her a farmer's brain which cost $1000. "Too expensive," said
the farmer's wife. "Show me another brain."

So the surgeon brought out another sample. "Here is the brain of an
Edmonton businessman. He buys and sells, and never loses on a business
deal. The price is $10,000."

Said the farmer's wife–"It's overpriced."

Then the surgeon brought out a third brain. He told the farmer's wife,
"Here is our best sample. It costs $20,000."

"But why does it cost so much?" asked the farmer's wife.

"Oh," said the surgeon. "That's easy. The brain has never been used.
It is the brain of an Ottawa politician."

Keynote speech to the Annual Meeting of the National Farmers Union, Edmonton, Alberta, December 7, 1976.

The Farmers Movement as Upsurge and Downswing

About 15 years ago, when I was research director for the old Centre for Community Studies in Saskatoon, we brought out from Montreal a graduate student named Jim McCrorie. We asked him to look into the history of the Saskatchewan farmers movement, and to get involved with the Saskatchewan Farmers Union, in a sympathetic way. McCrorie came up with a landmark report. It was entitled, *In Union is Strength*. What it said was this: the farmers' movement goes through a cycle of upsurge and downswing, every few years.

The upsurge is caused by the continuing exploitation of farmers by the capitalist corporations of Toronto, English Montreal, and the USA. Downswings occur when there are temporary price rises for farm products, and when there are other counteracting or diversionary factors. But the potential of upsurge is always present, because the farmers are an underdog group in Canada, with little political clout; because they have an awareness that they are very low on the totem pole of power in Canada; because they know they are exploited by the banks, the farm machinery companies, and the other great corporations of central Canada. Inevitably, underdogs fight back.

Now we must remind ourselves of certain on-going, long-run trends that adversely affect the political clout of farmers. For some decades, farms have been getting larger and the number of farmers has been decreasing. In 1963, farmers were 10.2 percent of the Canadian employed labour force; in 1972, only 5.8 percent. That's around a 50 percent drop. Likewise, the number of farms in Canada, since 1951, has rapidly declined.

This means the continuing social erosion of the countryside. It means the over-urbanization and over-centralization of Canadian society. It means the spread of big-city impersonality and hostilities and alienation. It contributes to the sharp rise of prices in urban land and housing, as people pile up in the cities.

The chief mechanism of the farmer's undoing is the cost-price squeeze. The farmer buys in markets controlled by monopolistic corporations, which charge what the traffic will bear, and more. But the farmer sells in markets wherein he does not control prices, and wherein there are many competing producers.

If we look at the income distribution in Canada, which has not changed much over the last 25 years according to Ian Adam's *Real Poverty Report*, we see that the farmer is one of those deprived groups, along with the Indians, the aged, women, the working poor, the Quebecers—which permit the existence of the rich minority—the corporate elite.

So far, I have said nothing new. You have heard all this before. Looking back, the picture is discouraging. It seems to point to the submergence of the independent family-farm population. The federal Task Force Report on Agriculture, issued just seven years ago, makes clear, ever so clear, that the federal policy is geared to the continued wipe-out of the family farm and the small community. Federal policy favours the spread of corporate farming, the profits of agribusiness like the big meatpackers, the flour millers, and the chain supermarkets. These big agribusiness corporations are often American-owned or controlled.

The New Situation in Canada

So far, we have been looking back, and the scene is discouraging. But in fact, a new scenario is emerging in Canada. We have the opportunity of a new people's upsurge, including farmers, labour unions, native peoples, consumers and so on – if only we can muster our forces.

The great victory of the Parti Québecois on November 15 must be taken into account by all of us. The momentous sweep of René Lévesque is as much cause as effect. Its roots go back to the conquest of New France in 1759 by a minority British Force. Quebec ever since has been a colony, an internal colony, of English Canada. Today, English Canada is an economic and cultural colony of the USA. But Quebec is a double colony – first of English Canada, then of the USA. Therefore, Quebec fights back twice as hard against its exploiters.

There is nothing more important that I can say to you this morning than to repeat again the basic dynamic of modern history: underclasses fight back against their overclass exploiters. Likewise, underdog hinterland groups fight back against their metropolitan bosses – and by bosses I mean the board members of corporations – mainly American.

And that is right where we are today. All over the world, the underdogs are standing up and fighting back. Look at Pakistan and Bangladesh. Look at Rhodesia. Look at South Africa. And – hear this – look at Scotland and Wales in the United Kingdom. Above all, look at ourselves in Canada.

Everywhere you look, the underdog groups of the world are fighting back. And that is just where we are today, in Canada. A new upsurge is underway. The farmers should be a part of this. But farmers must seek allies, and become part of a Canadian people's coalition.

There are two aspects of the new situation in Canada. The first is the landmark victory of René Lévesque and the Parti Québecois. The second, and I believe the more important, is the suicidal obsession of the Ottawa federalist Establishment – mainly the ruling Liberal Party.

The Debacle of Canadian Federalism, i.e., "Continentalism"

Let me now speak to you as one who has tried to read history, but not to be snowed by it.

For the last 50 years, the position of the Federal liberals has been "continentalist," that is, "snuggle up to the USA." Be a good colony to the Americans. Invite the Americans to buy up our resources and industries at a cheap price. Join the North American market – and we all know who is going to win that unequal contest.

The cover-up of the federal liberals has been – to parade as defenders of Canadian unity.

Sounds great, doesn't it?

Well, we have some new inputs. Second thoughts are in order.

In 1759, New France was conquered by a minority English Force. The conquest reflected events in western Europe, where the main show was a seven-year war between England and France. Quebec became an internal colony of Canada for two centuries. And Canada itself throughout its history has been a colony of foreign imperialisms – first France, then England, and now, since World War II, the USA.

But Quebec was a double colony. A generation ago, the French Canadians in Quebec were the blue-collar workers, while the English were the bosses and the owners. Francophones had to learn English to get jobs. This meant that they were competing for jobs and promotions in their second language – a severe handicap. They remained hewers of wood and drawers of water in their own home province.

However, in the past generation, a new situation has emerged in Quebec. The education system has greatly expanded, and also modernized. Instead of a very few upper-class Francophones getting a traditional education in Catholic philosophy, theology, law, etc. – large numbers of Quebec young people have gone into commerce, science, and engineering. They are bent on getting their share of the better jobs in Quebec. They are determined that the language of work in Quebec shall be French. And that is happening.

Let us remember that Quebec has always treated its language minorities better than the other provinces have done. Now that Quebec is tightening up its language policy, we cannot complain. They are just doing what the rest of us have always done.

In recent years, the key program of Pierre Trudeau to keep control of Quebec has been bilingualism in the important public services. That program today is in tatters. And why did it fail? It failed in English Canada partly because learning French made no sense to a great many anglophone Canadians, and partly because it was seen as a threat to the vested interests and job security of certain predominantly anglophone groups like the airline pilots. Bilingualism failed in Quebec because it did nothing about the real issues in Quebec—political and economic domination.

And that is also the reason why federalism is failing in this country—because it deals only with very limited aspects of our society, the public sector, and largely ignores the all-important private sector. It is the private sector that makes most of the key decisions in our country about investment, about production, about prices, and about employment. It is the private sector which has since World War II sold us out to the American empire. Ottawa and most of the provinces have basically co-operated with this sell-out. But the key decisions have been made in the board-rooms of the great corporations. They have been made on the basis of one yard-stick—the private profits of the corporations and of the handful of people who control those corporations. Many of those corporations are foreign-controlled.

I say that it is no longer acceptable to entrust the dominant role in our economic policy to the board-rooms of corporate capitalism. There is a very simple reason for this conclusion. Corporate capitalism no longer works in the public interest, if indeed it ever did.

All over the capitalist world, corporate capitalism is faltering. Canada, the USA, Australia, Japan, England, Italy—look where you will. The order of the day is inflation, rising unemployment, monetary crises, and stagnation. Governments cannot bail us out, because they lack the power so to do. The boards of the great corporations are, in a very real sense, their own ultimate law.

Here then, is the real crisis of Canadian federalism. Quebec is only a symptom, a small part of the whole picture. I do not know whether Quebec will separate from Canada. I do believe that decision should be made by the people who live in Quebec, free of coercion and free of scare propaganda. I know that Quebec is a real nation, as Alberta (for example) is not. Quebec has its own language, its religion, its history of supression and survival, its literature, its shared mythologies. Nations are born and forged in struggle.

If Quebec ever decides for independence, we can negotiate a customs union, a property settlement, and so on. But real political independence requires economic independence. Today, neither Quebec nor Canada has genuine economic independence. That is yet to be achieved.

The Parti Québecois is a social democratic party, not a socialist party. That is, it stands, like the NDP, for limited reforms within the framework of capitalism. I do not think such policies will prove adequate. But of one thing I am certain: on November 15, 1976, both Quebec and Canada turned an historic corner. Things will never be quite the same in Canada or in Quebec, ever again. The Canadian Establishment, the corporate elite (largely Anglophone) and the Ottawa federal apparatus, and the provincial governments too–all of which serve the corporate elite–that Establishment is shaken to its foundations. Now, as never before, we in Anglophone Canada can talk about our problems and our options. We can face up to our constricting situation. We can get out of the ruts into which the phony "federalism" of Ottawa (aided and abetted by the provinces) has forced us.

Four False Myths of Canadian Politics

If we are going to look realistically at our options, we must see Canadian society as it is. We must rid ourselves of certain illusions.

1. The first false myth is the belief that governments in Canada are impartial mediators among the several interest groups. This is sometimes true. And governments always require a certain scope and autonomy. But basically, the function of governments in capitalist societies is to serve the long-run interests of the corporate elites. A good example is the present federal effort to control wages and prices. Most of the clamp-down has come on wages, which were threatening to cut into profits.

2. The second false myth is a restatement of the first. The second myth is, that governments act in the interests of all Canadians. All too often, they act in the interest of foreign monopolistic corporations. You will be hearing more on this point tomorrow, from Edmonton publisher Mel Hurtig, a leading Canadian nationalist.

3. The third false myth is that the key decisions regarding investment, pricing, production, and employment can safely be left to the corporate elite, acting on the basis of their own profits. Never, not ever!

4. The fourth and last false myth is that profits and economics are adequate measures of the people's welfare. I do not say that economics should be ignored. But there are social yardsticks that must be taken into account. For example, it is the economics of corporate capitalism that has dictated the depopulation and the social erosion of our countrysides and the over-urbanizing of our people in a few giant cities. As a further example, there is mounting evidence that our over-centralized and over-urbanized high-technology society is not viable. Shortages of key resources, waste and pollution, increasing big-city alienation, the technological explosion, the population explosion–above all, the widening gap between rich and poor, both within nations and among nations– all these and other factors compel us to face up to drastic changes in our way of life. There is no way that the world can be, or ought to be, "automobilized."

What is to be Done?
Co-Operatives for Use, Instead of Corporations for Profit

In the short run, farmers as farmers must keep on doing what they have been doing for many years: pursue the quest for orderly marketing, defend the social worth of the family farm, and the integrity of the small community.

But in the longer run—and that means today—we must recognize that farmers are a small minority in Canada. Allies must be found; coalitions must be formed with labour unions, consumers, native Indians, small business people.

The common enemy is corporate capitalism. In part, this calls for liberation from the American empire. But only in part. It also calls for liberation from Canadian corporate capitalism.

Our positive aim must be to build in Canada a viable and humane social community. That is why I say to you that we must invoke a new, democratic and massive social movement in this country, dedicated to the nationalization of the biggest corporations, and to their conversion to co-operatives, run by their workers and their customers, decentralized wherever possible, and absolutely committed to production for social use instead of private profit.

This is the answer, the only effective answer, to inflation, unemployment, waste of our resources, and the rip-off of consumers by means of artificial scarcities induced by middlemen and speculators (as in housing).

An important step toward ending regional disparities, and poverty in Canada, is a guaranteed annual income for every Canadian, on a generous basis. The present average per capita Gross National Product in Canada is about $6000. If we take half of that, or even two-thirds, in services such as medicare, education, production of essential goods and so on—we can afford a much more equitable income distribution than we now have.

We need a new deal for our native people. A good first step would be to recognize their land claims in the far north.

There are many progressive measures, such as a public land bank, already set out in your 1975 Policy Statement, and your 1976 resolutions. I need not refer to them here. Let me conclude by emphasizing four tasks that urgently confront us.

The first is the liberation of Canada and Canadians from the power of the great corporations, many of them foreign. The second is the establishment, by democratic means, of a national policy of comprehensive social planning for use rather than for profit. Much of the world is already committed to some form of this. I believe that we can survive only by taking that step ourselves.

The third task before us is decentralization. Every country works out its own particular format and life-style. We all want more self-determination, more say in the policies that affect our lives. We want less bureaucracy, less secrecy. While we must have a public and national framework for co-ordinating our society, we need to ensure wide participation and in-puts from the grassroots. I suggest that the unique Canadian contribution to history is to rebuild our national community on the basis of co-operatives.

Finally, the fourth task is organization to carry out these policies. Talk to your neighbours, decide what sort of country you want, form study groups, and link up these groups across the nation. Both Social Credit in Alberta and the CCF in Saskatchewan came to power partly on the basis of "study groups." Only they were not simply study groups. They were people organizing and shaping a new political and social consciousness. We can do this again. But this time it must be on a national level.

If we are to construct a social order that is both viable and humane, we must send a people's government to Ottawa that will really serve all the people equally, instead of the vested interests.

Thank you all.

President's Message:

Simon Fraser University (SFU)

THE 1975 ANNUAL GENERAL MEETING mandated the Board of the Canadian Sociology and Anthropology Association (CSAA) to strengthen the censure and boycott of SFU, unless SFU satisfactorily reinstated the seven dismissed faculty. To encourage SFU to negotiate, the Canadian Association of University Teachers (CAUT) last winter lifted its boycott temporarily until July 1, 1975. No settlement was achieved; the CAUT boycott was reimposed on July 1.

However, negotiations continued between CAUT and SFU. In early October, 1975, I received from CAUT a copy of a proposed agreement. SFU offered two reinstatements (Potter, Aberle). A third, Leggett, was declared competent to teach in a university (he is associate professor with tenure at Rutgers!!), and was promised "fair and impartial consideration by normal appointment procedures," should he ever apply for a post at SFU.

On the premise that "the current academic marketplace is highly competitive and only those with PhDs or equivalent are considered for regular university appointments at asst. prof. level and above," the remaining four of the dismissed faculty were offered up to $9600/yr for up to two years to upgrade their academic qualifications. An additional $1000 each would be made available to CAUT for external evaluations of the four. If evaluations were positive, the four could apply to SFU for posts, and be assured of "fair and impartial consideration by normal university procedures."

The derogatory nature of this proposal for five of the seven is obvious.

Reprinted by permission. *Bulletin* of Société Canadienne de Sociologie et d'Anthropologie / Canadian Sociology and Anthropology Association, Number 39, February 1976. The author was president of CSAA 1975–1976.

Four of the five now hold, or have held since their dismissal by SFU, university appointments. One is an assistant professor at Toronto. Moreover, I am informed that SFU this year, as in past years, has continued to hire non-PhDs.

The SFU promise of "fair and impartial consideration" in the view of CSAA, and in view of the SFU record, totally lacks credibility.

Finally, CSAA legal counsel (Wright, Chivers & Co., Edmonton) advised us that the question of competence should not have been raised by SFU, nor entertained by CAUT. Common sense supports this position. They were qualified when hired, in SFU's judgement. And incompetence was not alleged by SFU when it dismissed them.

I was able to get copies of this draft proposal to most CSAA board members just before the Oct. 20 mail strike. No one supported it. All seven SFU victims rejected it. On Oct. 29, I wired CAUT that CSAA rejects the proposed settlement, with reasons as above.

The Second SFU Offer. I received a copy of this—another 6-foot telex—on Nov. 24, with a request for CSAA comments. (You must remember that CSAA is not a party to the negotiations.) This proposal improved on the first, but followed the same pattern.

Two reinstatements were offered. (This is nothing new: even SFU President Strand tried five years ago to retain Aberle and Potter on staff, while dumping the other five.) Nothing firm and enforceable was offered to the other five, with respect to reinstatements.

The junior four were offered "research grants" of up to $9600/yr for up to two years; plus evaluation as before. Or they could apply after one year but before two years, following signing of an agreement between SFU and CAUT, for evaluation; if the evaluation was positive, they could apply for an SFU post by "normal university appointment procedures."

"Outstanding charges" filed in 1969 against the dismissed faculty would be withdrawn. This is a large gain over the October proposal, which withdrew only the charges against Professor Wheeldon. But it omits charges laid or implied in 1970–71. And neither proposal said anything about withdrawing charges against Saghir Ahmad, deceased after dismissal.

Treatment of the five dismissed SFU faculty not guaranteed offers of reinstatement thus remained derogatory. All seven dismissed faculty attacked the proposal.

On Nov. 29–30, the CAUT negotiating committee presented the proposal to the CAUT Board and CAUT Council. The Board rejected the draft 13–7; the Council, 27–22, after all-day debates. On behalf of CSAA, I appeared briefly before each meeting to urge rejection. The censure and boycott by both CAUT and CSAA remain in effect.

CAUT and CSAA. The two boycotts are separate. CSAA makes an independent judgment of any settlement proposed by CAUT. We have no part in negotiations, unfortunately, and we have had great difficulty in getting information about the negotiations from CAUT, even on a confidential basis. We are now asking that CSAA have a representative on the CAUT negotiating committee, for this case only.

The CSAA Position. Because the chairman of the SFU Department of Sociology/Anthropology vaguely threatened CSAA with legal action when he appeared before the May, 1975, Board meeting, the Board authorized retention of legal counsel. This has been very helpful. We have evolved a partly new settlement pattern which we have suggested to CAUT as constructive and fair to all parties. Here it is.

1. SFU should withdraw all charges ever filed against the Eight, including the late Saghir Ahmad. (This is 90% won already.)

2. SFU should offer firm and enforceable reinstatements to all Seven, with details of rank and timing to be negotiated, and no more silly talk about upgrading qualifications. But many of the Seven might elect not to return to SFU: on advice of counsel, I contacted all Seven. Only the Seven, of course, can decide, when they have firm offers. But I think that reinstatement may prove to be an unacceptable token.

3. Additionally, therefore, we suggest $30,000 compensation to all Eight (including the estate of the late Saghir Ahmad), whether or not each of the Seven accepts reinstatement. We have already won a good part of this suggestion: SFU has acknowledged wronging the dismissed faculty, and that the latter have been "dislocated" and "disadvantaged." For the junior four, SFU has offered about $20,000 on a conditional basis. Our counsel describes this as thinly disguised compensation. We have only to make it unconditional and across the board.

If some of the Seven wish not to accept compensation, I suggest donating it to a Sahir Ahmad Memorial Fund for Progressive Education, terms of reference to be set by the contributors.

4. SFU should agree that none of its staff or administrators will ever issue any statements about any of the Seven, either positive or negative. Hopefully, this might reduce the flow of allegations of hounding and blacklisting by SFU administrators.

Points 1 and 2 above are not negotiable. After years of reaffirming CAUT and CSAA demands for seven firm offers of reinstatement, neither CSAA nor CAUT can afford to compromise on this aspect. As protective organizations, we would lose all credibility.

But neither can we afford, as an organization, to settle for an apology and offers of reinstatement that are likely to be rejected. Therefore, compensation becomes essential, for loss of professional credibility. Otherwise, any university could fire anyone, wait a few years, apologize, and escape scot-free.

CSAA is a Protective Association. CSAA's first responsibility is to its members and to the Canadian academic community. We do not speak for the dismissed Seven, though we take them into account. As much as anyone, we want SFU to be reintegrated into the academic world – but only on a basis acceptable to our traditions of academic freedom and the redress of past SFU injustices. This is not mere idealistic rhetoric. We face potentially severe conditions in Ontario and other universities where staff lay-offs loom. These could easily become political purges like SFU, especially if we accept a sell-out settlement with SFU.

Future Prospects. Even had CAUT accepted its inadequate settlement and lifted its boycott, CSAA could have sustained its own boycott. Our boycott has been quite effective, though not perhaps as effective as it might become. I am moving again (as I did last summer) to gain the renewed support of our sister associations abroad. Recently the executive of the British Sociological Association discussed the SFU case and voted to support the CSAA position.

Our job is to tighten the boycott of SFU. Our Professional Ethics committee will shortly present new member-discipline by-laws allowing sanctions against those members who, having a choice, accept posts at censured Canadian universities.

SFU appears to have committed two errors: a prominent role in negotiations has been given to hardline administrators some of whom were associated with the original firings. Secondly, it seems to have been agreed within SFU that no reinstatement will be imposed on any department. Ordinarily, this is a laudable principle of faculty autonomy. But in this case it shelters the vested interests of some faculty who have profited from the agonies of the dismissed; and it enlists those who joined the SFU staff despite the boycott. In my view, the collective guilt of the institution outweighs the career interests of individual faculty.

In the foregoing remarks, I imply no lack of integrity on the part of CAUT negotiators and officers. A great effort was put forward, especially by the chairman of the CAUT Academic Freedom & Tenure committee, the chief negotiator. It is easy to see, from an Olympian over-view, how protracted and difficult negotiations could lead to an insensible drawing-together by the negotiators, beyond the limits of an acceptable compromise. I can even understand why CAUT, faced with a tough negotiating situation, preferred to by-pass CSAA. I cannot accede to this, of course. Justice and the self-interest of all parties require another run at the problem.

Canada in the 1980s

THANK YOU Dr. Abucar. I think after Dr. Abucar's introduction I should leave immediately while I am still ahead.

I have lived for the last twenty-two years on the Prairies, in Saskatchewan and Alberta. It is always a pleasure to come to British Columbia and see a different landscape, the people are always very friendly and it is kind of an escape. But it is also coming back. As Dr. Abucar just said, welcome to the hinterland. Well, I come from the hinterland, too, and that's important.

Now, I am quite willing to be interrupted anytime if you want to discuss a point, just stick your hand up. Otherwise, I'll run about 30 minutes, try to hit some highlights, and we can have a dialogue after that.

I think the first thing that we need to ask in looking into the 1980s, and in asking ourselves what are the options for Canada in the 1980s, is how did we get here? The first thing to do is to recognize that we have to look at the total situation which is relevant to us. And that's not always easy to pick out. But quite clearly, in the pessimistic view which I am about to set forth, the important picture is the global picture. And we look at this global picture in terms of the totality, which is divided into oppositions. The interaction or resolution of these oppositions leads, in time, to basic change. And that's all that metropolis-hinterland really is. The metropolis is the big city, the boardrooms in the big city, the overclass groups, the elites of economics and politics. These elites exploit the hinterlands, the underclass groups. Then the underclass hinterland groups, sooner or later (and it may take some time), find out that they're being exploited. They start to fight back. In many ways that is the history of the Prairies and of British Columbia since at least 1900.

A public lecture sponsored by the Okanagan Regional College Sociology Department, Vernon, B.C., March 6, 1980. Attendance: 140. (Taped and typed verbatim.)

In the global picture, let's just try to keep these points in the background. We have three capitalist complexes: Japan, Western Europe, North America, and they are strongly competing with each other. In fact, Western Europe and Japan in the last, say decade or two decades, in many respects have surpassed the North American complex in industrial efficiency and productivity. And tragic as it may sound, they have surpassed us because they lost the second World War. Their capital plant was destroyed; they rebuilt it in the newest possible terms. But our own plant, especially Canada, is increasingly obsolete and stagnating. Yet even Japan and Western Europe are now moving into a stagnation phase. We seem to have come to the end of a generation of expansion since World War II. There is a theory of long cycles, thirty, fifty, sixty years, associated with the name Kondratiev. Perhaps we have now come to the end of one of those long cycles. All three of these big business, capitalist complexes are tending toward stagnation and inflation. What the economists do is to combine those two terms, stagnation plus inflation, into stagflation. OK?

Now, there is another phase to the constriction of the world's capitalist situation and that is the spread of Third World, independent countries. Zimbabwe is the latest. Some of these Third World countries have gone socialist. And when we talk of socialist countries we have to talk in the plural, just as we talk about capitalism in the plural. For all of these 10 to 12 socialist countries, 14 maybe now, are quite different among themselves. It is not accurate to think that they are simply offshoots of Moscow or of Peking; that's not the case at all.

In the larger North American scene, to get back a little closer to home, the Americans still have the same kind of problem, a problem of stagnation and inflation. Still, I think, they must be considered resilient. They have a great resilience. It took capitalism 500 years to get where it is now. Whatever comes next, at the moment looks like socialism. But it may be different 100 or 200 years from now. Certainly we are looking at 100 to 200, perhaps 300 years, assuming, and this is a great big if, that the bombs don't start to drop. I think they are going to start to drop in the very near future. I used to tell my classes, 5 or 10 years ago, that I felt that most people in this room will not be alive in 25 or 30 years. I would say now 10 or 15 years, and I rather think it may be more like 5 or 10, instead of 10 or 15. I am not saying these things because I want to shock you, I am not saying these things because I like the prospects, but I think you have to look at what is the real situation so far as we can see, so that we can try to be realistic.

On the Canadian scene, in the 1980s, we can look back to a generation of relative business expansion. We've had half a dozen recessions during that period, that's about standard, but there was that push toward an increase in markets and in the labour force which has been buoyant. But that prospect, I think, has ended, or is tapering off. We have reached a plateau. Something basic has changed in the last 5 or 6 or 8 or 10 years.

Canada is, at least politically, a sovereign state. It is not sovereign economically, it is an appendage of the American empire. This is something that we have to keep in mind, and something we have to face up to. We have taken it for granted, they tell us it is a great thing. I don't think that it is. And I speak to you as an ex-American of 20 or some 22 years standing up here.

The country is furthermore a collection of regions, and this is unique in Canada. We have one really industrialized region and that is southern Ontario. We have only a few pockets of industry elsewhere. All the other regions, the Maritimes, the Atlantic provinces, Quebec (except for the St. Lawrence Valley near Montreal and Quebec City), Northern Ontario (which is quite different from southern Ontario and should not be grouped with southern Ontario at all), the Prairies, British Columbia, the Far North—these other regions are primarily based on resources: timber, wheat, oil, fish, things like that. They export basically these resources; the processing is done elsewhere to a very large extent, mainly south of the border. When we export raw materials, you should always keep in mind that we export jobs.

Now here we are with this condition. We've plateaued out into a combination of unemployment and stagnation. The unemployment is up officially to 9 percent. Any statistician will tell you it should be at least 40 to 50 percent higher, mainly because of the way the survey is conducted. It is conducted in such a way as to minimize the actual unemployment level. Those unemployed who have dropped out of active job-seeking in discouragement are not counted. Hence we've got probably 13 or 14 percent unemployment right now.

In the Great Depression of the 1930s our unemployment level was 25 percent. The other thing is, we are now using maybe 75–80 percent of our plant capacity. We have idle capacity, in other words, as well as unemployed people. In the 1930s, the idle-plant capacity reached 50 percent. So we still have a way to go before we get into a real big depression, but we are edging, you know, near and nearer the brink. This is one of the disadvantages of American economic domination. When their economy gets a mild cold, they sneeze, but we get double pneumonia up here.

There's another aspect. It isn't just a matter of economics, inflation, unemployment—serious as those things are. I should like to read you just a line from a book called *Industry in Decline* by Richard Starkes, published just a year and a half ago. There is a very good summing up here. He says, "The problem here is that Canada doesn't just face the traditional conflicts between management and labour, between big business and small, or between the public and private sectors; it also faces the crippling problems associated with the Canadian confederation." This opens up a whole new prospect. It's a unique feature of Canada, now. Confederation started of course in 1867. It worked well, I would say, till about 1930. Even after World War II it worked pretty well because of the world-wide boom, at least for the North American, Western Europe and Japanese economies. But I think it is safe to say now that the present state of Confederation is one of advanced senility. The whole political scene, I think, has run out of gas.

Peter Newman, who is the editor of *Macleans Magazine* and a very good journalist, put it quite well in the middle of December, 1979. He said in his weekly editorial, just inside the front cover, that we have now had a new election thrust upon us; we face that election in a dismal state. It took Trudeau 11 years to show that he could not govern, it took Joe Clark 7 months to get to the same point. There are no political initiatives, he went on to say, except in Quebec, and I would add also among the native peoples, the Dene and some of the other native groups. The New Democratic Party, for better or worse, doesn't get off the ground.

In view of this general situation, we have to ask, do we not have really a basic trouble with the system as a whole, with the entire structure of Canadian society? It is not a question of the fault of any particular politician or of any particular party. We're all caught up in this critical situation, in this crisis.

As for the immediate prospects, as we look into the early 1980s, we're probably going to get very much the same budget from Trudeau that we got from Joe Clark. It will be dressed up to be a little more palatable. In a mass democracy, of course, you have to campaign with a certain populist bent. You make promises and then, after the election if you win it, you can say, well now, which ones do I have to keep in order to stay halfway credible? So there may be a few palliatives, you see, but fundamentally, where the pie that is being carved up among business men and among workers is not getting any bigger but is really tending to shrink, what we are going to see happening is the squeezing of the poor on behalf of the rich.

Some of the social effects of this squeeze will be, obviously, cutbacks in social services. There will be pressure on labour not to make tough demands for wage increases. In particular there will be an intensification of pressure on minorities. I know this concerns many of us. The envi-

ronmentalists are going to find it harder and harder to get public funds
and public attention on measures to cut down on pollution and waste—
measures which we desperately need. Immigrants are going to find themselves the targets of scapegoating, there will be more hostility toward
East Indians, even Canadian Chinese, many of whom are second or third
generation in this country. I think the women's groups are going to be
increasingly hardpressed. It's the weaker groups, in other words, that
are going to pay the shot simply because they don't have as much power
as big business and big government.

And there's one very serious danger here, and I fully expect to see
this sort of thing develop. That is that Ottawa in particular would try
to play off one region against another. It would be a serious mistake to
fall for that. In Alberta, there's a great deal of antipathy, hostility toward
Quebec; I'm told there is here also in British Columbia. That is most
unfortunate, because really it is Quebec that is setting the example for
the rest of the country. We have much more in common with Quebec
here in the West than we have not in common. Of course, we have our
differences.

I have said for some years, at least a dozen, that the real leader of
the Opposition in Canada is René Lévesque. When I first started saying
that in 1968, people just laughed. Well, they're not laughing much now.
And whoever succeeds Lévesque as Premier of Quebec is not going to
make much difference. I think Quebec will tilt in the same direction
if Claude Ryan is the premier. It is not a matter of personalities, it is
a matter of the basic forces of history. Regardless of how the referendum
comes out, I give Quebec 5 to 20 years to go entirely independent.

Alberta is feeling the pinch now with the return of Trudeau. I attend
sometimes Teachers' Conventions as a resource person. I've been to a
couple since the February 18th election. Many teachers say that the day
after and the second day after February 18, 1979, their pupils came back
to school, of course reflecting their parents, showing extreme frustration with the return to power of Trudeau.

I have little doubt if he gets half a chance, that Trudeau will give us
the War Measures Act again against Quebec as he did in October 1970.
Having looked into that a bit, I am quite conviced that the events of
October, 1970, were half, at least half, rigged by the highest authorities
in the land. The "October Crisis" was phony, a "whiff of grapeshot"
aimed at the Quebec independence movement by a few top Ottawa
policy-makers who blamed the affair on the tiny F.L.Q. (Front de Liberation de Québec).

As people begin to suffer, and that's what we are looking at, most
of us, with unemployment, inflation, scapegoating of different minori-

ties and scapegoating among the different regions of Canada—as we feel all these pressures; as they get more serious and as people suffer more, there is one hopeful aspect. That is, that when enough people suffer enough they start to think.

Some of them start to fight back; you see resistance. And this is the whole idea of the metropolis-hinterland theory. Maybe toward the middle of the 80s, perhaps the later 80s, we can look toward various attempts to start counter-actions to find new ideas, to come up with some new economic policies, a new constitution. These can only come from the grass roots. They are not likely to come from most of our political leaders. Maybe Quebec is the exception, I don't know.

One of the things we're going to have to do is to face up to American domination. I believe in self-determination for Quebec without scare propaganda and without coercion, but I think that if and when Quebec edges further and further out of Confederation (and as I said it is already halfway out) the thing we have to face up to is ourselves as English Canadians, Anglophone/Canadians: what we have to face up to, that is to say, is our domination by the American empire. It's a real question in my mind whether English Canada is a nation or not. I have the gravest doubts. But in the struggles which are coming I think we can become a nation, because nations are really born out of struggle.

Facing up to the Americans, gradually getting back control of our natural resources, that is the place to begin. There is a solution in sight that looks reasonable, a reasonable basis for a new national policy. That solution has three components, three parts: one is we progressively start with the regions—more power to the provinces—and they start with their resources, they take control of those resources, and they start processing those resources themselves instead of shipping everything down to California.

There's the second point, a massive effort toward what we call research and development. We can only pay for this R & D, as they call it, by the profits we get from the sale of our natural resources. We'll have to continue to sell, you see, for maybe quite some time. But we've got to aim eventually at finding economic manufactures in which we can be competitive and which we can sell first to our own people and then to people abroad. Above all, we have to diversify our trading partners. We send 75–80 percent of our manufactures to the U.S.A.; that's got to stop. Instead of learning French so much (and I have no objection to that in principle) it makes as much sense to learn Spanish or Japanese or Chinese as a second language so that we can develop trade with those countries. We really have to put a lot of study into foreign trade. We have to learn how to package things, how to label them, we have to ne-

gotiate with them; we have to go there and speak their language if we
want to be effective. On the Prairies we are very conscious of the fact
that we sell a tremendous amount of wheat to the People's Republic of
China. But we buy hardly anything from China. That cannot continue.
The Australians or the Argentinians will beat us out one of these days.

As I said, we take control of our resources. That's our capital, that
is our money in the bank. Secondly, massive research and development
effort. Thirdly, gradually emerging from the R & D effort, some new
industries in the regions—and not just in the big cities. It's time we
stopped expanding places like Edmonton and Toronto and Vancouver.
We should be putting our industries in the smaller places. I am quite
convinced that one of these days we are going to have to reconstruct
our countryside.

Overall, here we really have to ask, and start right now, what sort
of a society do we want? Although I have considerable sympathy for a
good many of our premiers, regardless of party, I think basically we are
not going to get the answers from the politicians. We are going to get
them from ourselves.

Let me mention one or two things. For one, this process of an increased role for the public sector. Yesterday in the Vancouver *Sun* I read
a story in the Business Section about the British Columbia Resources
Investment Corporation. It just took over a fairly small but still substantial chunk of Kaiser Resources Limited and Macmillan Bloedel, with the
full support of the management of both of those companies. That's the
kind of thing I have in mind: cooperation between the provincial governments and their crown corporations on the one hand, and the private
sector on the other, at least in the short run.

Another good example of that is Petro-Canada. We got Petro-Canada
thanks primarily to Venezuela, where we get much of our oil for the
East part of the country, anyway. In 1974 or 1975, they said, "We don't
want to deal with private corporations, we want to have a State corporation with which to deal." So we got Petro-Canada. Trudeau bowed.

That was and is the kind of thing I think we are going to see much
more of in the future. In Alberta we've got the Alberta Energy Corporation, in Saskatchewan there is Sask Oil and there's the potash corporation,
the name of which escapes me at the moment. Premier Blakney took
over one potash company. He borrowed the money, note this, he borrowed the money to pay for it from the Americans. And he took the
best corporation, he took the biggest one; he has got half the potash
production in the province in the people's pocket right now. Potash is
subject, of course, to cycles of boom and bust. Right now prices are
good. It's not as good as oil. You can make anything from a barrel of

oil, you just need a good chem lab. You can make all kinds of plastics, fabrics and so on. We're starting to do that in Alberta. We've got to do a lot more, but we're starting.

This sort of development is not an easy process. We make a lot of mistakes at first. The public sector, the crown corporations, has to acquire the expertise and the practice. For example, right here in British Columbia is one of the biggest boo-boos that you could possibly imagine: the deal over the Columbia River. That was a big sellout back in 1960.

In Manitoba there was the Churchill Forest Industries. The province, (the premier was Tory Duff Roblin) gave the contract to a very mysterious group of Swiss financiers who were never investigated. The province put up all the money, they got none of the control. Now if you can imagine a more stupid deal than that, it is very hard. Finally when the government changed, the NDP cancelled out the contract, but it was a tremendous loss. Saskatchewan had a similar experience in a pulp mill around Prince Albert. The late premier Ross Thatcher started that; it too, had to be scrapped.

There was the Bricklin car in New Brunswick. It had a few engineering kinks, I think. They were gradually working those out. They had trouble getting capital, but the province was behind it. One of the big obstacles, however, was the fact that Ontario would not give them a license to sell that car. And why? Because, of course, Ontario assembles motor cars and they were not anxious to have this other product. They said to New Brunswick, stay with your resources. In other words, stay a hinterland for the rest of your life. But that doesn't have to last.

Earlier in this speech I mentioned two world trends that are bound to affect Canada in the 1980s. One is the growth of the socialist bloc; the other is the spreading crisis of poverty in the Third World. Let me say something more about each one. My awareness of both is based as much on my travels as on library study. Even more, in fact.

The socialist bloc is growing in economic, political and social importance, and that means military importance, too. Industrial economies need central planning as guidelines, with provisions for local modification in both planning and execution, and indeed all socialist countries at least in practice have dual economies. But the overall principle is and must be benefit of all and not the profit of a few. No socialist nation has equality of incomes, though all have moved significantly in that direction.

I suggest to you that the stresses of a transition to socialism are likely to exceed the stresses of a mature socialism.

Above all, as I have told my students for years, Utopia is nowhere. Yet some places are better than others with regard to the people's wel-

fare. And the main forces making for socialism are the inherent contradictions of capitalism – the inequities and the poverty and the unemployment and the selfishness. I expect these trends to continue in the 1980s.
The world is moving toward socialism, whether we like it or not. If the
human race has a viable future – and I am extremely doubtful about
that – it will be a socialistic future, whatever islands of private enterprise
survive.

The socialist world is far from monolithic. Local, regional and national differences loom large. In 1977 at the Warsaw airport I found free
pamphlets in several languages outlining the vodka problem in Poland.
Though the Poles follow Soviet models in large-scale industry, they retain small-scale agriculture – high-cost and State-subsidized. Every few
years the State tries to cut subsidies and raise food prices, but people
take to the streets and the State backs down.

By contrast, Romania follows Soviet models in both industry and agriculture. But it pursues an independent foreign policy in important respects. Romania was instrumental in facilitating the first visit of Nixon
to China in 1972. Tito in Yugoslavia had to walk a tightrope among his
own ethnic and religious groups, and also manage to keep the Soviet
dogma of socialist unity and conformity at arm's length.

But the USSR has slowly mellowed over time, despite occasional back-
sliding. Having emerged from a backward peasant condition only in the
1930s, the Eastern bloc understands much better than the capitalist countries the problems of building an industrial society in a short time on
a pre-industrial social base. For there were two Russian revolutions:
1917–21, and the collectivization-industrialization drives starting with the
five-year Plans in 1929. The second was doubtless far more painful than
the first. Fourteen capitalist powers invaded Russia during the first revolution. (Canada sent 5000 troops at British behest.) Frank Lorimer, an
American demographer, estimated a "population deficit" of 28 million
between the 1897 and 1926 censuses, mostly attributable to the era of
World War I and the ensuing Civil War. (*Population of the Soviet Union*,
League of Nations, 1946, ch. 3). For the 1927–39 period, Lorimer more
tentatively estimates 5.5 million, mentioning collectivization, rapid industrialization, and nomad settlement as factors. (ch. 9). The official his-
tory, *Great Patriotic War of the Soviet Union* (Moscow, 1974), estimates
World War II losses at 20 million fatalities (ch. 22) USA losses in World
War II were barely half a million.

Ladies and Gentlemen, the Soviet figures just cited are incompre-
hensible to North Americans. I do not believe that the Soviets are para-
noid. Rather, they respond rationally to their life experiences of the last
three generations. By contrast, we in North America have little grasp

of what modern war means. The USA has had no serious war since its Civil War of 1861–65. In the 1898 Spanish war, in World Wars I and II, the USA came in late, took light casualties, and picked up most of the imperialist loot. Ever since 1917, except for a brief part of World War II, the Americans have generated a consistent stream of Soviet-bashing. As a collectivity, ignoring individual exception, they are the most ignorant people in the modern world. Canadians are but little better. The Americans do not understand their own history, let alone anyone else's.

In 1977 I visited Auschwitz, a former death house and concentration camp in what today is southern Poland. Now it is a museum. I passed a grim day there. Ten million victims, including six million Jews, met their deaths in German-run camps like Auschwitz. It gave me a faint idea of what War II was like. I was in that war, but only around the edges. But only since the war have I come to recognize the main outlines of what really happened.

Most of the serious fighting was on the Eastern front. The Western front was disgracefully delayed: a sizable body of American opinion shared the view of President H. Truman—let the Nazis and the Soviets destroy each other. Use of the atomic bombs against Japan was entirely unnecessary in 1945. I was reading intelligence despatches at that time, based on Okinawa. Japan was already utterly defeated. The atomic bombs were to scare the Soviets, who entered the war against Japan (as agreed by the allied leaders) exactly three months after victory in Europe.

If you look at the Soviet military forces, they are very strong in close. But they lack the long-range striking power of the Americans. I think the Soviet stance is basically defensive. In my view, the USSR made a mistake to go into Afghanistan in 1979. They may regret this some day. Of course, it is possible that they were suckered into that invasion by American CIA probing from Pakistan, which is a tinderbox of ethnic hostilities. I travelled through that region in the early 1970s.

Let us remember that the Soviets backed away from the Cuban missile crisis in 1962. Let us also recall that it was not simply the "Marxian key" that carried the USSR to victory in World War II; it was ancient and deep-rooted Russian nationalism. Stalin in early 1931, speaking to a group of Soviet executives who were asking for a slower rate of collectivization and industrialization, said, "We are 50 to 100 years behind the advanced countries. We must make good this lag in 10 years. Either we do it or they crush us." (I. Deutscher, *Stalin*, Oxford, 1949, 328) Ten years later came the Nazi invasion.

Many books have been written about the history and sociology of revolutions, which are invariably barbarous. It is useless to blame individual leaders for excesses that are due on a deeper level to the "forces of history." Moreover, in the case of the Russian revolution, the Soviet people paid the extra heavy penalties of "going first" into socialism. Thorstein Veblen used this concept in another connection, but surely it applies here. Later revolutions in China and Cuba have paid lesser penalties, however grievous.

I will mention also the overnight transformation of "White Russian" refugees in 1941. They immediately organized the Russian War Relief to send used clothes, medicine and cash. I watched in amazement these hitherto anti-Soviet people energetically going about their new roles. Many were prominent professionals and artists. But in this crisis they became Russian nationalists. And since then I have studied Soviet military history over recent centuries. Time and again, despite their inferiority on paper, they have defeated stronger enemies.

One more point I must touch upon: Canada in the 1980s will face the rising crisis of the Third World. Poverty of incredible proportions will confront us, especially in Africa, southeast Asia and Latin America. Most of these nations, with few exceptions, are experiencing large population growth and decreasing per capita resources. Famines, epidemics and social violence can be anticipated on an intensifying scale. Thus far, the capitalist nations show no adequate response to this prospect. Greed is still the name of the game. In many Third World States, the rulers spend more on arms to keep their own people oppressed than they spend on desperately needed food. Not infrequently, those rulers have dependent or client relationship with the trans-national corporations, mostly American. The latter wish to keep the Third World unchanged in order to harvest raw materials and cheap labour for the benefit of their own profits.

Let me read you three lines from a poem, "Lycidas" by John Milton, written in the 17th century. The lines are cited in John Brunner's science-fiction masterpiece, *The Sheep Look Up*. Brunner is an American writer, and I am a science-fiction buff. "The hungry sheep look up and are not fed, but, swollen with wind and the poisonous mist they draw, rot inwardly and foul contagion spread." I bought the last copy of Brunner in Kelowna this morning. Take it from me: a good journalist or a good science-fiction writer is worth a dozen academics.

Brunner's book deals with how a high-technology society might run down. I do not believe that our high-technology society is indefinitely viable. You cannot automobilize the world, nor should we even if we could. It is not socially desirable. I say this of both capitalist and socialist countries. With our waste, pollution, using up of nonrenewable resources, our spreading drug problem (at least in the USA)—how can we say that industrial society is indefinitely viable? Not to mention the arms race, which is clearly out of control. Each super-power can destroy the other in 30 minutes, many times over. Yet the pinheads in the Pentagon think they can win a nuclear war, so they resolutely dismiss all Soviet appeals for disarmament. The ancient Greeks had a word for this: Whom the gods would destroy, they first make mad.

My friends, we live in a mad world. In London there is a small institute making a last-minute effort to produce an intermediate technology. The inspiration of that institute is Edgar Schumacher's book, *Small Is Beautiful.* He says, if you want to build a factory, make it small. If you want to build a town, build it small. Sensible, perhaps, but I think it is too late to avert disaster. In China, judging from my four visits there during the 1970s, they aspire to bicycles, not motor cars. How long that will last, I do not know. But China and Tanzania seem now to be close to the philosophy of Schumacher.

What Canada faces in the 1980s depends mainly on global factors. But we live our lives mainly in terms of local conditions. We can reasonably be sure that the three capitalist complexes – Europe, Japan and North America – will become ever sharper competitors with each other. The arms race will sail on toward disaster. Socialism will spread. The unintended results of industrialism, like waste and pollution and exhaustion of non-renewable resources, will move inexorably to destroy us. We do not see these things in any sort of meaningful whole. But other species have disappeared from this planet. Why should we expect no such catastrophe for the human race?

There is at least one bright spot: Castro's Cuba. He founded socialism, created educational and health services, and employment too, for all – right under the Yankee noses. There is no utopia in Cuba, but a viable socialist society is in place. Yet some Cubans are moving into the fast lane with their new small motor cars. Castro is a great orator and original thinker. The new Cuba is his monument. But Cuba cannot escape the worldwide approach of nuclear disaster.

For the Americans still have learned nothing. Looking at all the angles, I am driven to the conclusion that the greatest threat to peace and survival comes from the United States of America.

Now, folks, let us have a discussion.

QUESTION: Do you think Quebec can survive without the rest of Canada?

DAVIS: In the short runs, five or ten years, we'd have problems. But let me recall the example of Norway, which was under Sweden after the Napoleonic wars. They went independent in 1905. There was a lot of big talk about holding them by force; but in the end no shots were fired.

The immediate result was an outburst of expansive economic activity in Norway that lasted until 1914, the first World War. Granted: Norway is different from Canada. But if we put our shoulders to the wheel, we could do that too. Maybe this means that large changes must come in a package of mutually consistent reforms: one step alone doesn't work. But I think Quebec, both in its own interest and in the interest of anglophone Canada, should be encouraged to go independent. We could all benefit from ending the endless bickering that has gone on ever since the 1760 conquest.

QUESTION: It might be suicide for any politician to advocate that approach; maybe that's why they don't do it.

DAVIS: Well, you may be right. But if we don't do it, we are facing progressing de-industrialism, increased unemployment and inflation. And I ask you, how long can we stand that?? Do we dare to find out? Maybe that's why I'm here. (Laughter)

QUESTION: How do we persuade people to follow this policy?

DAVIS: Good question. I've thought a lot about that myself. I don't have a blueprint. I know somehow we have to win wide public support; get enough people to understand. The universities won't be much help. We need a popular charismatic leader like Tommy Douglas. With mass support, we could do something. But in the present situation we are back with a government of has-beens; the official opposition in Ottawa is a bunch of never-weres; and the minority party, the NDP, isn't getting off the ground. Is it possible to look forward to a democratic process? Only time will tell. If that doesn't work, it's a cinch someone will try something else. You know, people will stand just so much suffering. They won't stand still to have their noses rubbed on a grindstone.

Friends, you have been very patient with me. I shall always remember this beautiful town of Vernon, and its people so friendly. My message has been heavy and complex, and not very happy. I think I have talked long enough, and there's all that wine and cheese on the side tables. (Warm applause)

Selected Public Letters
1972–1980

Anti-Hutterite Law Rapped

To the Editor:

For the informative articles (Dec. 21) and the editorial stand (editorials Dec 6, 10, 13 and 22) by The Journal on the Hutterite issue, you deserve the strongest public support and commendation. The discriminatory Communal Property Act should be promptly repealed by the Alberta legislature.

The essence of the matter is the on-going decline of our rural communities. This decline would continue whether or not Hutterites are present. Yet the Hutterites are used as scapegoats.

Merchants in small places are losing customers; churches and other local organizations are losing members. Hutterites make most of their large purchases in big-city markets. So do other big farmers. Hutterites keep to themselves which is their right.

An unmentioned issue is land. Farms in the West are becoming larger and fewer. Many hardpressed farmers need more land if they are to increase their volume and keep up. Hutterites can sometimes put cash on the barrel for extra land; many other farmers cannot.

My 13 years in Saskatchewan and Alberta have convinced me that Hutterites are a net asset, both to local communities and to the two provinces. Hutterite communities pay local taxes; they contribute to local causes when invited tactfully; they retail some of their produce to their neighbors at very reasonable prices. Above all, they stand for something, let the chips fall where they may.

Edmonton Journal
January 5, 1972

Are The Hutterites Merely Scapegoats?

To the Editor:

Your editorial, "Hutterite taxes," in *The Journal* of Dec. 13, was far below your usual standard. You upheld a federal court ruling that Hutterite colonies must pay income

taxes. A more uninformative editorial would be hard to find.

You did not point out (though your news columns of Nov. 23 did) that the Supreme Court of Canada exempted the Darius-Leut colonies from personal income taxes. You failed to explain that the federal government then sought corporate income taxes from each colony. You failed to say that the three groups of Hutterite colonies (only two of which have colonies in Alberta) have been treated as a divide and rule exercise by the federal government. You failed to say that the present court proceeding refers to corporate income taxes.

Above all, you failed to give any informative background concerning these matters. As one who supports a free Canadian press and who views with alarm the charges filed by the federal government against a Toronto newspaper for allegedly violating the Official Secrets Act, I think you owe your readers a better exposition of the issues.

The pursuit of the Hutterites by the present federal government is another example of the disintegration – moral and political – of the government of the day (May its reign be even shorter than present signs indicate.)

By contrast, the Alberta government, whatever its other failings – and they are indeed many, as your recent editorials have well documented – has done better by the Hutterite colonies than has the Ottawa regime. In 1972, Alberta repealed its clearly discriminatory Communal Property Act, which limited land sales to Hutterites in certain respects.

In August, 1977, Hutterite colonies in Alberta numbered 94. They included less than 7,000 persons. They operated some 722,000 acres. The average colony owned 6,920 acres and rented another 760 acres or 7,680 acres in all (source: Alberta consultant on communal property, municipal affairs)

In 1946, Hutterite colonies in Alberta owned about one percent of the province's arable land. In 1972, those colonies owned or operated about 1.5 percent. That is no threat at all (source: Alberta Select Committee of the Assembly, report on communal property, 1972).

So what really is going on?

First, the countryside is being socially eroded and economically drained by outside vested interests: the charter banks, the big farm machine agencies, and the big buyers of farm products – chain stores like the supermarkets (U.S. owned very often) – to mention no others. Some day we must rebuild our rural areas.

Second yet more important, a religious minority is being used as a scapegoat. This has happened before in Canada: the Mormons, the Ukrainians, the Japanese, the francophone Catholics – among others. Not least among the others is the dismal record of Canada against native Indian religions.

Are there some ways out of this dead-end bureaucratic conformity implied by your Dec. 13 editorial? Let us dialogue.

The government of Alberta may have set a precedent in the proceeding against the Mennonites last year. The court ruled that the Mennonites had the right to run their local school. The provincial government very wisely chose not to appeal that case.

In its total lack of wisdom, the federal government of the day has gone after the Hutterites. Perhaps the province of Alberta should intervene *amicus curiae* (friend of the court) in favor of the Hutterite colonies.

Above all, I point out that no one can win against the Hutterite moral stance: empires have crumbled before the power of conscience.

We need a disinterested and public review of the tax status of church property of all sects and denominations.

Should not the government of Canada allow taxpayers to stipulate that their taxes should not be directed to war-oriented expenditures? Why not? We can learn from the Hutterites.

Edmonton Journal
December 23, 1978

Our Vote Helps West to Fight Piggies Ottawa and Ontario

To the Editor:

Have the four western premiers blundered by urging Quebec to vote "No" in the May 20 referendum?

Great struggles now are shaping up between Ottawa and the provinces over the division of natural resource revenues. The provinces own the resources. Ottawa claims a big cut based on federal control of interprovincial and international trade.

Alberta vs. Ottawa on oil pricing is only one of the clashes. B.C. and Ottawa are snarling over coal development. Newfoundland, our poorest province, has some off-shore oil that may ease its burdens. Ottawa is now trying to grab that back, despite the 1979 ill-fated PC federal government commitment to concede off-shore rights to provinces. Ottawa is also reneging in part on its commitment to help develop a new port facility at Prince Rupert, B.C. There is a lot more.

Quebec, of course, is a special case. Conquered in 1760 by a minority British army as a sideshow of a great European war between France and England, Quebec has survived. It has made several thrusts towards autonomy, with echoes increasingly towards independence.

Quebec is a nation because it has a common territory with many resources, both natural and human. Its population is educated and ambitious. It has a common language – French – for more than 80 percent of its population. It has a shared history of oppression by the English: troops were sent into Quebec during both world wars, and again in October, 1970. Louis Riel was hanged in Regina in 1885 by the anglophone federal government. White supporters of the Metis uprising were never even charged.

Great efforts have been made by the English to assimilate the French. Inside Quebec, those efforts have failed.

More than a decade ago, the Bilingual-Bicultural Royal Commission pointed out there are two majorities in Canada: franco-phone in Quebec, anglophone outside Quebec. That division will not change.

In today's referendum, the one significant aspect is the division of the francophone vote. If the "Yes" side wins the francophone vote, the tilt of Quebec towards independence will continue. It is the younger people who lean towards independence.

We should not confuse the francophone vote with the total vote. The one-sixth non-francophone vote will be heavily "No." The English, Jewish, Italian, Cree and other communities will all vote "No." They could assure a total "No" vote. That would be misleading.

The real crisis in Canada does not lie in Quebec. It lies in English Canada. English Canada has yet to show that it is a nation with the political will to survive. The 1867 Confederation worked well – for the business elites of southern Ontario and English Montreal. It ran out of gas by the 1930s.

Confederation was based on western agricultural settlement. Continentalism followed, based on American penetration of Ontario manufacturing and of all provincial natural resources. That connection now has also run out of gas. The American economy is in increasingly desperate straits.

There is only one Canadian way out. The provinces must recapture their resources, mount a massive search and development operation, learn to process their products, diversify their trading partners. Ottawa is defending a dead horse – the hegemony of stagnating southern Ontario manufacturing (largely American branch plants), and the obsolete domination of American multinationals. And that provincial initiative is ongoing and vigorous. Hardly a day passes without an announcement in the business pages noting new provincial initiatives.

So we come back to the provincial premiers of the western provinces meeting at Lethbridge and urging a "No" vote in the Quebec referendum. How suicidal can they get? Ottawa is desperate; it stands for a de-

funct option—cuddle up to southern Ontario and the U.S. multinationals.

Consider the worst possibilities. Quebec,
on any pretext, will get the War Measures
Act. A *Journal* article (November 29, 1979)
sketches the probably phoney nature of the
October, 1970, crisis. The other provinces
will get a takeover on the grounds of national emergency re their oil resources.

And here are the western premiers biting Ottawa's bullet on the Quebec referendum.

The western provinces need Quebec, inside or outside of Confederation. Indeed,
Quebec would be more helpful to the West

if it were outside. The block of 75 Liberal
federal MPs would be gone. We in the West
could then cope with piggy Ontario on equal
terms. We could tell piggy Ottawa where to go.

At the very least, the four western premiers should have taken a stance in favor
of neutrality—self determination for Quebec.
Instead, the western premiers endorsed the
Ottawa option. Divide and rule.

Ottawa must be laughing all the way to
the bank.

Edmonton Journal
May 20, 1980

They Understand Us Too Well

To the Editor:

That Ottawa doesn't understand the West
is a widespread theme often voiced in these
parts. It appears in your story of the disillusionment of the president of the Canada
West foundation [AR, June 27]. I believe this
theme is erroneous and dangerous. Ottawa
understands the West all too well. So do
the business elites of southern Ontario and
English Montreal which Ottawa serves and
cuddles. Not to realize this is to invite self-
destructive half-measures on the part of western business and political leaders.

We must also recognize that the Central-
Canadian Establishment, including the governments that front for it in Queens Park
and Ottawa, is in a desperate condition.
It faces mounting stagnation, inflation and
unemployment. Its unofficial policy of
"continentalism"—selling Canada to U.S.
corporations—is clearly disastrous . . .

There is only one Canadian way out of
our economic miseries: expanding provincial initiatives, working closely with regional
business interests to gear up massive research
and development efforts, to learn to process our own resources and to industrialize
our resource economies. One precondition
is to build our own regional rail net and
set our own freight rates. How else can we
escape from the "doctrine of fair discrimination?" This is the principle which per-

mits central Canadian interests to charge
those arbitrarily high freight rates in the West
which for decades have effectively prevented
industrialization in the western provinces . . .

Ottawa and the central-Canadian Establishment are backs to the wall in desper-
ation. The pro-American policy is running
out of gas. Quebec is still straining to get
out of Confederation . . . And all the resource provinces are straining at their leashes
to lessen decisively their dependence on
central Canada.

We shall never do that so long as we are
lulled asleep by such ideas as "Ottawa doesn't
understand the West." It is we who don't
understand the power structure and fatal
dilemma of central Canada. Now is the time
to go for the jugular. Forget that nonsense
about joining the U.S. What we need is less
U.S. influence, not more. We need a loose
confederation with the other resource regions and with Quebec in or out of confederation. Ottawa cannot afford to make
a single large concession to the West, to
Quebec, or the Atlantic provinces.

If we are going to escape from the stifling
embrace of central Canada, we are going
to have to think big—a lot bigger than we
are now thinking.

Alberta Report
July 18, 1990

Canadians Must Combat Their Racism

To the Editor:

The Journal of July 18 reported the beating of an East Indian cab-driver late at night by six male passengers. He was a U. of A. law student, cab-driving part-time to pay for his education.

This red-necked hooliganism by whites needs to be analysed and countered, not merely deplored.

Racism is endemic in Canadian society. It dates from the conquest of North American natives by West European invaders. That conquest was rationalized by claims of racial or biological superiority.

Today the tide is reversing. White supremacy is challenged the world around. Racism is now reduced to a scapegoating mechanism. The real crisis lies in shortages of housing and jobs. Because of inherited attitudes, it is easy to blame visible minorities like East Indians for taking our houses and jobs.

To counter this pathology, public and private programs need strengthening. The recent experience of the Chinese communities in Canada is instructive. A national TV program last autumn alleged that foreign-born Chinese students were taking over Canadian campuses. In response, Chinese communities have organized a national defence organization in every major Canadian city. It was greeted with approval a few weeks ago by a "victory banquet" attended by city and provincial officials. The TV network has apologized. The "Chinese foreigners" it showed on its program turned out to be Canadian citizens of one or more generations.

The East Indian communities could profit from this experience. But, more is needed from many public and private agencies. I recognize that much is already being done to push for multicultural contacts, understanding and appreciation, with wide media support. This isn't enough. The ongoing recession will sharpen inter-group tensions in the next few years. The basic problems of unemployment and inflation are not being faced by governments in Canada.

It is most disquieting to see the obtuseness of the Alberta provincial government in this regard. It cannot perceive that prosperity as well as recession generates social pathologies: racism, child abuse, wife-beating, rape, inter-group conflict. Yet, the professionals and other civil servants in the employ of this government are entirely capable of supplying the necessary stepped-up and improved programs.

But, they seem not to be considered by the Alberta cabinet. The Alberta Individual's Rights Protection Act, one of the most tepid in Canada, was this spring further weakened by provincial government interference. The Alberta Human Rights Commission is a shambles because of a rash of recent staff resignations.

To top it all off, we appear to be in for a major strike by provincial government employees, whose wage increases for several years have been less than the rate of cost of living inflation.

This government, regardless of its overwhelming majority, seems increasingly out of touch with Albertans. One is reminded of the self-induced fall of the government of the late Premier Ross Thatcher of Saskatchewan, a decade ago. That government steadily and blindly alienated nearly every major provincial organization and interest group in Saskatchewan. Perhaps the present Alberta government may still pull up its socks.

Edmonton Journal
26 July, 1980

Sovereignty-Association

To the Editor:

Alberta Report's coverage of Ottawa versus provincial rights has been excellent. What surprises is the reluctance to draw the obvious conclusion: the future of Canada lies in sovereignty-association. It is not separatism, but a loose coalition of provinces negotiating directly with one another among themselves.

Confederation and Macdonald's National Policy were designed to benefit southern Ontario and English Montreal business interests. The West was prevented from industrializing by Ottawa's control of freight rates and interest rates.

But metropolitan domination eventually generates its own antidotes. Under-dog hinterlands move into cycles of resistance. They organize to improve their lot.

Sovereignty-association is the only way out. All the resource-based provinces must learn how to process their resources and diversify their economies. The provincial universities and research institutes alone can help them do this. Our unemployed Ph.D.'s can be put to work. The four western provinces, for example, could build their own railroad from Churchill to Prince Rupert and set their own freight rates.

Sovereignty-association would get rid of Ottawa's narrow version of bilingualism. We need to encourage Canadians to learn a second language – but any language is acceptable.

Sovereignty-association must include our native people. They, like us, have to get out from under a parasitical Ottawa bureaucracy.

Ferment in the West has not produced the necessary imaginative and charismatic leadership. Are the western premiers fearful? Can Ottawa's desperate bluffs destroy us all? All three federal parties are moribund, led by politicians oriented to southern Ontario. We hinterlanders can't live with that.

The best of our choices is sovereignty-association.

What does the Ottawa dinosaur offer? Continued constriction in favour of archaic vested interests, led by phony Quebec Mafia – Trudeau and Co. – and hangers-on like Alberta defector Coutts (just defeated in Toronto, thank heaven). Ottawa offers us a dead end.

What shall be our answer?

Alberta Report
September 11, 1980

Resource Game Won't Stop Until Catastrophe Strikes

To the Editor:

In the currently escalating battle between Ottawa and the resource-based provinces, especially the West and Newfoundland, the truth is now coming to light. Ottawa and the stagnating industrial complex it cuddles in Southern Ontario are desperate.

Ottawa has two power bases, both eroding. The first is Quebec. The May 20 referendum changed nothing basic; Quebec's departure from Confederation may take longer than some Quebecers expected. What temporarily carried the day last May 20 was the 19 percent non-francophones: the English, Italians, Jews, Crees, Portuguese and so on. Those groups are a permanent minority in

Quebec; they cannot indefinitely prevail against majority rule.

Ottawa's second power base is the only real industrial sector in Canada, Southern Ontario. It is an American branch-plant complex, but head offices in the U.S. are closing down their Canadian subsidiaries. Thousands of workers with 15 to 35 years of service are being laid off. They have little chance of reemployment in most cases and little prospect of reasonable severance agreements. It is the deindustrialization of Southern Ontario.

We have had innumerable warnings of the impending catastrophe. Nearly a decade ago, the Science Council of Canada, a federally funded research and advisory agency, published studies calling attention to Canada's progressive loss of research-and-development capacity to the U.S. head offices. No industrial complex can survive without a strong R and D effort.

It seems all too clear that most of our present federal and provincial political leaders will not be of much use in the disaster before us. What we need is a provincial, grassroots and interprovincial process of rewriting our national constitution – minus Ottawa. Ottawa is rapidly becoming an octopus.

Not one of the present three federal parties can offer leadership in this deepening crisis. Not one of them dares to speak frankly or tell the Canadian people what is really wrong with being a colony of a declining and decrepit American economic empire. And, let us not forget that the American influence is not simply economic. It is also political, cultural and military.

Anglophone Canada today is a scarecrow in rags, pretending to be a respectable middle-level power. The only political initiatives now emerging in "Canada" (a geographic term) come from Quebec and from our native Indians and Inuit. All of those initiatives deserve our thanks and support. They will be our way out, too.

But westward – look – the land is brightening.

The greatest risk in the West (and in Newfoundland) is that the present crop of politicians is still half-tied by the inherited and ossified slogans of the past. Present issues will not be settled by premiers' annual conferences. The premiers have no mandate for a new constitution. During elections, western premiers run against Ottawa, but this is a dead end.

Yet, the basic interests of the western provinces lie in hog-tying Ottawa. The political will seems to be developing in the West, but in a very ambivalent and weak manner. The economic conditions demand a strong provincial initiative in business and developmental enterprises. Regardless of ideologies, that initiative is emerging, willy-nilly. (This means more Crown corporations, especially provincial.)

The western provinces and Newfoundland – the underdogs – need dialogues, grassroots to local and provincial officials and vice versa. Such matters cannot be decided by meetings of premiers.

A new deal can be worked out in the hinterland provinces, among the underdogs. It will involve a major provincial initiative. Research and development can only be financed by the provinces and the universities, loosely co-ordinated. We shall need a diversification of Canada's foreign trade, away from the U.S. and towards other developing countries. We should encourage Canadians to learn a second language such as Spanish, Ukrainian, Japanese, or Chinese.

Quebec outside of Confederation will probably be happier, and so will we. With Quebec gone an alliance can be set up, and Ottawa can be exposed in all its "divide and con" irrelevancies. There may be a place even for Ottawa, at a reduced level, and shorn of its present role as a pack-rat thief.

Edmonton Journal
Friday, August 22, 1980

Autonomy Needed More Than Equality

To the Editor:

Journal news columns report (June 19) that the federal Parliament is moving to eliminate sexist discrimination from the Indian Act. Currently Treaty Indian men who marry non-Indian women retain their Indian status, with attendant benefits, however minimal, regarding health and education. Their children likewise. But Indian women who marry non-Indians lose their treaty status; so do their children.

The federal Minister of Indian Affairs has

tabled legislation in Parliament to reduce these discriminations against Treaty Indian women. That will please white middle-class feminists. The latter are out of touch with Indian realities, unfortunately.

This is not the way to go. A wider perspective is necessary.

The real problem is native property. As collectivities, with few exceptions, natives are the poorest of the poor. The cause is imperialist exploitation by the French and English for three centuries.

These collectivities now face a potential influx of 23,000 women and perhaps 40,000 children. An appalling prospect.

Daylight appears at the end of the tunnel. I refer to the Penner Report, October, 1983. Indian Self-Government, House of Commons. It is a landmark study.

Give the Indians self-government, says the report. Give them sole legislative rights over the reserves, plus grants of Crown land, plus negotiated subsidies until they get on their feet. Subsurface resources must be included.

Other countries are far ahead of Canada in minorities policy. It is disgraceful for Canada to lag behind Australia, Greenland and Scandinavia. Not to mention northeast Siberia, documented by Canadian writer Farley Mowat in Sibir. Even the U.S.A. seem to be doing better than Canada.

A new deal for Indian First Nations (treaty) must include Inuit and Metis. It can best begin in the N.W.T., where natives have a 70 percent majority. And natives must decide who is a native.

Edmonton *Journal*
June 26, 1984

The Open Forum: World Hunger Cause

Mankind are an incorrigible race. Give them but bugbears and idols—it is all that they ask.   WILLIAM HAZLITT

TO THE EDITORS:

Prof. Klopfer's "World Hunger" (June–July 1984 issue) blames world hunger on overpopulation. Instead of care packages, he says, we should offer contraceptives. This is a serious distortion. People in Third World peasant societies are not poor because they have large families; they have large families because they are poor. Family-planning campaigns, including free contraceptives, have failed in south-east Asia. Why? Because the Indian peasant on his patch of land knows that his survival requires a large family. To survive, he needs two or three adult sons. Yet half his children will die by age five. Half will be females, less desirable than males. To get two or three adult males will take eight or ten births. Sons mean an unpaid family labor force, supporters in neighborhood disputes, and help in the father's old age. The peasant is entirely rational as well

as traditional in rejecting contraception. Verification may be found in *Myth of Population Control*, by M. Mamdani (New York, 1972), a careful analysis, extendable to much of the Third World.

Klopfer mentions China as an exception, but he does not tell why. He is right: China has decisively reduced its birth rate. But this happened as part of a package of mutually consistent social and economic reforms: land reform, wide extension of health and education services—all in a planned economy context. China now has retirement plans, for example, and a widespread limited guaranteed annual income. India has nothing. That "horrendous" growth in China mentioned by Klopfer is not due to large families, but to the age structure: there are many families in the reproductive age category. This is temporary. China has encouraged contraception for thirty years.

The solution to hunger in the Third World is revolution, not condoms.

The Churchman
December, 1984

Discrimination Generates Poverty

To the Editor:

The birthday of Rev. Martin Luther King, an American black reformer assassinated in Tennessee in 1968, is a good time to take stock.

King was murdered soon after he linked racial discrimination with poverty. That tore it. But he was right. Discrimination generates poverty.

Let's not forget that Canada does little better. Can anyone be proud of the way we treated Canadian Indians and Inuit, not to mention other minorities? Anti-Semitism is covertly rampant in Canada.

The human race is doing badly. After a lifetime of teaching, study and travel, I doubt we shall survive. Even worse, we do not deserve to survive. The universe will be well rid of us. I say this with great grief.

Utopia is nowhere, I concluded years ago. I have been to China, the U.S.S.R., Cuba, India, England, Japan, Mexico and the U.S. But what do I most remember? Saskatchewan in the great days of Tommy Douglas, the greatest orator in North America.

Like Martin Luther King, Tommy Douglas was a churchman, a minister. But those two could not save us. They could point the way, but we could not follow.

Edmonton, *Journal*
February 2, 1986

Western Media and the Beijing Massacre of June 4, 1989

To the Editor:

A dense fog shrouds events in China because of the colossal western ignorance of Chinese history. The western media and bumbling leaders have stampeded to fill the ignorance gap with anti-Chinese propaganda.

This is the road to war, not peace.

On June 5 a *Journal* Opinion page carried three articles, all inflammatory. The lead editorial was, Chinese gov't loses its people: two Southam columns were headed, China's brutal tyrants, and Freedom of press worth defending. This line is sweeping all western nations.

I have seen two realistic insights in this flood of China-bashing, both in *The Journal*. One was by Prof. Lung-kee Sun, visiting University of Alberta (China's camouflaged coup, June 8), who listed other bloody incidents in the present generation; the other quoted Prof. Leslie Green ("Western media incited Chinese – U of A prof," June 9). "What we are seeing is the struggle of a dying government . . . not a system . . ." Right on.

For more than 2,000 years China has relied on periodic rebellions to clean out incompetent regimes. Not all rebellions were relevant or successful. They were first explained to the West by a perceptive British civil servant in China. In 1856 T. T. Meadows wrote. *The Chinese and Their Rebellions.* "Disinterested interference of one nation with another has never taken place. But we are being summoned to interference with the Chinese in the cause of humanity. Periodic rebellions are necessary to the well-being of China."

He was urging the West, in vain, not to interfere with the great Taiping uprising of 1849–65. China was then weak, being carved up by imperialist western nations. He forecast that interference would bring a strong nationalistic regime hostile to the West. So it did, in 1949. "The Chinese people have stood up," proclaimed Mao Tse-tung. The imperialists were expelled.

In Chinese eyes the students are contaminated by western influence. They proved this by choosing the U.S. Statue of Liberty for their symbol—very un-Chinese. A Chinese tank quite naturally knocked it over.

The lessons for the West are clear. China is a nuclear power. What happens in China, however messy, is the sole concern of China. The Cold War is not over, despite Mikhail Gorbachev. Socialism confronts capitalism; a nuclear war cannot be won. Time to sound the alarm.

Edmonton *Journal*
June 14, 1989

Quebec In Depth

The 1970 "October Crisis" Twenty-one Years Later

ON OCTOBER 5, 1970, the British Trade Commissioner in Montreal was kidnapped by a circle or "cell" of the Front de Liberation du Quebec (FLQ). The kidnappers demanded that an FLQ Manifesto be read on the air: this was done. They also required the release of the handful of other FLQ members in jail for various bombings in federal mailboxes, but that was refused. The Commissioner was held prisoner for two months, then released in a deal whereby the kidnappers and their families were flown to Cuba, plane supplied by courtesy of the Canadian Army. Sounds fishy? It was fishy.

On October 10 came the kidnapping of Pierre Laporte, Quebec Minister of Labour, allegedly by another cell. Five days later, the Quebec Government asked the Ottawa cabinet for military aid, after behind-the-scenes pressure from Ottawa to do so. The War Measures Act was invoked on October 16. Next day the body of Laporte was found in a car trunk parked on the military airport of St. Hubert in southeast Montreal. The airfield was chain-fenced and under tight military guard: how the car got there has never been explained. But the victim had been murdered.

The FLQ. This was a fringe group, one of several that arose in the "Quiet Revolution" of the 1960s. They featured various mixes of Quebec nationalism, anticolonialism and anti-English sentiments. Some displayed socialist ideas. Most looked for some sort of economic association with the rest of Canada once Quebec had achieved autonomy or independence. The FLQ had no central organization or fixed membership; people seem to have come and gone. The philosophical theme-setter is generally taken to have been Pierre Vallieres, author of *White Niggers of America* (Editions Parti pris, Montreal, 1968 in French; English trans. Monthly Review Press, New York, 1971). The FLQ was active in Montreal from 1963 to 1971, credited with "over 200 bombings." (*Canadian Encyclopedia*, 1988)

The 1914 War Measures Act.   This is a Canadian federal statute authorizing Cabinet rule by decree in time of "war, invasion or insurrection real or apprehended." It has been activated in World Wars I and II in the face of Quebec unrest concerning conscription: many Quebecers saw these wars as imperialistic ventures by Britain and France. Though francophones, Quebecers now saw themselves as North Americans, not as transplanted Europeans or transplanted Frenchmen. The Act has been invoked only against Quebec.

The Act can be invoked by one man – the Prime Minister. Given the rules on Cabinet secrecy and Party discipline, no member of Parliament (MP) would dare to challenge the Prime Minister in time of "crisis." The Prime Minister was Pierre Trudeau (actually he has six names), born in 1919 into an affluent elitist family, with a Scottish mother and a francophone father. He was educated at the Jesuit college Jean-de-Brébeuf, the Université de Montréal, Harvard, London, trained as a constitutional lawyer, widely travelled.

The bottom-line question is this: in October, 1970, were there any genuine grounds for expecting an insurrection in Quebec? Clearly the answer is an unqualified and resounding NO.

The Real Nature of the October Crisis.   In essence the "crisis" with its activation of the War Measures law was a "whiff of grapeshot" aimed at the legitimate movement for Quebec independence, especially at the rapidly growing new Parti Quebecois. Founded in 1968 by the merger of two small separatist groups and led by the charismatic René Lévesque, the Parti Quebecois spearheaded a mushrooming trend toward independence, drawing support from several other Quebec mass organizations. On April 29, 1970, the provincial election was handily swept by the federalist Liberal Party under R. Bourassa with 72 of 108 seats. But the Parti Quebecois won 24 per cent of the vote, which translated into a mere seven seats in the Quebec National Assembly.

On May 7, 1970, the Canadian Prime Minister set up a Strategic Operations Centre (SOC) which included politicians, Royal Canadian Mounted Police (RCMP), high military officers and a few others, all carefully screened. The East Block War Room was set up about the same time in the Parliament buildings complex. The SOC room was at 67 Sparks St., Ottawa, five minutes walk from the War Room. The SOC remained secret until 1975, when Canadian Broadcasting researchers discovered and revealed the facts.

The scapegoat or "fall guy" in this picture was of course the FLQ. The authorities infiltrated the FLQ, kept surveillance on known and suspected independence sympathizers, and provoked "incidents" which were then blamed on those provoked.

Indeed, the chief target was not simply the FLQ, but Quebec and the Quebecois in general–Canadian public opinion in general–and certain key elements high in the United States and the North Atlantic Treaty Organization (NATO) power structures that are responsible for safeguarding Western Capitalism. It was important to show the American Central Intelligence Agency that the Northern frontier was in safe hands, for example, and not a "northern Cuba."

Preparing the Minefield for the Quebec Independence Movement. "In the sixties, military planners in the U.S. and Canada began drafting fictitious scenarios for insurrections, civil disturbances . . . In 1970, the Canadian forces came up with Operation Essai (French for 'Test') . . . Through a planned provocation, it was designed to meet three objectives. These were: perfecting the repressive machinery across the country; centralizing all the available data on subversion; . . . and bolstering Canadian unity by disorganizing and dislocating as much as possible the groups promoting Quebec nationalism." (Pierre Vallieres, *Assassination of Pierre Laporte*, Lorimer, Toronto, 1977, p. 31; footnote ref. to the 1975 CBC researchers who "obtained the information from high-ranking military sources.")

The integration of the Army, Navy and Airforce branches of the Canadian military in 1966 led to a Mobile Command responsible for all future operations within Canada. Command headquarters were set up in southern Montreal at the St. Hubert military air base (*ibid*, p. 33). The strangled body of Pierre Laporte would be found near the Mobile Command HQ on the St. Hubert airfield on October 17, 1970.

Police forces were also active in counter-agitation and infiltration activities. Information was computerized and fed only to proven hard-line officials, thus by-passing officials deemed too "soft" on separatist tendencies. A Combined Anti-Terrorist (CAT) squad had been organized in 1964. The Montreal police broke up two attempted kidnappings in February and June, 1970. More were expected in the fall. In October, 1970, the public impression was fostered that the authorities were caught unprepared and flat-footed. The very opposite was true. The FLQ walked into a hidden minefield. Its dozen or 15 activists were all known to and watched by police agents.

But the military and police authorities were after far bigger game than the shadowy FLQ. They sought to administer a hard lesson to the mainstream of the Quebec independence movement. However, the Parti Quebecois avoided the trap by consistently attacking the violent tendencies of the FLQ fringe.

The Round-up of "Suspects." On October 16 at 0400 the War Measures Act was proclaimed. Eventually 497 persons were rounded up; 435 were soon released without charges; 32 more persons had their charges dropped in mid-1971. Sixteen persons were sentenced in connection with the Laporte murder; four faced charges of murder and/or kidnapping. One of the four was acquitted after four trials but was finally sentenced as an accessory. Two were convicted of murder, and one was convicted of kidnapping. All four were variously cited for contempt during their court proceedings because they disrupted their courtrooms or refused to testify for the Crown. A dozen other persons were convicted of lesser charges than murder and kidnapping. (*ibid*, 187–188)

Both the Quebec and the federal cabinets met with internal dissidence before they could agree on invoking the War Measures Act. An inside look at the federal cabinet is now available in the partial publication of the diary of the late Don Jamieson, Minister of Transport. This disclosure, appropriately entitled "Overkill," appeared in the April, 1988 issue of *Saturday Night*. The over-emotional federal Minister was Jean Marchand: he expressed highly exaggerated rumours of infiltration of the Quebec Government by the FLQ, along with baseless allegations of possible FLQ assassinations and bombing demolitions of buildings. The Prime Minister as usual was low-key in Cabinet meetings on the crisis wherein he was "essentially a listener." Trudeau said that the federal Government had been asked to intervene by the governments of Quebec and Montreal City; he went no further than these basic facts. On October 18 the RCMP Commissioner told the Cabinet he "had no evidence" that "an insurrection was being planned." (*ibid*, *Saturday Night*)

Now, in 1991, we can re-evaluate the *Saturday Night* article in the light of Pierre Vallieres' *Assassination of Pierre Laporte* (1977). Is it not perfectly clear that the Prime Minister was orienting mainly to the SOC rather than to his Cabinet? Indeed, the Cabinet was something of a "loose cannon" during the October crisis: it had to be neutralized or at least kept under wraps. The real information and key decisions were being made in the SOC, still a secret operation.

On February 11, 1991, the Canadian Press circulated a write-up of information on the October crisis based on Cabinet documents obtained under the Access to Information Act. They confirm that several Cabinet members did not believe that an insurrection threatened Quebec. The Prime Minister and Jean Marchand, however, wanted to make raids on the FLQ to forestall "opinion makers in Quebec," quickly. The War Measures Act was the easiest way to do that. (Edmonton *Journal*, February 11, 1991)

The Balance Sheet for the October Crisis, Short-run and Long-run. It was of course a managed or contrived affair, created primarily by the top brass in the Prime Minister's Office (PMO), the military, RCMP–anglophone elitists seeking to discredit in the eyes of Quebec and Canada (not to mention certain key American elements)–the movement for Quebec independence or some other form of special status for Quebec. The driving spark was the concealed hatred of the Prime Minister for any departure from the principle of equal status and rights and responsibilities for all the provinces and for all Canadians, led and enforced by a strong central government in Ottawa.

In the short run, then, the October ploy was wildly successful. The public was shocked by the first kidnapping on October 5. When the second kidnapping happened five days later, Canada panicked from coast to coast. On October 16 the War Measures Act was invoked by the federal Cabinet, banning the FLQ and suspending civil liberties. The discovery of the body of Laporte on October 17 was the final blow; in the eyes of a great majority of Canadians, it justified the War Measures Act. This was a short-run emotional conclusion. Some English Canadians thought–mistakenly as it turned out–that the October Crisis and the War Measures Act would settle the "Quebec question" once and for all. The murder of Laporte was perfectly timed to reinforce SOC machinations.

In the longer run, therefore, the "whiff of grapeshot" fired at the Quebec separatist movements by the top federalist authorities in October, 1970, was a net failure. Indeed, in my hindsight judgment, the shot boomeranged back onto those who fired it. The FLQ quickly evaporated, but the FLQ was more a symptom than a basic cause of the ancient antipathy between English and French Canada. After a few short years of relative inactivity, the Quebec movement toward separatism revived; the ferment of the 1960s flared up again. Only six years after the 1970 October crisis, René Lévesque and the Parti Quebecois won a decisive victory in Quebec on November 15, 1976, perhaps several years sooner than they would have without the 1970 fireworks.

Both the 1970 federal Minister of Justice (John Turner) and Quebec Premier Robert Bourassa later conceded that the invocation of the War Measures Act was meant to rally public support rather than to confront "an apprehended insurrection." A 1991 Canadian Press release said federal Cabinet ministers "openly challenged then-prime minister Trudeau, who was stopped short of pushing through even tougher measures." (Edmonton *Journal*, February 11)

The troops patrolling Montreal streets went home on January 4, 1971. Over the next four years, the trials of the four FLQ activists charged with complicity in the Laporte murder and kidnapping took place. Given the hysteria of the times, and the fact that the higher courts (Queen's Bench) are an arm of the federal government—the objectivity of these trials seems dubious.

"Firmly convinced that Quebec was not entitled to any form of 'special status' within Confederation, the federal government 'sacrificed' Laporte to achieve its basic ends. These were, in effect, to subject the Quebec government to federal dictates and to eliminate the 'separatist threat.'" (Vallieres, op. cit. 1977, p. 172)

This comes across as a fair appraisal. But then—Who really killed Pierre Laporte?

Quebec In History

New France: Explorations and Settlements. France showed interest in the New World belatedly, compared to the other West European nations. Explorations were made upstream along the St. Lawrence River in the 16th century, but mostly during the 17th century when settlements were established. The original attraction was fishing off Newfoundland, but soon the fur trade, especially beaver pelts for gentlemen's hats in Europe, became highly profitable. Pelts could be had for cheap glass trinkets and iron pots and old muskets—not to mention "firewater"—rotgut whisky and rum.

Even earlier, Spain had invaded Central and South America, where gold and silver loot was rich indeed, and attractive to pirates and licensed "privateers" (there was little difference between them) of other west European States. Portugal was into Brazil. The British had thirteen colonies along the east coast of North America, and from 1670 the Hudson's Bay Company held a nominal trading monopoly in Rupert's Land—all the land draining into Hudson's Bay from the Rocky Mountains eastward through central Canada. The English Queen Elizabeth I (reigned 1558–1603) invested funds in British privateers.

Vast land claims were usually staked out in terms of major river basins. Thus La Salle reached the Mississippi delta in 1682 and claimed the entire Mississippi-Missouri-Ohio basin for France, which in turn ceded it to Spain in the 1763 Treaty of Paris. But France got it back in 1800 by a secret treaty with Spain. In 1803 Napoleon sold Louisiana to the United States for $15 million in order to keep the huge region out of British hands.

Today about a million francophones live in the southern half of the State of Louisiana–White, Black and Indian Creoles, and Cajuns–the latter descended from the few thousand New Brunswick Acadians exiled by the British in 1755; many made their way back later. We should mention also Antonine Maillet (b. 1929), leading novelist and informal voice of the Acadians today; she won the prestigious Prix Goncourt about 1980, and became an immediate literary success in France. Acadians do not see themselves as Quebecois. In 1986 one-third of New Brunswick's 710,000 people were francophones. Quebec is 83 percent francophone.

Besides the exploration and settlement activities, New France pursued efforts to convert the native Indians to Catholicism, but without much success.

The Conquest of New France by England. This landmark event was a by-product of the great war between England and France, 1754–1763. Quebec City fell first in 1759; both field commanders, Montcalm and Wolfe, were fatalities of that battle on the Plains of Abraham. Montreal was captured about a year later. We shall outline the next two centuries using as our chief guide *Quebec-Canada: A New Deal.* This is a "white paper" issued by the Government of Quebec in 1979 to explain its views on present problems and future policies to resolve those problems. The subtitle is "The Quebec government proposal for a new Partnership between Equals: Sovereignty-Association." It may well be the most important political statement made in Canada since the 1867 Confederation.

The Conquest left Quebec under colonial rule. Many of its francophone upper class returned to France. The "habitants" were left with their local governments, parishes and forests. The British in 1774 passed the Quebec Act, allowing the use of French language and carrying on the civil law of France. Though the British in the long run pressed for assimilation of the French, in 1774 the former were hoping for some French support in the looming rebellion of the American colonies.

The Land System that prevailed from 1627 to 1854 in New France/ Quebec had a feudal nature. An administrative company represented the Crown; it allocated seigneuries to influential settlers, who in turn assigned narrow strips or *rangs* to tenants called "habitants." A seigneur was responsible for granting *rangs* to tenants, who paid dues to the seigneur. A seigneury was usually about 3 by 10 miles; a *rang* might be 4 or 5 acres wide and 40 or 45 acres deep, the narrow side fronting on a river, with the back end on a road. Access was easy in both summer and winter, and any stretch of road that had to be plowed open in winter was short. The seigneur could operate a local court, and run a grinding mill that tenants had to use. He could charge rents and fees in cash or in kind. The State regulated the relationships between seigneur and habitant. Seventy-five or 80 per cent of the population lived on seigneurial land until the mid-19th century. The seigneur also granted hunting, fishing and woodcutting licenses. Land around a seigneury might be held by a parish or a municipality. A religious institution could be granted a seigneury in return for educational and hospital services. All in all, this system of small farms and local services made for close-knit and reasonably efficient communities until the industrial revolution began to develop. (*Canadian Encyclopedia*, 1988)

Unsettled lands were divided into townships, and were sold. The *rang* pattern prevailed in the St. Lawrence, Richelieu and Chaudiere basins. (See *National Geographic* map of Quebec, March, 1991.)

The 1791 Constitutional Act. In response to a surge of British immigrants from the American colonies (now independent), this act divided Canada into two parts: Lower Canada (the southern part of contemporary Quebec) and Upper Canada (west from Lower Canada around the north shores of the Great Lakes to Fort William, but south of Rupert's Land). In both provinces, elected Assemblies were granted, but the Governors appointed by London had veto powers. That issue came to a head in the uprisings of 1837.

The Rebellions of 1837. In Lower Canada (Quebec) the French Canadians held a majority in the population, especially in the countryside, and in the elected Assembly. About 1826 Louis Joseph Papineau organized the Parti Patriote, which demanded that the Assembly control taxes and public spending. In the 1830s came a depression and a new influx of British immigrants, most of whom went to the cities, and who imported cholera: The French got blamed. In 1832 at an election riot, British soldiers shot three French Canadians. The British Governor vetoed the Patriote demands in the Assembly, which then refused to vote any funds for the Government. Next, the Governor dissolved the Assembly. In the new Assembly the Parti Patriote won 77 of 88 seats and a 90 percent sweep of the election vote. The same demands were again rejected and the Assembly was once more dissolved. The cleavages sharpened: urban-rural, Protestant-Catholic, upper class vs. middle and farming class, but above all—English vs. French. British troops arrived from abroad. In November and December, 1837, civil war broke out. Six of the seven battles were in the Richelieu valley south and south-east of Montreal. The Patriotes won the first one at St. Denis, which was sacked and burned a week later by the British troops. A year later the Patriotes won at Beauharnois–but nowhere else.

From London came a new Governor, Lord Durham. His mediation efforts failed. After he departed for London, more fighting began in November, 1838. But though the Patriotes fought fiercely, they were no match for British regular troops. In the two campaigns, 325 fatalities (including 27 soldiers) occurred. Twelve Patriotes were hanged, 58 were exiled to Australia. Many farms and houses were burned. Irregular British volunteers went on a rampage of destructive arson. Papineau fled to Paris, and other leaders made off to the United States, where they had considerable moral support.

The rising in Upper Canada, led by William Lyon Mackenzie, was a much smaller affair: the French-English cleavage, a prime dynamic in Lower Canada, was not a factor in the York (Toronto) outbreak. The latter was a class struggle against the oligarchy created by the Constitution Act of 1791, but it was entirely an Anglophone show. A reformist republican won the Assembly in 1828 and in 1834, but lost in 1836 when a number of moderates were defeated. This gave the more radical William Lyon Mackenzie his opening to lead the reformers. The economic depression and crop shortages of 1837 precipitated extra-Assembly agitation. When the Upper Canada Governor sent his British troops to Lower Canada in November, 1837, Mackenzie gathered about 1000 men from areas north of Toronto, with numbers of supporters from American migrants and from dissenting (non-Anglican) churches. There was marching back and forth: each side ran away from the other at least once. A separate uncoordinated rising occurred at Brantford. All these events happened in December, 1837. In 1838 the rebels organized raids from the United States border during the next few months, but they lacked the intensity of partisan feeling that motivated and unified the French Canadians in Lower Canada. In Upper Canada the ultra-tories remained in power. Mackenzie escaped to the United States.

The Act of Union, 1840. As recommended by Lord Durham's 1839 report, the British Parliament in 1840 created the United Province of Canada, effective in 1841. Details of a new regime were arranged during the next seven years; "Responsible Government" was the official aim and slogan. The extremists on both sides gave way to more moderate voices. But the aim of assimilation of the French–Durham described them as "a people with no literature and no history"–totally alienated the educated French. Unification was the means of avoiding a prospective francophone majority in Lower Canada. It also presented a stronger Canadian front against the bumptious anti-British and anti-monarchical Americans.

As passed by the British House of Commons, the Act of Union set up a single Parliament with equal representation for each of the two Canadas, Upper and Lower, and with a merger of their public debts. For Lower Canada this deal was one-sided: there was a larger population in French Canada but a higher debt in Upper Canada. The French language was forbidden in official government proceedings, but in 1849 French was restored. Over the next few years, several knotty problems were ironed out. Not the least of the favorable influences was the return of economic prosperity. But the French remained – oppressed.

The 1867 Act of Confederation. By the 1860s economic and political forces were making the 1840 Union obsolete. Upper Canada – or Canada West – in particular had gained population, and was thinking about westward expansion and railroads. The United States was already recognized as an aggressive neighbour, having seized Texas and the states to the west including California, 1845–48. In the same vein, the American purchase of Alaska from the Russian Empire in 1867 for $7.2 millions sent a shiver of apprehension through some Canadian leaders.

The four British colonies of Nova Scotia, New Brunswick, Prince Edward Island and Newfoundland were ambivalent. To P.E.I. its rail-building debt made the prospect of financial aid from a new and larger Dominion of Canada attractive. Nova Scotia waffled; indeed it was two-thirds against Confederation, but that was not discovered until after Confederation was proclaimed on July 1, 1867. Later that year 65 percent of Nova Scotians voted no, but its pro-Confederation leaders had the "marriage" already signed and sealed. New Brunswick went along when a pro-Confederation government replaced an anti-Confederation regime in 1866. Newfoundland, however, flatly refused to join until 1949. Not for nothing is Newfoundland known in Canadian history as "The Rock."

Quebec had bitter criticisms against the Union of 1840: its language was restricted, and it felt increasingly surrounded by an expanding sea of English people. Confederation offered some basic relief: it would recover its capital, Quebec City; it would have its own Legislature once again; and it could count on substantial French representation in the Ottawa federal Cabinet and Parliament. So Quebec went along with confederation.

What seems to have won the day for Confederation was a series of Fenian raids by Irish-Americans in the United States. The Fenian movement was aimed at freeing Ireland from English rule. By 1865 the Fenians had raised a half-million dollars and had enrolled 10,000 Civil War veterans. One Fenian faction reasoned that attacking England was impractical, so why not take a few swipes at Britain's North American colonies?

An 1866 raid against New Brunswick collapsed in April; another in June, 1866, crossed the Niagara frontier, won a skirmish against the local militia, then skipped back over the border. A few days later a group crossed from Vermont at Missisquoi Bay and stayed for two days before leaving Quebec. There were two more ventures into Quebec in 1870, and one into Manitoba in 1871, where Louis Riel raised local troops to repel the intrusion. The main effect of the 1866 raids was to help tip Maritime opinion in favour of Confederation.

Confederation was planned at Charlottetown, P.E.I. in September, 1864, and at Quebec City a month later. The final legislation for the British Parliament was worked out in London early in the winter of 1867, passed into law on March 29, and proclaimed by Queen Victoria on July 1 – the latter date is now observed as Canada's National Day.

Not until 1964 – a century later – did Canada manage to agree upon its own flag, after six months of heated debate mostly among the anglophone Members of Parliament. Some of them wanted to have a British-type flag. Yet Confederation and the "National Policy" that grew out of it developed a certain inner momentum, even a touch of euphoria.

The National Policy included western settlement by farmers, a transcontinental railroad that would carry Ontario manufactures to western settlers and western grain to eastern markets and ports, a high protective tariff, shunting the Indians onto wasteland reservations, and a cheap-land policy to attract settlers westward. Western settlement was also a defense against American intrusion, as Prime Minister Macdonald saw the matter.

Nonetheless, in the over-riding scenario of Confederation, there is another side. Confederation was not only successful development; it was also an accumulation of contradictions still waiting to be resolved. What about our Native Peoples? What about Quebec and Canada-without-Quebec? What about the economic, cultural and political domination of Canada by the United States-after-Iraq? Perhaps above all, what about the festering cancer of poverty, both within Canada and among the other world nations?

The 1885 Northwest Rebellion: Quebec and Louis Riel. Manitoba was admitted to Confederation in 1870, when a majority of its population was Metis and Indian. Hence French-language rights were operative, although by the early 1890s Anglos were predominant and the use of French was suppressed in the legislature and schools. The chief population centre was the Red River settlement where fur-trading posts had been established since 1738 at Fort Garry (Winnipeg). Louis Riel, a French Metis, was born in 1844; his grave is in the Cathedral cemetery in St. Boniface, now a francophone suburb of Winnipeg.

Riel was educated at St. Boniface and at the Collége de Montréal, where he studied for the priesthood. In 1869, with the transfer of Rupert's Land to Canada looming, friction arose between the Métis and officials sent in from Ontario. The Métis sent the officials back to the East, drew up grievance and demand lists; Riel emerged as head of a Provisional Government. Some Protestant activists were jailed; one (Thomas Scott, a surveyor) was courtmartialled and executed in March, 1870. This enraged the Ontario Protestant lodges. With British troops on the way west, Riel slipped out of the Red River settlement to the United States. In 1873 and again in 1874 he was elected to the Canadian Parliament, but was expelled from the House on a motion put by the Ontario leader of the Orange lodges. He was treated briefly for mental illness in Quebec and then moved to Montana as a trader and later a teacher.

In mid-1884, a Métis delegation from Batoche, Saskatchewan, visited Riel to invite his aid for Métis settlements along the South Saskatchewan River about 60 miles northeast of Saskatoon. The Indians were starving because the buffalo were all but gone; the Métis feared the loss of their small farms. In March, 1885, a Provisional Government was organized at Batoche with Riel as President and Gabriel Dumont as military commander. Prime Minister Sir John Macdonald set troops in motion westward. The first skirmish took place on March 26 when a force of Northwest Mounted Police and anglophone volunteers, about 100 in all, clashed with a Métis force at Duck Lake near Batoche. The police lost about a dozen personnel; the Métis about half that number. The police withdrew to Prince Albert.

Early in April, 1885, marauding Cree and Assiniboines attacked and killed about a dozen White men northwest of Battleford, Saskatchewan. The chiefs restrained their warriors from further depredations, as they did in most of the engagements. But British General Middleton had to subdivide his forces. The main British column moved northward from Qu'Appelle; a second started from Swift Current for the Battleford area; a third hiked from Calgary north to Edmonton, where it turned eastward for the Lloydminster district on the Saskatchewan border.

On April 24, Gabriel Dumont ambushed Middleton's column at Fish Creek a few miles south of Batoche. Three days of heavy fighting brought no change in the battlelines, until two British officers led an unplanned charge on Batoche. The Métis were running out of ammunition. Riel surrendered; Dumont escaped to the United States.

Meanwhile the second British column was ambushed at Cut Knife Hill just northwest of Battleford. Chief Poundmaker persuaded the Indians not to pursue the fleeing British, so casualties were light. The third column from Calgary via Edmonton caught up with a large Indian force at Frenchman's Butte east of Lloydminster. The Indians were entrenched in strong positions–too strong to attack. The two forces shot at each other on May 28 for several hours from a distance, then both sides retreated.

Not all the Métis or Indians supported the uprising: inherited hostility toward the Plains Cree kept the Woods Cree, the Blackfoot and the Blood neutral. Those Whites who had agitated on the Métis' behalf quickly changed sides when the shooting started; no Whites were charged by the authorities after the uprising ended.

Chiefs Poundmaker and Big Bear got three years in penitentiary. Wandering Spirit, a Frog Lake war chief, and seven other Indians were hanged at Battleford on November 2. Many others got conditional discharges or sentences up to seven years.

And Louis Riel? Tried and convicted at Regina, he was hanged on November 16, 1885. His execution could easily have been commuted. But Prime Minister John A. Macdonald and his Tory racist Cabinet decided to "let the law take its course." If Riel was a villain in Tory eyes, he was an instant hero in Quebec. Wilfrid Laurier, a future Prime Minister of Canada (1896–1911) and of course a Quebec Liberal Party member, made bitter attacks on the Riel sentence, thereby helping his career significantly. (*Canadian Encyclopedia*) Riel won his case–beyond the grave. (See especially J. K. Howard, *Strange Empire of Louis Riel*, Toronto, Swan edition, 1965.)

The Mercier Regime in Quebec. Honoré Mercier became Premier of Quebec, 1887–1891. He was a Quebec nationalist and Liberal who rode to power on the coat-tails of Louis Riel. As Premier, he pressed for railway building and colonization of unsettled lands in Quebec. He called the first conference of Premiers since the 1867 Confederation, and he led them in a struggle for greater provincial autonomy in administrative and fiscal matters. Late in 1891 Mercier was removed from office by the Quebec Lt.-Governor, an anglophone appointee of the English authorities in Ottawa. Though Mercier was promptly re-elected, his party was not.

Confederation was a victory for English-Canadian centralizers over the provincial-rights interests of francophone Quebec. One important response of Quebecers since the mid-19th century was emigration to small settlements in the West and to the mill-towns of New England. Mercier attempted to direct some of that emigration into the unsettled areas within Quebec. Migration out of Quebec meant assimilation into English-speaking North America. That has become a prime fear of Quebec nationalists.

Farms and businesses in Quebec remained small, except for the minority of large enterprises owned mainly by English and later by American corporations. Montreal in the mid-19th century consisted of anglophones and francophones about equally; by the 1986 census anglophones
were down to approximately 10 per cent. But it was an economically
dominant minority—that is, it included a disproportionately large number of economic policy-makers.

Anti-Conscription Agitation in Quebec. In the late stages of both
World War I and World War II, the Canadian Army ran short of manpower, obtained on a volunteer basis. Conscription became necessary
as the European wars took their toll of casualties. Conscription was
strongly supported by Canadian anglophones, and strongly resisted by
Quebec francophones. As the 1979 Quebec White Paper put the issue:

> In 1914, despite firm and virtually unanimous opposition from Quebec,
> Canada entered the war. When in addition Ottawa imposed conscription,
> Quebec rose in revolt: crowds poured into the street and conscripts hid;
> the demonstrations were severely repressed and the conscripts hunted
> down. . . .
>
> The Second World War gave rise to another crisis between Quebec and
> Canada. Quebec was opposed to conscription. Ottawa submitted the is-
> sue to a general referendum: English Canada answered with an over-
> whelming YES, while Francophones categorically said NO. Conscription
> was ordered. (*Quebec-Canada: A New Deal*, p. 11)

The 1949 Asbestos Strike. This bitter strike lasting five months is seen
by some writers as a turning point between the old and the new Quebec.
Though Quebec Premier Duplessis and his Provincial Police, as well as
local authorities, came down hard on the strikers, the Archbishop of
Quebec eventually mediated a settlement. The strikers won much of
what they sought. Perhaps their most significant gain was a recognized
place in the Quebec labour relations scene: the organized working class
now as never before had to be taken into account.

By contrast, in 1903 Monsignior Bruchesi wrote as follows in the Dio-
cese of Montreal: "Men will not change by one iota from what God has
decreed and Christ has upheld. To the end of time, then, God's creatures
will be divided into two great classes, the class of the rich and the class
of the poor . . . You cannot reasonably demand that the wages of the
laborer be continually increased, while his working hours are reduced
at the same time . . . Think of Heaven; then thou shalt receive thy eternal
reward . . . We advise the workers to submit patiently to their condition,
their eyes turned toward Heaven, their future home." (Cited in Pierre

E. Trudeau, ed: *The Asbestos Strike*, Toronto: James Lewis & Samuel, 1974, pp. 45–46.)

Such sentiments were obsolete a half-century later. The asbestos strike began in mid-February, 1949, and lasted into July. On May 1, Msgr. Joseph Charbonneau, Archbishop of Montreal, gave a sermon in Notre Dame Cathedral.

> The newspapers next day reported his words as follows: "The working class is a victim of a conspiracy to crush the working class . . . The Church has a duty to intervene. We want to have peace in our society, but we do not want to see the working class crushed. We are more attached to man than to capital. This is why the clergy decided to intervene. They want to see that justice and charity are respected, and it is their wish that more attention be paid to human beings than to the interests of money." (*Le Devoir*, May 2, 1949)
>
> In each of the dioceses the bishops ordered that collections be taken up at the doors of the churches until the end of the conflict. The amount of these contributions reached the impressive figure of $167,558.24. (*ibid*, p. 211, "The Church and the Conflict," by Gerard Dion, Department of Industrial Relations, Laval University.)

For another insightful comment on the Church in mid-twentieth-century Quebec, we may turn to Miriam Chapin, born in Vermont, graduate of the University of Vermont, a resident of Montreal from 1932, and correspondent in Quebec for the *Christian Science Monitor* from 1946.

> The clergy react to the demands for modern education, for higher wages, for more freedom of thought. They too are French Canadians. The Church is a national church. It takes its authority direct from Rome; it has always stood off interference from the Irish priests who make up the hierarchy in the United States and Ontario . . . Archbishop Charbonneau of Montreal was one of those who try to push the Church toward the side of Labour . . . Yet the changes Msgr. Charbonneau advocated are slowly being made, forced by public demand. (*Quebec Now*, New York: Oxford University Press, 1955, pp. 65, 67)

Shortly after the 1949 asbestos strike, Msgr. Charbonneau, in response to wire-pulling in Rome by Quebec Premier Duplessis, was transferred to a chaplaincy in Victoria, British Columbia, "for reasons of health." From Victoria he told an inquiring reporter (probably M. Chapin–AKD) that he "never felt better in his life."

In the 1950s *Cité Libre*, a social democratic magazine published by young francophone intellectuals (Pelletier, Trudeau et al.) began to appear. But the reactionary influence of Premier Maurice Duplessis (1890–1959) and his patronage machine blocked any serious changes until the "Quiet Revolution" of the 1960s and the appearance of the Parti Quebecois in the 1970s. Visible change, it appears, runs in irregular cycles. Duplessis blocked basic change during his lifetime. He dominated Quebec from 1944 to his death in 1959. In 1958 he tossed 50 (mainly francophone) seats to the Saskatchewan anglophone Conservative Prime Minister, John Diefenbaker, in order to work off his accumulated grudges against the federal Liberals. With the utmost care, Duplessis chose the local candidates and allocated their campaign funds. His power vehicle was the provincial Parti Union Nationale, which disappeared as a governing party in April, 1970. Its power base was small business, the rural areas and unorganized labour. (See Conrad Black, *Duplessis*, Toronto: McClelland & Stewart, 1977.)

The Future of Quebec

Hardening Lines between English Canada and Quebec. The "dirty tricks" aspect of the 1970 October Crisis has been analyzed at the beginning of this paper. They failed to stop the separatist movement: the Parti Quebecois won the 1976 election with 41 percent of the popular vote, and 71 of 110 seats in the Assembly. René Lévesque's Government brought major reforms in auto insurance, dental insurance for children, the charter of the French language, among others. But he pointed for a referendum on negotiating sovereignty-association in 1980, and lost: the vote was 40 percent YES, and 60 percent NO. In that campaign, Trudeau intervened with a massive billboard display and several passionate speeches. The public fear of losing their federal pensions was especially highlighted, even though the PQ said it would pick up all such pensions. Despite this loss, the PQ won the 1981 election by a margin even larger than in 1976: 49 percent of the popular vote translated into 80 of 110 Assembly seats. An economic recession set in. Premier Lévesque in 1984 announced that the election would not be waged on any separatist issue. This led to serious internal defections, and PQ lost the 1985 election. In 1989, however, the PQ began to recover: 40 percent of the vote and 29 of 125 seats. The most significant change has been the changeover of elements of the business class to support the PQ.

A small event shows a great deal—sometimes. The auto number plates of Quebec used to carry the slogan, "La Belle Province." The PQ Government changed that to, "Je me souviens"–I remember. From the historical pages above, we know that Quebec has a number of bitter memories and humiliations to recall, ever since the Conquest of 1760.

In June, 1990, a First Ministers' Conference (the Prime Minister and the 10 provincial Premiers) held behind closed doors broke down over

the "Meech Lake Accord" of 1987. No previous constitutional conference or measures had ever been taken in secrecy. Responsibility for the
Meech fiasco belonged solely to the Prime Minister, whose popularity
in the Gallup polls had fallen to an unbelievable and unprecedented 12
percent. Though elected to the House of Commons from a Quebec con-
stituency and fluent in French, the PM is no Quebecois–he is Irish. He
kisses whatever Blarney Stone will add to his popularity–he is the ultimate yuppie, a seeker after upward mobility at any cost. His image is
not one of principled political leadership, despite an allegedly surgically
lowered voice (inspired perchance by Henry Kissinger?)–his image is
that of a weathervane spinning in the winds. And the wind to which
he is most susceptible blows from Washington. Unfortunately the Canadian Constitution does not provide for impeachment or recall of top
public policymakers. Quebec Premier Mercier, called by some the first
leader of Quebec nationalism, was removed from office in 1891 by the
Crown representative Lt.-Governor of Quebec, a voice obviously of the
anglophone Establishment in Canada at that time. (Mercier was
promptly re-elected.) But what further sanction is available against a Son
of Ananias who repeatedly in the eyes of a majority of Canadians violates
the national interests of Canada? A charge of treason? A popular revolution? An ambassadorship to Lower Slobovia?

Asked on a TV newscast in 1991 how she would characterize the PM
in one word, an executive of a national women's-rights lobbying organization unhesitatingly replied, "Insincere." Well spoken.

Quebec and Canada-Minus-Quebec: Two Nations. Are they really "two
solitudes" as Hugh MacLennan suggested in his 1945 novel, *Two Solitudes*
(Toronto, Collins Pub. Co.)? Yes, they are. But near–neighbour nations
do not necessarily become solitudes. Why did that happen to English
Canada and Quebec?

It came about in large part because English Canada did not recognize
Quebec as a nation. Instead, English Canada, born in the military conquest of New France in 1760, pressed–in vain–for assimilation of the
francophones. Today in 1991, more than two centuries later, English Canada refuses to see Quebec as a nation. In anglophone mythology, Quebec is one of ten provinces, the other nine being anglophone, and all
should be treated alike (more or less) by the central Government. So
runs the mythology.

In historical fact, however, Lower Canada/Quebec as a collectivity has
gained an occasional windfall benefit from the 1760 Conquest, as traced
in the preceding pages. The 1774 Quebec Act granted French civil law
and strengthened Catholic religious scope. British governors already had

allowed the use of the French language. The 1791 Constitutional Act set up elected Assemblies for both Lower and Upper Canada, but the British-appointed governors from England had veto powers. In 1837–38 these conditions generated uprisings in both Lower and Upper Canada, soon stamped out by British troops. The 1840 Act of Union imposed restrictions on the French language, a single Parliament for both colonies, and onerous pressures for assimilation of francophones. Conferation in 1867 brought some relative relief, but it ensured a minority status for the Quebecois. The Riel affair in 1885 further antagonized francophone feelings. In the twentieth century the War Measures Act was invoked against Quebecers on three occasions.

By 1991, the Quebec movement for sovereignty-association had set off "Save Canada" agitations in English Canada. They are basically backward-looking, hence regressive – so far. No public anglophone figure or authority has acknowledged that Quebec is a nation, or that Quebec has a long history of grievances.

What is a nation? Here is one of the best-known formulations, linked to a perspective of change.

"A nation is a historically constituted, stable community of people, formed on the basis of a common language, territory, economic life, and psychological make-up manifested in a common culture." (Joseph Stalin, *Marxism and the National Question*, New York: International Publishers, 1942, p. 12). The original date of this statement is 1912–13. It lends itself to comparative case studies: see for example the paper on Ibn Khaldun and the concept of *asabia* – intense group feeling – earlier in this volume.

If English Canada cannot come up with a creative redefinition of Canadian realities, Quebec has already done so. It is: sovereignty-association. That is both a method and a program. English Canada will have to recognize Quebec as a nation, and then negotiate as sovereign equals.

Do nations have to become solitudes? Certainly not. They cannot afford such a risk, especially with near-neighbours. Mutual problems require negotiations of varying extent and frequency. It is far more economical – and more interesting – to develop the potential promise of sovereignty-association than to confront the spectres of stagnation and civil war.

For his germinal perception that Canada is developing into two unilingual countries, we are greatly indebted to Richard J. Joy, *Languages in Conflict*, (Toronto: McClelland and Stewart, 1967). History is confirming his insights. Only one major change has emerged to modify his conclusions: the upturn of the Quebec birthrate in the late 1980s. But his fundamental argument is still intact: two unilingual communities are materializing in Canada.

Demographic Insights

Five regional groupings are widely used to describe Canada. (See Table 1.) They are arbitrary, of course, but data is classified according to provincial boundaries and we must begin there. Yet much of northern and western Ontario, let us say from North Bay to Kenora—about 750 miles as the crow flies—is Canadian-Shield hinterland: rocky, scrubby trees, a few mines, many lakes, a few villages and Indian reserves. This immense region north of the Great Lakes Huron and Superior is more like Manitoba than southern Ontario. Similarly, the northern half of the Prairie region is sparsely populated "bush country"—a few mines and settlements—in sharp contrast to the agricultural and urbanized southern half; it is part of Canada North, regardless of the official east-west boundary line at 60 degrees north latitude.

Table 1

Population Overview, by Province, 1986 Census
(east to west, rounded)

Region, Province	Population (thousands)	%
Atlantic Canada, 9%		
Newfoundland	568	2.2
Prince Edward Island	127	0.5
Nova Scotia	873	3.5
New Brunswick	710	2.8
Central Canada, 62%		
Quebec	6,540	25.8
Ontario	9,114	35.9
Prairies, 17%		
Manitoba	1,071	4.2
Saskatchewan	1,010	4.0
Alberta	2,375	9.4
British Columbia, 11%		
British Columbia	2,889	11.4
North, 0.3%		
Yukon Territory	24	0.1
Northwest Territories	52	0.2
Total	25,353	100.0

Source: *Canada Year Book, 1990*, Ottawa, Statistics Canada, p. 2–19; derived and rounded.

Perhaps the most misleading classification is the linking of Quebec and Ontario provinces as "Central Canada." This device obscures the uniqueness of Quebec, but it suits the interests of the anglophone majority, especially the federal bureaucracy. For our analytical purpose, however, the categories "Quebec" and "Canada-minus-Quebec" are in certain respects more appropriate, that is to say, more precise.

Table 2 validates the point made in the preceding paragraph: the first two columns are the relevant data. The third "All Canada" column merely fudges the contrast so clearly evident in the first two columns—Quebec is a different country from the rest of Canada with respect to mother tongue or language. The importance of language in social life and in the self-images of individuals can hardly be overstated. In this key aspect of collective consciousness, Quebec is not "just another province" of that geographic territory labeled "Canada" on the maps of North America. To compare Quebec with "All Canada" is statistically absurd, because Quebec is included in both.

Other Comparative Indices. Religious affiliation is like Mother Tongue—an index of cleavage between Quebec and the rest of Canada when the data is re-arranged. The traditional arrangement, for example, shows a nearly even balance between Protestant and Catholic in the 1981 Census of Canada—41 percent and 47 percent respectively (*Canadian Encyclopedia*, vol. 3, p. 1851: Edmonton, Hurtig, 1988). Instead, let us use as our key categories—QUEBEC and CANADA-WITHOUT-QUEBEC. (The 1986 Census had no question on religion.)

Table 3 indicates that Canada-minus-Quebec is basically Protestant, although Protestants are subdivided into numerous denominations. "Other" includes Eastern Orthodox, Jewish, Islamic, Hindu, Sikh and Buddhist (each of them 1.5 percent or much less). Roughly half of

Table 2

Mother Tongue in Canada, 1986

(language first learned in childhood, and still understood)

Mother Tongue	Quebec (%)	Canada-minus-Quebec (%)	All Canada (%)
French	83	6	25
English	11	80	62
Other	6	14	14
Total	100	100	101

Source: *Canada Year Book, 1990*, derived from Table 2.15; rounded.

Table 3
Canadian Religious Affiliation, 1981
(percent, rounded)

	Catholic	Protestant	Other	Total
Quebec	88%	6%	5%	99%
Canada-minus-Quebec (omits Yukon & NWT)	35	60	6	101

Source: 1981 Census of Canada.

"Other" consists of "no religion"–most evident in Ontario westward to the Pacific.

Besides Quebec, one other province has a Roman Catholic majority: New Brunswick. But unlike Quebec, New Brunswick has a two-thirds anglophone majority and a one-third francophone minority (1986 Census). These latter are the "Acadians," for the most part, though there has been a small influx from Quebec. As a summer visitor in 1965, I found the Acadians noticeably less aggressive than the Quebecois. However, another visit in 1982 revealed a change: a majority of single-family houses with a yard had new flagpoles with large chiefly yellow flags, in the area around Moncton, seat of the Université de Moncton, where French is the language of instruction. Moncton is called the informal cultural capital of the francophones in New Brunswick.

New Brunswick is the only Canadian province that is officially bilingual. In the 1960s, an Acadian Premier, Louis Robichaud, during his 10-year incumbency led a reform movement roughly similar in certain respects to the "Quiet Revolution" in adjoining Quebec. His regime ex-

Table 4
Canadian Religious Affiliation, 1981
(percent)

	Catholic	Protestant	Other	Total
Quebec	88%	6%	5%	99%
New Brunswick	54	43	3	100
Canada-minus-Quebec- and-New-Brunswick	31	54	15	100

Source: Census of Canada cited in *Canadian World Almanac* for 1989 (Toronto: Global Press, 1988, p. 405).

Table 5
Summary of Basic Vital Statistics

	Quebec	Canada-minus-Quebec
Crude birth rate		
1982	14.0	16.0
1986	13.0	15.4
Crude death rate		
1982	6.7	7.4
1986	7.2	7.6
Net natural increase		
1982	7.3	8.6
1986	5.8	7.8

(Note: Crude birth (death) rate is number of births (deaths) per 1000 population. Net natural increase is the difference between them. Migration is ignored.)
Source: *Canada Year Book 1990*, p. 2–33 and 2–34, Statistics Canada.

panded opportunities for Acadians in public administration and education. He also widened the scope of public services and the Université de Moncton.

We do not see New Brunswick, however, as a separate nation like Quebec. New Brunswick comes across as a part of English Canada, despite its obvious – and often attractive – differences from both Quebec and English Canada.

The relevant finding shown in Table 5 is the decline of the Quebec Net Natural Increase compared to that of Canada-minus-Quebec. This is very disturbing to Quebec nationalists, especially to their leaders.

In 1988–89, Quebec enacted a fertility policy: a grant of $500. for each

Table 6
Total Fertility Rate
(for all orders and all mothers 15–44 years old)

Year	Quebec	Rest of Canada	Year	Quebec	Rest of Canada
1981	1611.1	1736.9	1985	1451.1	1765.6
1982	1513.1	1759.0	1986	1431.8	1754.0
1983	1479.5	1763.9	1987	1426.1	1741.0
1984	1475.3	1731.5	1988	1488.2	1711.5

(Note: A fertility rate relates births to women aged 15–45 or 15–49, by 5-year subgroups.)
Source: *Report on the Demographic Situation in Canada, 1990*, November, Ottawa: Statistics Canada, Table 10, p. 23.

first child and second child; then for each third and later child, a grant of $3000 paid quarterly ($375) over two years. In the next fiscal year, 1989–90, bonuses were raised. The second child gets a second $500 on his/her first birthday; and the third-and-later children get the quarterly $375 for three years instead of two–totalling $4500 in place of the original $3000.

The following evaluation, suitably cautious, yet possibly a landmark, is from the *Report on the Demographic Situation in Canada*, 1990, November, Ottawa: Statistics Canada, pp. 23–24.

> There has been an increase of almost 10 percent in first order [first birth– AKD] fertility for all age-groups in Quebec that has not occurred in the rest of Canada. As for higher order births, especially the closely observed third order, levels are very low and continue to drop both in Quebec and in the rest of Canada.

Infant Mortality Rates. This refers to deaths per thousand live births per year. Because infants are especially vulnerable to life-threatening stresses during the first year of life, this rate is widely accepted as an index of health and social conditions in a society. Male infants are at higher risk than females by several years, but we will use here an average of both sexes' mortality.

Table 7 shows in sketchy form the trend of infant mortality rates since 1926 in Canada. Here are some comparative rates chosen at random. (Source: 1990 World Population Data Sheet, Population Laboratory, Sociology Department, University of Alberta. Rounded.)

Mexico 50   Brazil 63   Saudi Arabia 71   Iraq 67   India 95   China 37
USSR   29   USA   10   Sweden   6   Cuba 12   Egypt 90   Japan   5

Clearly, the Canadian record is, in world terms, enviable indeed. Only Japan and Sweden are doing better, in the preceding list.

Table 7

Infant Mortality Rate, Canada

(both sexes, rounded)

1926	101	1966	23
1936	68	1976	14
1946	48	1986	8
1956	32		

Source: *ibid*, table 3–3, pp. 3–18; derived.

Table 8
1987 Infant Mortality Rate, By Provinces
(both sexes, rounded)

Quebec		Canada-minus-Quebec	
7.1		7.6	

Provinces (except Quebec)			
Newfoundland	7.6	Saskatchewan	9.1
Prince Edward Island	6.6	Alberta	7.5
Nova Scotia	7.4	British Columbia	8.6
New Brunswick	7.0	Yukon Territory	10.5
Ontario	6.6	Northwest Territory	12.5
Manitoba	8.4		
		All Canada	7.3

Source: Canada Centre for Health Information, *Health Reports 1990*, vol. 2, pp. 60–61; Ottawa, Statistics Canada.

Table 8 shows that Quebec has an infant death rate perceptibly below that of the rest of Canada treated as one collectivity.

Table 9 indicates a small difference between life expectancies (at birth) in Quebec, and in the rest of Canada treated as one collectivity. Life expectancy is a little less for Quebec than for the rest of Canada, by one year or less, for males and females and both sexes. The contrast between males and females, however, is approximately 7 or 8 years.

Urban–Rural Differences, 1986. The 1986 Census of Canada shows the following:

Quebec Population	78% urban	22% rural
Canada-minus-Quebec	74% urban	26% rural

This is not a great difference, but it is one that demographers always check out.

Table 9
Life Expectancy at Birth, 1981
(years)

	Males	Females	Both Sexes
Quebec	71	79	75
Canada-minus-Quebec	72	79.4	75.7

Source: *1989 Canada World Almanac*, Global Press, Agincourt, Ontario, pp. 67–70.

Unemployment, 1982–1987. This six-year average is of course all-important as an index of social and economic well-being.

	Average	Range	
Quebec	12.2%	high 13.9 (1983)	low 10.3 (1987)
Canada-minus-Quebec	11.7%	12.6 (1984)	11.1 (1987)

(These figures are from *1990 Canada Year Book*, Ottawa, Statistics Canada, 1988, 5–22, derived.) The consistently highest province is Newfoundland with a six-year average of 19.3; Saskatchewan has the lowest–7.4. Seen collectively, the provinces from Quebec eastward plus British Columbia, show the higher rates; from Ontario westward through Alberta they run perceptibly lower.

A Demographic Summary. Most of the demographic comparisons within Canada show two urban-industrial societies that do not greatly differ from each other. Their infant mortality rates are two of the lowest in the world. Quebec trails in total fertility, but an interesting effort to raise that rate is just recently underway. The child bonuses do not nearly equal the cost of raising children to age 18; there are other factors, some intangible. But Quebec may have turned around its declining fertility rate, at least temporarily.

Two of the foregoing demographic tables, however, are highly significant for the futures of both Quebec and Canada-minus-Quebec: mother tongue and religion. Quebec is 83 percent francophone in mother tongue: Canada-minus-Quebec is 80 percent anglophone. This is a decisive contrast. It assures at the very least a deep and lasting ambivalence in both countries. Several generations of Quebecers have had to learn English to get work in the English owned and/or operated business enterprises—because the Anglophone minority in Quebec is disproportionately a managerial elite. In the mid- or late 1970s, the tactless Ottawa anglophone government offered an extension course on "How to Speak English without a French accent." It was a slap in the face of every francophone, and of many anglophones of good will toward Quebec. Further, the incident is a stunning revelation of the underlying relationships and persisting assumptions that prevail in the political and economic domination of Quebec by English Canada since the conquest of 1760.

The Trudeau bilingualism policy embodied in the Official Languages Act of 1969 was intended to bridge the chasm between the two language groups in the area of public federal services. French immersion classes (taught in French) across Canada in primary schools were partly funded by federal grants, where affordable and parentally supported. But the francophone communities, except in Quebec and New Brunswick, were small in other provinces—about five percent in Ontario and Manitoba, and only one or two percent in the rest. Yet many anglophone families (mine for example) were glad to enroll their children in French-immersion classes. Alberta, often stereotyped as a "redneck" province, teaches school in six languages: overwhelmingly in English, of course, but also in French, with token cases of German, Ukrainian, Cree and Hebrew.

But the basic trend has been toward the emergence of two unilingual nations: anglophone and francophone. In essence the bilingual thrust has failed. A second-language skill is of great value for fostering all sorts of interests. But if Canada and Quebec are to develop as a trading nation in Spanish America or the Far East, a much wider variety of linguistic and cultural knowledge is necessary. The day when the English-speaking world could maintain its snobbish intolerance by saying—"If you want to talk to me, speak English"—those days are gone in a global economy, whether recognized or not. It is not enough to learn Chinese for business reasons; it is also necessary to acquire a broad understanding of Chinese history, geography and culture.

In addition to mother tongue, the above tables on religion (3 and 4) are of major importance. Quebec is 88 percent Catholic (1981) and only 6 percent Protestant; Canada-minus-Quebec is 35 percent Catholic and 60 percent Protestant. Religious differences generated ferocious wars in the Middle Ages and early modern times. Even today, religious cleavages are prone to heat up in conflict situations. Religious intolerance requires constant counteraction in public life.

Let us now turn to the difficult problem of clarifying some of the future options of Quebec and Canada-minus-Quebec.

The Looming Options

The future of a society is shaped by its past and by the external influences to which it is subjected. Before we look ahead, we must remind ourselves in outline form of the primacy of a longer, wider and deeper view that seeks to link organically (so to say) the past, the present and the future in comparative perspectives.

Toward that end, we shall consider the landmark paper, "The Epic of Greater America," by the late Professor Herbert E. Bolton (1870–1953), of Berkeley, California. This essay was the author's presidential address to the American Historical Association, given at Toronto in December, 1932. It made a "profound impression" then and since (*Encyclopedia Brittannica* 1985). It is reprinted in H. E. Bolton, *Wider Horizons of American History*, Indiana, University of Notre Dame Press, 1967.

Bolton's central theme was the necessity of viewing national histories of New World States in a hemispheric context. Nowadays we would seek a global rather than a hemispheric setting. But in 1932, Bolton's hemispheric vision was a potential bombshell.

> European history cannot be learned from books dealing alone with England, or France, or Germany, or Italy, or Russia ... In my own country the study of thirteen English colonies and the United States in isolation has obscured many of the larger factors in their development, and helped to raise up a nation of chauvinists. (*ibid*, p. 2)

When I was educated in the public schools of northern New England in the 1930s, I was taught that the "American Revolution" meant the uprising of the 13 English colonies, 1775–1783. Only after I read Bolton did I realize that the factual span of the "American Revolution" in hemispheric terms was 1776–1826. During that era all the major New World colonies of west European imperialist States attained their political independence, more or less. Economic domination or indirect colonialism had yet to be recognized and dealt with; that would await the coming of J. Hobson, Marx-Lenin-Stalin, Chairman Mao and numerous others. It was Bolton who reminded us that Spain and Portugal dominated and battled for the New World, which centered in Latin America. Until the late 18th century, the dominant metropolis in the New World was Mexico City; the earliest universities were those at Lima and Mexico City (1551) – not Harvard (1636) or Yale (1701). Britain had some 30 colonies in the New World, not 13. The fate of the Western Hemisphere reflected the endless spate of European wars. The conquest of New France by England in 1760 was but a sideshow of the bitter Franco-British war of 1754–63. At the decisive final battle of Yorktown in 1781, "the French soldiers, almost equal to the Americans in number, stood like a rock against the attempts of Cornwallis to break the cordon of besieging armies." (Charles and Mary Beard, *The Rise of American Civilization*, New York, Macmillan, 1930, p. 279.) The French fleet clinched the surrender of Cornwallis and his British army.

Curiously, in his 1932 hemispheric account of the American Revolution, 1776–1826, Bolton does not mention Quebec, still a colony of English Canada. That omission was certainly not due to ignorance. Perhaps he was "too polite" to put the boot to his Toronto anglophone hosts.

A generation before Bolton, another son of Wisconsin, Frederick Jackson Turner (1861–1932), had published a famous paper on the "Significance of the Frontier in American History." Turner read it at the annual meetings of the American Historical Association at Chicago, 1893. Amer-

ican social institutions, he argued, owe more to the influences of the
frontier as it moved westward than to European factors. First came the
explorers, then hunters and trappers, agricultural settlers, finally factory
towns and State administrative structures. Always there was free land
and river accesses to the west to nurture individualism, escape the bonds
of inherited customs—until about 1890. By then the free land was largely
gone, the Indian tribes were driven onto reservations or simply destroyed.

Turner saw the frontier as a source of "perennial rebirth." A broader
view would be to include as well the dark aggressive side of American
social evolution. For example, the Indians nearest the pioneering trading
posts got firearms—and firewater—sooner than did the more distant
tribes, with one-sidedly murderous results. The expansive bent of American life, once the frontier free land ran out, fostered a racist, white-
supremicist nationalism—a readymade ideology for imposing on the rest
of the world a virulent American imperialism with a self-appointed mis-
sionary zeal for world domination. Even as the domestic frontier van-
ished, the United States targeted the decrepit Spanish Empire (1898), the
resources and cheap labor of China and indeed of the entire Third
World. This is monopoly capitalism, American version, not merely a frontier epic. It is metropolis vs. hinterland, overclass vs. underclass. It is
class struggle on a global basis. Harnessed to that is an out-of-control
technological development, one aspect of which is military. The world
in 1991 is ringed with American military bases. Has the American eagle
become a vulture? To what end?

Turner's key essays are available in his *Frontier in American History*,
New York: Henry Holt and Co., 1921. For Canada, *The Fur Trade in
Canada* (by Harold Innis, Univ. of Toronto Press, rev. ed., 1956) is
indispensable.

*Quebec as One of Several New World Colonies Emerging from Coloni-
alism.* From Bolton, we must bear in mind the wider view: that the
main European colonies in the New World hemisphere won their political independence by 1826. Another key Bolton insight is that Spain and
Portugal dominated the regions of Central and South America—
Hispanic America—where the more advanced native peoples had
already achieved a series of town-based empires and a technology that
produced portable wealth in gold and silver. Settlements in North America were, so to say, second-choice pickings, even though they were supplemented by piracy of Spanish treasure ships on the high seas by
England and France.

Hence Quebec moved belatedly toward autonomy and independence. Why? The 1760 Conquest of New France by England impelled

a number of elite francophone leaders to return or move to France. French Canada became Habitant country: rural, largely self-sufficient, agricultural. Commerce and top political administration were British spheres. The Roman Catholic Church, deeply opposed to the development of urban-industrial commerce, reinforced the rural way of life into the twentieth century. The 1949 Asbestos strike signalled the arrival of fundamental changes in francophone Quebec. Earlier signals for several decades had marked that long-emerging transformation: the migration of many working-class Quebecers to the mills of New England textile towns, for example. Migration out of Quebec for employment opportunities meant deculturation for the francophone migrants. That dual penalization for Quebecers has been important in feeding the independence drive.

The Weakness in the Quebec Economy. The nature of the economy places overemphasis on light industry.

> The growth in demand for consumer goods provided the impetus for the growth of light consumer goods industries—boots and shoes, bakeries, tailors and clothiers, tanneries, textiles, tobacco products, butter and cheese and furniture . . . a dependence on low growth and low technology industries subject to fierce competition from low-wage, underdeveloped countries . . . The percentage of the labour force in heavy industry and the growth sectors of manufacturing is about half the Ontario level . . . It means a constrained growth in opportunities for the young and—since the expansion of education facilities in the early 1960s—for well-trained Francophones who are not willing to give up their language and culture to seek advancement elsewhere. (*Regional Disparities*, by Paul Phillips, Toronto: Lorimer, 1982, pp. 31–35)

This passage conveys an outline sketch of the enormous task of nation-building facing Quebec. That task will never be undertaken by Canada as now constituted—if only because of the central premise of Canada since Confederation in 1967—ten provinces (only four in 1867) that demand to be treated in a roughly equal manner. History shows great holes in that premise, yet the premise still lives. Especially since the June, 1990 federal debacle of Meech Lake, which promised to recognize Quebec as a "distinct society" and to grant the means to realize that distinctiveness—one thing has been clear: the other nine provinces will NEVER support any such deal. Never, not ever.

The Bottom Line, the Basic Crux. There are two crises in Canada—the crisis of the future of Quebec, and the crisis of the future of Canada-minus-Quebec. Neither can be resolved or substantially ameliorated within Confederation, or within a "restructured" Canadian federation.

For the stark underlying reality is this: Canada is a series of regions with varying natural resources and conflicting interests. The only substantial industrial sector lies in southern Ontario and extends down the St. Lawrence—the "Golden Triangle" so-called—Toronto-Ottawa, and English Montreal. This is the area of American branch-plant heavy industry, largely owned or controlled by corporations based for the most part in the United States. That industrial sector has been hit very hard by the depression of the 1980s–1990s.

Canada's largest province is Ontario. Its estimated 1990 population was 9.7 million, or 27.5 percent of the estimated total 1990 Canadian population of 26.6 million (1990 *Encyclopedia Britannica Yearbook*). In September, 1990, Ontario astounded everyone by electing a New Democratic Party (NDP) provincial government. The 130 seats were divided as follows: NDP 74, Liberals 36, Tories 20.

The Reasons for American Economic Penetration. Important among these reasons is the high Canadian tariff of 1879, a major ingredient of the National Policy dating roughly from the 1867 Confederation. A branch plant in Canada also gave access to British Empire customs preference. Profit repatriation was another motive for direct investment from abroad. (See Privy Council Task Force Report, *Foreign Ownership and the Structure of Canadian Industry*, by University of Toronto economist Melville Watkins, Ottawa, 1968.) On the cost side to the receiving country is the threat to national sovereignty.

Quebec's Option for Sovereignty-Association. What does Quebec mean by this concept? The best guideline is the Quebec Government White Paper, *Quebec-Canada: A New Deal*, issued in 1979 during the latter part of Premier René Lévesque's first term in office.

> Sovereignty is the power to make decisions autonomously, without being subject in law to any superior or exterior power, which implies that the sovereign state has full jurisdiction over a given territory . . .

> The sovereign state may, however, of its own accord and without giving up its sovereignty, agree to limit its scope or to delegate part of it in certain specific fields.

> Thus, for two states linked by an agreement or parties to an association, the joint exercise of their sovereignty would necessarily be reflected in reciprocal concessions. In the case that concerns us, any limitation that Quebec would agree to impose on the exercise of its sovereignty would entail, in return, the corresponding limitation, accepted by Canada, of its own sovereignty.

> In a federal system, sovereignty is shared by two powers one of which, the central power, has priority. Consequently, citizens are ruled by two

governments, two sets of laws and two court systems; there are two kinds of elections, one to elect the central parliament (the House of Commons, in Ottawa) the other to elect a local parliament (the National Assembly, in Quebec); there are also two taxation systems. On the other hand, there is a single customs tariff, a single currency and a single international personality.

Under the formula proposed by the Government of Quebec, sovereignty would reside entirely in the state of Quebec, so that Quebecers would be ruled by a single government and would pay taxes only to Quebec. Because of the association, Quebec and Canada would continue to share a single customs tariff and a single currency. Each partner, however, would have its own international personality.

In legal terms, the difference between the two formulas could be stated this way: at present, the relations between Quebec and Canada are ruled by a Constitution that divides powers between two governments, only one of which, the federal government, has an international personality; in the formula proposed by the government of Quebec, both Quebec and Canada would have an international personality, and their relations would be ruled not by a constitution, but by a treaty of association. (*Quebec-Canada: A New Deal*, Gouvernement du Quebec, Conseil Executif, Quebec City, 1979, pp. 50–51)

As examples of modern associations of sovereign states, the following are among the sixteen cases listed. Others could have been added. The European Economic Community; Benelux (Belgium, Holland, Luxembourg); Nordic Council (Iceland, Norway, Sweden, Denmark, Finland); Central American Common Market (five small countries).

The link between *sovereignty* and *association* makes Quebec a special case, in contrast to the earlier revolutions in Central and South America. In northwestern regions of South America, Simon Bolivar the Liberator (1783–1830) led revolutions in Venezuela, Colombia, Ecuador and Peru. Other key leaders established independent regimes in Mexico, Brazil, Chile and Argentina about the same time. Those national states were heavily military in character. Quebec experienced a military conquest in 1760, but Britain was mainly pre-occupied with imperial wars in Europe. However, British presence in Canada had a restraining effect upon American aggressive tendencies aimed northward, at least in the 19th century. The War of 1812–14 was a spanking – more or less – of American forces by the British-Canadian troops, including a sea raid up Chesapeake Bay by the British fleet that burned the American White House in Washington in 1814. International boundaries did not change in the 1814 peace treaty. Two weeks later, unaware of the peace, a U.S. army won a major victory over the British at New Orleans.

Opinion Poll of Two Business Communities, 1991. The *Globe and Mail* Report on Business for April, 1991, published an article, "Duelling in the Dark." Using a professional polling firm, the *Globe and Mail* and *Magazine Affaires Plus* jointly sent out 6000 questionnaires: 3000 to Quebec business executives and 3000 to business men outside Quebec. The number returned was 1711; we are not told how many from each category. The results showed sharp differences between Quebecers and non-Quebecers.

	Quebecers (%)	Non-Quebecers (%)
Favor Quebec sovereignty	80	22
Oppose Quebec sovereignty	20	76
For new negotiations	17	53
For status quo	3	25
For sovereignty association	72	12
For Quebec independence	7	9

The importance of this poll is the great change among Quebec executives since 1980. In that earlier referendum, both Quebec and non-Quebec businessmen were united in strong opposition to any change in the status of Quebec in Canada. Not so in 1991.

The English reject "any form of special status for Quebec." (*ibid*, p. 30)

"Will Quebec become a sovereign state?" Quebec respondents answered 95% YES: Non-Quebec respondents said 61% YES.

"If Quebec votes YES in a referendum, should Canada recognize that new status?" French executives said YES—95%; English executives—61%, YES. [Stunning!—AKD]

Both groups of respondents agreed on the need for a free trade pact between Canada and Quebec; they split on the questions of a common currency and a common central bank, and on responsibility for defense. Many in both groups expressed exasperation with Ottawa politicians. As a resident of Alberta myself, I understand that feeling very well. Further, Alberta sells a considerable amount of beef in Quebec, and Albertans certainly want to hang onto that market. There are reciprocal trade needs from Quebec.

Many aspects of Quebec's relations with other Canadian provinces will not change much, if at all. This is an important point to remember.

Civil War between Quebec and Canada-without-Quebec?? Let us look at this worst-possible scenario. Yes, it could happen. A hardening trend is apparent between Quebec and the rest of Canada. More important, the current depression is worsening: unemployment is 10.5 percent (April, 1991), and edging upwards. The grass-roots are smouldering.

Scapegoating is to be expected: minorities will suffer unless organized to resist.

The economic and related social developments that bring on this downward spiral in the standard of living of the masses are inherent in the context of monopolistic capitalism. Socialistic economies are likewise affected, to the extent that they wish to trade with, and emulate – the materialistic aspects of capitalism.

But what I am challenging is the viability of urban-industrial society, capitalist or socialist – though I see the superiority of the socialist world in understanding the structure and evolution of modern societies. Understanding, however, is not enough. There must be action–experiments– second thoughts–inputs from all factions – but then decisive action.

But given the understanding, however rough, the socialist approach offers the nearest thing to a total overview of any social system in its historical context. But that context is ever-changing. Orthodoxy, therefore, in any concrete case, may be a negative influence. But in emergencies, people in a crisis situation often resort to demands for orthodoxy. That may be either a retarding or a progressive influence.

The USSR, the Peoples Republic of China, and the Republic of Cuba are examples of progressive developments – in the net – and despite the immense handicaps they experienced from their specific heritages from feudalism, and from foreign capitalist intrusions. In brief, they have suffered and erred, as well as succeeded. And national survival is the bottom line.

The Necessity of Basic Change in Both Quebec and Canada-without-Quebec. Let us be clear – this is a shared necessity. The infrastructures of each country are in dire need of much rehabilitation – the roads, schools, housing stocks, transport systems, recreational facilities, environmental recovery.

All these essentials cost money. They all require comprehensive planning and coordination. They add up to a massive attack on the greatest paradox of urban-industrial societies: poverty in the midst of plenty.

This is not merely an economic problem. Bread we must have, but not just bread. The problem is social and cultural as well. Not all persons wish to live in an urban-industrial community. According to the 1986 Census, about 3 percent of the total Canadian population (that total is roughly 25.3 million) or some 712,000 persons have native origins (*Canada Yearbook, 1990*, Ottawa, tables 2.1 and 2.18). "Native origin" includes persons reporting Indian, Métis or Inuit origin, or mixes thereof, or mixes of "native" and "non-native." They live mostly in the western provinces and the Northwest Territory. There are large unknowns in this picture, especially with regard to the number of "Métis." But the present point is—some of these people are beginning to unite in voluntary pressure-group organizations. They want larger reserves and some form of sovereignty thereon; they must be accommodated. "Native land-claims" is a topic beyond the scope of this book, except to note the intensifying problem, hitherto dodged or ignored by Canadian governments. The rising of the Mohawks in the mid-summer of 1990 at Oka near Montreal is only one of numerous signs of tension between Natives and other Canadian public and private interest groups and power structures.

After all, when the Caucasians invaded and took over Canada three centuries ago, they stole the country from the aboriginals already established there centuries before the Europeans arrived. Something is due to the Natives. The 1990 Hollywood film, "Dances with Wolves," should clarify the issues we are discussing here, in passing.

A perceptive column by Andre Picard appeared in the *Globe and Mail* for March 28, 1991. It is based on a study commissioned by Quebec and carried out by Secor Consultants.

> There has been, in a single generation, a massive shift in the English-French power relationship in the province. Montreal, 1986 population 2.9 million, once dominated by an English business class, now has a confident and unabashedly francophone business elite. Major corporations headed by francophone Quebecers, virtually non-existent two decades ago, are now the norm rather than the exception. Following the lead of Hydro-Quebec and the Caisse de depot et placement du Quebec, the provincial pension fund manager, business is now conducting its affairs in French. More important, there are signs of hope for Montreal, notably the burgeoning aerospace industry, which has already created 40,000 new jobs in the area . . .
>
> More than 200,000 anglophones have left the city in the past 15 years . . . A disproportionate number of these residents were business leaders . . . The language of work has changed, but processes (of manufacturing infrastructure) remain inefficient and buildings continue to crumble, particularly in the working-class areas of the city, such as the east end and the southwestern part of the island . . .
>
> Secor said that in the long term, the costs of *francization* will be absorbed, and modernization will occur.

Similar remarks could be made about nearly every sizable North American city. The achievements, the problems—they go together. They dialectically interact. They bring changes—plusses and minusses, from many viewpoints. Yet basic changes do emerge.

The social history of a city is of course reflected in its architecture.

From the southeast, one approaches the city, lying just east of the joining of the Ottawa and St. Lawrence rivers. The long rocky hill behind the city is Mount Royal, rising 763 feet above sea level. The towers of the St. Joseph Oratory and the University of Montreal peer over the left skyline. Near the summit is the giant cross, illuminated at night. In the downtown area east part of the city below the hill, is a sea of towers. On one is a huge "Q"–headquarters of Quebec-Hydro–the new Quebec–lighted at night. This first megaproject, begun with the nationalization of hydro power by René Lévesque as Quebec Minister of Natural Resources in 1962, and expanded to the James Bay dams later, is the dream and vehicle of Quebec's breakthrough to a splendid independent future.

"Vive le Québec libre!" shouted General Charles de Gaulle of France, on July 24, 1967, standing on the balcony of Montreal City Hall. The crowd in the street below him cheered wildly, but the federal authorities in Ottawa were not amused–they hustled the General home to France. But the famous visitor had said aloud what many people in Quebec had been thinking for years.

I heard that historic shout on the radio in Calgary, where I was living on a rented acreage on the northwest fringe of the city. Nine years in western Canada had made me realize that Canada is not simply ten provinces. More significant is the fact that Canada is Two Nations and a series of contending regions. How long will it take us to recognize and adjust to those over-riding realities? I wondered then in the summer of 1967, that bright summer of Expo 67 in Montreal, as I sat on "Carol's Rock" near the top of Nose Hill gazing up the Bow River valley and the rugged Kananaskis Range 50 miles away. The rocky outcrop, named in my household for my oldest daughter Carol–bless her–was a fine vantage place for quiet reflections. Now of course, twenty-four years have gone by. Nose Hill is plastered with modern bungalows. But the Quebec question still remains.

Is it not high time to resolve that issue? Quebec is moving. The crisis is now more of an Anglo-Canadian than a Quebec crisis.

The danger comes from the "Rest of Canada." In recent weeks the American President has visited Ottawa, and has advised Canadians to "stay together." No matter that we never asked for his advice. After all, the American military juggernaut has left the Middle East far worse off than it was before the 1991 blitz. Why listen to the Americans?

Uncertainties flood the domestic Canadian scene. The depression is worsening. The most unpopular federal regime in Canadian history sits in Ottawa, desperate for a face-saving gesture in order to cling to power. Are we going to get the War Measures Act again? Aimed once more at Quebec?

Justice and common sense say NO. Help Quebec—and thereby the Rest of Canada—to realize sovereignty-association. Few belligerent noises—so far—have surfaced in English Canada. But the situation is dicey, to say the least. A lead editorial in the March 31, 1991, Edmonton *Journal* runs as follows: "Without Quebec there is no Canada." That is sheer nonsense, of course. It embodies an attitude that is negative—it opens the door to a destructive avalanche of unforeseeable and unintended disasters. It shows that English Canada, rather than Quebec, may over-react. And who can say where the fatal avalanche may lead?

Let us cite two lines from China's greatest modern poet.

> Nothing is hard in this world
> If you dare to scale the heights.
>
> *Reascending Chingkangshan*, by Mao Tse-tung, 1965
> (Peking, Foreign Languages Press, 1976)

A Lament for English Canada

In 1965, Professor George P. Grant (1918–1988) published his brilliant elegy, *Lament for a Nation: The Defeat of Canadian Nationalism* (Toronto: McClelland and Stewart, 97 pages). Toronto-born, educated at Queens and Oxford, Grant was a prominent figure in the Canadian anglophone intelligentsia. But he was more than that, as a philosopher, because his analytical apparatus was critical, even iconoclastic.

The immediate historical context of *Lament for a Nation* was the 1957–63 federal Tory regime. John G. Diefenbaker (1895–1979) of Prince Albert, Saskatchewan, was Prime Minister—the first Conservative-Party Head of Government between 1935 and 1984—except for the 9-month term of Joe Clark, 1979–80. The latter was a minority Government: Clark thought he could hold his office by governing "as if he had a majority;" that delusion was short-lived.

The question posed by Grant is—Why was Diefenbaker the Western populist, elected by a landslide, so unceremoniously dumped as Prime Minister in 1963, and as Conservative Party leader in 1967?

Not all the answers to this question are to be found in *Lament for a Nation*. Indeed, Grant deals only with the fall of Diefenbaker as Prime Minister; the Party Leadership affair was still in the future when Grant published his book in 1965. But that would show the same pattern: a concerted attack on Diefenbaker, fueled by the media and orchestrated by members of both major political parties, not just by the Opposition Liberals.

There are of course several objective factors in the troubled leadership career of "Dief the Chief," as he was called. An economic recession set in early in the 1960s, for which the Government got blamed. In 1959 came the cancellation of the Avro Arrow, likely the finest fighter aircraft ever built in North America. Its engine, fire-control and missile systems were Canadian-designed. Yet the Diefenbaker Government cancelled the project in 1959, thereby wrecking the Canadian military aircraft industry (*Canadian Encyclopedia*, 1988, Hurtig, Edmonton). A documentary film run on Canadian TV two or three years ago argues that the blueprints and possibly the fifth and last prototype model found their way south. The Americans as a result sold their fighters to Canada, instead of vice versa.

Finally, Diefenbaker never really understood regional power structures in Canada; he was blissfully blind to Quebec realities. His public speeches can be summed up as–One Canada–a standing affront, though unintended, to the emerging new Quebec.

Let us see what George Grant has to say about some of these matters.

> After 1940 it was not in the interests of the economically powerful to be nationalists. Most of them made more money by being the representatives of American capitalism and setting up the branch plants . . . Capitalism is a way of life based on the principle that the most important activity is profit-making. That activity led the wealthy in the direction of continentalism. They lost nothing essential to the principle of their lives in losing their country. It is this very fact that has made capitalism the great solvent of all tradition in the modern era. That is why liberalism is the perfect ideology for capitalism. It demolishes those taboos that restrain expansion . . .

> The only Canadians who had a profoundly different tradition from capitalist liberalism were the French Canadians, and they were not generally taken into decision-making unless they had foregone these traditions. Their very Catholicism did not lead the best of them to be interested in the managerial, financial and technical skills of the age of progress. (Op. cit. pp. 47–48)

Marx made the more general points about the achievements and the impact of capitalism on a society in Part I of the 1848 *Manifesto*, doubtless on a grander scale. But Grant is dealing with a particular case 125 years later. It is not easy to analyze and objectify the complexities of a concrete social order for the members of that order. Nonetheless his task is well done. One point demands correction: the prime barrier today between Quebec and the rest of Canada is language, not religion. Before the "Quiet Revolution," the reverse was true.

The Saving Role of Sovereignty-Association for Quebec and English-Canada and the Assembly of First Nations

Sovereignty-Association as defined previously (pp. 454–455) could prove to be an effective joint solution, a gate-opener, for both Quebec and anglophone Canada. Further down the road, it might even become a sigificant guideline for resolving Native land claims with Canada's First Nations. Not to mention possibly relevant implications for the USSR and perestroika, and for Yugoslavia. The list could go on and on.

Wrote George Grant in 1965: "A nation does not remain a nation only because it has roots in the past . . . There must be a thrust of intention into the future." (*ibid*, p. 12)

"Thrust" means a dynamic motivating force. Surely it is clear by now to the readers of these pages that "Canada" is a multi-cultural entity, a "community of communities." It is absurd, for example, to pretend that "Canada" on a political level is ten standardized provinces plus two or three territories. (The Northwest Territory (NWT) is in the process of being subdivided; the new territory will be Nunavut in the eastern Arctic region, home of a few thousand Inuit. When that process is completed, there will be three territories: Yukon, NWT, and Nunavut. Three collective personalities, sharing much, yet each unique.)

"Canada" is two major nations – Quebec and English Canada. In addition "Canada" includes a third category of Native "First Nations" still sorting themselves out, yet differing significantly from the bourgeois structures and cultures of English Canada and Quebec.

Socially and politically and economically, Quebec and English Canada and the First Nations Assembly (perhaps eventually including Status Indians, Métis and Inuit) should negotiate and operate in matters of common concern as three equal personalities.

The present stirrings in English Canada and in certain Quebec circles seem bound to fail their efforts to find a new constitutional pattern along the lines of the prevailing system. They will fail because they aim to compromise that which cannot be compromised. The thrust of Quebec for sovereignty will not fit into the inherited institutional orthodoxy upheld by the federal regime in Ottawa. Nor will the aspirations of the First Nations.

No matter that the current Prime Minister of Quebec is at heart a federalist and a compromiser (Robert Bourassa). He has the Parti Quebecois breathing down his neck. The PQ Leader of the Opposition is Jacques Parizeau (b. 1930), a very determined supporter of sovereignty-association, a distinguished economist, former Minister of Finance in the René Lévesque PQ Government, and experienced in public policy formulation.

We cite George Grant once again. "The keystone of a Canadian nation is the French fact; the slightest knowledge of history makes this platitudinous. English-speaking Canadians who desire the survival of their nation have to cooperate with those who seek the continuance of Franco-American civilization." (*ibid*, p. 20) This insight needs broadening to include the First Nations.

John Diefenbaker completely failed to perceive this basic truth. At heart he was a strong nationalist: he stood up to the American demand that Canada accept nuclear arms despite massive pressures from US President John Kennedy and his own Canadian military. (When Diefenbaker was defeated in 1963, his Liberal successor, Lester Pearson, promptly accepted nuclear warheads for Bomarc missiles.) Diefenbaker also incurred the wrath of the Americans in the Cuban missile crisis of October, 1962, by delaying for two or three days an American demand to go on instant red alert when Kennedy announced a naval blockade of Cuba to force recall of Soviet missiles from Cuba. In fact, the Canadian Cabinet had good reason to hesitate: the U.S. Bay of Pigs fiasco in April, 1961, and the strong Soviet military presence just over the North Pole were ample basis for thinking twice about the dangers inherent in American hotheaded belligerence.

Quebec sovereignty-association is not a threat to the rest of Canada. It is a saving and positive asset, provided that Ottawa does not descend to scare propaganda or panic us into civil war. From Diefenbaker's 1960 Human Rights Charter, entrenched in 1982 in the Constitution as the Charter of Rights and Freedoms, Canada enjoys strong civil rights—for individuals. What is woefully lacking is provision for the rights of collectivities. Now, in 1991, is the time to meet that need. The outcome is highly uncertain. English Canada is beset with a dangerous number of frustrated and discredited Tory politicians; all three major federal Parties have many anglophone leaders; a spark from almost anywhere could ignite and fan a redneck thrust against Quebec. That is not the way to go.

Vive le Québec libre! Vive le Canada anglais! Long live the First Nations! All must live together in peace and freedom, but not in institutional uniformity.

» «

Is this achievable? Possibly. Or is it utopian? Probably. The outcome depends partly on chance—factors not controllable—and partly on political will which must be organized to accomplish basic changes. Can this happen—in Canada? No one can say.

Yet history is full of cases of fundamental changes. In 1905, Norway

(1990 pop. est. 4.2 m.) and Sweden (8.5 m.) peacefully separated and prospered. Switzerland (6.7 m.) successfully combines three different ethnic-linguistic communities: German, French and Italian (65, 18, and 10 percent respectively, with several small groups accounting for the remaining 7 percent).

We can draw other examples from large nations as well as small ones. Who would have anticipated that China, the world's most populous State (1.2 billion in 1990), could emerge from its mid-19th-century prostration to become today a Great Power? Or that the USSR, in ruins after the 1917–21 civil war and invasions by 14 capitalist countries, would recover to build the first socialist State and defeat during World War II the most massive military assault in history?

Then what is so impossible about Quebec and English Canada transcending their inherited contradictions—without civil war—by means of sovereignty-association?

Quebec at least is facing its uncertain future, aware of its internal factions and ambivalence, but in the net planning and edging toward something more promising. But English Canada, likewise ambivalent, still faces backward, well aware of the present depression and political scandals in several provinces and huge loss of credibility and confidence in Ottawa. However, English Canada so far seems apathetic about its economic and cultural dependence upon the USA, and reluctant to confront its mounting crisis with Quebec and above all with itself.

Two minor incidents illuminate the dilemma of English Canada. In April, 1991, a western provincial Premier visited the Prime Minister of Quebec to threaten economic sanctions if Quebec persisted in separating—sanctions such as refusal to accept a new Quebec currency (should that materialize: no measure of that sort has been proposed by either Quebec or the Parti Quebecois opposition); and a denial of western markets to Quebec dairy products (in fact, that denial is beyond the powers of a provincial premier). Whatever, the hostile spirit of that visit is all too clear. That it was a blunder, likely to have an effect opposite from that intended, has been widely voiced in the Canadian media.

The second incident was a visit of four or five citizens from a small Alberta town to a small Quebec town. The visit lasted several days. None of the Westerners could speak French, but enough Quebecers could speak English to establish communication. Opposed to Quebec separation when they went to Quebec, the Western people returned with their minds changed. "We now believe that we can live with sovereignty-association," they said.

The first incident is destructive; the second, constructive.

Clearly, the basic relationships of Quebec and English Canada are bound to change. That the coming of sovereignty-association will entail stresses in the short run but mutual benefits in the long view—is a reasonable conclusion. The past supports it; the present demands it; may the future realize its promise.

But will this happen sooner, or later? No one can say. At least five of Canada's ten provinces are likely to change their governments in their next provincial elections, and so too is the Federal Government. All six are right-wing Tory. They will tend to seek a scapegoat—doubtless a campaign of coercion and scare propaganda against Quebec. The real enemy, of course, is the on-going and still worsening capitalist depression dominated by American trans-national corporations. But it is much safer to attack Quebec sovereignty-association. "Save Canada" will be the slogan of the day. With such a dust storm as camouflage, the cutbacks in public service programs and civil-servant staffs, already underway, can be continued.

"Divide and rule."

The Fury Across Canada. "There is fury in the land against the Prime Minister," says Keith Spicer, chairman of the federally appointed Citizens Forum on Canada's future. "Since hearings started in January, 1991, nearly 100 percent of the comments about the PM's leadership were negative. Public hearings were held across Canada for six months. "Is the PM the problem? Can a politician so disliked solve the unity question?" (Edmonton *Journal*, June 28 and 29, 1991).

For his critical suggestions on this paper, I am greatly indebted to Mr. Georges Vafakis of Montreal. A.K.D.

Index

Vafakis, Georges (Montreal), 465

Vallieres, Pierre, on 1970 Laporte affair, 427

Variance, concept of, 350

Vassar College, xiv

Veblen, Thorstein, thesis on, xi; general, 19, 21, 63–64; exhibition (University of Vermont), xv; on taxonomic constructs, 49; on Marxian elements, 50, 150; on orthodox economics, 54; relevance for sociology, 54; on neutrality, 57; life of, 69–79; bibliography, 77–78; supplementary works on, 78–79; education, 69–70; on Darwinism, 71, 73; institutions, 71; Marxian similarities, 71, 154; culture-lag, 72–73; writings, 69–78; influence, 76 & ff.; on waste in national budgets, 128; task of democracy, 130; "Veblen Once More," 149 & ff.; W. D. Howells on, 154; racism, 154; major works of, 156; U.S. dementia praecox, 156–157; end game syndrome (since Veblen's time), 158; on industrialism, 158; limitations of, 159; on overlapping cultures, 170; on universities as bureaucracies, 196; on "going first," 259; 262; 264; 274; on capitalist defects, 278–279; on social analysis and research, 300, 311; on philosophical anarchism, xi, 338; 386, 388

Vernon, B. C., 402, 414

Vietnam War, xx–xxi, 20, 104; and U.S. policy, 137, 148, 179; U.S. and Vietnam, 385

Wallace, George, 20, 129

Wallace, Henry, "progressive capitalism," 33, 153

War, capitalist dependence on, 46

War and Peace (–Tolstoy), 137, 215

War Measures Act (1970), 406, 426, 429; (–again?), 459

Warner, W. Lloyd, 51, review of, 226–227

Waterbury, Vermont (R. L. Duffus), 6

Watkins, Melville H., 123, 144, 350, 360, 365–366, 369; on *Foreign Ownership and Structure of Canadian Industry* (1968), 454

Wax, Murray L., on Indian Americans (review), 251–254

Weber, Max, on "rationalization," 17, 124; on culture-bearing elite, 48; Parsons on rationalization, 49; Weber's view of historical forces, 50; on China, 83; as source

for Naegele, 121–122; 141; 264–265; and Marx, 265; as ideologist, 276–283; on Protestant ethic theory of capitalist development, 276; influences on Lipset, Hagen, McClelland, et al., 276; and capitalist societies, 276; reification in, 278; on governmental aids to capitalism, 278–279; parochialism of, 283; 327 (note 6)

Western Association of Sociology and Anthropology (Canada), 10, 276

Western Washington State College and University, xvi, 314, 320

Wheat, in Canada, 330; Fowke on, 339; 341, 370 & ff. (See also Sask. wheat)

White, Leslie, 51, 73

Whitman, Walt, xv, xix, 18; "When Lilacs Last . . .," 18, 142

Whyte, W. F., *Street Corner Society*, 61; in *Canadian Society*, 122

Williams, William A., 19, 21, 25, 112, 120, 130, 132, 140, 148, 157, 319, 327 (note 8), 359, 362, 367

Willmott, Don E., studies of Esterhazy, 9–10, 24; on Community Council role, 312

Winspear, A. D., on dialectic in Greek thought, 255

Wittfogel on China, 83

Wolfe, Samuel, 8, 249

Wood, Kerry, on prairie settlement, 340

Woodsworth, J. S., McNaught on, 338–339; CCF leaders as preachers, 344

World history, 3-phase (obsolete), 60

World view, holistic (AKD), ix

Worsley, P. M., in urban Indian studies (Sask.), 320

Wright, Jim F. C., 3, 8, 112; on prairie settlement, 339; 352, 365

Wright, Quincy (*Study of War*), 158, 168, 214

Yale University (Veblen, 1884), 69

Yefremov, Ivan, on steppe nomads (*Andromeda*), 168; as optimist, 168

York University, Toronto, 356

Zakuta, L., on Agrarian Socialism in Ontario, 337

Zayas, A. M. de, on East European relations, 195

Zimmerman, Carle (Harvard), 149